PORTFOLIO CONSTRUCTION

CFA® Program Curriculum
2026 • LEVEL III CORE • VOLUME 2

WILEY

©2025 by CFA Institute. All rights reserved. This copyright covers material written expressly for this volume by the editor/s as well as the compilation itself. It does not cover the individual selections herein that first appeared elsewhere. Permission to reprint these has been obtained by CFA Institute for this edition only. Further reproductions by any means, electronic or mechanical, including photocopying and recording, or by any information storage or retrieval systems, must be arranged with the individual copyright holders noted.

CFA®, Chartered Financial Analyst®, AIMR-PPS®, and GIPS® are just a few of the trademarks owned by CFA Institute. To view a list of CFA Institute trademarks and the Guide for Use of CFA Institute Marks, please visit our website at www.cfainstitute.org.

This publication is designed to provide accurate and authoritative information in regard to the subject matter covered. It is sold with the understanding that the publisher is not engaged in rendering legal, accounting, or other professional service. If legal advice or other expert assistance is required, the services of a competent professional should be sought.

All trademarks, service marks, registered trademarks, and registered service marks are the property of their respective owners and are used herein for identification purposes only.

CONTENTS

Contents

How to Use the CFA Program Curriculum

The CFA® Program exams measure your mastery of the core knowledge, skills, and abilities required to succeed as an investment professional. These core competencies are the basis for the Candidate Body of Knowledge (CBOK™). The CBOK consists of four components:

> A broad outline that lists the major CFA Program topic areas (www.cfainstitute.org/programs/cfa/curriculum/cbok/cbok)

> Topic area weights that indicate the relative exam weightings of the top-level topic areas (www.cfainstitute.org/en/programs/cfa/curriculum)

> Learning outcome statements (LOS) that tell you the specific knowledge, skills, and abilities you should gain from each curriculum topic area. You will find these statements at the start of each learning module and lesson. We encourage you to review the information about the LOS on our website (www.cfainstitute.org/programs/cfa/curriculum/study-sessions), including the descriptions of LOS "command words" on the candidate resources page at www.cfainstitute.org/-/media/documents/support/programs/cfa-and-cipm-los-command-words.ashx.

> The CFA Program curriculum that candidates receive access to upon exam registration.

Therefore, the key to your success on the CFA exams is studying and understanding the CBOK. You can learn more about the CBOK on our website: www.cfainstitute.org/programs/cfa/curriculum/cbok.

The curriculum, including the practice questions, is the basis for all exam questions. The curriculum is selected/developed specifically to provide candidates with the knowledge, skills, and abilities reflected in the CBOK.

CFA INSTITUTE LEARNING ECOSYSTEM (LES)

Your exam registration fee includes access to the CFA Institute Learning Ecosystem (LES). This digital learning platform provides access to all the curriculum content and practice questions. The LES is organized as a series of learning modules consisting of short online lessons and associated practice questions. This tool is your source for all study materials, including practice questions and mock exams. The LES is the primary method by which CFA Institute delivers your curriculum experience. Here, you will find additional practice questions to test your knowledge, including some interactive questions.

DESIGNING YOUR PERSONAL STUDY PROGRAM

An orderly, systematic approach to exam preparation is critical. You should dedicate a consistent block of time every week to reading and studying. Review the LOS both before and after you study curriculum content to ensure you can demonstrate the knowledge, skills, and abilities described by the LOS and the assigned learning module. Use the LOS as a self-check to track your progress and highlight areas of weakness for later review.

Successful candidates report an average of more than 300 hours preparing for each exam. Your preparation time will vary based on your prior education and experience, and you will likely spend more time on some topics than on others.

ERRATA

The curriculum development process is rigorous and involves multiple rounds of reviews by content experts. Despite our efforts to produce a curriculum that is free of errors, we must make corrections in some instances. Curriculum errata are periodically updated and posted by exam level and test date on the Curriculum Errata webpage (www.cfainstitute.org/en/programs/submit-errata). If you believe you have found an error in the curriculum, you can submit your concerns through our curriculum errata reporting process found at the bottom of the Curriculum Errata webpage.

OTHER FEEDBACK

Please send any comments or suggestions to info@cfainstitute.org, and we will review your feedback thoughtfully.

Portfolio Construction

1

Overview of Equity Portfolio Management

by James Clunie, PhD, CFA, and James Alan Finnegan, CAIA, RMA, CFA.

James Clunie, PhD, CFA, is at Jupiter Asset Management (United Kingdom). James Alan Finnegan, CAIA, RMA, CFA (USA).

LEARNING OUTCOMES

Mastery	The candidate should be able to:
☐	describe the roles of equities in the overall portfolio
☐	describe how an equity manager's investment universe can be segmented
☐	describe the types of income and costs associated with owning and managing an equity portfolio and their potential effects on portfolio performance
☐	describe the potential benefits of shareholder engagement and the role an equity manager might play in shareholder engagement
☐	describe rationales for equity investment across the active management spectrum
☐	discuss considerations in choosing a benchmark for an equity portfolio

INTRODUCTION

1

Equities represent a sizable portion of the global investment universe and are often a primary component of investors' portfolios. Rationales for investing in equities include potential participation in the growth and earnings prospects of an economy's corporate sector as well as an ownership interest in a range of business entities by size, economic activity, and geographical scope. Publicly traded equities are generally more liquid than other asset classes and thus enable investors to easily monitor price trends and trade securities at low costs.

This reading provides an overview of equity portfolio management. In the next section, we discuss the roles of equities in a portfolio. Then, we examine the equity investment universe, including several ways investors segment that universe. We will also cover the income and costs for an equity portfolio, as well as shareholder engagement between equity investors and investee companies. In addition, we will discuss equity investment across the active management spectrum and considerations for benchmark selection for equity strategies, including for index-based strategies. A summary of key points completes the learning module.

2   THE ROLES OF EQUITIES IN A PORTFOLIO

☐ | describe the roles of equities in the overall portfolio

Equities play several roles in an overall portfolio, including providing such benefits as capital appreciation, dividend income, diversification with other asset classes, and a potential hedge against inflation. In addition to these benefits, client investment considerations play an important role for portfolio managers when deciding to include equities in portfolios.

Capital Appreciation

Long-term returns on equities, driven predominantly by capital appreciation, have historically been among the highest among major asset classes. Exhibit 1 shows geometric, annualized real returns on equities, bonds, and bills—both globally and in various regions—from 1900 to 2022. Equities outperformed both bonds and bills during this period across the world.

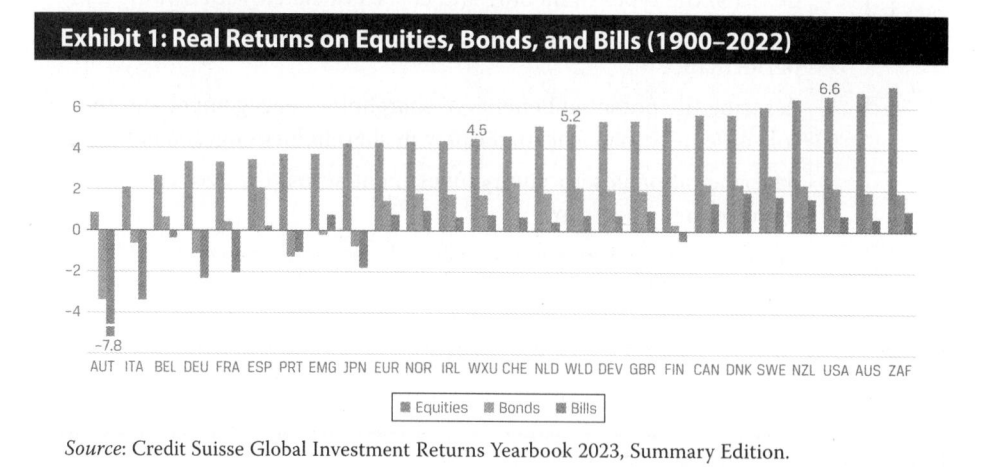

Exhibit 1: Real Returns on Equities, Bonds, and Bills (1900–2022)

Source: Credit Suisse Global Investment Returns Yearbook 2023, Summary Edition.

Equities tend to outperform other asset classes during periods of strong economic growth, and they tend to underperform other asset classes during weaker economic periods. Capital (or price) appreciation of equities often occurs when investing in companies with growth in earnings, cash flows, and/or revenues—as well as in companies with competitive success. Capital appreciation can occur, for example, in growth-oriented companies, such as small technology companies, as well as in large, mature companies where management successfully maintains profitability.

Dividend Income

The most common source of income for an equity portfolio is dividends. Companies may choose to distribute free cash flows as dividends rather than reinvest in projects, particularly when suitable projects do not exist or do not have returns greater than investors' required rate of return. Large, well-established corporations often provide dividend payments that increase in value over time, although there are no assurances that dividend payments from these corporations will grow or even be maintained. In addition to dividends on common stock (common dividends), preferred dividends can provide dividend income to those shareholders owning preferred shares.

Dividends have represented a significant component of long-term total returns for equity investors. Over shorter periods of time, however, the proportion of equity returns from dividends (reflected as dividend yield) can vary considerably relative to capital gains or losses. Exhibit 2 illustrates this effect of dividend returns relative to annual total returns on the S&P 500 Index from 1930 through 2021. Since 1990, the dividend yield on the S&P 500 has been in the 1%–3% range; thus, the effect of dividends can clearly be significant during periods of weak equity market performance, such as during the first decade of the 21st century, when price returns were negative. Also note that the dividend yield may vary considerably by sector.

Exhibit 2: S&P 500 Dividend Contribution (1930–2022)

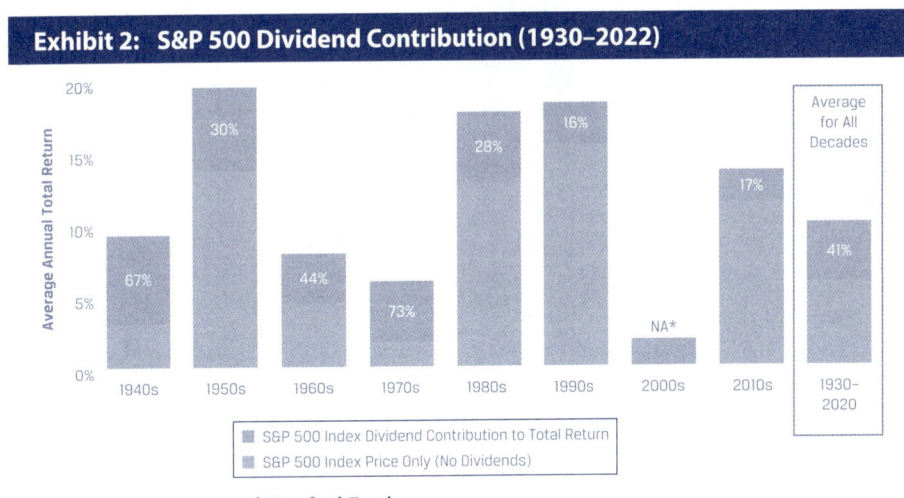

Sources: Morningstar and Hartford Funds.

Diversification with Other Asset Classes

Individual equities have unique characteristics, although the correlation of returns among equities is often high. In a portfolio context, however, equities can provide meaningful diversification benefits when combined with other asset classes (assuming less-than-perfect correlation). Recall that a major reason why portfolios can effectively reduce risk (typically expressed as standard deviation of returns) is that combining securities whose returns are less than perfectly correlated reduces the standard deviation of the diversified portfolio below the weighted average of the standard deviations of the individual investments. The challenge in diversifying risk is to find assets that have a correlation much lower than +1.0.

Exhibit 3 provides a correlation matrix across various global equity indexes and other asset classes using total monthly returns for the 20 years ended 31 October 2021. The correlation matrix shows that during this period, various broad equity indexes and, to a lesser extent, country equity indexes were highly correlated with each other. Conversely, both the broad and country equity indexes were considerably less correlated with indexes in other asset classes, notably Treasury bonds, investment-grade bonds, and gold. Overall, Exhibit 3 indicates that combining equities with other asset classes can result in portfolio diversification benefits.

It is important to note that correlations are not constant over time. During a long historical period, the correlation of returns between two asset classes may be low, but in any given period, the correlation can differ from the long term. Correlation estimates can vary based on the capital market dynamics during the period when the correlations are measured. During periods of market crisis, correlations across asset classes and among equities themselves often increase and reduce the benefit of diversification. As with correlations, volatility (standard deviation) of asset class returns may also vary over time.

Exhibit 3: Correlation Matrix, 20 Years Ended 31 October 2021

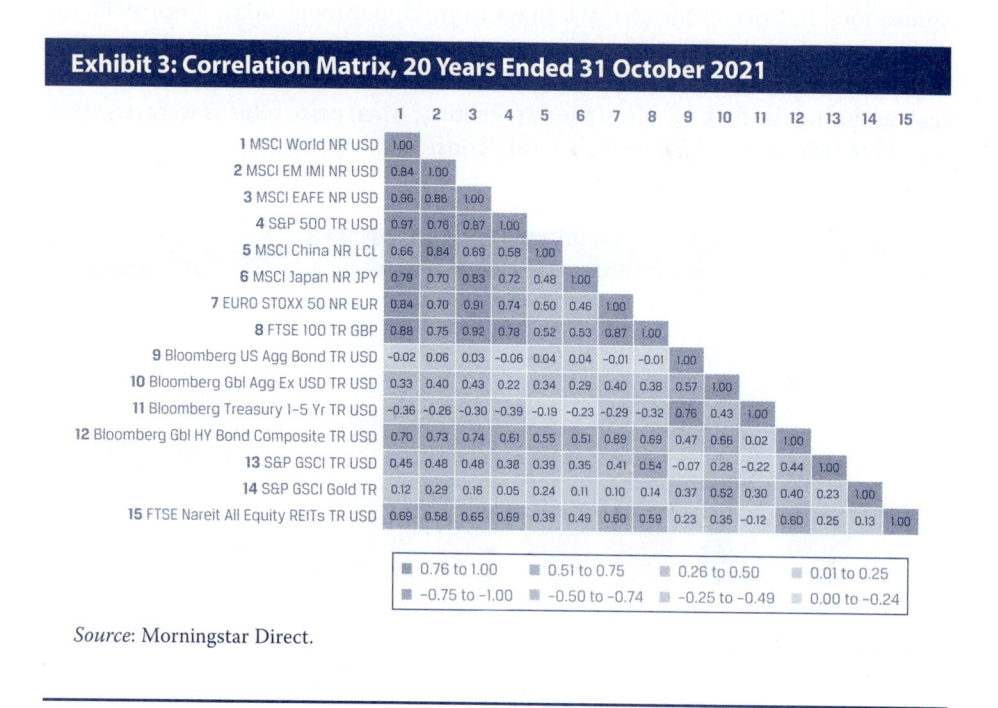

	1	2	3	4	5	6	7	8	9	10	11	12	13	14	15
1 MSCI World NR USD	1.00														
2 MSCI EM IMI NR USD	0.84	1.00													
3 MSCI EAFE NR USD	0.96	0.86	1.00												
4 S&P 500 TR USD	0.97	0.76	0.87	1.00											
5 MSCI China NR LCL	0.66	0.84	0.69	0.58	1.00										
6 MSCI Japan NR JPY	0.79	0.70	0.83	0.72	0.48	1.00									
7 EURO STOXX 50 NR EUR	0.84	0.70	0.91	0.74	0.50	0.46	1.00								
8 FTSE 100 TR GBP	0.88	0.75	0.92	0.78	0.52	0.53	0.87	1.00							
9 Bloomberg US Agg Bond TR USD	−0.02	0.06	0.03	−0.06	0.04	0.04	−0.01	−0.01	1.00						
10 Bloomberg Gbl Agg Ex USD TR USD	0.33	0.40	0.43	0.22	0.34	0.29	0.40	0.38	0.57	1.00					
11 Bloomberg Treasury 1–5 Yr TR USD	−0.36	−0.26	−0.30	−0.39	−0.19	−0.23	−0.29	−0.32	0.76	0.43	1.00				
12 Bloomberg Gbl HY Bond Composite TR USD	0.70	0.73	0.74	0.61	0.55	0.51	0.69	0.69	0.47	0.66	0.02	1.00			
13 S&P GSCI TR USD	0.45	0.48	0.48	0.38	0.39	0.35	0.41	0.54	−0.07	0.28	−0.22	0.44	1.00		
14 S&P GSCI Gold TR	0.12	0.29	0.16	0.05	0.24	0.11	0.10	0.14	0.37	0.52	0.30	0.40	0.23	1.00	
15 FTSE Nareit All Equity REITs TR USD	0.69	0.58	0.65	0.69	0.39	0.49	0.60	0.59	0.23	0.35	−0.12	0.60	0.25	0.13	1.00

■ 0.76 to 1.00	■ 0.51 to 0.75	■ 0.26 to 0.50	■ 0.01 to 0.25
■ −0.75 to −1.00	■ −0.50 to −0.74	■ −0.25 to −0.49	■ 0.00 to −0.24

Source: Morningstar Direct.

Hedge against Inflation

Some individual equities or sectors can provide some protection against inflation, although the ability to do so varies. For example, certain companies may be successful at passing along higher input costs (such as raw materials, energy, or wages) to customers. This ability to pass along costs to customers can protect a company's or industry's profit margin and cash flow and can be reflected in its stock prices. As another example, companies in sectors that produce broad-based commodities (e.g., oil or industrial metals producers) can more directly benefit from increases in commodity prices. Although individual equities or sectors can protect against inflation, the success of equities as an asset class in hedging inflation has been mixed. Certain empirical studies have shown that real returns on equities and inflation have positive correlation over the long term, but the degree of correlation typically varies by country and is dependent on the time period assessed. For severe inflationary periods, such as periods with an annual inflation rate over 5%, studies have shown that real returns on equities and inflation have been *negatively* correlated. Therefore, the asset class's efficacy as an inflation hedge may fail when it is most needed.

Client Considerations for Equities in a Portfolio

The inclusion of equities in a client's portfolio is driven by their goals and needs. A client's investment considerations are typically described in an investment policy statement (IPS), which establishes, among other things, return objectives, risk tolerance, constraints, and unique circumstances. By understanding these client considerations, a financial adviser or wealth manager can determine whether—and what amount of—equities should be in a client's portfolio.

Equity investments are often characterized by such attributes as growth potential, income generation, risk and return volatility, and sensitivity to various macroeconomic variables (e.g., GDP growth, interest rates, and inflation). As a result, a portfolio manager can adapt such specific factors to an equity investor's investment goals and risk tolerance. For example, a risk-averse and conservative investor may prefer some exposure to well-established companies with strong and stable cash flow that pay meaningful dividends. Conversely, a growth-oriented investor with an aggressive risk tolerance may prefer smaller companies with greater growth potential.

Wealth managers and financial advisers often consider the following investment objectives and constraints when deciding to include equities (or asset classes in general, for that matter) in a client's portfolio:

- *Risk objective* addresses how risk is measured (e.g., in absolute or relative terms); the investor's willingness to take risk; the investor's ability to take risk; and the investor's specific risk objectives.

- *Return objective* addresses how returns are measured (e.g., in absolute or relative terms); this term refers to stated return objectives.

- *Liquidity requirement* is a constraint in which cash is needed for anticipated or unanticipated events.

- *Time horizon* is the time period associated with an investment objective (e.g., short term, long term, or some combination of the two).

- *Tax concerns* include tax policies that can affect investor returns; for example, dividends may be taxed at a different rate than capital gains.

- *Legal and regulatory factors* are external factors imposed by governmental, regulatory, or oversight authorities.

- *Unique circumstances* are an investor's considerations other than liquidity requirements, time horizon, or tax concerns that may constrain portfolio choices. These considerations may include environmental, social, and governance (ESG) issues or religious preferences.

Clients' interest in ESG and sustainable investing has grown. With regard to equities, these considerations often determine the suitability of certain sectors or individual company stocks for designated investor portfolios. Historically, ESG approaches used by portfolio managers have largely represented **negative screening** (or exclusionary screening) and **positive screening** or **best-in-class** approaches. Negative screening refers to the practice of excluding certain sectors or companies that deviate from accepted standards in such areas as human rights or environmental concerns. Positive screening attempts to identify companies or sectors that score most favorably with regard to ESG-related risks and/or opportunities. For example, a negative screening approach may involve excluding oil and gas producers from consideration for a client's portfolio strategy, while a positive screening approach may overweight companies and industries with strong governance practices, such as an independent board chair. Rather than screening, however, as of 2020, the largest sustainable investment strategy globally was ESG integration, which is the inclusion of ESG considerations in financial analysis and investment decisions (GSIA 2020).

The goals of ESG integration are to reduce financial risks and/or enhance financial returns by identifying and valuing risks or opportunities that are not typically identified and valued. ESG integration begins with identifying relevant ESG information for sector, industry, and company research and evaluating its financial materiality. Financially material ESG information is then used alongside traditional financial information to inform an analyst's valuation and recommendation to buy, hold, or sell a security. Just as with traditional equity analysis, a variety of tools and methods exist for integrating ESG information into the analytical process, and analysts must choose the ones they believe are most appropriate for their analysis.

GUIDANCE AND CASE STUDIES FOR ESG INTEGRATION

CFA Institute and the United Nations–supported Principles for Responsible Investment (PRI) initiative published a best practice report ("Guidance and Case Studies for ESG Integration: Equities and Fixed Income") and three regional reports—one for the Americas (AMER), one for Asia Pacific (APAC), and one for Europe, the Middle East, and Africa (EMEA)—to help investors understand how they can better integrate ESG factors into their equity, corporate bond, and sovereign debt portfolios. This report contains many case studies of ESG integration and introduces an ESG Integration Framework as a reference for practitioners. The following two cases are brief excerpts from that report.

Adjusting Revenue and Margins

In "Evaluating ESG Impact on Revenue and Margins," AGF Investments Inc. illustrates how ESG information can be used to adjust forecasted financials. In this case study, Company A is a global leader in specialty chemicals that has positioned itself to profit from trending consumer preferences for sustainable products. Company A recently shifted from purchasing petrochemicals for use as a product base to manufacturing its own product base using naturally sourced, renewable raw materials. AGF analysts project that the shift to in-house manufacturing and use of renewable materials will reduce costs from purchasing petrochemicals and managing hazardous waste materials. Analysts also project that consumers will pay a premium for Company A's sustainable products versus competitors' petrochemical-based products, which will increase annual revenue growth by 30 bps. Analysts estimate that the cost savings plus increased revenue over the next five years will result in a 100 bp improvement to EBIT (earnings before interest and taxes).

Adjusting the P/E Multiple

The case study "Valuation Adjustment According to Environmental Regulations" demonstrates the use of ESG information to adjust the P/E multiple.

In this example, analysts at E Fund Management Co., Limited, believed that new pollution regulations in China would be strictly enforced and developed a four-factor framework to score companies in affected industries on environmental protection factors. The case study compares the evaluation of Y Chemical and H Corporation. After scoring the companies, analysts concluded that H Corporation had a greater environmental risk than Y Chemical. Analysts were unable to estimate the projected environmental protection costs for the two companies, so they chose to discount the target P/E for H Corporation to a

P/E of 20 versus the industry average P/E of 23.7 (trailing 12 months). Analysts believed that H Corporation was overpriced due to its environmental risks not being recognized by the market and thus would have a negative return.

Source: CFA Institute and the PRI, "Guidance and Case Studies in ESG Integration: Equities and Fixed Income" (2018). www.cfainstitute.org/-/media/documents/survey/guidance-case-studies -esg-integration.pdf.

Two other approaches to ESG investing are **thematic investing** and **impact investing**. Thematic investing refers to investing in companies with positive exposure to ESG megatrends, such as clean energy, green technology, sustainable agriculture, gender diversity, or affordable housing. Global economic development has raised the demand for energy at the same time as increased greenhouse gas emissions are widely believed to negatively affect the earth's climate. Similarly, rising global living standards and industrial needs have created a greater demand for water along with the need to prevent drought or increase access to clean drinking water in certain regions of the world. While these themes are based on trends related to environmental issues, social issues—such as access to affordable health care and nutrition—are also of interest.

Impact investing is a related approach that seeks to achieve targeted social or environmental objectives along with measurable financial returns through engagement with a company or by direct investment in projects or companies. An example would include investing in products or services that help achieve 1 (or more) of the 17 Sustainable Development Goals (SDGs) launched by the United Nations in 2015, such as "SDG 6: Clean Water and Sanitation—Ensure availability and sustainable management of water and sanitation for all" and "SDG 11: Sustainable Cities and Communities—Make cities and human settlements inclusive, safe, resilient and sustainable." Impact investing is a relatively smaller segment of the broader sustainable and responsible investing market.

ROLES OF EQUITIES

1. Alex Chang, Lin Choi, and Frank Huber manage separate equity portfolios for the same investment firm. Chang's portfolio objective is conservative in nature, with a regular stream of income as the primary investment objective. Choi's portfolio is more aggressive in nature, with a long-term horizon and with growth as the primary objective. Finally, Huber's portfolio consists of wealthy entrepreneurs who are concerned about rising inflation and wish to preserve the purchasing power of their wealth.

   Discuss the investment approach that each portfolio manager would likely use to achieve his or her portfolio objectives.

   Solution

   Given that his portfolio is focused on a regular stream of income, Chang is likely to focus on companies with regular dividend income. More specifically, Chang is likely to invest in large, well-established companies with stable or growing dividend payments. With a long-term horizon, Choi is most interested in capital appreciation of her portfolio, so she is likely to focus on companies with earnings growth and competitive success. Finally, Huber's clients are concerned about the effects of inflation, so he will likely seek to invest in shares of companies that can provide an inflation hedge. Huber would likely seek companies that can successfully pass on higher input costs to their customers, and he may also seek commodity producers that may benefit from rising commodity prices.

3   EQUITY INVESTMENT UNIVERSE

> ☐ | describe how an equity manager's investment universe can be segmented

Given the extensive range of companies in which an equity portfolio manager may invest and the range of clients' risk and return objectives, an important task for the manager is to segment the universe by grouping companies according to similar characteristics. This segmentation enables portfolio managers to better evaluate and analyze their equity investment universe, and it can help with portfolio diversification. Several approaches to segmenting the equity investment universe are discussed in the following sections.

Segmentation by Size and Style

A popular approach to segmenting the equity universe incorporates two factors: (1) size and (2) style. Size is typically measured by market capitalization and often categorized by large cap, mid cap, and small cap. Style is typically classified as value, growth, or a combination of value and growth (typically termed "blend" or "core"). In addition, style is often determined through a "scoring" system that incorporates multiple metrics or ratios, such as price-to-book ratios, price-to-earnings ratios, earnings growth, dividend yield, and book value growth. These metrics are then typically "scored" individually for each company, assigned certain weights, and then aggregated. The result is a composite score that determines where the company's stock is positioned along the value–growth spectrum. A combination of growth and value style is not uncommon, particularly for large corporations that have both mature and higher-growth business lines.

Exhibit 4 illustrates a common matrix that reflects size and style dimensions. Each category in the matrix can be represented by companies with considerably different business activities. For example, both a small, mature metal fabricating business and a small health care services provider may fall in the Small Cap Value category. An example of how several listed companies are categorized as of February 2023 is shown in Exhibit 5. In practice, individual stocks may not clearly fall into one of the size/style categories and classification is dynamic, so these are best thought of as guidelines rather than a strict taxonomy.

Exhibit 4: Equity Size and Style Matrix

	Style		
	Value	Blend	Growth
Large			
Mid			
Small			

Source: Morningstar.

	Style		
	Value	**Blend**	**Growth**
Large	Samsung Electronics Co. Ltd.	Tencent	Meituan
Mid	Schroders PLC	Gedeon Richter	Ocado PLC
Small	Hawaiian Airlines	National Beverage Corp.	WeWork Inc.

Exhibit 5: Equity Size and Style, Example Classifications as of February 2023

Source: Morningstar.

Segmentation by size/style can provide several advantages for portfolio managers. First, portfolio managers can construct an overall equity portfolio that reflects desired risk, return, and income characteristics in a relatively straightforward and manageable way. Second, given the broad range of companies in each segment, segmentation by size/style results in diversification across economic sectors or industries. Third, active equity managers—that is, those seeking to outperform a given benchmark portfolio— can construct performance benchmarks for specific size/style segments. Generally, large investment management firms may have sizable teams dedicated toward specific size/style categories, while small firms may specialize in a specific size/style category, particularly mid-cap and small-cap companies, seeking to outperform a standard benchmark or comparable peer group.

The final advantage of segmentation by size/style is that it allows a portfolio to reflect a company's maturity and potentially changing growth/value orientation. Specifically, many companies that undertake an IPO (initial public offering) are small and in a growth phase, and thus they may fall in the small-cap growth category. If these companies can successfully grow, their size may ultimately move to mid-cap or even large cap, while their style may conceivably shift from high growth to value or a combination of growth and value (e.g., a growth and income stock). Accordingly, over the life cycle of companies, investor preferences for these companies may shift increasingly from capital appreciation to dividend income. In addition, segmentation also helps fund managers adjust holdings over time—for example, when stocks that were previously considered to be in the growth category mature and possibly become value stocks. The key disadvantages of segmentation by size/style are that the categories may change over time and may be defined differently among investors.

Segmentation by Geography

Another common approach to equity universe segmentation is by geography. This approach is typically based on the stage of markets' macroeconomic development and wealth. Common geographic categories are *developed markets, emerging markets,* and *frontier markets.* Exhibit 6 demonstrates the commonly used geographic segmentation of international equity indexes according to MSCI. MSCI classifies countries as developed, emerging, or frontier according to a holistic framework that considers economic development, size and liquidity, and accessibility criteria, such as openness to foreign equity ownership. Other major index providers—such as FTSE, Standard & Poor's, and Russell—provide similar types of international equity indexes.

Geographic segmentation is useful to equity investors who have considerable exposure to their domestic market and want to diversify by investing in global equities. A key weakness of geographic segmentation is that investing in a specific market (e.g., market index) may provide lower-than-expected exposure to that market. As an example, Nestle, Roche, and Novartis together account for over half of the MSCI

Switzerland Index, but Switzerland accounts for less than 2% of each company's sales. Another key weakness of geographic segmentation is potential currency risk when investing in different global equity markets.

Exhibit 6: MSCI International Equity Indexes (as of January 2023)

Developed Markets

Americas	Europe and Middle East	Pacific
Canada	Austria	Australia
United States	Belgium	Hong Kong SAR
	Denmark	Japan
	Finland	New Zealand
	France	Singapore
	Germany	
	Ireland	
	Israel	
	Italy	
	Netherlands	
	Norway	
	Portugal	
	Spain	
	Sweden	
	Switzerland	
	United Kingdom	

Emerging Markets

Americas	Europe, Middle East, and Africa	Asia Pacific
Brazil	Czech Republic	Chinese mainland
Chile	Egypt	India
Colombia	Greece	Indonesia
Mexico	Hungary	South Korea
Peru	Kuwait	Malaysia
	Poland	Philippines
	Qatar	Taiwan region
	Saudi Arabia	Thailand
	South Africa	
	Turkey	
	United Arab Emirates	

Frontier Markets

Europe and CIS[1]	Africa	Middle East	Asia
Croatia	Kenya	Bahrain	Bangladesh
Estonia	Mauritius	Jordan	Pakistan
Iceland	Morocco	Oman	Sri Lanka
Lithuania	Nigeria		Vietnam
Kazakhstan	Tunisia		
Romania	WAEMU[2]		
Serbia			
Slovenia			

Notes: The following markets are not included in the developed, emerging, or MSCI frontier indexes but have their own market-specific indexes: Argentina, Jamaica, Panama, Trinidad and Tobago, Bosnia Herzegovina, Bulgaria, Malta, Russia, Ukraine, Botswana, Zimbabwe, Lebanon, and Palestine.
[1]*CIS:* Commonwealth of Independent States (formerly the USSR).
[2]*WAEMU:* West African Economic and Monetary Union, also known by its French acronym UEMOA,

which consists of the following countries: Benin, Burkina Faso, Ivory Coast, Guinea-Bissau, Mali, Niger, Senegal, and Togo.

Segmentation by Economic Activity

Economic activity is another characteristic that portfolio managers may use to segment the equity universe. Most equity classification systems group companies into industries/sectors using a *market-oriented* approach, grouping companies based on the markets they serve, the way revenue is earned, and the way customers use companies' products.

The four main commercial global classification systems, which were discussed earlier in the curriculum, are (1) the Global Industry Classification Standard (GICS); (2) the Industrial Classification Benchmark (ICB); (3) the Thomson Reuters Business Classification (TRBC); and (4) the Russell Global Sectors Classification (RGS). These classification systems help standardize industry definitions so that portfolio managers can compare and analyze companies and industries/sectors. In addition, the classification systems are useful in the creation of industry performance benchmarks.

Exhibit 7 compares the four primary classification systems. Each system is classified broadly and then increasingly more granularly to compare companies and their underlying businesses.

Exhibit 7: Primary Sector Classification Systems

Level/System	GICS	ICB	TRBC	RGS
1st	11 Sectors	10 Industries	10 Economic Sectors	9 Economic Sectors
2nd	24 Industry Groups	19 Super Sectors	28 Business Sectors	33 Sub-Sectors
3rd	68 Industries	41 Sectors	54 Industry Groups	157 Industries
4th	157 Sub-Industries	114 Sub-Sectors	136 Industries	Not Applicable

Sources: Thomson Reuters, S&P/MSCI, FTSE/Dow Jones.

To illustrate how segmentation of the classification systems may be used in practice, Exhibit 8 demonstrates how GICS, perhaps the most prominent classification system, sub-divides selected sectors—in this case, Consumer Discretionary, Consumer Staples, and Information Technology—into certain industry group, industry, and sub-industry levels.

Exhibit 8: GICS Classification Examples

Sector	Consumer Discretionary	Consumer Staples	Information Technology
Industry Group Example	Automobiles and Components	Food, Beverage, and Tobacco	Technology Hardware and Equipment
Industry Example	Automobiles	Beverages	Electronic Equipment, Instruments, and Components
Sub-Industry Example	Motorcycle Manufacturers	Soft Drinks	Electronic Manufacturing Services

Source: MSCI.

As with other segmentation approaches mentioned previously, segmentation by economic activity enables equity portfolio managers to construct performance benchmarks for specific sectors or industries. Portfolio managers may also obtain better industry representation (diversification) by segmenting their equity universe according to economic activity. The key disadvantage of segmentation by economic activity is that the business activities of companies—particularly, large ones—may include more than one industry or sub-industry.

SEGMENTING THE EQUITY INVESTMENT UNIVERSE

1. A portfolio manager is initiating a new fund that seeks to invest in the Chinese robotics industry, which is experiencing rapidly accelerating earnings. To help identify appropriate company stocks, the portfolio manager wants to select an approach to segment the equity universe.

   Recommend which segmentation approach would be most appropriate for the portfolio manager.

   Solution

   Based on his desired strategy to invest in companies with rapidly accelerating (growing) earnings, the portfolio manager would most likely segment his equity universe by size/style. The portfolio manager would most likely use an investment style that reflects growth, with size (large cap, mid cap, or small cap) depending on the company being analyzed. Other segmentation approaches, including those according to geography and economic activity, would be less appropriate for the portfolio manager given the similar geographic and industry composition of the Chinese robotics industry.

Segmentation of Equity Indexes and Benchmarks

Segmentation of equity indexes or benchmarks reflects some of or all the approaches previously discussed in this section. For example, the MSCI Europe Large Cap Growth Index, the MSCI World Small Cap Value Index, the MSCI Emerging Markets Large Cap Growth Index, and the MSCI Latin America Midcap Index combine various geographic, size, and style dimensions. This combination of geography, size, and style also sometimes applies to individual countries—particularly those in large, developed markets.

A more focused approach to segmentation of equity indexes uses industries or sectors. Because many industries and sectors are global in scope, the most common types of these indexes are composed of companies in different countries. Examples include the following:

- Global Natural Resources—the *S&P Global Natural Resources Index* includes 90 of the largest publicly traded companies in natural resources and commodities businesses across three primary commodity-related sectors: agribusiness, energy, and metals and mining.

- Worldwide Oil and Natural Gas—the *MSCI World Energy Index* includes the large-cap and mid-cap segments of publicly traded oil and natural gas companies in the developed markets.

- Multinational Financials—the *Refinitiv Global Financials Index* includes the 100 largest publicly traded companies in the global financial services sector as defined by the TRBC classification system.

Finally, some indexes reflect specific investment approaches, such as ESG investing. Such ESG indexes are made up of companies that reflect certain considerations, such as sustainability or impact investing.

INCOME ASSOCIATED WITH OWNING AND MANAGING AN EQUITY PORTFOLIO

4

☐ describe the types of income and costs associated with owning and managing an equity portfolio and their potential effects on portfolio performance

Dividends are the primary source of income for equity portfolios. In addition, some portfolio managers may use securities lending or option-writing strategies to generate income. On the cost side, equity portfolios incur various fees and trading costs that adversely affect portfolio returns. The primary types of income and costs are discussed in this section.

Dividend Income

Investors requiring regular income may prefer to invest in stocks with large or frequent dividend payments, whereas growth-oriented investors may have little interest in dividends. Taxation is an important consideration for dividend income received, particularly for individuals. Depending on the country where the investor is domiciled, where dividends are issued, and the type of investor, dividends may be subject to withholding tax and/or income tax.

Beyond regular dividends, equity portfolios may receive **special dividends** from certain companies. Special dividends occur when companies decide to distribute excess cash to shareholders, but the payments may not be maintained over time. **Optional stock dividends** are another type of dividend in which shareholders may elect to receive either cash or new shares. When the share price used to calculate the number of stock dividend shares is established before the shareholder's election date, the choice between a cash or stock dividend may be important. This choice represents "optionality" for the shareholder, and the optionality has value. Some market participants, typically investment banks, may offer to purchase this "option," providing an additional, if modest, source of income to an equity investor.

Securities Lending Income

For some investors, **securities lending**—a form of collateralized lending—may be used to generate income for portfolios. Securities lending can facilitate short sales, which involve the sale of securities the seller does not own. When a securities lending transaction involves the transfer of equities, the transaction is generally known as **stock lending** and the securities are generally known as *stock loans*. Stock loans are collateralized with either cash or other high-quality securities to provide some financial protection to the lender. Stock loans are usually open-ended in duration, but the borrower must return the shares to the lender on demand.

Stock lenders generally receive a fee from the stock borrower as compensation for the loaned shares. Most stock loans in developed markets earn a modest fee, approximately 0.2%–0.5% on an annualized basis. In emerging markets, fees are typically higher, often 1%–2% annualized for large-cap stocks. In many equity markets, certain stocks—called "specials"—are in high demand for borrowing. These specials can earn fees that are substantially higher than average (typically 5%–15% annualized), and in cases of extreme demand, they could be as high as 25%–100% annually. However, such high fees do not normally persist for long periods of time.

In addition to fees earned, stock lenders can generate further income by reinvesting the cash collateral received (assuming a favorable interest rate environment). However, as with virtually any other investment, the collateral would be subject to market risk, credit risk, liquidity risk, and operational risk. The administrative costs of a securities lending program, in turn, will reduce the collateral income generated. Dividends on loaned stock are "manufactured" by the stock borrower for the stock lender; that is, the stock borrower ensures that the stock lender is compensated for any dividends that the lender would have received had the stock not been loaned.

Index funds are frequent stock lenders because of their large, long-term holdings in stocks. In addition, because index funds merely seek to replicate the performance of an index, portfolio managers of these funds are normally not concerned that borrowed stock used for short-selling purposes might decrease the prices of the corresponding equities. Large, actively managed pension funds, endowments, and institutional investors are also frequent stock lenders, although these investors are likely more concerned with the effect on their returns if the loaned shares are used to facilitate short selling. The evidence on the impact of stock lending on asset prices has, however, been mixed (see, for example, Kaplan, Moskowitz, and Sensoy 2013).

Ancillary Investment Strategies

Additional income can be generated for an equity portfolio through a trading strategy known as **dividend capture**. Under this strategy, an equity portfolio manager purchases stocks just before their ex-dividend dates, holds these stocks through the ex-dividend date to earn the right to receive the dividend, and subsequently sells the shares. Once a stock goes ex-dividend, the share price should, in theory, decrease by the value of the dividend. In this way, capturing dividends would increase portfolio income, although the portfolio would—again, in theory—experience capital losses of similar magnitude. However, the share price movement could vary from this theoretical assumption given income tax considerations, stock-specific supply/demand conditions, and general stock market moves around the ex-dividend date.

Selling (writing) options can also generate additional income for an equity portfolio. One such option strategy is writing a *covered call*, whereby the portfolio manager already owns the underlying stock and sells a call option on that stock. Another option strategy is writing a *cash-covered put* (also called a *cash-secured put*), whereby the portfolio manager writes a put option on a stock and simultaneously deposits money equal to the exercise price into a designated account. Under both covered calls and cash-covered puts, income is generated through the writing of options, but clearly the risk profile of the portfolio would be altered. For example, writing a covered call would limit the upside from share price appreciation of the underlying shares.

EQUITY PORTFOLIO INCOME

1. Isabel Cordova is an equity portfolio manager for a large multi-national investment firm. Her portfolio consists of several dividend-paying stocks, and she is interested in generating additional income to enhance the

portfolio's total return. Describe potential sources of additional income for Cordova's equity portfolio.

Solution

Cordova's primary source of income for her portfolio would likely be "regular" and, in some cases, special dividends from those companies that pay them. Another potential source of income for Cordova is securities (stock) lending, whereby eligible equities in her portfolio can be loaned to other market participants, including those seeking to sell short securities. In this case, income would be generated from fees received from the stock borrower as well as from reinvesting the cash collateral received. Another potential income-generating strategy available to Cordova is dividend capture, which entails purchasing stocks just before their ex-dividend dates, holding the stocks through the ex-dividend date to earn the right to receive the dividend, and subsequently selling the shares. Selling (writing) options, including covered call and cash-covered put (cash-secured put) strategies, is another way Cordova can generate additional income for her equity portfolio.

COSTS ASSOCIATED WITH OWNING AND MANAGING AN EQUITY PORTFOLIO

5

☐ | describe the types of income and costs associated with owning and managing an equity portfolio and their potential effects on portfolio performance

Management Fees

Management fees are typically determined as a percentage of the funds under management (an *ad-valorem* fee) at regular intervals. For actively managed portfolios, the level of management fees involves a balance between fees that are high enough to fund investment research but low enough to avoid detracting too much from investor returns. Management fees for actively managed portfolios include direct costs of research (e.g., remuneration and expenses for investment analysts and portfolio managers) and the direct costs of portfolio management (e.g., software, trade processing costs, and compliance). For index-based portfolios, management fees are typically low because of lower direct costs of research and portfolio management relative to actively managed portfolios.

Investment managers typically present a standard schedule of fees to a prospective client, although actual fees can be negotiated between the manager and investors. For a fund, fees are established in the prospectus, although investors could negotiate special terms (e.g., a discount for being an early investor in a fund).

Performance Fees

In addition to management fees, portfolio managers sometimes earn performance fees (also known as incentive fees) on their portfolios. Performance fees are generally associated with hedge funds and long/short equity portfolios, rather than long-only portfolios. These fees are an incentive for portfolio managers to achieve or outperform return objectives, to the benefit of both the manager and investors. As an example, a performance fee might represent 10%–20% of any capital appreciation in a portfolio that exceeds some stated annual absolute return threshold (e.g., 8%). Several performance fee structures exist, although performance fees tend to be "upwards only"; that is, fees are earned by the manager when performance objectives are met, but fund investors are not reimbursed when performance is negative. However, performance fees could be reduced following a period of poor performance. Fee calculations also reflect high-water marks. A **high-water mark** is the highest value, net of fees, that the fund has reached. The use of high-water marks protects clients from paying twice for the same performance. For example, if a fund performed well in a given year, it might earn a performance fee. If the value of the same fund fell the following year, no performance fee would be payable. Then, if the fund's value increased in the third year to a point just below the value achieved at the end of the first year, no performance fee would be earned because the fund's value did not exceed the high-water mark. This basic fee structure is used by many alternative investment funds and partnerships, including hedge funds.

Administration Fees

Equity portfolios are subject to administration fees. These fees include the processing of corporate actions, such as rights issues; the measurement of performance and risk of a portfolio; and voting at company meetings. Generally, these functions are provided by an investment management firm itself and are included as part of the management fee.

Some functions, however, are provided by external parties, with the fees charged to the client in addition to management fees. These externally provided functions include the following:

- *Custody fees* paid for the safekeeping of assets by a custodian (often a subsidiary of a large bank) that is independent of the investment manager
- *Depository fees* paid to help ensure that custodians segregate the assets of the portfolio and that the portfolio complies with any investment limits, leverage requirements, and limits on cash holdings
- *Registration fees* that are associated with the registration of ownership of units in a mutual fund

Marketing and Distribution Costs

Most investment management firms market and distribute their services to some degree. Marketing and distribution costs typically include the following:

- Costs of employing marketing, sales, and client servicing staff
- Advertising costs
- Sponsorship costs, including costs associated with sponsoring or presenting at conferences
- Costs of producing and distributing brochures or other communications to financial intermediaries or prospective clients
- "Platform" fees, which are costs incurred when an intermediary offers an investment management firm fund services on the intermediary's platform of funds (e.g., a "funds supermarket")
- Sales commissions paid to such financial intermediaries as financial planners, independent financial advisers, and brokers to facilitate the distribution of funds or investment services

When marketing and distribution services are performed by an investment management firm, the costs are likely included as part of the management fee. However, those marketing and distribution services that are performed by external parties (e.g., consultants) typically incur additional costs to the investor.

Trading Costs

Buying and selling equities incur a series of trading (or transaction) costs. Some of these trading costs are explicit, including brokerage commission costs, taxes, stamp duties, and stock exchange fees. In addition, many countries charge a modest regulatory fee for certain types of equity trading.

In contrast to explicit costs, some trading costs are implicit in nature. These implicit costs include the following:

- Bid–offer spread
- Market impact (also called price impact), which measures the effect of the trade on transaction prices
- Delay costs (also called slippage), which arise from the inability to complete desired trades immediately because of order size or lack of market liquidity

In an equity portfolio, total trading costs are a function of the size of trades, the frequency of trading, and the degree to which trades demand liquidity from the market. Unlike many other equity portfolio costs, such as management fees, the total cost of trading is generally not revealed to the investor. Rather, trading costs are incorporated into a portfolio's total return and presented as overall performance data. One final trading cost relates to stock lending transactions that were previously discussed. Equity portfolio managers who borrow shares in these transactions must pay fees on shares borrowed.

Investment Approaches and Effects on Costs

Equity portfolio costs tend to vary depending on their underlying strategy or approach. As mentioned previously, index-based strategies tend to charge lower management fees than active strategies primarily because of lower research costs. Index-based equity portfolios also tend to trade less frequently than actively managed equity portfolios, with trading in index-based portfolios typically involving rebalancing or changes to index constituents. Index funds, however, do face a "hidden" cost from potential predatory trading. As an illustration, a predatory trader may purchase (or sell short) shares prior to their effective inclusion (or deletion) from an index, resulting in price movement and potential profit for a predatory trader. Such predatory trading strategies can be regarded as a cost to investors in index funds, albeit a cost that is not necessarily evident to a portfolio manager or investor.

Some active investing approaches "demand liquidity" from the market. For example, in a momentum strategy, the investor seeks to buy shares that are already rising in price (or sell those that are already falling). In contrast, some active investing approaches are more likely to "provide liquidity" to the market, such as deep value strategies (i.e., those involving stocks that are deemed to be significantly undervalued). Investment strategies that involve frequent trading and demand liquidity are, unsurprisingly, likely to have higher trading costs than long-term, buy-and-hold investment strategies.

6   SHAREHOLDER ENGAGEMENT

> ☐ | describe the potential benefits of shareholder engagement and the role an equity manager might play in shareholder engagement

Shareholder engagement refers to the process whereby investors actively interact with companies. Shareholder engagement often includes voting on corporate matters at general meetings as well as other forms of communication (e.g., quarterly investor calls or in-person meetings) between shareholders and representatives of a company. Generally, shareholder engagement concerns issues that can affect the value of a company and, by extension, an investor's shares.

When shareholders engage with companies, several issues may be discussed, including the following:

- *Strategy*—a company's strategic goals, resources, plans for growth, and constraints. Also of interest may be a company's research, product development, culture, sustainability and corporate responsibility, and industry and competitor developments. Shareholders may ask the company how it balances short-term requirements and long-term goals and how it prioritizes the interests of its various stakeholders.

- *Allocation of capital*—a company's process for selecting new projects as well as its mergers and acquisitions strategy. Shareholders may be interested to learn about policies on dividends, financial leverage, equity raising, and capital expenditures.

- *Corporate governance and regulatory and political risk*—including internal controls and the operation of the company's audit and risk committees.

- *Remuneration*—compensation structures for directors and senior management, incentives for certain behaviors, and alignment of interests between directors and shareholders.

- *Composition of the board of directors*—succession planning, director expertise and competence, culture, diversity, and board effectiveness.

Benefits of Shareholder Engagement

Shareholder engagement can provide benefits for both shareholders and companies. From a company's perspective, shareholder engagement can assist in developing a more effective corporate governance culture. In turn, shareholder engagement may lead to better company performance to the benefit of shareholders (as well as other stakeholders).

Investors may also benefit from engagement because they will have more information about companies or the sectors in which companies operate. Such information may include a company's strategy, culture, and competitive environment within an industry. Shareholder engagement is particularly relevant for active portfolio managers. By contrast, index-based fund managers are primarily focused on tracking a given benchmark or index while minimizing costs to do so. Any process, such as shareholder engagement, that takes up management time (and adds to cost) would detract from the primary goal of an index-based manager. This would be less of an issue for very large index-based portfolios, where any engagement costs could be spread over a sizable asset base.

Investors who do not pursue engagement can still benefit from the shareholder engagement of others as so-called free riders. Specifically, assume that a portfolio manager using an active strategy actively engages with a company to improve its operations and was successful in increasing the company's stock price. The manager's actions in this case improved the value of his portfolio and also benefited other investors who own the same stock in their portfolios. Investors who did not participate in shareholder engagement benefited from improved performance but without the costs necessary for engagement.

In addition to shareholders, other stakeholders of a company may also have an interest in the process and outcomes of shareholder engagement. These stakeholders may include creditors, customers, employees, regulators, governmental bodies, and certain other members of society (e.g., community organizations and citizen groups). These other stakeholders can gain or lose influence with companies depending on the outcomes of shareholder engagement. For example, employees can be affected by cost reduction programs requested by shareholders. Another example is when creditors of a company are affected by a change in a company's vendor payment terms, which can impact the company's working capital and cash flow. Such external forces as the media, the academic community, corporate governance consultants, and proxy voting advisers can also influence the process of shareholder engagement.

Shareholders that also have non-financial interests, such as ESG considerations, may also benefit from shareholder engagement. However, these benefits are difficult to quantify. Empirical evidence relating shareholder returns to a company's adherence to corporate governance and ESG practices is mixed. This mixed evidence could be partly attributable to the fact that a company's management quality and effective ESG practices may be correlated with one another. As a result, it is often difficult to isolate non-financial factors and measure the direct effects of shareholder engagement.

Disadvantages of Shareholder Engagement

Shareholder engagement is time consuming and can be costly for both shareholders and companies. Second, pressure on company management to meet near-term share price or earnings targets could be made at the expense of long-term corporate decisions. Third, engagement can result in selective disclosure of important information to a certain subset of shareholders, which could lead to a breach of insider trading rules while in possession of specific, material, non-public information about a company. Finally, conflicts of interest can result for a company. For example, a portfolio manager could engage with a company that also happens to be an investor in the manager's portfolio. In such a situation, a portfolio manager may be unduly influenced to support the company's management so as not to jeopardize the company's investment mandate with the portfolio manager.

The Role of an Equity Manager in Shareholder Engagement

Active managers of equity portfolios typically engage, to some degree, with companies in which they currently (or potentially) invest. In fact, investment firms in some countries have legal or regulatory responsibilities to establish written policies on stewardship and/or shareholder engagement. Engagement activities for equity portfolio managers often include regular meetings with company management or investor relations teams. Such meetings can occur at any time but are often held after annual, semi-annual, or quarterly company results have been published.

Larger investment firms may also employ an analyst (or team of analysts) that focus on ESG issues. They work in conjunction with traditional investment analysts on shareholder voting and other engagement topics.

Activist Investing

Activist investing is a distinct and specialized version of engagement. Activist investors (or activists) specialize in taking stakes in companies and creating change to generate a gain on their investment. Hedge funds are among the most common activists, possibly because of the potential for, in many cases, high performance fees. In addition, because hedge funds are subject to limited regulation, have fewer investment constraints, and can often leverage positions, these investors often have more flexibility as activists.

Engagement through activist investing can include meetings with management, shareholder resolutions, letters to management, presentations to other investors, and media campaigns. Activists may also seek representation on a company's board of directors as a way of exerting influence. Proxy contests are one method used to obtain board representation. These contests represent corporate takeover mechanisms in which shareholders are persuaded to vote for a group seeking a controlling position on a company's board of directors. Social media and other communication tools can help activists coordinate the actions of other shareholders.

Voting

The participation of shareholders in general meetings, also known as general assemblies, and the exercise of their voting rights are among the most influential tools available for shareholder engagement. General meetings enable shareholders to participate in discussions and to vote on major corporate matters and transactions that are not delegated to the board of directors. By engaging in general meetings, shareholders can exercise their voting rights on major corporate issues and better monitor the performance of the board and senior management.

Proxy voting enables shareholders who are unable to attend a meeting to authorize another individual (e.g., another shareholder or director) to vote on their behalf. Proxy voting is the most common form of investor participation in general meetings. Although most resolutions pass without controversy, sometimes minority shareholders attempt to strengthen their influence at companies via proxy voting. Occasionally, multiple shareholders may use this process to collectively vote their shares in favor of or in opposition to a certain resolution.

Some investors use external proxy advisory firms, such as Institutional Shareholder Services and Glass Lewis, that provide voting recommendations and reduce research efforts by investors. Portfolio managers need not follow the recommendations of proxy advisers, but these external parties can highlight potential controversial issues. An investor's voting instructions are typically processed electronically via third-party proxy voting agents.

When an investor loans shares, the transaction is technically an assignment of title with a repurchase option; that is, the voting rights are transferred to the borrower. The transfer of voting rights with stock lending could potentially result in the borrower having different voting opinions from the lending investor. To mitigate this problem, some stock lenders recall shares ahead of voting resolutions to enable exercise of their voting rights. The downside of this action would be the loss of stock lending revenue during the period of stock loan recall and potential reputation risk as an attractive lender. Investors, in some cases, may borrow shares explicitly to exercise the voting rights attached. This process is called *empty voting*, whereby no capital is invested in the voted shares.

SHAREHOLDER ENGAGEMENT

1. An investor manages a fund with a sizable concentration in the transportation sector and is interested in meeting with senior management of a small aircraft manufacturer. Discuss how the investor may benefit from

> his or her shareholder engagement activities, as well as from the shareholder engagement of other investors, with this manufacturer.
>
> **Solution**
>
> The investor may benefit from information obtained about the aircraft manufacturer, such as its strategy, allocation of capital, corporate governance, remuneration of directors and senior management, culture, and competitive environment within the aerospace industry. The investor may also benefit as a "free rider," whereby other investors may improve the manufacturer's operating performance through shareholder engagement—to the benefit of all shareholders. Finally, if the investor has non-financial interests, such as ESG, he or she may address these considerations as part of shareholder engagement.

EQUITY INVESTMENT ACROSS THE ACTIVE MANAGEMENT SPECTRUM

7

☐ | describe rationales for equity investment across the active management spectrum

The debate over index-based and active management of equity portfolios has been a longstanding one in the investment community. In reality, the decision between index-based and active management is not an "either/or" (binary) alternative. Instead, equity portfolios tend to exist on a spectrum, ranging from portfolios that closely track a broad, market-capitalization-weighted index to concentrated portfolios of a few equity securities. In some cases, portfolios may resemble a "closet index" in which the portfolio is advertised as actively managed but is essentially an index fund. For an equity manager (or investment firm), there are several considerations for positioning a portfolio along the spectrum.

Confidence to Outperform

An active investment manager typically needs to be confident that she can adequately outperform her benchmark. This determination requires an understanding of the manager's equity investment universe, a competitive analysis of other managers that have a similar investment universe, and appropriate resources (e.g., research staff and access to information).

Client Preference

For equity portfolio managers, client preference is a primary consideration when deciding between index-based or active management. Portfolio managers must assess whether their strategies will attract sufficient funds from clients to make the initiatives viable. Another consideration reflects investors' beliefs regarding the potential for active strategies to generate positive alpha. For example, in some equity market categories, such as large-cap/developed markets, companies are widely known and have considerable equity analyst coverage. For such categories, investors often believe that potential alpha is substantially reduced because all publicly available information is efficiently disseminated, analyzed, and reflected in stock prices.

Exhibit 9 illustrates the prevalence of index-based and active management in US open-end mutual funds and exchange-traded funds (ETFs) by Morningstar equity category. Nearly all assets under management (AUM) in some categories, such as foreign small/mid-cap growth, are managed on an active basis. Other categories, such as large-cap blend, are predominantly managed using an index-based approach.

Exhibit 9: Passive versus Active Equities in US Open-End Mutual Funds and ETFs

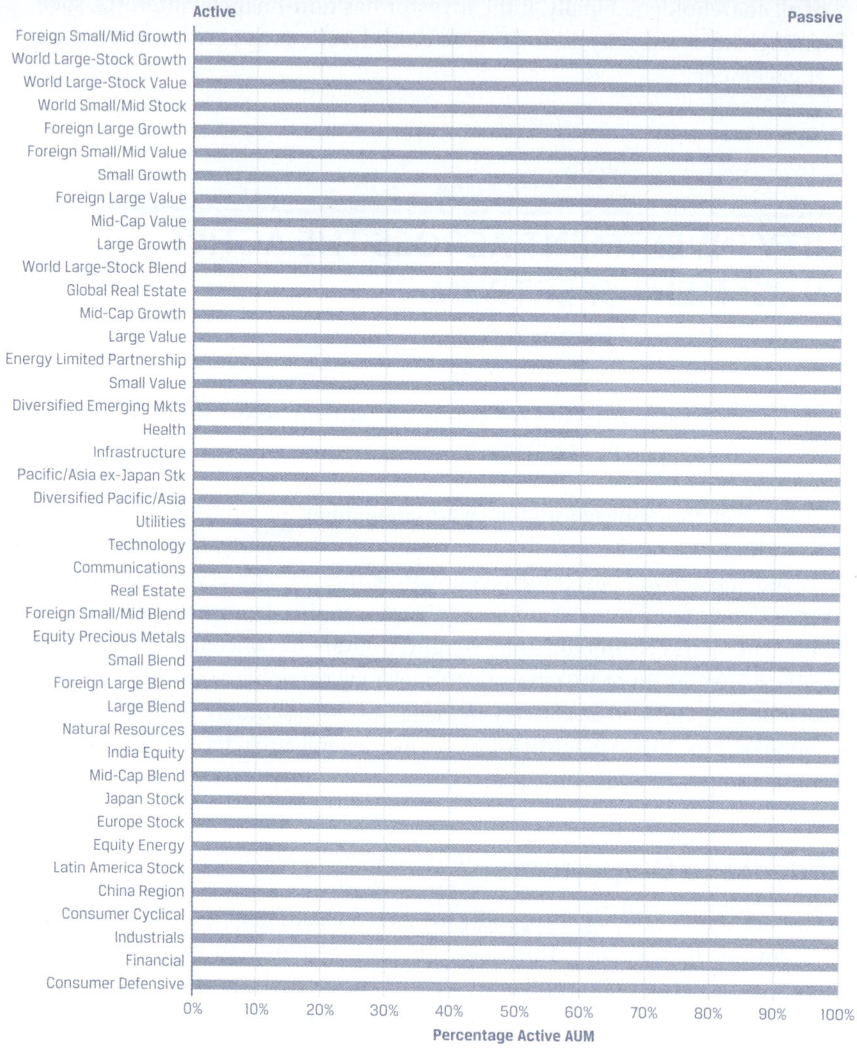

Source: Morningstar Direct. Data as of 31 October 2021.

Suitable Benchmark

An investor or equity manager's choice of benchmark can play a meaningful role in the ability to attract new funds. This choice is particularly relevant in the institutional equity market, where asset owners (and their consultants) regularly screen new managers in desired equity segments. As part of the selection process in desired equity segments, active managers normally must have benchmarks with sufficient liquidity of underlying securities (thus maintaining a reasonable cost of trading). In addition, the number of securities underlying the benchmark typically must be broad enough to generate sufficient alpha. For this reason, many country or sector-specific investment strategies (e.g., consumer defensive companies) are index based.

Client-Specific Mandates

Client-specific investment mandates, such as those related to ESG considerations, are typically managed actively. This active approach occurs because index-based management may not be particularly efficient or cost effective when managers must meet a client's desired holdings (or holdings to avoid). For example, a mandate to avoid investments in companies involved in certain "unacceptable" activities (e.g., the sale of military technology or weapons, tobacco/alcohol, or gambling) requires ongoing monitoring and management. As part of this *exclusionary* (or *negative*) *screening* process, managers need to determine those companies that are directly, as well as indirectly, involved in such "unacceptable" industries. Although ESG investing is typically active, there are a growing number of index-based ESG investment vehicles available.

Risks/Costs of Active Management

As mentioned previously, active equity management is typically more expensive to implement than index-based management. Additionally, "key person" risk is relevant for active managers if the success of an investment manager's firm is dependent on one or a few individuals ("star managers") who may potentially leave the firm.

Taxes

Compared with active strategies, index-based strategies generally have lower turnover and generate a higher percentage of long-term gains. An index fund that replicates its benchmark can have minimal rebalancing. In turn, active strategies can be designed to minimize tax consequences of gains/income at the expense of higher trading costs. One overall challenge is that tax legislation differs widely among countries.

ACTIVE MANAGEMENT SPECTRUM

1. James Drummond, an equity portfolio manager, is meeting with Marie Goudreaux, a wealthy client of his investment firm. Goudreaux is very cost conscious and believes that equity markets are highly efficient. Goudreaux also has a narrow investment focus, seeking stocks in specific country and industry sectors.

   Discuss where Goudreaux's portfolio is likely to be positioned along the active management spectrum.

   Solution

   Goudreaux's portfolio is likely to be managed using an index-based approach. Because she believes in market efficiency, Goudreaux likely believes that Drummond's ability to generate alpha is limited. Goudreaux's cost consciousness also supports index-based management, which is typically less expensive to implement than active management. Finally, Goudreaux's stated desire to invest in specific countries and sectors aligns with index-based approaches.

Advantages of Index-Based Equity Strategies

Many studies over decades support the use of index-based strategies for equities. Renshaw and Feldstein (1960) observed that the returns of professionally managed portfolios trailed the returns on the principal index of that time, the Dow Jones Industrial Average. They also concluded that the index would be a good basis for what they termed an "unmanaged investment company." French (2008) found that the cost of index-based investing is lower than the cost of active management.

Further motivation for index-based investing comes from studies that examine the return and risk consequences of security selection versus asset allocation. Brinson, Hood, and Beebower (1986) found a dominant role for asset allocation rather than security selection in explaining return variability. With index-based investing, portfolio managers eschew the idea of security selection, concluding that the benefits do not justify the costs.

The efficient market hypothesis gave credence to investors' interest in indexes by theorizing that stock prices incorporate all relevant information—implying that after costs, the majority of active investors could not consistently outperform the market. With this backdrop, investment managers began to offer strategies to replicate the returns of stock market indexes as early as 1971.

Index-based management requires substantially fewer personnel, fewer technological resources, and less time spent on analysis and management than active management. Consequently, index-based management fees are generally much lower than fees charged by active managers. This fee differential represents the most significant and enduring advantage of index-based management.

Another advantage is that managers seeking to track an index can generally achieve their objective. Index-based managers model their clients' portfolios to the benchmark's constituent securities and weights as reported by the index provider, in essence replicating the benchmark. The skill of an index-based manager is apparent in the ability to deliver risk-adjusted returns and explain their performance to clients. Gross-of-fees performance among index-based managers tends to be similar, so much of the industry views them as undifferentiated apart from their scope of offerings and client-servicing capabilities.

8   BENCHMARK SELECTION

> ☐   discuss considerations in choosing a benchmark for an equity portfolio

Successful investors choose their performance benchmarks with care. It is surprising that investors who spend countless hours analyzing the investment process and past performance of an active management strategy may accept a strategy based on a benchmark index without question. A comprehensive analysis of the creation methodology and performance of an index is just as important to investors as the analysis of an active strategy.

Indexes for Index-Based Strategies

For an index to become the basis for an equity investment strategy, it must meet three initial requirements. It must be rules based, transparent, and investable.

Examples of rules include criteria for including a constituent stock and the frequency with which weights are rebalanced. An active manager may use rules and guidelines, but it is often impossible for others to replicate the active manager's decision process. Index rules, in contrast, must be objective, consistent, and predictable.

Transparency may be the most important requirement because index-based managers expect to understand the rules underlying their investment choices. Benchmark providers disclose the rules used and constituents in creating their indexes without any black-box methodologies, which assures investors that indexes will continue to represent the intended strategy.

Equity index benchmarks are investable when their performance can be replicated in the market. For example, the FTSE 100 Index is an investable index because its constituent securities can be purchased easily on the London Stock Exchange. In contrast, most investors cannot track hedge fund-of-funds indexes, such as the HFRI series of indexes, because of the difficulty of buying the constituent hedge funds. Another example of a non-investable index is the Value Line Geometric Index, which is a multiplicative average price. The value of the index is obtained by multiplying the prices and taking a root corresponding to the number of stocks. This index is not useful for investing purposes because it cannot be replicated.

Certain features of individual securities make them non-investable as index constituents. Many stock indexes "free-float adjust" their shares outstanding, which means that they count only shares available for trade by the public, excluding those shares that are held by founders, governments, or other companies. When a company's shares that are floated in the market are a small fraction of the total shares outstanding, trading can result in disproportionate effects. Similarly, stocks for which trading volume is a small fraction of the total shares outstanding are likely to have low liquidity and commensurately high trading costs. Many indexes consequently require that stocks have float and average shares traded above a certain percentage of shares outstanding.

Equity index providers include CRSP, FTSE Russell, Morningstar, MSCI, and S&P Dow Jones. These index providers publicize the rules underlying their indexes, communicate changes in the constituent securities, and report performance. For a fee, they may also provide data to investors who want to replicate the underlying basket of securities.

Index providers have taken steps to make their indexes more investable. One key decision concerns when individual stocks will migrate from one index to another. As a stock increases in market capitalization over time, it might move from small-cap to mid-cap to large-cap status (or in the opposite direction if the stock decreases in market capitalization). Some index providers have adopted policies intended to limit stock migration problems and keep trading costs low for investors who replicate indexes. Among these policies are buffering and packeting. **Buffering** involves establishing ranges around breakpoints that define whether a stock belongs in one index or another. As long as stocks remain within the buffer zone, they stay in their current index. For example, the MSCI USA Large Cap Index contains the 300 largest companies in the US equity market. But a company currently in the MSCI USA Mid Cap Index must achieve a rank as the 200th largest stock to move up to the Large Cap Index. Similarly, a large-cap constituent must shrink and be the 451st largest stock to move down to the Mid Cap Index. Size rankings may change almost every day with market price movements, so buffering makes index transitions a more gradual and orderly process.

The effect of buffering is demonstrated with the MSCI USA Large Cap Index during the regularly scheduled May 2016 reconstitution. The MSCI USA Large Cap Index consists of stocks of US-based companies that meet the criterion to be considered for large cap. Further, the MSCI USA Large Cap Index is intended to represent the largest 70% of the market capitalization of the US equity market.

At each rebalance date, MSCI sets a cutoff value for the smallest company in the index and then sets the buffer value at 67% of the cutoff value. During the May 2016 rebalance, the cutoff market capitalization (market cap) of the smallest company in the index was USD15,707 million; so, the buffer value was USD10,524 million, or approximately USD10.5 billion.

Whole Foods Market, a grocery store operating primarily in the United States that was publicly traded before its acquisition by Amazon.com, had experienced a drop in market value from USD15.3 billion in May 2015 to USD10.4 billion in May 2016. The drop in value put the market cap of Whole Foods Market at a lower value than the acceptable buffer. That is, Whole Foods Market was valued at USD10.4 billion, which was below the buffer point of USD10.5 billion. Per the stated rules, Whole Foods Market was removed from the MSCI USA Large Cap Index and was added to the MSCI USA Mid Cap Index.

Packeting involves splitting stock positions into multiple parts. Let us say that a stock is currently in a mid-cap index. If its capitalization increases and breaches the breakpoint between mid-cap and large-cap indexes, a portion of the total holding is transferred to the large-cap index but the rest stays in the mid-cap index. On the next reconstitution date, if the stock value remains large cap and all other qualifications are met, the remainder of the shares are moved out of the mid-cap index and into the large-cap index. A policy of packeting can keep portfolio turnover and trading costs low. The Center for Research in Security Prices (CRSP) uses packeting in the creation of the CRSP family of indexes.

Considerations When Choosing a Benchmark Index

The first consideration when choosing a benchmark index is the desired factor exposures, which is driven by the objectives and constraints in the investor's investment policy statement (IPS). For equity portfolios, the choices to be made include the geographic market segment (broad versus sectors, domestic versus international), size (large, mid, or small market capitalization), style (value, growth, or blend/core), and other constituent characteristics (e.g., high or low momentum, low volatility, and quality) that are considered risk factors. These are the same factors discussed earlier in equity investment universe segmentation.

The choice of geographic market depends on the investor's circumstances. The investor's domicile, risk tolerance, liquidity needs, and legal considerations all influence the decision. For example, the decision will proceed differently for an Indian institutional investor than for a US-based individual investor. In India, while there are 7,000 listed equity securities, the domestic equity universe is less than one-tenth the size of the US equity market by market capitalization, making the Indian investor more likely to invest globally. But a domestic investment does not carry with it the complexities of cross-border transactions.

Market history and empirical studies show that small-cap stocks tend to be riskier and provide a higher long-term return than large-cap stocks, so size is an important consideration. To the extent that a benchmark's return is correlated with this risk factor, the benchmark has exposure to the size factor.

Size classifications range from mega-cap to micro-cap. Classifications are not limited to individual size categories. For example, many indexes seek to provide equity exposure to both small- and mid-cap companies ("smid-cap" indexes). Investors who desire exposure across the capitalization spectrum may use an "all-cap" index. Such indexes do not necessarily contain all stocks in the market; they usually just combine representative stocks from each of the size ranges. Note that a large-cap stock in an emerging market may have the same capitalization as a small-cap stock in a developed country. Accordingly, index providers usually classify company capitalizations in the context of the local market environment.

Equity benchmark selection also involves the investor's preference for exposure on the growth versus value style spectrum. Growth stocks exhibit such characteristics as high price momentum, high P/Es, and high EPS growth. Value stocks, however, may exhibit high dividend yields, low P/Es, and low price-to-book value ratios. Depending on their basic philosophy and market outlook, investors may have a strong preference for growth or value.

Exhibit 10 shows the number of available total-return equity indexes in various classifications available worldwide. Broad market exposure is provided by nearly 79% of all indexes. Developed market indexes are about four times as common as emerging market indexes. The majority of total-return global equity indexes cover the all-cap space or are otherwise focused on large-cap and mid-cap stocks. total-return global equity indexes cover the all-cap space or are otherwise focused on large-cap and mid-cap stocks.

Exhibit 10: Characteristics of Total-Return Global Equity Indexes

Total-return global equity indexes	14,650
Broad market indexes	11,559
Sector indexes	1,171
Not classified	1,920
Of the 14,650 total-return global equity market indexes:	
Developed markets	8,415
Emerging markets	2,210
Developed and emerging markets	4,006
Not classified	194
Of the 14,650 total-return global equity market indexes:	
All-cap stocks	6,806
Large-cap stocks	1,038
Large-cap and mid-cap stocks	5,766
Mid-cap stocks	216
Mid-cap and small-cap stocks	132
Small-cap stocks	682
Not classified	10

Source: Morningstar Direct, October 2021.

Once the investor has settled on the market, capitalization, and style of benchmark, the next step is to explore the method used in constructing and maintaining the benchmark index.

Index Construction Methodologies

Equity index providers differ in their stock inclusion methods, ranging from **exhaustive** to **selective** in their investment universes. Exhaustive stock inclusion strategies are those that select every constituent of a universe, while selective approaches target only those securities with certain characteristics. The FT Wilshire 5000 Index has perhaps the most exhaustive set of constituents in the US market. This market-cap-weighted index includes approximately 5,000 publicly traded stocks from across the market-cap spectrum. In contrast, the S&P 500 Index embodies a selective approach and aims to provide exposure to US large-cap stocks. Its constituent securities are selected using a committee process and are based on both size and broad industry affiliation.

The weighting method used in constructing an index influences its performance. One of the most common weighting methods is market-cap weighting. Each constituent company's weight in the index is calculated as its market capitalization divided by the total market capitalization of all constituents of the index. In the development of the capital asset pricing model, the capitalization-weighted market portfolio is mean–variance efficient, meaning that it offers the highest return for a given level of risk. To the extent a capitalization-weighted equity index is a reasonable proxy for the market portfolio, the tracking portfolio may be close to mean–variance efficient.

A further advantage of the capitalization-weighted approach is that it reflects a strategy's investment capacity. A cap-weighted index can be thought of as a liquidity-weighted index because the largest-cap stocks tend to have the highest liquidity and the greatest capacity to handle investor flows at a manageable cost. Many investor portfolios tend to be biased toward large-cap stocks and use benchmarks that reflect that bias.

The most common form of market-cap weighting is free-float weighting, which adjusts each constituent's shares outstanding for closely held shares that are not generally available to the investing public. The process to determine the free-float-adjusted shares outstanding relies on publicly available information to determine the holders of the shares and whether those shares would be available for purchase in the marketplace. One reason to adjust a company's share count is that strategic holdings by governments, affiliated companies, founders, and employees are seldom traded. Another less common reason is to account for limitations on foreign ownership of a company; these limitations typically represent rules that are generally set up by a governmental entity through regulation.

Adjusting a company's shares outstanding for float can be a complex task and often requires an index provider to work with the issuer's shareholder services unit or to rely on analytical judgements. Although all data used in determining a company's free-float-adjusted shares outstanding are public information, the various index providers often report a different number of float-adjusted shares outstanding for the same security based on methodological differences.

In a *price-weighted* index, the weight of each stock is its price per share divided by the sum of all share prices in the index. A price-weighted index can be interpreted as a portfolio that consists of one share of each constituent company. Although some price-weighted indexes, such as the Dow Jones Industrial Average and the Nikkei 225, have high visibility as indicators of day-to-day market movements, price-weighted investment approaches are not commonly used by portfolio managers. A stock split for any constituent of the index complicates the index calculation. The weight in the index of the stock that split decreases, and the index divisor decreases as well. With its divisor changed, the index ceases to be a simple average of the constituent stocks' prices. For price-weighted indexes, the assumption that the same number of shares is held in each component stock is a shortcoming, because very few market participants invest in that way.

Equally weighted indexes produce the least-concentrated portfolios. Such indexes have constituent weights of $1/n$, where n represents the number of stocks in the index. Equal weighting of stocks in an index can be considered a naive strategy because it does not show preference toward any single stock, but the reduction of single-stock concentration risk and slowly changing sector exposures make equal weighting attractive to many investors.

As noted by Zeng and Luo (2013), broad market equally weighted indexes are factor indifferent and the weighting randomizes factor mispricing. Equal weighting also produces higher volatility than cap weighting, one reason being that it imparts a small-cap bias to the portfolio. Equal weights deviate from market weights most dramatically for large-cap indexes, which contain mega-cap stocks. Constrained market-cap ranges, such as those of mid-cap indexes, even if market weighted, tend to have relatively uniform weights.

Equally weighted indexes require regular rebalancing because immediately after trading in the constituent stocks begins, the weights are no longer equal. Most index providers use a regular reweighting schedule. Standard & Poor's offers the S&P 500 Index in an equally weighted format and rebalances the index to equal weights once each quarter. Therein would appear to lie a misleading aspect of equally weighted indexes: For a 91-day quarter, the index is not equally weighted (albeit, modestly so) for 90/91 = 99% of the time.

Another drawback of equal weighting is its limited investment capacity. The smallest-cap constituents of an equally weighted index may have low liquidity, which means that investors cannot purchase a large number of shares without causing price changes. Zeng and Luo (2013) addressed this issue by assuming that 10% of shares in the cap-weighted S&P 100 and S&P 500 and 5% of shares in the cap-weighted S&P 400 and S&P 600 indexes are currently held in cap-weighted indexing strategies without any appreciable liquidity problems. They then focused on the smallest-cap constituent of each index as of December 2012, and they determined the value that 10% (5%) of its market capitalization represents. Finally, they multiplied this amount by the number of stocks in the index to estimate the total investment capacity for tracking each of the S&P equally weighted equity indexes. Zeng and Luo's estimates are shown in Exhibit 11.

Exhibit 11: Estimated Investment Capacity of Equally Weighted (EW) Equity Indexes

Index	Capitalization Category	Estimated Capacity
S&P 100 EW	Mega-cap	USD176 billion
S&P 500 EW	Large-cap	USD82 billion
S&P 400 EW	Mid-cap	USD8 billion
S&P 600 EW	Small-cap	USD2 billion

Source: Zeng and Luo (2013).

Qin and Singal (2015) showed that equally weighted portfolios have a natural advantage over cap-weighted portfolios. To the extent that any of the constituent stocks are mispriced, equally weighted portfolios will experience return superiority as the stock prices move up or down toward their correct intrinsic value. Because of the aforementioned need to rebalance back to equal weights, Qin and Singal found that the advantage largely vanishes when taxes and transaction costs are considered. However, based on their results, tax-exempt investors could experience superior returns from equal weighting.

Other non-cap-weighted indexes are weighted based on such attributes as a company's or stock's fundamental characteristics (e.g., sales, income, or dividends). Discussed in more detail later, fundamental weighting delinks a constituent stock's portfolio weight from its market value. The philosophy behind fundamental weighting is that although stock prices may become over- or undervalued, the market price will eventually converge to a level implied by the fundamental attributes.

Market-cap-weighted indexes and fundamentally weighted indexes share attractive characteristics, including low cost, rule-based construction, transparency, and invest-ability. Their philosophies, however, are different. Market-cap-weighted portfolios are based on the efficient market hypothesis, while fundamentally weighted indexes look to exploit possible inefficiencies in market pricing.

An important concern in benchmark selection relates to how concentrated the index is. In this case, the concept of the effective number of stocks, which is an indication of portfolio concentration, can provide important information. An index that has a high degree of stock concentration or a low effective number of stocks may be relatively undiversified. Woerheide and Persson (1993) showed that the Herfindahl–Hirschman Index (HHI) is a valid measure of stock-concentration risk in a portfolio, and Hannam and Jamet (2017) demonstrated its use by practitioners. The HHI is calculated as the sum of the constituent weightings squared, as shown in Equation 1:

$$\text{HHI} = \sum_{i=1}^{n} w_i^2, \tag{1}$$

where w_i is the weight of stock i in the portfolio.

The HHI can range in value from $1/n$, where n is equal to the number of securities held, to 1.0. An HHI of $1/n$ would signify an equally weighted portfolio, and a value of 1.0 would signify portfolio concentration in a single security.

Using the HHI, one can estimate the effective (or equivalent) number of stocks, held in equal weights, that would mimic the concentration level of the chosen index. The effective number of stocks for a portfolio is calculated as the reciprocal of the HHI, as shown in Equation 2:

$$\text{Effective number of stocks} = \frac{1}{\sum_{i=1}^{n} w_i^2} = 1/\text{HHI}. \tag{2}$$

Malevergne, Santa-Clara, and Sornette (2009) demonstrated that cap-weighted indexes have a surprisingly low effective number of stocks. Consider the NASDAQ 100, a US-based market-cap-weighted index consisting of 100 stocks. If the index were weighted uniformly, each stock's weight would be 0.01 (1%). In May 2017, the con-stituent weights ranged from 0.123 for Apple, Inc., to 0.0016 for Liberty Global plc—a ratio of 77:1. Weights for the top five stocks totaled almost 0.38 (38%), a significant allocation to those securities. Across all stocks in the index, the median weight was 0.0039 (that is, 0.39%). The effective number of stocks can be estimated by squaring the weights for the stocks, summing the results, and calculating the reciprocal of that figure. The squared weights for the NASDAQ 100 stocks summed to 0.0404, the reciprocal of which is $1/0.0404 = 24.75$, the effective number of stocks. Thus, the 100 stocks in the index had a concentration level that can be thought of as being equivalent to approximately 25 stocks held in equal weights.

EFFECTIVE NUMBER OF STOCKS

1. A market-cap-weighted index contains 50 stocks. The five largest-cap stocks have weights of 0.089, 0.080, 0.065, 0.059, and 0.053. The bottom 45 stocks represent the remaining weight of 0.654, and the sum of the squares of those weights is 0.01405. What are the portfolio's Herfindahl–Hirschman Index and effective number of stocks held?

Solution

The stocks, their weights, and their squared weights are shown in Exhibit 12.

Exhibit 12: Calculations for Effective Number of Stocks

Stock	Weight	Squared Weight
1	0.089	0.00792
2	0.080	0.00640
3	0.065	0.00423
4	0.059	0.00348
5	0.053	0.00281
Stocks 6–50	0.654	Sum of squared weights for Stocks 6–50: 0.01405
Total for Stocks 1–50	1.000	0.03889

The HHI is shown in the final row: 0.03889. The reciprocal of the HHI is $1/0.03889 = 25.71$. Thus, the effective number of stocks is approximately 26. The fact that the portfolio weights are far from being a uniform 2% across the 50 stocks makes the effective number of stocks held in equal weights less than 26.

The stock market crises of 2000 and 2007 brought heightened attention to investment strategies that are defensive or volatility reducing. For example, some income-oriented investors are drawn to strategies that weight benchmark constituents based on the dividend yield of each stock. Volatility weighting calculates the volatility of each constituent stock and weights the index based on the inverse of each stock's relative volatility. A related method produces a minimum-variance index using mean–variance optimization.

Exhibit 13 shows the various methods for weighting the constituent securities of broad-based, non-industry-sector, total-return global equity indexes.

Exhibit 13: Equity Index Constituent Weighting Methods

Weighting Method	Number of Indexes
Market-cap, free-float adjusted	11,211
Market-cap weighted	1,362
Multi-factor weighted	442

Weighting Method	Number of Indexes
Equal weighted	715
Dividend weighted	357

Source: Morningstar Direct, October 2021.

Another consideration in how an index is constructed involves its periodic rebalancing and reconstitution schedule. Reconstitution of an index frequently involves the addition and deletion of index constituents, while rebalancing refers to the periodic reweighting of those constituents. Index reconstitution and rebalancing create turnover. The turnover for developed-market, large-cap indexes that are infrequently reconstituted tends to be low, while benchmarks constructed using stock selection rather than exhaustive inclusion have higher turnover. As seen in Exhibit 14, both rebalancing and reconstitution occur with varied frequency, although the former is slightly more frequent.

Exhibit 14: Index Rebalancing/Reconstitution Frequency for Broad Global Equity Market Total-Return Indexes

Frequency	Rebalancing	Reconstitution
Daily	18	25
Monthly	624	42
Quarterly	9,354	4,389
Semi-annually	1,328	6,235
Annually	2,925	3,102
As needed	147	33

Note: The totals for the Rebalancing and Reconstitution columns differ slightly, as does the index total in Exhibit 14.
Source: Morningstar Direct, October 2021.

The method of reconstitution may produce additional effects. When reconstitution occurs, index-tracking portfolios, mutual funds, and ETFs will want to hold the newly included names and sell the deleted names. The demand created by investors seeking to track an index can push up the stock prices of added companies while depressing the prices of the deleted ones. Research shows that this produces a significant price effect in each case. Depending on the reconstitution method used by index publishers, arbitrageurs may be able to anticipate the changes and front-run the trades that will be made by index-based managers. In some cases, the index rules are written such that the decision to add or remove an index constituent is voted on by a committee maintained by the index provider. Where a committee makes the final decision, the changes become difficult to guess ahead of time. In other cases, investors know the precise method used for reconstitution, so guessing is often successful.

Chen, Noronha, and Singal (2004) found that constituent changes for indexes that reconstitute using subjective criteria are often more difficult for arbitrageurs to predict than indexes that use objective criteria. Even indexes that use objective criteria for reconstitution often announce the changes several weeks before they are implemented. Stocks near the breakpoint between small-cap and large-cap indexes are especially vulnerable to reconstitution-induced price changes. The smallest-cap stocks in the Russell 1000 large-cap index have a low weight in that cap-weighted index. After any of those stocks are demoted to the Russell 2000 small-cap index, they are likely to have some of the highest weights. Petajisto (2010) showed that the process of moving in that direction tends to be associated with increases in stock prices, while movements into the large-cap index tend to have negative effects. He also concluded that transparency in reconstitution is a virtue rather than a drawback.

A final consideration is investability. As stated earlier, an effective benchmark must be investable in that its constituent stocks are available for timely purchase in a liquid trading environment. Indexes that represent the performance of a market segment that is not available for direct ownership by investors must be replicated through derivative strategies, which, for reasons explained later in the curriculum, may be sub-optimal for many investors.

SUMMARY

- Equities can play several roles in an overall portfolio, including providing such benefits as capital appreciation, dividend income, diversification with other asset classes, and a potential hedge against inflation.

- The inclusion of equities in a portfolio can be driven by a client's goals or needs. Portfolio managers often consider the following investment objectives and constraints when deciding to include equities (or asset classes in general, for that matter) in a client's portfolio: *risk objective*, *return objective*, *liquidity requirement*, *time horizon*, *tax concerns*, *legal and regulatory factors*, and *unique circumstances*.

- Investors often segment the equity universe according to (1) size and style, (2) geography, and (3) economic activity.

- Sources of equity portfolio income include dividends, securities lending fees and interest, dividend capture, covered calls, and cash-covered puts (or cash-secured puts).

- Sources of equity portfolio costs include management fees, performance fees, administration fees, marketing/distribution fees, and trading costs.

- Shareholder engagement is the process whereby companies engage with their shareholders. The process typically includes voting on corporate matters at general meetings and other forms of communication, such as quarterly investor calls or in-person meetings.

- Shareholder engagement can provide benefits for both shareholders and companies. From a company's perspective, shareholder engagement can assist in developing a more effective corporate governance culture. In turn, shareholder engagement may lead to better company performance to the benefit of shareholders (as well as other stakeholders).

- Disadvantages of shareholder engagement include costs and time involved, pressure on a company to meet near-term share price or earnings targets, possible selective disclosure of information, and potential conflicts of interest.

- Activist investors (or activists) specialize in taking stakes in companies and creating change to generate a gain on the investment.

- The participation of shareholders in general meetings, also known as general assemblies, and the exercise of their voting rights are among the most influential tools available for shareholder engagement.

- The choice of using active or index-based management is not an "either/or" (binary) decision. Investors may decide to position their portfolios across the active management spectrum based on their confidence in outperforming, client preference, suitable benchmarks, client-specific mandates, risks/costs of active management, and taxes.

- Many active equity portfolio managers are unsuccessful at beating benchmarks and have charged high management fees. Consequently, index-based strategies have increased in popularity.

- Selection of a benchmark is driven by the equity investor's objectives and constraints as presented in the investment policy statement. The benchmark index must be rule-based, transparent, and investable. Specific important characteristics include the domestic or foreign market covered, the market capitalization of the constituent stocks, where the index falls in the value–growth spectrum, and other risk factors.

- The equity benchmark index weighting scheme is another important consideration for investors. Weighting methods include market-cap weighting, price weighting, equal weighting, and fundamental weighting. Market-cap weighting has several advantages, including the fact that weights adjust automatically.

- Index rebalancing and reconstitution policies are important features. Rebalancing involves adjusting the portfolio's constituent weights after price changes, mergers, or other corporate events have caused those weights to deviate from the benchmark index. Reconstitution involves deleting names that are no longer in the index and adding names that have been approved as new index members.

REFERENCES

Brinson, Gary P., L. Randolph Hood, and Gilbert L. Beebower. 1986. "Determinants of Portfolio Performance." *Financial Analysts Journal* 42 (4): 39–44.

Chen, Honghui, Gregory Noronha, and Vijay Singal. 2004. "The Price Response to S&P 500 Index Additions and Deletions: Evidence of Asymmetry and a New Explanation." *Journal of Finance* 59 (4): 1901–30.

French, Kenneth R. 2008. "Presidential Address: The Cost of Active Investing." *Journal of Finance* 63 (4): 1537–1573.

GSIA. 2020. "*Global Sustainable Investment Review 2020.*" www.gsi-alliance.org/.

Hannam, Richard and Frédéric Jamet. 2017. "*IQ Insights: Equal Weighting and Other Forms of Size Tilting.*" SSGA white paper (January).

Kaplan, Steven, Tobias Moskowitz, and Berk Sensoy. 2013. "The Effects of Stock Lending on Security Prices: An Experiment." *Journal of Finance* 68 (5): 1891–936.

Malevergne, Yannick, Pedro Santa-Clara, and Didier Sornette. 2009. "Professor Zipf Goes to Wall Street." *Working Paper Series (National Bureau of Economic Research)* 15295 (August).

Petajisto, Antti. 2010. "*The Index Premium and Its Hidden Cost for Index Funds.*" Working paper, NYU Stern.

Qin, Nan and Vijay Singal. 2015. "*Investor Portfolios When Stocks Are Mispriced: Equally-Weighted or Value-Weighted?*" Working paper, Virginia Tech.

Renshaw, Edward F. and Paul J. Feldstein. 1960. "The Case for an Unmanaged Investment Company." *Financial Analysts Journal* 16 (1): 43–46.

Woerheide, Walt and Don Persson. 1993. "An Index of Portfolio Diversification." *Financial Services Review* 2 (2): 73–85.

Zeng, Liu and Frank Luo. 2013. "*10 Years Later: Where in the World Is Equal Weight Indexing Now?*" White paper, Standard & Poor's.

PRACTICE PROBLEMS

The following information relates to questions 1-8

Three years ago, the Albright Investment Management Company (Albright) added four new funds—the Barboa Fund, the Caribou Fund, the DoGood Fund, and the Elmer Fund—to its existing fund offering. Albright's new funds are described in Exhibit 1.

Exhibit 1: Albright Investment Management Company New Funds	
Fund	**Fund Description**
Barboa Fund	Invests solely in the equity of companies in oil production and transportation industries in many countries.
Caribou Fund	Uses an aggressive strategy focusing on relatively new, fast-growing companies in emerging industries.
DoGood Fund	Investment universe includes all US companies and sectors that have favorable environmental, social, and governance (ESG) ratings and specifically excludes companies with products or services related to aerospace and defense.
Elmer Fund	Investments selected to track the S&P 500 Index. Minimizes trading based on the assumption that markets are efficient.

Hans Smith, an Albright portfolio manager, makes the following notes after examining these funds:

Note 1   The fee on the Caribou Fund is a 15% share of any capital appreciation above a 7% threshold and the use of a high-water mark.

Note 2   The DoGood Fund invests in Fleeker Corporation stock, which is highly rated in the ESG space, and Fleeker's pension fund has a significant investment in the DoGood Fund. This dynamic has the potential for a conflict of interest on the part of Fleeker Corporation but not for the DoGood Fund.

Note 3   The DoGood Fund's portfolio manager has written policies stating that the fund does not engage in shareholder activism. Therefore, the DoGood Fund may be a free rider on the activism by these shareholders.

Note 4   Of the four funds, the Elmer Fund is most likely to appeal to investors who want to minimize fees and believe that the market is efficient.

Note 5   Adding investment-grade bonds to the Elmer Fund will decrease the portfolio's short-term risk.

Smith discusses means of enhancing income for the three funds with the junior analyst, Kolton Frey, including engaging in securities lending or writing covered calls. Frey tells Smith the following:

Statement 1 Securities lending would increase income through reinvestment of the cash collateral but would require the fund to miss out on dividend income from the lent securities.

Statement 2 Writing covered calls would generate income, but doing so would limit the upside share price appreciation for the underlying shares.

1. The Barboa Fund can be *best* described as a fund segmented by:

    A. size/style.

    B. geography.

    C. economic activity.

2. The Caribou Fund is *most likely* classified as a:

    A. large-cap value fund.

    B. small-cap value fund.

    C. small-cap growth fund.

3. The DoGood Fund's approach to the aerospace and defense industry is *best* described as:

    A. positive screening.

    B. negative screening.

    C. thematic investing.

4. The Elmer fund's management strategy is:

    A. active.

    B. index.

    C. blended.

5. Based on Note 1, the fee on the Caribou Fund is *best* described as a:

    A. performance fee.

    B. management fee.

    C. administrative fee.

6. Which of the following notes about the DoGood Fund is correct?

    A. Only Note 2

    B. Only Note 3

    C. Both Note 2 and Note 3

7. Which of the notes regarding the Elmer Fund is correct?

    A. Only Note 4

B. Only Note 5

C. Both Note 4 and Note 5

8. Which of Frey's statements about securities lending and covered call writing is correct?

A. Only Statement 1

B. Only Statement 2

C. Both Statement 1 and Statement 2

The following information relates to questions 9-11

Evan Winthrop, a senior officer of a US-based corporation, meets with Rebecca Tong, a portfolio manager at Cobalt Wealth Management. Winthrop recently moved his investments to Cobalt in response to his previous manager's relative underperformance and high expenses.

Winthrop resides in Canada and plans to retire there. His annual salary covers his current spending needs, and his vested defined benefit pension plan is sufficient to meet retirement income goals. Winthrop desires exposure to global equity markets with a focus on low management costs and minimal tracking error to any index benchmarks. The fixed-income portion of the portfolio may consist of laddered maturities with a home-country bias.

Tong proposes using an index-based equity strategy and reviews the most important requirements for an appropriate benchmark. With regard to investable indexes, Tong tells Winthrop the following:

Statement 1   A free-float adjustment to a market-capitalization-weighted index lowers its liquidity.

Statement 2   An index provider that incorporates a buffering policy makes the index more investable.

Winthrop asks Tong to select a benchmark for the equity allocation that holds all sectors of the Canadian equity market and to focus the portfolio on highly liquid, well-known companies. In addition, Winthrop specifies that any stock purchased should have a relatively low beta, a high dividend yield, a low P/E, and a low price-to-book ratio (P/B).

9. Which of Tong's statements regarding equity index benchmarks is correct?

A. Only Statement 1

B. Only Statement 2

C. Both Statement 1 and Statement 2

10. To satisfy Winthrop's benchmark and security selection specifications, the equity index benchmark Tong selects should be:

A. small capitalization with a core tilt.

B. large capitalization with a value tilt.

    C. mid-capitalization with a growth tilt.

11. What is a problem with Winthrop's benchmark preference?

    A. The geographic limitation to Canadian equities

    B. The exclusion of fixed-income securities given Winthrop's significant exposure

    C. The inclusion of all sectors

SOLUTIONS

1. C is correct. The Barboa Fund invests solely in the equity of companies in the oil production and transportation industries in many countries. The fund's description is consistent with the production-oriented approach, which groups companies that manufacture similar products or use similar inputs in their manufacturing processes.

   A is incorrect because the fund description does not mention the firms' size or style (i.e., value, growth, or blend). Size is typically measured by market capitalization and often categorized as large cap, mid-cap, or small cap. Style is typically classified as value, growth, or a blend of value and growth. In addition, style is often determined through a "scoring" system that incorporates multiple metrics or ratios, such as price-to-book ratios, price-to-earnings ratios, earnings growth, dividend yield, and book value growth. These metrics are then typically "scored" individually for each company, assigned certain weights, and then aggregated.

   B is incorrect because the fund is invested in many countries, which indicates that the fund is not segmented by geography. Segmentation by geography is typically based on the stage of countries' macroeconomic development and wealth. Common geographic categories are developed markets, emerging markets, and frontier markets.

2. C is correct because the fund focuses on new companies that are generally classified as small firms, and the fund has a style classified as aggressive. A widely used approach to segment the equity universe incorporates two factors: size and style. Size is typically measured by market capitalization and often categorized as large cap, mid-cap, or small cap. Style is typically classified as value, growth, or a blend of value and growth.

3. B is correct. The DoGood fund excludes companies based on specified activities (e.g., aerospace and defense), which is a process of negative screening. Negative, or exclusionary, screening refers to the practice of excluding certain sectors or companies that deviate from accepted standards in such areas as human rights or environmental concerns.

   A is incorrect because positive screening attempts to identify companies or sectors that score most favorably regarding ESG-related risks and/or opportunities. The restrictions on investing indicate that a negative screen is established.

   C is incorrect because thematic investing focuses on investing in companies in a specific sector or following a specific theme, such as energy efficiency or climate change. The DoGood Fund's investment universe includes all companies and sectors that have favorable ESG ratings (no specific sectors or screens) but with specific exclusions.

4. B is correct. The fund is managed under the assumption that the market is efficient, and investments are selected to mimic an index. Compared with active strategies, index strategies generally have lower turnover and generate a higher percentage of long-term gains. An index fund that replicates its benchmark can have minimal rebalancing.

5. A is correct. Performance fees serve as an incentive for portfolio managers to achieve or outperform return objectives, to the benefit of both the manager and investors. Several performance fee structures exist, although performance fees tend to be "upward only"; that is, fees are earned by the manager when performance objectives are met, but fund investors are not reimbursed when performance is negative. Performance fees could be reduced, however, following a

period of poor performance. Fee calculations also reflect high-water marks. As described in Note 1, the fee for the Caribou Fund is a 15% share of any capital appreciation above a 7% threshold, with the use of a high-water mark, and is therefore a performance fee.

B is incorrect because management fees include direct costs of research (such as remuneration and expenses for investment analysts and portfolio managers) and the direct costs of portfolio management (e.g., software, trade processing costs, and compliance). Management fees are typically determined as a percentage of the funds under management.

C is incorrect because administrative fees include the processing of corporate actions, such as rights issues and optional stock dividends; the measurement of performance and risk of a portfolio; and voting at company meetings. Generally, these functions are provided by an investment management firm itself and are included as part of the management fee.

6. B is correct because the fund becomes a free rider if it allows other shareholders to engage in actions that benefit the fund, and therefore Note 3 is correct. Investors benefit from the shareholder engagement of others under the so-called free-rider problem. Specifically, assume that a portfolio manager using an active strategy actively engages with a company to improve its operations and was successful in increasing the company's stock price. The manager's actions in this case improved the value of his portfolio and also benefited other investors that own the same stock in their portfolios. Those investors that did not participate in shareholder engagement benefit from improved performance but without the costs necessary for engagement.

Note 2 is incorrect because a conflict of interest arises on the part of the DoGood Fund if it owns shares of a company that invests in the fund. Conflicts of interest can result for a company. For example, a portfolio manager could engage with a company that also happens to be an investor in the manager's portfolio. In such a situation, a portfolio manager may be unduly influenced to support the company's management so as not to jeopardize the company's investment mandate with the portfolio manager.

7. A is correct. For index-based portfolios, management fees are typically low because of lower direct costs of research and portfolio management relative to actively managed portfolios. Therefore, Note 4 is correct.

Note 5 is incorrect because the predictability of correlations is uncertain.

8. B is correct. Writing covered calls also generates additional income for an equity portfolio, but doing so limits the upside from share price appreciation of the underlying shares. Therefore, Statement 2 is correct.

A is incorrect because dividends on loaned stock are "manufactured" by the stock borrower for the stock lender; that is, the stock borrower ensures that the stock lender is compensated for any dividends that the lender would have received had the stock not been loaned. Therefore, Statement 1 is incorrect. Frey is incorrect in stating that the funds would miss out on dividend income on lent securities.

9. B is correct. The three requirements for an index to become the basis for an equity investment strategy are that the index be (a) rule based, (b) transparent, and (c) investable. Buffering makes index benchmarks more investable (Statement 2) by making index transitions a more gradual and orderly process.

A is incorrect because basing the index weight of an individual security solely on the total number of shares outstanding without using a free-float adjustment may make the index less investable. If a stock market cap excludes shares held by founders, governments, or other companies, then the remaining shares more accurately reflect the stock's true liquidity. Thus a free-float adjustment (Statement 1) to a market index more accurately reflects its actual liquidity (it does not lower its liquidity). Many indexes require that individual stocks have float and average shares traded above a certain percentage of shares outstanding.

10. B is correct. To address Winthrop's concerns (sector diversification, liquidity, risk, dividend yield, P/E, and P/B), the benchmark should consist of large-capitalization stocks with a value tilt. A large-capitalization index contains the largest-cap stocks, which tend to have the highest liquidity. Value stocks tend to exhibit high dividend yields and low P/E and P/B ratios.

A is incorrect because small-capitalization stocks tend to be riskier than large-capitalization stocks. Winthrop has a preference for low-beta (low-risk) stocks.

C is incorrect because a growth index will not address Winthrop's preference for a low P/E. Growth stocks exhibit such characteristics as high price momentum, high P/Es, and high EPS growth.

11. A is correct. Winthrop desires exposure to global equity markets, so the equity benchmark should be global as well—for example, the MSCI All Country World Index.

B is incorrect because Winthrop was stating a preference for the benchmark for his equity allocation. Including fixed income would be inappropriate.

C is incorrect because including all sectors is appropriate because his investment strategy includes all sectors.

2

Overview of Fixed-Income Portfolio Management

by Bernd Hanke, PhD, CFA, and Brian J. Henderson, PhD, CFA.

Bernd Hanke, PhD, CFA, is at Global Systematic Investors LLP (United Kingdom). Brian J. Henderson, PhD, CFA, is at the George Washington University (USA).

LEARNING OUTCOMES

Mastery	The candidate should be able to:
☐	discuss roles of fixed-income securities in portfolios and how fixed-income mandates may be classified
☐	describe fixed-income portfolio measures of risk and return as well as correlation characteristics
☐	describe bond market liquidity, including the differences among market sub-sectors, and discuss the effect of liquidity on fixed-income portfolio management
☐	describe and interpret a model for fixed-income returns
☐	discuss the use of leverage, alternative methods for leveraging, and risks that leverage creates in fixed-income portfolios
☐	discuss differences in managing fixed-income portfolios for taxable and tax-exempt investors
☐	describe liability-driven investing
☐	describe the strategy of cash flow matching
☐	describe construction, benefits, limitations, and risk–return characteristics of a laddered bond portfolio

INTRODUCTION

1

Investors often seek regular income from their investments as well as a predetermined date when their capital will be returned. Fixed-income investments offer both.

Fixed-income instruments include a broad range of publicly traded securities (such as commercial paper, notes, and bonds traded through exchanges as well as OTC) and non-publicly traded instruments (such as loans and private placements). Individual loans or fixed-income obligations may be bundled into a pool of assets supporting such instruments as asset-backed securities and covered bonds. Fixed-income portfolio managers combine these diverse instruments across issuers, maturities, and jurisdictions to meet the various needs of investors. We discuss the different roles of fixed-income securities in portfolios and explain the two main types of fixed-income mandates—liability-based mandates and total return mandates—as well as bond market liquidity. We also provide an overview of portfolio measures, instruments, and vehicles used in fixed-income portfolio management and introduce a model of how a bond position's total expected return can be decomposed.

We explain liability-driven investing in fixed-income investing by demonstrating how to best structure a fixed-income portfolio when considering both the asset and liability sides of the investor's balance sheet. We introduce the idea of structuring a bond portfolio to match the future cash liabilities that have bond-like characteristics. Asset–liability management (ALM) strategies are based on the concept that investors incorporate both rate-sensitive assets and liabilities into the portfolio decision-making process. When the liabilities are given and assets are managed, liability-driven investing (LDI), a common type of ALM strategy, may be used to ensure adequate funding for an insurance portfolio, a pension plan, or an individual's budget after retirement. The techniques and risks associated with LDI are introduced and then expanded to cover both cash flow and duration-matching techniques and multiple liabilities. This strategy, known as immunization, may be viewed simply as a special case of interest rate hedging.

2   ROLES OF FIXED-INCOME SECURITIES IN PORTFOLIOS

	discuss roles of fixed-income securities in portfolios and how fixed-income mandates may be classified

Fixed-income securities serve important roles in investment portfolios, including diversification, regular cash flows, and possible inflation hedging. We will briefly review the roles in turn.

Diversification Benefits

Fixed-income investments can provide diversification benefits when combined with other asset classes in a portfolio. Recall that a major reason portfolios can effectively reduce risk is that combining securities whose returns are not perfectly correlated (i.e., a correlation coefficient of less than +1.0) provides risk diversification. Lower correlations are associated with higher diversification benefits and lower risk. The challenge in diversifying risk is to find assets with correlations much lower than +1.0.

Correlations between fixed-income and equity securities vary, but adding fixed-income exposure to portfolios that include equity securities is usually an effective way to obtain diversification benefits. Fixed-income investments may also provide risk reduction because of their low correlations with other asset classes, such as real estate and commodities. Exhibit 1 shows the correlation between the S&P 500 Index and various fixed-income categories based on total returns (monthly) over a 20-year period ending in December 2019.

Exhibit 1: Total Return Correlations between US Fixed Income and Equities

	Fixed-Income Indexes						
	US Aggregate	10Y US Treasury	US Corporate Bonds	Global Aggregate	US TIPS	US High Yield	Emerging Market (USD)
S&P 500	−0.09	−0.30	0.20	0.15	0.02	0.63	0.51

Note: Bloomberg Barclays Indices are shown.
Source: Bloomberg.

Exhibit 2 shows the divergent performance of US equities and bonds from the end of 2019 to the end of March 2020. For example, bonds outperformed equities amid the fears over the global COVID-19 pandemic in Q1 2020.

Exhibit 2: Returns of S&P 500 vs. 10-Year Treasuries, 12 December 2019–31 March 2020

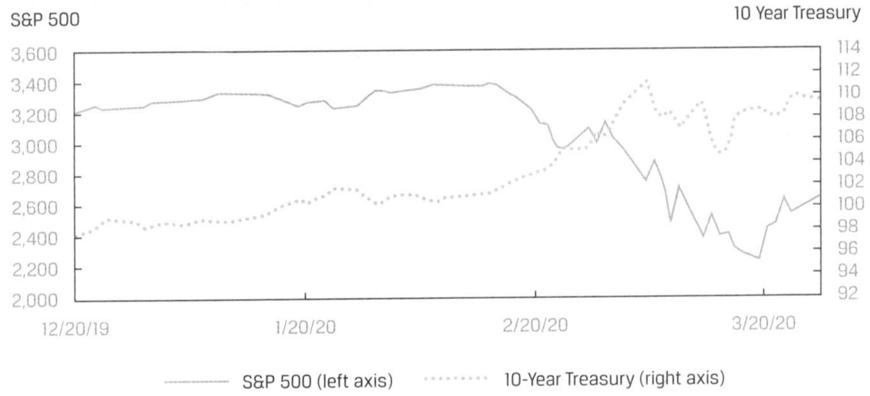

Note: Daily data; constant-maturity 10-year Treasuries used.

Within the fixed-income asset class, the correlation between fixed-income indexes will be driven largely by the interest rate component (i.e., duration) and by geography. Rate changes can explain a significant amount of movement in fixed-income securities prices. The credit component or credit spread will likely result in diversification given differences in sectors, credit quality, and geography. For example, investment-grade securities may exhibit less correlation with below-investment-grade securities and with emerging market securities and equities. The rate component of the return can be isolated by calculating correlations using excess returns (this is more meaningful when evaluating returns across fixed-income sectors). Exhibit 3 shows correlations on an excess return basis between various fixed-income indexes.

Exhibit 3: Excess Return Correlations of Barclays Bloomberg Indices over a 20-Year Period

	US Aggregate	US Corporate	Global Aggregate	US High Yield	Emerging Market (USD)
US Aggregate	1.00				
US Corporate	0.93	1.00			
Global Aggregate	0.88	0.86	1.00		
US High Yield	0.86	0.84	0.76	1.00	
Emerging Market (USD)	0.79	0.76	0.74	0.80	1.00

Notes: Bloomberg Barclays Indices shown. Based on monthly data over 20 years ending December 2019.
Source: Bloomberg.

Importantly, correlations are not constant over time. During a long historical period, the average correlation of returns between two asset classes may be low, but in any period, the correlation can differ from the average correlation. During periods of market stress, investors may exhibit a "flight to quality" by buying safer assets, such as government bonds (increasing their prices), and selling riskier assets, such as equity securities and high-yield bonds (lowering their prices). These actions may decrease the correlation between government bonds and equity securities, as well as between government bonds and high-yield bonds. At the same time, the correlation between riskier assets, such as equity securities and high-yield bonds, may increase.

Note that similar to correlations, volatility (standard deviation) of asset class returns may also vary over time. If interest rate volatility increases, bonds, particularly those with long maturities, can exhibit higher near-term volatility relative to the average volatility over a long historical period. The standard deviation of returns for lower-credit-quality (high-yield) bonds can rise significantly during times of financial stress because as credit quality declines and the probability of default increases, investors often view these bonds as being more similar to equities.

Exhibit 4 shows the annual returns of the S&P 500 versus the Bloomberg Barclays US Corporate High Yield Index over a 20-year period ending in December 2019. It illustrates how the fixed-income sector and equities can behave in a similar way. Recall that both asset classes are strongly linked to the issuer's business performance and fundamentals. Over the 20-year period, the average return was 7.96% and 6.26% for the high-yield index and the S&P 500, respectively, and the standard deviation was 15.54% and 17.02%, respectively. The correlation was 0.69.

Exhibit 4: Relationship between S&P 500 and High-Yield Returns

Percentage (%)

High-Yield Index

S&P 500

11/1999   11/2019

Benefits of Regular Cash Flows

Fixed-income investments typically produce regular cash flows for a portfolio. Regular cash flows allow investors—both individual and institutional—to meet known future obligations, such as tuition payments, pension obligations, and payouts on life insurance policies. In these cases, future liabilities can be estimated with some reasonable certainty. Fixed-income securities are often acquired and "dedicated" to funding those future liabilities. In dedicated portfolios, fixed-income securities are selected with cash flows matching the timing and magnitude of projected future liabilities.

It is important to note that reliance on regular cash flows assumes that no credit event (such as an issuer missing a scheduled interest or principal payment) or other market events (such as a decrease in interest rates that causes an increase in prepayments of mortgages underlying mortgage-backed securities) will occur. These events may cause actual cash flows of fixed-income securities to differ from expected cash flows. If any credit or market event occurs or is forecasted to occur, a portfolio manager may need to adjust the portfolio.

Inflation-Hedging Potential

Some fixed-income securities can provide a hedge for inflation. Bonds with floating-rate coupons can protect interest income from inflation because the market reference rate should adjust for inflation over time. The principal payment at maturity is unadjusted for inflation. Inflation-linked bonds provide investors with valuable inflation-hedging benefits by paying a return that is directly linked to an index of consumer prices and adjusting the principal for inflation. The return on inflation-linked bonds, therefore, includes a real return plus an additional component that is tied directly to the inflation rate. All else equal, inflation-linked bonds typically exhibit lower return volatility than conventional bonds and equities do because the volatility of the returns on inflation-linked bonds depends on the volatility of *real*, rather than *nominal*, interest rates. The volatility of real interest rates is typically lower than the volatility of nominal interest rates that drive the returns of conventional bonds and equities.

Many governments in developed countries and some in developing countries have issued inflation-linked bonds, as have financial and non-financial corporate issuers. For investors with long investment horizons, especially institutions facing long-term liabilities (for example, defined benefit pension plans and life insurance companies), inflation-linked bonds are particularly useful.

Adding inflation-indexed bonds to diversified portfolios of bonds and equities typically results in superior risk-adjusted real portfolio returns. This improvement occurs because inflation-linked bonds can effectively represent a separate asset class since they offer returns that differ from those of other asset classes and add to market completeness. Introducing inflation-linked bonds to an asset allocation strategy can result in a superior mean–variance-efficient frontier.

ADDING FIXED-INCOME SECURITIES TO A PORTFOLIO

Mary is anxious about the level of risk in her portfolio because of a recent period of increased equity market volatility. Most of her wealth is invested in a diversified global equity portfolio.

She contacts two wealth management firms (Firm A and Firm B) for advice. In her conversations with each adviser, she expresses her desire to reduce her portfolio's risk and to have a portfolio that generates a cash flow stream with consistent purchasing power over her 15-year investment horizon.

The correlation coefficient of Mary's diversified global equity portfolio with a diversified fixed-coupon bond portfolio is −0.10 and with a diversified inflation-linked bond portfolio is 0.10. The correlation coefficient between a diversified fixed-coupon bond portfolio and a diversified inflation-linked bond portfolio is 0.65.

The adviser from Firm A suggests diversifying half of her investment assets into nominal fixed-coupon bonds. The adviser from Firm B also suggests diversification but recommends that Mary invest 25% of her investment assets in fixed-coupon bonds and 25% in inflation-linked bonds.

---

1. Evaluate the advice given to Mary by each adviser based on her stated desires regarding portfolio risk reduction and cash flow stream. Recommend which advice Mary should follow, making sure to discuss the following concepts in your answer:

   a. Diversification benefits

   b. Cash flow benefits

   c. Inflation-hedging benefits

   Solution

   Advice from Firm A:

   Diversifying into fixed-coupon bonds would offer substantial diversification benefits in lowering overall portfolio volatility (risk) given the negative correlation of −0.10. The portfolio's volatility, measured by standard deviation, would be lower than the weighted sum of standard deviations of the diversified global equity portfolio and the diversified fixed-coupon bond portfolio. The portfolio will generate regular cash flows because it includes fixed-coupon bonds. This advice, however, does not address Mary's desire to have the cash flows maintain purchasing power over time and thus serve as an inflation hedge.

   Advice from Firm B:

   Diversifying into both fixed-coupon bonds and inflation-linked bonds offers additional diversification benefits beyond that offered by fixed-coupon bonds only. The correlation between diversified global equities and inflation-linked bonds is only 0.10. The correlation between nominal fixed-coupon bonds and inflation-linked bonds is 0.65, which is also less than 1.0. The portfolio will generate regular cash flows because of the inclusion of fixed-coupon and inflation-linked bonds. Adding the inflation-linked bonds helps at least partially address Mary's desire for consistent purchasing power over her investment horizon.

Which Advice to Choose:

Based on her stated desires and the analysis given, Mary should follow the advice provided by Firm B.

Classifying Fixed-Income Mandates

The previous section covered the roles of fixed-income securities in portfolios and the benefits these securities provide. When investment mandates include an allocation to fixed income, investors need to decide how to add fixed-income securities to portfolios. Fixed-income mandates can be broadly classified into liability-based mandates and total return mandates. Exhibit 5 provides a broad overview of the different types of mandates, splitting the universe into two broad categories—liability-based mandates and total return mandates.

Exhibit 5: Fixed-Income Mandates

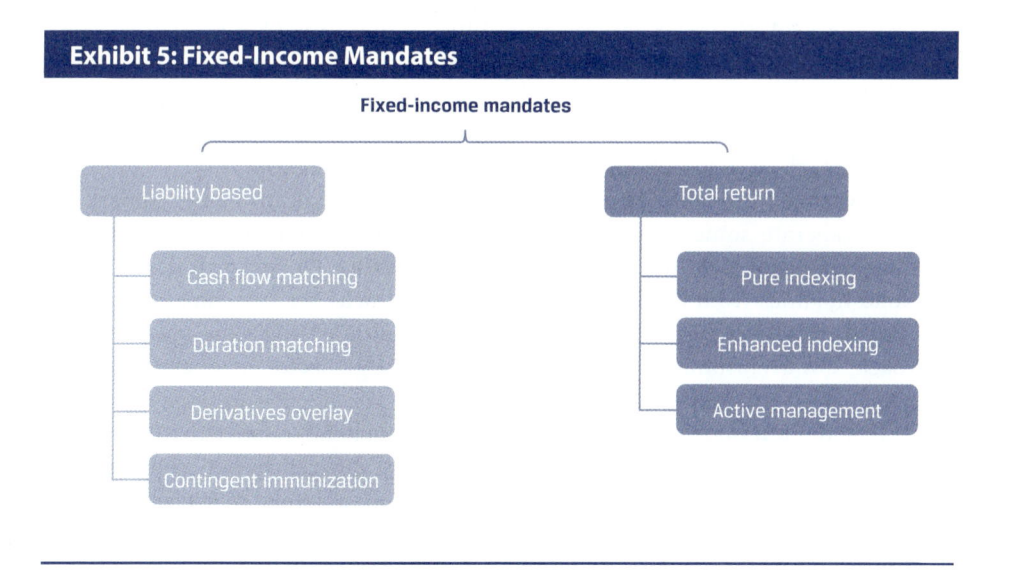

Liability-Based Mandates

Liability-based mandates are investments that take an investor's future obligations into consideration. Liability-based mandates are managed to match or cover expected liability payments (future cash outflows) with future projected cash inflows. As such, they are also referred to as asset/liability management (ALM) or mandates that use liability-driven investments (LDIs). These types of mandates are structured in a way to ensure that a liability or a stream of liabilities (e.g., a company's pension liabilities or those projected by insurance companies) can be covered and that any risk of shortfalls or deficient cash inflows is minimized. **Cash flow matching** is an immunization approach that attempts to ensure that all future liability payouts are matched precisely by cash flows from bonds or fixed-income derivatives. **Duration matching** is an immunization approach that is based on the duration of assets and liabilities. Ideally, the liabilities being matched (the liability portfolio) and the portfolio of assets (the bond portfolio) should be affected similarly by a change in interest rates. The mandates may use futures contracts (such as in a derivatives overlay) and, as in the case of **contingent immunization**—a hybrid approach that combines immunization with an active management approach when assets exceed the present value of liabilities—may allow for active bond portfolio management. Such liability-based mandates, which will be covered in detail later, are important because of their extensive use by such entities as pension plans and insurance companies.

Total Return Mandates

Total return mandates are generally managed to either track or outperform a market-weighted fixed-income benchmark, such as the Bloomberg Barclays Global Aggregate Bond Index. They are used by many types of investors, including individuals, foundations, endowments, sovereign wealth funds, and defined contribution retirement plans. Liability-based and total return mandates exhibit common features, such as the goal to achieve the highest risk-adjusted returns (or perhaps the highest yields to maturity) given a set of constraints. The two types of mandates, however, have fundamentally different objectives. A common total return approach is **pure indexing**. It attempts to replicate a bond index as closely as possible and is sometimes referred to as "full replication." Under this approach, the targeted **active return** (portfolio return minus benchmark return, also known as "tracking difference") and **active risk** (annualized standard deviation of active returns, also known as the benchmark **tracking risk** or tracking error) are both zero. In practice, even if the active risk is zero, the realized portfolio return will almost always be lower than the corresponding index return because of trading costs and management fees. We will explain the limitations of this approach later, in our coverage of index-based strategies.

An **enhanced indexing approach** maintains a close link to the benchmark but seeks to generate some outperformance relative to the benchmark. As with the pure indexing approach, in practice, enhanced indexing allows small deviations in portfolio holdings from the benchmark index but tracks the benchmark's primary risk factor exposures very closely (particularly duration). Unlike the pure indexing approach, however, minor risk factor mismatches (e.g., sector or quality bets) are used in enhanced indexing.

Active management allows larger risk factor mismatches relative to a benchmark index. These mismatches may cause significant return differences between the active portfolio and the underlying benchmark. Most notably, portfolio managers may take views on portfolio duration that differ markedly from the duration of the underlying benchmark. To take advantage of potential opportunities in changing market environments, active managers may incur significant portfolio turnover—often considerably higher than the underlying benchmark's turnover. Active portfolio managers normally charge higher management fees than pure or enhanced indexing managers charge.

Exhibit 6 summarizes the key features of the total return approaches.

Exhibit 6: Total Return Approaches: Key Features

	Pure Indexing	Enhanced Indexing	Active Management
Objective	Match benchmark return and risk as closely as possible	Modest outperformance (generally 20–30 bps) of benchmark while active risk is kept low (typically around 50 bps or lower)	Higher outperformance (generally around 50 bps or more) of benchmark and higher active risk levels
Portfolio weights	Ideally the same as benchmark or only slight mismatches	Small deviations from underlying benchmark	Significant deviations from underlying benchmark
Target risk factor profile	Aims to match risk factors exactly	Most primary risk factors are closely matched (in particular, duration)	Large risk factor deviations from benchmark (in particular, duration; note that some active strategies do not take large risk factor deviations and focus on high idiosyncratic risk)
Turnover	Similar to underlying benchmark	Slightly higher than underlying benchmark	Considerably higher than underlying benchmark

Fixed-Income Mandates with ESG Considerations

Some fixed-income mandates include a requirement that environmental, social, and governance (ESG) factors be considered during the investment process. When considering these factors, an analyst or portfolio manager may look for evidence of whether the portfolio contains companies whose operations are favorable or unfavorable in the context of ESG and whether such companies' actions and resource management practices reflect a sustainable business model. For example, the analyst or portfolio manager may consider whether a company's activities involved significant environmental damage, instances of unfair labor practices, or lapses in corporate governance integrity. For companies that do not fare favorably in an ESG analysis, investors may assume that these companies are more likely to encounter future ESG-related incidents that could cause serious reputational and financial damage to the company. Such incidents could impair a company's credit quality and result in a decline in both the price of the company's bonds and the performance of a portfolio containing those bonds.

THE CHARACTERISTICS OF DIFFERENT TOTAL RETURN APPROACHES

1. A consultant for a large corporate pension plan is looking at three funds (Funds X, Y, and Z) as part of the pension plan's global fixed-income allocation. All three funds use the Bloomberg Barclays Global Aggregate Bond Index as a benchmark. Exhibit 7 provides the characteristics of each fund and the index. Identify the approach (pure indexing, enhanced indexing, or

active management) that is *most likely* used by each fund and support your choices by referencing the information in Exhibit 7.

Exhibit 7: Characteristics of Funds X, Y, and Z and the Bloomberg Barclays Global Aggregate Bond Index

Risk and Return Characteristics	Fund X	Fund Y	Fund Z	Bloomberg Barclays Global Aggregate Bond Index
Average maturity (years)	8.61	8.35	9.45	8.34
Modified duration (years)	6.37	6.35	7.37	6.34
Average yield to maturity (%)	1.49	1.42	1.55	1.43
Convexity	0.65	0.60	0.72	0.60
Quality				
AAA	41.10	41.20	40.11	41.24
AA	15.32	15.13	14.15	15.05
A	28.01	28.51	29.32	28.78
BBB	14.53	14.51	15.23	14.55
BB	0.59	0.55	1.02	0.35
Not rated	0.45	0.10	0.17	0.05
Maturity Exposure				
0–3 years	21.43	21.67	19.20	21.80
3–5 years	23.01	24.17	22.21	24.23
5–10 years	32.23	31.55	35.21	31.67
10+ years	23.33	22.61	23.38	22.30
Country Exposure				
United States	42.55	39.44	35.11	39.56
Japan	11.43	18.33	13.33	18.36
France	7.10	6.11	6.01	6.08
United Kingdom	3.44	5.87	4.33	5.99
Germany	6.70	5.23	4.50	5.30
Italy	4.80	4.01	4.43	4.07
Canada	4.44	3.12	5.32	3.15
Other	19.54	17.89	26.97	17.49

Notes: Quality, maturity exposure, and country exposure are shown as a percentage of the total for each fund and the index. Weights do not always sum to 100 because of rounding. Historical data used as of February 2016.

Source: Barclays Research.

Solution

Fund X most likely uses an enhanced indexing approach. Fund X's modified duration and convexity are very close to those of the benchmark but still differ slightly. The average maturity of Fund X is slightly longer than that of the benchmark, whereas Fund X's average yield to maturity is slightly higher than that of the benchmark. Fund X also has deviations in quality, maturity exposure, and country exposure from the benchmark, providing further

> evidence of an enhanced indexing approach. Some of these deviations are meaningful; for example, Fund X has a relatively strong underweighting in Japan.
>
> Fund Y most likely uses a pure indexing approach because it provides the closest match to the Bloomberg Barclays Global Aggregate Bond Index. The risk and return characteristics are almost identical for Fund Y and the benchmark. Furthermore, quality, maturity exposure, and country exposure deviations from the benchmark are very minor.
>
> Fund Z most likely uses an active management approach because risk and return characteristics, quality, maturity exposure, and country exposure differ markedly from the index. The difference can be seen most notably with the mismatch in modified duration (7.37 for Fund Z versus 6.34 for the benchmark). Other differences between Fund Z and the index exist, but a sizable duration mismatch provides the strongest evidence of an active management approach.

FIXED-INCOME PORTFOLIO MEASURES

3

☐ | describe fixed-income portfolio measures of risk and return as well as correlation characteristics

We first provide a brief review of fixed-income risk and return measures introduced in earlier lessons (Exhibit 8).

Exhibit 8: Bond Risk and Return Measures

Macaulay duration (MacDur)	Macaulay duration is a weighted average of the time to receipt of the bond's promised payments, where the weights are the shares of the full price that correspond to each of the bond's promised future payments.
Modified duration (ModDur)	The Macaulay duration statistic is divided by one plus the yield per period, which estimates the percentage price change (including accrued interest) for a bond given a change in its yield to maturity.
Effective duration (EffDur)	The sensitivity of the bond's price to a change in a benchmark yield curve (i.e., using a parallel shift in the benchmark yield curve (ΔCurve). Effective duration is essential to the measurement of the interest rate risk of a complex bond where future cash flows are uncertain.
Key rate duration (KeyRatDur, also called *partial duration*)	A measure of a bond's sensitivity to a change in the benchmark yield curve at a specific maturity point or segment. Key rate durations help identify "shaping risk" for a bond or a portfolio—that is, its sensitivity to changes in the shape of the benchmark yield curve (e.g., the yield curve becoming steeper or flatter or showing more or less curvature).

Empirical duration	A measure of interest rate sensitivity that is determined from market data—that is, run a regression of bond price returns on changes in a benchmark interest rate (for example, the price returns of a 10-year euro-denominated corporate bond could be regressed on changes in the 10-year German bund or the 10-year Euribor swap rate).
Money duration	A measure of the price change in units of the currency in which the bond is denominated. Money duration can be stated per 100 of par value or in terms of the bond's actual position size in the portfolio. Commonly called "dollar duration" in the United States.
Price value of a basis point (PVBP)	An estimate of the change in a bond's price given a 1 bp change in yield to maturity. PVBP "scales" money duration so that it can be interpreted as money gained or lost for each basis point change in the reference interest rate.
	Also referred to in North America as the "dollar value of an 0.01" (pronounced *oh-one*) and abbreviated as DV01. It is calibrated to a bond's par value of 100; for example, a DV01 of $0.08 is equivalent to 8 cents per 100 points. (The terms PVBP and DV01 are used interchangeably; we will generally use PVBP, but DV01 has the same meaning).
	A related statistic to PVBP, sometimes called "basis point value" (or BPV), is the money duration times 0.0001 (1 bp).
Convexity	A second-order effect that describes a bond's price behavior for larger yield movements. It captures the extent to which the yield/price relationship deviates from a linear relationship.
	If a bond has positive convexity, the expected return of the bond will be higher than the return of an identical-duration, lower-convexity bond if interest rates change.
	This price behavior is valuable to investors, and therefore, a bond with higher convexity might be expected to have a lower yield to maturity than a similar-duration bond with less convexity.
	Nominal convexity calculations assume that the cash flows do not change when yields to maturity change.
Effective convexity (EffCon)	A curve convexity statistic that measures the secondary effect of a change in a benchmark yield curve. A pricing model is used to determine the new prices when the benchmark curve is shifted upward (PV+) and downward (PV−) by the same amount (ΔCurve), holding other factors constant.

Exhibit 8 provides a reminder of convexity and why it is valuable. It is likely to be even more valuable when interest rate volatility is expected to increase. This dynamic tends to drive changes in the shape of the yield curve: As convexity becomes more valuable, investors will bid up prices on the longer-maturity bonds (which have more convexity), and the long end of the curve may decline or even invert (or invert further), increasing the curvature of the yield curve. A helpful heuristic for understanding convexity is that for zero-coupon (option free) bonds, the following are true:

- Macaulay durations increase linearly with maturity: A 30-year zero-coupon bond has three times the duration of a 10-year zero-coupon bond. Convexity is approximately proportional to duration squared; therefore, a 30-year zero-coupon bond has about nine times the convexity of a 10-year zero-coupon bond.

- Coupon-paying bonds have more convexity than zero-coupon bonds: A 30-year coupon-paying bond with a duration of approximately 18 years has more convexity than an 18-year zero-coupon bond. The more widely dispersed a bond's cash flows are around the duration point, the more convexity it will exhibit. For this reason, a zero-coupon bond has the lowest convexity of all bonds of a given duration.

SCALING CONVENTIONS

Convexity statistics must always be interpreted carefully because there is no convention for how they should be presented. When calculating the impact of convexity in approximating returns, the proper accounting for the scaling of convexity is important. Note that some data vendors report the convexity statistic divided by 100, whereas other applications may use the "raw" number.

Portfolio Measures of Risk and Return

Building on the measures of risk and return that apply to individual fixed-income securities, we now provide an overview of measures of risk and return applicable to portfolios of fixed-income securities. We will then illustrate their use in fixed income in a portfolio management scenario and refer to them in the subsequent coverage of liability-driven investing and total return strategies.

Bond portfolio duration is the sensitivity of a portfolio of bonds to small changes in interest rates. Recall that it can be calculated as the weighted average of time to receipt of the aggregate cash flows or, more commonly, as the weighted average of the individual bond durations of the portfolio.

Modified duration of a bond portfolio indicates the percentage change in the market value given a change in yield to maturity. If the modified duration of a portfolio is 15, then for a 100 bp increase or decrease in yield to maturity, the market value of the portfolio is expected to decrease or increase by about 15%. Modified duration of a portfolio comprising j fixed-income securities can be estimated as

$$\text{AvgModDur} = \sum_{j=1}^{J} \text{ModDur}_j \left(\frac{MV_j}{MV} \right),$$

where MV stands for market value of the portfolio and MV_j is the market value of a specific bond.

Convexity of a bond portfolio can be a valuable tool when positioning a portfolio. Importantly, it is a second-order effect; it operates behind duration in importance and can largely be ignored for small yield changes. When convexity is added with the use of derivatives, however, it can be extremely important to returns. This effect will be demonstrated later. Negative convexity may also be an important factor in a bond's or a portfolio's returns. For bonds with short option positions embedded in their structures (such as mortgage-backed securities or callable bonds) or portfolios with short option positions, the convexity effect may be large. For a portfolio comprising j fixed-income securities, it can be estimated as

$$\text{AvgConvexity} = \sum_{j=1}^{J} \text{Convexity}_j \left(\frac{MV_j}{MV} \right).$$

Adding convexity to a portfolio is not costless. Portfolios with higher convexity are most often characterized by lower yields to maturity. Investors will be willing to pay for increased convexity when they expect yields to change by more than enough to cover the amount given up in yield to maturity. Convexity is more valuable when yields to maturity are more volatile. A portfolio's convexity can be altered by shifting the maturity/duration distribution of bonds in the portfolio, by adding individual bonds with the desired convexity properties, or by using derivatives.

Effective duration and convexity of a portfolio are the relevant summary statistics when future cash flows of bonds in a portfolio are contingent on interest rate changes.

$$\text{Effective Duration(EffDur)} = \frac{(PV_-) - (PV_+)}{2(\Delta \text{Curve})(PV_0)}.$$

$$\text{Effective Convexity(EffCon)} = \frac{(PV_-) + (PV_+) - 2(PV_0)}{(\Delta \text{Curve})^2 (PV_0)}.$$

Spread duration is a useful measure for determining a portfolio's sensitivity to changes in credit spreads. Duration indicates the percentage price effect of an interest rate change on a bond, and spread duration measures the effect of a change in yield spread on a bond's price. Spread duration provides the approximate percentage increase (decrease) in bond price expected for a 1% decrease (increase) in credit spread.

Duration times spread (DTS) is a modification of the spread duration definition to incorporate the empirical observation that spread changes across the credit spectrum tend to occur on a *proportional percentage* basis rather than being based on *absolute* basis point changes. This measure, reviewed in detail in a later lesson, weights the spread duration by a factor equal to the current credit spread, increasing the magnitude of expected price changes for a given change in spread.

Portfolio dispersion captures the variance of the times to receipt of cash flows with respect to the duration. It is used in measuring interest rate immunization for liabilities. Whereas Macaulay duration is the weighted *average* of the times to receipt of cash flows, dispersion is the weighted *variance*. It measures the extent to which the payments are spread out around the duration. Convexity is affected by the dispersion of cash flows. Higher cash flow dispersion leads to an increase in convexity.

Correlations between Fixed-Income Sectors

Correlation characteristics refer to the interplay between benchmark rates, spreads, and such factors as currencies. Correlations between fixed-income sectors within a market are likely to be higher than those across markets given country-specific factors, such as central bank policy, economic growth, and inflation. In developed economies, investment-grade securities with a low probability of default are highly correlated with interest rate changes in the sovereign yield curve. Below-investment-grade securities are affected more by changes in spread than by changes in general interest rates and often exhibit stronger correlations with equity markets. Recall that correlations between interest rates and spreads can often be negative. As the economy worsens, interest rates fall and spreads widen, and the reverse occurs when the economy improves. Correlations for global government bonds will be partly driven by changes in interest rates but also by changes in local currency exchange rates.

Use of Measures of Risk and Return in Portfolio Management

We now provide an overview of how portfolio measures may be used by fund managers to reflect their views.

Portfolio Duration in Total Return Mandates

Total return mandates that are actively managed often use a top-down approach to establish the large risk factors in a portfolio combined with a bottom-up approach of individual security selection. The analytics discussed earlier can be used to measure and manage the macroeconomic risk factors in the portfolio. Portfolio managers develop or use a forecast of the direction of the economy and an assessment of the current business, political, and regulatory environment to develop themes that can be reflected in the portfolio. On the basis of expectations for changes in interest rates and the shape of the yield curve, portfolio managers can adjust the duration of a portfolio to reflect their view. For example, if the portfolio manager expects interest rates to rise and the yield curve to steepen, she would reduce the exposure of the portfolio to longer-dated bonds relative to the benchmark, which would reduce portfolio duration. If her view materialized as expected, all else equal, the fund would outperform the benchmark, resulting in active excess returns.

Managing Credit Exposure Using Spread Duration

Portfolio managers often use the spread duration measures introduced earlier to gauge the portfolio's sensitivity to changes in credit spreads. A portfolio manager expecting credit spreads to narrow may wish to increase the spread duration in an actively managed portfolio. The manager may face constraints, such as a target duration, rating-based restrictions, or limits to derivatives use, as part of the investment mandate. A second way to increase the portfolio credit exposure is to reduce the average credit rating of the portfolio; for example, reduce A rated names and increase BBB rated credits. In this case, the duration times spread measure may be a more appropriate measure of portfolio value changes. These active portfolio management tools are addressed in more detail in a later lesson on credit strategies.

The single bond risk and return measures discussed previously at an aggregate level will determine the large risk factors for the portfolio. The portfolio manager will select securities as part of the portfolio construction process to achieve a targeted level of tracking error or active risk relative to a benchmark. The contribution to duration, convexity, spread duration, and DTS of a single bond to the portfolio is weighted by the market value of the position relative to the total market value of the portfolio. The portfolio manager will select a diversified universe of holdings to construct the portfolio in the manner he believes will optimize expected return and risk.

Relative Value Concept

Relative value is a key concept in the active management of fixed-income portfolios that describes the selection of the most attractive individual securities to populate the portfolio with, using ranking and comparing. Portfolio managers analyze and rank securities based on such considerations as valuation, issuer fundamentals, and market technical conditions (supply and demand). This analysis is carried out across sectors, issuers, and individual securities to select securities with the most attractive risk and return profiles. The portfolio manager will establish a time horizon over which the relative value analysis is applied. The single bond characteristics can be used to express an active position relative to the benchmark. For example, each bond has a distinct key rate duration (KeyRateDur) profile. If the portfolio manager wants to establish a bullet or barbell position as part of the active risk decision, bonds with a specific KeyRateDur profile will be selected. Similarly, the portfolio manager can select securities that in aggregate have more/less DTS than the benchmark if she is bullish/bearish on corporate bond spreads. The selection of the most attractive individual securities to populate the portfolio will apply relative value analysis to compare and rank securities. In the context of the efficient frontier, those securities that offer the most expected return for a given level of risk would offer the best relative value.

The positioning of the portfolio reflects the portfolio manager's total return expectations for the market and relative returns versus the benchmark, given his views about both the direction of interest rates and credit spread changes. Diversification considerations ensure that idiosyncratic risks are within acceptable risk parameters.

KNOWLEDGE CHECK

1. Which of the following best describes a measure of sensitivity to changes in yields to maturity for a portfolio of bonds with cash flows contingent on interest rate changes?

   A. Portfolio dispersion

   B. Modified duration

   C. Effective duration

   Solution

   C is correct. Effective duration is particularly relevant in scenarios where the cash flows from the bonds held in a portfolio are contingent on changes in interest rates.

---

2. Which of the following is a true statement about portfolio dispersion?

   A. It can be described as the variance of time to the receipt of cash flows.

   B. The higher the dispersion, the lower the convexity of the portfolio.

   C. It determines the portfolio's sensitivity to changes in credit spreads.

   Solution

   A is correct. Dispersion measures the variance of the time to receive cash flows from the fixed-income securities held.

---

4   BOND MARKET LIQUIDITY

☐ | describe bond market liquidity, including the differences among market sub-sectors, and discuss the effect of liquidity on fixed-income portfolio management

A liquid security is one that may be transacted quickly with little effect on the security's price. Fixed-income securities vary greatly in their liquidity.

Compared with equities, fixed-income markets are generally less liquid. The global fixed-income universe contains many individual bonds with varying features. Many issuers have multiple bonds outstanding with their own unique maturity dates, coupon rates, early redemption features, and other specific features.

An important structural feature affecting liquidity is that fixed-income markets are typically over-the-counter dealer markets. Search costs (the costs of finding a willing counterparty) exist in bond markets because investors may have to locate desired bonds. In addition, when either buying or selling, investors may have to obtain quotes from various dealers to obtain the most advantageous pricing. With limited, although improving, sources for transaction prices and quotes, bond markets are ordinarily less transparent than equity markets. Liquidity, search costs, and price transparency are closely related to the type of issuer and its credit quality. An investor is likely to find that bonds of a highly creditworthy government issuer are more liquid, have greater price transparency, and have lower search costs than bonds of, for example, a corporate issuer with lower credit quality.

Bond liquidity is typically highest immediately after issuance. For example, an on-the-run bond issue (the most recently issued bonds) of a highly creditworthy sovereign entity is typically more liquid than a bond with similar features—including maturity—that was issued previously (an off-the-run bond). On-the-run bonds also trade at narrow bid–ask spreads. This difference in liquidity is typically present even if the off-the-run bond was issued only one or two months earlier. One reason for this phenomenon is that soon after bonds are issued, dealers normally have a supply of the bonds in inventory, but as time goes by and bonds are traded, many are purchased by buy-and-hold investors. Once in the possession of such investors, those bonds are no longer available for trading.

Recall that liquidity typically affects bond yields to maturity. Bond investors require higher yields for investing in illiquid securities relative to otherwise identical securities that are more liquid. The higher yield to maturity compensates investors for the costs they may encounter if they try to sell illiquid bonds prior to maturity. These costs include the opportunity costs associated with the delays in finding trading counterparties as well as the bid–ask spread (which is a direct loss of wealth). The incremental yield to maturity investors require for holding illiquid bonds instead of liquid bonds is referred to as a *liquidity premium*. The magnitude of the liquidity premium normally varies depending on such factors as the issuer, the issue size, and time to maturity. For example, when a 10-year US Treasury bond shifts from on-the-run to off-the-run status, it typically trades at a yield to maturity several basis points above that of the new on-the-run bond.

Liquidity among Bond Market Sub-Sectors

Bond market liquidity varies across sub-sectors. These sub-sectors can be categorized by such key features as issuer type, credit quality, issue size, and maturity. The global bond market includes sovereign government bonds, non-sovereign government bonds, government-related bonds, corporate bonds, and securitized bonds (such as asset-backed securities and commercial mortgage-backed securities). Sovereign government bonds are typically more liquid than corporate and non-sovereign government bonds. Their superior liquidity relates to their large issuance size, use as benchmark bonds, acceptance as collateral in the repo market, and well-recognized issuers. Sovereign government bonds of countries with high credit quality and large issuance are typically more liquid than bonds of lower-credit-quality countries.

Corporate bonds are issued by many different companies and represent a wide spectrum of credit quality. For corporate bonds with low credit quality, it can be difficult to find a counterparty dealer with the securities in inventory or willing to take them into inventory. Bonds of infrequent issuers are often less liquid than the bonds of issuers with many outstanding issues because market participants are less familiar with companies that seldom issue debt. In addition, smaller issues are generally less liquid than larger issues because small bond issues are typically excluded from major bond indexes with minimum issue size requirements.

The Effects of Liquidity on Fixed-Income Portfolio Management

Liquidity concerns influence fixed-income portfolio management in multiple ways, including pricing, portfolio construction, and consideration of alternatives to bonds (such as derivatives).

Pricing

Sources for pricing of recent bond transactions—notably corporate bonds—are not always readily available. Note that price transparency is improving in some bond markets. In the United States, the Financial Industry Regulatory Authority's Trade Reporting and Compliance Engine (TRACE) and the Municipal Securities Rulemaking Board's Electronic Municipal Market Access (EMMA) are electronic systems that help increase transparency in corporate and municipal bond markets, and similar initiatives play a similar role elsewhere for corporate bonds traded on market exchanges, increasing pricing transparency. In most bond markets, however, the lack of transparency in corporate bond trading presents a challenge.

Because many bonds do not trade or trade infrequently, using recent transaction prices to represent current value is not practical. Reliance on last traded prices, which may be out of date and may not incorporate current market conditions, could result in costly trading decisions. The determinants of corporate bond value, including interest rates, credit spreads, and liquidity premiums, change frequently. One solution to the pricing problem is to use matrix pricing that makes use of observable liquid benchmark yields of similar maturity and duration as well as benchmark spreads of bonds with comparable times to maturity, credit quality, and sector or security type to estimate the current market yield and price.

Portfolio Construction

Investors' liquidity preferences directly influence portfolio construction. In constructing a portfolio, investors must consider the important trade-off between yield to maturity and liquidity. As mentioned previously, illiquid bonds typically have higher yields to maturity; a buy-and-hold investor seeking higher returns will often prefer less liquid bonds with higher yields to maturity. In contrast, investors who prefer greater liquidity will likely sacrifice returns and choose more liquid bonds with lower yields to maturity. Some investors may restrict their portfolio holdings to bonds within a certain maturity range. This restriction reduces the need to sell bonds to generate needed cash inflows. In such cases, the investors that anticipate their liquidity needs may give up the higher yield to maturity typically available to longer-term bonds. In addition to avoiding longer-term bonds, investors with liquidity concerns may also avoid small issues and private placements of corporate bonds.

A challenge in bond portfolio construction relates to the dealer market. Bond dealers often carry an inventory of bonds because buy and sell orders do not arrive simultaneously. A dealer is not certain how long bonds will remain in its inventory. Less liquid bonds are likely to remain in inventory longer than liquid bonds. A dealer provides bid–ask quotes (prices at which it will buy and sell) on bonds of its choice. Some illiquid bonds will not have quotes, particularly bid quotes, from any dealer. Several different factors determine the bid–ask spread. Riskier bonds often have higher bid–ask spreads because of dealers' aversion to hold those bonds in inventory. Because bond dealers must finance their inventories, the dealers incur costs in both obtaining funding and holding those bonds. Dealers seek to cover their costs and make a profit through the bid–ask spread, and therefore, the spread will be higher for illiquid bonds that are likely to remain in inventory longer.

A bond's bid–ask spread is also a function of the bond's complexity and how easily market participants can analyze the issuer's creditworthiness. Bid–ask spreads in government bonds are generally lower than spreads in corporate bonds or structured financial instruments, such as asset-backed securities. Conventional (plain vanilla) corporate bonds normally have lower spreads than corporate bonds with non-standard or complex features, such as embedded options. Bonds of large, high-credit-quality corporations that have many outstanding bond issues are the most liquid among corporate bonds, and thus they have relatively low bid–ask spreads compared with smaller, less creditworthy companies.

Illiquidity directly increases bid–ask spreads of bonds, which increases the cost of trading. Higher transaction costs reduce the benefits of active portfolio decisions and may decrease portfolio managers' willingness to adjust their portfolios to take advantage of opportunities that present themselves. As an example to quantify trading costs, if a corporate bond with a 15-year duration is being quoted by dealers with a 10 bp bid–ask spread, the cost impact to the portfolio is approximately 1.50% (0.0010 × 15 × 100 = 1.50%). The portfolio manager would buy the bond at $100, and when the portfolio is priced (typically at bid or the midpoint between the bid and the ask), the bond would have a value of $98.50, reducing the total portfolio return. This is the price that would be realized if the bond were sold, holding other factors constant. To mitigate trading costs, investors can participate in the primary or new issue market where bonds are typically issued at a discount to the price at which a similar issue trades in the secondary market.

KNOWLEDGE CHECK

1. Rank the following instruments from the usually most liquid to the least liquid:

   - Low-credit-quality corporate bond
   - Recently issued on-the-run sovereign bond issued by a high-credit-quality government
   - High-credit-quality corporate bond
   - Sovereign bond issued a year ago by a high-credit-quality government

   Solution

   - Recently issued on-the-run sovereign bond issued by a high-credit-quality government
   - Sovereign bond issued a year ago by a high-credit-quality government
   - High-credit-quality corporate bond
   - Low-credit-quality corporate bond

Alternatives to Direct Investment in Bonds

Because transacting in fixed-income securities may present challenges resulting from low liquidity in many segments of the fixed-income market, fund managers may use alternative methods to establish bond market exposures. The methods we outline are applicable across different fixed-income mandates. We will take a more in-depth look at the ones particularly relevant to passive and liability-driven mandates later as part of our coverage dedicated to such mandates. Next, we provide an overview of the most common methods—specifically, mutual funds, exchange-traded funds (ETFs), exchange-traded derivatives, and OTC derivatives. In considering direct versus indirect investments, the asset manager must weigh the ongoing fees associated with such instruments as mutual funds and ETFs against the bid–offer cost of direct investment in the underlying securities.

ETFs and mutual funds. These products provide an alternative to transacting in individual bonds. Mutual funds are pooled investment vehicles whose shares or units represent a proportional share in the ownership of the assets in an underlying portfolio. In the case of open-end mutual funds, new shares may be redeemed or issued at the fund's net asset value (NAV) established at the end of each trading day based on the fund's valuation of all existing assets minus liabilities, divided by the total number of shares outstanding. Bond mutual fund investors enjoy the advantage of being able to redeem holdings at the fund's NAV rather than needing to sell illiquid positions. The benefit from economies of scale is usually the overriding factor for smaller investors in their choice of a bond mutual fund over direct investment. Because bonds often trade at a minimum lot size of USD1 million or higher per bond, successful replication of a broad index or construction of a diversified actively managed portfolio could easily require hundreds of millions of dollars in investments. Therefore, the greater diversification across fixed-income markets achievable by a larger fund may be well worth the additional cost in terms of an upfront load in some instances and an annual management fee.

Although investors benefit from increased diversification, the fund must outline its stated investment objectives and periodic fees, but actual security holdings are available only on a retroactive basis. Unlike the underlying securities, bond mutual funds have no maturity date; the fund manager continuously purchases and sells bonds to track index performance, and monthly interest payments fluctuate based on fund holdings.

Exchange-traded funds share some mutual fund characteristics but have more tradability features. Investors benefit from greater bond ETF liquidity versus mutual funds given their availability to be purchased or sold throughout the trading day.

Exchange-traded derivatives. Futures and options on futures provide exposure to underlying bonds. Being exchange-traded, they involve financial instruments with standardized terms, documentation, and pricing traded on an organized exchange. Exchange-traded products also include interest rate products and options for interest rate–related ETFs.

OTC derivatives. Interest rate swaps are the most widely used OTC derivative worldwide and entail customized arrangements between two counterparties that reference an underlying market price or index. Some interest rate swaps are liquid, with multiple swap dealers posting competitive two-way quotes. In addition to interest rate swaps, fixed-income portfolio managers use inflation swaps, total return swaps, and credit swaps to alter their portfolio exposure. Because they trade over the counter, swaps may be tailored to an investor's specific needs.

A total return swap (TRS), a common over-the-counter portfolio derivative strategy, combines elements of interest rate swaps and credit derivatives. Similar to an interest rate swap, a total return swap involves the periodic exchange of cash flows between two parties for the life of the contract. Unlike an interest rate swap, in which counterparties exchange a stream of fixed cash flows versus a floating-rate benchmark such as the MRR (the market reference rate) to transform fixed assets or liabilities to a variable exposure, a TRS has a periodic exchange based on a reference obligation that is an underlying equity, commodity, or bond index. Exhibit 9 outlines the most basic TRS structure. The **total return receiver** receives both the cash flows from the underlying index and any appreciation in the index over the period in exchange for paying the MRR plus a predetermined spread. The **total return payer** is responsible for paying the reference obligation cash flows and return to the receiver but will also be compensated by the receiver for any depreciation in the index or default losses incurred by the portfolio.

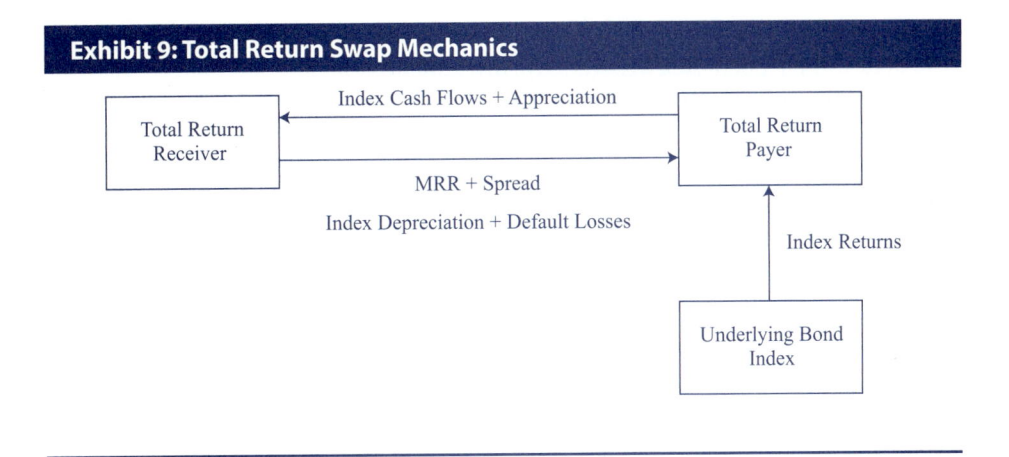

Exhibit 9: Total Return Swap Mechanics

The TRS transaction is an over-the-counter derivative contract based on an ISDA (International Swaps and Derivatives Association) master agreement. This contract specifies a notional amount, periodic cash flows, and final maturity, as well as the credit and other legal provisions related to the transaction. The historical attractiveness of using TRS stemmed from the efficient risk transfer on the reference obligation from one counterparty to another on a confidential basis without requiring the full cash outlay associated with the mutual fund or ETF purchase. In fact, another way to think of the TRS is as a synthetic secured financing transaction in which the investor (the total return receiver) benefits from more-advantageous funding terms faced by a dealer (typically the total return payer) offering to facilitate the transaction.

The potential for both a smaller initial cash outlay and lower swap bid–offer costs compared with the transaction costs of direct purchase or use of a mutual fund or ETF are the most compelling reasons to consider a TRS to add fixed-income exposure. As a funding cost arbitrage transaction, the TRS can allow investors to gain particular access to subsets of the fixed-income markets, such as bank loans or high-yield instruments for which cash markets are relatively illiquid or the cost and administrative complexity of maintaining a portfolio of these instruments is prohibitive for the investor.

That said, several considerations may offset these benefits in a few instances:

- The investor does not legally own the underlying assets but, rather, has a combined synthetic long position in the market and the credit risk of the index that is contingent on the performance of the total return payer. The total return receiver must both perform the necessary credit due diligence on its counterparty and face the rollover risk at maturity of having the ability to renew the contract with reasonable pricing and business terms in the future.

- Structural changes to the market and greater regulatory oversight, particularly capital rules affecting dealers, have raised the cost and increased the operational burden of these transactions because of the need to collateralize mark-to-market positions frequently and within a shorter timeframe.

A MODEL FOR FIXED-INCOME RETURNS

5

☐ | describe and interpret a model for fixed-income returns

Investors often have views on future changes in the yield curve and structure or restructure their portfolios accordingly. Investment strategies should be evaluated in terms of expected returns rather than just yields to maturity. A bond's yield to maturity provides an incomplete measure of its expected return. Instead, expected fixed-income returns consist of several different components in addition to yield to maturity. Examining these components leads to a better understanding of the driving forces behind expected returns—on individual bonds and fixed-income portfolios. The focus is on *expected* as opposed to *realized* returns, which may be decomposed in a similar manner.

Decomposing Expected Returns

Decomposing expected fixed-income returns allows an investor to differentiate among several important return components. At the most general level, expected returns, denoted as $E(R)$, can be decomposed (approximately) in the following manner:

$E(R) \approx$ Coupon income

$+/-$ Rolldown return

$+/- E(\Delta$Price due to investor's view of benchmark yield)

$+/- E(\Delta$Price due to investor's view of yield spreads)

$+/- E(\Delta$Price due to investor's view of currency value changes),

where $E(...)$ represents effects on expected returns based on expectations of the item in parentheses and Δ represents "change." The decomposition holds only approximately and ignores taxes (note that some of the material on decomposing expected returns has been adapted from Hanke and Seals (2010).

Coupon Income

Coupon income is the income that an investor receives from coupon payments relative to the bond's price and interest on reinvestment income. Assuming there is no reinvestment income, coupon income equals a bond's annual current yield.

Coupon income (or Current yield) = Annual coupon payment/Current bond price.

Rolldown Return

The rolldown return, sometimes referred to as "rolldown and carry return," results from the bond "rolling down" the yield curve as the time to maturity decreases (see Exhibit 10), assuming zero interest rate volatility. Bond prices change as time passes even if the market discount rate remains the same. As time passes, a bond's price typically moves closer to par. This price movement is illustrated by the constant-yield price trajectory, which shows the "pull to par" effect on the price of a bond trading at a premium or a discount to par value. If the issuer does not default, the price of a bond approaches par value as its time to maturity approaches zero.

Exhibit 10: Rolling down the Yield Curve Effect

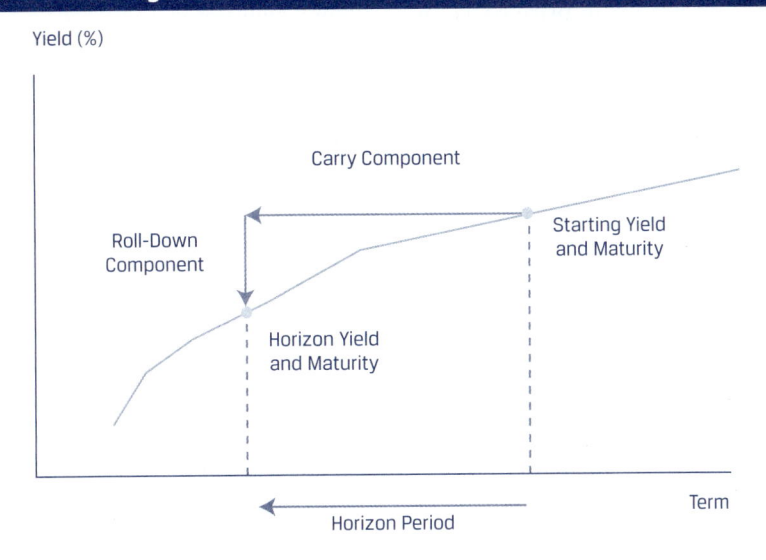

The rolldown return equals the bond's percentage price change assuming an unchanged yield curve over the strategy horizon. Bonds trading at a premium to their par value will experience capital losses during their remaining life, and bonds trading at a discount relative to their par value will experience capital gains during their remaining life.

To compute the rolldown return, the bond has to be revalued at the end of the strategy horizon assuming an unchanged yield curve. Then the rolldown return is as follows:

$$\text{Rolldown return}$$
$$= \frac{\left(\text{Bond price}_{End\text{-}of\text{-}horizonperiod} - \text{Bond price}_{Beginning\text{-}of\text{-}horizonperiod}\right)}{\text{Bond price}_{Beginning\text{-}of\text{-}horizonperiod}}.$$

The sum of the coupon income and the rolldown return may be referred to as the bond's *rolling yield*.

Views of Benchmark Yields

The expected change in price based on investor's views of benchmark yields to maturity and the term structure of yield volatility reflects an investor's expectation of changes in yields to maturity and yield volatility over the investment horizon. This expected change is zero if the investor expects yield curves and yield volatility to remain unchanged. Assuming the investor does expect a change in the yield curve, this expected return component is computed as follows:

$E(\Delta$Price based on investor's views of yields and yield volatility)

$$= (-\text{ModDur} \times \Delta\text{Yield}) + [\tfrac{1}{2} \times \text{Convexity} \times (\Delta\text{Yield})^2],$$

where ModDur is the modified duration of a bond, ΔYield is the expected change in yield to maturity, and Convexity reflects the second-order effect of the price–yield relationship. Note that for bonds with embedded options, the duration and convexity measures used should be effective duration and effective convexity. Also, in contrast to fixed-coupon bonds, floating-rate notes have a modified duration that is largely due to spread changes, as described in detail later.

Views of Yield Spreads

The expected change in price based on investor's views of yield spreads reflects an investor's expectation of changes in market credit spreads over the investment horizon. When economic or credit conditions are improving, spreads are typically said to tighten, thereby reducing the required yield to maturity on the bond. Deteriorating conditions would conversely result in higher required yields to maturity. This component of expected return reflects general market conditions rather than any spread changes due to issuer-specific (or idiosyncratic) risk and is computed as follows:

$E(\Delta$Price based on investor's views of yield spreads)

$$= (-\text{ModSpreadDur} \times \Delta\text{Spread}) + [\frac{1}{2} \times \text{Convexity} \times (\Delta\text{Yield})^2].$$

Yield spreads can also fluctuate because of idiosyncratic risk. Credit migration refers to credit quality changes that may result in an issuer downgrade or upgrade. This can result in either lower spreads for higher ratings or higher spreads for lower ratings affecting the expected return on bonds. Higher-quality credits tend to have low probabilities of default but can experience changes in bond prices due to an anticipated or actual migration. The price impact is calculated in the same way as noted previously for market changes in yield to maturity. Note that investors face price declines on non-defaulted bonds if spreads widen. Yearly default rates can vary significantly and are more severe for speculative-grade (high-yield) issues.

Views of Currency Value Changes

If an investor holds bonds denominated in a currency other than her home currency, she also needs to factor in any expected fluctuations in the currency exchange rate or expected currency gains or losses over the investment horizon. The magnitude and direction of the change in the exchange rate can be based on a variety of factors, including the manager's own view, results from surveys, or a quantitative model output. It can also be based on the exchange rate that can be locked in over the investment horizon using currency forwards.

Return measured in functional currency terms (domestic currency returns of foreign currency assets) can be shown as $R_{DC} = (1 + R_{FC})(1 + R_{FX}) - 1$ for a single asset or

$$R_{DC} = \sum_{i=1}^{n} \omega_i (1 + R_{FC,i})(1 + R_{FX,i}) - 1$$

for a portfolio, where R_{DC} and R_{FC} are the domestic and foreign currency returns expressed as a percentage, R_{FX} is the percentage change of the domestic currency versus the foreign currency, and ω_i is the respective portfolio weight of each foreign currency asset (in domestic currency terms), with the sum of ω_i equal to 1. In the context of the return decomposition framework, R_{DC} simply combines the third factor, $E(\Delta$Price due to investor's view of benchmark yield), and the fifth factor, $(+/- E(\Delta$Functional currency value), in the expected fixed-income return model.

DECOMPOSING EXPECTED RETURNS

1. Ann Smith works for a US investment firm in its London office. She manages the firm's British pound–denominated corporate bond portfolio. Her department head in New York City has asked Smith to make a presentation on next year's total expected return of her portfolio in US dollars and the components of this return. Exhibit 11 shows information on the portfolio and Smith's expectations for the next year. Expected return (for the bond portfolio) and its components are on an annualized basis, and any

potential coupons are assumed to be paid annually. Calculate the total expected return of Smith's bond portfolio, assuming no reinvestment income.

Exhibit 11: Portfolio Characteristics and Expectations

Notional principal of portfolio (in millions)	£100
Average bond coupon payment (per £100 par value)	£2.75
Coupon frequency	Annual
Investment horizon	1 year
Current average bond price	£97.12
Expected average bond price in one year (assuming an unchanged yield curve)	£97.285
Average bond convexity in one year	18
Average bond modified duration in one year	3.70
Expected average benchmark yield-to-maturity change	0.26%
Expected change in spread (spread expected to narrow in this scenario)	−0.10%
Expected currency losses (£ depreciation versus US$)	0.50%

Solution

The portfolio's coupon income is 2.83%. The portfolio has an average coupon of £2.75 on a £100 notional principal and currently trades at £97.12. The coupon income over a one-year horizon is 2.83% = £2.75/£97.12.

In one year's time, assuming an unchanged yield curve and zero interest rate volatility, the rolldown return is 0.15% = (£97.285 − £97.12)/£97.12.

The rolling yield, which is the sum of the coupon income and the rolldown return, is 3.00% = 2.98% + 0.15%.

The expected change in price based on Smith's views of benchmark yields to maturity is −0.96%, calculated as follows: The bond portfolio has a modified duration of 3.70 and a convexity statistic of 18. Smith expects an average benchmark yield-to-maturity change of 0.26%. Smith expects to incur a decrease in prices and a reduction in return based on her rate view. The expected change in price based on Smith's views of yields to maturity and yield spreads is thus −0.0096 = (−3.70 × 0.0026) + [½ × 18 × (0.0026)^2]. So, the expected reduction in return based on Smith's rate view is 0.96%.

Smith expects an impact from the 0.1% change (narrowing in this scenario) in spread in her well-diversified investment-grade bond portfolio. The impact on the expected return is, therefore, 0.37% = [−3.70 × (−0.0010)] + [1/2 × 18 × (−0.0010)^2].

Smith expects the British pound, the foreign currency in which her bond position is denominated, to depreciate by an annualized 50 bps (or 0.5%) over the investment horizon against the US dollar, the home country currency. The expected currency loss to the portfolio is thus 0.50%.

The total expected return on Smith's bond position is 1.91%, as summarized in Exhibit 12.

Exhibit 12: Return Component Calculations

Return Component	Formula	Calculation
Coupon income	Annual coupon payment/Current bond price	£2.75/£97.12 = 2.83%
+ Rolldown return	$$\frac{\left(\text{Bond price}_{End-of-horizon\ period} - \text{Bond price}_{Beginning-of-horizon\ period}\right)}{\text{Bond price}_{Beginning-of-horizon\ period}}$$	(£97.285 – £97.12)/£97.12 = 0.17%
= Rolling yield	Coupon income + Rolldown return	2.83% + 0.17% = 3.00%
+/– E(ÄPrice* based on Smith's benchmark yield view)	$(-\text{ModDur} \times \Delta\text{Yield})$ $+ [\frac{1}{2} \times \text{Convexity} \times (\Delta\text{Yield})^2]$	(-3.70×0.0026) $+ [\frac{1}{2} \times 18 \times (0.0026)^2] = -0.96\%$
+/– E(ÄPrice due to investor's view of yield spreads)	$(-\text{ModDur} \times \Delta\text{Spread})$ $+ [\frac{1}{2} \times \text{Convexity} \times (\Delta\text{Spread})^2]$	$(-3.70 \times -0.0010) + [1/2 \times 18 \times (-0.0010)^2]$ $= 0.37\%$
+/– E(Currency gains or losses)	Given	–0.50%
= Total expected return		1.91%

Note that the change in price in the context of this example refers to the change in portfolio value.

Estimation of the Inputs

In the model for fixed-income returns discussed earlier, some of the individual expected return components can be more easily estimated than others. The easiest component to estimate is the coupon income. The return model's most uncertain individual components are the investor's views of changes in benchmark yields and yield spreads and expected currency movements. These components are normally based on purely qualitative (subjective) criteria, a quantitative model (including surveys), or a mixture of the two. Although a quantitative approach may seem more objective, there are several quantitative models that can be used, each with different methodologies associated with the underlying calculations.

Limitations of the Expected Return Decomposition

The return decomposition just described is an approximation; only duration and convexity are used to summarize the price–yield relationship. In addition, the model implicitly assumes that all intermediate cash flows of the bond are reinvested at the yield to maturity, which results in different coupon reinvestment rates for different bonds.

The model also ignores other factors, such as local richness/cheapness effects and potential financing advantages. Local richness/cheapness effects are deviations of individual maturity segments from the fitted yield curve, which were obtained using a curve estimation technique. Yield curve estimation techniques produce relatively smooth curves, and there are likely slight deviations from the curve in practice. There may be financing advantages to certain maturity segments in the repo market. The repo market provides a form of short-term borrowing for dealers in government securities who sell government bonds to other market participants overnight and buy them back, typically on the following day. In most cases, local richness/cheapness effects and financing advantages tend to be relatively small and are thus not included in the expected return decomposition model.

> **COMPONENTS OF EXPECTED RETURN**
>
> Kevin Tucker manages a global bond portfolio. At a recent investment committee meeting, Tucker discussed his portfolio's domestic (very high-credit-quality) government bond allocation with another committee member. The other committee member argued that if the yield curve is expected to remain unchanged, the only determinants of a domestic government bond's expected return are its coupon payment and its price.
>
> 1. Explain why the other committee member is incorrect, including a description of the additional expected return components that need to be included.
>
>   **Solution**
>
>   A bond's coupon payment and its price allow only its coupon income to be computed. Coupon income is an incomplete measure of a bond's expected return. For domestic government bonds, in addition to coupon income, the rolldown return needs to be considered. The rolldown return results from the fact that bonds are pulled to par as the time to maturity decreases, even if the yield curve is expected to remain unchanged over the investment horizon. Currency gains and losses would also need to be considered in a global portfolio. Because the portfolio consists of government bonds with very high credit quality, the view on yield spreads is less relevant for Tucker's analysis. For government and corporate bonds with lower credit quality, however, yield spreads would also need to be considered as additional return components.

LEVERAGE

6

☐ | discuss the use of leverage, alternative methods for leveraging, and risks that leverage creates in fixed-income portfolios

Leverage is the use of borrowed capital to increase the magnitude of portfolio positions, and it is an important tool for fixed-income portfolio managers. By using leverage, fixed-income portfolio managers may be able to increase portfolio returns relative to what they can achieve in unleveraged portfolios.

Managers often have mandates that place limits on the types of securities they may hold. Simultaneously, managers may have return objectives that are difficult to achieve, especially during low–interest rate environments. Through the use of leverage, a manager can increase his investment exposure and may be able to increase the returns to fixed-income asset classes that typically have low returns. The increased return potential, however, comes at the cost of increased risk: If losses occur, these would be higher than in unleveraged positions.

Using Leverage

Leverage increases portfolio returns if the securities in the portfolio have returns higher than the cost of borrowing. In an unleveraged portfolio, the return on the portfolio (r_p) equals the return on invested funds (r_I). When the manager uses leverage, however, the invested funds exceed the portfolio's equity by the amount that is borrowed.

The leveraged portfolio return, r_p, can be expressed as the total investment gains per unit of invested capital:

$$r_P = \frac{\text{Portfolio return}}{\text{Portfolio equity}} = \frac{r_I \times (V_E + V_B) - (V_B \times r_B)}{V_E},$$

where

V_E = Value of the portfolio's equity

V_B = Borrowed funds

r_B = Borrowing rate (cost of borrowing)

r_I = Return on the invested funds (investment returns)

r_p = Return on the levered portfolio

The numerator represents the total return on the portfolio assets, $r_I \times (V_E + V_B)$, minus the cost of borrowing, $V_B \times r_B$, divided by the portfolio's equity.

The leveraged portfolio return can be decomposed further to better identify the effect of leverage on returns:

$$r_P = \frac{r_I \times (V_E + V_B) - (V_B \times r_B)}{V_E}$$

$$= \frac{(r_I \times V_E) + [V_B \times (r_I - r_B)]}{V_E}$$

$$= r_I + \frac{V_B}{V_E}(r_I - r_B).$$

This expression decomposes the leveraged portfolio return into the return on invested funds and a portion that accounts for the effect of leverage. If $r_I > r_B$, then the second term is positive because the rate of return on invested funds exceeds the borrowing rate; in this case, leverage increases the portfolio's return. If $r_I < r_B$, then the second term is negative because the rate of return on invested funds is less than the borrowing rate; in this case, the use of leverage decreases the portfolio's return. The degree to which the leverage increases or decreases portfolio returns is proportional to the use of leverage (amount borrowed), V_B/V_E, and the amount by which investment return differs from the cost of borrowing, $r_I - r_B$.

Methods for Leveraging Fixed-Income Portfolios

Fixed-income portfolio managers have a variety of tools available to create leveraged portfolio exposures—notably, the use of financial derivatives and borrowing via collateralized money markets. Derivatives and borrowing are explicit forms of leverage. Other forms of leverage, such as the use of structured financial instruments, are more implicit. We provide a description of the most common ones.

Futures Contracts

Futures contracts embed significant leverage because they permit the counterparties to gain exposure to a large quantity of the underlying asset without having to transact in the underlying. Futures contracts can be obtained for a modest investment that comes in the form of a margin deposit. A futures contract's notional value equals the current value of the underlying asset multiplied by the multiplier, or the quantity of the underlying asset controlled by the contract.

The futures leverage is the ratio of the futures exposure (in excess of the margin deposit) normalized by the amount of margin required to control the notional amount. We can calculate the futures leverage using the following equation:

$$\text{Leverage}_{Futures} = \frac{\text{Notional value} - \text{Margin}}{\text{Margin}}.$$

Swap Agreements

An interest rate swap can be viewed as a portfolio of bonds. In an interest rate swap, the fixed-rate payer is effectively short a fixed-rate bond and long a floating-rate bond. When interest rates increase, the value of the swap to the fixed-rate payer increases because the present value of the fixed-rate liability decreases, and the floating-rate payments received increase. The fixed-rate receiver in the interest rate swap agreement effectively has a long position in a fixed-rate bond and a short position in a floating-rate bond. If interest rates decline, the value of the swap to the fixed-rate receiver increases because the present value of the fixed-rate asset increases, and the floating-rate payments made decrease.

Because interest rate swaps are economically equivalent to a long–short bond portfolio, they provide leveraged exposure to bonds; the only capital required to enter into swap agreements is collateral required by the counterparties. Collateral for interest rate swap agreements has historically occurred between the two (or more) counterparties in the transaction. Increasingly, collateral for interest rate and other swaps occurs through central clearinghouses.

Repurchase Agreements

Repurchase agreements (repos) are an important source of short-term financing for fixed-income security dealers and other financial institutions, as evidenced by the trillions of dollars of repo transactions that take place annually. In a repurchase agreement, a security owner agrees to sell a security for a specific cash amount while simultaneously agreeing to repurchase the security at a specified future date (typically one day later) and price. Repos are thus effectively collateralized loans. When discussing a repo, the transaction normally refers to the borrower's standpoint; from the standpoint of the lender (such as a money market fund), these agreements are referred to as **reverse repos**. Exhibit 13 illustrates the transaction.

The interest rate on a repurchase agreement, called the **repo rate**, is the difference between the security's selling price and its repurchase price. For example, consider a dealer wishing to finance a EUR15 million bond position with a repurchase agreement. The dealer enters an overnight repo at a repo rate of 5%. We can compute the price at which she agrees to repurchase this bond after one day as the EUR15 million value today plus one day of interest. The interest amount is computed as follows:

Dollar interest = Principal amount × Repo rate × (Term of repo in days/360).

Continuing with the example, the dollar interest is EUR2,083.33 = EUR15 million × 5% × (1/360). Thus, the dealer will repurchase the bond the next day for EUR15,002,083.33.

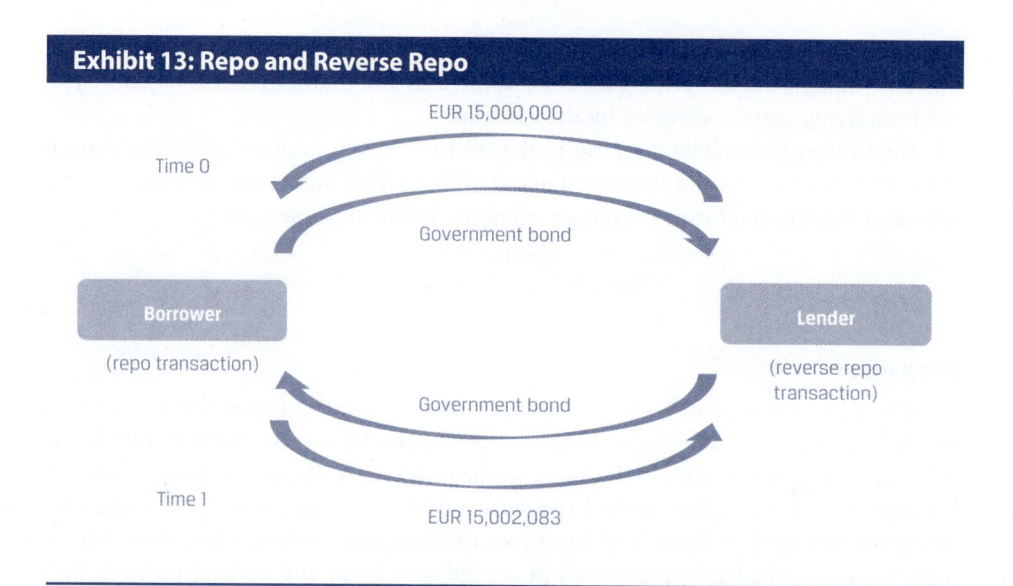

Exhibit 13: Repo and Reverse Repo

The term, or length, of a repurchase agreement is measured in days. Overnight repos are common, although they are often rolled over to create longer-term funding. A repo agreement may be cash driven or security driven. Cash-driven transactions feature one party that owns bonds and wants to borrow cash, as in the foregoing example. Cash-driven transactions usually feature "general collateral"—securities commonly accepted by investors and dealers, such as Treasury bonds. In a security-driven transaction, the lender typically seeks a particular security. The motives may be for hedging, arbitrage, or speculation.

Credit risk is a concern for the counterparty that lends capital in a repo agreement. Protection against a default by the borrower is provided by the underlying collateral bonds. Additional credit protection comes from the "haircut," the amount by which the collateral's value exceeds the repo principal amount. For example, haircuts for high-quality government bonds typically range from 1% to 3% and are higher for other types of bonds. The size of the haircut serves to not only protect the lender against a potential default by the borrower but also to limit the borrower's net leverage capacity. Generally, the size of the haircut increases as the price volatility of the underlying collateral increases.

Repos are categorized as bilateral repos or tri-party repos, depending on the way they are settled. Bilateral repos are conducted directly between two institutions, and settlement is typically conducted as "delivery versus payment," meaning that the exchanges of cash and collateral occur simultaneously through a central custodian (for example, the Depository Trust Company in the United States). Bilateral repos are usually used for security-driven transactions. Tri-party repo transactions involve a third party that provides settlement and collateral management services. Most cash-motivated repo transactions against general collateral are conducted as tri-party repo transactions.

Security Lending

Security lending is another form of collateralized lending and is closely linked to the repo market. The primary motive of security lending transactions is to facilitate short sales, which involve the sale of securities the seller does not own. A short seller must borrow the securities he has sold short to deliver them upon trade settlement. Another motive for security lending transactions is financing, or collateralized borrowing. In a financing-motivated security loan, a bond owner lends the bond to another investor in exchange for cash.

Security lending transactions are collateralized by cash or high-credit-quality bonds. In the United States, most transactions feature cash collateral, although in many other countries, highly rated bonds are used as collateral. Typically, security lenders require collateral valued more than the value of the borrowed securities when bonds are used as collateral. For example, if high-quality government bonds are used as collateral, the lender may require bonds valued at 102% of the value of the borrowed securities. The extra 2% functions in the same way as the haircut in the repo market, providing extra protection against borrower default. The collateral required will increase if lower-quality bonds are used as collateral.

In security lending transactions with cash collateral, the security borrower typically pays the security lender, typically a long-only investment fund, a fee equal to a percentage of the value of the securities loaned. For securities that are readily available for lending, that fee is small. The security lender earns an additional return by reinvesting the cash collateral. In cases where the security loan is initiated for financing purposes, the lending fee is typically negative, indicating that the security lender pays the security borrower a fee in exchange for its use of the cash.

When bonds are posted as collateral, the income earned on the collateral usually exceeds the security lending rate; the security lender (who is in possession of the bonds as collateral) usually repays the security borrower a portion of the interest earned on the bond collateral. The term **rebate rate** refers to the portion of the collateral earnings rate that is repaid to the security borrower by the security lender. This relationship can be expressed as follows:

Rebate rate = Collateral earnings rate − Security lending rate.

When securities are difficult to borrow, typically because there is high demand to short those securities, the rebate rate may be negative, which means the fee for borrowing the securities is greater than the return earned on the collateral. In this case, the security borrower pays a fee to the security lender in addition to foregoing the interest earned on the collateral.

There are important differences between repurchase agreements and security lending transactions. Unlike repurchase agreements, security lending transactions are typically open-ended. The security lender may recall the securities at any time, forcing the borrower to deliver the bonds by buying them back or borrowing from another lender. Similarly, the borrower may deliver the borrowed securities back to the lender at any time, forcing the lender, or its agent, to return the collateral (cash or bonds) and search for another borrower.

Risks of Leverage

Leverage alters the risk–return properties of an investment portfolio. A heavily leveraged portfolio may incur significant losses even when portfolio assets suffer only moderate valuation declines.

Leverage can lead to forced liquidations. If the value of the portfolio decreases, the portfolio's equity relative to borrowing levels is reduced and the portfolio's leverage increases. Portfolio assets may be sold to pay off borrowing and reduce leverage. If portfolio assets are not liquidated, then the overall leverage increases, corresponding to higher levels of risk. Decreases in portfolio value can lead to forced liquidations even if market conditions are unfavorable for selling—for example, during crisis periods. The term "fire sale" refers to forced liquidations at prices that are below fair value because of the seller's need for immediate liquidation. Reducing leverage, declining asset values, and forced sales have the potential to create spiraling effects that can result in severe declines in values and reduction in market liquidity.

Additionally, reassessments of counterparty risk typically occur during extreme market conditions, such as during the 2008–09 Global Financial Crisis. During periods of financial crisis, counterparties to short-term financing arrangements, such as credit lines, repurchase agreements, and security lending agreements, may withdraw their financing. These withdrawals undermine the ability of leveraged market participants to maintain their investment exposures. Thus, leveraged investors may be forced to reduce their investment exposure at exactly the worst time—that is, when prices are depressed.

USING LEVERAGE IN A FIXED-INCOME PORTFOLIO

1. Arturo manages a mutual fund that is benchmarked to the Global Aggregate Bond Index. He currently has a bullish view of the global economy and believes corporate bond spreads are attractive. He is bearish on US Treasury interest rates given his economic growth forecast and expects rates to increase. The fund's US corporate bond holdings have a duration of seven years. He believes the best opportunities are in emerging market securities, and he is bullish on Brazilian rates, expecting them to decrease. The fund has experienced strong inflows recently and is fully invested. Arturo is evaluating ways to potentially increase the fund's total return by creating leveraged fixed-income exposures.

   Given Arturo's plan to leverage exposures in his fund, discuss how he would achieve his objectives and identify the strategy risks.

   Solution

   The mutual fund is fully invested; therefore, Arturo needs to use leverage to potentially increase his returns. His bearish view on US Treasury interest rates would require that he reduce the fund's seven-year duration contributed by the US corporate bond holdings. He can sell the number of futures contracts on US Treasuries, whose notional value and associated duration would offset the duration of the corporate bonds to his new target duration. Doing so would allow him to retain exposure (spread duration) to the corporate bonds, whose spreads may contract as the economy grows while shedding the interest rate exposure, since he believes rates will rise, adversely affecting bond prices.

   Arturo's bullish view on Brazilian rates can be expressed by entering into a receive fixed-rate, pay floating-rate swap on Brazilian rates. The fund will effectively have the equivalent of a fixed-rate bond that will appreciate in price if his view that Brazilian interest rates will fall materializes.

   Both the short US Treasury futures and long Brazilian interest rate swap positions are leveraged since the only capital used is the collateral required by the counterparties. The risk to the leveraged strategy is that if Arturo's view on either position turns out to be incorrect, losses are magnified. This may also require positions to be closed and assets sold to cover the losses, which may occur at an inopportune time if the markets have sold off.

FIXED-INCOME PORTFOLIO TAXATION

7

☐ | discuss differences in managing fixed-income portfolios for taxable and tax-exempt investors

A tax-exempt investor's objective is to achieve the highest possible risk-adjusted returns net of fees and transaction costs. A prudent taxable investor needs to also consider the effects of taxes on both expected and realized net investment returns.

The investment management industry has traditionally made investment decisions based on pretax returns as though investors are tax exempt (such as pension funds in many countries; see Rogers [2006]). Most of the world's investable assets, however, are owned by taxable investors, who are concerned with after-tax, rather than pretax, returns.

Taxes may differ among investor types, among countries, and based on income source, such as interest or capital gains. In many countries, pension funds are exempt from taxes, but corporations generally have to pay tax on their investments. Many countries make some allowance for tax-sheltered investments that individuals can use (up to certain limits). These types of tax shelters generally offer either an exemption from tax on investment income or a deferral of taxes until an investor draws money from the shelter (usually after retirement). Such shelters allow returns to accrue on a pretax basis until retirement, which can provide substantial benefits. In a fixed-income context for taxable investors, coupon payments (interest income) are typically taxed at the investor's normal income tax rate. Capital gains, however, may be taxed at a lower effective rate than an investor's normal income tax rate. In some countries, income from special types of fixed-income securities, such as bonds issued by a sovereign government, a non-sovereign government, or various government agencies, may be taxed at a lower effective rate, or even not taxed.

Specific tax rules vary among jurisdictions. Any discussion of the effect of taxes on investor returns—and, therefore, on how portfolios should optimally be managed for taxable investors—is especially challenging if it needs to apply on a global level. Although accounting standards have become more harmonized globally, any kind of tax harmonization among countries is not likely to occur anytime soon. An investor should consider how taxes affect investment income in the country where the income is earned and how the investment income is treated when it is repatriated to the investor's home country. Treaties between countries may affect tax treatment of investment income. Taxes are complicated and can make investment decisions difficult. Portfolio managers who manage assets for taxable individual investors, as opposed to tax-exempt investors, need to consider a few issues.

Principles of Fixed-Income Taxation

Although tax codes differ among jurisdictions, there are certain principles that most tax codes have in common regarding taxation of fixed-income investments:

- The two primary sources of investment income that affect taxes for fixed-income securities are coupon payments (interest income) and capital gains or losses.

- In general, tax is payable only on capital gains and interest income that have been received. In some countries, an exception to this rule applies to zero-coupon bonds. Imputed interest that is taxed throughout a zero-coupon bond's life may be calculated. This method of taxation ensures that tax is paid over the bond's life and that the return on a zero-coupon bond is not taxed entirely as a capital gain.

- Capital gains are frequently taxed at a lower effective tax rate than interest income.

- Capital losses generally cannot be used to reduce sources of income other than capital gains. Capital losses reduce capital gains in the tax year in which they occur. If capital losses exceed capital gains in the year, they can often be "carried forward" and applied to gains in future years; in some countries, losses may also be "carried back" to reduce capital gains taxes paid in prior years. Limits on the number of years that capital losses can be carried forward or back typically exist.

- In some countries, short-term capital gains are taxed at a different (usually higher) rate than long-term capital gains.

An investor or portfolio manager generally has no control over the timing of when coupon income is received, and the related income tax must be paid. However, he or she can generally decide the timing of the sale of investments and, therefore, has some control over the timing of realized capital gains and losses. This control can be valuable for a taxable investor because it may be optimal to delay realizing gains and related tax payments and to realize losses as early as possible. This type of tax-driven strategic behavior is referred to as tax-loss harvesting.

Key points for managing taxable fixed-income portfolios include the following:

- Selectively offset capital gains and losses for tax purposes.

- If short-term capital gains tax rates are higher than long-term capital gains tax rates, then be judicious when realizing short-term gains.

- Realize losses considering tax consequences. They may be used to offset current or future capital gains for tax purposes.

- Control turnover in the fund. In general, the lower the turnover, the longer capital gains tax payments can be deferred.

- Consider the trade-off between capital gains and income for tax purposes.

Investment Vehicles and Taxes

The choice of investment vehicle often affects how investments are taxed at the final investor level. In a pooled investment vehicle (sometimes referred to as a *collective investment scheme*), such as a mutual fund, interest income is generally taxed at the final investor level when it occurs—regardless of whether the fund reinvests interest income or pays it out to investors. In other words, for tax purposes the fund is considered to have distributed interest income for tax purposes in the year it is received even if it does not actually pay it out to investors. Taxation of capital gains arising from the individual investments within a fund is often treated differently in different countries.

Some countries, such as the United States, use what is known as *pass-through treatment* of capital gains in mutual funds. Realized net capital gains in the underlying securities of a fund are treated as if distributed to investors in the year that they arise, and investors need to include the gains on their tax returns. Other countries, such as the United Kingdom, do not use pass-through treatment. Realized capital gains arising within a fund increase the net asset value of the fund shares that investors hold. Investors pay taxes on the net capital gain when they sell their fund shares. This tax treatment leads to a deferral in capital gains tax payments. A UK portfolio manager's decisions on when to realize capital gains or losses do not affect the timing of tax payments on capital gains by investors.

In a separately managed account, an investor typically pays tax on realized gains in the underlying securities at the time they occur. The investor holds the securities directly rather than through shares in a fund. For separately managed accounts, the portfolio manager needs to consider tax consequences for the investor when making investment decisions.

Tax-loss harvesting, which we defined earlier as deferring the realization of gains and realizing capital losses early, allows investors to accumulate gains on a pretax basis. The deferral of taxes increases the present value of investments for the investor.

MANAGING TAXABLE AND TAX-EXEMPT PORTFOLIOS

A bond portfolio manager needs to raise €10,000,000 in cash to cover outflows in the portfolio she manages. To satisfy her cash demands, she considers one of two corporate bond positions for potential liquidation: Position A and Position B. For tax purposes, capital gains receive pass-through treatment; realized net capital gains in the underlying securities of a fund are treated as if distributed to investors in the year that they arise. Assume that the capital gains tax rate is 28% and the income tax rate for interest is 45%. Exhibit 14 provides relevant data for the two bond positions.

Exhibit 14: Selected Data for Two Bonds

	Position A	Position B
Current market value	€10,000,000	€10,000,000
Capital gain/loss	€1,000,000	–€1,000,000
Coupon rate	5.00%	5.00%
Remaining maturity	10 years	10 years
Income tax rate	45%	
Capital gains tax rate	28%	

The portfolio manager considers Position A to be slightly overvalued and Position B to be slightly undervalued. Assume that the two bond positions are identical regarding all other relevant characteristics. How should the portfolio manager optimally liquidate bond positions if she manages the portfolio for the following investors?

1. How should the portfolio manager optimally liquidate bond positions if she manages the portfolio for tax-exempt investors?

   Solution

   The taxation of capital gains and capital losses has minimal consequences for tax-exempt investors. Consistent with the portfolio manager's investment views, the portfolio manager would likely liquidate Position A, which she considers slightly overvalued, rather than liquidating Position B, which she considers slightly undervalued.

2. How should the portfolio manager optimally liquidate bond positions if she manages the portfolio for taxable investors?

   Solution

   All else equal, portfolio managers for taxable investors should have an incentive to defer capital gains taxes and realize capital losses early (tax-loss harvesting) so that losses can be used to offset current or future capital

> gains. Despite the slight undervaluation of the position, the portfolio manager might want to liquidate Position B because of its embedded capital loss, which will result in a lower realized net capital gain being distributed to investors. This decision assumes that there are no other capital losses in the portfolio that can be used to offset other capital gains. Despite the slight overvaluation of Position A, its liquidation would be less desirable for a taxable investor because of the required capital gains tax.

8   LIABILITY-DRIVEN INVESTING

☐ | describe liability-driven investing

Let us start with the example of a 45-year-old investor who plans to retire at age 65 and who would like to secure a stable stream of income thereafter. It is quite probable that he currently has a diversified portfolio that includes bonds, equities, and possibly other asset classes. Our focus here is on the fixed-income portion of his overall portfolio. We will assume that the investor builds the bond portfolio (immediately) and will add to it each year. Upon retirement, he plans to sell the bonds and buy an annuity that will pay a fixed benefit for his remaining lifetime. This investor's initial 20-year time horizon is critical to identifying and measuring the impact on retirement income arising from future interest rate volatility, and it forms the initial frame of reference for understanding and dealing with interest rate risk.

More generally, the frame of reference is in the form of a balance sheet of rate-sensitive assets and liabilities. In the example of the 45-year-old investor, the asset is the growing bond portfolio, and the liability is the present value of the annuity that the investor requires to satisfy the fixed lifetime benefit.

Liability-Driven Investing vs. Asset-Driven Liabilities

Liability-driven investing (LDI) and asset-driven liabilities (ADL) are special cases of ALM. The key difference is that with ADL, the assets are given, and the liabilities are structured to manage interest rate risk; whereas with LDI, which is much more common, the liabilities are given, and the assets are managed. As an example of LDI, a life insurance company acquires a liability portfolio based on the insurance policies underwritten by its sales force. Another example involves the future employee benefits promised by a defined benefit pension plan, which create a portfolio of rate-sensitive liabilities. In each circumstance, the liabilities are defined and result from routine business and financial management decisions. The present value of those liabilities depends on current interest rates (as well as other factors). A life insurance or pension manager will use the estimated interest rate sensitivity of plan liabilities as a starting point when making investment portfolio decisions. This process often requires building a model for the liabilities.

With ADL, the asset side of the balance sheet results from a company's underlying businesses, and the debt manager seeks a liability structure to reduce interest rate risk. One example might be a leasing company with short-term contracts that chooses to finance itself with short-term debt. The company is aiming to match the maturities of its assets and liabilities to minimize risk. Alternatively, a manufacturing company might identify that its operating revenues are highly correlated with the business cycle. Monetary policy is typically managed so there is positive correlation between interest rates and the business cycle. Central banks lower policy rates when the economy is weak and raise them when it is strong. Therefore, this company has a natural preference for variable-rate liabilities so that operating revenue and interest expense rise and fall together.

Types of Liabilities

An LDI strategy starts with analyzing the size and timing of the entity's liabilities. Exhibit 15 shows a classification scheme for this analysis.

Exhibit 15: Classification of Liabilities

Liability Type	Amount of Cash Outlay	Timing of Cash Outlay	Examples	
Type I	Known	Known	Traditional fixed-income bond with no embedded options	← MacDur, ModDur, money duration, and the PVBP can be used to measure the interest rate sensitivity
Type II	Known	Uncertain	Callable and putable bonds Term life insurance policy (timing of death unkown)	
Type III	Uncertain	Known	Floating-rate note-interest payments depend on future interest rates Inflation-protected securities-amounts of interest and principal payments tied to inflation	Effective duration needed to estimate interest rate sensitivity. Calculated using a model for: • Uncertain amount and/or timing of the cash flows • Initial assumption about the yield curve
Type IV	Uncertain	Uncertain	Property and casualty insurance (weather events difficult to predict)	

Note that effective duration is needed with Types II, III, and IV liabilities, based on initial assumptions about the yield curve. Then, the yield curve is shifted up and down to obtain new estimates for the present value of the liabilities. We demonstrate this process later for the sponsor of a defined benefit pension plan, which is another example of an entity with Type IV liabilities.

EXAMPLE 1

Modern Mortgage, a savings bank, decides to establish an ALCO (asset–liability committee) to improve risk management and coordination of its loan and deposit rate–setting processes. Modern's primary assets are long-term, fixed-rate, monthly payment, fully amortizing residential mortgage loans. The mortgage loans are prime quality and have loan-to-value ratios that average 80%. The loans are pre-payable at par value by the homeowners at no fee. Modern also holds a portfolio of non-callable, fixed-income government bonds (considered free of default risk) of varying maturities to manage its liquidity needs. The primary liabilities are demand and time deposits that are fully guaranteed by a government deposit insurance fund. The demand deposits are redeemable by check or debit card. The time deposits have fixed rates and maturities ranging from 90 days to three years and are redeemable before maturity at a small fee. The banking-sector regulator in the country in which Modern operates has introduced a new capital requirement for savings banks. In accordance with the requirement, contingent convertible long-term bonds are issued by the savings bank and sold to institutional investors. The key feature is that if defaults on the mortgage loans reach a certain level or the savings bank's capital ratio drops below a certain level, as determined by the regulator, the bonds convert to equity at a specified price per share.

As a first step, the ALCO needs to identify the types of assets and liabilities that comprise its balance sheet using the classification scheme in Exhibit 15. Type I has certain amounts and dates for its cash flows; Type II has known amounts but uncertain dates; Type III has specified dates but unknown amounts; and Type IV has uncertain amounts and dates.

1. Specify and explain the classification scheme for residential mortgage loans

   Solution

   Residential mortgage loans are Type IV assets to the savings bank. The timing of interest and principal cash flows is uncertain because of the pre-payment option held by the homeowner. This type of call option is complex. Homeowners might elect to prepay for many reasons, including sale of the property as well as the opportunity to refinance if interest rates come down. Therefore, a prepayment model is needed to project the timing of future cash flows. Default risk also affects the projected amount of the cash flow for each date. Even if the *average* loan-to-value ratio is 80%, indicating high-quality mortgages, some loans could have higher ratios and be more subject to default, especially if home prices decline.

2. Specify and explain the classification scheme for government bonds

   Solution

   Fixed-rate government bonds are Type I assets because the coupon and principal payment dates and amounts are determined at issuance.

3. Specify and explain the classification scheme for demand and time deposits

   Solution

   Demand and time deposits are Type II liabilities from the savings bank's perspective. The deposit amounts are known, but the depositor can redeem the deposits prior to maturity, creating uncertainty about timing.

4. Specify and explain the classification scheme for contingent convertible bonds

   Solution

   The contingent convertible bonds are Type IV liabilities. The presence of the conversion option makes both the amount and timing of cash flows uncertain.

MANAGING THE INTEREST RATE RISK OF MULTIPLE LIABILITIES

9

☐ | describe the strategy of cash flow matching

The principle of interest rate immunization applies to multiple liabilities in addition to a single liability. For now, we continue to assume that these are Type I cash flows in that the scheduled amounts and payment dates are known to the asset manager. In this section, we discuss two approaches to manage these liabilities:

- *Cash flow matching*, which entails building a dedicated portfolio of zero-coupon or fixed-income bonds to ensure that there are sufficient cash inflows to pay the scheduled cash outflows (a related concept, the so-called "laddered portfolio," also falls into the cash flow matching category of approaches);

- *Duration matching*, which extends the ideas of the previous section to a portfolio of debt liabilities.

Cash Flow Matching

A classic strategy to eliminate the interest rate risk arising from multiple liabilities is to build a dedicated asset portfolio of high-quality fixed-income bonds that, as closely as possible, matches the amount and timing of the scheduled cash outflows. "Dedicated" means that the bonds are placed in a held-to-maturity portfolio. A natural question is, if the entity has enough cash to build the dedicated bond portfolio, why not just use that cash to buy back and retire the liabilities? The answer is that the buyback strategy is difficult and costly to implement if the bonds are widely held by buy-and-hold institutional and retail investors. Most corporate bonds are rather illiquid, so buying them back on the open market is likely to drive up the purchase price. Cash flow matching can be a better use of the available cash assets.

A corporate finance motivation for cash flow matching is to improve the company's credit rating. The entity has sufficient cash assets to retire the debt liabilities, and dedicating the bonds effectively accomplishes that objective. Under some circumstances, a corporation might even be able to remove both the dedicated asset portfolio and the debt liabilities from its balance sheet through the process of accounting defeasance. Also called in-substance defeasance, accounting defeasance is a way of extinguishing a debt obligation by setting aside sufficient high-quality securities, such as US Treasury notes, to repay the liability.

Panel A in Exhibit 16 illustrates the dedicated cash flow matching asset portfolio. These assets could be zero-coupon bonds or traditional fixed-income securities. Panel B represents the amount and timing of the debt liabilities. The amounts are the sum of the coupon and principal payments of debt securities on a hypothetical balance sheet.

Exhibit 16: Cash Flow Matching

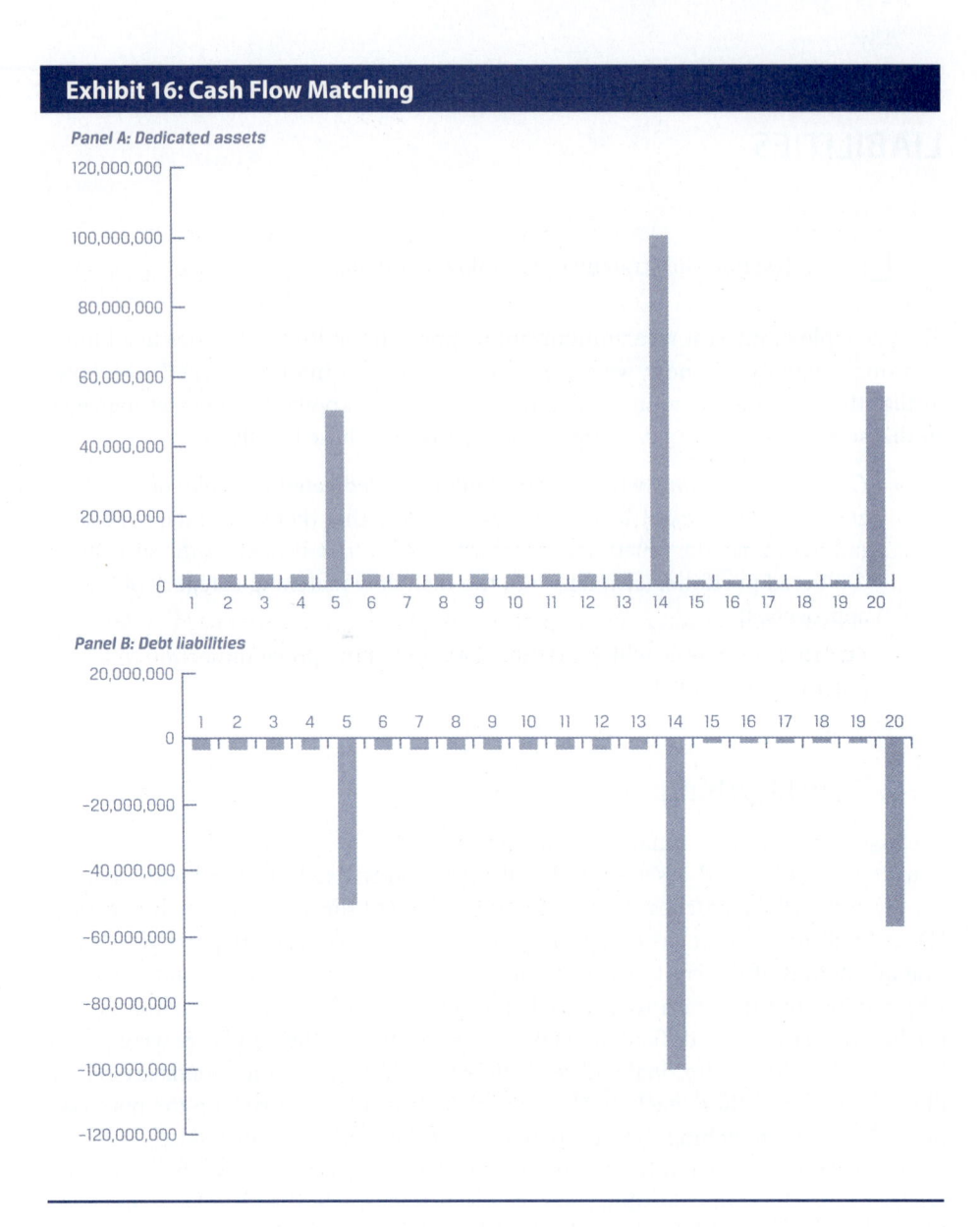

Panel A: Dedicated assets

Panel B: Debt liabilities

A concern when implementing this strategy is the *cash-in-advance constraint*. That means securities are not sold to meet obligations; instead, sufficient funds must be available on or before each liability payment date to meet the obligation. The design of traditional bonds—a fixed coupon rate and principal redemption at maturity—is a problem if the liability stream, unlike in Exhibit 16, is a level payment annuity. That scenario could lead to large cash holdings between payment dates and, therefore, cash flow reinvestment risk, especially if yields on high-quality, short-term investments are low (or worse, negative).

EXAMPLE 2

Alfred Simonsson is assistant treasurer at a Swedish lumber company. The company has sold a large tract of land and now has sufficient cash holdings to retire some of its debt liabilities. The company's accounting department assures Alfred that its external auditors will approve of a defeasement strategy if Swedish government bonds are purchased to match the interest and principal payments on the liabilities. Following is the schedule of payments due on the debt as of June Year 1 that the company plans to defease:

June Year 2	SEK3,710,000
June Year 3	SEK6,620,000
June Year 4	SEK4,410,000
June Year 5	SEK5,250,000

The following Swedish government bonds are available. Interest on the bonds is paid annually in May of each year.

Coupon Rate	Maturity Date
2.75%	May Year 2
3.50%	May Year 3
4.75%	May Year 4
5.50%	May Year 5

1. How much in par value for each government bond will Alfred need to buy to defease the debt liabilities, assuming that the minimum denomination in each security is SEK10,000?

Solution

The cash flow matching portfolio is built by starting with the last liability of SEK5,250,000 in June Year 5. If there were no minimum denomination, that liability could be funded with the 5.50% bonds due May Year 5 having a par value of SEK4,976,303 (= SEK5,250,000/1.0550). To deal with the constraint, however, Alfred buys SEK4,980,000 in par value. That bond pays SEK5,253,900 (= SEK4,980,000 × 1.0550) at maturity. This holding also pays SEK273,900 (= SEK4,980,000 × 0.0550) in coupon interest in May Year 2, 3, and 4.

Then move to the June Year 4 obligation, which is SEK4,136,100 after subtracting the SEK273,900 received on the 5.50% bond: SEK4,410,000 − SEK273,900 = SEK4,136,100. Alfred buys SEK3,950,000 in par value of the 4.75% bond due May Year 4. That bond pays SEK4,137,625 (= SEK3,950,000 × 1.0475) at maturity and SEK187,625 in interest in May Year 2 and Year 3. The net obligation in June Year 3 is SEK6,158,475 (= SEK6,620,000 − SEK273,900 − SEK187,625) after subtracting the interest received on the longer-maturity bonds. The company can buy SEK5,950,000 in par value of the 3.50% bond due May Year 3. At maturity, this bond pays SEK6,158,250 (= SEK5,950,000 × 1.0350). The small shortfall of SEK225 (= SEK6,158,475 − SEK6,158,250) can be made up because the funds received in May are reinvested until June. This bond also pays SEK208,250 in interest in May Year 2. Finally, Alfred needs to buy SEK2,960,000 in par value of the 2.75% bond due May Year 2. This bond pays SEK3,041,400 (= SEK2,960,000 × 1.0275) in May Year 2. The final coupon and principal, plus the interest on the 5.50%, 4.75%, and 3.50% bonds, total SEK3,711,175 (= SEK3,041,400 + SEK273,900 + SEK187,625 + SEK208,250). That amount is used to pay off the June Year 2 obligation of SEK3,710,000. Note that the excess could be kept in a bank account to cover the Year 3 shortfall.

In sum, Alfred buys the following portfolio:

Bond	Par Value
2.75% due May Year 2	SEK2,960,000
3.50% due May Year 3	SEK5,950,000

Bond	Par Value
4.75% due May Year 4	SEK3,950,000
5.50% due May Year 5	SEK4,980,000

The following chart illustrates the cash flow matching bond portfolio: Each bar represents the par amount of a bond maturing in that year plus coupon payments from bonds maturing in later years.

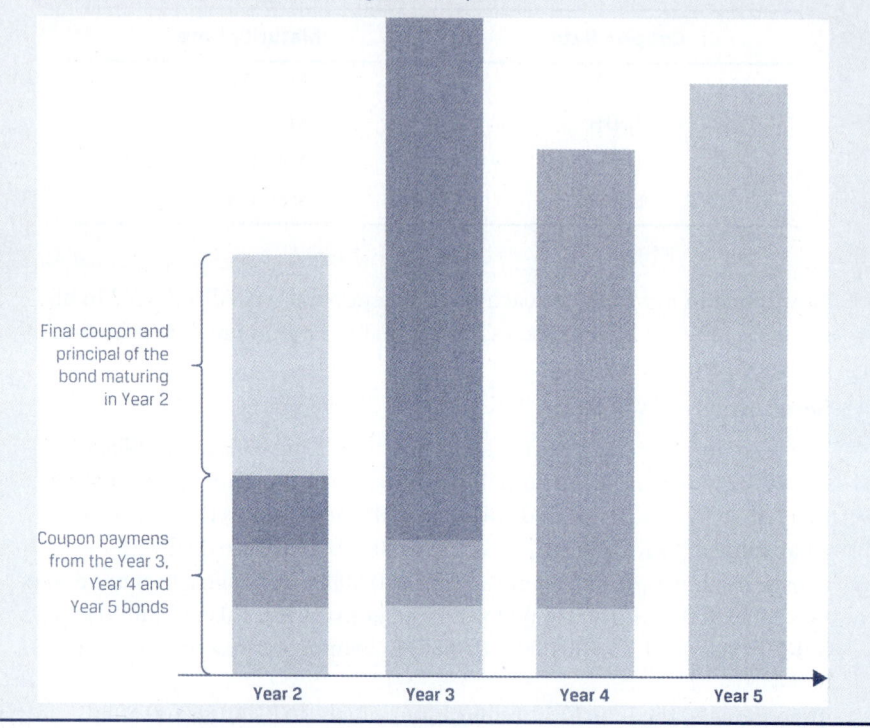

Final coupon and principal of the bond maturing in Year 2

Coupon paymens from the Year 3, Year 4 and Year 5 bonds

Year 2   Year 3   Year 4   Year 5

10   LADDERED PORTFOLIOS

☐ describe construction, benefits, limitations, and risk–return characteristics of a laddered bond portfolio

A popular fixed-income investment strategy in the wealth management industry is to build a "laddered" portfolio for clients. Exhibit 17 illustrates this approach, along with two other maturity-based strategies—a "bullet" portfolio and a "barbell" portfolio. The laddered portfolio spreads the bonds' maturities and par values evenly along the yield curve. The bullet portfolio concentrates the bonds at a particular point on the yield curve, whereas the barbell portfolio places the bonds at the short-term and long-term ends of the curve. In principle, each can have the same portfolio duration statistic and approximately the same change in value for a parallel shift in the yield curve. A non-parallel shift or a twist in the curve, however, leads to very different outcomes for the bullet and barbell structures. An obvious advantage to the laddered portfolio is protection from shifts and twists—the cash flows are essentially "diversified" across the time spectrum.

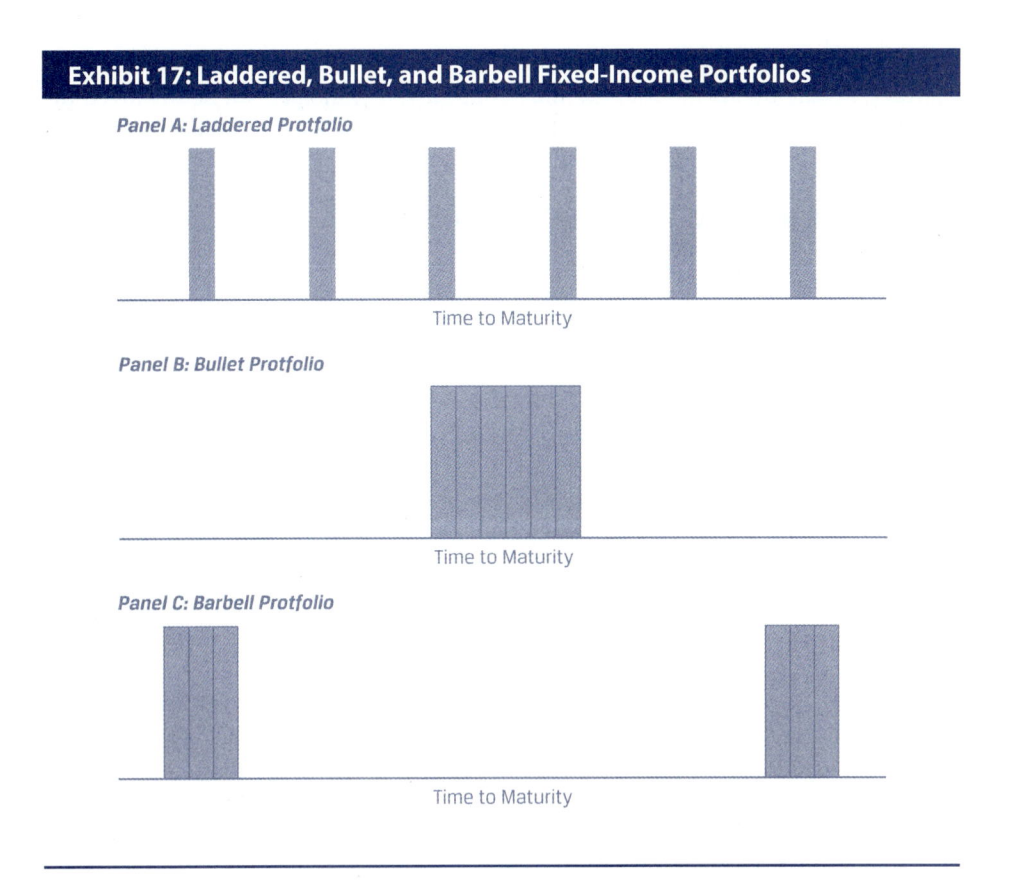

Exhibit 17: Laddered, Bullet, and Barbell Fixed-Income Portfolios

Panel A: Laddered Protfolio

Time to Maturity

Panel B: Bullet Protfolio

Time to Maturity

Panel C: Barbell Protfolio

Time to Maturity

Benefits of Using Laddered Portfolios

This "diversification" over time provides the investor a balanced position between the two sources of interest rate risk—cash flow reinvestment and market price volatility. Bonds mature each year and are reinvested at the longer-term end of the ladder, typically at higher rates than short-term securities. Over time, the laddered portfolio likely includes bonds that were purchased at high interest rates as well as low interest rates. Investors familiar with "dollar cost averaging" will see the similarity. In addition, reinvesting funds as bonds mature maintains the duration of the overall portfolio.

Another attractive feature to the laddered portfolio apparent in Exhibit 17 is in convexity. Convexity, technically, is the second-order effect on the value of an asset or liability given a change in the yield to maturity. Importantly, it is affected by the dispersion of cash flows, as indicated in the following equation:

$$\text{Immunized Portfolio Convexity} = \frac{\text{MacDur}^2 + \text{MacDur} + \text{Dispersion}}{(1 + \text{Cash flow yield})^2}.$$

If the three portfolios have the same duration (and cash flow yield), then the barbell clearly has the highest convexity and the bullet the lowest. The laddered portfolio will tend to have relatively high convexity because its cash flows by design are spread over the timeline. Compared with the barbell, the laddered portfolio has much less cash flow reinvestment risk.

In practice, perhaps the most desirable aspect of the laddered portfolio is in liquidity management. This aspect is particularly relevant if the bonds are not actively traded, as is the case for many corporate securities. As time passes, there is always a bond that is close to redemption. Its duration will be low so that its price is fairly stable even in a time of interest rate volatility. If the client needs immediate cash, the soon-to-mature bond makes for high-quality collateral on a personal loan or, for an institution, a repo contract. As the bonds mature, the final coupon and principal can be deployed for consumption or reinvested in a long-term bond at the back of the ladder.

Using ETFs to Build Laddered Portfolios

Another way for a wealth manager to build a laddered portfolio for a client is to use fixed-maturity corporate bond exchange-traded funds (ETFs). These ETFs have a designated year of maturity and credit risk profile—for instance, 2024 investment-grade corporate bonds. The passively managed, low-cost ETF seeks to replicate the performance of an index of, for instance, 50 held-to-maturity investment-grade corporate bonds that mature in 2021. As discussed in previous sections, the ETF manager can use a stratified sampling approach to track the index.

Suppose that in 2021, the wealth manager buys for the client roughly equal positions in the 2022 through 2029 fixed-maturity corporate bond ETFs. These purchases create a laddered portfolio that should provide the same benefits as holding the bonds directly—price stability in the soonest-to-mature ETF and greater convexity than holding more of a bullet portfolio. Moreover, the ETFs should be more liquid than positions in the actual bonds.

But laddered portfolios are not without limitations. For many investors, the decision to build a laddered bond portfolio should be weighed against buying shares in a fixed-income mutual fund, especially if the portfolio consists of a limited number of corporate bonds. Clearly, the mutual fund provides greater diversification of default risk. Moreover, actual bonds can entail a much higher cost of acquisition. If the entire investment needs to be liquidated, the mutual fund shares can be redeemed more quickly than the bonds can be sold, and likely at a better price.

EXAMPLE 3

Mr. Zheng is a Shanghai-based wealth adviser. A major client of his, the Wang family, holds most of its assets in residential property and equity investments and relies on regular cash flows from those holdings. Zheng recommends that the Wang family also have a laddered portfolio of Chinese government bonds. He suggests the portfolio shown in Exhibit 18, priced for settlement on 1 January 2021.

Exhibit 18: Zheng's Suggested Portfolio

Coupon Rate	Payment Frequency	Maturity	Flat Price	Yield (s.a.)	Par Value (CNY)	Market Value (CNY)
3.22%	Annual	26-Mar-22	101.7493	1.758%	10 million	10,422,826
3.14%	Annual	8-Sept-24	102.1336	2.508%	10 million	10,312,292
3.05%	Annual	22-Oct-26	101.4045	2.764%	10 million	10,199,779
2.99%	Semi-annual	15-Oct-29	101.4454	2.803%	10 million	10,208,611
					40 million	41,143,508

The yields to maturity on the first three bonds have been converted from a periodicity of one to two in order to report them on a consistent semi-annual bond basis, as indicated by "(s.a.)." The total market value of the portfolio is CNY41,143,508. The cash flow yield for the portfolio is 2.661%, whereas the market value-weighted average yield is 2.455%.

Most important for his presentation to the senior members of the Wang family is the schedule for the 30 cash flows:

1	26-Mar-21	322,000	16	8-Sep-24	10,314,000
2	15-Apr-21	149,500	17	15-Oct-24	149,500
3	8-Sep-21	314,000	18	22-Oct-24	305,000
4	15-Oct-21	149,500	19	15-Apr-25	149,500
5	22-Oct-21	305,000	20	15-Oct-25	149,500
6	26-Mar-22	10,322,000	21	22-Oct-25	305,000
7	15-Apr-22	149,500	22	15-Apr-26	149,500
8	8-Sep-22	314,000	23	15-Oct-26	149,500
9	15-Oct-22	149,500	24	22-Oct-26	10,305,000
10	22-Oct-22	305,000	25	15-Apr-27	149,500
11	15-Apr-23	149,500	26	15-Oct-27	149,500
12	8-Sep-23	314,000	27	15-Apr-28	149,500
13	15-Oct-23	149,500	28	15-Oct-28	149,500
14	22-Oct-23	305,000	29	15-Apr-29	149,500
15	15-Apr-24	149,500	30	15-Oct-29	10,149,500

1. Indicate the main points that Zheng should emphasize in this presentation about the laddered portfolio to senior members of the Wang family.

Solution

Zheng should emphasize three features of the portfolio:

High credit quality. Given that the family already has substantial holdings in residential property and equity, which are subject to price volatility and risk, investments in government bonds provide the Wang family with holdings in a very low-risk asset class.

Liquidity. The schedule of payments shows that coupon payments are received each year. These funds can be used for any cash need, including household expenses. The large principal payments can be reinvested in longer-term government bonds at the back of the ladder.

Yield curve diversification. The bond investments are spread out along four segments of the government bond yield curve. If they were concentrated at a single point, the portfolio would have the risk of higher yields at that point. By spreading out the maturities in the ladder formation, the portfolio has the benefit of diversification.

SUMMARY

- Fixed-income investments provide diversification benefits in a portfolio context. These benefits arise from the generally low correlations of fixed-income investments with other major asset classes, such as equities.
- Floating-rate and inflation-linked bonds can be used to hedge inflation risk.
- Fixed-income investments have regular cash flows, which is beneficial for the purposes of funding future liabilities.

- For liability-based fixed-income mandates, portfolio construction follows two main approaches—cash flow matching and duration matching—to match fixed-income assets with future liabilities.

- Total return mandates are generally structured to either track or outperform a benchmark.

- Total return mandates can be classified into various approaches according to their target active return and active risk levels. Approaches range from pure indexing to enhanced indexing to active management.

- Bond portfolio duration is the sensitivity of a portfolio of bonds to small changes in interest rates. It can be calculated as the weighted average of time to receipt of the aggregate cash flows or, more commonly, as the weighted average of the individual bond durations that comprise the portfolio.

- Modified duration of a bond portfolio indicates the percentage change in the market value given a change in yield to maturity. Modified duration of a portfolio comprising j fixed-income securities can be estimated as

$$\text{AvgModDur} = \sum_{j=1}^{J} \text{ModDur}_j\left(\frac{\text{MV}_j}{\text{MV}}\right),$$

  where MV stands for market value of the portfolio and MV_j is the market value of a specific bond in the portfolio.

- Convexity of a bond portfolio is a second-order effect; it operates behind duration in importance and can largely be ignored for small yield changes. When convexity is added with the use of derivatives, however, it can be extremely important to returns.

- Effective duration and convexity of a portfolio are the relevant summary statistics when future cash flows of bonds in a portfolio are contingent on interest rate changes.

- Spread duration is a useful measure for determining a portfolio's sensitivity to changes in credit spreads. It provides the approximate percentage increase (decrease) in bond price expected for a 1% decrease (increase) in credit spread.

- Duration times spread is a modification of the spread duration definition to incorporate the empirical observation that spread changes across the credit spectrum tend to occur on a *proportional percentage* basis rather than being based on *absolute* basis point changes.

- Portfolio dispersion captures the variance of the times to receipt of cash flows around the duration. It is used in measuring interest rate immunization for liabilities.

- Duration management is the primary tool used by fixed-income portfolio managers.

- Convexity supplements duration as a measure of a bond's price sensitivity for larger movements in interest rates. Adjusting convexity can be an important portfolio management tool.

- For two portfolios with the same duration, the portfolio with higher convexity has higher sensitivity to large declines in yields to maturity and lower sensitivity to large increases in yields to maturity.

- Interest rate derivatives can be used effectively to increase or decrease duration and convexity in a bond portfolio.

- Liquidity is an important consideration in fixed-income portfolio management. Bonds are generally less liquid than equities, and liquidity varies greatly across sectors.

- Liquidity affects pricing in fixed-income markets because many bonds either do not trade or trade infrequently.

- Liquidity affects portfolio construction because there is a trade-off between liquidity and yield to maturity. Less liquid bonds have higher yields to maturity, all else being equal, and may be more desirable for buy-and-hold investors. Investors anticipating liquidity needs may forego higher yields to maturity for more liquid bonds.

- Investors can obtain exposure to the bond market using mutual funds and ETFs that track a bond index. Shares in mutual funds are redeemable at the net asset value with a one-day time lag. ETF shares have the advantage of trading on an exchange.

- A total return swap, an over-the-counter derivative, allows an institutional investor to transform an asset or liability from one asset category to another—for instance, from variable-rate cash flows referencing the market reference rate to the total return on a particular bond index.

- A total return swap (TRS) can have some advantages over a direct investment in a bond mutual fund or ETF. As a derivative, it requires less initial cash outlay than direct investment in the bond portfolio for similar performance but carries counterparty risk.

- As a customized over-the-counter product, a TRS can offer exposure to assets that are difficult to access directly, such as some high-yield and commercial loan investments.

- When evaluating fixed-income investment strategies, it is important to consider expected returns and to understand the various components of expected returns.

- Decomposing expected fixed-income returns allows investors to understand the different sources of returns given expected changes in bond market conditions.

- A model for expected fixed-income returns can decompose them into the following components: coupon income, rolldown return, expected change in price based on investor's views of yields to maturity and yield spreads, and expected currency gains or losses.

- Leverage is the use of borrowed capital to increase the magnitude of portfolio positions. By using leverage, fixed-income portfolio managers may be able to increase portfolio returns relative to what they can achieve in unleveraged portfolios. The potential for increased returns, however, comes with increased risk.

- Methods for leveraging fixed-income portfolios include the use of futures contracts, swap agreements, repurchase agreements, structured financial instruments, and security lending.

- Taxes can complicate investment decisions in fixed-income portfolio management. Complications result from the differences in taxation among investor types, countries, and income sources.

- The two primary sources of investment income that affect taxes for fixed-income securities are coupon payments (interest income) and capital gains or losses. Tax is usually payable only on capital gains and interest income that have actually been received.

- Capital gains are frequently taxed at a lower effective tax rate than interest income. If capital losses exceed capital gains in the year, they can often be "carried forward" and applied to gains in future years.

- Structured fixed-income investing requires a frame of reference, such as a balance sheet, to structure the bond portfolio. This frame of reference can be as simple as the time to retirement for an individual or as complex as a balance sheet of rate-sensitive assets and liabilities for a company.

- Assets and liabilities can be categorized by the degree of certainty surrounding the amount and timing of cash flows. Type I assets and liabilities, such as traditional fixed-rate bonds with no embedded options, have known amounts and payment dates. For Type I assets and liabilities, such yield duration statistics as Macaulay, modified, and money duration apply.

- Type II, III, and IV assets and liabilities have uncertain amounts and/or uncertain timing of payment. For Type II, III, and IV assets and liabilities, curve duration statistics, such as effective duration, are needed. A model is used to obtain the estimated values when the yield curve shifts up and down by the same amount.

- Structural risk to immunization arises from some non-parallel shifts and twists to the yield curve. This risk is reduced by minimizing the dispersion of cash flows in the portfolio, which can be accomplished by minimizing the convexity statistic for the portfolio.

- For multiple liabilities, one method of immunization is cash flow matching. A portfolio of high-quality zero-coupon or fixed-income bonds is purchased to match as closely as possible the amount and timing of the liabilities.

- A motive for cash flow matching can be accounting defeasance, whereby both the assets and liabilities are removed from the balance sheet.

- A laddered bond portfolio is a common investment strategy in the wealth management industry. The laddered portfolio offers "diversification" over the yield curve compared with "bullet" or "barbell" portfolios.

- A laddered portfolio offers an increase in convexity because the cash flows have greater dispersions than a more concentrated (bullet) portfolio.

- A laddered portfolio provides liquidity in that it always contains a soon-to-mature bond that could provide high-quality, low-duration collateral on a repo contract if needed.

REFERENCES

Hanke, B. and G. Seals. 2010. *"Fixed-Income Analysis: Yield Curve Construction, Trading Strategies, and Risk Analysis."* CFA Institute online course.

Rogers, D. 2006. *Tax-Aware Investment Management: The Essential Guide.* New York: Bloomberg Press.

PRACTICE PROBLEMS

The following information relates to questions 1-6

Cécile is a junior analyst for an international wealth management firm. Her supervisor, Margit, asks Cécile to evaluate three fixed-income funds as part of the firm's global fixed-income offerings. Selected financial data for the funds Aschel, Permot, and Rosaiso are presented in Exhibit 1. In Cécile's initial review, she assumes that there is no reinvestment income and that the yield curve remains unchanged.

Exhibit 1: Selected Data on Fixed-Income Funds

	Aschel	Permot	Rosaiso
Current average bond price	$117.00	$91.50	$94.60
Expected average bond price in one year (end of Year 1)	$114.00	$96.00	$97.00
Average modified duration	7.07	7.38	6.99
Average annual coupon payment	$3.63	$6.07	$6.36
Present value of portfolio's assets (millions)	$136.33	$68.50	$74.38
Bond type*			
Fixed-coupon bonds	95%	38%	62%
Floating-coupon bonds	2%	34%	17%
Inflation-linked bonds	3%	28%	21%
Quality*			
AAA	65%	15%	20%
BBB	35%	65%	50%
B	0%	20%	20%
Not rated	0%	0%	10%
Value of portfolio's equity (millions)	$94.33		
Value of borrowed funds (millions)	$42.00		
Borrowing rate	2.80%		
Return on invested funds	6.20%		

*Bond type and quality are shown as a percentage of the total for each fund.

After further review of the composition of each of the funds, Cécile makes the following notes:

Note 1   Aschel is the only fund of the three that uses leverage.

Note 2   Rosaiso is the only fund of the three that holds a significant number of bonds with embedded options.

Margit asks Cécile to analyze liability-based mandates for a meeting with Villash Foundation. Villash Foundation is a tax-exempt client. Prior to the meeting,

Cécile identifies what she considers to be two key features of a liability-based mandate.

Feature 1   It matches expected liability payments with future projected cash inflows.

Feature 2   It can minimize the risk of deficient cash inflows for a company.

Two years later, Margit learns that Villash Foundation needs $5 million in cash to meet liabilities. She asks Cécile to analyze two bonds for possible liquidation. Selected data on the two bonds are presented in Exhibit 2.

Exhibit 2: Selected Data for Bonds 1 and 2

	Bond 1	Bond 2
Current market value	$5,000,000	$5,000,000
Capital gain/loss	$400,000	–$400,000
Coupon rate	2.05%	2.05%
Remaining maturity	8 years	8 years
Investment view	Overvalued	Undervalued
Income tax rate		39%
Capital gains tax rate		30%

1. Based on Exhibit 1, which fund provides the highest level of protection against inflation for coupon payments?

    A. Aschel

    B. Permot

    C. Rosaiso

2. Based on Exhibit 1, the rolling yield of Aschel over a one-year investment horizon is *closest* to:

    A. 2.56%.

    B. 0.54%.

    C. 5.66%.

3. The leveraged portfolio return for Aschel is *closest* to:

    A. 7.25%.

    B. 7.71%.

    C. 8.96%.

4. Based on Note 2, Rosaiso is the only fund for which the expected change in price based on the investor's views of yields to maturity and yield spreads should be calculated using:

    A. convexity.

    B. modified duration.

    C. effective duration.

5. Is Cécile correct with respect to key features of liability-based mandates?

    A. Yes.

    B. No, only Feature 1 is correct.

    C. No, only Feature 2 is correct.

6. Based on Exhibit 2, the optimal strategy to meet Villash Foundation's cash needs is the sale of:

    A. 100% of Bond 1.

    B. 100% of Bond 2.

    C. 50% of Bond 1 and 50% of Bond 2.

The following information relates to questions 7-12

Celia is chief investment officer for the Topanga Investors Fund, which invests in equities and fixed income. The clients in the fund are all taxable investors. The fixed-income allocation includes a domestic (US) bond portfolio and an externally managed global bond portfolio.

The domestic bond portfolio has a total return mandate, which specifies a long-term return objective of 25 basis points (bps) over the benchmark index. Relative to the benchmark, small deviations in sector weightings are permitted, such risk factors as duration must closely match, and tracking error is expected to be less than 50 bps per year. These features are typical of enhanced indexing.

The objectives for the domestic bond portfolio include the ability to fund future liabilities, protect interest income from short-term inflation, and minimize the correlation with the fund's equity portfolio. The correlation between the fund's domestic bond portfolio and equity portfolio is currently 0.14. Celia plans to reduce the fund's equity allocation and increase the allocation to the domestic bond portfolio. She reviews two possible investment strategies.

Strategy 1   Purchase AAA-rated fixed-coupon corporate bonds with a modified duration of two years and a correlation coefficient with the equity portfolio of –0.15.

Strategy 2   Purchase US government agency floating-coupon bonds with a modified duration of one month and a correlation coefficient with the equity portfolio of –0.10.

Celia realizes that the fund's return may decrease if the equity allocation of the fund is reduced. Celia decides to liquidate $20 million of US Treasuries that are currently owned and to invest the proceeds in the US corporate bond sector. To fulfill this strategy, Celia asks Dan, a newly hired analyst for the fund, to recommend specific Treasuries to sell and corporate bonds to purchase.

Dan recommends Treasuries from the existing portfolio that he believes are overvalued and will generate capital gains. Celia asks Dan why he chose only overvalued bonds with capital gains and did not include any bonds with capital losses.

Dan responds with two statements.

Statement 1   Taxable investors should prioritize selling overvalued bonds and always sell them before selling bonds that are viewed as fairly valued or undervalued.

Statement 2   Taxable investors should never intentionally realize capital losses.

Regarding the purchase of corporate bonds, Dan collects relevant data, which are presented in Exhibit 1.

Exhibit 1: Selected Data on Three US Corporate Bonds

Bond Characteristics	Bond 1	Bond 2	Bond 3
Credit quality	AA	AA	A
Issue size ($ millions)	100	75	75
Maturity (years)	5	7	7
Total issuance outstanding ($ millions)	1,000	1,500	1,000
Months since issuance	New issue	3	6

Celia and Dan review the total expected 12-month return (assuming no reinvestment income) for the global bond portfolio. Selected financial data are presented in Exhibit 2.

Exhibit 2: Selected Data on Global Bond Portfolio

Notional principal of portfolio (in millions)	€200
Average bond coupon payment (per €100 par value)	€2.25
Coupon frequency	Annual
Investment Horizon	1 year
Current average bond price	€98.45
Expected average bond price in one year (assuming an unchanged yield curve)	€98.62
Average bond convexity	22
Average bond modified duration	5.19
Expected average benchmark yield-to-maturity change	0.15%
Expected change in credit spread (widening)	0.13%
Expected currency gains (€ appreciation vs. $)	0.65%

Celia contemplates adding a new manager to the global bond portfolio. She reviews three proposals and determines that each manager uses the same index as its benchmark but pursues a different total return approach, as presented in Exhibit 3.

Exhibit 3: New Manager Proposals: Fixed-Income Portfolio Characteristics

Sector Weights (%)	Manager A	Manager B	Manager C	Index
Government	53.5	52.5	47.8	54.1
Agency/quasi-agency	16.2	16.4	13.4	16.0
Corporate	20.0	22.2	25.1	19.8
MBS	10.3	8.9	13.7	10.1

Risk and Return Characteristics	Manager A	Manager B	Manager C	Index
Average maturity (years)	7.63	7.84	8.55	7.56
Modified duration (years)	5.23	5.25	6.16	5.22
Average yield to maturity (%)	1.98	2.08	2.12	1.99
Turnover (%)	207	220	290	205

7. Which approach to its total return mandate is the fund's domestic bond portfolio *most likely* to use?

   A. Pure indexing

   B. Enhanced indexing

   C. Active management

8. Strategy 2 is *most likely* preferred to Strategy 1 for meeting the objective of:

   A. protecting against inflation.

   B. funding future liabilities.

   C. minimizing the correlation of the fund's domestic bond portfolio and equity portfolio.

9. Are Dan's statements to Celia that support Dan's choice of bonds to sell correct?

   A. Only Statement 1 is correct.

   B. Only Statement 2 is correct.

   C. Neither Statement 1 nor Statement 2 is correct.

10. Based on Exhibit 1, which bond *most likely* has the highest liquidity premium?

   A. Bond 1

   B. Bond 2

   C. Bond 3

11. Based on Exhibit 2, the total expected return of the fund's global bond portfolio is *closest* to:

   A. 0.90%.

   B. 1.66%.

   C. 3.76%.

12. Based on Exhibit 3, which manager is *most likely* to have an active management total return mandate?

A. Manager A

B. Manager B

C. Manager C

SOLUTIONS

1. B is correct. Permot has the highest percentage of floating-coupon bonds and inflation-linked bonds. Bonds with floating coupons protect interest income from inflation because the reference rate should adjust for inflation. Inflation-linked bonds protect against inflation by paying a return that is directly linked to an index of consumer prices and adjusting the principal for inflation. Inflation-linked bonds protect both coupon and principal payments against inflation.

   The level of inflation protection for coupons equals the percentage of the portfolio in floating-coupon bonds plus the percentage of the portfolio in inflation-linked bonds:

   Aschel = 2% + 3% = 5%.

   Permot = 34% + 28% = 62%.

   Rosaiso = 17% + 21% = 38%.

   Thus, Permot has the highest level of inflation protection, with 62% of its portfolio in floating-coupon and inflation-linked bonds.

2. B is correct. The rolling yield is the sum of the coupon income and the rolldown return. Coupon income is the sum of the bond's annual current yield and interest on reinvestment income. Cécile assumes that there is no reinvestment income for any of the three funds, and the yield income for Aschel will be calculated as follows:

   Coupon income = Annual average coupon payment/Current bond price

   = \$3.63/\$117.00

   = 0.0310, or 3.10%.

   The rolldown return is equal to the bond's percentage price change assuming an unchanged yield curve over the horizon period. The rolldown return will be calculated as follows:

   $$\text{Rolldown Returns} = \frac{\left(\text{Bond price}_{End-of-horizon\ period} - \text{Bond price}_{Beginning-of-horizon\ period}\right)}{\text{Bond price}_{Beginning-of-horizon\ period}}$$

   $$= \frac{(\$114.00 - \$117.00)}{\$117.00}$$
   $$= -0.0256, \text{ or } -2.56\%.$$

   Rolling yield = Coupon income + Rolldown return = 3.10% − 2.56% = 0.54%.

3. B is correct. The return for Aschel is 7.71%, calculated as follows:

   $$r_P = \frac{r_I \times (V_E + V_B) - V_B \times r_B}{V_E}.$$

   $$= r_I + \frac{V_B}{V_E}(r_I - r_B)$$

   $$= 6.20\% + \frac{\$42.00\ \text{million}}{\$94.33\ \text{million}}(6.20\% - 2.80\%)$$

   $$= 7.71\%.$$

4. C is correct. Rosaiso is the only fund that holds bonds with embedded options. Effective duration should be used for bonds with embedded options. For bonds with embedded options, the duration and convexity measures used to calculate the expected change in price based on the investor's views of yields to maturity and yield spreads are effective duration and effective convexity. For bonds without embedded options, convexity and modified duration are used in this calculation.

5. A is correct. Liability-based mandates are investments that take an investor's future obligations into consideration. Liability-based mandates are managed to match expected liability payments with future projected cash inflows. These types of mandates are structured in a way to ensure that a liability or a stream of liabilities can be covered and that any risk of shortfalls or deficient cash inflows for a company are minimized.

6. A is correct. The optimal strategy for Villash is the sale of 100% of Bond 1, which Cécile considers to be overvalued. Because Villash is a tax-exempt foundation, tax considerations are not relevant and Cécile's investment views drive her trading recommendations.

7. B is correct. The domestic bond portfolio's return objective is to modestly outperform the benchmark. Its risk factors, such as duration, are to closely match the benchmark. Small deviations in sector weights are allowed, and tracking error should be less than 50 bps per year. These features are typical of enhanced indexing.

8. A is correct. Floating-coupon bonds provide inflation protection for the interest income because the reference rate should adjust for inflation. The purchase of fixed-coupon bonds as outlined in Strategy 1 provides no protection against inflation for either interest or principal. Strategy 1 would instead be superior to Strategy 2 in funding future liabilities (better predictability as to the amount of cash flows) and reducing the correlation between the fund's domestic bond portfolio and equity portfolio (better diversification).

9. C is correct. Since the fund's clients are taxable investors, there is value in harvesting tax losses. These losses can be used to offset capital gains within the fund that will otherwise be distributed to the clients and result in higher tax payments, which decreases the total value of the investment to clients. The fund has to consider the overall value of the investment to its clients, including taxes, which may result in the sale of bonds that are not viewed as overvalued. Tax-exempt investors' decisions are driven by their investment views without regard to offsetting gains and losses for tax purposes.

10. C is correct. Bond 3 is most likely to be the least liquid of the three bonds presented in Exhibit 1 and will thus most likely require the highest liquidity premium. Low credit ratings, longer time since issuance, smaller issuance size, smaller issuance outstanding, and longer time to maturity typically are associated with lower liquidity (and thus a higher liquidity premium). Bond 3 has the lowest credit quality and the longest time since issuance of the three bonds. Bond 3 also has a smaller issue size and a longer time to maturity than Bond 1. The total issuance outstanding for Bond 3 is smaller than that of Bond 2 and equal to that of Bond 1.

11. B is correct. The total expected return is calculated as follows:

    Total expected return =

    Rolling yield

$+/- E$(Change in price based on investor's benchmark yield view)

$+/- E$(Change in price due to investor's view of credit spread)

$+/- E$(Currency gains or losses),

where Rolling yield = Coupon income + Rolldown return.

Return Component	Formula	Calculation
Coupon income	Annual coupon payment/Current bond price	€2.25/€;98.45 = 2.29%
+ Rolldown return	(Bond price$_{End\text{-}of\text{-}horizon\ period}$ − Bond price$_{Beginning\text{-}of\text{-}horizon\ period}$)/Bond price$_{Beginning\text{-}of\text{-}horizon\ period}$	(€98.62 − €98.45)/€98.45 = 0.17%
= Rolling yield	Coupon income + Rolldown return	2.29% + 0.17% = 2.46%
$+/- E$(Change in price based on investor's benchmark yield view)	$(-MD \times \Delta Yield) + [½ \times Convexity \times (\Delta Yield)^2]$	$(-5.19 \times 0.0015) + [½ \times 22 \times (0.0015)^2]$ = −0.78%
$+/- E$(Change in price due to investor's view of credit spread)	$(-MD \times \Delta Spread) + [½ \times Convexity \times (\Delta Spread)^2]$	$(-5.19 \times 0.0013) + [½ \times 22 \times (0.0013)^2]$ = −0.67%
$+/- E$(Currency gains or losses)	Given	0.65%
= Total expected return		**1.66%**

12. C is correct. The sector weights, risk and return characteristics, and turnover for Manager C differ significantly from those of the index, which is typical of an active management mandate. In particular, Manager C's modified duration of 6.16 represents a much larger deviation from the benchmark index modified duration of 5.22 than that of the other managers, which is a characteristic unique to an active management mandate.

3

Asset Allocation to Alternative Investments

by Adam Kobor, PhD, CFA, and Mark D. Guinney, CFA.

Adam Kobor, PhD, CFA, is at New York University (USA). Mark D. Guinney, CFA (USA).

LEARNING OUTCOMES

Mastery	The candidate should be able to:
☐	explain the roles that alternative investments play in multi-asset portfolios
☐	compare alternative investments and bonds as risk mitigators in relation to a long equity position
☐	compare traditional and risk-based approaches to defining the investment opportunity set, including alternative investments
☐	discuss investment considerations that are important in allocating to different types of alternative investments
☐	discuss suitability considerations in allocating to alternative investments
☐	discuss approaches to asset allocation to alternative investments
☐	discuss the importance of liquidity planning in allocating to alternative investments
☐	discuss considerations in monitoring alternative investment programs

INTRODUCTION

1

☐	explain the roles that alternative investments play in multi-asset portfolios

Asset allocation is a critical decision in the investment process. The mathematical and analytical processes inherent in contemporary asset allocation techniques are complicated by the idiosyncrasies of alternative investments. Approaches to incorporating alternative assets into the strategic asset allocation have developed rapidly as allocations to assets other than stocks and bonds have accelerated in the aftermath of the 2008 Global Financial Crisis. The term "alternative" understates the prominence of alternative investment allocations in many investment programs, because institutional and private clients have been increasingly turning to these investments not just to supplement traditional long-only stocks and bonds but also sometimes to replace them altogether. For example, the Yale Endowment and the Canada Pension Plan Investment Board both have close to 50% of their assets allocated to alternatives.[1] Although these two funds are admittedly outliers, between 2008 and 2017 most of the pension funds around the world substantially expanded their allocations to alternative asset classes. On average, pension funds in developed markets increased their allocation from 7.2% to 11.8% of assets under management (AUM) in 2017, a 63% increase.[2]

"Alternative" investment has no universally accepted definition. For the purposes of this reading, alternative investments include private equity, hedge funds, real assets (including energy and commodity investments), commercial real estate, and private credit.

The reading begins with a discussion of the role alternative assets play in a multi-asset portfolio and explores how alternatives may serve to mitigate long-only equity risk, a role traditionally held by bonds. We then consider different ways investors may define the opportunity set—through the traditional asset class lens or, more recently, using a risk- or factor-based lens. An allocation to alternatives is not for all investors, so the reading describes issues that should be addressed when considering an allocation to alternatives. We then discuss approaches to asset allocation when incorporating alternatives in the opportunity set and the need for liquidity planning in private investment alternatives. Finally, the reading discusses the unique monitoring requirements for an alternatives portfolio.

The Role of Alternative Investments in a Multi-Asset Portfolio

Allocations to alternatives are playing an increasing role in investor portfolios largely driven by the belief that these investments increase the risk-adjusted return expectations for their programs. Some allocations are driven by expectations of higher returns, while others are driven by the expected diversification (risk-reduction) benefits. In the aggregate, the portfolio's *risk-adjusted* return is expected to improve. Exhibit 1 provides a framework for how the common alternative strategies are generally perceived to affect the risk/return profile of a "typical" 60/40 portfolio of public stocks and bonds.

---

1 Boston Consulting Group (BCG), "The Rise of Alternative Assets and Long-Term Investing (March 2017).
2 See Ivashina and Lerner 2018.

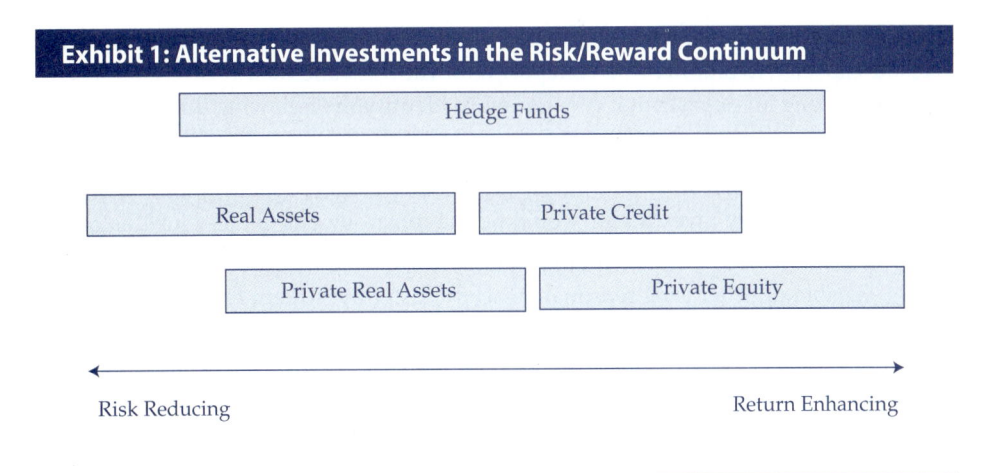

Exhibit 1: Alternative Investments in the Risk/Reward Continuum

Although we present a simplified view, real assets are generally believed to mitigate the risks to the portfolio arising from unexpected inflation. At the other end of the spectrum, venture capital investments (private equity) are expected to provide a sufficient return premium over public equities to compensate for their illiquidity risk and heightened operational complexity. Hedge funds, the least homogenous of strategies, span the spectrum from "risk reducing" or diversifying (many arbitrage strategies) to "return enhancing" (e.g., an activist fund that takes significant positions in public companies with the goal of improving performance through management changes, capital allocation policies, and/or company strategy).

Risk reduction can mean different things to different investors. Institutions may choose to add non-correlated strategies to their portfolios to reduce the volatility of the overall investment program. Private clients are frequently concerned with reducing only downside volatility—the "left tail" risk associated with significant public equity market drawdowns. An insurance pool whose liabilities are sensitive to inflation might benefit from real assets that could reduce its asset–liability mismatch. Exhibit 2 provides some guidance as to how an allocator might view alternative assets vis-à-vis traditional asset classes.

Exhibit 2: Illustrative Capital Market Assumptions

	Traditional Assets					Alternative Assets					
	Public Equities	**Cash**	**Govt Bonds**	**Broad Fixed Income**	**Private Credit**	**Hedge Funds**	**Commodities**	**Public Real Estate**	**Private Real Estate**	**Private Equity**
Expected Return (Geometric Average)	6.5%	2.0%	2.3%	2.8%	6.5%	5.0%	4.5%	6.0%	5.5%	8.5%
Volatility	17.0%	1.1%	4.9%	3.4%	10.0%	8.1%	25.2%	20.4%	13.8%	15.7%
Correlation with Equities	1.00	−0.12	−0.60	−0.41	0.70	0.83	0.21	0.60	0.37	0.81
Equity Beta	1.00	−0.01	−0.17	−0.08	0.40	0.40	0.31	0.72	0.30	0.74

Source: Authors' own data.

In the context of asset allocation, investors may categorize an asset class based on the role it is expected to play in the overall portfolio. The roles and their relative importance will vary among investors, but it is common to identify the following functional roles:

- *Capital growth*: This role may be a top priority for portfolios with a long-term time horizon and relatively high-return target. Usually, public and private equity investments would be the most obvious choices for this role.

- *Income generation*: Certain asset classes, like fixed income or real estate, are capable of generating reasonably steady cash flow stream for investors.

- *Risk diversification*: In the case of an equity-oriented portfolio, investors may seek assets that diversify the dominant equity risk. Real assets and several hedge fund strategies may fit here. Similarly, fixed-income investors may be interested in diversifying pure yield curve risk via private credit.

- *Safety*: Certain asset classes may play the role of safe haven when most of the risky asset classes suffer. Government bonds or gold may potentially play such roles in a well-diversified portfolio.

Exhibit 3 illustrates how each of the alternative assets is generally perceived to fulfill these functional roles.

Exhibit 3: The Role of Asset Classes in a Multi-Asset Portfolio

Asset Class		Capital Growth	Income	Diversifying Public Equities	Safety
Fixed Income and Credit	Governments		M	H	H
	Inflation-Linked		M	H	H/M
	Inv.-Grade Credit		M	H	M
	High-Yield Credit		H	M	
	Private Credit		H	M	
Equities	Public Equity	H	M		
	Private Equity	H	M	M	
Real Estate	Public Real Estate	M	H	M	
	Private Real Estate	M	H	M	
Real Assets	Public Real Assets (Energy, Metal, etc.)			H	
	Private Real Assets (Timber, etc.)	H	H	H	
Hedge Funds	Absolute Return		M	H	
	Equity Long/Short			M	

Notes: H = high/strong potential to fulfill the indicated role; M = moderate potential to fulfill the indicated role.

Exhibit 4 illustrates the potential contributions the various alternative strategies might make to a portfolio dominated by equity risk. Note that the graph illustrates the *average* investment characteristics of each asset class over some extended period of time. Some assets—gold, for example—may not consistently exhibit attractive *aggregate* characteristics compared to other strategies but may serve the portfolio well during many major market shocks.

Exhibit 4: Diversification Potential of Various Alternative Asset Classes

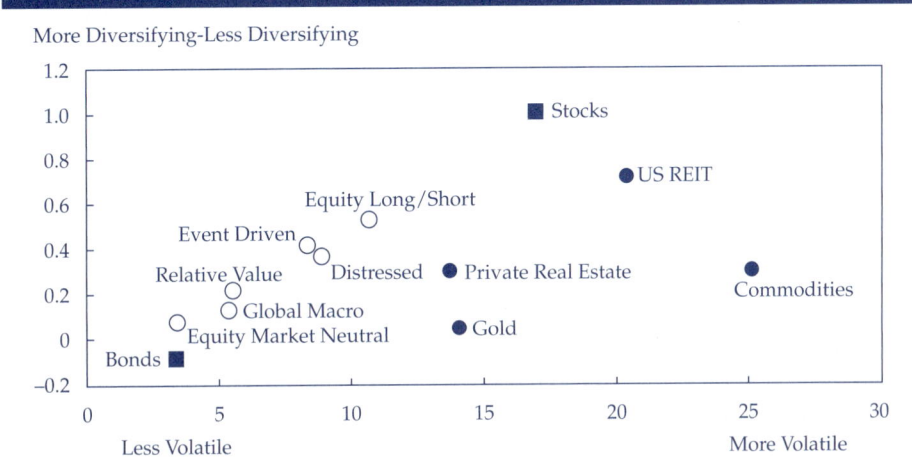

Sources: Bloomberg and authors' own data and calculations.

The Role of Private Equity in a Multi-Asset Portfolio

Private equity investments are generally viewed as a return enhancer in a portfolio of traditional assets. The expectation for a return premium over public equities stems from the illiquidity risk that comes with most forms of private equity investment. Because of the strong link between the fundamentals of private and public companies, there are limited diversification benefits when added to a portfolio that otherwise contains significant public equity exposure. Private equity volatility is not directly observable because holdings are not publicly traded. Assets tend to be valued at the lower of cost or the value at which the company raises additional capital or when ownership changes hands (e.g., through an initial public offering or a sale to a strategic buyer or to another private equity sponsor). Consequently, private equity indexes do not provide a true picture of the strategy's risk. For asset allocation exercises, volatility is often estimated using a public equity proxy with an adjustment to better represent the nature of the private equity program. For example, a proxy for early stage venture capital might be microcap technology companies. A proxy for buyout funds might start with the volatility of a geographically relevant large-cap equity index (e.g., S&P 500, Nikkei), which is then adjusted for relative financial leverage.

The Role of Hedge Funds in a Multi-Asset Portfolio

As illustrated in Exhibit 1, hedge funds span the spectrum from being risk reducers to return enhancers. Generally speaking, long/short equity strategies are believed to deliver equity-like returns with less than full exposure to the equity premium but with an additional source of return that might come from the manager's shorting of individual stocks. Short-biased equity strategies are expected to lower a portfolio's overall equity beta while producing some measure of alpha. Arbitrage and event-driven strategies, executed properly, look to exploit small inefficiencies in the public markets while exhibiting low to no correlation with traditional asset classes. However, most hedge fund arbitrage strategies involve some degree of "short volatility" risk. Because of this "short volatility" risk, the volatility in an arbitrage strategy is non-symmetrical; the aggregate volatility may look muted if the period from which the data are drawn does not include a market stress period. "Opportunistic" strategies (e.g., global macro and managed futures), although very volatile as stand-alone strategies, provide exposures not otherwise readily accessible in traditional stock and bond strategies.

The Role of Real Assets in a Multi-Asset Portfolio

This category includes timber, commodities, farmland, energy, and infrastructure assets. The common thread for these investments is that the underlying investment is a physical asset with a relatively high degree of correlation with inflation broadly or with a sub-component of inflation, such as oil (energy funds), agricultural products (farmland), or pulp and wood products (timber).

Timber investments provide both growth and inflation-hedging properties in a multi-asset portfolio. Growth is provided through the biological growth of the tree itself as well as through the appreciation in the underlying land value. Timber's inflation-hedging characteristics are derived from the unique nature in which the value of the asset is realized: If the market for timber products is weak, the owner of the asset can leave it "on the stump" waiting for prices to rise. While waiting, the volume of the asset increases—the tree continues to grow—and there is ultimately more of the asset to sell when prices recover. At the same time, the volatility of the timber asset rises; the market for more mature timber is more volatile, and the potential loss from pests and natural disasters rises.

Commodities investments (i.e., tradable commodities) fall into the following four categories:

- Metals (gold, silver, platinum, copper)
- Energy (crude oil, natural gas, heating oil, gasoline)
- Livestock and Meat (hogs, pork bellies, live cattle)
- Agricultural (corn, soybeans, wheat, rice, cocoa, coffee, cotton, sugar)

Although it is possible to own the commodity asset directly (e.g., corn, wheat, barrel of oil), most investors will invest in commodity derivatives (i.e., futures contracts) whose price is directly related to the price of the physical commodity. Investors generally own commodities as a hedge against a core constituent of inflation measures as well as a differentiated source of alpha. Gold and other precious metals are frequently owned directly because they are thought to be a good store of value in the face of a depreciating currency. Storage and insurance costs come with owning commodities directly.

Farmland investing involves two primary approaches. The higher return/risk strategy involves owning the farmland while providing the farmer a salary for tending and selling the crops. The investor retains the commodity risk and the execution risk. This approach requires a long time horizon and has high sensitivity to natural disasters and regulatory risk, such as trade disputes. In the other main approach, the investor owns the farmland but leases the property to the farmer. The farmer retains the risk for execution and commodity prices. If an investor pursues this second strategy, farmland is more like core commercial real estate investing than a real asset (commodity) strategy.

Energy investments consist of strategies that focus on the exploration, development, transportation, and delivery of energy (primarily oil and natural gas-based energy sources but also increasingly wind, hydroelectric, and solar) as well as all the ancillary services that facilitate energy production. Investors usually do not own the land that holds the minerals. Most energy investments are executed through call-down, private equity-style funds and are usually long-dated, illiquid holdings. Energy assets are generally considered real assets because the investor owns the mineral rights to certain commodities (e.g., natural gas, oil, methane) that can be correlated with certain inflationary factors. Master limited partnerships (MLPs) are another frequently used vehicle for energy investments. MLPs generally construct and own the pipelines that carry oil or natural gas from the wellhead to the storage facility. MLPs rarely take ownership of the energy assets. The companies charge a fee based on the volume of oil/natural gas they transport. This fee is often pegged to the Producer Price Index.

Infrastructure is a strategy that typically involves the construction and maintenance of public-use projects, such as building bridges, toll roads, or airports. Because of the illiquid nature of these assets, the holding period associated with these funds can be even longer than the typical illiquid strategy, with some lasting 20 years or longer. These assets tend to generate stable or modestly growing income, and the asset itself often requires minimal upkeep or capital expenditures once built. The revenue generated by the assets tends to have high correlation with overall inflation, though it is often subject to regulatory risks because governmental agencies may be involved in price setting with certain jurisdictions and assets.

The Role of Commercial Real Estate in a Multi-Asset Portfolio

Real estate investing involves the development, acquisition, management, and disposition of commercial properties, including retail, office, industrial, housing (including apartments), and hotels. Strategies range from *core,* the ownership of fully occupied properties and collecting rents, to *opportunistic,* ground-up property development (land acquisition, construction, and sale) and/or the purchase of distressed assets with the intent to rehabilitate them.

Real estate investments are believed to provide protection against unanticipated increases in inflation. Two fundamental attributes of real estate investment contribute to this inflation protection. Well-positioned properties frequently have the ability to increase rents in response to inflationary pressures, and the value of the physical buildings may increase with inflation (properties are often valued as a function of replacement cost). In this way, real estate contributes both income and capital gain potential to a portfolio. Building a diversified private commercial real estate program can be challenging for all but the largest and most sophisticated allocators. The public real estate market is a fraction of the size of the private real estate market, but it may be easier and cheaper to build a diversified real estate investment program in some geographies (e.g., United States, Europe) via the public markets. However, private real estate can offer exposures that are difficult if not impossible to achieve through publicly-traded real estate securities. Investing directly (or in a private fund) offers customization by geography, property type, and strategy (e.g., distressed, core, development).

The Role of Private Credit in a Multi-Asset Portfolio

Private credit includes distressed investment and direct lending. Although both strategies involve the ownership of fixed-income assets, their roles in an investment program are quite different. Direct-lending assets are income-producing, and the asset owner assumes any default or recovery risks. Direct-lending assets generally behave like their public market counterparts with similar credit profiles (i.e., high-quality, direct-lending assets behave like investment-grade bonds, and low-quality, direct-lending assets behave like high-yield bonds). Distressed debt assets have a more equity-like profile. The expected return is derived from the value of a company's assets relative to its debt. Illiquidity risks are high with both strategies. Direct-lending assets have no secondary market.

Direct-lending funds provide capital to individuals and small businesses that generally cannot access more traditional lending channels. Some loans are unsecured while others might be backed by an asset, such as a house or car. Direct lending is one of the least liquid debt strategies because there is typically no secondary market for these instruments. Investors in direct-lending strategies gain access to a high-yielding but riskier segment of the debt market that is not available via the traditional public markets.

Distressed funds typically purchase the securities of an entity that is under stress and where the stress is relieved through legal restructuring or bankruptcy. The investment can take the form of debt or equity, and in many strategies, the manager often takes an active role throughout the restructuring or bankruptcy. Because many investors are precluded from owning companies or entities that are in bankruptcy or default, managers of distressed funds are often able to purchase assets (usually the debt) at a significant discount. Experience with the bankruptcy process frequently distinguishes these managers from others. Although the asset is usually a bond, distressed investments typically have low sensitivity to traditional bond risks (i.e., interest rate changes or changes in spreads) because the idiosyncratic risk of the company itself dominates all other risks.

2   DIVERSIFYING EQUITY RISK

☐ | compare alternative investments and bonds as risk mitigators in relation to a long equity position

In this section, we examine the claim that alternative assets may be better risk mitigators than government bonds. To address this question, we must agree on *which* risks alternatives are said to mitigate and on *what* time horizon is relevant. If your investment horizon is short term, volatility may be the most important risk measure. If you are a long-term investor, not achieving the long-horizon return objective may be the most relevant concern.

Volatility Reduction over the Short Time Horizon

Let's look first at the short horizon investor and consider how alternative asset classes compare to bonds as a volatility reducer in an equity-dominated portfolio. Advocates of alternative investments as risk reducers sometimes argue that alternative investments' volatilities calculated based on reported returns are significantly lower than the volatility of public equities. An immediate technical challenge is that reported returns of many alternative asset classes need an adjustment called **unsmoothing** for proper risk estimation. (Various approaches have been developed to unsmooth a return series that demonstrates serial correlation. The specifics of those approaches are beyond the scope of this reading.) In the case of private investments, reported returns are calculated from appraisal-based valuations that may result in volatility and correlation estimates that are too low. (The underlying assumptions in most appraisal models tend to lead to gradual and incremental changes in appraised value that may not accurately capture the asset's true price realized in an actual transaction. The low volatility of the return stream may also dampen the reported correlation between the appraisal-based asset and the more volatile market-based asset.) Other factors may also contribute to underestimated risk across alternatives. For example, **survivorship bias** and **back-fill bias** (reporting returns to a database only after they are known to be good returns) in hedge fund databases can potentially lead to an understatement of downside risk. Additionally, a hedge fund "index" includes many managers whose returns exhibit low correlation; in the same way that combining stocks and bonds in a portfolio can be expected to lower overall portfolio volatility, so too does combining several hedge funds into an "index."

As an example, we build a hypothetical, equally-weighted index of long/short equity hedge funds with volatilities ranging from 6% to 11%. As shown in Exhibit 5, given the less-than-perfect correlation among the constituents of our index, the index volatility is only 4.9%:

Exhibit 5: Volatility Is Less Than the Sum of Its Parts

	Fund 1	Fund 2	Fund 3	Fund 4	Fund 5	Combined
Volatility	10.9%	6.5%	8.5%	9.7%	8.1%	**4.9%**
Correlation						
Fund 1		−0.02	0.14	0.00	0.15	
Fund 2			0.27	0.39	0.29	
Fund 3				0.25	−0.03	
Fund 4					0.14	

Exhibit 6 shows the correlations of fixed-income and alternative asset classes to public equities based on observed market data over 1997–2017. We also show each asset class's estimated equity beta. To estimate correlations and betas, we used unsmoothed return data for alternative asset classes. We discuss unsmoothing of returns in more detail in a later section.

Exhibit 6: Fixed-Income's and Alternative's Equity Beta and Correlation with Equities

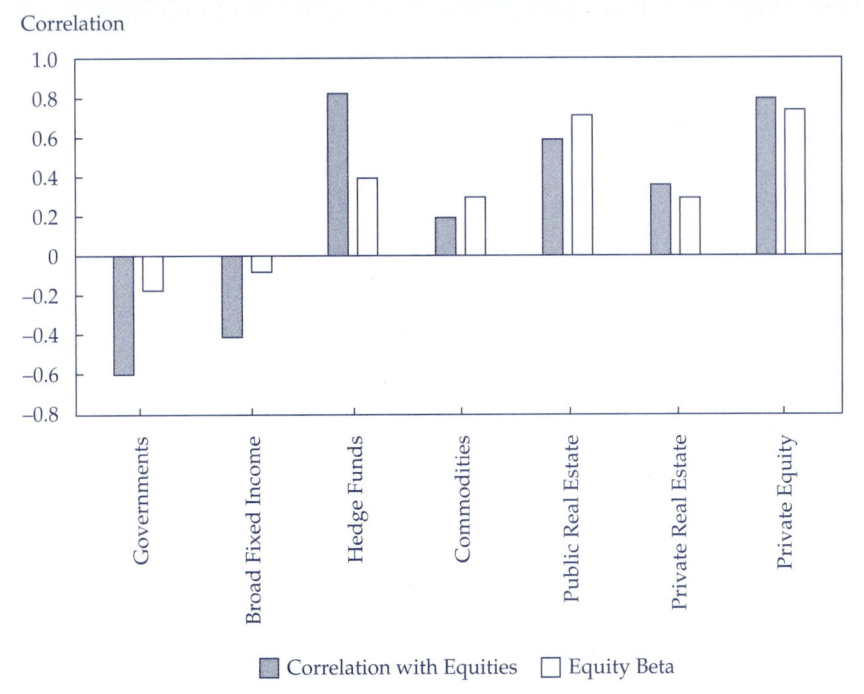

Sources: Bloomberg and authors' own data and calculations.

Most of the alternative investment categories had positive, but less than perfect, correlation with equities. Although certain alternatives (e.g., commodities, particularly gold) may rally during a public equity market downturn, other alternative investments—like hedge funds, private credit, or private equities—also experience drawdowns at the same time the equity market falls. Hedge funds and private equities have a correlation co-efficient with equities over +0.8, and this indicates a fairly strong positive relationship between public equities and these alternative investments.

Government bonds, however, have a −0.6 estimated correlation with equities, which indicates a negative relationship of moderate strength. This is consistent with the tendency for government bonds to serve as a risk haven during "risk-off" or "flight to quality" episodes.

Although correlation and beta have the same sign and are statistically interrelated, we have to remember that they quantify two different things. The correlation coefficient quantifies the strength of a linear relationship between two variables, thus playing a crucial role in portfolio diversification: The lower the correlation, the stronger the asset's diversification power. Beta, however, measures the response of an asset to a unit change in a reference index; for example, equity beta measures how various assets would respond to a 1% rise of public equities. Hedge funds' beta is estimated at around 0.4; thus, we would expect a 0.4% return (excluding manager alpha) from hedge funds if equities rose by 1%. Hedge funds' relatively low beta (0.4) and high correlation (+0.8) means that hedge funds' rise or fall is milder than those of public equities in magnitude, but this directional relationship is fairly strong in a statistical sense. Commodities also have an equity beta of similar positive magnitude (0.3), but their correlation with equities is much weaker (+0.2); so, we can expect that a much bigger portion of commodity price changes would be driven by factors unrelated to the equity markets.

In Exhibit 7, we compare the total return volatility of public equities (black bar) with volatilities of portfolios comprised of 70% equity and 30% other asset classes. Using 20 years of data, the volatility of public equities is estimated at approximately 17%. A portfolio allocated 70% to equity and 30% to cash would imply a portfolio volatility of 11.9% (70% × 17%). Portfolios of 70% equities and 30% any of the alternative asset classes also reduces portfolio volatility relative to an all-equity portfolio, but the lowest volatility of 11.1% could be achieved by combining equities with government bonds because of the negative correlation between these two asset classes.

Exhibit 7: Volatility of Portfolios Comprised of 70% Equities and 30% Other Asset Class

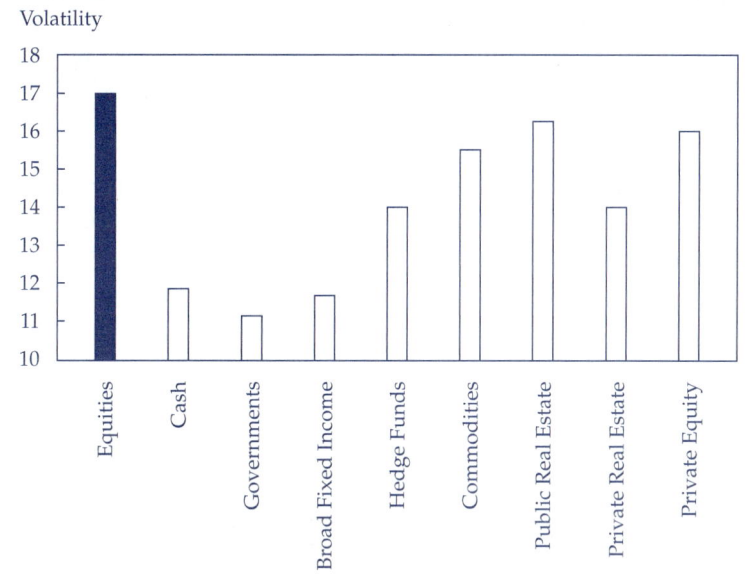

Sources: Bloomberg and authors' own data and calculations.

Bear in mind, however, that this analysis is based on 20 years of returns ending in 2017, a period that was characterized by a persistent negative equity–bond correlation. Because there was limited inflation in developed markets over this period, economic growth prospects were the dominant influence on asset prices. Positive growth surprises are good for equities (better earnings outlook) and negative for bonds (potential central bank rate increases). If inflation becomes a threat, bonds' risk mitigation power could erode. Exhibit 8 looks at the US equity–bond correlation since the 1950s. As the chart suggests, the correlation between US equities and government bonds was, in fact, positive in the 1970s through the 1990s when inflation was also more elevated.

Exhibit 8: Long-Term Historical Equity–Bond Correlation and Inflation

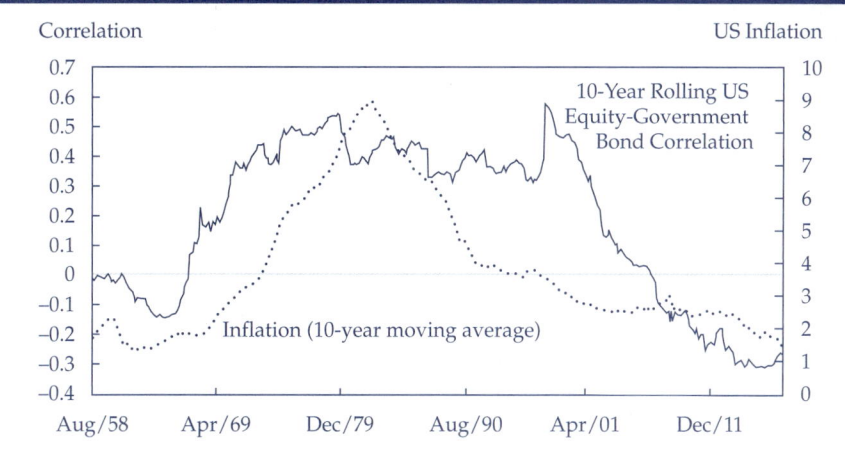

Sources: Bloomberg and the authors' own data and calculations.

Risk of Not Meeting the Investment Goals over the Long Time Horizon

Volatility is not always the most relevant risk measure. An endowment portfolio is often focused on generating a total return equal to at least the spending rate, say 5%, plus inflation to preserve real value of capital over a long time horizon. When bond yields are very low, the likelihood of meeting the investment objective would be reduced given a heavy allocation to bonds, simply because the portfolio's value would likely grow more slowly than the rate implied by the spending rate and inflation. Exhibit 9 illustrates this point: We show the probability of achieving a 5% real (7.1% nominal[3]) return over various horizons up to 10-years for three 70% equity/30% other asset class portfolios. We used quarterly rebalancing. Although allocating the 30% "other" to government bonds would lead to the greatest reduction in portfolio volatility, government bonds also have lower expected return compared to hedge funds and private equity (see Exhibit 2).

Exhibit 9: The Probability of Achieving Investment Objectives over the Longer Time Horizon

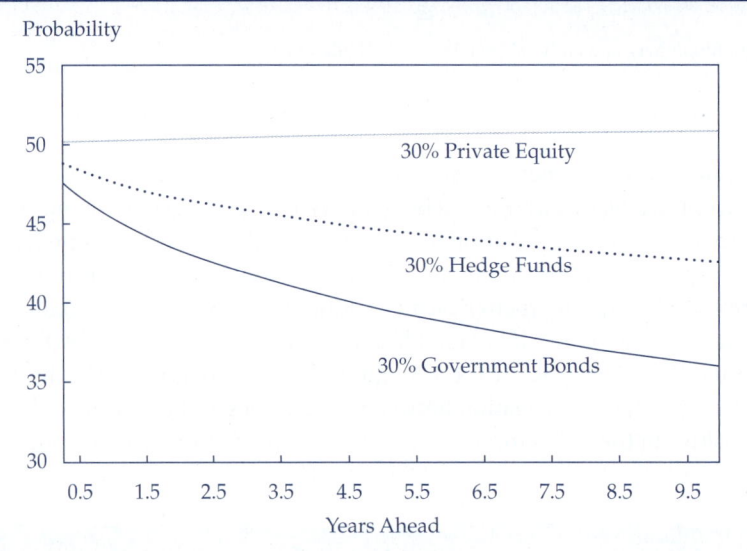

Note: Portfolios comprised of 70% equities and 30% other asset classes.

Source: Authors' calculations.

The 70% public equities/30% government bond portfolio has an expected return of 5.7%[4], below the nominal return target of 7.1%. The 70% public equities/30% private equities portfolio has an expected geometric return of 7.2%, slightly over the return target. Both portfolios' expected returns are 50th percentile returns; there is a 50% probability that this is the return that would be realized over time. Thus, the 70% public equities/30% private equities portfolio, with a nominal expected return of 7.2%, has slightly better than a 50% probability of meeting the 7.1% nominal return target. The 70% public equities/30% government bond portfolio, with an expected return less than the nominal return target, therefore has less than a 50% probability of meeting

---

3 By using the Fisher equation to combine the 5% real return and 2% inflation: $(1 + 5\%) * (1 + 2\%) - 1 = 7.1\%$.
4 Note that geometric expected return is approximated as the expected arithmetic return minus half of the investment's variance. Thus, portfolio expected geometric return is not simply the weighted average of the asset classes' expected geometric returns because portfolio variance benefits from diversification.

the required return. Why does the 70% public equities/30% private equities portfolio maintain its 50%+ probability of meeting the return target over time while the probability that the 70% public equities/30% government bond portfolio meets the return target declines over time? As the time horizon lengthens, return accumulation (compounding) becomes more and more important. In a simplified way, return accumulates proportionally with time, whereas volatility scales with the square root of time. Thus, as we lengthen the time horizon, the gap between the cumulative return target and the expected return accumulation widens faster than the range of possible portfolio return outcomes. As a result, the likelihood of a low-returning portfolio catching up to the target return declines over time.

To summarize, bonds have been a more effective volatility mitigator than alternatives over shorter time horizons, but over long horizons, a heavy allocation to bonds would reduce the probability of achieving the investment goal. It is important to emphasize that volatility and the probability of achieving the target return are two very different dimensions of risk. Volatility addresses interim fluctuations in portfolio return, whereas achieving a return target takes on increasing importance as we expand the time horizon over multiple years. Both risks are important, especially for a program that is distributing 7% of assets per year as in this example. Although the 30% allocation to private equity increases the chance of meeting the expected return, a severe and sustained short-term drawdown in the public equity markets could significantly handicap the fund's ability to achieve its long-term return objectives. This is why drawdowns (related to volatility) need to be considered and managed.

EXAMPLE 1

Mitigating Equity Risk by Allocating to Hedge Funds or Bonds

The investment committee of a major foundation is concerned about high equity valuations and would like to increase the allocation either to hedge funds or to high-grade, fixed-income assets to diversify equity risk. As the risk manager of this foundation:

1. Discuss the justifications and the limitations of using bonds to mitigate equity risk.

Solution:

- Supporting argument: Bonds have exhibited negative correlation and beta to equities in a low inflation environment, so as long as inflation stays at or below average historical levels, this negative equity–bond correlation should lead to the highest reduction in portfolio volatility.

- Limitations: The negative stock/bond correlation may be temporary, and amid high inflation the stock/bond correlation could turn positive. Furthermore, if bonds' expected return is low, a heavy allocation to bonds may reduce the probability of achieving the foundation's long-term return objectives.

2. Discuss the justifications and the limitations of using hedge funds to mitigate equity risk.

Solution:

- Supporting argument: With an equity beta of around 0.4 (see Exhibit 2), hedge funds would reduce an equity-dominated portfolio's overall beta. With higher expected returns than bonds, an allocation to hedge funds would make achieving the long-term return target more feasible.

- Limitations: Although a well-constructed hedge fund portfolio may reduce portfolio volatility and beta, hedge funds are often highly actively managed, levered investment strategies, and individual hedge funds may suffer significant and permanent losses during turbulent times.

3   TRADITIONAL APPROACHES TO ASSET CLASSIFICATION

☐ | compare traditional and risk-based approaches to defining the investment opportunity set, including alternative investments

In this section, we consider how traditional approaches to asset allocation can be adapted to include alternative investments and how investors can apply risk-based approaches to incorporate alternatives in their asset allocation. This reading extends the asset allocation framework introduced in earlier readings on asset allocation. Although the ultimate goal of meeting the investment objectives subject to the relevant constraints remains the same, investors often face several analytical and operational challenges when introducing alternative asset classes.

Traditional Approaches to Asset Classification

When defining asset classes for the traditional approaches to asset allocation, investors may group and classify alternative assets along several dimensions. Two common approaches (in addition to the growth–income–diversification–safety roles described earlier) are with respect to the liquidity of the asset class and with respect to asset behavior under various economic conditions.

A Liquidity-Based Approach to Defining the Opportunity Set

Certain alternative investments, like REITs or commodity futures, are highly liquid and can be easily traded in public markets. Private investments, however, are highly illiquid and usually require long-term commitments (more than 10 years) from the investors. Of course, there are differences among various private asset classes in this respect as well: Private equity investments may require longer than a 10-year commitment, while the term of a private credit fund can be shorter, say 5 to 8 years. Although public equity and private equity may be similar asset classes from the fundamental economic point of view, they differ significantly in their liquidity characteristics.

The long investment horizon and the lack of liquidity in many of the alternative asset classes make it difficult to accurately characterize their risk characteristics for purposes of the asset allocation exercise. One approach to dealing with this issue is to make the initial asset allocation decision using only the broad, liquid asset classes in which the underlying data that drive risk, return, and correlation assumptions are robust (e.g., stocks, bonds, and real estate). A second iteration of the asset allocation exercise would break the equity/fixed-income/real estate asset allocation down further by using the asset groupings as shown in Exhibit 10, which illustrates a possible categorization of asset classes that incorporates their broad liquidity profile.

Exhibit 10: Major Asset Class Categories

	Equity & Equity-Like	Fixed Income & Fixed Income-Like	Real Estate
Marketable/Liquid	Public Equity Long/Short Equity Hedge Funds	Fixed Income Cash	Public Real Estate Commodities
Private/Illiquid	Private Equity	Private Credit	Private Real Estate Private Real Assets

An Approach Based on Expected Performance under Distinct Macroeconomic Regimes

Investors may also categorize asset classes based on how they are expected to behave under different macroeconomic environments, and investors may assign roles to them in a broad macroeconomic context:

- *Capital growth assets* would be expected to benefit from healthy economic growth. Public and private equities would belong to this category.
- *Inflation-hedging assets*—so-called "real assets" such as real estate, commodities, and natural resources but also inflation-linked bonds—would be expected to outperform other asset classes when inflation expectations rise or actual inflation exceeds expectations.
- *Deflation-hedging assets* (e.g., nominal government bonds) would be expected to outperform most of the other asset classes when the economy slows and inflation becomes very low or negative.

In Exhibit 11, we illustrate how investors may think about the expected performance of various asset classes in a broad macroeconomic context. Each asset class is positioned along the continuum to illustrate the macroeconomic environment in which we would expect it to generate strong performance. Such mapping is usually based on both historical experience and qualitative judgment. Considering the fundamental economic drivers of asset classes could help investors construct portfolios that are better diversified and more robust under various economic conditions and scenarios.

Exhibit 11: Asset Classes Grouped by the Macroeconomic Environment under Which They Would Be Expected to Generate Strong Performance

		Inflation Environment		
		Deflation	Moderate Inflation	High Inflation
Economic Environment	High Growth		Public Equity Private Equity High-Yield Bonds Private Credit	Real Estate Commodities
	Low Growth/ Recession	Government Bonds		Inflation-Linked Bonds Gold

Source: Authors' data.

Exhibit 12 illustrates the average quarterly total return of various asset classes and alternative strategies under stronger and weaker economic growth environments between 1997 and 2017, a period of low to moderate inflation in developed markets.

Exhibit 12: Historical Asset Class Performance under Stronger and Weaker Economic Growth Periods (1997–2017)

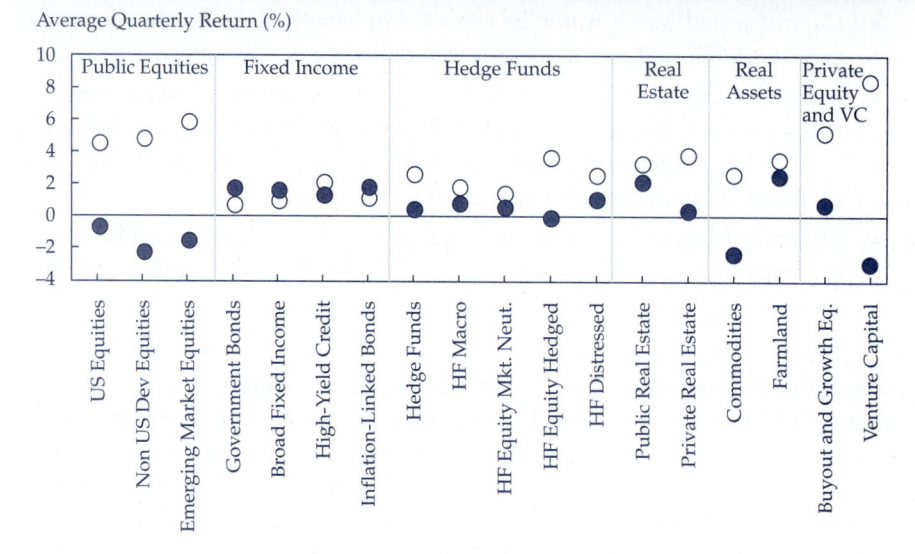

Notes: Strong and weak economic periods were determined using quarterly GDP data. Strong growth periods were those quarters when GDP growth exceeded the average GDP growth through the full historical sample.

Sources: The exhibit is based on the authors' calculations. Index data is based on the following. US Equities: Russell 3000; Non-US Developed Market Equities: MSCI EAFE USD Net unhedged; Emerging Market Equities: MSCI Emerging Markets Net USD unhedged; Governments: Bloomberg Barclays US Treasury Index; Broad Fixed Income: Bloomberg Barclays US Aggregate; High Yield: Bloomberg Barclays US Corporate High Yield; Inflation-Linked Bonds: Bloomberg Barclays US Government Inflation-Linked Bonds Index; Hedge Funds: HFRI; Public Real Estate: Dow Jones Equity REIT Index; Private Real Estate: NCREIF Property Index; Commodities: S&P GSCI Total Return Index; Farmland: NCREIF Farmland Index; Buyout and Growth Equities: Cambridge Associates US Private Equity Index; Venture Capital: Cambridge Associates US Venture Capital Index.

Public and private equities, hedge funds, and commodities posted strong returns amid strong economic growth conditions and weaker returns amid weaker economic conditions. Commodities exhibit a bigger disparity between returns in periods of stronger and weaker growth than does the hedge fund category.

Within fixed income, government bonds posted higher returns during periods of weaker economic growth—when investors likely reallocated from risky assets to safer assets. On the other hand, high-yield bonds (and potentially private credit, if we assume a behavior pattern similar to that of high-yield bonds) performed well during periods of stronger economic growth but posted lower returns during weaker economic periods, likely because of concerns about weakening credit quality.

Understanding how various asset classes behave under distinct macroeconomic regimes enables investors to tailor the asset allocation to align with their fundamental goals or to mitigate their fundamental risks. If the investment portfolio has a specific goal, such as hedging inflation risk, then it would be logical to build a portfolio that is dominated by asset classes that are expected to perform best amid rising inflation. Even if the portfolio's goal is to generate high return over the long run, combining "growth" asset classes with "inflation-hedging" or "deflation-hedging" asset classes could make the asset allocation more resilient to changing economic and market conditions. This approach can be extended to macroeconomic scenario analysis and stress testing when the analyst evaluates how various asset allocation options would perform under conditions of high or low economic growth and/or inflation, and it can identify which economic conditions would hurt the investment portfolio the most.

RISK-BASED APPROACHES TO ASSET CLASSIFICATION

4

☐ | compare traditional and risk-based approaches to defining the investment opportunity set, including alternative investments

When we assign traditional and alternative asset classes to certain functional roles in the portfolio, or when we assess how different asset classes would perform under distinct macroeconomic regimes, we can also easily realize that many traditional and alternative asset classes share similar characteristics that can result in high correlations. We may put public equities in the same functional bucket as private equity, and we may expect elevated default rates from high-yield bonds and private credit during recessionary environments.

Exhibit 13 compares the betas of various traditional and alternative asset classes to global equities. The chart clearly shows that private equity and venture capital asset classes have global equity betas similar to public equites. On the other hand, betas of various hedge fund strategies differ significantly. Hedge fund returns, in aggregate, had a beta of 0.4. However, global macro or equity market-neutral strategies had betas as low as 0.1. The long/short "equity hedged" strategy's beta is estimated to be much higher, around 0.5, which is consistent with its long equity bias.

Exhibit 13: Global Equity Beta of Various Asset Classes, 1997–2017

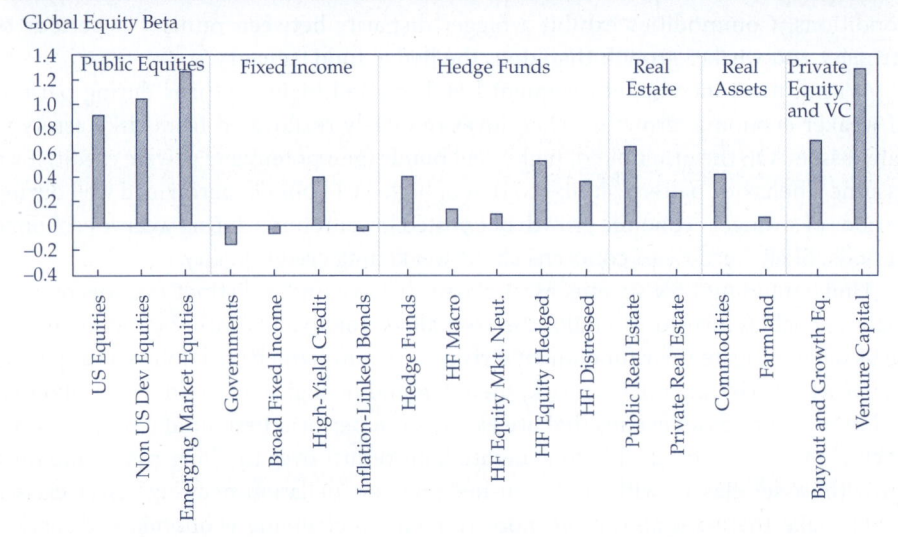

Note: Betas were estimated as a regression slope of representative index returns relative to the global equity return stream over the time period 1997–2017.

Sources: Authors' calculations; index data sources are the same as those in Exhibit 12.

Many investors have begun to view asset allocation through a risk factor lens to capture these similarities. In this section, we extend the risk factor asset allocation framework introduced in earlier readings to alternative investments using the following risk factors:

- *Equity market return*: representative of the general direction of global equity markets, and investors may also refer to this as the best market proxy for "growth."

- *Size*: excess return of small-cap equities over large-cap equities.

- *Value*: excess return of value versus growth stocks (*negative* factor sensitivity = *growth* bias.

- *Liquidity*: the Pastor–Stambaugh liquidity factor[5]—a market-wide liquidity measure based on the excess returns of stocks with large sensitivity to changes in aggregate liquidity (less-liquid stocks) versus stocks with less sensitivity to changing liquidity (more-liquid stocks).

- *Duration*: sensitivity to 10-year government yield changes.

- *Inflation*: sensitivity to 10-year breakeven inflation changes obtained from the inflation-linked bond markets.

- *Credit spread*: sensitivity to changes in high-yield spread.

- *Currency*: sensitivity to changes in the domestic currency versus a basket of foreign currencies.

This framework can easily be extended further to other risk factors, like momentum or volatility.

Exhibit 14 illustrates risk factor sensitivities of various traditional and alternative investment strategies using a construct as discussed by Naik, Devarajan, Nowobilski, Page, and Pedersen (2016). The parameters in the table are regression coefficients based on 20 years of historical data. Quarterly index returns representing each asset class were regressed on the risk factors listed previously. Note that for conventional

---

5 For more details on Pastor–Stambaugh liquidity factors, see Naik et al. (2016).

reasons we changed the signs of the "nominal duration" and "credit spread" sensitivities: The 4.2 duration of broad fixed income, for example, means that this asset class would experience an approximate 4.2% decline in response to a 100 bps increase in the nominal interest rates.

Exhibit 14: Factor Sensitivity Estimates across Various Asset Classes

Asset Classes	Equity	Size	Value	Liquidity	Nominal Duration	Inflation	Credit Spread	Currency	R-squared
US Equities	1.0								1.00
Non-US Dev Equities	0.9							0.7	0.86
Emerging Mkt Equities	1.1	0.5						0.5	0.66
Government Bonds					4.8				0.96
Broad Fixed Income					4.2		0.6		0.89
High-Yield Credit					4.1		4.2		0.95
Inflation-Linked Bonds					6.6	7.0			0.82
Hedge Funds	0.3	0.1					0.6		0.74
HF Macro	0.2	0.2			1.9	3.1	−0.9	0.1	0.28
HF Equity Mkt. Neut.	0.1								0.14
HF Equity Hedged	0.5								0.72
HF Distressed	0.1	0.2					1.8		0.72
Commodities						18.0		0.8	0.36
Public Real Estate	0.9				4.6	0.9			0.38
Private Real Estate	0.2			0.1		2.4			0.20
Buyout & Growth Equities	0.6	0.2	−0.3	0.1					0.70
Venture Capital	0.8	0.6	−1.8	0.2					0.38

Note: Only statistically significant slopes are displayed in the exhibit. Sources are the same as those for Exhibit 12.

In a risk factor-based asset allocation framework, the factors represent the systematic risks embedded in the selected asset classes and investment strategies. The primary systematic risk factors would fully, or almost fully, explain the behavior of broad, passive traditional public asset classes. There should be a relatively larger portion of unexplained risk in the alternative asset classes. This arises from such issues as the appraisal-based valuation in real estate, the idiosyncratic risks in the portfolio companies of private equity funds, or the idiosyncratic risks in hedge funds resulting from active management. (This last one is logically intuitive if you subscribe to the belief that returns generated by hedge fund strategies should be primarily driven by *alpha* rather than systematic risk factors.)

The extension of the risk factor framework to alternative asset classes allows every asset class to be described using the same framework. Investors can therefore more clearly understand their sources of investment risk and identify the intended and unintended tilts and biases they have in the portfolio. Furthermore, a risk factor framework enables investors to more efficiently allocate capital and risk in a multi-dimensional framework (i.e., a framework that seeks to do more than simply achieve the highest return at a given level of volatility). If an investor, for example, would like to increase the portfolio's inflation risk-mitigating exposure, decomposing this specific risk factor from inflation-linked bonds, real estate, or commodity asset classes could help the investor to identify the asset classes and exposures that are most likely to facilitate that goal.

Risk factor-based approaches improve upon the traditional approaches in identifying the investment opportunity set but do have certain limitations. As mentioned earlier, a small set of systematic risk factors is insufficient to describe the historical return stream of alternative asset classes. Note that all non-zero-risk factor coefficients displayed in the table are statistically significant based on their t-statistics. Although our eight illustrative factors fit the total return history of traditional asset classes with r-squared statistics of 0.8–1.0, the r-squared ratios for alternative investments are lower, ranging between 0.3 and 0.7. Increasing the number of risk factors would certainly improve the goodness of fit, but too many factors could make the risk factor-based asset allocation framework difficult to handle and interpret. In addition, certain risk factor sensitivities can be quite volatile, making a "point in time" factor-based definition of an asset class a poor descriptor of the class's expected behavior. For example, the aggregate hedge fund inflation beta typically fluctuates in the range of 0.3 to 0.4, while the inflation beta of commodities fluctuates much more widely.[6]

EXAMPLE 2

Applying Risk Factors for Inflation Hedging

1. The CIO (chief investment officer) of the United Retired Workers Plan would like to reduce inflation risk in the portfolio. Based on the data displayed in Exhibit 14, which asset classes would you recommend as potential inflation-hedging tools?

Solution:

Commodities and inflation-linked bonds have the highest factor sensitivity to inflation, so they are the most obvious candidates. Real estate (both public and private) also has some potential to protect against inflation. Based on the data presented, macro hedge fund strategies also exhibited a positive inflation beta, but given their active nature, further analysis may be needed before choosing them as inflation-hedging vehicles.

2. The CIO is not only concerned about inflation but also rising interest rates. Which alternative asset classes would you recommend for consideration?

Solution:

Commodities and private real estate would be the likely asset classes to hedge against rising interest rates, given their zero-factor sensitivity to nominal duration. Some of the hedge fund strategies also show zero-factor sensitivity to duration, but the relationship may not hold true in the future given the actively managed nature of hedge funds. Although Exhibit 14 indicates equity strategies (both public and private) also show little to no sensitivity to rising interest rates (duration) bonds and equities have been more highly correlated in the past.

---

6 For further detail on expanding asset allocation to risk allocation, we refer to Naik et al. (2016) and Cambridge Associates LLC (2013).

Illustration: Asset Allocation and Risk-Based Approaches

Let's look at an example of how a risk-based approach may enhance traditional asset allocation. In Exhibit 15, we show two investment portfolios, Portfolio A and Portfolio B, that have exactly the same high-level asset allocations. However, the underlying investments in the two portfolios are quite different. The fixed-income assets in Portfolio A are government bonds, while the fixed-income assets in Portfolio B are high-yield bonds. Hedge fund investments in Portfolio A are represented by very low equity beta market neutral strategies, while Portfolio B is invested in the higher beta long/short equity hedge funds. Similarly, Portfolio B's investments in real assets and private equity have higher risk than those in Portfolio A.

Exhibit 15: Traditional Asset Allocation and Risk Contribution Comparison						
Broad Asset Classes	**Asset Allocation**		**Underlying Investments**		**% Contribution to Risk**	
	Portfolio A	**Portfolio B**	**Portfolio A**	**Portfolio B**	**Portfolio A**	**Portfolio B**
Fixed Income	20%	20%	Government Bonds	High-Yield Bonds	−6.5%	7.6%
Public Equities	20%	20%	US Equities	Non-US Developed Equities	51.4%	18.2%
Hedge Funds	20%	20%	Equity Market Neutral	Long/Short Equity	5.4%	11.1%
Real Assets	20%	20%	Inflation-linked bonds	REITs	0.7%	13.2%
Private Equity	20%	20%	Buyout	Venture Capital	48.9%	49.8%
Total	**100%**	**100%**				
				Expected Return	**5.3%**	**8.8%**
				Volatility	**5.9%**	**16.5%**
				Equity Beta	**0.30**	**0.79**

Notes: The percentage contribution to risk is a result of three components: the asset allocation to a specific asset, its volatility, and its correlation with the other assets. For fixed income, the contribution to total risk is negative in the case of Portfolio A because government bonds have negative correlations with other asset classes; however, it is positive in the case of Portfolio B because high-yield bonds have positive correlations with the other asset classes.
Source: Authors' calculations.

As a result of these major differences between nominally similar broad asset allocations, it is not surprising that Portfolio B has higher volatility, beta, and expected return compared to Portfolio A. Let's look more closely at the risk contribution of each of the asset classes:

Portfolio A.

The majority of the risk in Portfolio A comes from public and private equity. Hedge funds contribute approximately 5% to the total risk, and fixed income actually reduces risk because government bonds had negative correlations with public equities in our historical data sample.

Portfolio B.

Private equity explains about half of the total portfolio risk of Portfolio B. (In this portfolio, the private equity allocation is represented by the higher risk venture capital.) Public equities, hedge funds, and real assets each contribute roughly the same to the total risk of the portfolio. This is consistent with the equity-like characteristics of the underlying assets in the portfolio. The long/short equity hedged strategy has an equity beta of around 0.5, and REITs have an equity beta of 0.9. In Portfolio B, fixed income contributes positively to total risk, consistent with high-yield bonds' positive correlation with equities over the time series.

Although the nominal asset allocations of the two portfolios are the same, the risk profile and the risk allocation among asset classes are significantly different. Let's go one step further and apply the risk factor sensitivities of Exhibit 14 to our hypothetical portfolios. Exhibit 16 shows the absolute contribution to total portfolio risk by risk factor. This approach moves beyond the borders of asset classes and aggregates the equity risk factor embedded in public equities, private equities, venture capital, and REITs into a single-factor contribution. Both portfolios are highly dominated by exposure to equity risk. Portfolio A's total risk is almost fully explained by the exposure to the equity factor, while about 70% of Portfolio B's total risk comes from the equity risk factor alone. Portfolio B also has exposure to the size and value factors, driven by the allocation to venture capital. Finally, we can also see that although Portfolio B is not directly investing in government bonds, some risk mitigation benefit still arises from the low "duration" component of high-yield bonds and REITs.

Exhibit 16: Absolute Contribution to Total Risk by Risk Factors

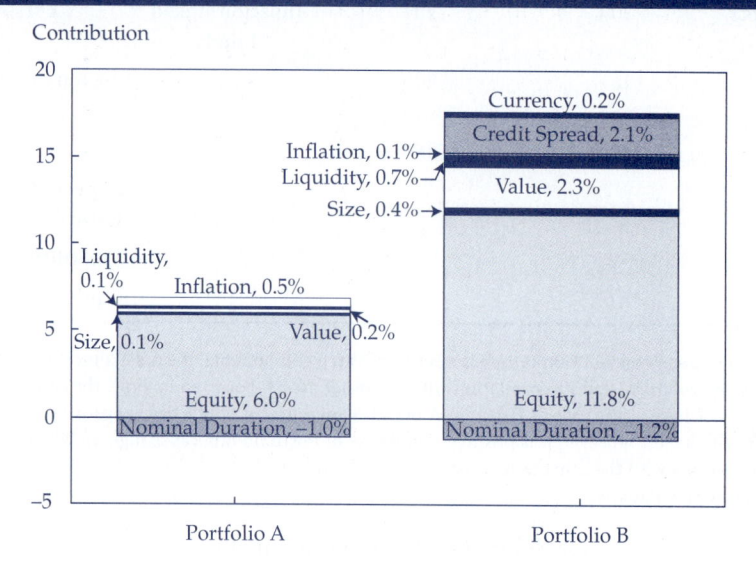

This is an extreme example (the two portfolios have vastly different expected returns), but it is useful to illustrate how factor sensitivities can be used to explore the underlying risk exposures in seemingly similar asset allocations.

Comparing Risk-Based and Traditional Approaches

Investors often employ multiple approaches in setting their asset allocation for a portfolio that includes alternative investments. When applying these various approaches, investors must consider their strengths and limitations.

Main strengths of traditional approaches:

- *Easy to communicate.* Listing the roles of various asset classes is intuitive and easy to explain to the decision makers, who often have familiarity with the traditional asset class-based approach. Scenario analyses based on historical or expected behavior of various asset classes under different macroeconomic conditions can help to introduce quantitative aspects of the portfolio's expected performance and risk and substantiate the asset allocation proposal.

- *Relevance for liquidity management and operational considerations.* Public and private asset class mandates have vastly distinct liquidity profiles. Thus, although private and public equity would have a lot of commonality in their risk factor exposures, they would be positioned very differently from a liquidity management perspective. Similarly, investors must implement the target asset allocation by allocating to investment managers. The traditional categorization of asset classes may be necessary to identify the relevant mandates—what portion of the equity portfolio she would like to allocate to equity-oriented hedge funds rather than to long-only equity managers.

Main limitations of traditional approaches:

- *Over-estimation of portfolio diversification.* Without a proper analytical framework for assessing risk, investors may have a false sense of diversification. An allocation spread across a large number of different asset classes may appear to be very well diversified, when, in fact, the underlying investments may be subject to the same underlying risks.

- *Obscured primary drivers of risk.* Investments with very different risk characteristics may be commingled under the same asset class category. For example, government bonds and high-yield bonds may both be classified as "fixed income," but each has distinct risk characteristics.

Risk-based approaches are designed to overcome some of these limitations.

Key benefits of risk-based approaches:

- *Common risk factor identification.* Investors are able to identify common risk factors across all investments, whether public or private, passive or active.

- *Integrated risk framework.* Investors are able to build an integrated risk management framework, leading to more reliable portfolio-level risk quantification.

Key limitations of risk-based approaches:

- *Sensitivity to the historical look-back period.* Empirical risk factor exposure estimations may be sensitive to the historical sample. For example, the duration of a bond portfolio or the beta of a diversified equity portfolio could be reasonably stable, but the estimated inflation sensitivity of real assets can change rapidly over time. Thus, the analyst has to be cautious when interpreting some of the risk factor sensitivities, such as the "inflation beta" of commodities.

- *Implementation hurdles.* Establishing a strategic target to different risk factors is a very important high-level decision, but converting these risk factor targets to actual investment mandates requires additional considerations, including liquidity planning, time and effort for manager selection, and rebalancing policy.

- *Determining which risk factors should be used and how to measure them in different asset classes.* One drawback with risk-based approaches is the decision on which risk factors to use is somewhat subjective and how these factors are measured can also be subjective. For example, if using a liquidity factor, should it be measured by the Pastor-Stambaugh metric or by some other metric?

  This issue is highlighted by noting that in Level III *Hedge Fund Strategies*, hedge fund returns are analyzed via a conditional factor model using just four risk factors: equities, credit, currencies, and volatility. These risk factors were selected as they are deemed to provide a reasonably broad cross-section of risk exposures for the typical hedge fund, and each of the factor returns can be realized through relatively liquid instruments.

  In sum, a limitation of risk-based approaches is the potential subjectivity embedded in their implementation.

5   RISK CONSIDERATIONS, RETURN EXPECTATIONS, AND INVESTMENT VEHICLE

☐ | discuss investment considerations that are important in allocating to different types of alternative investments

In addition to the risk, return, and correlation characteristics relevant to the decision to invest in the alternative asset classes, many operational and practical complexities must be considered before finalizing a decision to invest. It is essential that the investor be fully aware of these complexities: Failure to grasp these differences between traditional and alternative investments can derail an investment program. The primary factors to consider include:

- properly defining risk characteristics;
- establishing return expectations;
- selection of the appropriate investment vehicle;
- operational liquidity issues;
- expense and fee considerations;
- tax considerations (applicable for taxable entities); and
- build vs. buy.

Risk Considerations

Mean–variance optimization (MVO), widely used in modeling asset allocation choices, cannot easily accommodate the characteristics of most alternative investments. MVO characterizes an asset's risk using standard deviation. Standard deviation is a one-dimensional view of risk and an especially poor representation of the risk characteristics of alternative investments—where assets suffer some degree of illiquidity, valuations may be subjective, and returns may be "chunky" and not normally distributed. The non-standard deviation risks are usually accommodated in an MVO framework by assigning a higher standard deviation than might be derived solely by looking at the historical returns of the asset class.

Most approaches to asset allocation assume that the portfolio's allocation to an asset class is always fully invested. Although this is not an assumption that is limited to alternatives, the problem is exaggerated with the private alternative strategies where it could take several years for capital to be invested and where capital is returned to the investor as investments are sold. Thus, it is rare that the *actual* asset allocation of a program with a significant exposure to alternatives will mirror the *modeled* asset allocation. This suggests that the investor must carefully (and continually) monitor the program's aggregate exposures to ensure that the risks are in line with the strategic asset allocation. A case in point: Some investors over-allocated to private equity, real-estate, and other call-down funds prior to 2008 in order to more quickly reach their asset allocation targets. Many of these investors then found themselves in a situation where they were receiving capital calls for these commitments during 2008 and 2009, a period where their public assets had lost considerable value and liquidity and cash were scarce. Some investors had to reduce distributions, sell illiquid investments in the secondary market at severely discounted prices, and/or walk away from their fund commitments, thereby forfeiting earlier investments.

Although every strategy (and, by extension, each individual fund) will have its own unique risk profile, we provide two examples of the complications that might be encountered when modelling an allocation to alternative investments.

Short-only strategy:

A short-biased fund can provide strong diversification benefits, lowering a portfolio's aggregate exposure to the equity risk factor; however, a short-only fund has a risk profile quite unlike a long-only equity fund. Most investors understand that a long-only equity fund has theoretically infinite upside potential and a downside loss bounded by zero (assuming no leverage). A short-biased or short-only fund has the opposite distribution. A short-selling strategy is capped on its upside but has unlimited downside risk.

Option payouts:

Some hedge fund strategies will structure their trades as call options either by owning call options outright or by synthetically replicating a call option (e.g., convertible bond arbitrage in which the manager goes long the convertible bond, short the equity for the same underlying, and hedges the interest rate risk). If executed properly, the fund would have limited downside but unlimited upside. It is difficult, if not impossible, to accurately model such a return profile by looking simply at a fund's historical standard deviation or other risk metrics, especially if the fund's track record does not encompass a full market cycle.

Return Expectations

Given the limited return history of alternative investments (relative to stocks and bonds) and the idiosyncratic nature of alternative investment returns, no single accepted approach to developing the return expectations required in an asset allocation exercise exists. One approach that can be applied with some consistency across asset classes is a "building blocks" approach: Begin with the risk-free rate, estimate the return associated with the factor exposures relevant to the asset class (e.g., credit spreads, level and shape of the yield curve, equity, leverage, liquidity), apply an assumption for manager alpha, and deduct appropriate fees (management and incentive) and taxes. Where the portfolio already contains an allocation to alternative investments, the underlying money managers can be helpful in estimating exposures and return potential. The portfolio's current positions can be characterized by their known exposures, rather than through a generic set of exposures that may not be truly representative of the program's objectives for the asset class exposure. Say, for example, that the investor's hedge fund program deliberately excludes long/short equity hedge funds because the investor chooses to take equity risk in the long-only portion of the portfolio. The return (and risk) characteristics of this hedge fund allocation would be very different from those of a broad-based allocation to hedge funds, which typically has a significant weight to long/short equity funds.

Investment Vehicle

Most alternative investments are implemented through a private (limited) partnership that is controlled by a general partner (GP), the organization and individuals that manage the investments. The asset owner becomes a limited partner (LP) in the private partnership. The main rationale for using the limited partnership format is that it limits the investor's liability to the amount of capital that she has contributed; she is not responsible for the actions of or the debts incurred by the GP. The investor may invest directly into a manager's fund or through a fund of funds, a private partnership that invests in multiple underlying partnerships. Larger investors may also consider making co-investments alongside a manager into a portfolio company, or they may make direct private equity investments on their own.

Private limited partnerships are the dominant investment vehicle for most alternative investments in private equity, real estate, private credit, and real assets. In the United States, hedge funds will tend to employ two structures: a limited partnership (typically Delaware-based) or an offshore corporation or feeder fund (possibly based in the Cayman Islands, Bermuda, or the British Virgin Islands) that usually feeds into an underlying limited partnership (i.e., feeder fund). European hedge funds tend to register their vehicles in Ireland or Luxembourg[7] as a public limited company, a partnership limited by shares, or a special limited partnership.

There are growing opportunities to invest in alternatives using mutual funds, undertakings for collective investment in transferable securities (UCITS), and/or separately managed accounts (SMAs), although the strategies implemented through these more-liquid vehicles are unlikely to have the same risk/return profile as their less-liquid counterparts. The requirements and demands of a broader investor base have made mutual funds, UCITS, and SMAs increasingly popular. We describe the structure, benefits, and drawbacks of each of these vehicles.

Direct investment in a limited partnership:

An investor with the necessary scale and expertise can purchase limited partnership interests directly from the GP. GPs have broad discretion to select and manage the underlying investments and will typically invest a portion of their capital in the fund alongside the limited partners. Because each limited partnership follows its own distinct investment strategy, the investor must often invest in multiple partnerships to diversify idiosyncratic risk. In order to maintain the limited liability shield afforded by the limited partnership structure, the investor must not become too involved in the operation of the fund itself.

---

7 See Eurekahedge, "2016 Key Trends in Global Hedge Funds" (August 2016).

Funds of funds (FOFs):

Many investors lack the necessary scale and investment/operational expertise to access, evaluate, and develop a diversified alternative investment program. An FOF pools the capital of these investors, allowing them to achieve an allocation to an asset class that would otherwise be unobtainable. An FOF manager will typically specialize in a certain alternative strategy, such as Asian private equity funds, and may invest in either many or just a handful of underlying funds. The FOF manager is responsible for sourcing, conducting due diligence on, and monitoring the underlying managers. Using an FOF simplifies the investor's accounting and reporting: Capital calls from the underlying funds are frequently consolidated into a single capital call by the FOF, and investors receive a single report consolidating the accounting and investment results of all the underlying funds. The FOF manager does charge additional fees for these services. Investors in an FOF also lose a degree of flexibility to customize their exposures.

SMAs/funds of one:

As large institutions and family offices increased capital allocated to the alternative investment space, many of them demanded more-favorable investment terms and conditions than those offered to smaller investors. Some alternative investment managers, interested in accessing these large pools of capital, have agreed to offer investment management services to these clients through a highly customizable SMA. SMAs have very high minimum investments and pose greater operational challenges for both the manager and the investor. In instances where an SMA is impractical, fund managers have created a "fund of one"—a limited partnership with a single client. These funds have many of the same benefits as an SMA but can be easier to implement. (For example, an SMA requires that the *investor* must be approved by each of the counterparties to any derivatives contracts. In a fund of one, GPs must obtain and maintain these approvals, which is something that they do in the ordinary course of running their investment businesses.)

SMAs and funds of one cannot generally avail themselves of the alignment of interests that arises from the investment of GP capital alongside that of the LPs. When other clients are invested in the GP's primary investment vehicles at the GP's standard fees and to which the GP has committed some of its own capital, there is a risk that the GP favors these other funds in allocating capital-constrained investment opportunities.

Mutual funds/UCITS/publicly traded funds:

A number of open-ended mutual funds and UCITS seek to replicate some alternative investment strategies, particularly hedge funds. Nominally, these allow smaller investors to access asset classes that would otherwise be unavailable to them. It should be noted, however, that these vehicles often operate with regulatory restrictions that limit the fund manager's ability to implement the investment strategy offered via their primary investment vehicle. Accordingly, the investor must be cautious in considering whether the track record achieved in the manager's primary investment vehicle is representative of what might be achieved in a mutual fund, UCIT, or other publicly-traded vehicle. For example, a mutual fund that offers daily liquidity is unlikely to be a suitable investment vehicle for a distressed or activist investment fund, where the time horizon to realize investment returns may be one to two years. This "liquid-alt" space grew significantly following the Global Financial Crisis.

6   LIQUIDITY

☐ | discuss investment considerations that are important in allocating to different types of alternative investments

Traditional assets are generally highly liquid, and the vehicles that are typically used by investors to access the asset class (e.g., separate accounts or daily valued commingled funds, such as mutual funds and UCITS) typically do not impose additional liquidity constraints. That is not the case with many alternative assets, where both the vehicle and the underlying instruments may expose the investor to some degree of liquidity risk. We address liquidity risks at the fund and security level separately.

Liquidity Risks Associated with the Investment Vehicle

The most common vehicle employed by alternative asset managers is the private limited partnership previously described. (Some investors will invest via an offshore corporate structure used for certain tax and regulatory reasons. This offshore corporation is typically a "feeder" fund—a vehicle that channels investors' assets to the master limited partnership.) The private placement memorandum (PPM) details the subscription and redemption features of the partnership. Liquidity provisions differ across asset classes but are substantially similar within asset classes. Exhibit 17 details the typical liquidity considerations associated with investing in a private limited partnership. SMA liquidity provisions may be negotiated directly with the manager.

Exhibit 17: Typical Liquidity Provisions for Alternative Investment Vehicles

	Subscription	Redemption	Lock-Up
Hedge Funds	▪ Typically accept capital on a monthly or quarterly basis.	▪ Quarterly or annual redemptions with 30 to 90 days' notice required. ▪ May be subject to a gate limiting the amount of fund or investor assets that can be redeemed at any one redemption date. ▪ 10% holdback of the redemption amount pending completion of the annual audit.	▪ Typically one year in the US; shorter in Europe. ▪ Redemptions prior to the lock-up period may be permitted but are subject to a penalty, typically 10%.
Private Equity, Private Credit, Real Estate, and Real Asset Funds	▪ Funds typically have multiple "closes." The final close for new investors is usually one year after the first close. Committed capital is called for investment in stages over a 3-year investment period.	▪ No redemption provisions. Fund interests may be sold on the secondary market, subject to GP approval. ▪ Distributions paid as investments are realized over the life of the fund. Unrealized assets may be distributed in kind to the LP at fund termination.	▪ Typical 10-year life, with GP option to extend fund term 1 to 2 years.

Secondary markets:

Although fund terms may prevent investors from redeeming early, a small but growing secondary market for many alternative funds exists. Some brokers will match sellers and buyers of limited partnership interests, and some secondary funds' main objective is to buy limited partnership interests from the original investor. These transactions typically occur at a significant discount to the net asset value (NAV) of the fund and usually require the GP to approve the transaction.

Understanding a drawdown structure:

Private equity/credit, private real estate, and real asset funds typically call investors' capital in stages as fund investments are identified. This investment period is specified in the PPM and typically ranges from three to five years from the initial capital call. Thus, although an investor may have committed a specified percentage of the portfolio to an asset class, the allocation may not be fully funded until some point well into the future. We will illustrate the drawdown structure for a single fund using a hypothetical commitment to a real estate fund:

The Chan Family Partnership commits €5,000,000 to Uptown Real Estate LP. The fund has a three-year investment period. When fully invested, Uptown expects to hold 12 to 15 properties. The capital call schedule for Uptown may look something like this:

- Year 1: €1,500,000 of the €5,000,000 committed is called, covering three investments
- Year 2: €2,500,000 is called, covering six investments
- Year 3: €500,000 is called, covering two investments
- Year 6: €2,000,000 is distributed by Uptown Real Estate
- More distributions in subsequent years

Expanding on this example, Exhibit 18 shows how the cash flows for our hypothetical fund might operate throughout the fund's life.

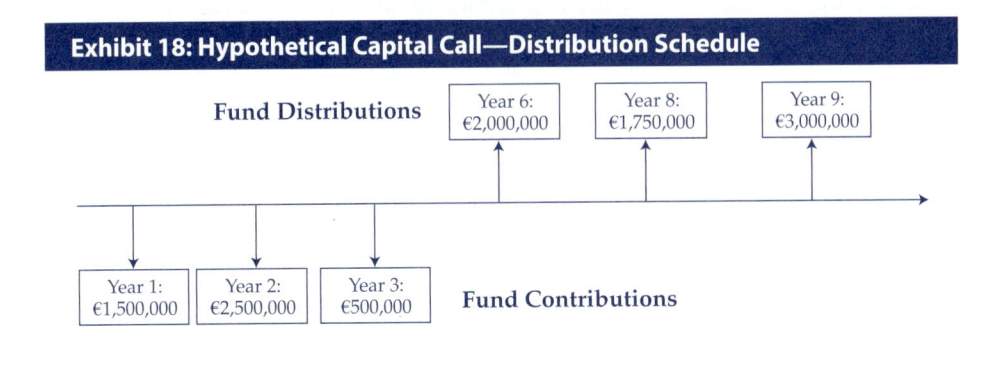

Exhibit 18: Hypothetical Capital Call—Distribution Schedule

Fund Distributions

| Year 6: €2,000,000 | Year 8: €1,750,000 | Year 9: €3,000,000 |

Fund Contributions

| Year 1: €1,500,000 | Year 2: €2,500,000 | Year 3: €500,000 |

In reality, most funds will have several capital calls in a year. It is also possible that a fund may make a distribution before the final capital call occurs. Because of the highly uncertain liquidity profile of call down (or drawdown) funds (private equity/credit, real estate/real assets), it is incumbent on the investor to plan for multiple contingencies. Funds may end up calling significantly less capital than the investor assumed or may call capital at a faster pace than planned. Capital may be returned to the investor more quickly or more slowly than originally anticipated. Each of these scenarios could result in investors being under or over their target allocations. Critically, investors will want to verify that they have suitable liquidity, such that even under adverse conditions they are able to meet their capital calls. Investors who are unable to meet their capital calls may be required to forfeit their entire investment in the fund (or such other penalties as may be specified in the PPM).

The capital commitment/drawdown structure also presents potential opportunity costs for the investor. Returning to Exhibit 18, having committed €5,000,000 to Uptown Real Estate LP, the Chan Family Partnership is obligated to meet the GP's capital calls but must address the opportunity cost of having the committed capital invested in lower-returning liquid (cash) assets pending the capital call—or face the risk of having insufficient assets available to meet the capital call if the funds were invested in another asset class that has experienced a loss in the interim. Also note that only €4,500,000 of the €5,000,000 commitment was called before distributions began.

Liquidity Risks Associated with the Underlying Investments

The investor must be aware of any potential mismatch between the fund terms and the liquidity profile of the underlying instruments held by the fund. This is particularly important if the investor is negotiating fund terms or if other investors have terms that may be different from his own. Because the private market funds rarely offer interim liquidity, this problem most often arises in hedge funds. We provide a few examples of the issues an investor may encounter.

Equity-oriented hedge funds:

The majority of assets in a typical equity-oriented hedge fund are liquid, marketable securities compatible with monthly or quarterly fund-level liquidity terms. Short positions may be notably less liquid than long positions, so funds that make greater use of short selling will have correspondingly lower overall liquidity. This should be taken into consideration when evaluating the potential for a liquidity mismatch between the fund's terms and the underlying holdings. Some otherwise liquid hedge fund strategies may own a portion of their holdings in illiquid or relatively illiquid securities. The GP may designate these securities as being held in a "side pocket." Such "side-pocketed" securities are not subject to the fund's general liquidity terms. The redeeming investor's pro rata share of the side pocket would remain in the fund and be distributed at such time as the fund manager liquidates these assets, which could take quarters or even years to accomplish. If the percentage of assets held in side pockets is large, this could render the fund's liquidity terms irrelevant. The investor must evaluate the illiquidity challenges inherent in the underlying holdings, including side pockets, in order to estimate a liquidity profile for the total portfolio.

Event-driven hedge funds:

Event-driven strategies, by their nature, tend to have longer investment horizons. The underlying investments in a merger arbitrage strategy, for example, are generally liquid, but the nature of the strategy is such that returns are realized in "chunks." It is in the manager's and the investor's interests to ensure that the liquidity terms provide the necessary flexibility to execute the investment thesis. A hedge fund focused on distressed investing is dealing with both the "workout" horizon (the time frame over which the negotiations between the creditors and the company are being conducted) and the lesser liquidity of the distressed assets. The fund terms for a distressed strategy are likely to be much longer than other hedge fund strategies. (In fact, many distressed funds choose to organize in a private equity fund structure.)

Relative value hedge funds:

Many relative value hedge funds will invest in various forms of credit, convertibles, derivatives, or equities that have limited or at least uncertain liquidity characteristics. Many funds will include provisions in the fund documents to restrict redemptions under certain scenarios so that they are not forced to sell illiquid securities at inopportune moments. Without such provisions, the fund manager may be forced to sell what securities they *can* (i.e., the more liquid holdings) rather than the securities that they *want.* This could have the unfortunate consequence of leaving remaining investors in the fund holding a sub-optimally illiquid portfolio. On the other hand, funds that deal in managed futures or similar instruments may have very flexible terms (daily or weekly liquidity, only a few days notification, etc.). This was a scenario many hedge fund managers faced during the Global Financial Crisis as investors made significant redemption requests to meet their own cash needs. The liquid funds were disproportionately affected as investors sought to raise cash wherever they could find it.

Leverage:

A fund's use of leverage and its agreements with counterparties providing the leverage can also affect the alignment between fund terms and the investment strategy. If a strategy is levered, lenders have a first claim on the assets. The lenders' claims are superior to those of the LPs, and the lenders have preferential liquidity terms; most lenders can make a margin call on stocks, bonds, or derivatives positions with just two days' notice. Given that margin calls are most likely to happen when the markets (and/or the fund) are stressed, the LPs' liquidity can evaporate as the most-liquid positions in the portfolio are sold to meet margin calls. The need to de-lever and sell assets to meet margin calls will typically result in a lower return when the market eventually recovers.

FEES AND EXPENSES, TAX CONSIDERATIONS, AND OTHER CONSIDERATIONS | 7

In addition to management fees of 0.5% to 2.5% of assets and incentive fees of 10% to 20% of returns, investments in alternative assets often entail higher expenses passed through to or paid directly by the investor. These fees can result in a significant variation between the gross and net of fee returns. Consider a hedge fund that was earning a 3% gross quarterly return (12.6% annualized). After deducting a 2% management and a 20% incentive fee, accrued quarterly, the net return at year-end is just 8.2%.

Fees can have a larger impact on the difference between gross and net returns for such call-down-type fund structures as private equity funds, where the management fee is charged on *committed* capital, not invested capital. If the manager is slow to deploy capital, there can be a pronounced J-curve effect (negative IRRs in the early years) that can be difficult to overcome (the adage 'it takes a 100% return to recover from a 50% loss').

In addition, most alternative investment funds will pass through normal fund expenses, including legal, custodial, audit, administration, and accounting fees. For smaller funds, these additional costs can add up to another 0.5%. Larger funds can spread these same costs out over the larger asset base, and the pass-through to investors is likely to be in the range of 0.05% to 0.20% of assets. Some of these expenses have a limited life (e.g., the capitalized organizational expenses), so the impact can vary over time. Funds may also pass through to investors costs associated with acquiring an asset, including the due diligence costs and any brokerage commissions paid. A careful evaluation of the fund's offering documents is essential to understanding the all-in cost of an investment in alternatives.

Tax Considerations

For taxable investors, the tax implications associated with many alternatives can have a significant impact on their relative attractiveness. In many instances, a tax inefficient strategy, one that generates substantial short-term gains or taxable income, can significantly erode the anticipated return benefits. This arises frequently with many hedge fund strategies, especially those funds and fund companies where tax-exempt investors dominate the client base and the fund manager may be insensitive to tax efficiency. Vehicle selection becomes an important tool to mitigate potential tax consequences. For example, certain Asia-based investors may use European or other offshore vehicles that feed into US strategies in order to mitigate US tax withholding. Conversely, some funds benefit from preferential tax treatment that might add to its relative attractiveness.

Here are a few examples of these tax considerations:

- The US tax code has provisions that favor real estate, timber, and energy investments. Timber sales, for example, are taxed at lower capital gains rates rather than as ordinary income and may benefit from a depletion deduction. Commercial and residential building assets can be depreciated according to various schedules, with the depreciation offsetting income received on those assets. Some oil and natural gas royalty owners may benefit from a depletion deduction, offsetting income generated from the sale of the oil or gas.

- Some alternative investment strategies can generate unrelated business income tax (UBIT). UBIT arises when a US tax-exempt organization engages in activities that are not related to the tax-exempt purpose of that organization. Since most tax-exempt entities seek to mitigate (if not avoid) taxes, they will want to verify whether such a fund might generate UBIT and, if so, whether the fund manager has an offshore vehicle that may shield the investor from such income.

- The taxable investor faces additional costs and operational hurdles because of the more complex tax filings. Some taxable investors must estimate their expected annual income, including income that is derived from investments. Deriving an accurate estimate can be a challenge. Unfortunately, if the mis-estimation is large enough it might result in tax penalties.

Tax considerations, like fees, will affect the return assumptions used in the asset allocation exercise.

Other Considerations

Although smaller investors seeking to build a diversified alternative investment program are generally constrained to use an intermediary, such as a fund of funds, large investors have the opportunity to build a program in-house and must decide whether this approach is appropriate given their governance structure. Key questions to explore in evaluating the options include the following:

- What is the likelihood that the investor can identify and gain access to the top-tier managers in the investment strategy?

    Truly differentiated strategies and top-tier managers are notoriously capacity constrained, which tends to limit the amount of assets they can reasonably manage without negatively affecting investment returns. Fund managers who recognize this problem frequently limit the number of investors that they allow into their fund and may close their doors to new clients or capital. This can make it extremely difficult for investors to find and access top-tier managers. Investors who are subject to public disclosure requirements may be rejected by a manager who believes that success is based on a proprietary informational edge that could be eroded through these required public disclosures. Many studies on alternative assets have concluded that it may not be worth the costs and resources required to be successful in this space if investors do not have access to top-tier funds.

■ What is the likelihood that the investor will be accorded the access needed to conduct effective due diligence on an investment strategy?

It is not enough to know when or if to invest with a fund manager; it is equally, if not more, important to be able to determine when to terminate the relationship. Having poor to no access to the key decision makers within the organization could make it difficult to ascertain if the conditions have changed such that a redemption is warranted. The situation could be even worse if other clients have good (or preferential) access to the fund manager, which might result in their redeeming early, leaving other, less-informed investors subject to gates or other more-restrictive redemption terms that could be triggered.

■ What skills and resources does the investor have in-house to evaluate and monitor an alternative investment program?

This question is evaluated through a consideration of the cost tradeoffs, the investment expertise of in-house staff, the desire to tailor an investment program to investor-specific wants and needs, and the degree of control.

- Cost is typically the overriding factor in the decision to build a program in-house or buy an existing off-the-shelf product. The all-in costs of compensation, benefits, rent, technology, reporting, travel, overhead, and other miscellaneous expenses associated with managing an alternative investments program can far exceed the costs associated with running a traditional asset portfolio. However, very large organizations may be able to justify the costs of building in-house teams.

- Investors seeking to leverage a manager's expertise through co-investments and other direct investment opportunities must build an in-house team with the expertise to evaluate specific securities and deals and must provide the infrastructure needed to support those efforts.

- Investors who require highly customized investment programs might be poorly served by consultants or FOFs who typically gain scale and margin by providing solutions that can be broadly applied to a large number of clients. For example, an endowment that wants their alternative investment program to consider environmental, social, and governance (ESG) factors (i.e., socially responsible investing) may have a difficult time finding an investment consultant who can deliver on the client's specific ESG requirements. Or, a family office that wants to emphasize tax-efficient angel investments might need to hire in-house resources in order to find and supervise these more specialized investments.

- Those investors who desire a high degree of control and/or influence over the implementation of the investment program are more likely to have this need met through an in-house program.

EXAMPLE 3

Considerations in Allocating to Alternative Investments

The investment committee (IC) for a small endowment has decided to invest in private equity for the first time and has agreed upon a 10% strategic target. The internal investment team comprises the CIO (chief investment officer) and two analysts. The IC asks the CIO to recommend an implementation plan at the next meeting.

1. What are the options the CIO should include in her report as it relates to vehicles, and what factors might influence the recommendation?

Solution:

The primary considerations for the CIO include the size of the private equity allocation, the team's expertise with private equity, and the available resources. Because this is a small endowment, it may be difficult to commit enough capital to achieve an adequate level of diversification. The size of the fund's investment team is also likely to be a concern. Unless there are financial resources to add a private equity specialist and/or employ an outside consultant, the fund-of-funds route would likely be the optimal vehicle(s) to implement a diversified private equity program.

2. The IC provided no guidance as to expectations for when the investment program should reach its 10% target weight. What additional information should the CIO gather before presenting her plan of action?

Solution:

The CIO should factor in the cash flows and anticipated liquidity profile of the overall endowment in considering the speed with which they would commit to a significant PE program. If, for example, the foundation is embarking on a capital campaign and anticipated distributions are small over the next few years, then commitments may be accelerated after factoring in an appropriate vintage year diversification. (Because private investment returns are very sensitive to the fund's vintage year, it is common for investors to build up to a full allocation over a period of years, called vintage year diversification.) However, if the rest of the investment program is heavily exposed to illiquid investments (e.g., real estate, certain hedge fund strategies) and anticipated distributions to fund operating expenses are high, the CIO may want to commit at a slower pace.

EXAMPLE 4

Considerations in Allocating to Alternative Investments

A $100 million client of a family office firm has requested that all public securities investments meet certain ESG criteria. The ESG ratings will be provided by an independent third-party firm that provides a rating for most public equities and some fixed-income issuers. Moreover, the family would like to dedicate a percentage of assets to support an "environmental sustainability" impact theme.

1. Which alternative investment strategies may not be suitable for this client given the ESG requirements?

Solution:

Because the ESG criteria apply to all public securities, most hedge fund strategies would be precluded because they are typically owned in a commingled vehicle, such as a limited partnership or a mutual fund where transparency of holdings is limited and the investor has no influence over the composition of the underlying portfolio. Separate account strategies are available for certain large portfolios, but it is unlikely that a $100 million client would be eligible for a custom portfolio that would be allocating only a small asset base to any particular fund.

2. What additional information might the family office firm require from the client in order to meet the environmental sustainability threshold?

Solution:

The client and the manager would need to agree on a clear definition of environmental sustainability and the types of investments that might qualify for this theme. It is unlikely that most hedge funds, private credit, energy, or infrastructure strategies would be considered to positively impact environmental sustainability. The most likely candidates for consideration could be timber, sustainable farmland, and clean-tech funds under the venture capital category.

SUITABILITY CONSIDERATIONS

8

☐ | discuss suitability considerations in allocating to alternative investments

Alternative investments are not appropriate for all investors. We discuss briefly several *investor* characteristics that are important to a successful alternative investment program.

Investment Horizon

Investors with less than a 15-year investment horizon should generally avoid investments in private real estate, private real assets, and private equity funds. An alternative investment program in private markets may take 5 to 7 years to fully develop and another 10 to 12 years to unwind, assuming no new investments are made after the 7-year mark. Even a 10-year horizon may be too short to develop a robust private alternative investment program.

Other strategies can tolerate a shorter investment focus. Many hedge fund strategies that focus on public equities or managed futures have much shorter lock-ups (on the order of months or not at all). Some strategies can be entered and exited in shorter time frames, and the purchase or sale of limited partnership interests on the secondary market may be used to shorten the entry and exit phases of the process.

However, the alternative investment program has a higher likelihood of success if the investor adopts a long-horizon approach coupled with an understanding of the underlying investment processes.

Expertise

A successful alternative investment program requires that the investor understand the risks entailed and the market environments that drive success or failure of each of the strategies. Understanding the breadth of the alternative investment opportunities and the complexity of strategies within each alternative class requires a relatively high level of investment expertise. Even if the investor is highly experienced, the risk of information asymmetry between the limited partner (LP) and the general partner (GP) is always there. A pension fund without full-time investment staff, or an individual without the resources to hire an adviser with a dedicated alternative investments team, is unlikely to have the investment expertise necessary to implement a successful alternative investment program.

Additionally, the investment philosophy of the asset owner (or its overseers) must be consistent with the principles of alternative investments. An investor whose investment philosophy is rooted in a belief that markets are fundamentally efficient may struggle to embrace an alternative investment program, where success is predicated on active management. A mismatch in philosophy could very well be a set up for failure when the alternative investments underperform traditional asset classes.

Governance

A robust investment governance framework ensures that an alternative investment program is structured to meet the needs of the investor. The following are hallmarks of a strong governance framework suitable to an alternative investment program:

- The long- and short-term objectives of the investment program are clearly articulated.
- Decision rights and responsibilities are allocated to those individuals with the knowledge, capacity, and time required to critically evaluate possible courses of action.
- A formal investment policy has been adopted to govern the day-to-day operations of the investment program.
- A reporting framework is in place to monitor the program's progress toward the agreed-on goals and objectives.

Investors without a strong governance program are less likely to develop a successful alternative investment program.

Transparency

Investors must be comfortable with less than 100% transparency into the underlying holdings of their alternative investment managers. In real estate, private equity, and real asset funds, the investor is typically buying into a "blind pool"—committing capital for investment in a portfolio of as-yet-unidentified assets. During the course of investment due diligence, the investor may have looked at the assets acquired in the manager's previous funds, but there is no assurance that the new fund will look anything like the prior funds. Hedge fund managers are generally reluctant to disclose the full portfolio to investors on an ongoing basis. Even if you were to have access to the full underlying portfolio, it is rarely apparent where the true risk exposures lie without a detailed understanding of the investment themes the manager is pursuing.

Reporting for alternative funds is often less transparent than investors are accustomed to seeing on their stock and bond portfolios. Generally, no legal requirements mandate the frequency, timing, and details of fund reporting for private investment partnerships. For many illiquid strategies (real estate/assets, private equity/credit), reporting is often received well past month- or quarter-end deadlines that investors are accustomed to with their traditional investments.

A typical hedge fund report, usually available on a quarterly basis, may detail performance, top 10 holdings, and some general commentary on the capital markets as well as some factors that influenced fund performance. The hedge fund manager may also provide a risk report that broadly outlines the major risk exposures of the fund. There is no commonality among the risk reports provided from fund to fund. This hampers an investor's efforts to develop a picture of aggregate risk exposure. Clients with separately managed accounts have access to portfolio holdings and may be able to produce their own risk reporting with a common set of risk metrics.

Private equity funds will provide more transparency into portfolio holdings, but the private equity fund report is unlikely to "slice-and-dice" the exposures by geography, sector, or industry. The investor must gather the additional information needed to develop a fuller exposure of the portfolio's risk exposures and progress toward meeting expectations. Private equity managers typically provide an abbreviated quarterly report with a more detailed annual report following the completion of the fund's annual audit.

This lack of transparency can shield questionable actions by GPs. In 2014, the US Securities and Exchange Commission found that more than 50% of private equity firms had collected or misallocated fees without proper disclosure to their clients.[8] This study and subsequent lawsuits have increased transparency within the industry, although the industry remains opaque at many levels.

Reporting for private real estate funds commonly consists of a quarterly report with details on the fund's size, progress in drawdowns, realizations to date, and valuations of unrealized investments as well as market commentary relevant to the fund's strategy. Reports typically include details on each investment such as the original acquisition cost(s), square footage, borrowing details (e.g., cost of debt, leverage ratios, and debt maturity dates), and fundamental metrics regarding the health of the properties (e.g., occupancy rates and, if appropriate, the estimated credit health of tenants). Often there is qualitative commentary on the health of the property's submarket, on anticipated next steps, and on the timing of realization(s). Reports are typically issued with a one-quarter lag to allow sufficient time to update property valuations. Annual reports, which frequently require updated third-party appraisals, may not be available until the second quarter following year end.

Investors should ensure that funds use independent administrators to calculate the fund and LPs' NAV. These administrators are also responsible for processing cash flows, including contributions, fee payments, and distributions that are consistent with the fund documents. The use of independent administrators is common practice among hedge funds. It is relatively uncommon for a fund investing in illiquid strategies (e.g., private equity/credit, real estate/natural resources) to use an independent administrator. Funds that do not use third-party administrators have wide discretion in valuing assets. In the midst of the Great Financial Crisis, it was not uncommon for two different private equity firms with ownership interests in the same company to provide very different estimates of the company's value.

The lack of transparency common with many alternative investments can challenge risk management and performance evaluation. High-quality alternative investment managers will engage an independent and respected accounting firm to perform an annual audit of the fund; the audit report should be available to the LPs.

---

8 Andrew Ceresney, "Keynote Address: Private Equity Enforcement," Securities Enforcement Forum West (12 May 2016).

Regulatory requirements for mutual funds and UCITS funds require such standardized information as costs, expected risks, and performance data. Additional information may also be available on a periodic basis. Information provided to one investor should be available to all shareholders. These rules have been interpreted by some mutual fund/UCITS managers to mean that they cannot provide more-detailed, non-standardized information given the complexity of sharing it with a broad audience. This can possibly restrict the level of transparency certain shareholders can obtain for these vehicles.

EXAMPLE 5

Suitability Considerations in Allocating to Alternative Investments

The Christian family office is concerned with investor or manager fraud and so will invest only in separately managed accounts (SMAs).

1. What are the benefits and drawbacks to the use of SMAs?

Solution:

Although an SMA allows for greater transparency and control of capital flows (the manager does not generally have the authority to distribute capital from the client account), it has several potential disadvantages: 1) SMAs are not available or appropriate for many alternative strategies; thus, the requirement to invest via an SMA may limit the ability to develop an optimal alternative investment program. 2) A manager cannot invest alongside the client in the client's SMA. This may reduce the alignment of interest between the manager and the client and may give rise to conflicts of interest as trades are allocated between the SMA and the manager's other funds.

2. The 75-year-old patriarch of the Christian family would like to consider a significant private equity allocation in a trust that he oversees on behalf of his youngest daughter. This would be the first alternative investment commitment made with any of the family's assets. The daughter is 40 years old. She will receive one-half of the assets outright upon his death. The remainder of the assets will be held in trust subject to the terms of the trust agreement. List some of the reasons why private equity may or may not be appropriate for this trust.

Solution:

- Successful private equity investment requires a long time horizon. Given the patriarch's age, it is likely that half of the trust's assets will be distributed before the private equity program has had time to mature. This may lead to an unintended doubling in the size of the private equity allocation.

- The patriarch has no experience investing in alternative assets. Unless he is willing to commit the time, money, and effort and engage an outside adviser with the relevant expertise and access to top-tier funds, the likelihood of a successful private equity investment program would be low.

- Because the beneficiary of the trust is relatively young, the time horizon of the investment likely matches the profile of the underlying investor. It may be appropriate for the trust to invest in long-dated private equity assets, provided the investment is sized appropriately and the necessary expertise has been retained.

ASSET ALLOCATION APPROACHES AND STATISTICAL PROPERTIES AND CHALLENGES

9

☐ | discuss approaches to asset allocation to alternative investments

We mentioned earlier that one approach to determining the desired allocation to the alternative asset classes is to make the initial asset allocation decision using only the broad, liquid asset classes and do a second iteration of the asset allocation exercise incorporating alternative assets. After first addressing the challenges in developing risk and return assumptions for alternative asset classes, we then discuss three primary approaches that investors use to approach this second iteration.

1. *Monte Carlo simulation.* We discuss how Monte Carlo simulation may be used to generate return scenarios that relax the assumption of normally distributed returns. We illustrate how simulation can be applied to estimate the long-term risk profile and return potential of various asset allocation alternatives, and, in particular, we evaluate whether various asset allocation alternatives would satisfy the investor's ultimate investment objectives.

2. *Optimization techniques.* Mean–variance optimization (MVO) typically over-allocates to alternative asset classes, partly because risk is underestimated because of stale or infrequent pricing and the underlying assumption that returns are normally distributed. Practitioners usually address this bias towards alternatives by establishing limits on the allocations to alternatives. Optimization methods that incorporate downside risk (mean–CVaR optimization) or take into account skew may be used to enhance the asset allocation process.

3. *Risk factor-based approaches.* Risk factor-based approaches to alternative asset allocation can be applied to develop more robust asset allocation proposals.

These analytical techniques complement each other, and investors frequently rely on all of them rather than just using one or the other. Monte Carlo simulation can provide simulated non-normal (fat-tailed) data for a mean–CVaR optimization, but simulation can also be applied to analyze the long-term behavior of various asset allocation alternatives that are the results of portfolio optimization.

Statistical Properties and Challenges of Asset Returns

Alternative investments present the modeler with a number of analytical challenges. These two are particularly relevant in the asset allocation process:

1. Appraisal-based valuations used in private alternative investments often lead to stale and/or artificially smoothed returns. Volatility and other risk measures estimated based on these smoothed time series would potentially understate the actual, fundamental risk.

2. Although even the public asset classes can exhibit non-normal return distributions, skewness and fat tails (excess kurtosis) are more pronounced with many of the alternative investment strategies. Leverage, sensitivity to the disappearance of liquidity, and even the asymmetric nature of performance fees all contribute to additional skewness and excess kurtosis among alternative investments. This option–payoff style quality can undermine a simplistic statistical approach.

Asset allocators use various analytical approaches to mitigate the impact of these challenges.

Stale Pricing and Unsmoothing

Appraisal-based valuation is common in private real estate and private equity. The valuation parameter assumptions in the appraisal process change quite slowly. This has a smoothing effect on reported returns and gives the illusion that illiquid assets' performance is much less volatile than that of public marketable assets with similar fundamental characteristics. This issue also affects hedge funds in which the manager invests in illiquid or less-liquid assets whose valuations are updated infrequently or are using models with static valuation assumptions. These artificially smoothed returns can be detected by testing the return stream for serial correlation. If serial correlation is detected and found statistically significant, the analyst needs to unsmooth the returns to get a more accurate representation of the risk and return characteristics of the asset class we are modelling.

To illustrate unsmoothing, we use a simple approach described by Ang (2014). Exhibit 19 illustrates the reported quarterly return history of the Cambridge Associates Private Equity Index, as well as the unsmoothed series.[9] The annualized volatility estimated using the reported quarterly return data and scaling using the square root of time convention is 9.5%.[10] The widely accepted rule of scaling by the square root of time, however, is based on the assumption of serially uncorrelated, normally-distributed returns. In our example, the serial correlation of the quarterly reported private equity returns is 0.38, which, given the number of observations, is significant with a t-statistic of 4.09. Because our returns are serially correlated, we want to unsmooth the returns to get a better estimate of volatility. The volatility calculated on the unsmoothed return series is 14.0%, significantly higher than the volatility estimated from the unsmoothed data.

---

9 We used the following formula to unsmooth the report total return time series:

$r_{t,\text{unsmoothed}} = (r_{t,\text{reported}} - s \times r_{t-1,\text{reported}})/(1-s),$

where s denotes the estimated serial correlation of the time series.

10 To scale volatility estimates to a longer (or shorter) time horizon, the volatility can be multiplied by the square root of time. For example, if we know the quarterly volatility and want an annual volatility estimate, we would multiply the quarterly volatility estimate by the square root of 4. (This scaling convention assumes price changes are independent and returns are not serially correlated over time.)

Exhibit 19: C|A Private Equity Index Quarterly Returns

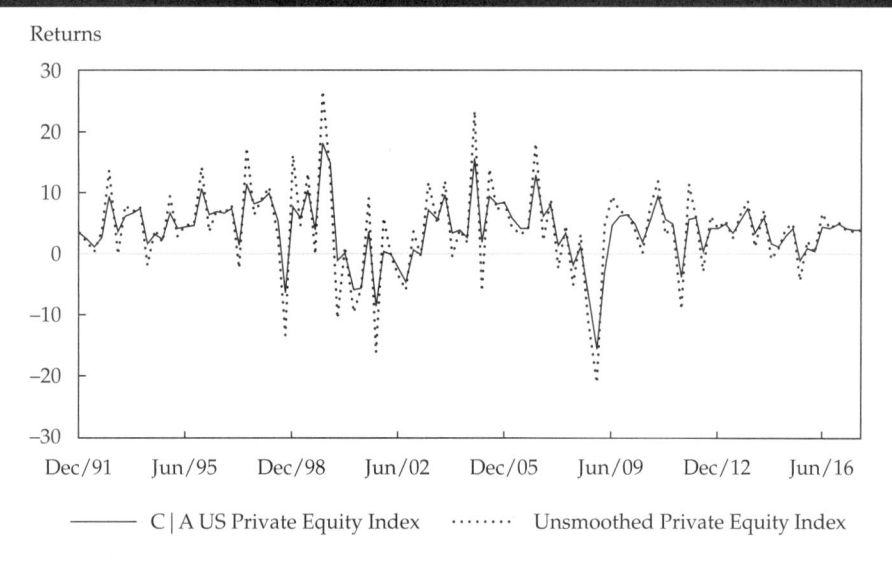

Returns

——— C | A US Private Equity Index ········ Unsmoothed Private Equity Index

Exhibit 20 illustrates serial correlation and volatility estimates based on quarterly returns of a broad range of asset classes. Although the serial correlation of public marketable asset classes is generally low, private asset classes and some hedge fund strategies have higher serial correlations that indicate stronger smoothing effects. The higher the serial correlation in the reported return series, the larger the difference between the volatility based on the unsmoothed and reported (smoothed) return data. The impact of smoothing is the highest in the case of private investments, as suggested by the serial correlation for private real estate (0.85) and private equity (0.38). The unsmoothed volatility of private real estate is, in fact, three times the volatility that we would estimate based on the reported returns. Given the serial correlation evident in private alternative strategies, it is not surprising that the distressed hedge fund strategy exhibits higher serial correlation (0.36) than other hedge fund strategies.

Exhibit 20: The Effect of Serial Correlation on Volatility

Quarterly Data Dec. 1997–Sept. 2017	Serial Correlation	Volatility (reported returns)	Volatility (unsmoothed)
US Equities	0.03	17.0%	17.7%
Non-US Developed Market Equities	0.08	19.2%	20.8%
Emerging Market Equities	0.17	26.2%	30.8%
Governments	−0.01	4.9%	4.9%
Broad Fixed Income	0.02	3.4%	3.5%
High-Yield Credit	0.34	10.0%	14.3%
Inflation-Linked Bonds	0.12	5.0%	5.7%
Hedge Funds—Aggregate	0.15	8.1%	9.5%
HF Macro	0.08	5.4%	5.9%
HF Equity Market Neutral	0.17	3.5%	4.1%
HF Equity Hedged	0.19	10.7%	13.1%
HF Distressed	0.36	8.9%	13.0%
Commodities	0.14	25.2%	28.8%

Quarterly Data Dec. 1997–Sept. 2017	Serial Correlation	Volatility (reported returns)	Volatility (unsmoothed)
Public Real Estate	0.15	20.4%	24.0%
Private Real Estate	0.85	4.6%	13.8%
Private Equity	0.38	10.7%	15.7%

Skewness and Fat Tails

A common and convenient assumption behind asset pricing theory, as well as models applied for asset allocation and risk analytics, is that asset returns are normally distributed. Both academic researchers and practitioners are widely aware of the limitations of this assumption, but no standard quantitative method to replace this assumption of normality exists. Skewness and excess kurtosis, or so-called "fat tails," in the distributions of empirically observed asset returns may lead to underestimated downside risk measures in the case of both traditional and alternative asset classes. Non-normality of returns, however, can be more severe in private alternative asset class and certain hedge fund strategies than in most of the traditional asset classes.

In Exhibit 21, we show skewness and excess kurtosis parameters calculated based on 20 years of unsmoothed quarterly return data of various public and alternative asset classes. We also show 95% quarterly conditional value at risk (CVaR) estimates based on the assumption of normally distributed asset returns, as well as based on the observed (actual) distributions. Positive skewness indicates smaller downside risk potential, while negative skewness indicates greater downside risk potential. Excess kurtosis (i.e., a kurtosis parameter exceeding 3) similarly points toward greater downside risk than would be apparent from the numbers calculated using the assumption of normally-distributed returns. The observed (actual) CVaR estimates typically exceed the normal distribution-based CVaR figures when kurtosis is high and skewness is negative. Equity market-neutral hedge funds and private real estate have the biggest *relative* differences between the 95% normal distribution CVaR and the observed CVaR (columns C and D divided by column C). Both of these strategies have negative skewness and fairly high excess kurtosis. It's interesting to note that distressed hedge funds similarly have high kurtosis and negative skewness, but the difference in tail risk measures becomes mainly visible at the 99% confidence level, where the extreme but infrequent losses may occur.

Exhibit 21: Normal Distribution Assumption and Observed Downside Risk Measures

	(A)	(B)	(C)	(D)	(E)	(F)
Unsmoothed Quarterly Data Dec. 1997–Sept. 2017	Skewness	Excess Kurtosis	95% CVaR (Normal Distribution)	95% CVaR (Observed)	99% CVaR (Normal Distribution)	99% CVaR (Observed)
US Equities	−0.51	0.43	−15.3%	−17.7%	−20.3%	−23.9%
Non-US Dev Equities	−0.19	0.29	−18.9%	−19.8%	−24.8%	−20.7%
Emerging Mkt Equities	−0.23	−0.03	−28.2%	−25.4%	−37.0%	−27.7%
Governments	0.59	0.39	−3.5%	−3.2%	−4.9%	−4.0%
Broad Fixed Income	−0.05	−0.41	−2.1%	−2.4%	−3.1%	−3.1%
High-Yield Credit	0.18	6.14	−7.9%	−9.8%	−10.8%	−19.7%
Inflation-Linked Bonds	−0.32	1.08	−4.2%	−4.2%	−5.8%	−8.1%
Hedge Funds	−0.17	1.69	−7.6%	−8.6%	−10.3%	−9.7%

Unsmoothed Quarterly Data Dec. 1997–Sept. 2017	(A) Skewness	(B) Excess Kurtosis	(C) 95% CVaR (Normal Distribution)	(D) 95% CVaR (Observed)	(E) 99% CVaR (Normal Distribution)	(F) 99% CVaR (Observed)
HF Macro	0.36	0.85	−4.3%	−4.1%	−6.0%	−5.1%
HF Equity Market Neutral	−1.17	3.55	−2.9%	−3.9%	−4.1%	−5.4%
HF Equity Hedged	0.08	2.24	−10.8%	−10.6%	−14.5%	−12.7%
HF Distressed	−1.25	3.52	−10.8%	−11.1%	−14.5%	−16.9%
Commodities	−0.71	1.62	−28.4%	−30.6%	−36.6%	−50.6%
Public Real Estate	−0.88	4.60	−20.9%	−24.5%	−27.7%	−40.2%
Private Real Estate	−2.80	9.62	−11.3%	−15.4%	−15.3%	−27.9%
Private Equity	−0.46	2.05	−12.2%	−15.7%	−16.7%	−22.6%

Source: Authors' calculations.

To further illustrate the impact of non-normality on the downside risk, in Exhibit 22 we compare the ratio of observed to normal CVaR measures with the skewness and excess kurtosis. Although the skewness or excess kurtosis alone doesn't fully explain the relative difference between observed and normal 95% CVaR (positive skewness may compensate high excess kurtosis or vice versa), we can see the evidence that higher kurtosis or more negative skewness usually increases the likely severity of any tail risk.

Exhibit 22: The Impact of Skewness and Kurtosis on Tail Risk

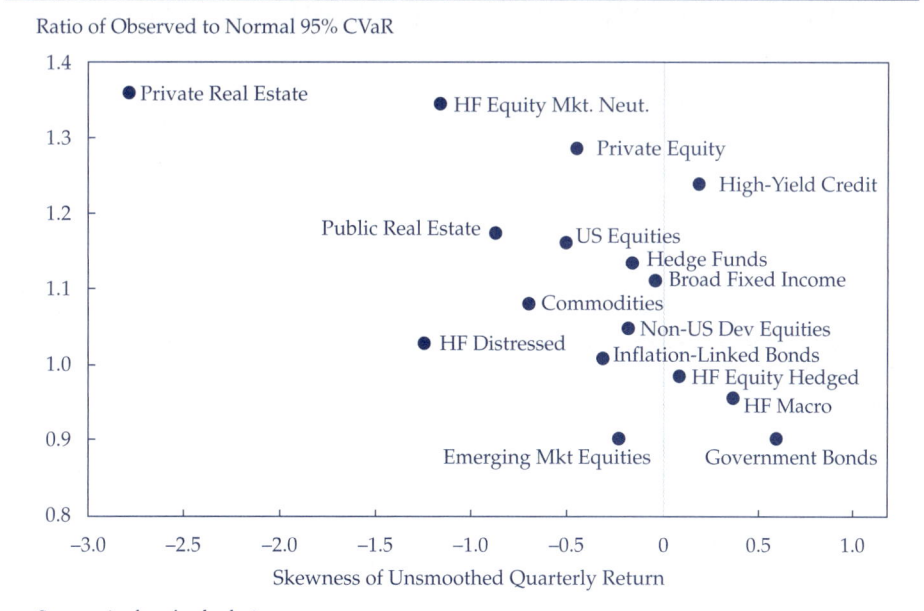

Source: Authors' calculations.

Analysts can choose to incorporate non-normality into their analyses in a few different ways. The most obvious and straightforward choice is to use empirically observed asset returns instead of working with the normal distribution. Still, in private investments where we typically have only quarterly return data, the analyses may be subject to serious limitations. Even with 20 years of quarterly return data, we have only 80 data points (and the industry has changed significantly over this time, further straining the validity of the data).

With sufficient data, analysts and researchers can capture the effects of fat tails by using advanced mathematical or statistical models:

- Time-varying volatility models (e.g., stochastic volatility), which assume that volatility is not constant over time but changes dynamically, can be used.

- Regime-switching models capture return, volatility, and correlation characteristics in different market environments (bull/bear or low volatility and moderate correlation vs. high volatility and elevated correlation). The combination of two or more normal distributions with different average returns, volatilities, and correlations could capture skewed and fat-tailed distributions.

- Extreme value theory and other fat-tailed distributions can be used when the analyst wants to focus on the behavior in the tails.

Although no single and uniformly accepted approach exists to address all of these quantitative challenges to the asset allocation exercise, a sound asset allocation process will do the following:

1. Adjust the observed asset class return data by unsmoothing the return series if the autocorrelation is significant.

2. Determine whether it is reasonable to accept an assumption of normal return distributions, in which case mean–variance optimization is appropriate to use.

3. Allow you to choose an optimization approach that takes the tail risk into account if the time series exhibits fat tails and skewness and if the potential downside risk would exceed the levels that would be observed with a normal distribution.

10 MONTE CARLO SIMULATION

Monte Carlo simulation can be a very useful tool in asset allocation to alternative investments. In this section, we discuss two applications of this modeling approach. First, we discuss how we can simulate risk factor or asset return scenarios that exhibit the skewness and kurtosis commonly seen in alternative investments. Second, we illustrate simulation-based risk and return analytics over a long time horizon in a broad asset allocation context.

At a very high level, we can summarize the model construction process in the following steps:

1. Identify those variables that we would like to randomly generate in our simulation. These variables may be asset class total returns directly, or risk factors, depending on the model.

2. Establish the quantitative framework to generate realistic random scenarios for the selected asset class returns or risk factors. Here, the analyst faces several choices, including the following:

   a. What kind of time-series model are we using? Will it be a random walk? Or will it incorporate serial correlations and mean-reversion-like characteristics?

    b. What kind of distribution should we assume for the shocks or innovations to the variables? Is normal distribution reasonable? Or, will we use some fat-tailed distribution model instead?

    c. Are volatilities and correlations stable over time? Or, do they vary across time?

3. If using a risk factor approach, convert the risk factors to asset or asset class returns using a factor-based model. In this reading, all our illustrations are based on linear factor models, but certain asset types with optionality need more-sophisticated models to incorporate non-linear characteristics as well.

4. Further translate realistic asset class return scenarios into meaningful indicators. We can simultaneously model, for example, the investment portfolio and the liability of a pension fund, enabling us to assess how the funding ratio is expected to evolve over time. Or, in the case of an endowment fund, we can assess whether certain asset allocation choices would improve the probability of meeting the spending rate target while preserving the purchasing power of the asset base.

Simulating Skewed and Fat-Tailed Financial Variables

A fairly intuitive way of incorporating non-normal returns into the analysis is to assume that there are two (or more) possible states of the world. Individually, each state can be described by using a normal distribution (*conditional normality*), but the combination of these two distributions will not be normally distributed.[11] Next, we show a fairly simplified application for the public equities and government bonds. Note that the same approach can be applied to more asset classes as well, or it can be applied to risk factor changes rather than asset class returns.

    For this illustration, we assume that the capital markets can be described by two distinct regimes—a "quiet period" (Regime 1) and a high-volatility state (Regime 2). Exhibit 23 shows the quarterly return history of the US equities and government bonds as well as the model's more volatile regimes (the gray-shaded periods). It is easy to see that the Global Financial Crisis—and such earlier crisis periods as the 1997 Asian currency contagion, the 1998 Russian ruble crisis and LTCM meltdown, and the 2002 tech bubble burst—all belong to the high-volatility regimes. The mean return and volatility statistics for the full period as well as each of the two regimes can be found in Exhibit 24. Equities outperformed government bonds over the full observation period, and it's interesting to see how dynamics changed between the quiet to the volatile periods. In the quiet period (Regime 1), equities outperformed bonds by around 4.6% quarterly, whereas in the volatile period (Regime 2), government bonds outperformed equities by more than 5%. The total return volatilities also jumped dramatically when the market switched from quiet to volatile periods. In addition, the correlation between equities and bonds was near zero during the quiet period but turned significantly negative (about −0.6) during the volatile period. Finally, we estimate that the low-volatility Regime 1 prevailed 62% of the time and the high-volatility Regime 2 prevailed 38% of the time.

---

11 The estimation process of such models is beyond the scope of this reading. Readers interested in additional details are referred to Hamilton (1989) and Kim and Nelson (1999).

Exhibit 23: US Equities and Government Bonds Return History and Identification of High-Volatility Regimes

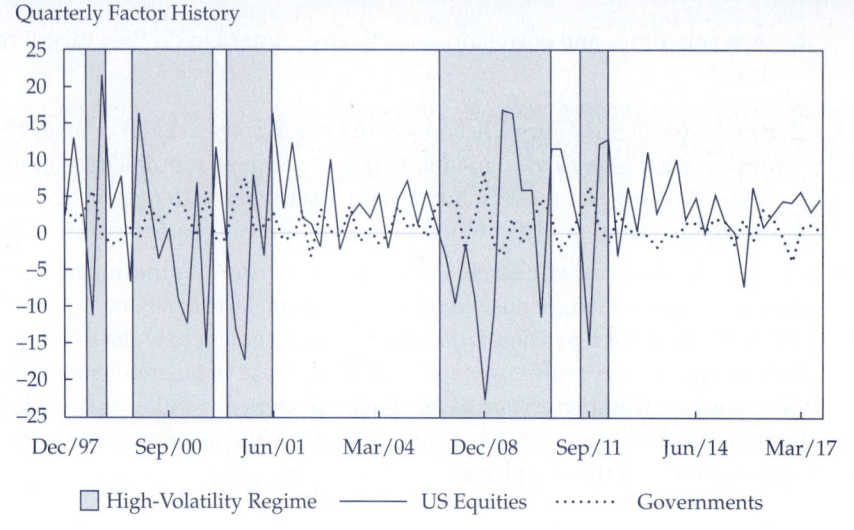

Quarterly Factor History

☐ High-Volatility Regime   —— US Equities   ········ Governments

Source: Authors' calculations.

Exhibit 24: Return Statistics (1997–2017)

	Equities	Government Bonds
Quarterly Average Return	2.1%	1.2%
Quarterly Return Volatility	8.5%	4.5%
Skewness	−0.5	0.6
Kurtosis	0.4	0.4
Average Return in Regime 1	5.1%	0.5%
Average Return in Regime 2	−3.1%	2.4%
Volatility in Regime 1	5.5%	1.9%
Volatility in Regime 2	13.7%	3.8%
Correlation in Regime 1	0.0	
Correlation in Regime 2	−0.6	

If we want to capture only skewness and fat tails in a simulation framework, we just need the normal distribution parameters of the distinct regimes and the overall state probabilities of either Regime 1 or Regime 2. Then, the analyst would generate normally distributed random scenarios based on the different means and covariances estimated under the two (or more) regimes with the appropriate frequency of the estimated probability of being the quiet or hectic regimes. This mixture of high- and low-volatility normal distributions would lead to an altogether skewed and fat-tailed distribution of asset class return or risk factor changes. In practice, some may build a more dynamic, multi-step simulation model for a longer time horizon, in which case it's also important to estimate the probability of switching from one regime to another.

Exhibit 25 shows histograms of equity returns, overlaid with the fitted normal distribution and the combined distributions from our regime-switching model. As the chart illustrates, the combination of two normal distributions improves the distribution fit and introduces some degree of skewness and fat-tail characteristics.

Exhibit 25: Normal and Fat-Tailed Distribution Fit for US Equity Quarterly Returns

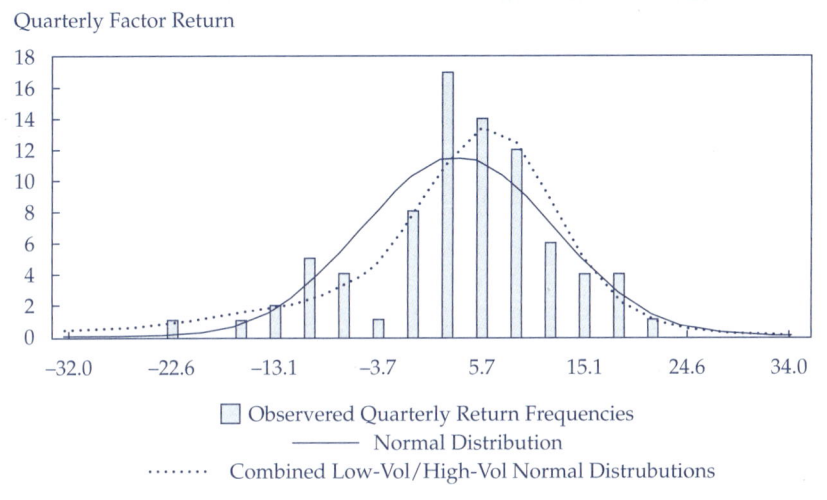

Quarterly Factor Return

☐ Observed Quarterly Return Frequencies
——— Normal Distribution
········ Combined Low-Vol/High-Vol Normal Distrubutions

Source: Authors' calculations.

Several variations of regime-switching models are available. We have used a very basic set-up to illustrate the additional richness a regime-switching model can bring to the analysis. We could also apply a similar approach if we were to build asset classes using risk factors. We could overlay the non-normal distributions of the risk factors on the relevant asset class returns.[12]

Simulation for Long-Term Horizon Risk Assessment

We will now work through a practical application of Monte Carlo simulation in the context of asset allocation over a long time horizon. We simulate asset class returns in quarterly steps over a 10-year time horizon.[13] Such models exhibit some degree of mean-reversion and also capture dynamic interactions across risk factors or asset classes over multiple time periods.

The volatilities, correlations, and other parameters of the time series model are estimated based on the past 20 years of unsmoothed asset class return data. The expected returns for the selected asset classes (shown in Exhibit 26), however, are not based on historical average returns but are illustrative, forward-looking estimates. Note that these return expectations mostly assume passive investments in the specific asset class and don't include the possible value-added from (or lost through) active management. Hedge funds are the exception, of course, because by definition hedge

---

12 In this reading, we assume that various asset classes have constant risk factor sensitivities over time, an assumption that can be relaxed in practice. For example, Berkelaar, Kobor, and Kouwenberg (2009) present time-varying risk factors for various hedge fund strategies in a similar Monte Carlo simulation framework.
13 To ensure that we not only capture short-horizon risks but also properly assess long-term asset return behavior characteristics, we capture the linear interdependencies among multiple time series by working with a vector-autoregressive model.

funds are actively managed investment strategies rather than a true stand-alone asset class. The expected returns are also generally assumed to be net of fees to make them comparable across asset classes.

Asset class-level expected returns are critically important to an asset allocation exercise. Return expectations should be reflective of the current market conditions—including valuations, levels of interest rates, and spreads. Setting return expectations requires a combination of objective facts (e.g., the current yield and spread levels) and judgment (how risk factors and valuation ratios might change from the current levels over the relevant time horizon).

Exhibit 26: Asset Class Expected Returns

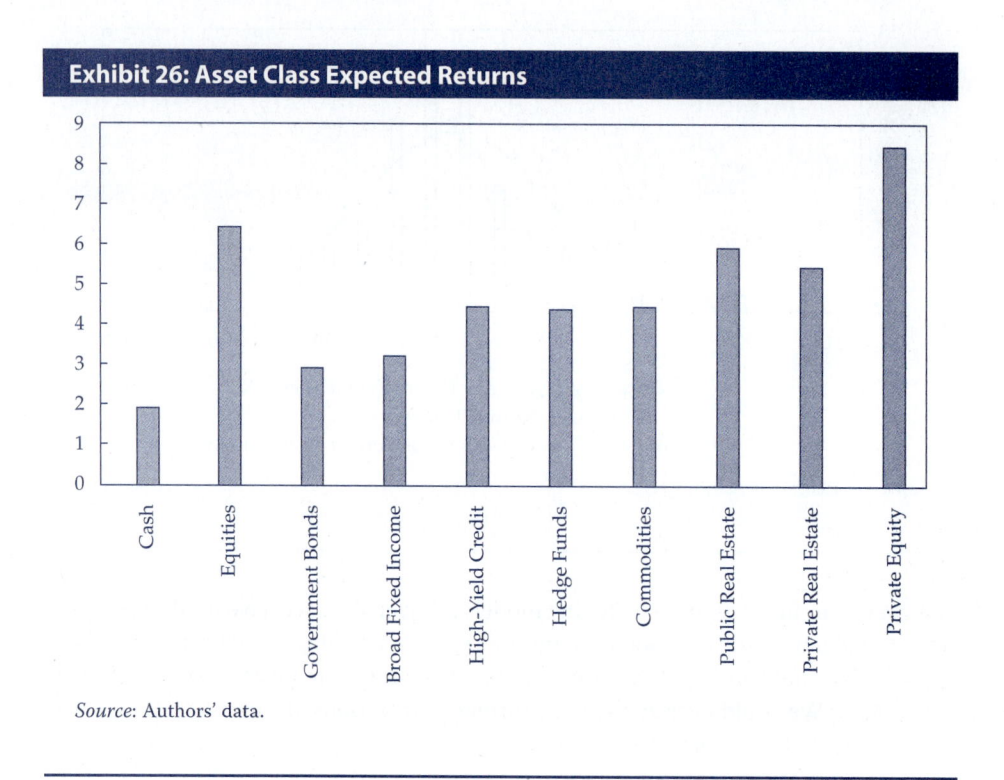

Source: Authors' data.

In this example, we compare three possible portfolios:

- A portfolio 100% invested in government bonds
- A portfolio allocated 50% to global public equities and 50% to broad fixed income
- A diversified "endowment portfolio" allocated 40% to global public equities, 15% to fixed income, 20% to broad hedge funds, 15% to private equity, 5% to private real estate, and 5% to commodities

Exhibit 27 shows the risk and return statistics for the three portfolios. VaR and CVaR downside risk measures focus over the shorter, quarterly, and 1-year time horizons. The worst drawdown and the cumulative annualized total return ranges are expressed over a 10-year time horizon.

Exhibit 27: Portfolio Risk and Return Estimates

	Government Bond Portfolio	50/50 Portfolio	Endowment Portfolio
Expected Geometric Return over 10 Years	2.3%	5.6%	7.0%
Annual Total Return Volatility	4.2%	6.6%	11.2%
95% VaR over Q/Q (quarter over quarter)	−3.1%	−2.9%	−4.6%
95% VaR over 1 Year	−5.2%	−4.2%	−9.1%
95% CVaR over Q/Q	−4.0%	−3.9%	−6.4%
95% CVaR over 1 Year	−6.9%	−6.6%	−13.1%
99% VaR over Q/Q	−4.5%	−4.6%	−7.5%
99% VaR over 1 Year	−7.9%	−8.1%	−15.6%
99% CVaR over Q/Q	−5.2%	−5.5%	−8.7%
99% CVaR over 1 Year	−9.2%	−10.3%	−18.7%
Worst Drawdown over 10 Years	−19.8%	−22.5%	−36.9%

10-Year Return Distribution	Government Bond Portfolio	50/50 Portfolio	Endowment Portfolio
5% Low	0.0%	2.3%	1.9%
25% Low	1.2%	4.2%	4.8%
50% (Median)	2.3%	5.6%	7.0%
75% High	3.1%	7.0%	9.1%
95% High	4.5%	9.0%	12.2%

From Exhibit 27, we see that the multi-asset endowment portfolio generates a significantly higher return than the portfolio exclusively invested in government bonds, albeit at much higher downside risk as measured by VaR, CVaR, or worst drawdown. This table alone, however, is insufficient to determine which investment alternative a particular investor should choose.

Consider the case of a university endowment fund. Let's assume that the investment objective is to support a 5% annual spending rate as well as to preserve the purchasing power of the asset base over the 10-year time horizon. We use the same simulation engine to generate the analytics of Exhibit 28. Here, we plot the expected cumulative total return within a +/− 1 standard deviation range together with the cumulative spending rate, as well as the spending rate augmented with inflation on a cumulative basis. The latter two variables represent the investment target, so we can meaningfully interpret the return potential of the two investment choices in the context of the investment objective. The 50% equities/50% government bond portfolio initially appeared to be a lower risk alternative in Exhibit 27, but Exhibit 28 shows that this choice is more likely to fall short of the return target, given that its median return of 5.6% is less than the nominal return target of approximately 7% (the 5% spending rate plus 2% inflation). At the same time, the endowment portfolio's 7% median return indicates that it would have a better chance of meeting the investment objective.

Exhibit 28: Cumulative Total Return Cones Simulated over a 10-Year Horizon

A. 50/50 Portfolio

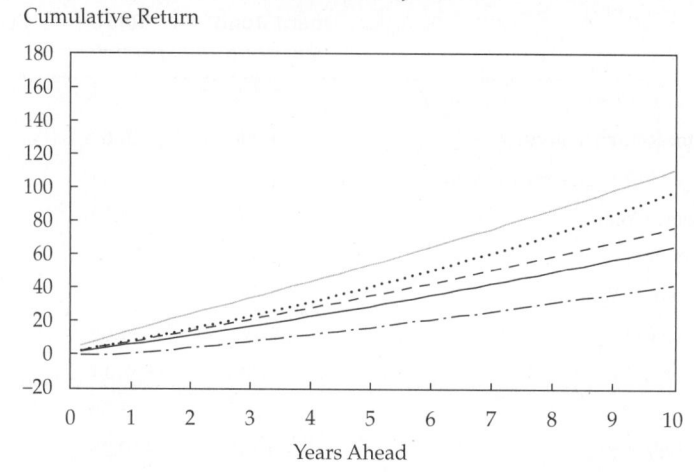

B. Endowment Portfolio

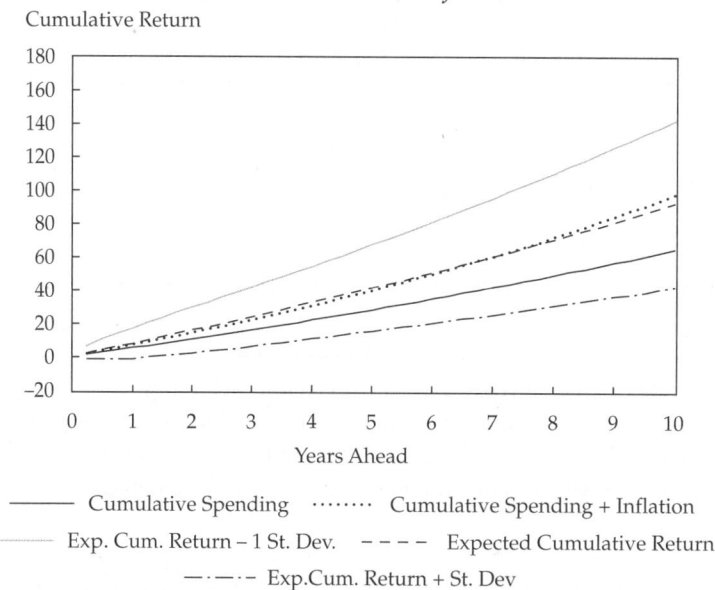

——— Cumulative Spending ········ Cumulative Spending + Inflation
——— Exp. Cum. Return – 1 St. Dev. – – – – Expected Cumulative Return
—·—·— Exp.Cum. Return + St. Dev

Exhibit 29 shows the probability of meeting the spending rate as well as the spending rate plus inflation at any point in time over the investment horizon. If risk is defined as the probability of falling short of meeting the return target (rather than the asset-only perspective of risk, volatility), the otherwise lower-risk 50% equities and 50% government bond portfolio becomes the higher risk alternative.

Exhibit 29: Estimated Probability of Achieving the Investment Goal

A.

Probability of meeting spending target

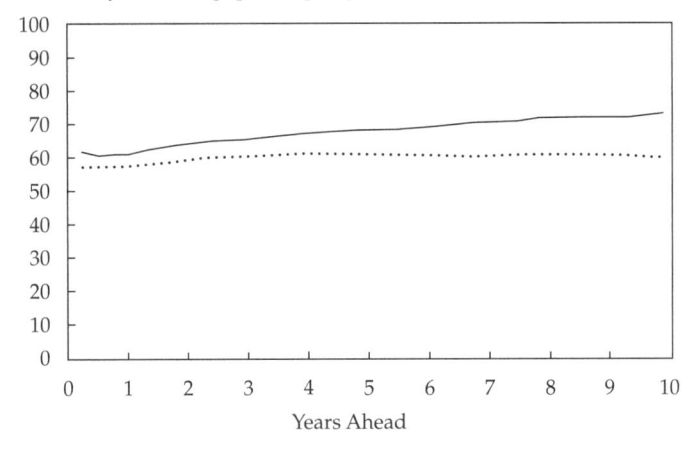

B.

Probability of meeting spending target plus inflation

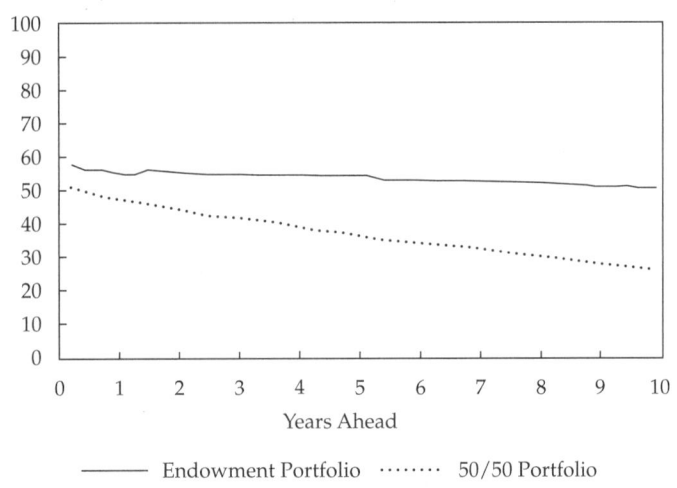

——— Endowment Portfolio   ········ 50/50 Portfolio

PORTFOLIO OPTIMIZATION

11

☐ | discuss approaches to asset allocation to alternative investments

Portfolio optimization for asset allocation has been covered in great detail in earlier readings. Here we focus on some special considerations for optimization in the context of alternative investments.

Mean–Variance Optimization without and with Constraints

We mentioned earlier that mean–variance optimization would likely over-allocate to alternative, mainly illiquid, asset classes given their higher expected returns and potentially underestimated risk. Some investors impose minimum and maximum constraints on various asset classes to compensate for this bias. Let's consider the ramifications of this approach.

Here, the input data for our optimization are comprised of the asset class expected returns depicted in Exhibit 26, while the covariance matrix is based on the unsmoothed asset class return history over the past 20 years. Exhibit 30 shows the optimized portfolio allocations generated by the mean–variance optimization without and with constraints. Each column in these bar charts represents an optimized portfolio allocation subject to a return target. The exhibit progresses from low-return targets on the left to high-return targets on the right. In total, we show 20 possible portfolio allocations first without and then with constraints.

By reviewing Panel B of Exhibit 30, we can see that the unconstrained portfolio allocations are dominated by cash and fixed income at the lower end of the risk spectrum, and private equity becomes the dominant asset class for higher risk portfolios. Optimization is quite sensitive to the input parameters: It's quite common to see allocations concentrated in a small number of asset classes. Thus, investors shouldn't take the unconstrained output as the "best" allocation. Small changes in the input variables could lead to large changes in the asset allocations.

Because investors would potentially reject the raw, concentrated output of unconstrained mean–variance optimization, we also ran a constrained optimization where we capped private equity and hedge fund allocations at 30% each, private real estate at 15%, and major public asset classes at 50% each. The resulting constrained allocations, shown in the Panel A of Exhibit 30, are less concentrated and appear to be more diversified.

Exhibit 31 depicts the mean–variance efficient frontiers corresponding to the optimized portfolio allocations of Exhibit 30. Note that both frontiers contain 20 dots, each representing an optimized portfolio. The numbers under each bar in Exhibit 30 identify the allocation associated with each of the dots on the efficient frontiers in Exhibit 31 (e.g., the allocation associated with portfolio 20 on the efficient frontier in Exhibit 31 is the one shown at the rightmost edge of Exhibit 30).

Exhibit 30: Unconstrained and Constrained Asset Allocations

A. Constrained Portfolios

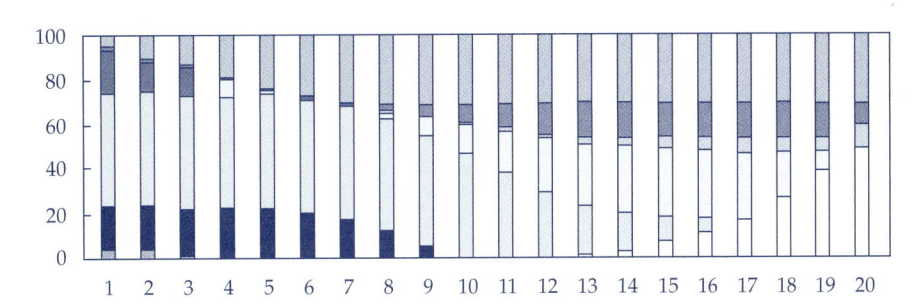

B. Unconstrained Portfolios

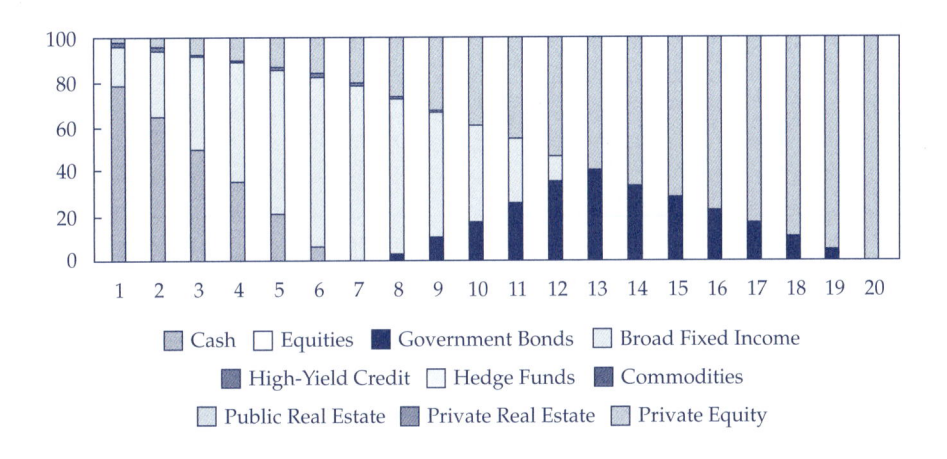

Legend: Cash · Equities · Government Bonds · Broad Fixed Income · High-Yield Credit · Hedge Funds · Commodities · Public Real Estate · Private Real Estate · Private Equity

Note that the constrained efficient frontier runs below its unconstrained peer (Exhibit 31). This is not unexpected, as we artificially prohibited the optimization from selecting the most efficient allocation it could get based on the available quantitative data.

Exhibit 31: Unconstrained and Constrained Mean–Variance Efficient Frontiers

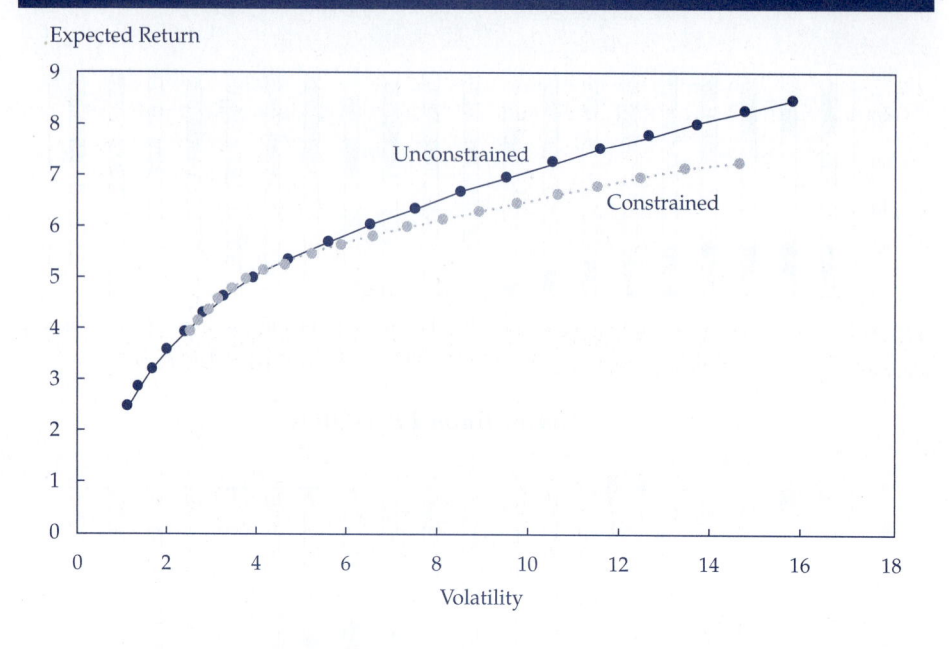

In practice, many investors are aware of the limits of the mean–variance framework—the possible underestimation of the true fundamental risks based on the reported returns of private investments—and they may also have in mind other constraints, such as capping illiquidity. Thus, introducing maximum and minimum constraints for certain asset classes may be a reasonable, although exogenous, adjustment to the quantitative optimization. However, not even constrained optimized allocations should be accepted without further scrutiny. In fact, similar volatility and expected return profiles can be achieved with a wide variety of asset allocations. So, although optimized portfolios may serve as analytical guidance, it's important to validate whether a change to an asset allocation policy results in a significant return increment and/or volatility reduction. Sometimes the results of a constrained optimization are largely driven by the constraints (especially if they are very tight). If that is the case, then the optimizer might not be able to perform its job due to the many (or very tight) constraints applied.

Mean–CVaR Optimization

Portfolio optimization can also improve the asset allocation decision through a risk management lens. An investor who is particularly concerned with the downside risk of a proposed asset allocation may choose to minimize the portfolio's CVaR rather than its volatility relative to a return target.[14] If the portfolio contains asset classes and investment strategies with negative skewness and long tails, the CVaR lens could materially alter the asset allocation decision. Minimizing CVaR subject to an expected return target is quantitatively much more complex than portfolio variance minimization: It requires a large number of historical or simulated return scenarios to properly incorporate potential tail risk into the optimization.[15]

---

14 Because we are optimizing allocation to asset classes, the CVaR tail risk measure quantifies *systematic* asset class level risks. Individual asset managers or securities may impose additional idiosyncratic risk when the asset allocation is implemented in practice.
15 Technical details are provided by Rockafellar and Uryasev (2000).

Our first illustration is applied to three hedge fund strategies: macro, equity market neutral, and long/short equity hedged. Our expected returns for the three strategies are 3.6%, 3.6%, and 6.0%, respectively. The observed return distribution for macro strategy is fairly normal, while equity market neutral exhibits negative skew and the highest kurtosis of these three strategies (see Exhibit 21).

Panels A and B of Exhibit 32 compare 20 possible portfolio allocations generated by the mean–variance and mean–CVaR optimizations, varying from low to high risk/ return profiles. The allocation to long/short equity hedged (the black bar) is similar under both the MVO and CVaR approaches. The macro strategy receives a much higher allocation using the CVaR approach than it does using the MVO approach.

Exhibit 32: Hedge Fund Allocations

A. Mean–Variance

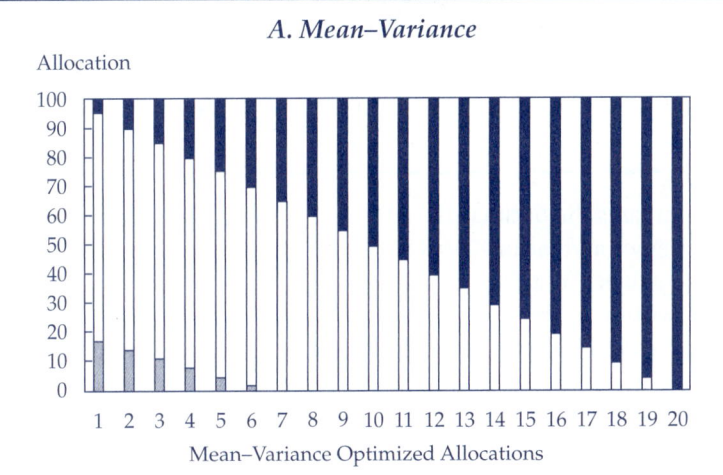

B. Mean–CVaR

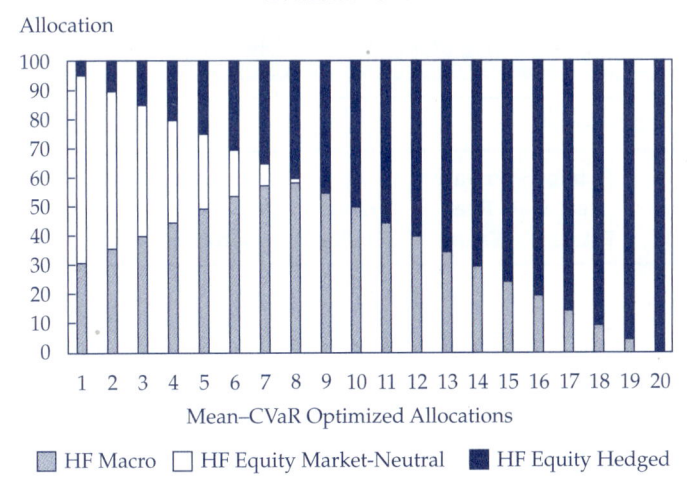

Exhibit 33 compares portfolio #12 from the mean–variance efficient frontier to portfolio #12 from the mean–CVaR efficient frontier. Both portfolios allocated 60% to the long/ short equity strategy. Under the CVaR-optimization approach, the remaining 40% of the portfolio is invested in global macro. Under the MVO approach, the remaining 40% of the portfolio is invested in equity market-neutral.

Let's compare the portfolio volatilities and downside risk measures. The mean– CVaR portfolio has higher volatility (7.8% vs 7.3%) but lower tail risk (–6.8% vs –7.7%). Exhibit 33 also shows a third portfolio, which evenly *splits* the 40% not allocated to equity-hedged between global macro and equity market neutral. The volatility of this portfolio lies between the two optimal portfolios. Although nominally more diversified than either of the #12 portfolios from the optimization, its CVaR is worse than that of the mean–CVaR optimized portfolio (but still better than that of the MVO portfolio). An investor may have qualitative considerations that warrant including this more-diversified portfolio among the options to be evaluated.

Exhibit 33: Mean–Variance and Mean–CVaR Efficient Hedge Fund Allocations

	Asset Allocation			Portfolio Characteristics			
	Macro	Equity Market Neutral	Long/Short Equity	Expected Return	Volatility	95% VaR	95% CVaR
Mean–Variance Optimal	0.0%	40.0%	60.0%	5.0%	7.3%	−3.7%	−7.7%
Mean–CVaR Optimal	40.0%	0.0%	60.0%	5.0%	7.8%	−4.1%	−6.8%
Combination	20.0%	20.0%	60.0%	5.0%	7.5%	−3.7%	−7.3%

Exhibit 34 compares the optimal allocations of a broad asset class portfolio through the mean–variance and mean–CVaR lenses. In this example, the optimal allocations were selected subject to a 6.8% expected return target. Both approaches allocated a significant portion of the portfolio to private equity and hedge funds (30% each). A notable difference, however, is in the allocation to public and private real estate. Where the MVO approach allocated 22% to the combined real estate categories, the CVaR approach allocated nothing at all to either real estate category. We can identify the reason for this by referring back to Exhibit 21: The public and private real estate categories are characterized by 99% CVaRs of −40.2% and −27.9%, respectively.

Exhibit 34: Mean–Variance and Mean–CVaR Efficient Multi-Asset Portfolios

	Asset Allocation						Portfolio Characteristics		
	Equities	Govt Bonds	Hedge Funds	Public Real Estate	Private Real Estate	Private Equity	Expected Return	Volatility	99% CVaR
Mean–Variance Optimal	18%	0%	30%	7%	15%	30%	6.8%	11.5%	−20.7%
Mean–CVaR Optimal	34%	6%	30%	0%	0%	30%	6.8%	12.1%	−15.6%

EXAMPLE 6

Asset Allocation Recommendation

The CIO (chief investment officer) of the International University Endowment Fund (the Fund) is preparing for the upcoming investment committee (IC) meeting. The Fund's annual asset allocation review is on the agenda, and the CIO plans to propose a new strategic asset allocation for the Fund. Subject to prudent risk-taking, the recommended asset allocation should offer

- the highest expected return and

- the highest probability of achieving the long-term 5% real return target.

The inflation assumption is 2%.

In addition, the risk in the Fund is one factor that is considered when lenders assign a risk rating to the university. The university's primary lender has proposed a loan covenant that would trigger a re-evaluation of the university's creditworthiness if the Fund incurs a loss greater than 20% over any 1-year period.

The investment staff produced the following tables to help the CIO prepare for the meeting.

	Asset Allocation						
Alterna-tive	Cash	Public Equity	Govt	Credit	Hedge Fund	Real Estate	Private Equity
A	5.0%	60.0%	30.0%	5.0%	0.0%	0.0%	0.0%
B	4.0%	50.0%	16.0%	5.0%	10.0%	5.0%	10.0%
C	2.0%	40.0%	8.0%	5.0%	18.0%	7.0%	20.0%
D	1.0%	30.0%	5.0%	4.0%	20.0%	10.0%	30.0%
E	2.0%	40.0%	3.0%	3.0%	15.0%	7.0%	30.0%
F	2.0%	50.0%	3.0%	0.0%	10.0%	5.0%	30.0%
G	1.0%	56.0%	3.0%	0.0%	10.0%	0.0%	30.0%

Portfolio Characteristics

						10-Year Horizon:		
Alternative	Expected Return	Volatility	1-Year 99% VaR	1-Year 99% CVaR	5th Percen-tile Return	95th Percentile Return	Probability of Meeting 5% Real Return	Probability of Purchas-ing Power Impairment
A	6.0%	9.0%	−12.4%	−15.0%	1.6%	10.5%	37.0%	7.1%
B	6.7%	10.3%	−14.6%	−17.3%	2.0%	11.4%	46.1%	4.3%
C	7.1%	11.1%	−15.8%	−18.8%	2.2%	12.2%	52.1%	3.2%
D	7.4%	11.5%	−16.3%	−19.4%	2.4%	12.6%	56.1%	2.5%
E	7.7%	12.3%	−17.4%	−20.6%	2.4%	13.2%	58.8%	2.8%
F	7.8%	13.0%	−18.5%	−21.8%	2.2%	13.7%	60.8%	3.6%
G	7.9%	13.5%	−19.3%	−22.7%	2.1%	14.1%	61.0%	4.0%

Notes:

- 1-year horizon 99% VaR: the lowest return over any 1-year period at a 99% confidence level (i.e., only a 1% chance to experience a total return below this threshold).

- 1-year horizon 99% CVaR: the expected return if the return falls below the 99% VaR threshold.

- 5th and 95th percentile annualized returns over a 10-year time horizon: a 90% chance that the annualized 10-year total return will fall between these two figures

- probability of purchasing power impairment[16]: as defined by the IC, the probability of losing 40% of the endowment's purchasing power over 10 years after taking gifts to the endowment, spending from the endowment, and total return into account.

1. Which asset allocation is *most likely* to meet the committee's objective and constraints?

Solution:

Portfolio D. Portfolios E, F, and G have 1-year, 99% CVaRs, which, if realized, would trigger the loan covenant. Portfolio D has the next highest probability of meeting the 5% real return target and the lowest probability of purchasing power impairment. Portfolios A, B, and C have lower probabilities of meeting the return targets and higher probabilities of purchasing power impairment.

12   RISK FACTOR-BASED OPTIMIZATION

Increasingly, investors believe that viewing investment decisions through a risk factor lens (e.g., growth, inflation, credit risk) may improve the investment process. Separating fundamentally similar investments, like public and private equities, into distinct asset classes ignores the probability that both are exposed to the same risk factors. In this section, we will work through an asset allocation example using a risk factor lens.

Let's assume that an investor starts the asset allocation exercise by first allocating the overall risk budget across the main risk factors.[17] Instead of setting expectations for distinct asset classes, she may start thinking about the return expectations and correlation of the fundamental risk factors. Exhibit 35 shows her return expectations for the risk factors described in Exhibit 14. In this illustration, the global equity risk factor (a practical proxy for macroeconomic-oriented "growth") is expected to generate the highest return. She expects the duration and value factors to generate negative returns because stronger economic growth fueled by advances in technology would lead to rising rates and better returns for growth stocks. She is concerned about rising inflation, so she has assigned a positive expected return to the inflation factor.

---

16 Similar measures of risk are proposed by Swensen (2009) in the context of endowment funds.
17 Approaches to asset allocation and portfolio construction are expanding as the understanding of risk factors is increasing. A risk parity approach to asset allocation, for example, would allocate total risk in equal portion to the selected risk factors.

Exhibit 35: Expected Factor Returns

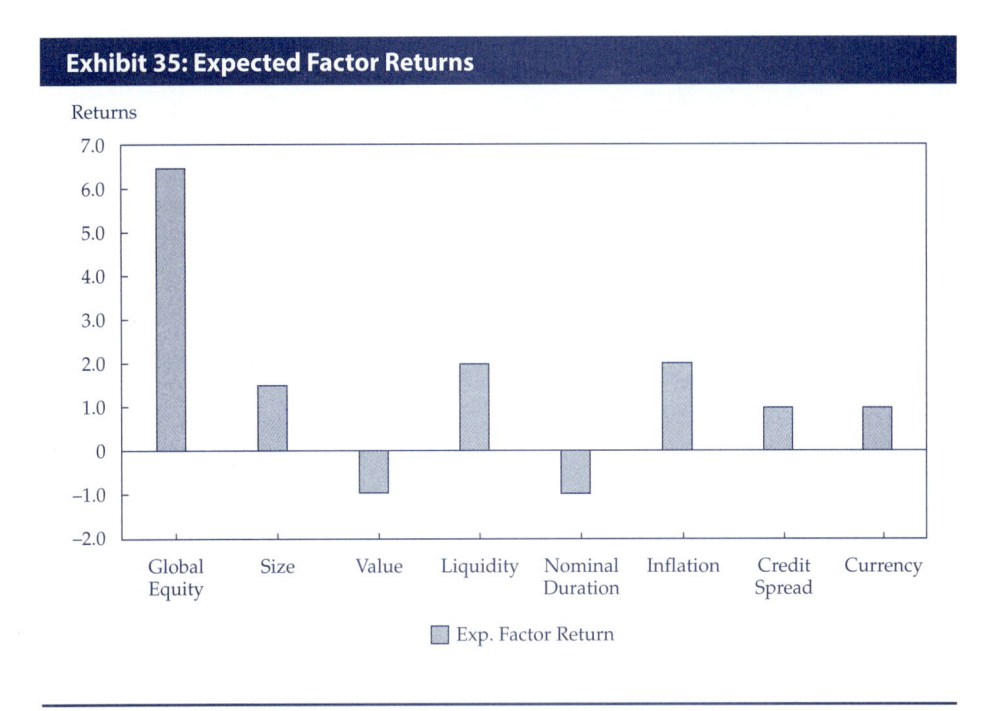

Returns

Exp. Factor Return

Using these returns and the historical factor volatilities and correlations, we can optimize the risk factor exposure by minimizing factor-implied risk subject to a total return target of 6.5%. The black bars in Exhibit 36 show these optimal factor exposures. Note that the target exposures of the value and nominal duration factors are positive, although the associated expected factor returns are negative. The model allocates to these factors for their diversification potential because they are negatively correlated with other risk factors. Duration and equity factors have a correlation of −0.6, whereas value and equity factors have a correlation of −0.3 based on the data used for this illustration.

We have established optimal risk factor exposures, so now we must implement this target using actual investments. Some investors may have access to only public market investments, while other investors may also have access to private illiquid investments. The gray and white bars in Exhibit 36 illustrate the two possible implementations of the target factor exposures. Portfolio 1 assumes the investor is limited to public market investments. Portfolio 2 uses both public market investments and private, illiquid investments. The portfolio allocation details are displayed in Exhibit 37.

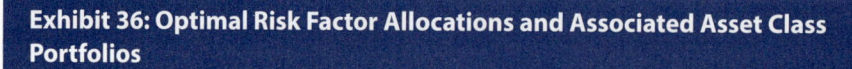

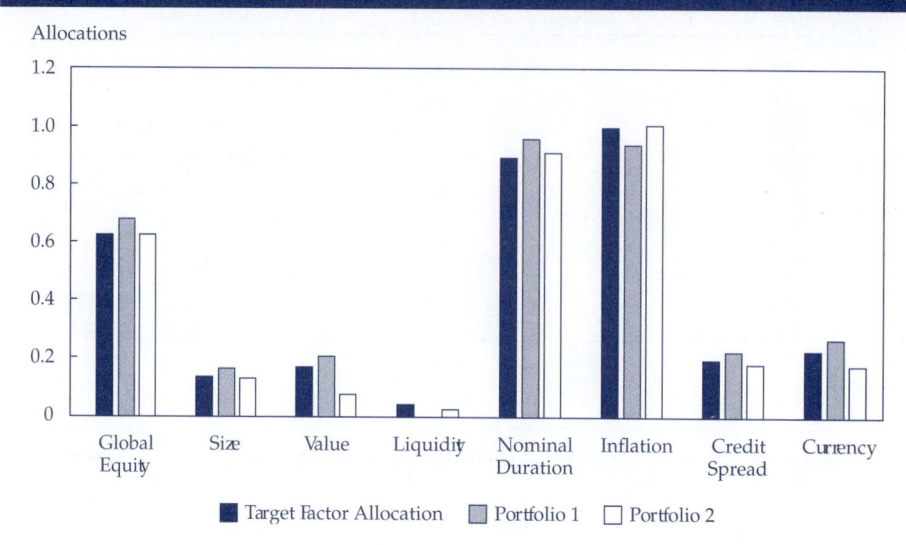

Exhibit 36: Optimal Risk Factor Allocations and Associated Asset Class Portfolios

Exhibit 37: Asset Class Portfolios Designed Based on Optimal Risk Factor Allocations

	Portfolio 1	Portfolio 2
Domestic Equities; *Value Tilt*	21.0%	13.0%
Non-Domestic Developed Market Equities; *Value Tilt*	21.0%	13.0%
Foreign Emerging Market Equities	21.0%	12.0%
Government Bonds	0.0%	5.0%
Broad Fixed Income	10.0%	0.0%
High-Yield Credit	2.0%	3.0%
Inflation-Linked Bonds	7.0%	0.0%
Hedge Funds	15.0%	10.0%
Commodities	3.0%	4.0%
Public Real Estate	0.0%	12.0%
Private Real Estate	0.0%	13.0%
Private Equity	0.0%	15.0%
Total	**100.0%**	**100.0%**
Expected Return	6.2%	6.9%
Volatility	13.5%	13.2%

Even though they have similar factor exposures, you can see some significant differences in the asset class allocations of the two portfolios. Portfolio 1 allocates 63% to public equities, whereas Portfolio 2 allocates 35% to public equities plus 15% to private equity for its higher return potential. Portfolio 1 allocates 18% to alternatives (15% in hedge funds and 3% in commodities, two of the most liquid alternative asset classes), while Portfolio 2 has allocated 54% to alternatives (10% hedge funds, 4% commodities, 12% public real estate, 13% private real estate, and 15% private equity). Portfolio 1 achieves its inflation sensitivity by allocating to inflation-linked bonds and commodities. Portfolio 2 achieves its desired exposure to the inflation factor through a combined allocation to real estate and commodities. The volatility of the two portfolios is similar, but Portfolio 2 is able to achieve a higher expected return given its ability to allocate to private equity.

Although a risk factor-driven approach is conceptually very elegant, we must mention a few caveats:

- While generally accepted asset class definitions provide a common language among the investment community, risk factors may be defined quite differently investor-to-investor. It's important to establish a common understanding of factor definitions and factor return expectations among the parties to an asset allocation exercise. This includes an agreement as to what financial instruments can be used to best match the factor exposures if they are not directly investable.

- Correlations among risk factors, just like correlations across asset classes, may dramatically shift under changing market conditions; thus, careful testing needs to be applied to understand how changing market conditions will affect the asset allocation.

- Some factor sensitivities are stable (like the nominal interest rate sensitivity of government bonds), while others are very unstable (like the inflation sensitivity of commodities). Factor sensitivities also need to be very carefully tested to validate whether the invested portfolio would truly deliver the desired factor exposures and not deliver unintended factor returns.

EXAMPLE 7

Selecting an Asset Allocation Approach

1. You have a new client who has unexpectedly inherited a substantial sum of money. The client is in his early 30s and newly married. He has no children and no other investible assets. What asset allocation approach is most suitable for this client?

Solution:

Mean–variance optimization with Monte Carlo simulation is most appropriate for this client. He has limited investment expertise, so your first responsibility is to educate him with respect to such basic investment concepts as risk, return, and diversification. A simple MVO approach supplemented with Monte Carlo simulation to illustrate potential upside and downside of an asset allocation choice is mostly likely to serve the asset allocation and investment education needs.

2. Your client is a tax-exempt foundation that recently received a bequest doubling its assets to €200 million. There is an outside investment adviser but no dedicated investment staff; however, the six members of the investment committee (IC) are all wealthy, sophisticated investors in their own right. The IC conducts an asset allocation study every three years and reviews the asset allocation at its annual meeting. The current asset allocation is 30% equities, 20% fixed income, 25% private equity, and 25% real estate. Three percent of assets are paid out annually in grants; this expenditure is covered by an annuity purchased some years ago. The foundation's primary investment objective is to maximize returns subject to a maximum level of

volatility. A secondary consideration is the desire to avoid a permanent loss of capital. What asset allocation approach is most suitable for this client?

Solution:

Given the sophistication and investment objectives of the IC members, using a mean–CVaR optimization approach is appropriate to determine the asset allocation. This client has a more sophisticated understanding of risk and will appreciate the more nuanced view of risk offered by mean–CVaR optimization. Given the portfolio's exposure to alternative investments, the asset allocation decision will be enhanced by the more detailed picture of left-tail risk offered by CVaR optimization (the risk of permanent loss) relative to mean–variance optimization. The lack of permanent staff and a once-per-year meeting schedule suggest that a risk factor-based approach may not be appropriate.

13   LIQUIDITY PLANNING

☐ | discuss the importance of liquidity planning in allocating to alternative investments

Earlier, we addressed various aspects of liquidity associated with investing in alternative asset classes. In this section, we focus on multi-year horizon liquidity planning for private investments.

When managing portfolios that contain allocations to alternative investments, managing liquidity risk takes on critical importance. We need to ensure sufficient liquidity to meet interim obligations or goals, which might include:

- periodic payments to beneficiaries (e.g., a pension fund's retirement benefit payments or an endowment fund's distributions to support operating expenses);

- portfolio rebalancing or funding new asset manager mandates; or

- fulfilling a commitment made to a private investment fund when the general partner makes the capital call.

Alternative investments pose unique liquidity challenges that must be explicitly addressed before committing to an alternative investment program. Private investments—including private equity, private real estate, private real assets, and private credit—represent the most illiquid components of an investment portfolio. Private investments usually require a long-term commitment over an 8- to 15-year time horizon. An investor contributes capital over the first few years (the investment period) and receives distributions in the later years. Combined with the call down (or drawdown) structure of a private investment fund, this creates a need to model a hypothetical path to achieving and maintaining a diversified, fully-invested allocation to private investments. Here we will explore the challenges with private investment liquidity planning with three primary considerations:

1. How to achieve and maintain the desired allocation.

2. How to handle capital calls.

3. How to plan for the unexpected.

Achieving and Maintaining the Strategic Asset Allocation

Strategic planning is required to determine the necessary annual commitments an investor should make to reach and maintain the long-term target asset allocation. Large private investors often use a liquidity forecasting model for their private investment programs. Here, we illustrate one such model based on work published by Takahashi and Alexander (2001). We also discuss private investment commitment pacing as an application of this model. This model is only one possible way to forecast private investment cash flows; investors may develop their own model using their own assumptions and experience.

We will illustrate this model with a hypothetical capital commitment (CC) of £100 million to a fund with a contractual term (L) of 12 years.

We begin by modeling the capital contributions (C) to the fund. Certain assumptions must be made regarding the rate of contribution (RC). We'll assume that 25% is contributed in the first year and that 50% of the remaining commitments are contributed in each of the subsequent years:

> Year 1: £100 million × 25% = £25 million
>
> Year 2: (£100 million – £25 million) × 50% = £37.5 million
>
> Year 3: (£100 million – £25 million – £37.5 million) × 50% = £18.75 million

and so on.

The capital contribution (C) in year t can be expressed with the following formula:

$$C_t = RC_t \times (CC - PIC_t) \tag{1}$$

where PIC denotes the already paid-in capital.

Alternatively, we can express this in words:

Capital Contribution

= Rate of Contribution × (Capital Commitment – Paid-in-Capital)

In practice, the investment period is often limited to a defined number of years; also, not all of the committed capital may be called.

The next step is to estimate the periodic distribution paid to investors. Distributions (D) are a function of the net asset value (NAV). From one year to the next, the NAV rises as additional capital contributions are made and as underlying investments appreciate. NAV declines as distributions are made (or as assets are written down).

If the partnership investment develops as anticipated, then the fund's IRR would be equal to this rate.

To estimate the expected annual distribution payments, we need to make an assumption about the pattern of distributions. For example, an analyst may assume that the fund does not distribute any money in Year 1 or Year 2 but distributes 10% of the prevailing net asset value in Year 3, 20% in Year 4, 30% in Year 5, and 50% of the remaining balance in each of the remaining years. In the case of real estate funds, it is also possible that there is a pre-defined minimum annual distribution rate (called the "yield"). Once the annual rates of distribution are determined, the annual amount distributed is calculated by the following formula:

$$D_t = RD_t[NAV_{t-1} \times (1 + G)] \tag{2}$$

where

$$RD_t = (t/L)^B, \tag{3}$$

$$NAV_t = [NAV_{t-1} \times (1 + G)] + C_t - D_t \tag{4}$$

Again, in words:

Distributions at time t

= Rate of Distribution at time t × [NAV at time t-1 × (1 + Growth Rate)], and

NAV at time t

= prior NAV × (1 + Growth Rate) + Capital Contribution − Distributions

In Exhibit 38, we display the forecasted annual capital contributions, outstanding commitment forecast, distributions, NAV, and cumulative net cash flow for a private investment fund with a 12-year life. We assume that 25% of the committed capital is contributed in the first year and that 50% of the remaining commitments are contributed in each of the subsequent years. Using a bow (B) parameter of 2.5, we set the RD_t distribution rates such that the yearly distribution rates would increase fairly gradually. We assume a 13% growth rate from the investments in this fund.

Exhibit 38: Expected Annual Contribution, Outstanding Commitment, Rate of Distribution, Annual Distribution, NAV, and Net Cash Flow of a Hypothetical Private Investment Fund

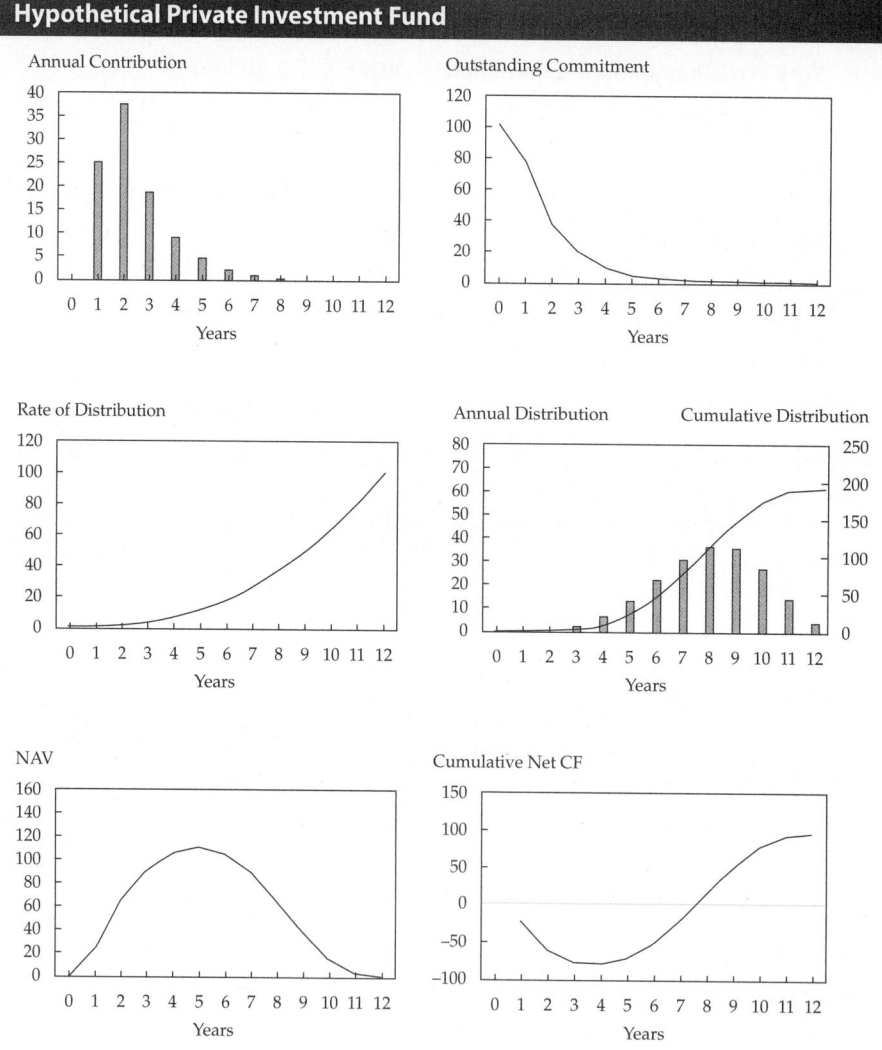

The corresponding annual RD_t rates are displayed in Exhibit 39.

Exhibit 39: Assumed Annual Distribution Rates (RD$_t$)

Year	1	2	3	4	5	6	7	8	9	10	11	12
Rate of Distribution	0%	1%	3%	6%	11%	18%	26%	36%	49%	63%	80%	100%

How does the shape of the expected rate of distribution influence NAV and the annual distribution amounts? For illustration purposes we can change our assumption of RD by setting the bow parameter (B) to 5.0, such that early year distribution rates are very low and start increasing in the second half of the fund's life. The new distribution rates are shown in Exhibit 40, and Exhibit 41 shows how distributions and the NAV would react to this change.

Exhibit 40: Alternative Assumed Annual Distribution Rates (RD$_t$)

Year	1	2	3	4	5	6	7	8	9	10	11	12
Rate of Distribution	0%	0%	0%	0%	1%	3%	7%	13%	24%	40%	65%	100%

Exhibit 41: Rate of Distribution, Expected Annual Distribution, NAV, and Cumulative Net Cash Flow with Back-Loaded Distributions

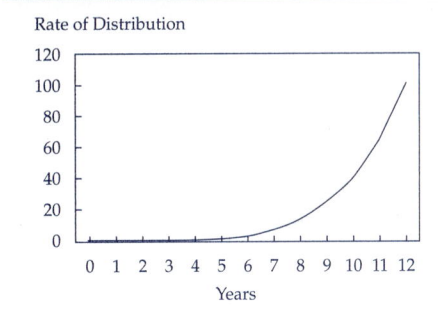
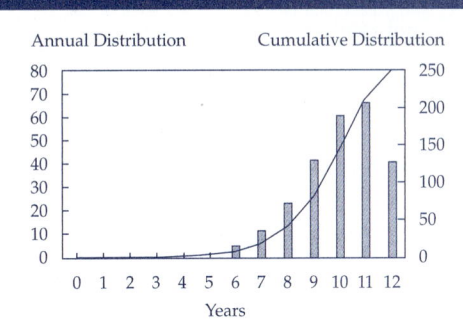
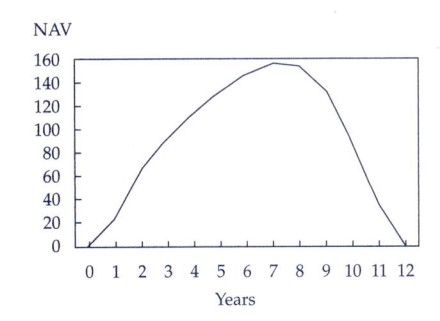
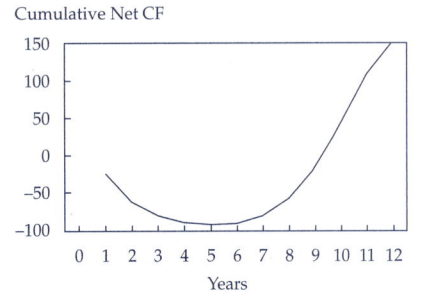

Although the annual capital contributions would not be affected, we can see that the lower distribution rate in the early years allows the NAV to grow higher. The cumulative net cash flow, however, would stay in the negative zone for a longer time.

EXAMPLE 8

Liquidity Planning for Private Investments

1. The NAV of an investor's share in a private renewable energy fund was €30 million at the end of 2020. All capital has been called. The investor expects a 20% distribution to be paid at the end of 2021. The expected growth rate is 12%. What is the expected NAV at year-end 2022?

Solution:

The expected NAV at year-end 2022 is €30,105,600. The expected distribution at the end of 2021 is €6.72 million [(€30 million x 1.12) x 20%]. The NAV at year-end 2022 is therefore (€30 million x 1.12) x (1 − 0.20) x 1.12 = €30,105,600.

An important practical application of such models is to help determine the size of the annual commitment an investor needs to make to reach the target allocation of an asset class over the coming years (i.e., investment commitment pacing).

Assume that we manage an investment portfolio of £1 billion and that our strategic asset allocation target for private equities is 20%. We currently do not have any private equity investment in the portfolio. We also must project the growth of the aggregate investment portfolio, because we want to achieve the 20% allocation based on the expected *future* value of the portfolio and of the private equity investment, not today's value. We assume an aggregate portfolio growth rate of 6% per year, including both net contributions and investment returns.

With these assumptions, and the private investment cash flow and NAV forecasting model discussed previously, the investor can determine the annual commitments needed to reach the overall target allocation. By using the same cash flow forecasting parameters as for the analysis in Exhibit 38, we can see that a £100 million commitment would lead the NAV to peak at around £110 million five years from now. A rough approximation could be the following: In five years, the total portfolio size would be £1 billion × $1.06^5 ≈ £1.338$ billion; so, at that point, the total private equity NAV should be approximately 20% × £1.338 billion=£268 million. Since we know that a £100 million commitment would lead to an NAV of £110 million in five years, we can extrapolate to arrive at the conclusion that a £243 million commitment today could achieve the goal.

However, this would result in a very concentrated private equity investment, with an NAV peaking in four to five years and then declining over the following years as distributions are made. A better practice is to spread commitments out over multiple years. A stable and disciplined multi-year commitment schedule leads to a more stable NAV size over time. It also achieves an important objective of diversifying exposure across vintage years. Thus, an investor can choose to commit a target amount of around £70 million per year over a period of four years (2017 through 2020) instead of concentrating the commitment in a single year. This schedule would bring the total private equity NAV to the target 20% level over five years. In Exhibit 42, we illustrate how the portfolio of private equity investments of different vintage years would build up over time. We also show how the total NAV would evolve beyond 2022 if no further capital commitment is made. As the chart suggests, the NAV would continue to grow through 2023 but would start to decline in later years as the 2017–2020 vintage private funds make distributions.

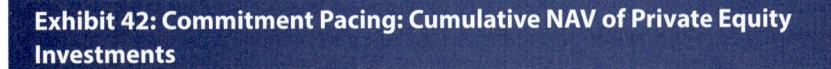

Exhibit 42: Commitment Pacing: Cumulative NAV of Private Equity Investments

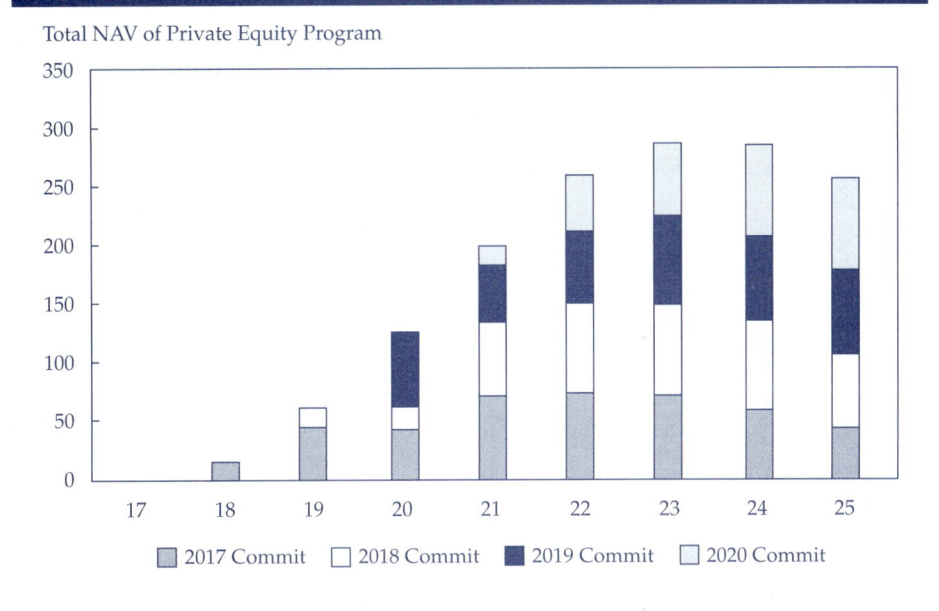

Total NAV of Private Equity Program

◼ 2017 Commit   ☐ 2018 Commit   ◼ 2019 Commit   ☐ 2020 Commit

In Exhibit 43, we show how private equity investments would grow as a proportion of the overall investment portfolio. As in the previous chart, we extend the forecast beyond 2022 to show the proportion of private equity investments will start to decline without further capital commitments after 2020.

Exhibit 43: Commitment Pacing: Private Equity NAV as % of the Total Portfolio

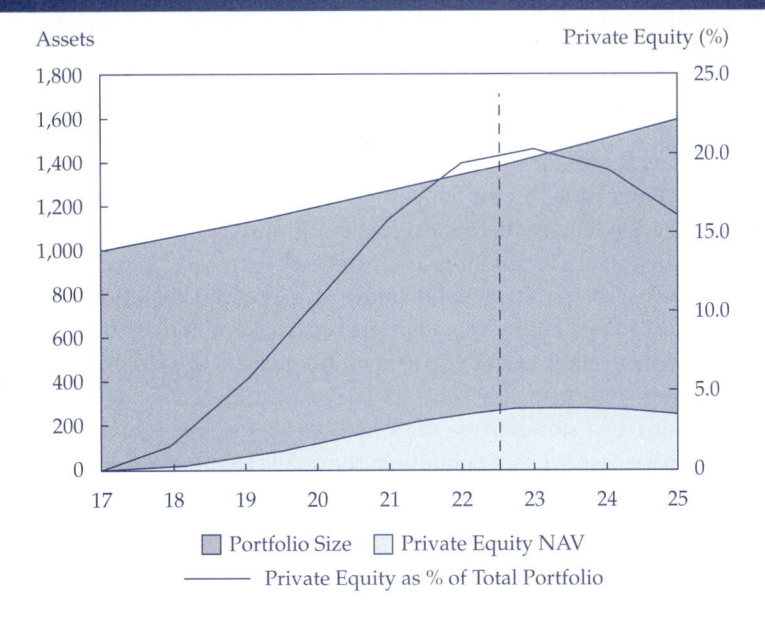

Assets   Private Equity (%)

◼ Portfolio Size   ☐ Private Equity NAV
—— Private Equity as % of Total Portfolio

The investor must review her pacing model forecast periodically, updating it as needed based on the actual commitments and transactions that have occurred and refreshing the assumptions for the future. If the investor plans to maintain a 20% allocation to private equity investments over the long run, she will clearly have to make ongoing commitments in the future, although at a slower pace once private equity is an established asset class in the portfolio.

To summarize, cash flow and pacing models enable investors to better manage their portfolio liquidity, set realistic annual commitment targets to reach the desired asset allocation, and manage portfolio beta in aggregate. Investors need to validate their model assumptions and evaluate how different parameter settings and liquidity stress scenarios could impact their investment portfolios.

14   PREPARING FOR THE UNEXPECTED

> discuss the importance of liquidity planning in allocating to alternative investments

The investor makes an up-front commitment of a certain dollar amount to a private investment fund, and the funds will typically be called (paid in) over a period of three to four years. In many cases, the general partner (GP) will never call the full amount of the capital commitment. The limited partner (LP) is obligated to pay the capital call in accordance with the terms agreed to with the GP, often within 30 days of receiving the call notification. However, it is not practical to keep all the committed (but not yet called) capital in liquid reserves given the opportunity cost of being out of the markets during the investment phase. Investors must develop a strategy for maintaining the asset allocation while waiting for the fund to become fully invested. Capital pending investment in a private equity fund is often invested in public equities as a proxy for private equities. A similar approach may be followed in the case of other private asset classes: The investor may consider high yield as a placeholder for pending private credit investments, REITs as a placeholder for private real estate investments, and energy stocks or commodity futures as a proxy for private real asset investments.

Preparing for the Unexpected

The liquidity-planning model described here addresses the key components of cash inflows and outflows, but the model results are clearly heavily dependent on the assumptions. The model parameters can be based purely on judgment, but a better practice would be to verify estimates and forecasts with a sample of representative private funds' historical experience. Obviously, the realized cash flows in the future are likely to differ from what the model predicted based on the assumed parameters. Thus, it is advisable to run the analysis using different sets of assumptions and under different scenarios. In a bear market, GPs may call capital at a higher pace and/or make distributions at a slower pace than had been expected. This suggests that in addition to the base case scenario planning, the analyst should develop an additional set of assumptions with faster capital calls and lower distribution rates.

If the fund is scheduled to begin liquidation when the investor's public market portfolio is performing poorly (as it did in the 2007–2008 period), it is likely that the GP will exercise his option to extend the fund life. If this happens, investors may find themselves with an asset allocation significantly different from target or being unable to meet the capital calls that were intended to be funded from the distributions. These contingencies should be modeled as part of stress testing the asset allocation.

EXAMPLE 9

Private Investments, Asset Allocation, and Liquidity Planning

The Endowment Fund of the University of Guitan (the Fund) has $750 million in assets. The investment committee (IC) adopted the following strategic asset allocation four years ago. Private investments are at the lower end of the permitted range. To reach the target allocation among private investments, the investment team has made several new commitments recently, and they expect capital calls over the coming year equal to approximately about 20% of the current private asset net asset value.

	Strategic Asset Allocation Target	Permitted Range	Current Asset Allocation (%)	Current Asset Allocation ($mil)
Cash	2%	0 to 5%	3%	22.5
Public Equities (including long/short equity)	35%	30 to 40%	35%	262.5
Government Bonds	5%	4 to 10%	7%	52.5
High-Yield Credit	3%	2 to 5%	5%	37.5
Hedge Funds (excluding long/short equity)	20%	17 to 23%	23%	172.5
Private Real Estate	10%	7 to 13%	8%	60.0
Private Real Assets	5%	3 to 7%	4%	30.0
Private Equity	20%	15 to 22%	15%	112.5
Total				$750 mil
Expected Return	7.1%			
Expected Volatility	11.1%			
99% CVaR	−18.8%			
Assumed Inflation Rate	2%			

The strategic asset allocation has a 52% probability of meeting the 5% real return target (4% spend rate, 1% principal growth, and 2% inflation).

At its last meeting, the endowment committee of the board approved a temporary increase in the spending rate, raising it from 4% to 5% for the next five years to support the university's efforts to reposition itself in the face of declining enrollments. The spending rate is calculated as a percentage of the Fund's trailing 5-year average value.

The CIO (chief investment officer) has produced a capital market outlook that will guide the fund's tactical asset allocation strategy for the next several quarters. Key elements of the outlook are:

- accommodative central bank policies are ending;
- equity valuation metrics have recently set new highs;
- the economic cycle is at or near its peak (i.e., there is a meaningful probability of rising inflation and a weaker economic environment over the next several quarters); and
- returns will quite likely be lower than what has been experienced over the past five years.

She also developed the following stress scenario based on her capital market outlook:

Return Stress Scenario	
Cash	2%
Public Equities (including l/s equity)	−30%
Government Bonds	−3%
High-Yield Credit	−10%
Hedge Funds (excluding l/s equity)	−8%
Private Real Estate	0%
Private Real Assets	10%
Private Equity	−10%

1. Identify and discuss the liquidity factors that the CIO should consider as she develops her portfolio positioning strategy for the next 12 to 24 months.

Solution:

- Given the market outlook, it is reasonable to assume cash flows into the fund from existing private investments will be negligible.
- The fund has next-12-month liabilities as follows:

    - Approximately $37.5 million to the university ($750 million x 5%). This is a high (conservative) estimate based on an assumption that the trailing 5-year average Fund value is less than the current $750 million.

    - Approximately $40.5 million in capital calls from private investment commitments (equally allocated across private real estate, private real assets, and private equity

    [($60m + $30m + $112.5m) × 20%]

    - Total liabilities next 12 months = $78 million
- Sources of immediate liquidity:

    - Cash = $22.5 million
    - Government bonds are at the midpoint of the permitted range. The allocation could be reduced from 7% to 4% and remain within the permitted range. This would free up $22.5 million ($750 million x 3%) of immediate liquidity. However, if the return scenario is realized (government bonds down 3%), then the government bond allocation will fall below the 4% minimum and additional rebalancing will be required.
    - $75.0 million in total (less than the $78 million liability)
- Other liquidity:

    - Public equities are at the midpoint of the permitted range. The allocation could be reduced from 35% to 30% and remain within the permitted range. This would free up $37.5 million ($750 million × 5%) for reinvestment in more-defensive asset classes or to meet anticipated liquidity needs. However, if the return scenario is realized (equities down 30%), then the equity allocation will fall below the 30% minimum and additional rebalancing will be required.

- High-yield credit is at the upper end of the allowed range. The allocation could be reduced from the current 5% to 2% or 3%, freeing up an additional $15 to $22.5 million. The limited liquidity in high-yield bond markets may make this challenging.

- The hedge fund allocation is at the upper end of the allowed range. The allocation could be reduced from the current 23% to something in the range of 17% to 20% (between the lower end of the band and the target allocation). However, given the required redemption notice (generally 60 to 90 days in advance of the redemption date), if the market weakens the hedge funds might invoke any gates allowed for in their documents.

  - Longer term, a temporary increase in the spending rate reduces the probability that the fund will meet its real return target. This objective would be further threatened if the inflation rate does rise as the CIO fears. The liquidity profile of the Fund's investments should prepare for the possibility that, in a bad year, they may be called upon to dip into capital to fund the spending obligation.

2. Recommend and justify a tactical asset allocation strategy for the Fund.

Solution:

  - The Fund should target the upper end of the ranges for cash and government bonds in light of the current high equity valuations, weakening economic outlook, and threat of rising inflation. Given rising inflation and interest rate concerns, she may also consider shortening the duration of the government bond portfolio.

  - The higher cash and bond allocation will also provide the liquidity buffer needed to meet the Fund's liabilities. Additional cash might be justified to fund the known payouts.

  - A high allocation to real estate could also be considered a defensive positioning, but the current 8% allocation may rise toward its 13% maximum, even without additional allocations, given the expected decline in the balance of the portfolio. In addition, tactical tilts in private asset classes are difficult to implement because it would take an extended time period to make new commitments and invest the additional capital.

  - The allocations to public equites and hedge funds could be reduced to fund the increases in cash and government bonds.

The following table summarizes the proposed allocation and looks at the likely end-of-year allocations if events unfold as forecast.

| | Allowed Ranges | | | Proposed Allocation | | | Allocation 12 Months Forward | |
	Lower Limit	Upper Limit	Current Allocation	%	$ (mil)	Expected Return Next 12 Months	%	$ (mil)
Cash	0%	5%	3%	10%	75	2%		0*
Public Equities	30%	40%	35%	30%	225	−30%	25%	157.50
Government Bonds	4%	10%	7%	10%	75	−3%	12%	72.75

	Allowed Ranges			Proposed Allocation			Allocation 12 Months Forward	
	Lower Limit	Upper Limit	Current Allocation	%	$ (mil)	Expected Return Next 12 Months	%	$ (mil)
High-Yield Credit	2%	5%	5%	5%	37.5	−10%	5%	33.75
Hedge Funds	17%	23%	23%	17%	127.5	−8%	19%	117.30
Private Real Estate	7%	13%	8%	8%	60	0%	12%	72.00
Private Real Assets	3%	7%	4%	5%	37.5	10%	8%	48.75
Private Equity	15%	22%	15%	15%	112.5	−10%	20%	123.75
Total				100%	$750.0		100%	$625.80

> * Cash paid to fund liabilities ($37.5 million to the university and $40.5 million to fund private investment capital calls. Additional cash needs funded from government bond portfolio.

15   MONITORING THE INVESTMENT PROGRAM

> ☐ | discuss considerations in monitoring alternative investment programs

The monitoring of an alternative investment program is time and labor intensive. Data are hard to come by and are not standardized among managers or asset classes. The analyst must spend a good amount of time gathering data and ensuring that the analysis is comparable across managers and asset classes. It is incumbent on the investor to both monitor the managers *and* the alternative investment program's progress toward the goals that were the basis for the investment in these assets.

Overall Investment Program Monitoring

When an investor makes a strategic decision to invest in alternative assets, specific goals are typically associated with the alternative investment program—return enhancement, income, risk reduction, safety, or a combination of the four. The goals may vary by asset class. A real estate program, for example, might be undertaken with the objective of replacing a portion of the fixed-income allocation—providing yield or income but also providing some measure of growth and/or inflation protection. The real estate program should be monitored relative to those goals, not simply relative to a benchmark.

We know that an alternative investment program is likely to take a number of years to reach fully-invested status. Is it reasonable to defer an assessment of the program until that point? Probably not. The investor must monitor developments in the relevant markets to ensure that the fundamental thesis underlying the decision to invest remains intact. Continuing with our real estate analogy, if real estate cap rates[18] fall to never-before-seen lows, what are the implications for the real estate's ability to continue to fulfill its intended role in the portfolio? Or if the managers hired within the real estate allocation allocate more to commercial office properties than was anticipated, what are the implications for the ability of real estate to fulfill the income-oriented goal? Only by monitoring the development of the portfolio(s) will the investor be able to adjust course and ensure that the allocation remains on track to achieve the goals established at the outset.

We also know that investor goals and objectives are subject to change. Perhaps a university experiences a persistent decline in enrollments and the endowment fund will be called upon to provide greater support to the university while it transitions to the new reality; what are the implications for a private equity program? Or what if the primary wage-earner in a two-parent household becomes critically ill; how might this affect the asset allocation? These types of events cannot be predicted, but it is important to continuously monitor the linkages between the asset allocation and the investor's goals, objectives, and circumstances. Particularly in the private markets— where changing course requires a long lead time and abruptly terminating an investment program can radically alter the risk and return profile of the portfolio—an early warning of an impending change can greatly improve the investor's ability to maintain the integrity of the investment program.

Performance Evaluation

Properly benchmarking an alternative investment strategy is a challenge that has important implications for judging the effectiveness of the alternative investment program. Many investors resort to custom index proxies (e.g., a static return premium over cash or equity index) or rely on peer group comparisons (e.g., Hedge Fund Research, Inc., Eurekahedge, Cambridge Private Equity Index). Both approaches have significant limitations.

Consider a private equity program benchmarked to the MSCI World Index plus 3%. This custom index may help frame the return expectation the investment committee holds with regard to its private equity assets, but it is unlikely to match the realized risk, return, and liquidity characteristics of the actual private equity program.

It is similarly challenging to develop a peer group representative of a manager's strategy given the high level of idiosyncratic risk inherent in most alternative investment funds. Existing providers follow vastly different rules in constructing these "benchmarks." They all have their own set of definitions (e.g., whether a fund is a credit fund or an event-driven fund), weighting methodology (asset weighted or equal weighted), method for dealing with potential survivorship bias, and other rules for inclusion (e.g., whether the fund is currently open or closed to new capital).

Exhibit 44 shows the returns from three different hedge fund index providers. An event driven fund that generated a 6% return over the relevant 5-year period might look attractive if evaluated relative to the Credit Suisse index, whereas it might look subpar if evaluated relative to the Eurekahedge index. Additionally, a manager's ranking within the peer group is affected as much by what *other* managers do as by his own actions. Clearly, peer group ranking is, at best, one small part of the overall benchmarking exercise.

---

18 The ratio of net operating income (NOI) to property asset value (the inverse of price/earnings).

Exhibit 44: The Trouble with Peer Groups

Strategy	Provider	3-Year Annualized Return (%)	5-Year Annualized Return (%)
		ending December 31, 2017	
Equity Hedge	HFRI	5.7	6.6
	Credit Suisse	4.3	7.1
	Eurekahedge	6.5	7.8
Event-Driven	HFRI	3.8	5.9
	Credit Suisse	0.8	3.7
	Eurekahedge	6.8	7.2
Global Macro	HFRI	0.6	0.7
	Credit Suisse	2.0	2.7
	Eurekahedge	−0.1	1.2

The timing and nature of reported alternative investment returns also pose challenges to monitoring the performance of alternative investment managers. For call-down strategies such as private equity, private real estate, and real assets, tracking and calculating performance might require different systems and methodologies. Private equity, credit, and real estate returns are typically reported using internal rates of return (IRRs) rather than time-weighted returns (TWR) as is common in the liquid asset classes. IRRs are sensitive to the timing of cash flows into and out of the fund. Two managers may have similar portfolios but very different return profiles depending on their particular capital call and distribution schedule. Investors have to be wise to the ways in which a manager can bias their reported IRR. Alternative metrics, such as multiple on invested capital (MOIC) have been developed to provide an additional frame of reference. (MOIC is a private equity measure that divides the current value of the underlying companies plus any distributions received by the total invested capital.)

Pricing issues also complicate performance evaluation of most alternative strategies. Stale pricing common in many alternative strategies can distort reported returns and the associated risk metrics. Betas, correlations, Sharpe ratios, and other measures must be interpreted with a healthy degree of skepticism.

Although performance measurement has its challenges with all asset classes, relying exclusively on any single measure with alternative investments increases the likelihood of inaccurate or misleading conclusions. With respect to the more illiquid investment strategies, judgment as to whether a given fund is meeting its investment objectives should be reserved until most or even all of the investments have been monetized, and capital has been returned to the investor. If capital is returned quickly (thereby possibly producing extraordinarily high IRRs), the investor may want to put greater emphasis on the MOIC measure. Similarly, funds that return capital more slowly than expected might want to put greater weight on the IRR measure. Even a fund with both a weak MOIC and a weak IRR need the measures to be put into context. An appropriate peer group analysis can help ascertain whether the "poor" performance was common across all funds of similar vintage (perhaps suggesting a poor investment climate) or whether it was specific to that fund. Likewise, a fund that posts strong performance may simply have benefited from an ideal investment period.

Perhaps the best way to gain performance insight beyond the numbers is to develop a qualitative understanding of the underlying assets. What are the manager's expectations at the time of acquisition? How does the manager plan to add value to the investment over the holding period? What is the manager's exit strategy for the investment? The investor can monitor how the investment develops relative to the initial thesis. This type of qualitative assessment can lead to a better understanding of whether the manager did well for the right reasons, whether the manager was wrong but for the right reasons, or whether the manager was just wrong.

Monitoring the Firm and the Investment Process

In addition to monitoring the portfolio, monitoring of the investment process and the investment management firm itself are particularly important in alternative investment structures where the manager cannot be terminated easily, and the assets transferred to another manager in which the investor has more confidence. What follows is a non-exhaustive list of issues that the investor will want to monitor:

- *Key person risk*: Most alternative investment strategies depend to a large extent on the skill of a few key investment professionals. These are what are known as "key persons." Key persons are typically specified in the fund documents, with certain rights allocated to the limited partners in the event a key person leaves the firm. It is important to ensure that these investment professionals remain actively involved in the investment process. There are also other employees of the investment manager whose departure may negatively affect the operation of the business or signal an underlying problem. If, for example, the chief operating officer or chief compliance officer leaves the firm, it is important to understand why and what effect it may have on the business. Finally, it is important to note that for quantitatively oriented strategies, key person risk is often reduced because the quantitative investment process remains in place even if a key person leaves.

- *Alignment of interests*: Alignment of interest issues range from the complexity of the organization, structure of management fees, compensation of the investment professionals, growth in assets under management (AUM), and the amount of capital the key professionals have committed to the funds that they are managing. The investor will want to verify that the money manager's interests remain closely aligned with their own. Has the manager withdrawn a significant portion of her own capital that had been invested alongside the limited partners? If so, why? Is the manager raising a new fund? If so, what safeguards are in place to ensure that the investment professionals are not unduly distracted with fundraising, firm administration, or unfairly concentrated on managing other funds? Is the opportunity set deep enough to support the additional capital being raised? Will the funds have shared ownership interest in a given asset? If so, what conflicts of interest may arise (e.g., the manager may earn an incentive fee in one fund if the asset is sold, while it may be in the best interest of the second fund to sell the asset at a later date).

- *Style drift*: Fund documents often give managers wide latitude as to their investment options and parameters, but it is incumbent on the investor to understand where the fund manager has a competitive advantage and skill and confirm that the investments being made are consistent with the manager's edge.

- *Risk management*: The investor should understand the manager's risk management philosophy and processes and periodically confirm that the fund is abiding by them. Where a fund makes extensive use of leverage, a robust risk management framework is essential.

- *Client/asset turnover*: A critical part of the ongoing due diligence process should include a review of clients and assets. A significant gain or drop in either may be a sign of an underlying problem. An unusual gain in assets could make it difficult for the investment professionals to invest in suitably attractive investments, potentially handicapping future performance. Conversely, significant client redemptions may force the money manager to sell attractive assets as he looks to raise cash. If this occurs during periods of market turmoil when liquidity in the market itself may be low, the manager may be forced to sell what he can rather than what he should in order to optimize performance. This could hurt the returns of non-redeeming clients and/or leave the remaining clients with illiquid holdings that might make it difficult for them to redeem in the future.

- *Client profile*: Investors will want to gauge the profile of the fund manager's other clients. Are the fund's other clients considered long-term investors, or do they have a history of redeeming at the first sign of trouble? Are they new to the alternative investment space and perhaps don't understand the nuances of the fund's strategy and risks? You may have a strong conviction in a money manager's skills, but the actions of others may affect your ability to reap the benefits of those skills. If too many of her other clients elect to redeem, the manager may invoke the gates allowed by the fund's documents or, at the extreme, liquidate the fund at what might be the worst possible moment. This was a common occurrence during 2008–2009, when investors sought to raise cash by redeeming from their more liquid fund managers. Even if a money manager weathers massive outflows, profitability and the ability to retain key talent may be at risk.

- *Service providers:* Investors will want to ensure that the fund manager has engaged independent and reputable third-party service providers, including administrators, custodians, and auditors. Although an investor may have performed extensive checks prior to investing, it is good practice to periodically verify that these relationships are intact and working well. If the service provider changes, the investor will want to understand *why*. Has the fund's AUM grown to a level that cannot be handled adequately by the current provider? Perhaps the service provider has chosen to terminate the relationship because of actions taken by the fund manager. Exploring the motivation behind a change in a service provider can uncover early warning flags deserving of further investigation.

EXAMPLE 10

Monitoring Alternative Investment Programs

1. The O'Hara family office determined that the illiquidity risk inherent in private investments is a risk that the family is ill-suited to bear. As a result, they decided several years ago to unwind their private equity program. There are still a few remaining assets in the portfolio. The CIO (chief investment officer) notices that the private equity portfolio has delivered outstanding performance lately, especially relative to other asset classes. He presents the data to his research staff and wants to revisit their decision to stop making new private equity investments. Explain why the investment results that prompted the CIO's comments should not be relied upon.

Solution:

With small, residual holdings, even a modest change in valuation can result in outsized returns; for example, a $2,000 investment that gets revalued to $3,000 would report a nominal return of 50%. The 50% return is not representative of private equity investment as a whole but is merely an artifact of the unwinding process. A more accurate picture of performance must consider the development of the fund IRR over time and consider other performance measures, such as the MOIC.

2. The ZeeZaw family office has been invested in the Warriors Fund, a relatively small distressed debt strategy, which has performed very well for a number of years. In a recent conversation with the portfolio manager, the CIO for ZeeZaw discovered that the Warriors fund will be receiving a significant investment from a large institution within the next few weeks. What are some of the risks that might develop with the Warriors Fund as a result of this new client? What are some other issues that the CIO might want to probe with the Warriors Fund?

Solution:

The CIO should investigate whether the fund manager is able to appropriately deploy this new capital consistent with the investment process and types of investments that contributed to the Warriors Fund success. Because the fund was relatively small, a very large influx of capital might force the portfolio manager to make larger investments than is optimal or more investments than they did before. Either change without the appropriate resources could undermine future success. Finally, a large influx of cash could dilute near-term performance, especially if the funds remain undeployed for a significant period of time.

SUMMARY

- Allocations to alternatives are believed to increase a portfolio's risk-adjusted return. An investment in alternatives typically fulfills one or more of four roles in an investor's portfolio: capital growth, income generation, risk diversification, and/or safety.

- Private equity investments are generally viewed as return enhancers in a portfolio of traditional assets.

- Long/short equity strategies are generally believed to deliver equity-like returns with less than full exposure to the equity premium. Short-biased equity strategies are expected to lower a portfolio's overall equity beta while producing some measure of alpha. Arbitrage and event-driven strategies are expected to provide equity-like returns with little to no correlation with traditional asset classes.

- Real assets (e.g., commodities, farmland, timber, energy, and infrastructure assets) are generally perceived to provide a hedge against inflation.

- Timber investments provide both growth and inflation-hedging properties.

- Commodities (e.g., metals, energy, livestock, and agricultural commodities) serve as a hedge against inflation and provide a differentiated source of alpha. Certain commodity investments serve as safe havens in times of crisis.

- Farmland investing may have a commodity-like profile or a commercial real-estate-like profile.

- Energy investments are generally considered a real asset as the investor owns the mineral rights to commodities that are correlated with inflation factors.

- Infrastructure investments tend to generate stable/modestly growing income and to have high correlation with overall inflation.

- Real estate strategies range from core to opportunistic and are believed to provide protection against unanticipated increases in inflation. Core real estate strategies are more income-oriented, while opportunistic strategies rely more heavily on capital appreciation.

- Bonds have been a more effective volatility mitigator than alternatives over shorter time horizons.

- The traditional approaches to defining asset classes are easy to communicate and implement. However, they tend to over-estimate portfolio diversification and obscure primary drivers of risk.

- Typical risk factors applied to alternative investments include equity, size, value, liquidity, duration, inflation, credit spread, and currency. A benefit of the risk factor approach is that every asset class can be described using the same framework.

- Risk factor-based approaches have certain limitations. A framework with too many factors is difficult to administer and interpret, but too small a set of risk factors may not accurately describe the characteristics of alternative asset classes. Risk factor sensitivities are highly sensitive to the historical look-back period.

- Investors with less than a 15-year investment horizon should generally avoid investments in private real estate, private real asset, and private equity funds.

- Investors must consider whether they have the necessary skills, expertise, and resources to build an alternative investment program internally. Investors without a strong governance program are less likely to develop a successful alternative investment program.

- Reporting for alternative funds is often less transparent than investors are accustomed to seeing on their stock and bond portfolios. For many illiquid strategies, reporting is often received well past typical monthly or quarter-end deadlines. Full, position-level transparency is rare in many alternative strategies.

- Three primary approaches are used to determine the desired allocation to the alternative asset classes:

  - Monte Carlo simulation may be used to generate return scenarios that relax the assumption of normally distributed returns.

  - Optimization techniques, which incorporate downside risk or take into account skew, may be used to enhance the asset allocation process.

  - Risk factor-based approaches to alternative asset allocation can be applied to develop more robust asset allocation proposals.

- Two key analytical challenges in modelling allocations to alternatives include stale and/or artificially smoothed returns and return distributions that exhibit significant skewness and fat tails (or excess kurtosis).

- Artificially smoothed returns can be detected by testing the return stream for serial correlation. The analyst needs to unsmooth the returns to get a more accurate representation of the risk and return characteristics of the asset class.

- Skewness and kurtosis can be dealt with by using empirically observed asset returns because they incorporate the actual distribution. Advanced mathematical or statistical models can also be used to capture the true behavior of alternative asset classes.

- Applications of Monte Carlo simulation in allocating to alternative investments include:

  1. simulating skewed and fat-tailed financial variables by estimating the behavior of factors and/or assets in low-volatility regimes and high-volatility regimes, then generating scenarios using the different means and covariances estimated under the different regimes; and

  2. simulating portfolio outcomes (+/– 1 standard deviation) to estimate the likelihood of falling short of the investment objectives.

- Unconstrained mean–variance optimization (MVO) often leads to portfolios dominated by cash and fixed income at the low-risk end of the spectrum and by private equity at the high-risk end of the spectrum. Some investors impose minimum and maximum constraints on asset classes. Slight changes in the input variables could lead to substantial changes in the asset allocations.

- Mean–CVaR optimization may be used to identify allocations that minimize downside risk rather than simply volatility.

- Investors may choose to optimize allocations to risk factors rather than asset classes. These allocations, however, must be implemented using asset classes. Portfolios with similar risk factor exposures can have vastly different asset allocations.

- Some caveats with respect to risk factor-based allocations are that investors may hold different definitions for a given risk factor, correlations among risk factors may shift under changing market conditions, and some factor sensitivities are very unstable.

- Cash flow and commitment-pacing models enable investors in private alternatives to better manage their portfolio liquidity and set realistic annual commitment targets to reach the desired asset allocation.

- An alternative investment program should be monitored relative to the goals established for the alternative investment program, not simply relative to a benchmark. The investor must monitor developments in the relevant markets to ensure that the fundamental thesis underlying the decision to invest remains intact.

- Two common benchmarking approaches to benchmarking alternative investments—custom index proxies and peer group comparisons—have significant limitations.

- IRRs are sensitive to the timing of cash flows into and out of the fund: Two managers may have similar portfolios but different return profiles depending on their capital call and distribution schedule.

- Pricing issues can distort reported returns and the associated risk metrics, such as betas, correlations, and Sharpe ratios.

- Monitoring of the firm and the investment process are particularly important in alternative investment structures where the manager cannot be terminated easily. Key elements to monitor include key person risk, alignment of interests, style drift, risk management, client/asset turnover, client profile, and service providers.

REFERENCES

Ang, A. 2014. *Asset Management: A Systematic Approach to Factor Investing.* New York: Oxford University Press. 10.1093/acprof:oso/9780199959327.001.0001

Berkelaar, A. B., A. Kobor, and R. R. P. Kouwenberg. 2009. "Asset Allocation for Hedge Fund Strategies: How to Better Manage Tail Risk." In *The VaR Modeling Handbook: Practical Applications in Alternative Investing, Banking, Insurance, and Portfolio Management*, ed. Gregoriou, Greg N. New York: McGraw-Hill.

Hamilton, J. D. 1989. "A New Approach to the Economic Analysis of Nonstationary Time Series and the Business Cycle." *Econometrica* 57 (2): 357–84. 10.2307/1912559

Ivashina, Victoria and Josh Lerner. 2018. "Looking for Alternatives: Pension Investments around the World, 2008 to 2017." Federal Reserve of Boston conference paper.

Kim, C. and C. R. Nelson. 1999. *State-Space Models with Regime Switching – Classical and Gibbs-Sampling Approaches and Applications.* Cambridge, MA: MIT Press.

Naik, V., M. Devarajan, A. Nowobilski, S. Page, and N. Pedersen. 2016. *Factor Investing and Asset Allocation – A Business Cycle Perspective.* Charlottesville, VA: CFA Institute Research Foundation.

Rockafellar, R. T. and S. Uryasev. 2000. "Optimization of Conditional Value at Risk." *Journal of Risk* 2 (3): 21–42. 10.21314/JOR.2000.038

Swensen, D. F. 2009. *Pioneering Portfolio Management: An Unconventional Approach to Institutional Investment.* New York: Free Press.

Takahashi, D. and S. Alexander. 2001. "*Illiquid Alternative Asset Fund Modeling.*" Yale School of Management (January).

PRACTICE PROBLEMS

The following information relates to questions 1-8

Kevin Kroll is the chair of the investment committee responsible for the governance of the Shire Manufacturing Corporation (SMC) defined benefit pension plan. The pension fund is currently fully funded and has followed an asset mix of 60% public equities and 40% bonds since Kroll has been chair. Kroll meets with Mary Park, an actuarial and pension consultant, to discuss issues raised at the last committee meeting.

Kroll notes that the investment committee would like to explore the benefits of adding alternative investments to the pension plan's strategic asset allocation. Kroll states:

Statement 1   The committee would like to know which alternative asset would best mitigate the risks to the portfolio due to unexpected inflation and also have a relatively low correlation with public equities to provide diversification benefits.

The SMC pension plan has been able to fund the annual pension payments without any corporate contributions for a number of years. The committee is interested in potential changes to the asset mix that could increase the probability of achieving the long-term investment target return of 5.5% while maintaining the funded status of the plan. Park notes that fixed-income yields are expected to remain low for the foreseeable future. Kroll asks:

Statement 2   If the public equity allocation remains at 60%, is there a single asset class that could be used for the balance of the portfolio to achieve the greatest probability of maintaining the pension funding status over a long time horizon? Under this hypothetical scenario, the balance of the portfolio can be allocated to either bonds, hedge funds, or private equities.

Park confirms with Kroll that the committee has historically used a traditional approach to define the opportunity set based on distinct macroeconomic regimes, and she proposes that a risk-based approach might be a better method. Although the traditional approach is relatively powerful for its ability to handle liquidity and manager selection issues compared to a risk-based approach, they both acknowledge that a number of limitations are associated with the existing approach.

Park presents a report (Exhibit 1) that proposes a new strategic asset allocation for the pension plan. Kroll states that one of the concerns that the investment committee will have regarding the new allocation is that the pension fund needs to be able to fund an upcoming early retirement incentive program (ERIP) that SMC will be offering to its employees within the next two years. Employees who have reached the age of 55 and whose age added to the number of years of company service sum to 75 or more can retire 10 years early and receive the defined benefit pension normally payable at age 65.

Exhibit 1: Proposed Asset Allocation of SMC Defined Benefit Pension Plan

Asset Class	Public Equities	Broad Fixed Income	Private Equities	Hedge Funds	Public Real Estate	Total
Target	45%	25%	10%	10%	10%	100%
Range	35%–55%	15%–35%	0%–12%	0%–12%	0%–12%	–

Kroll and Park then discuss suitability considerations related to the allocation in Exhibit 1. Kroll understands that one of the drawbacks of including the proposed alternative asset classes is that daily reporting will no longer be available. Investment reports for alternatives will likely be received after monthly or quarter-end deadlines used for the plan's traditional investments. Park emphasizes that in a typical private equity structure, the pension fund makes a commitment of capital to a blind pool as part of the private investment partnership.

In order to explain the new strategic asset allocation to the investment committee, Kroll asks Park why a risk factor-based approach should be used rather than a mean–variance-optimization technique. Park makes the following statements:

Statement 3   Risk factor-based approaches to asset allocation produce more robust asset allocation proposals.

Statement 4   A mean–variance optimization typically overallocates to the private alternative asset classes due to stale pricing.

Park notes that the current macroeconomic environment could lead to a bear market within a few years. Kroll asks Park to discuss the potential impact on liquidity planning associated with the actions of the fund's general partners in the forecasted environment.

Kroll concludes the meeting by reviewing the information in Exhibit 2 pertaining to three potential private equity funds analyzed by Park. Park discloses the following due diligence findings from a recent manager search: Fund A retains administrators, custodians, and auditors with impeccable reputations; Fund B has achieved its performance in a manner that appears to conflict with its reported investment philosophy; and Fund C has recently experienced the loss of three key persons.

Exhibit 2: Potential Private Equity Funds, Internal Rate of Return (IRR)

Private Equity Fund	Fund A	Fund B	Fund C
5-year IRR	12.9%	13.2%	13.1%

1. Based on Statement 1, Park should recommend:

    A. hedge funds.

    B. private equities.

    C. commodity futures.

2. In answering the question raised in Statement 2, Park would *most likely* recommend:

    A. bonds.

B. hedge funds.

C. private equities.

3. A limitation of the existing approach used by the committee to define the opportunity set is that it:

   A. is difficult to communicate.

   B. overestimates the portfolio diversification.

   C. is sensitive to the historical look-back period.

4. Based on Exhibit 1 and the proposed asset allocation, the greatest risk associated with the ERIP is:

   A. liability.

   B. leverage.

   C. liquidity.

5. The suitability concern discussed by Kroll and Park *most likely* deals with:

   A. governance.

   B. transparency.

   C. investment horizon.

6. Which of Park's statements regarding the asset allocation approaches is correct?

   A. Only Statement 3

   B. Only Statement 4

   C. Both Statement 3 and Statement 4

7. Based on the forecasted environment, liquidity planning should take into account that general partners may:

   A. call capital at a slower pace.

   B. make distributions at a faster pace.

   C. exercise an option to extend the life of the fund.

8. Based on Exhibit 2 and Park's due diligence, the pension committee should consider investing in:

   A. Fund A.

   B. Fund B.

   C. Fund C.

The following information relates to questions 9-13

Eileen Gension is a portfolio manager for Zen-Alt Investment Consultants (Zen-Alt), which assists institutional investors with investing in alternative investments. Charles Smittand is an analyst at Zen-Alt and reports to Gension. Gension and Smittand discuss a new client, the Benziger University Endowment Fund (the fund), as well as a prospective client, the Opeptaja Pension Plan (the plan).

The fund's current portfolio is invested primarily in public equities, with the remainder invested in fixed income. The fund's investment objective is to support a 6% annual spending rate and to preserve the purchasing power of the asset base over a 10-year time horizon. The fund also wants to invest in assets that provide the highest amount of diversification against its dominant equity risk. Gension considers potential alternative investment options that would best meet the fund's diversification strategy.

In preparation for the first meeting between Zen-Alt and the fund, Gension and Smittand discuss implementing a short-biased equity strategy within the fund. Smittand makes the following three statements regarding short-biased equity strategies:

Statement 1   Short-biased equity strategies generally provide alpha when used to diversify public equities.

Statement 2   Short-biased equity strategies are expected to provide a higher reduction in volatility than bonds over a long time horizon.

Statement 3   Short-biased equity strategies are expected to mitigate the risk of public equities by reducing the overall portfolio beta of the fund.

Gension directs Smittand to prepare asset allocation and portfolio characteristics data on three alternative portfolios. The fund's risk profile is one factor that potential lenders consider when assigning a risk rating to the university. A loan covenant with the university's primary lender states that a re-evaluation of the university's creditworthiness is triggered if the fund incurs a loss greater than 20% over any one-year period. Smittand states that the recommended asset allocation should achieve the following three goals, in order of priority and importance:

- Minimize the probability of triggering the primary lender's loan covenant.
- Minimize the probability of purchasing power impairment over a 10-year horizon.
- Maximize the probability of achieving a real return target of 6% over a 10-year horizon.

Smittand provides data for three alternative portfolios, which are presented in Exhibits 1 and 2.

Exhibit 1: Asset Allocation

Alternative Portfolio	Cash	Public Equity	Gov't.	Credit	Hedge Fund	Real Estate	Private Equity
A	4.0%	35.0%	6.0%	5.0%	20.0%	10.0%	20.0%
B	2.0%	40.0%	8.0%	3.0%	15.0%	7.0%	25.0%
C	1.0%	50.0%	3.0%	6.0%	10.0%	0.0%	30.0%

Exhibit 2: Portfolio Characteristics

Alternative Portfolio	1-Year 99% VaR	1-Year 99% CVaR	Probability of Meeting 6% Real Return (10-Year Horizon)	Probability of Purchasing Power Impairment (10-Year Horizon)
A	−16.3%	−19.4%	56.1%	2.5%
B	−17.4%	−20.6%	58.8%	2.8%
C	−19.3%	−22.7%	61.0%	4.0%

Notes:

- One-year horizon 99% VaR: the lowest return over any one-year period at a 99% confidence level

- One-year horizon 99% CVaR: the expected return if the return falls below the 99% VaR threshold

- Probability of purchasing power impairment: the probability of losing 40% of the fund's purchasing power over 10 years, after consideration of new gifts received by the fund, spending from the fund, and total returns

Gension next meets with the investment committee (IC) of the Opeptaja Pension Plan to discuss new opportunities in alternative investments. The plan is a $1 billion public pension fund that is required to provide detailed reports to the public and operates under specific government guidelines. The plan's IC adopted a formal investment policy that specifies an investment horizon of 20 years. The plan has a team of in-house analysts with significant experience in alternative investments.

During the meeting, the IC indicates that it is interested in investing in private real estate. Gension recommends a real estate investment managed by an experienced team with a proven track record. The investment will require multiple capital calls over the next few years. The IC proceeds to commit to the new real estate investment and seeks advice on liquidity planning related to the future capital calls.

9. Which asset class would *best* satisfy the Fund's diversification strategy?

   A. Private equity

   B. Private real estate

   C. Absolute return hedge fund

10. Which of Smittand's statements regarding short-biased equity strategies is *incorrect*?

    A. Statement 1

    B. Statement 2

    C. Statement 3

11. Based on Exhibit 2, which alternative portfolio should Gension recommend for the fund given Smittand's stated three goals?

    A. Portfolio A

    B. Portfolio B

    C. Portfolio C

12. Which of the following investor characteristics would *most likely* be a primary-concern for the plan's IC with respect to investing in alternatives?

    A. Governance

    B. Transparency

    C. Investment horizon

13. With respect to liquidity planning relating to the plan's new real estate investment, Gension should recommend that the fund set aside appropriate funds and invest them in:

    A. 100% REITs.

    B. 100% cash equivalents.

    C. 80% cash equivalents and 20% REITs.

The following information relates to questions 14–15

Inge Greslo is an adviser with an investment management company and focuses on asset allocation for the company's high-net-worth investors. She prepares for a meeting with Maarten Pua, a new client who recently inherited a $10 million portfolio solely comprising public equities.

Greslo meets with Pua and proposes that she create a multi-asset portfolio by selling a portion of his equity holdings and investing the proceeds in another asset class. Greslo advises Pua that his investment objective should be to select an asset class that has a high potential to fulfill two functional roles: risk diversification and capital growth. Greslo suggests the following three asset classes:

- Public real estate

- Private real assets (timber)

- Equity long/short hedge funds

14. **Determine** which asset class is *most likely* to meet Pua's investment objective. **Justify** your response.

   - Public real estate
   - Private real assets (timber)
   - Equity long/short hedge funds

15. Five years after her first meeting with Pua, Greslo monitors a private real estate investment that Pua has held for one year. Until recently, the investment had been managed by a local real estate specialist who had a competitive advantage in this market; the specialist's strategy was to purchase distressed local residential housing properties, make strategic property improvements, and then sell them. Pua is one of several clients who have invested in this opportunity.

   Greslo learns that the specialist recently retired and the investment is now managed by a national real estate company. The company has told investors that it now plans to invest throughout the region in both distressed housing and commercial properties. The company also lengthened the holding period for each investment property from the date of the initial capital call because of the complexity of the property renovations, and it altered the interim profit distribution targets.

   Discuss the qualitative risk issues that have *most likely* materialized over the past year.

The following information relates to questions 16-18

The Ælfheah Group is a US-based company with a relatively small pension plan. Ælfheah's investment committee (IC), whose members collectively have a relatively basic understanding of the investment process, has agreed that Ælfheah is willing to accept modest returns while the IC gains a better understanding of the process Two key investment considerations for the IC are maintaining low overhead costs and minimizing taxes in the portfolio. Ælfheah has not been willing to incur the costs of in-house investment resources.

Qauhtèmoc Ng is the investment adviser for Ælfheah. He discusses with the IC its goal of diversifying Ælfheah's portfolio to include alternative assets. Ng suggests considering the following potential investment vehicles:

   - Publicly traded US REIT
   - Relative value hedge fund
   - Tax-efficient angel investment

Ng explains that for the relative value hedge fund alternative, Ælfheah would be investing alongside tax-exempt investors.

16. **Determine** which of the potential investment vehicles *best* meets the investment considerations for Ælfheah. **Justify** your response. **Explain** for *each* investment not selected why the investment considerations are not met.

   - Publicly traded US REIT
   - Relative value hedge fund
   - Tax-efficient angel investment

17. Ng and the IC review the optimal approach to determine the asset allocation for Ælfheah, including the traditional and risk-based approaches to defining the investment opportunity set.

    Determine which approach to determine the asset allocation is *most appropriate* for Ælfheah. **Justify** your response.

    - Traditional
    - Risk based

18. The following year, Ng and the IC review the portfolio's performance. The IC has gained a better understanding of the investment process. The portfolio is meeting Ælfheah's liquidity needs, and Ng suggests that Ælfheah would benefit from diversifying into an additional alternative asset class. After discussing suitable investment vehicles for the proposed alternative asset class, Ng proposes the following three investment vehicles for further review:

    - Funds of funds (FOFs)
    - Separately managed accounts (SMAs)
    - Undertakings for collective investment in transferable securities (UCITS)

    Determine the investment vehicle that would be *most appropriate* for Ælfheah's proposed alternative asset class. **Justify** your response.

The following information relates to questions 19–20

Mbalenhle Calixto is a global institutional portfolio manager who prepares for an annual meeting with the investment committee (IC) of the Estevão University Endowment. The endowment has €450 million in assets, and the current asset allocation is 42% equities, 22% fixed income, 19% private equity, and 17% hedge funds.

The IC's primary investment objective is to maximize returns subject to a given level of volatility. A secondary objective is to avoid a permanent loss of capital, and the IC has indicated to Calixto its concern about left-tail risk. Calixto considers two asset allocation approaches for the endowment: mean–variance optimization (MVO) and mean–CVaR (conditional value at risk) optimization.

19. **Determine** the asset allocation approach that is *mostsuitable* for the Endowment. **Justify** your response.

    - MVO
    - Mean–CVaR optimization

20. Calixto reviews the endowment's future liquidity requirements and analyzes one of its holdings in a private distressed debt fund. She notes the following about the fund:

    - As of the most recent year end:
      - The NAV of the endowment's investment in the fund was €25,000,000.
      - All capital had been called.

- At the end of the current year, Calixto expects a distribution of 18% to be paid.
- Calixto estimates an expected growth rate of 11% for the fund.

Calculate the expected NAV of the fund at the end of the current year.

SOLUTIONS

1. C is correct. Real assets (which include energy, infrastructure, timber, commodities, and farmland) are generally believed to mitigate the risks to the portfolio arising from unexpected inflation. Commodities act as a hedge against a core constituent of inflation measures. Rather than investing directly in the actual commodities, commodity futures may be incorporated using a managed futures strategy. In addition, the committee is looking for an asset class that has a low correlation with public equities, which will provide diversification benefits. Commodities are regarded as having much lower correlation coefficients with public equities than with private equities and hedge funds. Therefore, commodities will provide the greatest potential to fulfill the indicated role and to diversify public equities.

2. C is correct. When projecting expected returns, the order of returns from highest to lowest is typically regarded as private equities, hedge funds, bonds. Therefore, the probability of achieving the highest portfolio return while maintaining the funded status of the plan would require the use of private equities in conjunction with public equities. In addition, private equities have a high/strong potential to fulfill the role of capital growth. Fixed-income investments are expected to have a high/strong potential to fulfill the role of safety.

3. B is correct. A traditional approach has been used to define the opportunity set based on different macroeconomic conditions. The primary limitations of traditional approaches are that they overestimate the portfolio diversification and obscure the primary drivers of risk.

4. C is correct. With the introduction of the early retirement incentive plan (ERIP), the defined benefit pension plan will likely be called upon to make pension payments earlier than originally scheduled. As a result, the near term liquidity of the plan is the greatest risk arising from the addition of the alternative asset classes (e.g., private equities, hedge funds, and real estate). Investments in alternatives, such as private equities, can take upwards of five years to reach a full commitment and potentially another decade to unwind.

5. B is correct. The pension plan's investment in private equities via a blind pool presents the prospect that less than perfect transparency will be associated with the underlying holdings of the alternative asset manager. Capital is committed for an investment in a portfolio of assets that are not specified in advance. In addition, reporting for alternative funds is often less transparent than investors are accustomed to seeing on their stock and bond portfolios.

6. C is correct. Statement 3 is correct because risk factor-based approaches to asset allocation can be applied to develop more robust asset allocations. Statement 4 is correct because a mean–variance optimization typically overallocates to the private alternative asset classes, partly because of underestimated risk due to stale pricing and the assumption that returns are normally distributed

7. C is correct. Park notes that the current macroeconomic environment could lead to a bear market within a few years. Liquidity planning should take into account that under a scenario in which public equities and fixed-income investments are expected to perform poorly, general partners may exercise an option to extend the life of the fund.

8. A is correct. Fund A should be selected based on both quantitative and quali-

tative factors. Fund A has a five-year IRR (12.9%) that is slightly lower than, but comparable to, both Fund B (13.2%) and Fund C (13.1%). Given the sensitivity to the timing of cash flows into and out of a fund associated with the IRR calculation, however, the final decision should not be based merely on quantitative returns. It is also important to monitor the investment process and the investment management firm itself, particularly in alternative investment structures. Considering the qualitative factors identified by Park, Fund A is the only fund with a strong, positive factor: It benefits from service providers (administrators, custodians, and auditors) with impeccable reputations. Fund B seems to be experiencing style drift, which suggests that the returns are not consistent with the manager's advertised investment edge (hence, a negative factor). Fund C has experienced the departure of key persons, which puts future fund returns in jeopardy (hence, a negative factor).

9. C is correct. An absolute return hedge fund has a greater potential to diversify the fund's dominant public equity risk than either private equity or private real estate. Absolute return hedge funds exhibit an equity beta that is often less than that of private equity or private real estate. Also, absolute return hedge funds tend to exhibit a high potential to diversify public equities, whereas equity long/short hedge funds exhibit a moderate potential to fulfill this role.

   A is incorrect because although private equity provides moderate diversification against public equity, an absolute return hedge fund has a greater potential to do so. The primary advantage of private equity is capital growth.

   B is incorrect because private real estate provides only moderate diversification against public equity, whereas absolute return hedge funds have a greater potential to do so. The primary advantage of private real estate is income generation.

10. B is correct. While bonds reduce the probability of achieving a target return over time, they have been more effective as a volatility mitigator than alternatives over an extended period of time.

    A is incorrect because Statement 1 is correct. Short-biased strategies are expected to provide some measure of alpha in addition to lowering a portfolio's overall equity beta.

    C is incorrect because Statement 3 is correct. Short-biased equity strategies help reduce an equity-dominated portfolio's overall beta. Short-biased strategies are believed to deliver equity-like returns with less-than-full exposure to the equity premium but with an additional source of return that might come from the manager's shorting of individual stocks.

11. A is correct. Among the three portfolios, Portfolio A minimizes the probability of triggering the primary lender's loan covenant, which is the highest-priority goal, because it has the lowest one-year 99% CVaR, −19.4%. Portfolio A also has the lowest probability of purchasing power impairment over a 10-year horizon (2.5%). While Portfolio A has the lowest probability of achieving a real return target of 6% over a 10-year horizon (56.1%), that is the least important goal to be met. Therefore, Gension should recommend Portfolio A for the fund.

    B is incorrect because Portfolio B has a one-year 99% CVaR of −20.6%, which crosses the loan covenant threshold of a 20% loss. Portfolio A is the only one that satisfies the most important goal and is the portfolio least likely to trigger the loan covenant. Since Portfolio B does not achieve the most important goal of minimizing the probability of triggering the primary lender's loan covenant, Portfolio B should not be the recommended portfolio.

    C is incorrect because despite the fact that Portfolio C has the highest probability of meeting the 6% real return over a 10-year horizon, 61.0%, it also has a one-year 99% CVaR of −22.7% and thus the highest probability of triggering the loan covenant. Portfolio A is the only one that satisfies the most important goal and is the portfolio least likely to trigger the loan covenant. Since Portfolio C does not achieve the most important goal of minimizing the probability of triggering the primary lender's loan covenant, Portfolio C should not be the recommended portfolio.

12. B is correct. As a public pension fund that is required to provide detailed reports to the public, a primary concern for the IC is transparency. Investors in alternative investments must be comfortable with less than 100% transparency in their holdings. Private equity funds often necessitate buying into a "blind pool." Although an investor can look at the assets acquired in a manager's previous funds, there is no assurance that future investments will exactly replicate the previous funds.

A is incorrect because the IC has a formal investment policy, as well as an in-house team with experience in alternatives and the knowledge and capacity to critically evaluate alternative investments.

C is incorrect because the IC has a long-term investment horizon. While investors with less than a 15-year horizon should generally avoid investing in alternatives, the IC has a 20-year investment horizon that should easily accommodate an investment in private equity.

13. A is correct. REITs are most appropriate for funds committed to private real estate investments since they will have the most similar return and risk characteristics and will help maintain the strategic asset allocation of the plan. Although cash equivalents have less volatility over a short-term horizon, they are less likely to meet the plan's long-term return objectives.

B is incorrect because the opportunity cost of being out of the markets over the next few years during the capital call period makes cash equivalents an inappropriate investment. Although cash equivalents have lower volatility, which is often desirable over a short-term period, they will not help the plan meet its long-term return objectives.

C is incorrect because, although REITs will have the return and risk characteristics most similar to private real estate, a 20% allocation is not large enough to achieve the plan's long-term return objectives. The 80% allocation to cash equivalents will greatly affect the return, making the plan less likely to meet the long-term return objectives.

14. Private real assets (timber) is *most likely* to meet Pua's investment objective.

- Timber exhibits a low correlation with public equities and can fulfill the functional role of risk diversification.

- Timber provides high long-term returns and can fulfill the functional role of capital growth.

    Private real assets (timber) is the asset class most likely to meet Pua's objective. Private real assets, such as timber, tend to exhibit a low correlation with public equities and therefore have a high potential to fulfill the functional role of risk diversification in Pua's current all-equity portfolio. In addition, timber has a high potential to fulfill the functional role of capital growth in the portfolio since growth is provided by the underlying biological growth of the tree as well as through appreciation in the underlying land value.

    Compared with timber, public real estate as an asset class would likely offer less opportunity for capital growth and lower diversification benefits. Also, equity long/short hedge funds as an asset class would provide a moderate degree of risk diversification in Pua's all-equity portfolio but do not carry significant capital growth potential.

15.

- Pua's investment has been affected by key person risk as shown by the effect of the management change.

- Style drift has occurred as shown by the change from a local to a regional investment strategy and the expansion of the investment strategy to include commercial properties.

- The risk of the investment has changed owing to the added complexity of the property renovations.

- The longer holding periods and the change in interim profit distribution targets will affect this investment.

- Client/asset turnover following the management change may now affect the performance of the investment.

- The management change may alter the client profile, which could have a negative effect on investment performance.

Qualitative considerations can lead to a better understanding of the revised strategy for the investment and whether this investment remains suitable for Pua. Pua's investment has been affected by key person risk as shown by the management change from the local manager to a national company. Style drift has occurred as shown by the change from a local to a regional investment strategy and the expansion of the strategy to include commercial properties.

The risk of the investment has changed because of the added complexity of the renovations, and monitoring the company's risk management will be important for Greslo as she manages Pua's portfolio. Monitoring of the private real estate investment has revealed discrepancies in the new management strategy of the national company relative to the initial investment strategy of the local manager, including the longer holding periods and the changed interim profit distribution targets. Client/asset turnover following the management change may now significantly affect the performance of the investment. Finally, the change in management may alter the client profile, which could have a negative effect on investment performance.

16. Publicly traded US REIT *best* meets the investment considerations for Ælfheah. The publicly traded US REIT offers tax advantages to Ælfheah from the depreciation of its US real estate assets. The depreciation would help offset income received on those assets. In addition, the REIT would not require an in-house management team; thus, Ælfheah can maintain low overhead costs.

The relative value hedge fund is unlikely to be a tax-efficient strategy for Ælfheah. This tax inefficiency is seen frequently with many hedge fund strategies, especially those funds and fund companies where tax-exempt investors dominate the client base. The fund manager may be insensitive to tax considerations for a taxable investor such as Ælfheah.

The tax-efficient angel investment is a specialized investment that will require a highly customized investment approach. Researching and managing this type of investment will require an in-house team to locate and supervise these more specialized investments. Adding these resources would increase overhead costs and violate the IC's investment consideration of maintaining low overhead costs.

17. The traditional approach to determine the asset allocation is *most appropriate* for Ælfheah.

- The traditional approach is more appropriate since describing the roles of various asset classes is intuitive.

- This approach will be easier for Ng to explain to the IC, whose members have only a basic understanding of the investment process.
- This approach will make it easier to identify relevant mandates for the portfolio's alternative investments.
- Since Ælfheah seeks to maintain low overhead costs, the risk-based approach would not be appropriate.

  The traditional approach is more appropriate for Ælfheah. The IC is less sophisticated in its understanding of alternative investments but may have some familiarity with the traditional asset class-based approach. Listing the roles of various asset classes will be more intuitive and easy for Ng to explain to the IC.

  The traditional approach has relevance for the IC's liquidity and operational considerations. This approach will make it easier to identify relevant mandates for the alternative investments in the portfolio. The traditional approach also will allow the IC to obtain a better understanding of how various asset classes behave so that Ng can tailor the asset allocation to address any concerns. The traditional approach will be easier to implement, and the IC does not want to add costly in-house resources, which would likely be necessary with the risk-based approach.

18. FOFs is the the investment vehicle that would be *most appropriate* for Ælfheah's proposed alternative asset class.

    - An FOF would allow Ælfheah to co-invest with other investors in alternative investment opportunities for which Ælfheah might otherwise be too small to participate.
    - An in-house team would not be necessary to review and maintain an FOF, which uses an outside manager.
    - Ælfheah is unlikely to meet the very high minimum investment of an SMA, which may also require enhanced in-house investment resources.
    - Ælfheah does not need the higher liquidity of UCITS, which have a less attractive risk/return profile for Ælfheah's relatively small-sized portfolio.

      An FOF is the most appropriate investment vehicle for Ælfheah. This vehicle allows Ælfheah to co-invest alongside other investors in order to participate in alternative investment opportunities for which it would otherwise be too small to participate. An expert in-house team would not be necessary to review and maintain the types of investments in an FOF since this investment vehicle uses an outside manager.

      SMAs are available for certain large portfolios, such as those of large family offices or foundations, but it is unlikely that Ælfheah would meet the very high minimum investment requirement. This type of investment poses greater operational challenges for the investor; thus, an SMA may require enhanced in-house investment resources. UCITS are less appropriate for Ælfheah since its liquidity needs are being met. Ælfheah should instead invest in a vehicle that offers lower liquidity with a more attractive risk/return profile. Also, UCITS have regulatory restrictions that can make them more difficult for a fund manager to implement the desired investment strategy.

19. Mean–CVaR optimization is the asset allocation approach that is *most suitable*

for the Endowment.

- Mean–CVaR will better address the IC's concern about left-tail risk (the risk of a permanent capital loss).
- If the portfolio contains asset classes and investment strategies with negative skewness and long tails, CVaR optimization could materially alter the asset allocation decision.

    Given the IC's investment objectives for the endowment, using a mean–CVaR optimization approach is more suitable for determining the asset allocation. The IC has 36% of its portfolio invested in alternative assets, 19% in private equity, and 17% in hedge funds. Thus, the IC has a more sophisticated understanding of risk and will appreciate the more nuanced view of risk offered by mean–CVaR optimization. The portfolio has exposure to alternative investments, and the IC is concerned about left-tail risk (the risk of a permanent loss of capital), as indicated to Calixto. Thus, the asset allocation decision will be enhanced by the more detailed understanding of left-tail risk offered by mean–CVaR optimization relative to MVO. MVO cannot easily accommodate the characteristics of most alternative investments. MVO characterizes an asset's risk using standard deviation. Standard deviation, a one-dimensional view of risk, is a poor representation of the risk characteristics of alternative investments for which asset returns may be not normally distributed. MVO typically over-allocates to alternative asset classes, partly because risk is underestimated because of stale or infrequent pricing and the underlying assumption that returns are normally distributed.

    An investor particularly concerned with the downside risk of a proposed asset allocation may choose to minimize the portfolio's CVaR rather than its volatility relative to a return target. If the portfolio contains asset classes and investment strategies with negative skewness and long tails, CVaR optimization could materially alter the asset allocation decision.

20. The expected NAV of the fund at the end of the current year is €22,755,000, calculated as follows:

    First, the expected distribution at the end of the current year is calculated as

    Expected distribution

    = [Prior-year NAV × (1 + Growth rate)] × (Distribution rate).

    Expected distribution = [(€25,000,000 × 1.11) × 18%] = €4,995,000.

    Therefore, the expected NAV of the fund at the end of the current year is

    Expected NAV

    = Prior-year NAV × (1 + Growth rate) + Capital contributions − Distributions.

    Expected NAV = (€25,000,000 × 1.11) + 0 − €4,995,000 = €22,755,000.

An Overview of Private Wealth Management

LEARNING OUTCOMES

Mastery	The candidate should be able to:
☐	discuss the different types of individual wealth and how wealth is created and distributed globally
☐	evaluate how changes in human capital, financial capital, and economic net worth across the financial stages of an individual's life influence their financial decision making
☐	justify how returns, risks, objectives, and constraints for individuals relate to their human and financial capital
☐	evaluate how various types of taxes imposed on individual investors and the impact of inflation influence investment decisions
☐	discuss the differences between private and institutional clients and formulate an appropriate Investment Policy Statement for private clients

INTRODUCTION

1

Private wealth management combines financial planning and investment management to help individual investors, particularly **high-net-worth individuals (HNWIs)** and **ultra-high-net-worth individuals (UHNWIs)**, manage their **wealth**. This service encompasses several interconnected processes including personalized financial planning, specialized investment and financial advice, portfolio management, and advising on wealth management, tax planning, and estate planning matters.

Over the past 40 years global wealth has increased significantly, and private wealth management has become an integral, vital service offered by financial institutions, banks, asset management firms, and specialized advisors. This reading uses terms like "private wealth managers," "wealth managers," "managers," and "advisors" interchangeably and refers to their individual investors as "private clients" or, simply, "clients."

Private wealth management is a highly tailored service and involves close collaboration between the wealth manager and the client to define, plan for, and achieve financial objectives. Wealth managers work with clients to understand their financial goals, risk tolerance, and investment preferences, typically focusing on one or more of the interconnected processes listed above. They establish a complete picture of the client's personal and financial circumstances including assets, liabilities, income, and expenses. In developing comprehensive financial plans, wealth managers are supported by tax advisory, estate planning, wealth transfer, and multigenerational planning expertise.

The primary objective of private wealth managers is to maximize after-tax wealth while considering the client's goals, risk tolerance, and portfolio constraints. Private wealth managers can add value in various ways, such as purchasing undervalued securities, selling overpriced securities, and improving asset allocations. Efficient tax management is essential, as taxes can significantly impact net performance for the taxable investor. Tax rates, especially for HNWIs, can greatly influence returns and typically have a more substantial effect than portfolio management costs. Moreover, private wealth managers can offer retirement strategies, charitable giving and philanthropic advising, and client education on various financial matters when needed. This underscores the comprehensive approach to private wealth management.

This reading presents a framework for private wealth management based on a life-cycle view of human capital. Section 1 introduces the concept of wealth in a global context. Section 2 discusses the life-cycle view of human capital and its influence on investment decision making. Section 3 examines individual investors' return and risk considerations, including their objectives and constraints. Section 4 addresses the impact of taxation and inflation on investment decision making. Finally, Section 5 concludes the reading by exploring the unique features of individual investors, their investment plans, and investment policy statements.

LEARNING MODULE OVERVIEW

- Net worth refers to the value of all assets owned by an individual, minus any liabilities or debts. Sources of wealth include accumulated after-tax income from personal and business assets and intergenerational wealth transfers.

- Following World War II, global growth was boosted by new technology, more competition, government policies that supported businesses, and, in some cases, privatization of public services. The growth of free market capitalism, fewer regulatory obstacles, easier access to investment capital, and an increase in entrepreneurship and new businesses greatly encouraged global economic growth and wealth creation. The increase in the value of assets and financial innovations also played a role.

- The global expansion of free markets in recent decades pushed global per capita wealth higher, especially in lower middle income and low income economies.

- However, wealth inequality measures indicate increasing levels of inequality across global populations, with greater disparities in developed markets. While there is more wealth, there is also more wealth inequality.

- Individual investors and institutional investors have different time horizons, tax structures, liquidity needs, investment knowledge and research capabilities, decision-making processes, access to investment opportunities, and roles in the market.

- Individual investors in developed and emerging markets have different levels of access to financial information, different investment opportunities available to them, different investment preferences, and different regulatory environments.

- The **wealth life cycle** of an individual investor typically consists of seven phases: the education phase, the early career phase, the career development phase, the peak accumulation phase, the preretirement phase, the early retirement phase, and the late retirement phase.

- Human capital is the net present value of an individual's future expected labor income. Economic balance sheets include the human capital of an individual and provide a more comprehensive view of an individual's wealth. Individual wealth and asset composition tend to evolve throughout their lifetime, with financial wealth typically increasing as the horizon to build human capital declines.

- Consequently, as individuals approach retirement, the value of their assets and investments tends become a more significant portion of their aggregate human capital.

- Individuals need to diversify their income and risk sources during the wealth accumulation phase to decouple it from their human capital.

- Wealthier individuals in retirement may focus less on covering costs and more on fulfilling philanthropic goals, transferring wealth, and achieving other long-term financial objectives.

- Models for quantifying wealth, such as human capital calculations, are useful but may not fully capture the complexities of real-life situations.

- The impact of inflation on investment returns can vary based on the investment horizon. Investors should focus on preserving their long-term purchasing power, not just nominal returns.

- Assessing a client's risk tolerance involves understanding their willingness and ability to bear financial risk. Risk tolerance questionnaires are commonly used, but they have limitations and should be supplemented with in-depth discussions that can yield valuable insights about the individual's risk tolerance and investment approach.

- Clients often have multiple financial goals, and their risk tolerance may vary for each. Goals can be either planned (like retirement or specific purchases) or unplanned (like unexpected expenses).

- In most jurisdictions, different tax rates apply to different types of investment returns: interest, dividends, and capital gains or losses. Some tax systems impose a wealth tax, which function similarly to income taxes by reducing after-tax returns and accumulations.

- Tax drag, or the negative effect of taxes on after-tax returns, increases with higher investment returns and longer investment horizons.

- Deferral of taxes, often applied to capital gains, helps accumulate returns without tax drag until they are realized. The benefit of tax deferral compounds over time and can outweigh a lower tax rate over time. Investments with deferred capital gains taxation can be more tax efficient than those with annually taxed returns.

- Tax-advantaged investment vehicles help mitigate the impact of taxes on investment returns by offering tax deferrals, reduced tax rates, or tax exemptions, enabling investors to retain more returns for reinvestment and growth over time.

- Portfolio returns originate from various sources and are subject to different tax rates, which must be considered for portfolio management.
- Inflation affects future purchasing power and can change consumption patterns throughout an individual's life cycle. Solely focusing on nominal returns can distort the perception of an investment's real, after-tax, long-term performance.
- By considering the joint effects of taxes and inflation, investors can make informed decisions and choose investments for the most favorable long-term outcomes.
- An investment policy statement (IPS) documents a client's specific investment goals, risk tolerance, investment time frame, and constraints and reflects the mutual understanding of the investment manager's mandate.
- The IPS defines the investment process, clarifies the advisor's fiduciary duty, and is updated regularly to accommodate changes in the client's situation or market conditions.
- The main components of an IPS are the client's background and investment objectives, investment program parameters, portfolio asset allocation ranges, portfolio management processes, and duties and responsibilities of the involved parties.

2   WEALTH IN A GLOBAL CONTEXT

☐ | discuss the different types of individual wealth and how wealth is created and distributed globally

The first section focuses on the concept of wealth, sources of wealth and income, and the distribution of wealth across the world.

Defining Wealth

Typically, wealth refers to the value of all the assets owned by an individual less any liabilities or debts owed, as shown in Exhibit 1. There are various approaches to categorizing asset types, but the following offers a comprehensive view of different sources of wealth, excluding human capital, which we will discuss later.

Exhibit 1: Aggregate Wealth

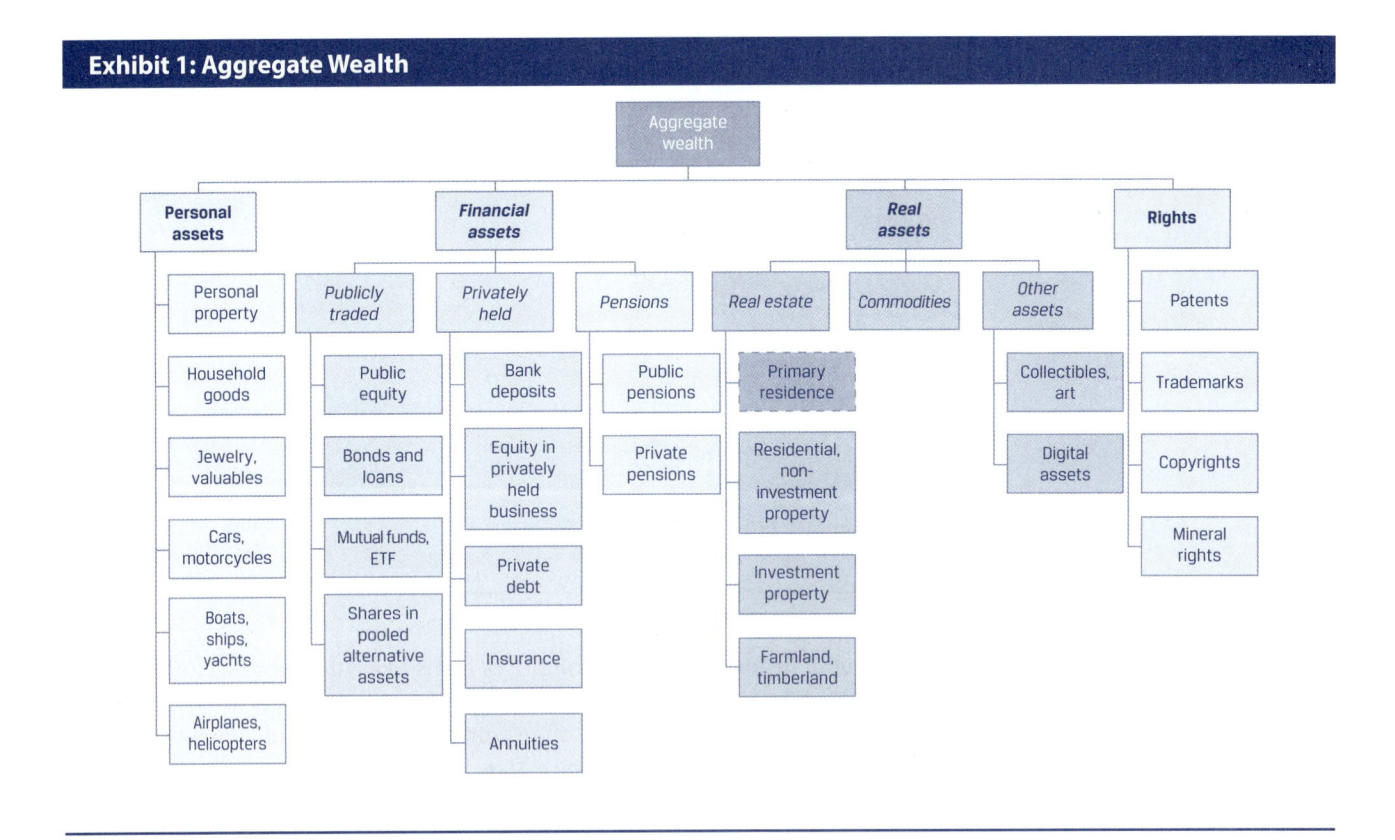

To determine someone's wealth, it is necessary to differentiate among various definitions of wealth. Exhibit 2 breaks down wealth into distinct components including personal, financial, real assets, and rights.

Exhibit 2: Components of Wealth

	Personal property	Financial assets			Real assets			Rights
		Publicly traded	Privately held	Pensions	Real estate	Commodities	Other assets	
Aggregate wealth	√	√	√	√	√	√	√	√
Financial wealth		√		√				
Real wealth					√	√	√	√
Productive wealth			√		√	√		√
Liquid wealth		√					√	
Investable wealth		√						

An individual's **aggregate wealth** is the total value of all assets owned, encompassing personal property, financial assets, real assets, and rights. **Net worth** is the difference between assets and liabilities whose values are relatively easy to measure, such as publicly traded investments, privately held assets, real estate, and debts, as illustrated in Exhibit 3.

This representation excludes intangible assets like copyrights, digital rights, and other nontangible assets, claims, or rights, which can be a significant part of wealth but are not included here because of their uncertain market value, complex valuation, and limited liquidity.

Exhibit 3: Net Worth

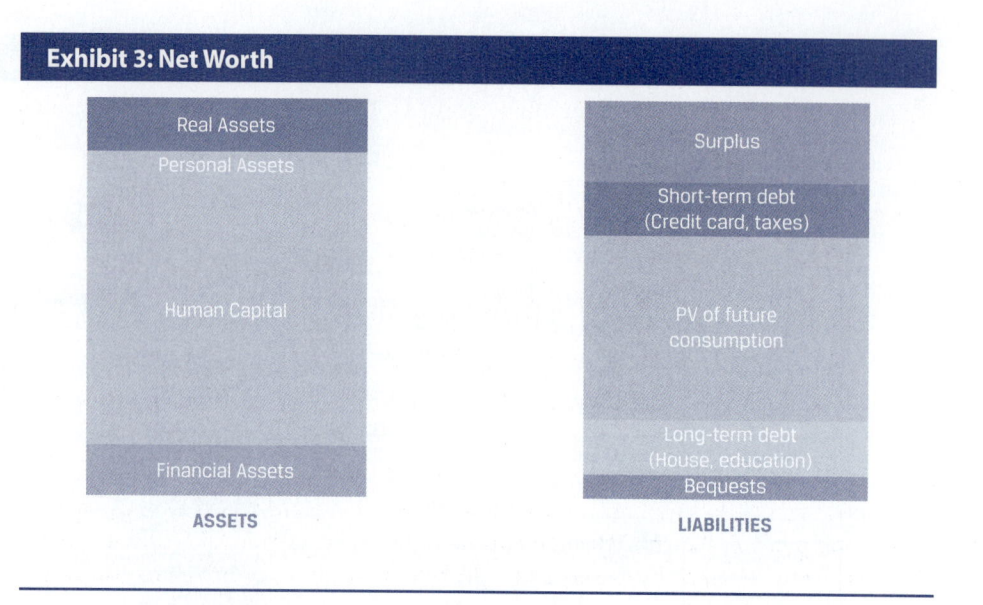

- ***Personal property*** typically comprises items like automobiles, clothes, furniture, and personal residences. Generally, **personal assets** are not expected to appreciate in value and are often worth more to the individual than their current fair market value. Some assets, like real estate and collectibles (jewelry, wine, stamps, and artwork), could be considered "mixed" assets with both personal and real asset characteristics. Some consider primary residential property as a personal property. Others would consider secondary residential properties as investments. For simplicity, we categorize primary residential property as a real asset.

- *Financial wealth* comprises all financial assets, such as publicly traded equity, debt, and investments in pooled vehicles like mutual funds, and alternative assets like hedge funds, private equity, and private debt investments. Financial wealth excludes direct ownership in non–publicly traded businesses like family businesses. Financial assets are often the easiest to identify and include both tangible investment assets and less tangible assets like accrued pensions. One criterion for subdividing financial assets is marketability: publicly traded, non–publicly traded, or privately held. Portfolio management has traditionally concentrated on publicly traded financial assets, overlooking privately held assets such as annuities, insurance, and business assets.

- *Real wealth* refers to tangible assets typically including real estate, commodities, and other owned assets and excluding both personal property and financial assets. Real assets, especially a primary residence, may be the largest asset owned by an individual. For example, in Germany, approximately half of households own a home, whereas in China, the number is closer to 90%. To purchase a home, most individuals obtain a mortgage, a loan secured by the property, which is frequently the largest fixed obligation of homeowners. The use of debt to purchase homes magnifies the impact of home value changes on homeowners' equity and net worth.

- *Productive wealth* reflects assets that can be used to generate income through production and business operations, such as a business directly owned by an individual or a family. For many wealthy individuals, productive wealth constitutes the largest portion of their aggregate wealth. Investing for business owners involves unique considerations, as their total capital may be closely tied to their business's overall performance (i.e., if the business does poorly, it affects not only the value of the business but also the owner's earnings). The value of business assets may vary based on market conditions and will often correlate with other financial assets within a household portfolio.

- *Liquid, available, or cash wealth* refers to assets that can be easily converted into cash, typically including publicly traded equity and debt in addition to cash and cash equivalents, bank deposits, or ready cash held on hand.

- **Investable wealth** refers to financial and other assets that are readily available for investment and is typically a subset of financial assets. Private wealth management often focuses primarily on investable wealth.

- **Investable net worth** is the sum of liquid assets, such as savings and investment accounts, and less short-term liabilities such as credit card debt.

- *Economic net worth* extends net worth to include claims to future assets that can be used for consumption, such as the individual's human capital and pension benefits. **Human capital** is the present value of future income streams adjusted by the actuarial probability of survival, wage growth, and a discount rate that reflects occupational income risk. A large part of an individual's wealth may be attributable to pensions, different types of retirement plans offered across the globe. Pensions can be offered by employers or government programs. Forms of retirement plans vary. Common forms include employee-directed savings plans, in which the contribution amounts and investments are controlled by the individual, or traditional defined benefit pension plans that guarantee some level of retirement benefits typically based on past wages. Government pensions are like employer pension plans but are generally more secure (in countries with low inflation and a high degree of creditworthiness). Because pension benefits typically accrue over time, only their vested value should be recognized in current wealth calculations; moreover, because they are claims on future cash payments, their value can be hard to estimate, and they are not as liquid as other financial assets. When we refer to economic net worth in this reading, we refer to the more holistic accounting of resources that can be used to fund future consumption for the purpose of financial planning over the life cycle.

The simplest balance sheet for an individual includes recognizable marketable assets (investment portfolio, retirement portfolio, real estate, and other tangible and intangible items of value) and liabilities (mortgage debt, credit card debt, auto loans, business or other debts guaranteed by the individual, and student loans). Such a simple balance sheet or statement of net worth is depicted in the case study below.

Valuing publicly traded investments and homeowners' equity is relatively straightforward. For example, an individual with a home valued at EUR1 million and a EUR900,000 mortgage only has EUR100,000 in equity. However, the human capital of an individual is influenced by hard-to-quantify factors such as wage growth, income risk, and economic considerations. Two individuals with the same life expectancy, each earning EUR50,000 annually, may experience positive or negative events over time (unexpected wage growth, job loss, or other impacts to their income) that lead to significantly different wealth outcomes.

CASE STUDY

Taylor, Aiysha, and Chimwala: Traditional Balance Sheet

Assets for three clients across different wealth levels and asset distributions are:

- Taylor: Young professional with limited assets (age: 25)
- Aiysha: Established small business owner with substantial assets tied up in the business (age: 45)
- Chimwala: Entrepreneur who is about to sell a large private business (age: 55)

Balance Sheet as of 31 December 20X1 in Thousands of EUR

Assets and liabilities	Taylor Age 25	Aiysha Age 45	Chimwala Age 55
Liquid assets			
Checking account[a]	10	35	400
Savings account	20	100	500
Total liquid assets	**30**	**135**	**900**
Investment assets			
Taxable investment account	5	350	1,000
Retirement plan, private pension[b]	75	2,000	500
Tax advantaged investment account	75	750	1,500
Total investment assets	**155**	**3,100**	**3,000**
Personal property			
Apartment, house	-	1,000	300
Vacation home	-	500	250
Cars	-	500	100
House contents	10	150	200
Collectibles	-	300	50
Total personal property	**10**	**2,450**	**900**
Business assets			
Direct and / or indirect ownership in business or business interests[c]	-	5,000	25,000
Total assets (Aggregate worth)	*195*	*10,685*	*29,800*
Short-term liabilities			
Short-term debt, credit card debt	15	250	5
Total short-term liabilities	**15**	**250**	**5**
Long-term liabilities			
Education loans	300	500	-
Car loan	10	400	-
Home mortgage	-	500	-
Home equity loan	-	750	500
Business debt			

Assets and liabilities	Taylor Age 25	Aiysha Age 45	Chimwala Age 55
Business loans[d]	–	4,000	7,000
Total long-term liabilities	**310**	**6,150**	**7,500**
Total liabilities	*325*	*6,400*	*7,505*
Net worth	**(130)**	**4,285**	**22,295**
Investable net worth[e]	**100**	**1,200**	**3,000**
Investable net worth after the business is sold		2,200	21,000

[a] *As a transaction account, the checking account may not be considered as part of investable net worth*

[b] *Retirement plans may or may not be considered part of investable net worth, depending on the structure of the retirement plan*

[c] *The way assets are held can vary based on a company's structure, as they may be owned directly or indirectly through a suitable legal entity; valuation methods for privately held assets have been discussed earlier in the curriculum*

[d] *Corporate debt, as corporate equity, can be either direct or indirect, and it might be backed by the company's ultimate beneficial owner; valuing privately held liabilities can be simplified using the valuation adjustments previously explained*

[e] *Savings account and investment accounts, excluding pension*

This balance sheet presents the varied financial situations of three clients, each with different backgrounds and asset levels. A wealth manager can utilize this information to develop customized strategies for each client, addressing their distinct financial objectives and situations.

- Taylor, a young professional, has a limited amount of assets and liabilities. Most of the assets are liquid and investable, while the liabilities are short term. However, considering the significant educational debt load (which is not unusual for young professionals), Taylor currently has a negative net worth. Moreover, if Taylor's income grows as a result of the educational investment, then the negative net worth should disappear as the loans are repaid.

- Aiysha, a successful small business owner, has a higher net worth but also carries substantial debt, which consists of personal debt, mortgage debt, and business debt.

- Chimwala, an entrepreneur, boasts a remarkable net worth, but the assets are mostly locked up in business assets. Once the business is liquidated, Chimwala's assets will become liquid, realizing the value of the ownership as it is converted into investable assets.

For both Aiysha and Chimwala, the portion of total assets invested in their businesses is crucial, as equity and retained earnings constitute a significant part of their current wealth. The percentage of earnings they allocate as compensation influences their present consumption, while retaining earnings can enhance their businesses' cash flow, capital, and competitive standing.

Sources of Global Wealth

In the decades following World War II, economic growth around the world has been substantial, albeit geographically uneven and sometimes volatile. This history is described in the example box on global economic transformation below and illustrated in Exhibit 4.

This economic growth reflects fundamentally improved economic opportunities combining technological advances, increased economic and business competition, broad deregulation, business-friendly policies, privatization, and emphasis on entrepreneurship as an engine for growth, with changes in international trade that integrate different parts of the world. Other contributing factors to wealth creation have been positively trending asset price appreciation and the marginal but often anecdotally supported influx of accidental wealth through unexpected stardom. While we could consider windfalls from lottery earnings, gambling wins, inherited wealth, or court settlements as examples of such unforeseen wealth, it is critical to emphasize that these instances primarily involve wealth transfer rather than wealth generation.

Exhibit 4: GDP Growth for the World and Select Countries Measured by the Average Per Capita GDP between 1960 and 2022 in Constant 2010 USD

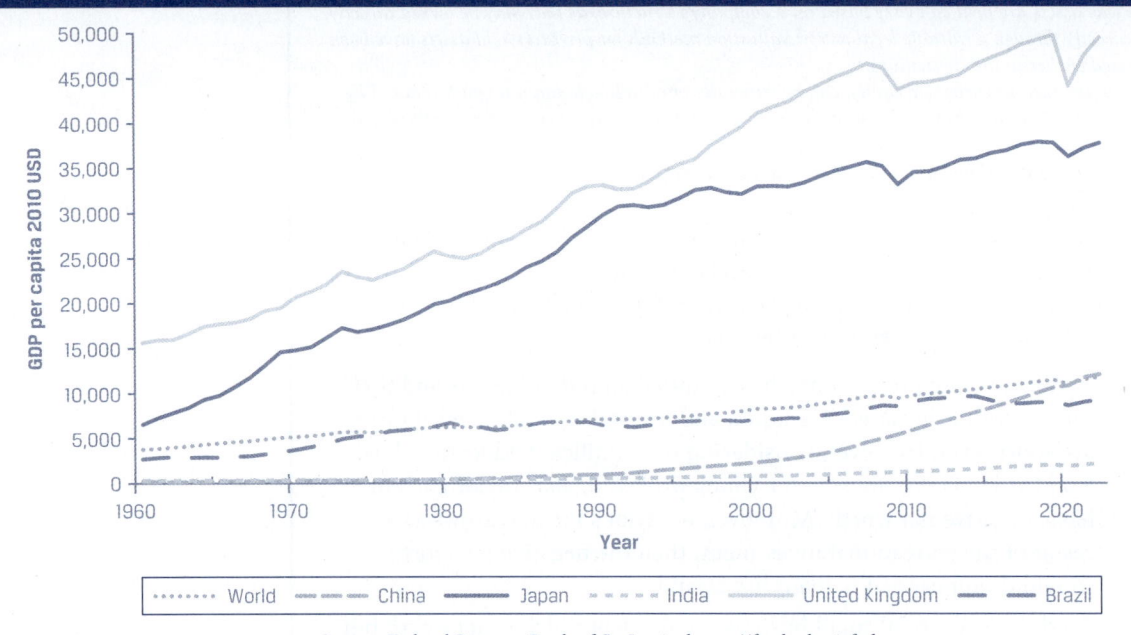

Source: Federal Reserve Bank of St. Louis, https://fred.stlouisfed.org.

THE GLOBAL ECONOMIC TRANSFORMATION

The global economic landscape fundamentally changed after World War II. The war brought about the collapse of the old colonial system, while technological breakthroughs spurred persistent productivity growth and increased international trade further accelerated economic growth. These political, economic, and commercial changes were transformative and led to a substantial rise in global wealth. Exhibit 5 shows the 10-year change in GDP per capita.

Exhibit 5: Decennial Change in GDP Per Capita in Selected Geographic Areas between 1950 and 2020

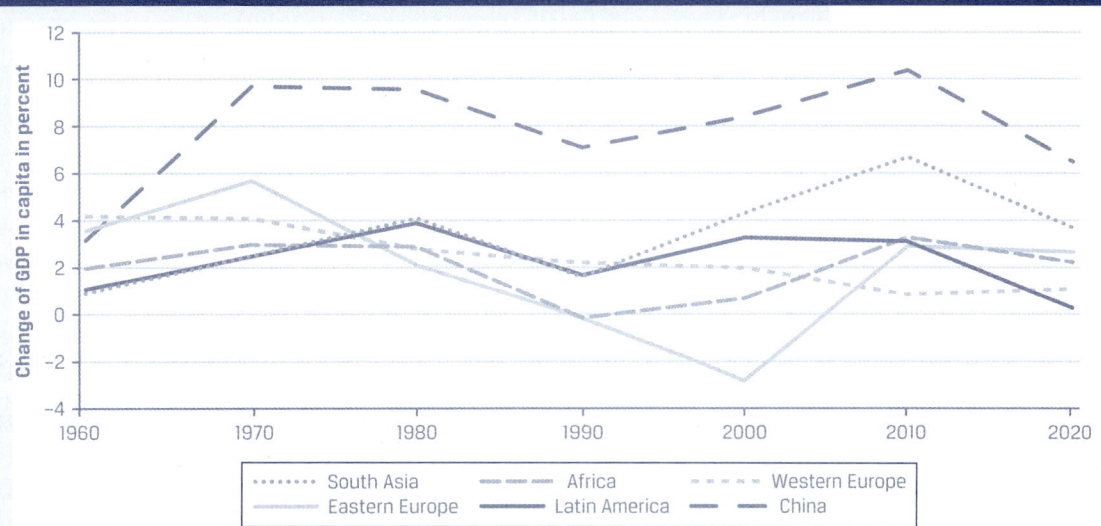

Source: World Bank Data, World Development Indicators (WDI), https://data.worldbank.org.

Decolonization played a key role in this transformation. European powers such as Britain and France could no longer maintain their colonial empires, leading to over 50 countries gaining independence from 1945 to 1960. Despite challenges such as political instability and social inequalities, this shift allowed new nations to control resources and industries, leading to economic expansion.

In South Asia, India and Bangladesh pursued economic strategies that led to both growth and challenges. India focused on developing heavy industries and infrastructure, achieving a 3.5% annual GDP growth rate from 1951 to 1980. Bangladesh, after initial struggles, saw wealth creation through the growth of its ready-made garment industry.

In Africa, countries faced different economic outcomes after decolonization. While nations like Botswana and Mauritius achieved significant economic growth through good governance and economic diversification, others, like Somalia and Nigeria, suffered because of various reasons including corruption and political instability.

Europe saw a division in economic paths, with Western Europe experiencing rapid growth through economic integration and Eastern Europe struggling under inefficient centrally planned economies. However, the fall of the Soviet Union in 1991 prompted market-oriented reforms leading to growth in Eastern Europe.

In Latin America, countries experienced varied economic outcomes based on state intervention, external influences, and policy effectiveness. While policies encouraging domestic market production initially led to growth, they eventually resulted in inefficiencies and hindered wealth creation. External actors and global economic shifts also significantly influenced the region's economic outcomes.

Economic opportunities are crucial in driving economic growth and wealth creation. After the fall of the Berlin Wall in 1989, market-oriented economic policies and increased cross-border competition boosted global economic capacity and spurred wealth creation. Advances in information technology and widespread adoption of many other new technologies led to unprecedented productivity growth. Increased trade flows between different parts of the world also contributed to growth.

The shift towards free market capitalism also played a significant role. Countries like the United Kingdom, former Soviet bloc nations, and Latin American countries such as Mexico and Brazil adopted aggressive privatization policies, transferring state-owned assets to private ownership. This improved efficiency and competitiveness across various industries and contributed to wealth creation.

Reductions in regulatory barriers, more access to funding and capital, and increased global connectivity and communication facilitated a surge in business formation.

The rise in entrepreneurship and business creation led to job creation, innovation, and economic growth in both developed and developing countries. These new ventures fostered a more competitive business environment, driving further advancements in technology and productivity and ultimately contributing to the global increase in wealth.

However, protracted economic growth has not been uniform worldwide nor has it translated into broader wealth creation across all segments of the society. A commonly advanced argument is that economic growth does not directly translate to income growth and that wealth growth does not directly reflect income growth, as shown in Exhibit 6. In fact, rapid economic growth can exacerbate income inequality, as the benefits mainly accrue to those who control the means of production, investable capital, and natural resources and can leverage their financial, social, political, and intellectual capital. High income concentration can reduce demand from the general population, further concentrating capital and wealth in the hands of the already wealthy. To counter these developments, policymakers can implement policies that promote competition, dismantle oligopolies and monopolies, and transfer wealth through taxation. Breaking up dominant market players reduces market entry barriers, fosters innovation, and provides opportunities for new businesses to grow. This process can stimulate job creation and promote a more equitable distribution of wealth.

Moreover, investing in education, building infrastructures, and improving both access to and the quality of healthcare can support long-term economic growth and benefit the broader population. This not only supports social mobility but also supports the workforce by giving individuals the skills necessary to compete globally. Both of these developments also support wealth creation and wealth accumulation. Nonetheless, almost all countries have benefited from economic growth.

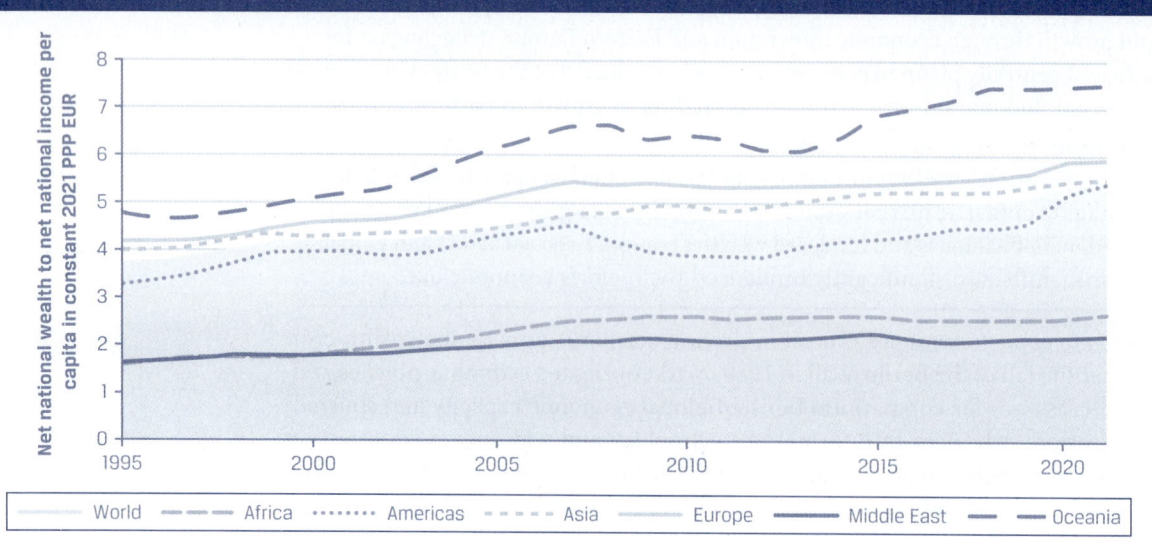

Exhibit 6: Net National Wealth to Net National Income Per Capita between 1995 and 2020 in Constant 2021 PPP EUR

Note: Net national wealth to net national income per capita is calculated in constant 2021 PPP EUR.

Source: World Income Inequality Database – WIID, 30 June 2022. https://www.wider.unu.edu/database/world-income-inequality-database-wiid.

Gains from economic growth are reflected in Credit Suisse's Global Wealth Report 2022 (Exhibit 7), which shows that global per capita wealth has increased over the past 20 years, most notably in the lower middle income and low income economies that account for 75% of the world's population and one-third of global GDP.

MEASURING NET WORTH

The lack of a universally accepted definition of net worth leads to different organizations using their own methodologies when calculating it. For example, Credit Suisse defines net worth or "wealth" of households as the value of financial assets plus real assets (mainly housing) owned by households, minus their debts. This resembles a household's balance sheet, listing owned items and their net value if sold. Credit Suisse's definition excludes private pension fund assets but includes state pension entitlements. It does not consider human capital or an individual's share in state-owned assets and debts, which are difficult to assign to individuals.

This definition may differ from academic research on wealth and income inequality, which can use varying metrics, methodologies, and models leading to different wealth and income levels. Additionally, estimates for the ultra-wealthy may rely on statistical approximations rather than census data. As a result, comparisons between different studies on wealth and income should be made cautiously, considering the specific definitions and methodologies used.

According to the World Bank's classification, in 2021, lower middle income economies had a gross national income (GNI) per capita ranging from USD1,036 to USD4,045. The upper middle income economies had a GNI per capita between USD4,046 and USD12,535. According to the same classification, China is an upper middle income economy. India is identified as a lower middle income economy. This classification highlights the connection between economic opportunities and accelerated wealth growth in rapidly developing countries. There are no countries classified as low income in Europe or North America, and all North American countries are considered high income countries.

Exhibit 7: Average Per Capita Wealth Growth in USD between 2000 and 2021 across Different Regions and Income Levels

Region/country	High income	Upper middle income	Lower middle income	Low income	Average growth
Africa	164%	165%	190%	210%	194%
Asia Pacific	107%	186%	192%	123%	159%
China		289%			289%
Europe	127%	229%	302%		154%
India			177%		177%
Latin America	88%	125%	149%	−18%	112%

Region/country	High income	Upper middle income	Lower middle income	Low income	Average growth
North America	113%				113%
Average	117%	170%	193%	187%	160%

Source: Credit Suisse Research Institute, Global Wealth Databook 2022. https://www.credit-suisse.com/media/assets/corporate/docs/about-us/research/publications/global-wealth-databook-2022.pdf. Data as of December 31, 2021.

Since the 1980s, *entrepreneurship* and new business formation has grown across the world. Entrepreneurs create new markets, disrupt old industries, and create jobs by incorporating new technologies, increasing access to capital and information, engaging in global trade and investments, and shifting attitudes for risk taking and innovation. Many entrepreneurs build and sell their business, thereby transferring real wealth to financial wealth. Increasingly, entrepreneurs drive economic growth by creating new products, services, and markets using the latest technological advances.

Asset price appreciation, especially in the United States and other developed markets, drove wealth growth over the past decades. Exhibit 8 shows the relationship between global stock market capitalization and global GDP. Between 1970 and the end of 2021, both the global stock market capitalization and global GDP grew by around 7%. The graph shows that global stock market capitalization and global GDP are highly positively correlated over the time period.

Exhibit 8: The Growth of Global Stock Market Capitalization and Global GDP in Current USD between 1970 and 2021

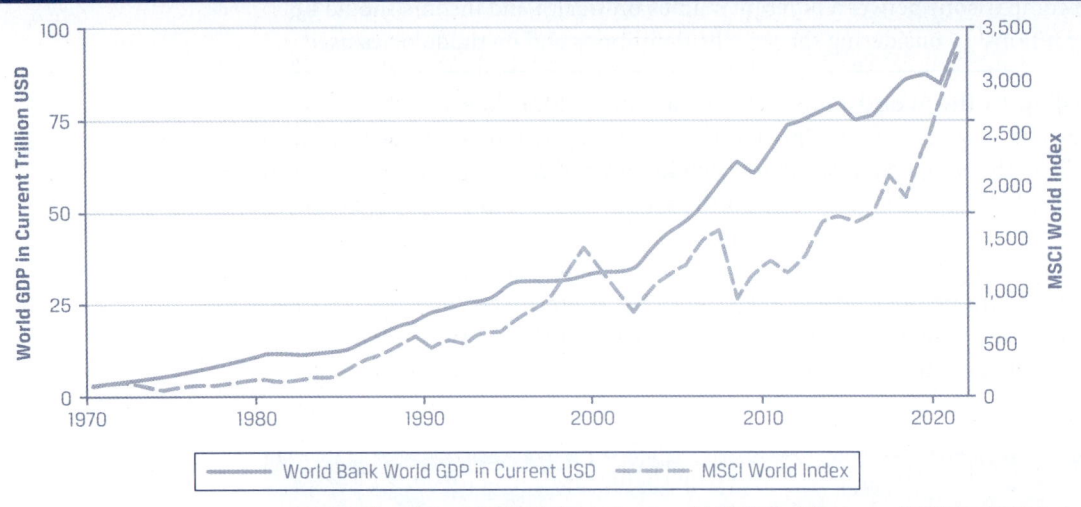

Source: Bloomberg. MXWO Index is the annual MSCI World Index and WGDPWRLD is the World Bank World GDP in Current USD.

Privatizing government assets, selling family-owned businesses, and initial public offerings contributed to this wealth increase. So did financial innovation and financial product development, which drove investments into commodity and real estate markets worldwide. Even though the public listing of a family-owned business reclassifies wealth (from privately held wealth to publicly held wealth, as the cash proceeds from sales can be invested in financial assets), wealth created through entrepreneurship and asset price appreciation remains the main source of wealth creation in most economies.

Furthermore, the significance of inheritance-related wealth transfers is predicted to increase in the future. However, this is not the creation of new riches, but rather the transfer of existing wealth between generations. In the coming decades, the Silent Generation (those born between 1925 and 1945) and the Baby Boomers (those born between 1946 and 1965) will transfer trillions of USD in wealth to subsequent generations through inheritances and gifts.

Finally, accidental wealth through large legal settlements and awards and lottery and gambling winnings is a small but anecdotally significant source of wealth. Gambling is not directly derived from productive work but can dramatically change an individual's financial status overnight. These sources of wealth may be less common, and they do not create new wealth, but they transfer existing wealth.

Much like lottery or gambling winnings, sudden fame can lead to a rapid accumulation of wealth for individuals who suddenly gain immense popularity or recognition in their respective fields such as entertainment, sports, or social media. However, unlike lottery winnings, sudden fame leads to wealth creation.

The global distribution of financial wealth, nonfinancial wealth, and indebtedness generally has remained stable over time across different regions. Here, nonfinancial wealth includes personal property and real assets but excludes human capital. Exhibit 9 shows the distribution of total wealth from 2000 and 2020. Although there are clear disparities among the drivers of wealth growth at the national level — reflecting, in part, differences in economic development, market structure, economic policy, and political preferences — there are some notable regional patterns.

Exhibit 9: Distribution of Total Wealth across the Globe

Region	Wealth type in percent	2000	2005	2010	2015	2020
Africa	Financial wealth	41	44	43	39	44
	Nonfinancial wealth	59	56	57	61	56
	Debts	9	11	11	8	7
Asia- Pacific	Financial wealth	50	52	50	50	50
	Nonfinancial wealth	50	48	50	51	50
	Debts	15	12	12	12	12
China	Financial wealth	36	37	41	43	44
	Nonfinancial wealth	64	63	59	57	56
	Debts	1	4	6	8	11
Europe	Financial wealth	49	43	41	45	45
	Nonfinancial wealth	52	57	59	56	55
	Debts	14	14	15	14	13
India	Financial wealth	24	24	24	22	24
	Nonfinancial wealth	76	76	76	78	76
	Debts	6	7	8	8	9
Latin America	Financial wealth	38	40	40	45	46
	Nonfinancial wealth	62	60	60	55	54
	Debts	10	9	12	11	11
North America	Financial wealth	67	62	68	71	72
	Nonfinancial wealth	33	38	32	29	29
	Debts	14	16	17	14	12
World	Financial wealth	55	51	51	53	54

Region	Wealth type in percent	2000	2005	2010	2015	2020
	Nonfinancial wealth	45	49	49	47	46
	Debts	14	14	14	12	12

Source: Credit Suisse Research Institute, Global Wealth Databook 2022. Data as of December 31, 2021. https://www.credit-suisse.com/media/assets/corporate/docs/about-us/research/publications/global -wealth-databook-2022.pdf.

Between 2000 and 2020, China experienced a significant increase in indebtedness, which may be due to its rapid economic growth and the need for credit to support that growth. In North America, financial wealth plays a crucial role, possibly because of a strong financial market performance, a widespread investment in financial assets, and an overall favorable investment and tax climate. Nonfinancial wealth is more important in India, consistently accounting for around 76% of total wealth from 2000 to 2020, which could be attributed to a cultural emphasis on holding tangible assets, such as real estate and gold, traditionally viewed as reliable stores of value in Indian culture. Finally, both Africa and India tend to accumulate relatively low levels of debt compared to other regions, with debts constituting 7% to 9% of total wealth in 2020. This may reflect limited access to credit financing, substantial underbanked populations, and a general cultural aversion to debt.

Exhibit 10 shows that global wealth is concentrated in North America and Europe, which in 2021 collectively accounted for close to 57% of total global wealth.

Exhibit 10: Wealth Distribution across Different Parts of the World at the End of 2021

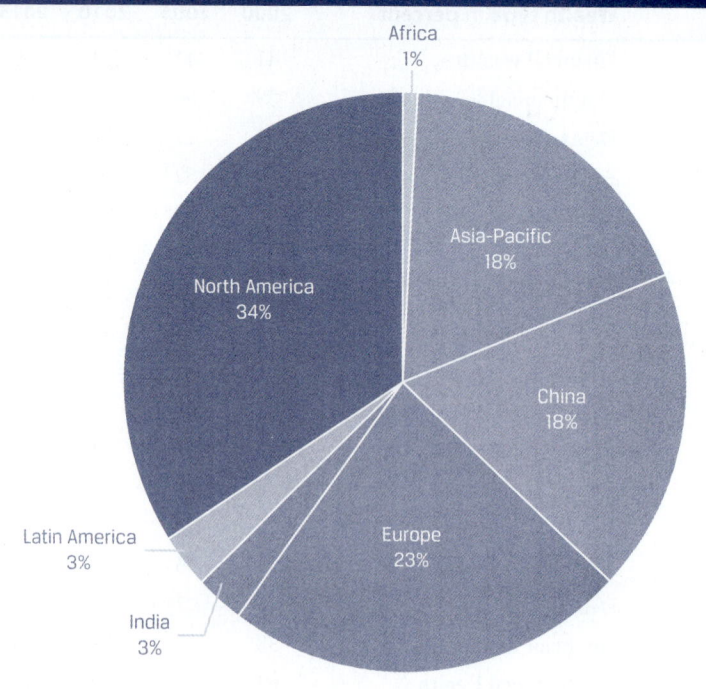

Source: Credit Suisse Research Institute, Global Wealth Databook 2022. Data as of December 31, 2021. https://www.credit-suisse.com/media/assets/corporate/docs/about-us/research/publications/ global-wealth-databook-2022.pdf.

In *North America*, the primary drivers of wealth are economic growth, largely fueled by business formation and entrepreneurship. Steady economic and productivity growth, along with positive financial market returns, have led to increased wealth levels. However, this wealth distribution has been unequal, primarily benefiting the more affluent segments of society. A significant factor contributing to this inequality is the prevalence of equity-based compensation for employees in publicly traded companies, such as professionals and executives. Additionally, successful business owners who have commercialized their ideas and sold their businesses to investors contribute to wealth creation. Accomplished professionals, athletes, and artists also play a role in generating wealth in North America.

In *Europe,* as in North America, economic growth has been a main driver of wealth creation. But unlike private business formation or "new money" in North America, it is "old money" that dominates Western European wealth. There are a substantial number of family-controlled medium- to large-sized businesses in Western Europe that typically remain privately held. But the main source of wealth is inherited wealth, primarily real estate.

In the formerly Communist Central and Eastern European countries, the significant structural economic change and privatization that followed the fall of the Soviet Union spurred immense wealth creation, helped by their ascendancy into the European Union, increased direct foreign investment, and investments in education. As these countries transitioned from communist to market-based economies through waves of privatization, many opportunists became wealthy quickly. Example 1 describes the changing fortunes of Czechia/Czech Republic and Slovakia (formerly Czechoslovakia) during this time. In many other formerly Communist countries with large natural resources and commodity-driven economies, there has been significant wealth creation that mainly benefitted a group of politically well-connected individuals.

EXAMPLE 1

The Changing Fortunes of Czechoslovakia, Czechia, and Slovakia

Czechoslovakia was one of the most prosperous European countries before World War II, with an estimated GDP per capita of approximately USD1,800 in 1938, the highest in Central Europe. It had a developed, diverse, and competitive industrial sector.

After World War II Czechoslovakia became a Communist state. Its economy became centrally planned, with state ownership of most of its businesses. The overall economic growth in Communist Czechoslovakia was slow, and living standards remained low, even though both educational opportunities and health care improved.

After the fall of Communism in 1989, the new regime started broad market-oriented economic reforms. Privatization began in 1991 and led to substantial job losses, particularly in industries that were not internationally competitive. Additionally, it also led to a few well-connected oligarchs controlling most of its economy. Allegations of corruption and cronyism were rampant, but the economic changes and privatization revitalized the economy and increased its overall competitiveness. Overall, the Czechoslovakian privatization process is considered a success. After 1993, when Czechoslovakia peacefully split into two independent countries, the Czech Republic (Czechia) and Slovakia, economic growth continued.

The *Asia-Pacific* region has experienced significant economic growth because of high economic growth rates, integration into global commerce, and financial development, which has resulted in considerable wealth accumulation. This growth has been fueled by a transformation from agrarian-based economies to industrialized ones focusing on manufacturing and services. A combination of domestic policies and focus on international trade drove this transformation. For instance, Japan, South Korea, and Singapore adopted an export-oriented strategy, attracting foreign investment, and investing in education and training to develop a globally competitive and highly skilled workforce. Both India and China also created considerable wealth. The region also has intense entrepreneurship across broad sectors including manufacturing, trade, and real estate development. That entrepreneurship in several Asian countries, where small and medium-sized enterprises drive economic growth, has made many entrepreneurs rich. Moreover, real estate development has also played a noticeable role in wealth creation. Finally, the high savings rates, relatively young and educated population, and substantive foreign direct investments all contribute to wealth accumulation.

In *Latin America*, the rapid growth and modernization of stagnant economies have resulted in a significant increase in personal wealth; however, the wealth is distributed relatively unequally. Several Latin American countries have some of the largest wealth and income inequalities. Enterprises and small business owners are also a source of wealth. However, sustained economic growth and political stability remain elusive in many Latin American nations.

In the *Middle East*, petroleum remains the main economic driver, having generated tremendous affluence. However, this wealth is extremely concentrated among a small number of families who have inherited their riches over multiple generations and control significant portions of national economies. Example 2 discusses a shift away from oil dependence, as Saudi Arabia is seeking to diversify its economy by investing its wealth into sectors that can continue to propel its economic growth, albeit at a lower rate.

EXAMPLE 2

The Saudi 2030 Vision

Because up to 40% of Saudi Arabia's GDP comes directly from oil revenue, in 2016 the country launched the Vision 2030 plan to reduce the country's reliance on oil, diversify its economy, and improve the quality of life for its citizens. The plan focuses on three main pillars.

The first pillar aims to create a tolerant, cohesive society that is committed to Islamic and national values and can support the growth of the economy.

The second pillar aims to develop new industries, attract foreign investment, and reduce the country's dependence on oil exports. The plan is to raise non–oil-related export sources of Saudi Arabia's GDP by 2030, specifically to raise the share of non-oil GDP from 16% to 50%. Because a fall in oil prices negatively affects the economy, such diversification reduces Saudi Arabia's dependence on oil as the main driver of its economy. To further reduce its reliance on oil, this plan also aims to increase foreign direct investment inflows from approximately 4% of GDP in 2019 to close to 6% by 2030. Through economic diversification, Saudi Arabia intends to insulate its economy from secular changes in the demand for oil, as the demand for oil is expected to slow down. Finally, the plan also seeks to transform Saudi Arabia into one of the world's 15 largest economies.

The third pillar aims to improve the education system, develop the health care sector, and create a more efficient and effective government. Additionally, the goal is to increase the international competitiveness of the educational sector, aiming to have five Saudi universities among the top 200 universities in international rankings. Moreover, the plans call to increase Saudi Arabian life expectancy to 80 years from 74 years.

A successful implementation of Vision 2030 could increase Saudi Arabia's geopolitical influence in the Middle East.

In recent years, *Africa* has witnessed a rather robust increase in wealth driven by revenues from oil and other commodities, the acceleration in GDP growth, the increase in foreign direct investment, the comparatively robust performance of local economies, and the relative appreciations of local currencies. Still, wealth remains concentrated among the ruling elite, executives, and professionals, as well as small and family-owned enterprises. Wealth in Africa is highly concentrated, with inequality levels comparable to those found in Latin America. Many African countries, such as Botswana, are pursuing policies to reduce their reliance on their core industries and diversify their economies as discussed in Example 3.

EXAMPLE 3

Botswana's Economic Diversification: Moving Beyond Diamonds

Botswana, as the world's top producer of gem diamonds, generates around 40% of the global output, and diamonds contribute to around 35% to its GDP. Botswana now aims to expand other sectors and diversify its economy by focusing on tourism, agriculture, and manufacturing.

Capitalizing on Botswana's diverse wildlife and natural beauty, tourism has grown in significance. In 2000, tourism accounted for approximately 6% of GDP. In 2019, it represented 13%. Because agriculture amounts to 2% of its GDP and is important to subsistence farmers, the government in Botswana has been enhancing both farming productivity and crop diversity. Finally, Botswana is also promoting investments in industries such as manufacturing, services, and technology to create jobs and foster economic growth.

Understanding growth in real wealth, particularly in countries or regions that have suffered extreme economic changes or otherwise are prone to significant exchange rate volatility, requires explicitly accounting for the impacts of inflation and variable exchange rates, as Example 4 on Argentina explains.

EXAMPLE 4

The Deceptive Rise of Wealth: Understanding the Difference between Nominal and Real Growth in Times of Crisis

Argentina has experienced several economic crises including sharp currency devaluations and hyperinflation. In the late 1980s, its annual inflation rate was almost 500%. In 2002, the inflation rate peaked at 41%. Hyperinflationary periods have significantly decreased the real purchasing power of Argentinians. Although the nominal wealth of Argentinians appeared to increase because of hyperinflation, the devaluation of the currency decreased the foreign currency value of their assets. Consequently, the real wealth decreased due to the hyperinflation.

Inflation Rate and Relevant USD Exchange Rates in Argentina 1987–2022

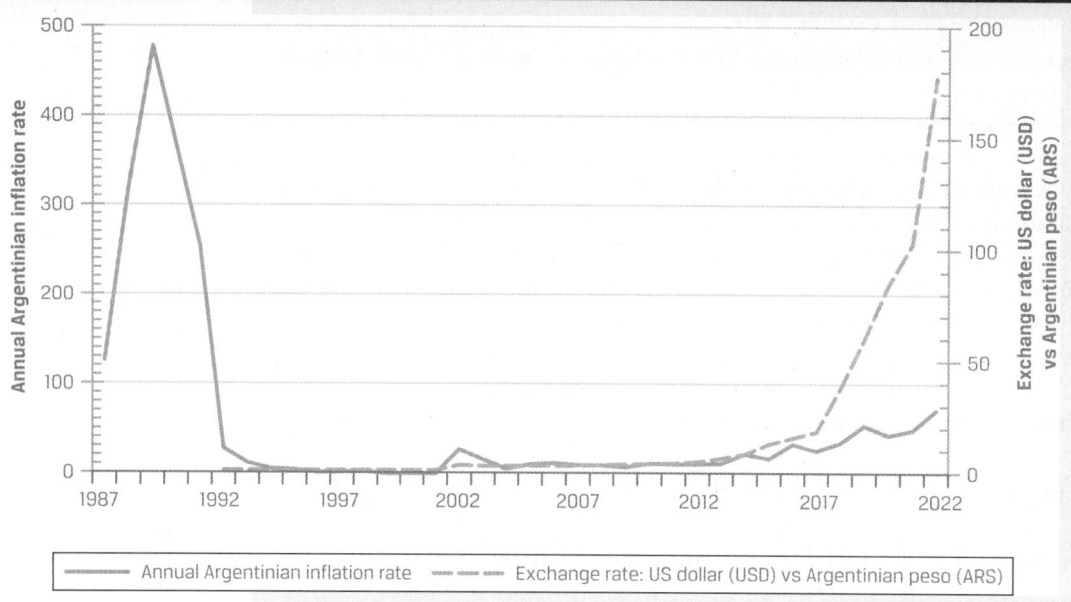

For instance, in 2001, the GDP per capita of Argentina was approximately USD7,100, but by 2002, it had fallen to approximately USD2,500 because of hyperinflation and currency devaluation. Moreover, the severe economic downturn that followed led to a negative real GDP growth rate of −11% in 2002, as depicted in the graph below. Furthermore, the poverty rate, measured by the proportion of the population living under USD5.50 per day, increased from 31% in 2001 to 44% in 2002.

GDP Per Capita in USD and GDP Growth in Argentina, 1986–2022

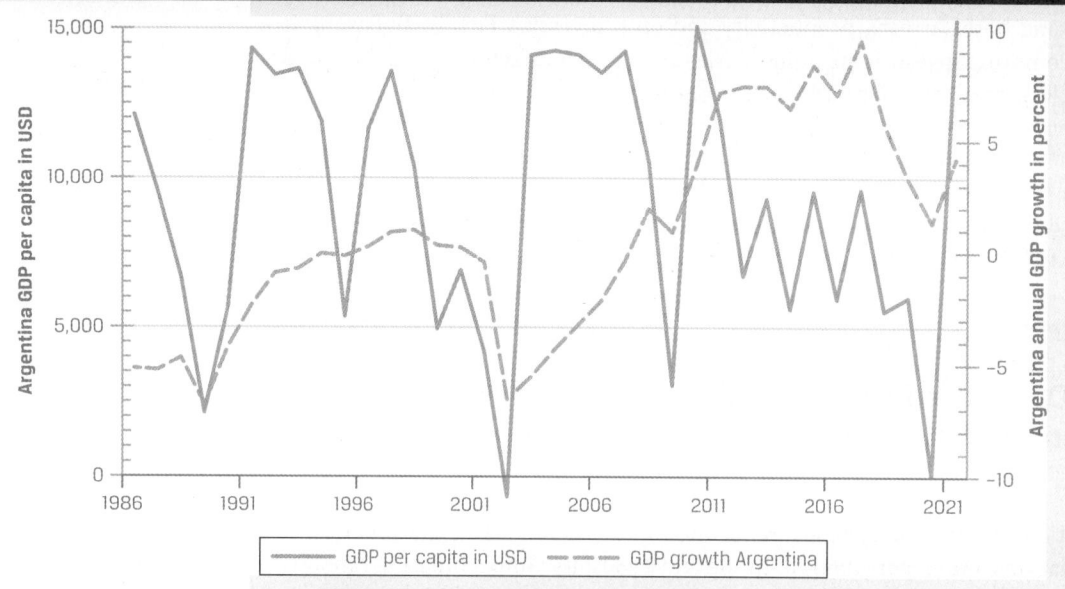

The currency devaluation during the economic crisis caused an illusion of increased wealth: someone with the equivalent of USD10,000 in the bank before the devaluation would have had the equivalent of around ARS10,000. After devaluation, the same dollar wealth would be worth around ARS30,000.

Although nominal wealth increased because of hyperinflation during the crisis, the real value of this wealth had actually decreased. The importance of factoring in inflation and exchange rates when analyzing wealth growth in markets or regions prone to extreme events or exchange rate volatility is underscored by this example.

Distribution of Global Wealth

Although the precise wealth levels across the world continuously evolve, driven by asset price, commodity price, and exchange rate dynamics, there are some persistent trends. First, wealth is unevenly distributed. Second, wealth is highly concentrated. Third, very few people hold large amounts of wealth. Fourth, the number of millionaires is increasing each year because the USD1 million cutoff point changes with economic growth rates, exchange rate fluctuations, and inflation. Understanding these trends helps wealth managers better serve their high-net-worth clients.

According to Credit Suisse, in 2021 the household wealth distribution across the global adult population of 5.3 billion shows that 2.8 billion people, or 53% of all adults, had wealth below USD10,000; 1% of the adults, or approximately 54 million people, had wealth exceeding USD1,000,000; see Exhibit 11.

Exhibit 11: Distribution of Global Wealth

	Africa	Asia Pacific	China	Europe	India	Latin America	North America	World
Number of adults in millions	690	1,257	1,111	589	916	453	282	5,299
Mean wealth per adult (in USD)	8,419	64,700	76,639	180,275	15,535	27,717	560,846	87,489
Median wealth per adult (in USD)	1,111	5,218	28,258	26,385	3,457	5,139	95,255	8,360
Distribution of adults by wealth range (USD) in percent								
Under 10,000	87	63	18	32	75	65	22	53
Between 10,000 and 100,000	12	26	67	36	23	30	29	34
Between 100,000 and 1,000,000	1	10	15	29	2	5	39	12
Over 1,000,000	0	1	1	3	0	0	10	1

Source: Credit Suisse Research Institute, Global Wealth Databook 2022. Data as of December 31, 2021. https://www.credit-suisse.com/media/assets/corporate/docs/about-us/research/publications/global-wealth-databook-2022.pdf.

Median global wealth is USD8,360, while the mean global wealth is USD87,489, as a few individuals with very high levels of wealth can greatly increase the average wealth while the median wealth remains relatively low. The global distribution of wealth can be shown by comparing the wealth of the top wealth groups compared to the average citizen and comparing the average citizen to those at the bottom of the wealth distribution. Exhibit 12 contains all wealth deciles to show the different distribution of wealth across different parts of the world. The top decile of individuals controls more wealth than the remaining 90% of the population. At the end of 2021, the bottom 50% of adults in the global wealth distribution controlled less than 1% of total global wealth.

Exhibit 12: Distribution of Global Wealth across Deciles

Geographic areas	Wealth share (%) per wealth population decile										Top percentile (1%)
	1	2	3	4	5	6	7	8	9	10	
Africa	−1	0	0	0	1	2	3	5	10	79	44
Asia Pacific	0	0	0	0	1	1	2	4	10	82	39
China	0	1	2	2	3	4	6	8	14	60	31
Europe	−1	0	0	1	1	2	5	9	16	68	30
India	−1	0	1	1	2	3	4	6	11	73	41
Latin America	−1	0	0	1	1	2	4	6	12	76	39
North America	−1	0	0	1	1	2	4	6	12	74	35
World	−1	0	0	0	1	1	2	4	10	82	46

Source: Credit Suisse Research Institute, Global Wealth Databook 2022. Data as of December 31, 2021. https://www.credit-suisse.com/media/assets/corporate/docs/about-us/research/publications/global -wealth-databook-2022.pdf.

The richest decile, the top 10% of the adults in the world, controls 82% of wealth, and the remaining 90% control 18%. For example, in the Asia-Pacific region, the top 1% of wealth holders have a wealth share of 39%, while the bottom 90% have a wealth share of 18%. In China, the top 10% of wealth holders have a wealth share of 60%, while the bottom 50% have a wealth share of 9%. Overall, the table shows that wealth is concentrated at the top decile, particularly in the top 1%, with the largest wealth share in most regions held by this group. The top 1% of the adult population controls 46% of the global wealth. In some regions, such as Africa and India, there are negative wealth shares in the lower wealth deciles, indicating that those groups have negative net worth.

The difference in entry points to different wealth deciles shows the regional differences in wealth and that, in many parts of the world, a notable number of individuals have negative net worth. In 2021, the minimum wealth to belong to the richest 10% of the world's adults was USD138,000, to belong to the richest 5%, USD296,000, and to the top 1%, USD1,147,000. There are notable regional and national differences for these cutoff points, as shown in Exhibit 13.

Exhibit 13: Minimum Wealth in USD to Qualify for a Wealth Decile

Geographic area	Minimum wealth of deciles (USD per adult)								
	2	3	4	5	6	7	8	9	10
Africa	−235	−14	172	576	1,111	1,988	3,323	5,978	12,692
Asia Pacific	−213	513	1,583	3,112	5,218	8,635	15,709	34,796	122,248
China	4,888	11,043	15,279	20,348	28,258	37,907	51,593	80,292	134,193
Europe	−266	3,386	8,929	15,044	26,385	57,074	114,292	200,285	397,553
India	−596	904	1,398	2,295	3,457	5,243	7,819	12,325	25,377
Latin America	−1,229	−541	580	2,576	5,139	8,015	13,122	22,055	48,597
North America	−13,302	8,563	22,428	58,948	95,255	156,896	255,099	468,151	909,331
World	−162	840	2,214	4,493	8,360	14,155	25,123	51,633	138,346

Source: Credit Suisse Research Institute, Global Wealth Databook 2022. https://www.credit-suisse.com/

media/assets/corporate/docs/about-us/research/publications/global-wealth-databook-2022.pdf.

These are threshold estimates to qualify for each of the deciles. Note that there are no estimates for the first decile.

The table shows that the minimum wealth of the different deciles varies greatly across regions. In Africa, for example, the poorest 10% have a maximum wealth of –USD235 per adult. This means that to be in the second-lowest wealth decile, one would have a maximum wealth of –USD235; they are net debtors, with their debts exceeding the value of their assets. In contrast, the wealthiest 10% in Africa have a minimum wealth of USD12,692 per adult.

The maximum wealth of the poorest 10% in North America, similarly, the entry threshold to the second decile of the wealth distribution, is –USD13,302 and is much lower than the maximum wealth of the poorest 10% in Asia Pacific, or –USD213. The minimum wealth of the wealthiest 10% is also much higher in North America than in other regions.

All the data demonstrates the extent of wealth inequality. All countries contain varying degrees of wealth inequality or income inequality. Wealth inequality is different from income inequality because income inequality looks at the distribution of income generated by society, and wealth inequality looks at the economic distribution of assets and their ownership and reinforces wide national wealth gaps.

The **Gini coefficient**, a more broad-based measure of inequality that focuses on the entirety of the wealth spectrum, confirms the skewness of the wealth distribution. It ranges from 0 to 1, where 0 represents perfect equality (everyone gets an equal share of the wealth) and 1 represents perfect inequality (one individual owns all the wealth). It compares the **Lorenz curve**, the cumulative percentage of wealth owned by each percentage of the population, with the line of perfect equality, where wealth is uniformly distributed across the population. Each percentage of the population owns an equal percentage of the wealth. Example 5 looks at how the Gini coefficient captures different types of wealth distribution.

EXAMPLE 5

Gini Coefficient

The Gini coefficient measures wealth inequality in a population. It ranges from 0 to 1, with 0 indicating a perfectly equal wealth distribution and 1 indicating maximum wealth inequality. Here are three examples:

Cumulative percentage of households	Cumulative percentage of wealth		
	Example 1 Perfect wealth distribution Gini coefficient = 0	Example 2 Low degree of wealth inequality Gini coefficient = 0.27	Example 3 High degree of wealth inequality Gini coefficient = 0.69
0%	0%	0%	0%
10%	10%	1%	1%
20%	20%	5%	2%
30%	30%	10%	3%
40%	40%	20%	4%
50%	50%	30%	6%
60%	60%	40%	7%
70%	70%	55%	10%
80%	80%	70%	20%

	Cumulative percentage of wealth		
Cumulative percentage of households	Example 1 Perfect wealth distribution Gini coefficient = 0	Example 2 Low degree of wealth inequality Gini coefficient = 0.27	Example 3 High degree of wealth inequality Gini coefficient = 0.69
90%	90%	85%	50%
100%	100%	100%	100%

Exhibit 14 shows these examples graphically.

Exhibit 14: Gini Coefficient and Wealth Distribution

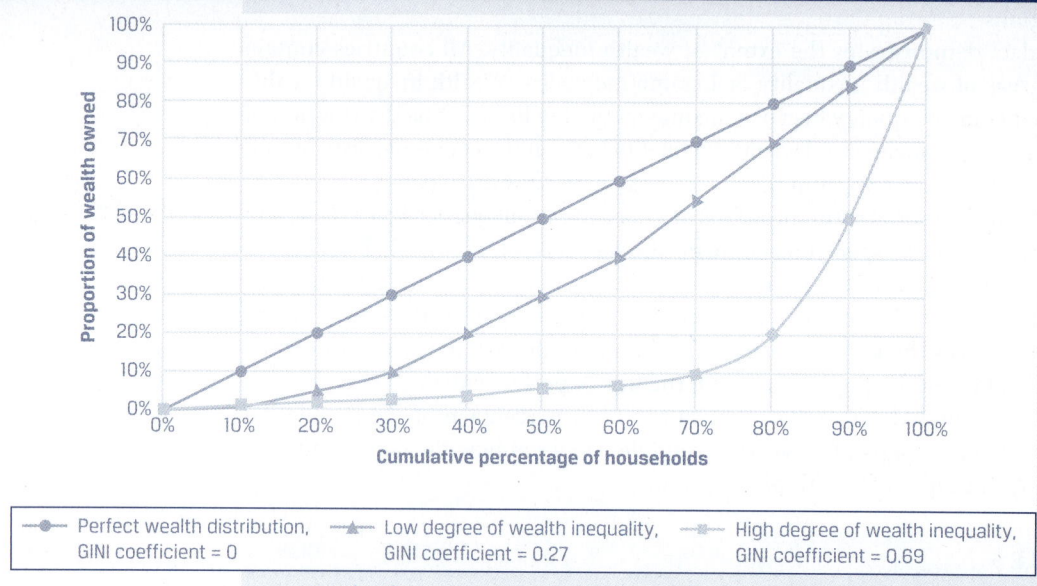

In the first example, the Gini coefficient is 0, which represents a perfectly equal wealth distribution. This means that every household in the population has the same amount of wealth. The area under the Lorenz curve is also 0, which indicates that the cumulative percentage of households and the cumulative percentage of wealth are the same. This can be an ideal situation for a society in terms of wealth equality.

In the second example, the Gini coefficient is 0.27, indicating a low degree of wealth inequality in the population. This means that the distribution of wealth is relatively even across the population, with a small percentage of households holding a disproportionate amount of wealth. The area under the Lorenz curve is also relatively small, indicating a smaller degree of inequality. In this situation, the mean wealth per household provides a more accurate representation of the economic status of the population, as there is less concentration of wealth in a small group of households.

In the third example, the Gini coefficient is 0.69, indicating a high degree of wealth inequality in the population. This means that a small percentage of households have a disproportionate amount of wealth compared to the rest of the population. The area under the Lorenz curve is also relatively large, indicating a large degree of inequality. In this situation, the mean wealth per household does not provide an accurate representation of the economic status of the population, as there is a significant concentration of wealth in a small group of households.

Long-term changes in Gini coefficients reveal trends in wealth inequality. When the Gini coefficients rise over time, wealth inequality worsens. Economic policies, technological advances, and demographic shifts can affect long-term change in Gini coefficients over time, as we can see in Exhibit 15. In a recession or depression, wealth becomes more concentrated among fewer people or households, raising the Gini coefficient. Looking at the global long-term changes between 2000 and 2020, the overall wealth distribution appears to have changed in several countries. Both the global financial crisis and the COVID-19 pandemic impacted wealth inequality. Many individuals in lower and middle income brackets experienced substantial financial hardships, job losses, and economic problems. Wealthier individuals, on average, fared better. The COVID-19 pandemic exacerbated this divide. Individuals in lower income brackets, usually employed in service-based industries, lost their jobs. Wealthier individuals, on the other hand, benefitted from surging stock markets and increased demand in certain technology-centric industries.

Although wealth inequality increased in both developed and developing markets, the gap is greater in the developed markets due to weaker social safety nets and greater income variability.

Exhibit 15: Trends in Gini Coefficients for Selected Countries between 2000 and 2020

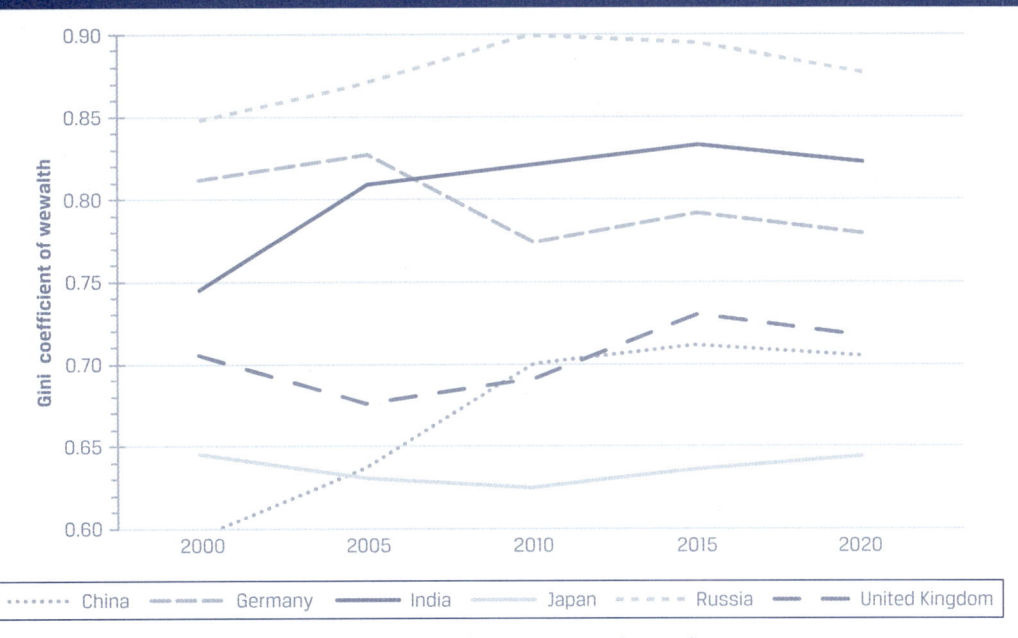

Source: Credit Suisse Research Institute, Global Wealth Databook 2022. Data as of December 31, 2021. https://www.credit-suisse.com/media/assets/corporate/docs/about-us/research/publications/global-wealth-databook-2022.pdf. Reported estimates.

Over time, changes in global wealth inequality reflect both shifts in the wealth inequality within countries and between countries. The rise of household wealth in many emerging markets has pushed overall global wealth inequality down. For instance, between 2000 and 2021, the average wealth in India increased by 9% annually and in China by 15%. At the same time, the average growth rate of wealth across the globe was 5%. The fact that average wealth levels in China are approaching global wealth levels suggests that global wealth distribution is becoming less unequal in aggregate.

Private wealth managers have traditionally categorized clients by wealth levels. Each wealth stratum presents unique demands, challenges, and opportunities from the wealth manager's perspective. These segments typically include mass-affluent and affluent clients in the top decile of the wealth pyramid, as well as wealthier clients such as HNWIs, very-high-net-worth individuals (VHNWIs), and UHNWIs, as shown in Exhibit 16.

Exhibit 16: Wealth Segments and the Number of Individuals (in Thousands) Belonging to Each of These Segments across the Globe

Wealth segment	Wealth range (in million USD)	North America	Europe	Asia Pacific	China	Latin America	India	Africa	World
High net worth (HNWI)	1–5	21,565	15,300	9,859	5,582	809	696	316	54,126
Very high net worth (VHNWI)	5–10	3,360	912	587	366	63	59	24	5,371
	10–50	1,706	442	279	210	38	37	11	2,723
Ultra-high net worth (UHNWI)	50–100	107	27	19	20	3	3	1	180
	100–500	38	14	10	11	2	2	1	77
	500+	2	2	1	1	1	-	-	7

Source: Credit Suisse Research Institute, Global Wealth Databook 2022. Data as of December 31, 2021. https://www.credit-suisse.com/media/assets/corporate/docs/about-us/research/publications/global -wealth-databook-2022.pdf. Numbers are rounded.

However, this segmentation method may not fully capture the sophistication and complexity of the guidance, investment planning, and financial, legal, and tax advice a client requires. Factors such as a client's legal and physical domicile, stage in their financial life cycle, demographics, income, wealth structure, asset class holdings, and values can influence service expectations, which may vary among clients with similar wealth levels.

Private wealth managers prioritize liquid or investable wealth over total wealth, as it provides an initial indication of a client's position in the wealth strata and their current and future service needs. For example, private wealth managers would offer different levels of services to a client with USD50 million that included an investment portfolio of USD3 million and a family business equity worth USD47 million, compared to a client with USD45 million in their investment portfolio and USD5 million in private real estate.

The UHNWI category typically consists of the upper half of decamillionaires, who have a net worth exceeding USD10 million, and includes the centimillionaires, with a net worth surpassing USD100 million. As per *Forbes*' 2022 calculations, there are around 2,300 billionaires worldwide, and to be among the top 500 richest individuals, an estimated net worth of USD5 billion is necessary.

Family offices play a vital role in managing UHNWIs' wealth. These private firms offer a range of wealth management services, including investment, tax, estate planning, and philanthropy management, tailored specifically to UHNWIs and their families' needs. The primary objective of family offices is to preserve and grow wealth across generations while tackling the unique challenges and opportunities associated with significant wealth. By possessing a deeper understanding of a family's values, goals, and legacy objectives, family offices can effectively address the complex financial needs of UHNWIs. This close relationship allows them to develop and execute long-term strategies aligned with the family's vision while navigating the complex legal, tax, and regulatory landscape linked to substantial wealth.

Furthermore, family offices often employ or collaborate with highly specialized professionals, such as legal advisors, accountants, and investment managers, to deliver a holistic wealth management approach. This comprehensive strategy ensures that all aspects of a family's wealth are considered and managed, encompassing investment management, risk mitigation, succession planning, and philanthropic activities. Exhibit 17 illustrates *Bloomberg*'s RICH <GO> function, displaying the richest individuals in the world.

Exhibit 17: RICH <GO> at *Bloomberg* as of October 31, 2023

It is worth looking at the size of the global UHNWI market to assess the potential revenues that accumulated wealth can generate in the following case study.

CASE STUDY

Sizing the Global UHNWI Market

This example estimates the potential revenue for the global UHNWI wealth management market based on assets under management–based fees. For assets between USD50 million and USD100 million, revenue is around 5 bp; for USD100 million and USD500 million, around 1 bp; and for assets over USD500 million, around 0.1 bp.

Region Data as of 2021	Individuals with wealth between USD50 m and 100 m	Individuals with wealth between USD100 m and 500 m	Individuals with wealth above USD500 m	Total number of UHNWIs	% of the world
United States	103,669	35,740	1,726	141,135	53.4
China	20,013	11,411	1,282	32,706	12.4
Germany	6,052	3,354	318	9,724	3.7
Canada	3,472	1,912	123	5,507	2.1
India	3,024	1,750	210	4,984	1.9
Japan	3,373	1,411	88	4,872	1.8
France	3,237	1,314	85	4,636	1.8
Australia	2,947	1,576	109	4,632	1.8
United Kingdom	2,787	1,278	110	4,175	1.6
Italy	2,574	1,253	103	3,930	1.5
Korea	2,450	1,319	117	3,886	1.5
Russia	2,134	1,488	253	3,875	1.5
Switzerland	2,115	987	92	3,194	1.2
Hong Kong SAR	1,790	1,139	127	3,056	1.2
Sweden	1,866	1,019	76	2,961	1.1
Taiwan Region	1,874	912	93	2,879	1.1
Spain	1,509	666	51	2,226	0.8
Brazil	1,238	749	95	2,082	0.8
Singapore	974	570	73	1,617	0.6
Netherlands	1,100	471	28	1,599	0.6

Source: Credit Suisse Research Institute, Global Wealth Databook 2022. Data as of December 31, 2021. https://www.credit-suisse.com/media/assets/corporate/docs/about-us/research/publications/global-wealth-databook-2022.pdf.

To estimate the average wealth within each range, we will use the midpoint of the specified intervals. For the USD50 million to 100 million range, we will use USD75 million as the average, for the USD100 million to 500 million range, USD300 million will serve as the average, and for individuals with wealth exceeding USD500 million, the average wealth is conservatively estimated at USD1 billion. Based on these calculations, the estimated revenue for the top 10 countries is approximately USD7.5 billion, while the combined revenue for all the mentioned countries is around USD8.5 billion.

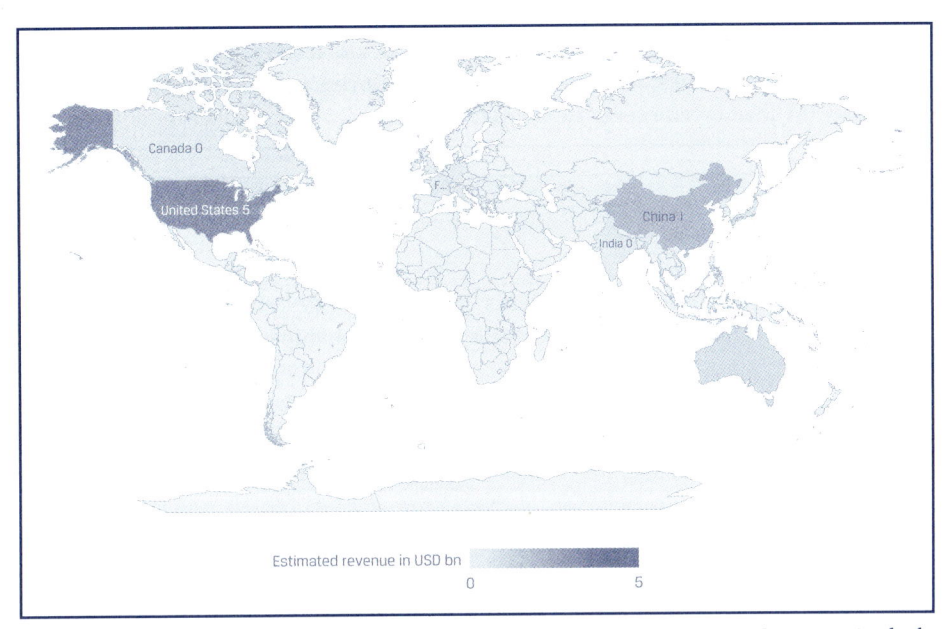

Estimated revenue in USD bn

Wealth inequality is a critical issue in contemporary society. One particularly contentious point centers on the tax obligations of UHNWIs and the phenomenon of wealthy individuals considering the move to tax-friendly jurisdictions.

THE MOBILITY OF HNWIS

Decisions made by HNWIs and their financial advisors significantly impact not only their personal wealth but also the economic and social fabric of their home countries. As wealth mobility increases, balancing the legitimate need for wealth preservation and legal protection with an ethical responsibility of contributing to societal well-being can come to the forefront.

HNWIs might perceive high taxes as unfairly punitive or as diminishing the incentive for wealth creation and entrepreneurial activities, and, consequently, they often consider moving their assets, legal residence, or both to jurisdictions with more tax-friendly policies, "tax havens." However, taxes may not be the only motivator.

Political risk is a significant concern and goes beyond direct expropriations. It can include changes in regulations, legal frameworks, taxation regimes, and discriminatory practices. Deteriorating rule of law and instances of physical violence, such as kidnappings, can all be substantial threats to their wealth and business operations and could compel them to relocate to places offering more legal protection, political stability, and predictability. Moreover, political risk is not limited to developing countries, as populist governments are elected in developed countries, as well.

Investors must consider these factors in their decision-making processes when assessing the situation in their home country, the country where they plan to seek domicile, and the physical and legal locations of their wealth.

Besides legal, economic, and political factors, there may be a crucial aspect wealthy individuals should consider. The wealth many wealthy individuals accumulate is often deeply intertwined with the resources and benefits available in their country. Elements such as the legal framework, the education system, regulatory and political structures, public infrastructure, and educational systems are often funded by taxpayers and play a significant role in creating an environment where businesses and entrepreneurship can thrive and generate wealth. Thus, prosperity often depends directly on the infrastructure and public goods that taxpayers finance.

> When the wealthy leave a country, that could trigger a chain reaction: shrinking tax revenues, reducing public expenditures, and potentially placing a heavier tax load on the remaining citizens.

QUESTION SET

1. Which of the following components of wealth best describes wealth associated with an individual's direct ownership of a business?

   A. Financial wealth

   B. Real wealth

   C. Productive wealth

   Solution:

   C is the correct response. Productive wealth reflects assets that can be used to generate income through production and business operations such as a business directly owned by an individual or a family. A is incorrect. as financial wealth comprises all financial assets but excludes direct ownership of businesses. B is incorrect, as real wealth refers to tangible assets such as real estate and commodities.

2. Contrast an individual's aggregate wealth and net worth.

   Solution:

   Aggregate wealth is the total value of all assets. Net worth reflects the value of assets minus the individual's liabilities. As such, an individual could conceivably have a very large value of assets versus a low net worth. This would happen if an individual were highly levered.

3. Discuss the factors that a private wealth management firm might consider with respect to identifying countries in which individuals are likely to have greater economic opportunities for income and wealth growth.

   Solution:

   Factors associated with greater economic opportunities and wealth growth within countries or regions include (1) technological advancements that contribute to productivity improvements; (2) shifts towards free market capitalism; (3) business privatization (transfers of state-owned assets to private ownership); (4) increases in business formation, especially entrepreneurial ventures that lead to job creation, innovation, and economic growth worldwide; and (5) economic and business deregulation. Additionally, asset price appreciation in real terms is a factor driving wealth growth in countries and regions.

4. Which of the following factors would typically result in a scenario where a region or country is experiencing economic growth, along with improvement in income and wealth inequality?

   A. The regional economy's growth is highly dependent on natural resources.

   B. Significant concentration of control of investable capital within a country.

> **C.** Regulatory effort within a country to dismantle monopoly businesses.
>
> **Solution:**
>
> C is the correct response. A country with a regulatory focus on breaking up monopolies may help promote improvements in income and wealth inequality. Both responses A and B make statements that would be more consistent with higher levels of income and wealth inequality.
>
> 5. A country's Gini coefficient for income distribution is currently 0.35 and was 0.25 10 years earlier. Which of the following responses best describes the level and change of the country's income inequality?
>
>   **A.** Income inequality is relatively low currently and has decreased over the last 10 years.
>
>   **B.** Income inequality is relatively low currently and has increased over the last 10 years.
>
>   **C.** Income inequality is relatively high currently and has improved over the last 10 years.
>
> **Solution:**
>
> B is the correct response. Gini coefficients range from zero to one, with a value of zero reflecting income equality. Income inequality is greater as the Gini coefficient moves higher. With a value closer to zero, 0.35 likely reflects relatively low levels of income inequality. But, as the coefficient has moved higher over the last 10 years, it indicates an increase in income inequality or a decrease in income equality in the country.

LIFE-CYCLE VIEW OF HUMAN CAPITAL

3

☐ | evaluate how changes in human capital, financial capital, and economic net worth across the financial stages of an individual's life influence their financial decision making

Large institutional investors, who typically invest capital on the behalf of their clients, differ from individual investors, who invest their own capital with some of the notable differences outlined in Exhibit 18.

Exhibit 18: Differences between Institutional and Individual Investors

Characteristics	Institutional	Individual
Purpose	Specific	Multiple
Investment objectives	Static	Dynamic
Number of liabilities	Many	Handful
Relative size of individual liabilities	Small	Variable
Time horizon	Long term/infinite	Multiple (for different objectives)
Asset size	Very large	Usually small

Characteristics	Institutional	Individual
Investment options	More access	Less access
Tax situation	Differing, often tax-exempt	Usually taxable and complex
Performance measurement	Index, benchmark	Shortfall meeting a goal or liability
Client sophistication	High	Low to average
Risk	Objective and quantifiable	Failing to meet a specific goal
Customization	Low to medium	High

Institutional investors, such as pension funds, endowments, insurance companies, hedge funds, and investment managers, actively allocate capital to generate returns aligned with their specific investment mandates. Sometimes these objectives are to meet their clients' financial obligations, who may be individual investors seeking long-term capital accumulation by investing with an investment manager.

Institutional investors secure, pool, and manage capital. Some institutional investors, such as pension funds and insurance companies, have long-term obligations towards their clients. These investors design and implement investment strategies to fulfill those obligations over long horizons, oftentimes decades. In executing their strategies, some institutional investors accumulate returns in a tax-aware manner, while others are tax exempt.

Institutional investors measure and evaluate their investment performance against defined indices or benchmarks and use risk measures, such as various measures of volatility, to quantify the risk that they take with client funds. Many large institutional investors have the resources to conduct extensive research and analysis to identify investment opportunities in various markets, sectors, and asset classes. Consequently, they invest across a diverse array of strategies. Here, because of their size, they benefit from economies of scale that reduces their expenses, which they can pass onto their clients. These lower expenses can benefit their clients, who do not have the same capital or professional research capabilities and who are willing to pay a fee to have their assets professionally managed by institutional investors.

Individual investors allocate their own, generally more limited capital to achieve multiple, sometimes conflicting, objectives: growing personal wealth, saving for retirement, buying a car or home, starting a business, or leaving a legacy for their heirs. Their time horizons combine short-, medium-, and long-term objectives. Some of their short-term financial goals may be only a few years away, while their longest-term objectives, such as funding retirement and enabling generational wealth transfer, are typically bookended by the natural human life span. Overall, individual investors manage multiple smaller liabilities, such as saving for a house or retirement, with different certainty throughout their lives. Additionally, these investment objectives (i.e., liabilities) are more likely to change or evolve over time as the family's situation changes. Because their resources are smaller, individuals typically have less access to various investment products or opportunities compared to institutional investors.

Because they are usually taxed on their investment income, capital gains, or dividends, individual investors' decisions may hinge on the tax implications of their investment choices. Since tax rates depend on their tax domicile, tax jurisdiction, and their level of income, individual investors may benefit from having some flexibility to manage the size and timing of their tax obligations. As a result, their tax situations can be more complex than those of institutions. Individual investors gauge their performance by their ability to meet their financial objectives. If they do not fulfill their financial goals or obligations, they have underperformed their objectives. It is worth emphasizing that, despite some of the additional complexities associated with private wealth management, clients are typically less sophisticated in a financial sense than institutional clients.

However, there are some individual investors, particularly UHNWIs, for whom investment strategies, objectives, and resources are more akin to those of a small or medium-size institution than those of an average individual investor. Most UHNWIs have large portions of their portfolios allocated to more complex investment strategies that require scale, such as tax-loss harvesting, and alternative investments such as private equity, infrastructure, and hedge funds that are normally not accessible to the average HNWI.

There are also differences between individual investors domiciled in developed markets and in emerging markets. Apart from the notable differences in wealth levels, distinctions in investment opportunities and market conditions also characterize the two groups. Many emerging market–domiciled investors seek to pursue wealth management services in developed markets to expand their investment alternatives. Conversely, investors domiciled in developed markets may seek out emerging market investment opportunities. Some pertinent differences in investment opportunities between developed and emerging markets are summarized in Exhibit 19.

Exhibit 19: Differences in Investment Opportunities

	Developed markets	Emerging markets
Markets	Large, active markets and multiple different investment alternatives	Smaller markets with limited investment alternatives
Access to information	High	Low
Regulation	Regulated market practices	Less regulated market practices

Compared to investors in emerging markets, individual investors in developed markets tend to have access to larger, active markets with more investment opportunities, have higher access to information, and benefit from more regulated market practices.

Developed markets offer large active financial markets with a range of different investment opportunities and investment alternatives. Their robust financial systems, mature capital markets, and enhanced transparency collectively promote long-term wealth accumulation. The established institutional structure in these markets, including access to premium financial information, grants investors a unique advantage for long-term wealth accumulation. Moreover, regulatory integrity in developed markets safeguards investors, fostering trust in the financial system.

Investors in emerging markets typically can only choose from a more limited array of investment alternatives, and the regulatory support for investments may not be as stringent as in developed markets. In many emerging markets, investors eschew investments in financial markets for familiar investment opportunities, such as private businesses owned by family members and friends, or in tangible assets such as real estate or gold for long-term wealth accumulation. Nonetheless, considering the size and development of emerging markets, there are more and more investors there who seek to diversify their investments.

The Wealth Life Cycle

Financial stages of life are a useful construct when thinking about financial goals, priorities, objectives, and constraints. The financial stages are often divided into seven periods, as Exhibit 20 shows.

Exhibit 20: The Seven Financial Stages of Life

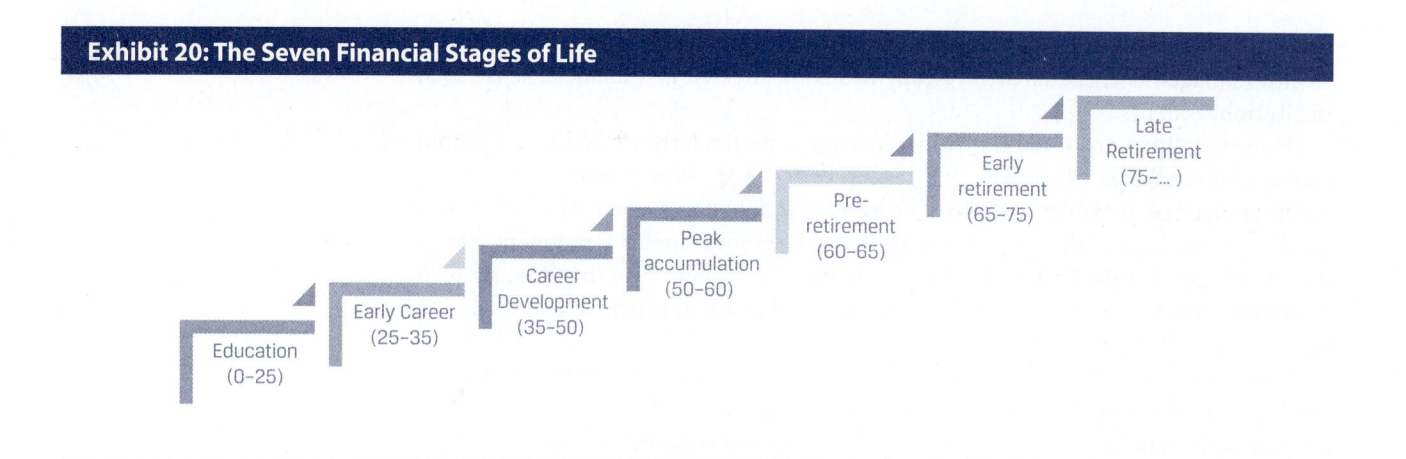

- The *education phase* occurs during the individual's education before entering the workforce. During this phase, individuals may be financially dependent on their parents or guardians and have little accumulated financial capital or focus on savings.

- The *early career phase* normally begins when an individual enters the workforce, usually in their late teens to early thirties. During this phase, individuals may marry, have young children, incur debt to purchase a home, and begin to save for their children's education expenses.

- The *career development phase* typically occurs during the ages of 35–50 and is a time of specific skill development, upward career mobility, and income growth. However, significant family and housing expenses during this phase may limit an individual's ability to save, with human capital representing a large proportion of total wealth.

- The *peak accumulation phase* typically begins during the ages of 50–60, when most people have reached maximum earnings and have the greatest opportunity for wealth accumulation. During this phase, individuals may accumulate funds for other goals and objectives, but retirement income planning and minimizing taxes are usually the primary focus.

- The *pre-retirement phase* consists of the few years preceding the planned retirement age, usually around 65 years of age. It is typically an individual's maximum career income and highest point of wealth accumulation. For those forced to retire due to injury or unemployment, this time may involve changing expectations and adapting to a lifestyle more commensurate with their wealth.

- The *early retirement phase* is the most active period of retirement and is when an individual is less likely to suffer from cognitive or mobility limitations. Even in retirement, it is important to continue taking an appropriate level of investment risk in portfolios to ensure asset growth.

- The *late retirement phase* is a complex phase because of its unknown duration. This uncertainty is known as **longevity risk**, the risk that an individual outlives their financial resources in retirement. Cognitive decline and physical activity and mobility limitations can present risks as well as concerns about the need for long-term health care and the need to care for disabled children.

The earlier part of the reading discussed the role of entrepreneurship in wealth creation. The case study below offers a perspective on how wealth managers can support social entrepreneurs throughout their professional and personal lives.

CASE STUDY

Saffron Threads: How Wealth Managers Support Entrepreneurs throughout Their Life Cycle

Arya is a 28-year-old social entrepreneur who decides to move to a Southeast Asian country to launch a sustainable clothing business, Saffron Threads. The business focuses on producing inclusive-size clothing that is environmentally conscious, while also empowering and educating rural women from marginalized communities.

To start her business, Arya receives initial seed capital from her family, as well as funds secured from the United Nations Development Programme (UNDP) and the International Finance Corporation (IFC). Arya's wealth manager, M.N. Thaler, a leading Swiss wealth management firm, through their network of specialized financial service providers helped her receive crucial financial advice on managing the seed capital, investing in the business, and mitigating risks.

As Arya's business grows, her wealth also increases, reaching CHF5 million. M.N. Thaler advises Arya to diversify her portfolio and raise additional capital for business expansion.

During Arya's peak accumulation phase in her early 50s, Saffron Threads employs hundreds of women, and Arya's wealth grows to CHF15 million. M.N. Thaler assists Arya with approaches that optimize her tax exposure and coordinates employee benefits with her investment and retirement plans.

As Arya enters the pre-retirement phase, her wealth has grown to CHF50 million. This is after selling her business to a private equity firm affiliated with M.N. Thaler. They ensure that the proceeds from the sale are invested wisely, considering Arya's long-term financial goals and retirement plans.

In the early retirement phase, Arya purchases a vineyard in Australia and runs it alongside a restaurant while supporting and empowering women and minorities through her new ventures. Together with M.N. Thaler, Arya explores various impact investing opportunities in Australia, identifying investments that not only generate returns but also make a positive impact on society and the environment.

In the late retirement phase, M.N. Thaler continues to manage Arya's financial resources. They consider the impact of cognitive decline and the potential need for long-term health care, adjusting Arya's investment portfolio and financial strategies accordingly.

Throughout Arya's entrepreneurial journey, M.N. Thaler has been a crucial partner in her financial life cycle, providing tailored services and advice at each stage of her wealth accumulation, business growth, and eventual retirement. Together, they demonstrate the power of impact investing in creating both financial and social returns, contributing to a more sustainable and equitable future.

Exhibit 21 shows the stylized relationship between the different stages of life and the economic wealth of the individual.

Exhibit 21: Wealth Accumulation across the Seven Financial Stages of Life

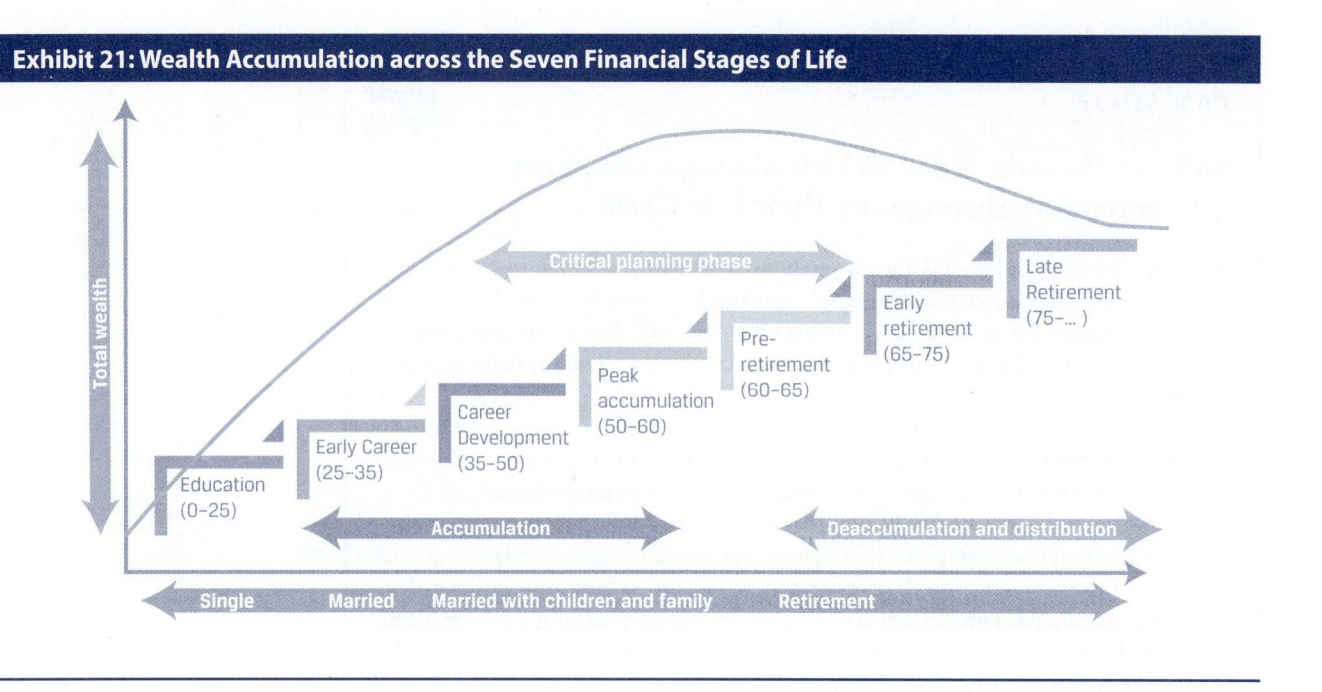

The wealth of an individual changes throughout one's lifetime, as does the underlying asset composition: financial wealth is accumulated as human capital declines. As human capital declines, consumption needs are increasingly met using accumulated financial, real, and personal assets.

The Economic Value of the Individual

Applying a traditional balance sheet view to quantify an individual's assets and liabilities fails to consider two important components: the value of human capital and the present value of future consumption needs.

An individual's **economic balance sheet**, or holistic extended family balance sheet, more comprehensively represents the assets available to fund life-cycle consumption, to preserve wealth, and to transfer wealth during their lifetime and at death. In this context, **surplus** replaces the concept of net worth in the economic balance sheet. It is the difference between the assets including human capital and liabilities including future consumption.

As Exhibit 22 shows, it supplements the traditional balance sheet with the net present value of an individual's expected future earnings and the present value of future consumption. This is particularly important when human capital is a significant share of the individual's overall wealth or when pension assets are considerable.

Exhibit 22: Economic Balance Sheet

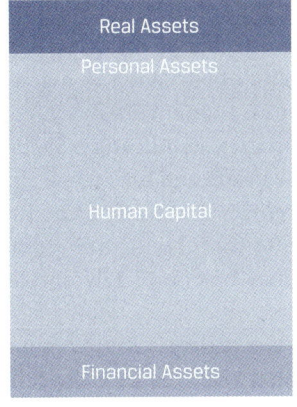

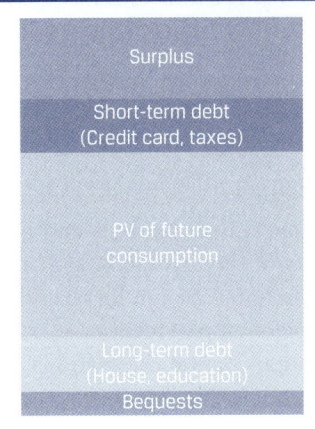

ASSETS

LIABILITIES

KNOWLEDGE CHECK: COMPARING FINANCIAL AND HUMAN CAPITAL

1. Describe human capital and financial capital.

   Solution:

   Human capital is an implied asset commonly defined as the mortality-weighted net present value of an individual's future expected labor income. Financial capital is explicit assets that include the tangible and intangible assets (outside of human capital) owned by an individual or household. For example, a home, a car, stocks, bonds, a vested retirement portfolio, and money in the bank are all examples of an individual's financial capital (or financial assets).

An economic balance sheet quantifies the optimal level of future consumption given nonconsumption goals and the individual's financial and other resources. This form of balance sheet allows an individual to anticipate how available resources can be used in the future to maximize the expected utility of future consumption. Human capital is calculated as the present value of future income streams adjusted by the actuarial probability of survival, wage growth, and a discount rate that reflects occupational income risk, as Equation 1 shows:

$$HC_0 = \sum_{t=1}^{N} \frac{p(s_t)\,w_{t-1}(1+g_t)}{(1+r_f+y)^t} \tag{1}$$

where

   $p(s_t)$ = the probability of surviving to year (or age) t

   w_{t-1} = the income from employment in period $t-1$

   g_t = the annual wage growth rate

   r_f = the nominal risk-free rate

   y = risk premium associated with occupational income volatility

   N = the length of working life in years

Human capital calculations in Equation 1 quantify wealth from all future earnings, $w_{t-1}(1 + g_t)$, an individual is expected to receive over their working lifetime, discounted to its current value, $(1 + r_f + y)^t$. The actuarial probability of survival, $p(s_t)$, refers to the likelihood that an individual will live to a certain age, based on mortality tables and statistical models. Mortality $p(s_t)$ is the probability of surviving to a given year (or age). The risk adjustment, y, based on occupational income volatility recognizes the fact that the income from different professions can vary significantly. Specifically, the overall stability of labor income for government workers and teachers is different from investment bankers and race car drivers. Moreover, it considers the inherent stability of the income stream as well as the possibility that the income stream will be interrupted by job loss, disability, or death that may be completely unrelated to the type of employment.

Human capital calculations quantify wealth, but the reality is more complicated than models. Income levels and growth rates, nominal risk-free rates, specific risk adjustments, and mortality can be modeled but are not easily estimated. The case study below computes human capital for a young professional in the early days of employment.

CASE STUDY

Taylor: Estimating Human Capital

Taylor is the hypothetical example of an early career individual used in the first case study from this reading. This example will illustrate how the relative value of various household assets changes over a lifetime. Taylor is 25 years old and just entered the workforce.

Taylor's initial salary is EUR20,000, which is expected to increase by 1.5% annually in real terms (inflation assumption is 2%) over the planned trajectory of 40 years, making the nominal growth rate, g, equal to approximately 3.5%, or, more specifically, 3.53% (i.e., (1.015) x (1.02) − 1). Since the choice of the career path generates a stable income flow, the income volatility is expected to be 1%. Taylor has no initial financial capital but designates 5% of the annual income into investment and savings.

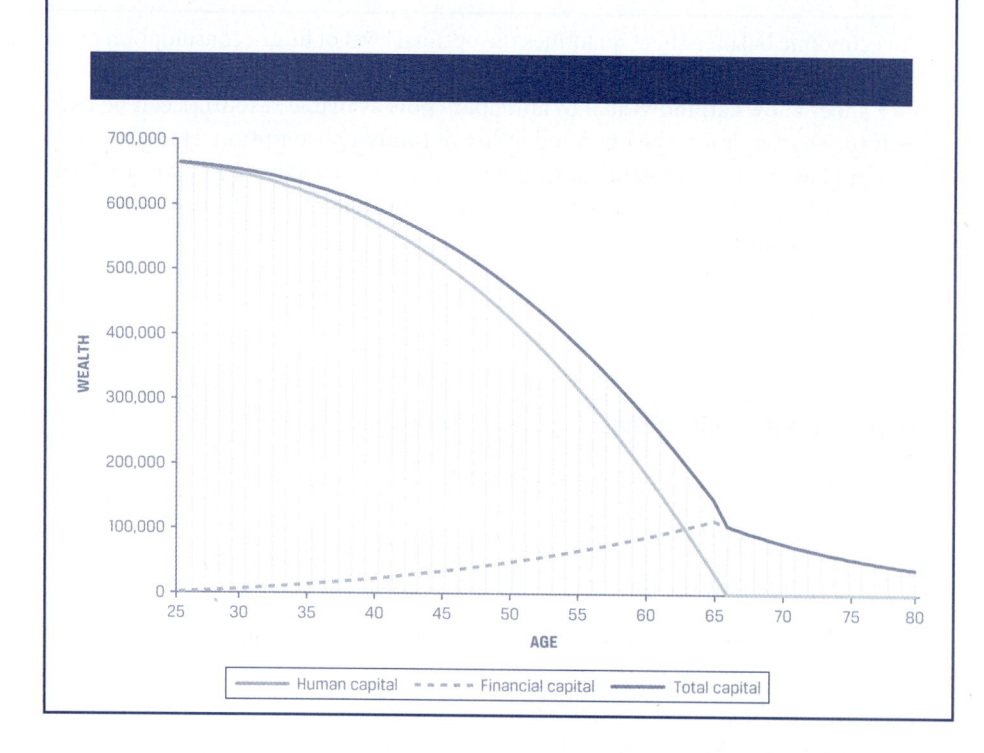

Considering a retirement age of 65 years and 15-year life expectancy beyond that (to 80) with an annual withdrawal of 10% of the available financial capital, the pattern of human capital used is calculated as:

Age	Human capital	Financial capital	Total capital
25	636,156	927	637,082
30	618,751	6,346	625,097
35	589,338	13,288	602,626
40	545,442	22,083	567,524
45	484,421	33,112	517,533
50	403,856	46,795	450,651
55	302,031	63,577	365,609
60	177,905	83,939	261,844
65	31,720	108,372	140,092
70	-	76,003	76,003
75	-	53,302	53,302
80	-	37,382	37,382

Human capital starts high and declines over time, while financial capital begins to accumulate during the working years. The table above provides annual estimates of human capital, financial capital, and total capital. At the start of the year when Taylor turns 25, the human capital is EUR636,156, financial capital amounts to EUR927, and the total capital equals EUR637,082. At the beginning of the year when Taylor turns 65 (or at the conclusion of Taylor's 64th year), the human capital value decreases to EUR31,720. However, the financial capital is EUR108,372, making the total capital amount to EUR140,092.

For the typical individual, the financial capital, or investment portfolio, represents a significant portion of wealth at the beginning of age 65, or retirement. The financial capital is often capital accumulated directly by the individual; a substantive proportion can be retirement savings, which may be self-directed or secured through an employer or a government run pension system. Private wealth management focuses on managing this financial capital.

As individuals progress through their lives, the value of their financial and other investments becomes more significant, particularly as they approach retirement. At this point, people tend to rely more on their investment portfolio to provide them with income in retirement. However, once individuals retire, the relative importance of their investment portfolio typically decreases. Instead, the remaining mortality-weighted net present value of benefits, such as pension benefits and the value of real estate such as their personal residence, become more crucial factors in determining their financial situation in retirement.

The mortality-weighted net present value of benefits is the total expected value of future retirement benefits adjusted for the likelihood of surviving to each future year of receipt and the time value of money. This calculation reflects the probability that individuals will live long enough to receive their retirement benefits and the potential impact of inflation on the value of those benefits. Meanwhile, the value of real estate can be a significant determinant of financial stability in retirement. For example, individuals can use the value of their personal residence to generate additional income by downsizing to a less expensive home or borrowing against the capital built up over the years through reverse mortgages, equity release mortgages, or similar products.

The case study below provides an example in which Taylor's total capital accumulation is estimated with some more realistic conditions: it includes investment in a primary residence and the existence of a pension system. These two are often the greatest sources of an individual's total wealth.

CASE STUDY

Taylor: Estimating Total Capital with Investments and Pensions

Expanding on the previous example, Taylor's purchases a home at age 30 that equals twice the annual income at that age, putting 5% of the value of the home as equity and borrowing the balance over 30 years. The real estate increases in value by 1% annually in real terms. Additionally, Taylor is also the beneficiary of a simple defined benefit pension plan that accumulates each year at 10% of income paid by the employer. The pension payments vest after 10 years. The pension payments during the decumulation phase will be adjusted for inflation.

With these changes, the human wealth is changed as well; more specifically, the trajectory is impacted by the purchase of a home and the accumulation of pension wealth.

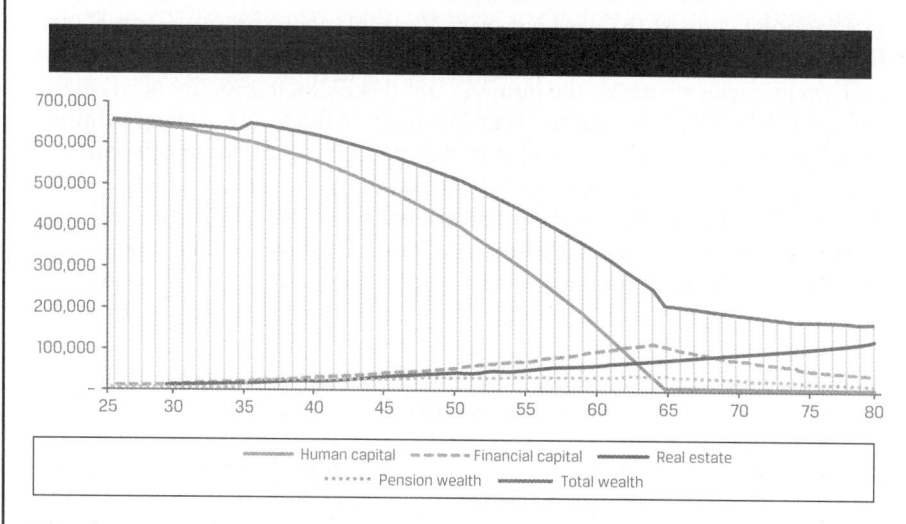

The change in relative wealth across the lifetime demonstrates the importance of real estate and pensions as a source of total wealth.

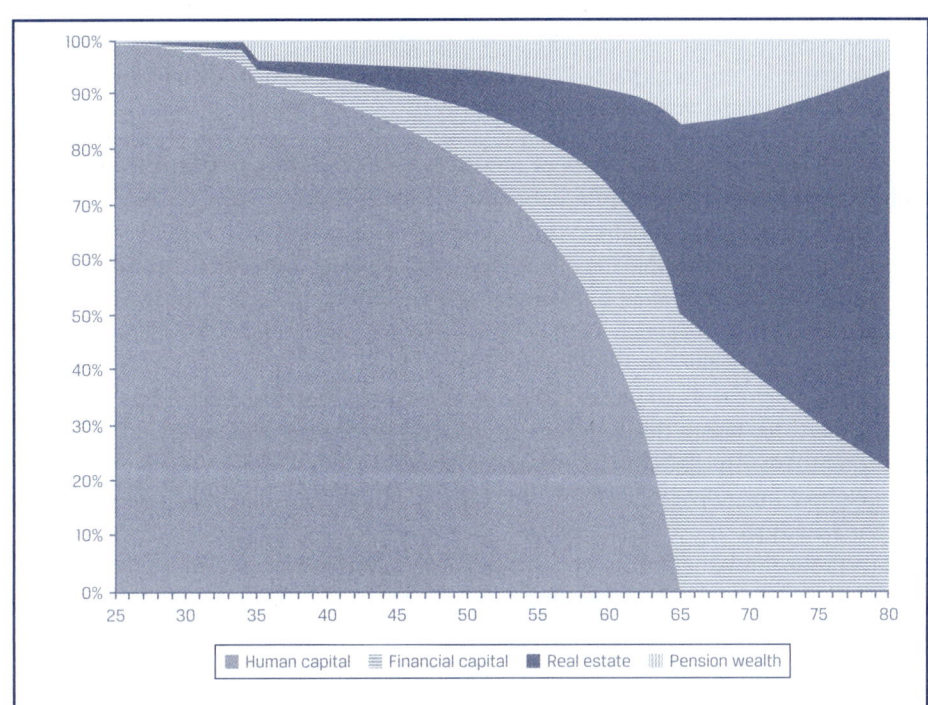

The table below provides annual estimates of human capital, financial capital, real estate value, pension wealth, and total capital.

Age	Human capital	Financial capital	Real estate	Pension wealth	Total wealth
25	636,156	927	0	0	637,082
30	618,751	6,346	2,032	0	627,129
35	589,338	13,288	8,897	20,158	631,681
40	545,442	22,083	16,458	22,095	606,077
45	484,421	33,112	24,767	24,186	566,486
50	403,856	46,795	33,880	26,363	510,894
55	302,031	63,577	43,860	28,473	437,941
60	177,905	83,939	54,768	30,333	346,945
65	31,720	108,372	66,676	31,722	238,490
70	0	76,003	79,656	24,859	180,518
75	0	53,302	93,787	17,487	164,576
80	0	37,382	109,152	9,692	156,226

Pension benefits and real estate investment do not impact Taylor's human capital at 25, which equals EUR637,082. The impact of the pension benefit increases Taylor's total capital when it vests after 10 years of work, at the age of 35. At the beginning of the year when Taylor turns 65 (or at the conclusion of Taylor's 64th year), the human capital value decreases to EUR31,720. However, the financial capital is EUR108,372, the real estate capital EUR66,676, and pension wealth EUR31,722, making the total capital amount to EUR238,490. By allocating some of the human capital income to residential real estate, the total capital at retirement has increased by the equity value of the residence.

> As pension benefits accumulate over time, their relative share increases closer to retirement and is expected to compensate for some of the loss of human capital that comes with retirement.

There are generally two types of pension systems: **defined contribution plans** and **defined benefit plans**. In a defined contribution plan, typically the employee, the employer, or both contribute to the employee's account. The employee assumes investment risk, and the final benefit is based on the performance of their investments. In contrast, in a defined benefit plan, the employer guarantees a monthly retirement benefit based on factors such as the employee's years of service, salary, and age. The employer is responsible for funding the plan and bears the investment risk to ensure there are enough assets to pay the benefits. Most public pension systems are defined benefit plans for which the government determines the benefit levels and bears the investment risk. The stability and predictability of defined benefit plans can reduce the incentive for individuals to save for retirement, as they may rely solely on their pension benefits.

Educational attainment and choice of career alternatives determine the value of human capital. An individual choosing a more lucrative, well-paying career or choosing entrepreneurship may realize a higher human capital. The case study below looks at the benefits of successful entrepreneurship, which is one of the main sources of wealth that is being created, and human capital.

CASE STUDY

Taylor: Entrepreneurship and Human Capital

Expanding on the previous examples, let us assume that Taylor decides to pursue a different career path: entrepreneurship. In exchange for a lower and more stable income stream from full time employment, Taylor, as an entrepreneur, expects to accumulate greater wealth at the expense of greater certainty and income stability.

This higher expected value and income volatility influences the aggregate wealth accumulation through greater estimated cash flows and higher discount rates and thus influences the value of human capital. The business grows rapidly and steadily. And, instead of retiring at age 65, Taylor sells the business and rolls over the proceeds into financial capital to use together with other accumulated pension wealth to finance consumption during the remainder of life. With these changes, total wealth is changed, as well.

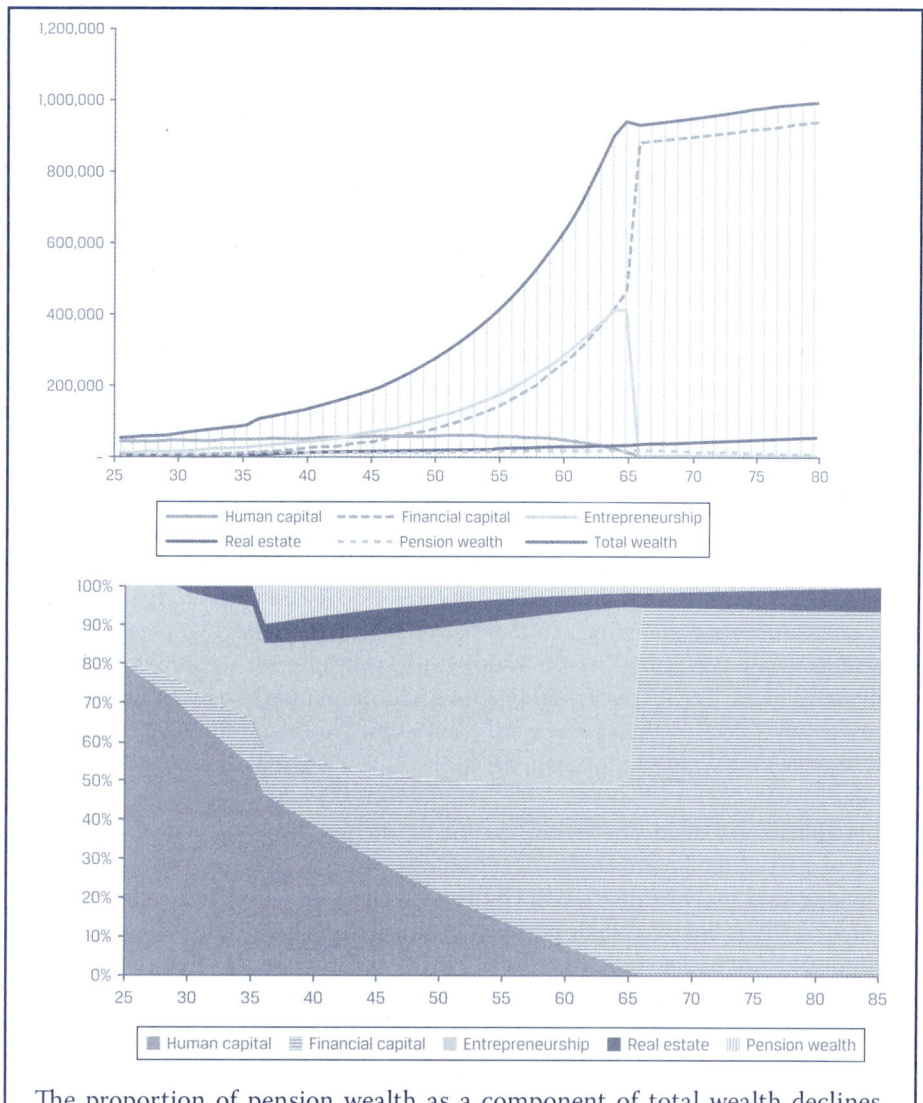

The proportion of pension wealth as a component of total wealth declines, and the considerable financial wealth that comes from the liquidation of the entrepreneurial activities continues to increase in value throughout the life.

For affluent individuals, pension wealth usually constitutes a small portion of their total wealth portfolio during retirement. The proportion of pension wealth in an individual's overall wealth portfolio depends on their unique circumstances. For instance, a 45-year-old full-time employee with EUR5 million in human capital, EUR1 million in pension benefits, and EUR1 million in financial assets will have different investment options compared to a 45-year-old entrepreneur with EUR10 million in human capital invested in their business, EUR1 million in pension benefits, and EUR1 million in financial assets.

The full-time employee's human capital is linked to their salary income, which is generally stable and predictable, while the entrepreneur's human capital is tied to their business, which has more uncertain and unpredictable cash flows. The volatility and growth of income in human capital calculations seeks to account for this difference. To diversify their human capital, pension benefits, and financial assets, individuals mainly have control over how their financial portfolios are invested and allocated. Consequently, during the accumulation phase, they should seek to allocate their investment portfolio to diversify their income and risk from human capital.

During the accumulation phase, a full-time employee with stable salary income should have an investment portfolio that balances the relative stability of their salary income and human capital through higher allocations to equities. In contrast, an entrepreneur's income from their business is more volatile and often more exposed to risks of a particular industry or sector, so their investment portfolio allocation should reflect these differences in risk and have a strong fixed-income allocation and, perhaps, relatively greater exposure to industries less correlated with their human capital.

This also has implications for the decumulation phase. For instance, in 20 years' time, the now 65-year-old retired employee and 65-year-old retired entrepreneur from the previous example will have different spending patterns throughout the rest of their lives. The retired employee, who has EUR4 million in wealth split evenly between financial wealth and pension wealth, will have different options compared to the retired entrepreneur, who possesses EUR40 million in financial wealth and EUR2 million in pension wealth. The retired employee will depend on their pension wealth, which needs to generate income for the remainder of their lifetime. As a result, their portfolio must both produce income and maintain purchasing power.

On the other hand, the pension wealth makes up a smaller portion of the entrepreneur's total wealth and therefore has limited influence on their ability to maintain their post-retirement spending for the rest of their life. Generally, pension wealth represents a low percentage of the total wealth portfolio for wealthier individuals during retirement. The focus of their portfolio allocation may be less about generating income to cover costs in their retirement years and more about fulfilling philanthropic goals, transferring wealth to future generations, and achieving other long-term financial objectives.

Individuals will need to consider means to safeguard the value of their pension wealth as part of the financial planning process. For example, a pension plan from a private employer may be impacted by company-specific risk, just like an entrepreneur's personal wealth is linked to their business. A private pension plan can be terminated, and a government backed public pension system can face shortfalls that cannot be met through increased taxes and contributions, all of which that can imperil the likelihood of repayment. The broad risk of insolvency is a significant concern that could lead to the loss of the benefits from an employer-based pension plan or an entrepreneur's financial wealth.

To reduce this risk from such equity-like or equity-linked sources of wealth, such as from a privately held business, investments in fixed-income instruments can be a viable option. However, this involves a trade-off between higher yet volatile returns and lower yet safer returns. Individuals need to determine whether this aligns with their financial objectives.

While the investment portfolio holds substantial importance for the typical individual at age 65 or retirement, it still represents less than 50% of the total economic wealth when considering other factors such as home equity, pension wealth, and human capital. As individuals move through retirement and spend their funds, the investment portfolio's relative share decreases. The remaining mortality-weighted net present value of benefits and real estate value, such as the individual's home, become the primary factors determining their financial situation during retirement.

While human capital calculations provide a framework for quantifying wealth, it is important to note that reality is more complex than models. For instance, estimating income levels and growth rates, nominal risk-free rates, specific risk adjustments, and mortality can be challenging. Particularly in the early stages of the life cycle, the potential loss of human capital is a significant risk factor.

QUESTION SET

1. Contrast performance measurement and the definition of risk for institutional investors and the typical individual investor.

   Solution:

   Institutional investors measure performance relative to defined indices or benchmarks, while individual investors assess performance based on the attainment of specific financial goals. For an institutional investor, a portfolio underperforms if its performance is less than the stated index or set benchmark. Institutional investors define risk with quantitative measures, such as volatility, beta, and so on. For an individual investor, a portfolio underperforms if the performance does not sufficiently meet a set goal. Individual investors define risk by the likelihood and consequences of failing to meet specific financial goals. Hence, risk and performance are closely linked.

2. Which of the following statements accurately characterizes the comparison between developed and emerging financial markets based on the given text?

   A. Both developed and emerging markets offer a similar array of investment opportunities and regulatory support for investments.

   B. Developed markets offer larger active financial markets and more stringent regulatory support compared to emerging markets.

   C. Emerging markets typically offer more diverse investment alternatives and better access to high quality financial information than developed markets.

   Solution:

   B is the correct response. Developed markets offer a wider range of investment alternatives and have a more stringent regulatory framework. This allows for a broader spectrum of investment choices and promotes trust in the financial system, offering investors a unique advantage for long-term wealth accumulation.

   Both statements A and C are incorrect. Developed markets offer a larger variety of investment opportunities and more robust regulatory support than emerging markets. Developed markets also offer better access to high-quality financial information. Also, emerging markets are characterized by a more limited array of investment alternatives compared to developed markets.

3. At what stage of the wealth life cycle does accumulated or total wealth typically achieve its maximum level?

   A. Peak accumulation

   B. Pre-retirement

   C. Early retirement

   Solution:

   B is the correct response. Pre-retirement years (typically from age 60–65) should be the period in which wealth reaches its maximum. Answer A is not correct, as wealth continues to grow during the peak accumulation years, and answer C is not correct, as the period of wealth deaccumulation begins at early retirement.

> 4. Contrast the most appropriate portfolio allocations to equities and fixed-income securities for the following two individuals in the accumulation phase of their wealth life cycles: an individual who works in a government job with stable income characteristics, and an individual who is pursuing an entrepreneurial career.
>
> **Solution:**
>
> The individual working in a government job with stable income characteristics is likely to allocate more to risky equity securities in their portfolio allocation as compared to the individual pursuing an entrepreneurial career. The entrepreneur's riskier future income stream is likely to cause a larger allocation to fixed-income securities as compared to the individual pursuing a government career with a less risky future income stream.

4   INDIVIDUAL INVESTORS: RETURN, RISK, AND OTHER OBJECTIVES AND CONSTRAINTS

☐   justify how returns, risks, objectives, and constraints for individuals relate to their human and financial capital

Nominal and Inflation-Adjusted Returns

For long-term individual investors, especially those saving for retirement, safeguarding their long-term purchasing power is more crucial than focusing solely on nominal returns. By considering purchasing power–adjusted returns, investors can make well-informed decisions about their investments and ensure that their financial objectives are achieved. The influence of inflation on investment returns can differ based on the investment horizon, and neglecting it may result in inaccurate conclusions about an investment's performance.

The fact that inflation diminishes the purchasing power of capital has significant consequences for investment management, portfolio construction, and purchasing power adjusted wealth accumulation. In the short term, inflation reduces purchasing power, affecting the value of returns and principal investments. Rising inflation rates can hinder individual investors' ability to invest effectively. Over the long term, the impact of inflation compounds, potentially leading to a significant decrease in the real, purchasing power– adjusted value of investments and potentially impeding individuals' capacity to accumulate enough wealth to meet their long-term financial goals or needs. For those in the decumulation phase who depend on their accumulated capital as their primary income source, investment returns that do not outpace inflation will result in a decline in their purchasing power. To protect against inflation, investors usually consider assets such as equities, real estate, and commodities, which have historically produced returns that surpass long-term inflation rates.

It is important to distinguish between beating inflation and hedging against inflation. Assets like equities over long periods tend to provide a return that outpaces inflation: the average annual return of the stock market over the past several decades has generally outperformed inflation. Equities perform especially well in real terms when inflation is low. However, equities can be quite volatile in the short term, and their returns may not outpace increasing or persistent inflation. Additionally, commodities, such as oil and gold, can see their prices outperform during inflationary periods but can also be seen to contribute to increased inflation. Hence, investing in these assets could be, at least for shorter periods, considered as a hedge against inflation. However, they do not always outperform persistent inflation, and their prices can, at times, be quite volatile.

Inflation-protected bonds issued by governments link the return to inflation and are designed to keep pace with inflation. Despite the existence of such **inflation-linked bonds**, most fixed-income instruments are not inflation linked. Additionally, real estate can serve as a hedge against inflation because the value of properties tends to rise over time along with the general price level. As inflation leads to a general increase in prices, the price of real estate often increases, as landlords may increase rents over time to keep up with inflation. This increasing income stream can keep pace with rising prices, but that is not always the case. Real estate prices can sometimes stagnate or even decrease during inflationary periods because of factors such as general economic uncertainty.

Risks

Individual investors face different types of risks that can affect their investment outcomes such as asset price and return volatility, drawdown risk, and the risk of not achieving financial objectives.

- Return volatility refers to the fluctuations in the value and returns of an investment over time and captures the likelihood that an investment may decline in value because of changes in market conditions, economic factors, or company-specific events. It impacts all asset classes.

- Drawdown risk is the risk of experiencing losses because of a decline in the value of an investment over a specific period and is the difference between the investment's peak value and its lowest point during a market downturn. This can be material either when an investor benchmarks the portfolio against achieving a certain financial goal and objective, or when an investor is forced to realize a loss. An investor who buys an exchange-traded fund (ETF) for ZAR90,000 that subsequently increases in value to ZAR100,000 and then drops in value to ZAR80,000 experiences a drawdown of ZAR20,000. A drawdown is not a realized loss; rather, it is a decline in value, a paper loss. A realized loss would only occur if the investor sold the ETF or if the ETF were used as collateral for a loan and there were suddenly a collateral shortfall that the investor could not address. The investor would then be forced to liquidate the asset to remain compliant with the loan covenants.

- The risk of not achieving financial objectives refers to the possibility that an investor will not achieve their planned financial goals because of a combination of possible factors including return shortfalls, market environment, and economic conditions, or because the investor did not dedicate enough capital to meet the goals.

Investors can reduce the impact of volatility and drawdown risk by diversifying across a range of different asset classes. All investors should review and adjust their investment strategies, portfolios, and asset allocations regularly, but it is particularly important for individual investors for whom the inherent risk is not achieving set financial objectives. For individual investors, inflation is a critical factor to consider when assessing the risk of not achieving financial objectives — meeting income needs. Purchasing power–adjusted returns also affect the volatility of an investment, as changes in inflation rates can impact market conditions and asset values and may also affect drawdown risk, as inflation can reduce the inflation-adjusted value of an investment.

Evaluating a private client's risk tolerance is a key step in the information-gathering process. The term risk tolerance usually describes a set of risk-related concepts. The following are some key terms used in this context:

- **Risk tolerance** refers to the level of risk an individual is willing and able to bear. Differently put, risk tolerance is the willingness to engage in a risky behavior in which possible outcomes can be negative. Risk tolerance is related to **risk aversion**, which is the degree of an investor's *unwillingness* to take risk.

- **Risk capacity** is the ability to bear financial risk. The key difference between risk capacity and risk tolerance is that risk capacity is more objective in nature, while risk tolerance relates to an attitude. Risk capacity is determined by the client's wealth, income, investment time horizon, liquidity needs, and other relevant factors. Clients with greater risk capacity can tolerate greater financial losses without compromising current or future consumption goals.

- Risk perception is the subjective assessment of the risk involved in the outcome of an investment decision. Unlike risk tolerance, risk perception — how a client perceives the riskiness of an investment decision or the investment climate — depends on the circumstances involved. Consequently, a wealth manager can help shape a client's risk perception. Risk perception varies considerably across individuals.

In practice, wealth managers often utilize questionnaires to assess clients' risk tolerances. The result of a risk tolerance questionnaire, typically a numerical score, is often used as an input in the investment planning process. The questionnaire in Exhibit 23 provides some common types of questions that may be found on a risk tolerance questionnaire.

Exhibit 23: Sample Questions from a Risk Tolerance Questionnaire

1. When you make investment decisions, on which of the following do you tend to focus?
   a. Always on the potential for gain
   b. Usually on the potential for gain
   c. Always on the potential for loss
   d. Usually on the potential for loss

2. Compared to your friends and family, are you:
   a. less willing to take risk?
   b. equally willing to take risk?
   c. more willing to take risk?

3. What potential percentage decline in your investment portfolio value over a one-year period are you willing to experience?
   a. 5%
   b. 10%
   c. 20%
   d. 30%
   e. More than 30%

4. Which of the following statements best describes your attitude about the performance of your investment portfolio over the next year?

    a. I can tolerate a substantial loss.

    b. I can tolerate a loss.

    c. I can tolerate a small loss.

    d. I would have a hard time tolerating a loss of any magnitude.

5. Suppose that you have made an investment that, because of a sudden broad market decline, has declined in price by 25%. Which of the following actions would you take?

    a. Sell all of the investment

    b. Sell a portion of the investment

    c. Hold the investment (take no action)

    d. Buy more of the investment

6. Suppose that you have access to two types of investments: one investment with low risk and low expected return and one with high risk and high expected return. Which of the following portfolio mixes would you select?

    a. 100% low risk/low return

    b. 75% low risk/low return and 25% high risk/high return

    c. 50% low risk/low return and 50% high risk/high return

    d. 25% low risk/low return and 75% high risk/high return

    e. 100% high risk/high return

7. Suppose that you are offered employment that involves the choice of a fixed salary, variable compensation that could be higher or lower than the fixed salary, or some mix of the two. Which of the following would you choose?

    a. Entirely fixed salary

    b. Mostly fixed salary

    c. Entirely variable compensation

    d. Mostly variable compensation

    e. An equal mix of the two

8. Which of the following best characterizes the time horizon for your primary investment goal?

    a. Less than 3 years

    b. 3 to 8 years

    c. 9 to15 years

    d. 16 to 20 years

    e. Greater than 20 years

Risk tolerance questionnaires have limitations. It is also unclear if they can accurately predict investor behavior. Relying solely on the results of such questionnaires to recommend investments or asset allocations for a client demands significant judgment and inevitably involves some guesswork by wealth managers. Academic research suggests that client questionnaires are highly subjective, which can lead to the manager's own risk perceptions influencing investment decision making on behalf of clients. Furthermore, studies have shown that the sequence and structure of questions can directly affect the responses.

The way losses are presented, either as a percentage (relative loss) or a currency amount (absolute loss), can result in different responses from the same person. Moreover, a question involving a small absolute loss on a smaller portfolio might elicit a different reaction compared to a question involving a large absolute loss on a larger portfolio, even if the relative losses are identical.

Risk tolerance conversations, which are more difficult to conduct than administering questionnaires, are more suitable for higher net worth clients and can yield valuable insights into the individual's risk tolerance, such as

- How much are the client's financial decisions influenced by friends or family members?

- What financial experiences have shaped the client's perspective? Individuals who lived through deep recessions, even in childhood, may bring that perspective to present-day investment decisions.

- What are the client's past (notable) investment mistakes and (celebrated) successes?

- What are the sources of the client's investment wealth? Individuals could achieve wealth through saving, investments, speculation, inheritance, business activities, a liquidity event (such as selling a privately held business), substantial real estate holdings, other less liquid assets (such as collectibles), or a combination of these various sources.

- How does the client evaluate investment risk? Individuals can think about investment losses in absolute or percentage terms.

Risk tolerance discussions enable wealth managers to educate clients about investment risks. A wealth manager may present a client with an array of portfolio options, each having different expected returns and expected levels of volatility. The client's selection from these options offers insights into their risk tolerance. This process is dynamic, as educating the client and gathering their feedback can reveal valuable information about their investment approach that may not be apparent from a risk tolerance questionnaire or a personality type assessment. Additionally, the dynamic aspect of risk tolerance conversations offers the client opportunities to learn about the complexities of investing and the associated risks.

Objectives

To this point, we have discussed a client's overall risk tolerance. Because clients often have multiple goals or objectives, their risk tolerance may vary for different goals. For example, a client may have a low risk tolerance with respect to larger near-term goals but a higher risk tolerance when it comes to longer-term goals. A challenge for wealth managers in managing client relationships is to satisfactorily address potentially conflicting risk tolerance levels.

Wealth managers assist their customers in formulating, prioritizing, and implementing their financial objectives, which may span a range of needs and desires, through goal prioritization and the implementation of investment strategies. Rather than being a one-time exercise, identifying client goals is an ongoing communication between wealth manager and client.

- **Planned goals** are those financial objectives that can be reasonably estimated or quantified at the onset and can be achieved within an expected time horizon. Such planned goals typically include retirement, specific purchases such as a primary residence, vehicle, or luxury item, family events such as weddings, education such as college or professional education, wealth transfer through gifts and bequests, and philanthropy.

- **Unplanned goals** are those related to unforeseen financial needs, and as such they are more difficult to quantify than planned goals because either the funding need or the timing of the financial need or both may not be estimated. Such unplanned goals typically include unexpected expenses such as property repairs that insurance may not cover fully, medical expenses not covered by the health care system or medical insurance, and similar expenses.

Planning for goals is among the more challenging areas of a client's financial profile, as they are sometimes poorly articulated. By quantifying goals, prioritizing goals, and adjusting to changing goals, wealth managers directly assist clients in identifying these financial objectives. For instance, the manager may conclude that a client's clearly stated retirement goals are unfeasible based on their assessment. In this case, the manager has the chance to develop specific, more realistic, and achievable client goals, which can further help the client quantify each goal and develop appropriate plans.

Wealth managers also assist clients with setting priorities when they have multiple parallel and conflicting objectives, such as launching a new business, purchasing a second home, and retiring to Provence, as illustrated in the case study below. A wealth manager should conduct periodic reviews of the client's financial circumstances, including their financial goals, in order to modify an investment strategy if there is any significant change in the goals and circumstances.

CASE STUDY

C.Y. Lee: Client Goals

Mr. C.Y. Lee is a managing director for the investment firm Acme & Bass, which is located in the Asia-Pacific region. Lee is 40 years old, is married, and has two children, ages 12 and 10. He and his family reside in a home that they own in Singapore. In a conversation with his wealth manager, Lee states that he wishes to fund the undergraduate tuition for his children to study abroad. Lee expects the tuition cost to be approximately GBP40,000 per child per year and annual living expenses an additional GBP40,000, or approximately a total of GBP640,000. Lee also wishes to fund his children's weddings at some point in the future. Lee also wants to provide for his and his wife's elderly and infirm relatives. Additionally, Lee is also concerned about the future health care expenses of his wife's parents and to what degree he and his wife may need to support them financially.

Because the education costs will occur in the next 5–10 years, Mr. Lee states that they are his top priority. The secondary goal is to provide financially for the welfare of their elderly relatives.

Lee anticipates working until age 65 and does not know how much he and his wife will need to fund their retirement lifestyle. He mentions his desire to purchase a flat in London and let (rent) it as part of their retirement plan. The flat would cost approximately GBP5 million.

Questions:

1. Identify Lee's planned goals.

   Answer:

   Lee's planned goals are (a) funding his children's education, (b) funding his children's weddings, (c) funding his and his wife's retirement, (d) purchasing and subsequently letting (renting) a flat in London, and e) providing financially for the welfare of elderly relatives.

2. Identify Lee's unplanned goals.

   Answer:

   Lee's unplanned goals relate to the future health care expenses of his wife's parents, as well as possible uninsured property repairs for the Lee's Singapore residence and, if purchased, their London flat.

3. Discuss the issue of goal quantification for Lee.

   Answer:

   Lee has quantified the education funding goal and the flat purchase. He and his wealth manager should work to estimate the cost of the weddings for Lee's children, the anticipated retirement lifestyle needs for Lee and his wife, and the cost of providing for the welfare of their elderly relatives. Understandably, the health care cost quantification may be difficult to achieve.

4. Discuss the issue of goal prioritization for Lee.

   Answer:

   Lee states that his first priority is education funding for his children. However, the timing of a need should not be the sole determinant of goal priority. If funding their children's education costs will leave Lee and his wife unprepared for retirement, for example, they may wish to reevaluate their priorities.

QUESTION SET

1. What distinguishes risk tolerance from risk capacity?

   Solution:

   Risk tolerance focuses on the willingness of the investor to take on risk, and if risk is taken on, the appropriate level of compensation is expected for the level of risk. Risk capacity focuses on how much investors can put at risk without affecting their current or future consumption.

2. Which of the following asset classes is least likely to provide protection against inflation?

   A. Equity securities

   B. Inflation-linked bonds

   C. Fixed-income securities

   Solution:

   C is the correct response. Fixed-income securities, except for inflation-linked bonds, are not considered as providing potential for inflation protections. The value of cash flows of fixed-income securities declines, in present value terms, as discount rates rise during periods of inflation. Because of this feature of fixed-income securities, they likely do not provide inflation protection.

   A is incorrect because equities are noted specifically for their ability to not only provide some degree of inflation protection but also to potentially provide returns that outpace inflation over the long term.

B is incorrect because inflation-linked bonds are structured to provide incremental cash flows that adjust with the inflation rate, so they are likely to provide protection against inflation.

3. Differentiate between an asset used as an inflation hedge and an asset that outpaces inflation in an investment strategy.

Solution:

An asset used as an inflation hedge protects the purchasing power during periods of inflation as their value or returns increase in line with or close to the inflation rate. Inflation-linked bonds may protect against inflation, but they do not necessarily provide real growth in value. An asset that outpaces inflation is expected to not only maintain its value during inflationary periods but also increase in value at a rate higher than the rate of inflation. Typically, equities, or stocks, fall into this category; however, this may not always be the case. Individual companies and broader market indexes can exhibit different behaviors, as some companies can often pass increased costs on to consumers during inflationary periods, leading to increased profits and thus increased stock prices. However, the overall market performance can lag, particularly when inflation is persistently high.

4. An individual investor is assessing three different risky investment portfolios with the following expected characteristics:

   - Portfolio A has an expected return of 8% with volatility of 20%.
   - Portfolio B has an expected return of 9% with volatility of 25%.
   - Portfolio C has an expected return of 10% with volatility of 30%.

   The risk-free rate is 4%. This investor can take on the risk associated with the highest risk portfolio and has been assessed as having low risk aversion. The investor chooses Portfolio A. Which one of the following concepts can lead the investor to choose Portfolio A?

   A. Risk tolerance
   B. Risk capacity
   C. Risk perception

   Solution:

   C is the correct response. Even though each of the portfolios offers the same return-to-risk trade-off (Sharpe ratio of each portfolio is 0.2), the investor has chosen the portfolio with the lowest risk. This choice implies that the investor has a subjective assessment (i.e., perception) that the higher risk portfolios are not attractive.

   A is incorrect because low risk aversion reflects high risk tolerance. B is incorrect because the investor has the capacity to invest in the highest risk portfolio.

5. A 40-year-old individual investor meets with a financial advisor and discusses two specific goals: university education for her two children (ages 6 and 8) and her retirement at age 60. She is very specific with her advisor that her children have the financial means to attend a top-tier private university. On the other hand, she is willing to accept a wide range of acceptable income

> levels during her retirement. Evaluate this investor's risk tolerance with respect to the two investment objectives discussed with the adviser.
>
> **Solution:**
>
> This investor is more likely to have lower risk tolerance with respect to meeting the goal of funding her children's future education expenses. Because she has a very specific type of institution in mind, her tolerance for not meeting this objective is likely low. On the other hand, she seems to be willing to accept a wide range of possible income levels in retirement, so her risk tolerance is likely to be high for this objective.

5 THE IMPACT OF TAXATION AND INFLATION

☐   evaluate how various types of taxes imposed on individual investors and the impact of inflation influence investment decisions

This section focuses on taxes that most directly affect tax planning for investments: specifically, taxes on investment income to individuals.

The tax systems in many countries are designed to encourage or discourage certain activities through tax incentives. Tax structures vary globally and can change as the needs and objectives of the governmental jurisdiction change. As the environment is dynamic, investment managers must comprehend the effects of various tax structures on investment returns and wealth. Instead of outlining specific country tax rules, this reading offers a framework to help managers understand and implement investment strategies in a changing environment where dissimilar tax situations may apply to different clients and clients' tax environments may shift over time.

In most tax jurisdictions, a tax rate structure is applied to ordinary income such as earnings from employment. Special categories of income, such as investment income (sometimes referred to as capital income for tax purposes), may be subject to other tax rates. Investment income (e.g., interest, dividends, distributions, or capital gains) is frequently taxed differently depending on the type of income and losses.

Exhibit 24 shows a simple and highly generalized schematic of how different components of investment returns can be taxed. Some components may be taxed as part of ordinary income, while others may be taxed at more advantageous rates. Certainly, investment income can also be taxed at a higher rate. Note that countries may choose to tax investment income separately from ordinary income and apply tax rates different from ordinary income tax rates. For example, as the right side of Exhibit 24 shows, dividends could be subject to a reduced tax rate or excluded from taxable income altogether.

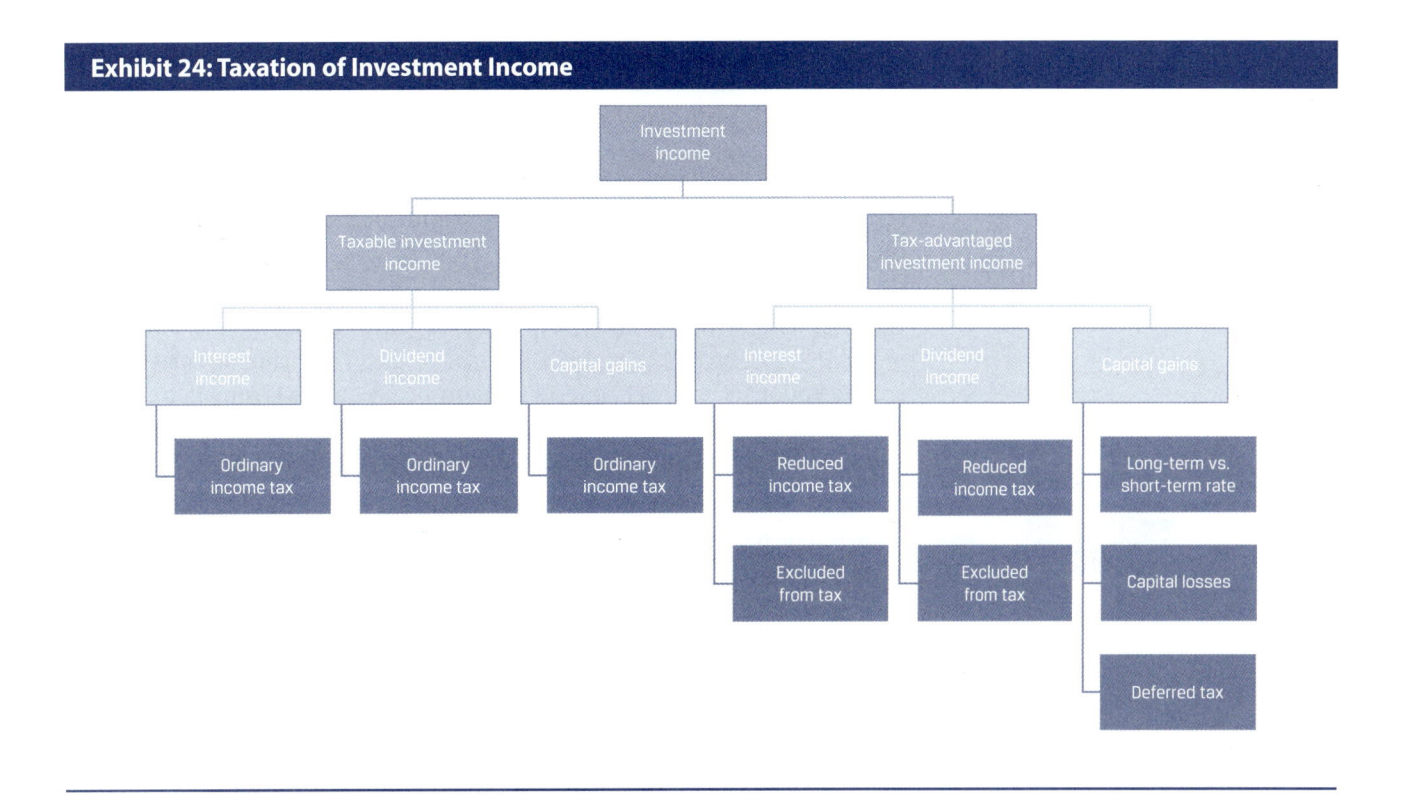

Exhibit 24: Taxation of Investment Income

- *Investment income* is often taxed based on the nature of the income: interest, dividends, or realized capital gains and losses.

- *Interest income and dividends* are typically taxed in the year they are received or on an annual basis. Some jurisdictions exclude certain types of interest income from taxation; others tax dividend income more advantageously.

- *Capital gains tax* is typically triggered when the asset is sold at an appreciated value. Some systems recognize the impact of capital losses, which can be used to offset capital gains taxes. Additionally, many systems allow for deferring the payment of capital income tax until a later date, which is a valuable option for the investor.

Most countries and their tax systems build on a progressive tax rate structure, in which higher income levels are taxed at increasingly higher rates. There are some countries where the tax system is flat, in which all income is taxed at the same rate regardless of the total income earned.

Taxes on Investment Income

Some tax systems tax investment incomes at the tax rates applicable to ordinary income (ordinary rates) unless special provisions exist that reduce the tax liability on investment income. Other tax systems have separate tax rates for investment income and ordinary income.

- For *interest income*, special provisions typically include exemptions for specific types of interest income, favorable tax rates, or exclusion amounts that allow a limited amount of interest income to be tax free. In some jurisdictions, inflation adjustments for fixed-income instruments may not be subject to taxation.

- For *dividend income*, special provisions typically include exemptions, special tax rates, or exclusions as mentioned for interest income. To address the issue of double taxation — since dividends are a distribution of company earnings that may have already been taxed — some tax systems (such as those in Australia) utilize tax credits. For instance, dividends can be taxed at standard rates, but individuals might be entitled to a credit for a portion of the taxes paid by the company.

- For *capital gains*, special provisions typically depend on the length of time the asset has been held, the type of asset, or other considerations. This form of taxation can be highly complex because of the ever-changing rules, rates, and exceptions. Generally, long-term gains receive more favorable treatment than short-term gains. The minimum holding period for long-term investments varies across jurisdictions and may also differ among asset classes.

Furthermore, different tax rates may apply to various types of assets. For instance, the sale of privately held and publicly traded equities might be taxed at different rates even if both positions have identical holding periods. Real estate often has unique tax rates compared to other asset classes, especially if the property is the taxpayer's primary residence. Additionally, tax systems may provide lifetime capital gains exemptions for individuals or establish thresholds under which accumulated capital gains are not subject to taxation. Finally, capital gains can be offset by capital losses, and the rules recognizing capital losses can be quite complex.

The case study below, Nataliia Kozlowska: Tax Rates and Tax Calculations, shows the basics of tax calculations commonly applied to ordinary income based on a progressive tax system. In a progressive tax system, the different tax brackets are graduated, and the **marginal tax rate** is the rate at which the highest level of income is taxed.

CASE STUDY

Nataliia Kozlowska: Tax Rates and Tax Calculations

Ms. Nataliia Kozlowska, a new client living in a jurisdiction with a progressive tax rate structure, expects to earn a taxable ordinary income of EUR700,000 this year. She additionally expects to receive investment income: EUR10,000 in interest income and EUR5,000 in dividend income.

The graduated tax rate structure in her jurisdiction is:

Taxable income (EUR)		Tax on column 1	Percentage on excess over column 1
Over	Up to		
0	30,000	—	5
30,000	60,000	1,500	10
60,000	90,000	4,500	15
90,000	250,000	9,000	20
250,000	500,000	41,000	30
500,000	1,000,000	116,000	40
1,000,000		316,000	50

Questions:

1. What is Ms. Kozlowska's marginal tax rate on her ordinary income?

   Answer:

   The marginal tax rate is the rate applied to the last EUR of income, which is the rate applicable to the income level that immediately follows the taxable income. In this case, the taxable income is EUR700,000, which falls under the next to last income bracket. Therefore, the applicable marginal tax rate would be 40%. If the taxable income exceeds EUR1,000,000, the marginal tax is 50% (i.e., for each additional unit of income, 50% will be taxed away).

2. What is Ms. Kozlowska's tax liability and average tax rate on her ordinary income?

   Answer:

   For incomes between EUR500,000 and EUR1,000,000, the tax rate is 40%. For the first EUR500,000, the tax is EUR150,000, and for the next EUR200,000 the tax rate is 40% x (EUR700,000 – EUR500,000) = EUR80,000. The total tax payable is then EUR150,000 + EUR80,000 = EUR230,000, and the average tax rate is 32.86%.

3. What is Ms. Kozlowska's total tax liability and average tax rate if all her investment income is taxed at the same rate as her ordinary income?

   Answer:

   Considering the expected investment income of EUR10,000 in interest income and EUR5,000 in dividend income, the total income is EUR715,000. For the first EUR500,000 in ordinary income tax, the tax is EUR150,000, and for the next EUR215,000, the tax rate is 40% x (EUR715,000 – EUR500,000) = EUR86,000. The total tax payable is then EUR150,000 + EUR86,000 = EUR236,000. Thus, 33.01% of the total income of EUR715,000 is paid in taxes.

4. What is Ms. Kozlowska's total tax liability if the first EUR5,000 in interest income is excluded from taxation and the remainder is subject to the income tax rate and her dividend income is taxed at 15%?

   Answer:

   In this scenario, the investment income is taxed differently than ordinary tax rates, as part of the interest income is excluded from ordinary income tax rates and dividend income is taxed at a lower rate than the marginal tax rate. Of the total interest income of EUR10,000, EUR5,000 is excluded from taxation. This means that the taxable income is reduced from EUR715,000 to EUR710,000 after accounting for the interest income exclusion. Two different tax rates apply to this taxable income.

   i. The ordinary income, which comprises the regular income (EUR700,000) and the taxable portion of the interest income (EUR5,000), is taxed according to the table above. Meanwhile, the dividend income of EUR5,000 is subject to a flat tax of 15%.

> **ii.** The ordinary income tax amounts to EUR150,000 for the first EUR500,000 and EUR82,000 for the remaining EUR205,000 (including the taxed portion of her interest income). This is calculated as 40% x (EUR705,000 − EUR500,000) = EUR82,000, resulting in a total income tax of EUR232,000.
>
> For the dividend income of EUR5,000, there is a 15% tax, equating to EUR750. In total, she pays EUR232,000 in ordinary income tax and EUR750 in investment income tax on the dividends, with a total tax liability of EUR232,750. She pays 32.55% of her total income of EUR715,000 in taxes, and her taxable income is EUR710,000.

Additionally, there are other important dimensions in tax planning for investments. Some countries permit the use of tax deferred savings and retirement accounts that typically

- delay taxation on investment returns within the account to some later date;
- may permit a deduction for contributions to the account that reduce taxable income; and
- may occasionally permit tax free distributions under certain circumstances.

Finally, there are tax systems that impose a wealth tax on the accumulation of wealth. These wealth taxes are usually levied annually, and because they are often set as a percentage of the wealth, they function the same way as income taxes do, by reducing after-tax returns and accumulations.

The Impact of Accrual Taxes on Investment Returns

Estimating the taxes on investment alternatives allows taxable investors to compare returns and wealth accumulations for different types of investments subjected to different tax rates and methods of taxation. **Accrual taxes** are levied and paid on a periodic basis, usually annually. **Deferred taxes** can be postponed until some future date.

When investment returns are subject to accrual taxes, the after-tax return is equal to the pretax return, R, multiplied by $(1 - t_x)$, where t_x represents the tax rate applicable to investment income. For simplicity, the investment's return is entirely taxed at a single uniform rate. Then, the amount of money accumulated for each unit of currency, invested for T years, assuming that returns (after taxes at rate t_x are paid) are reinvested at the same rate of return, R, is simply

$$FVIF_T = [1 + R(1 - t_x)]^T \tag{2}$$

Equation 2 is simply the future value interest factor (FVIF) based on an after-tax return. Comparing the accumulation with and without the impact of taxes gives the **tax drag**, the negative impact of taxes on an investment's net returns, reducing the overall performance and growth of an investment portfolio.

With accrual taxation, the tax drag on capital accumulation compounds over time. By contrast, when taxes on gains are deferred until the end of the investment horizon, the tax rate equals the tax drag on capital accumulation, as the case study involving Nataliia Kozlowska shows.

CASE STUDY

Nataliia Kozlowska: Accrual Taxes and Tax Drag

Ms. Nataliia Kozlowska is determining the impact of taxes on her expected investment returns and wealth accumulations. Ms. Kozlowska lives in a tax jurisdiction with a flat tax rate of 20%, which applies to all types of income and is taxed annually. Ms. Kozlowska expects to earn 7% per year on her investment over a 20-year time horizon and has an initial portfolio of EUR100,000.

Questions:

1. What is Ms. Kozlowska expected wealth at the end of 20 years?

   Answer:

   $$FV_t = \text{EUR}100,000 \times [1 + R(1 - t_x)]^T = \text{EUR}100,000 \times [1 + 0.07(1 - 0.20)]^{20}$$
   $$= \text{EUR}297,357.$$

2. What proportion of potential investment gains was consumed by taxes?

   Answer:

   Ignoring taxes, $FV = \text{EUR}100,000 [1 + 0.07]^{20} = \text{EUR}386,968$. The difference between this and the after-tax amount accumulated from above is EUR89,611(EUR386,968 – EUR297,357). The proportion of potential investment gains consumed by taxes was EUR89,611/EUR286,968 = 31%, which is greater than the 20% tax rate. The negative impact of taxes on the investment's net returns reduced the overall performance and growth of an investment by 31%. This proportion of potential investment gains is a measure of "tax drag".

As long as taxes can be delayed, the compounding effect of the tax drag can be neutralized, which increases long-term accumulation. Moreover, since longer-term capital gains can be taxed at a lower rate compared to shorter-term capital gains, the longer taxes can be delayed, the lower the loss of the accumulated increase in purchasing power.

The size of the tax drag is considerable enough to be a specific factor in making investment decisions. Exhibit 25 illustrates the impact of taxes on capital growth for various investment horizons and rates of return.

Exhibit 25: Proportion of Potential Investment Growth Consumed by Annual Taxes on Return

	Investment horizon in years (n)							
r(%)	5	10	15	20	25	30	35	40
1	0.30	0.31	0.31	0.32	0.33	0.33	0.34	0.34
2	0.31	0.32	0.33	0.34	0.35	0.36	0.37	0.38
5	0.32	0.35	0.37	0.40	0.43	0.46	0.48	0.51
10	0.34	0.39	0.45	0.50	0.55	0.60	0.64	0.68

	Investment horizon in years (n)							
r(%)	5	10	15	20	25	30	35	40
12	0.35	0.41	0.47	0.54	0.59	0.65	0.69	0.74
15	0.36	0.44	0.51	0.59	0.65	0.71	0.76	0.80
20	0.38	0.48	0.57	0.66	0.73	0.79	0.84	0.87

Note: The calculations assume a 30% annual tax rate assessed on investment returns.

According to Exhibit 25, tax drag has the following effects:

- When investment returns are taxed annually, the impact of taxes on capital growth is more significant than the nominal annual tax rate suggests.
- Over time, the negative consequences of taxes on capital growth compound, resulting in a growing gap between pretax and after-tax gains.
- As investment returns increase, tax drag also increases, assuming other factors remain constant.
- Both return and investment horizons have a multiplicative effect on tax drag related to future accumulations.

This implies that for fixed-income instruments, for which most or even all investment returns are subject to annual taxation, the effect of returns on tax drag is more substantial for longer investment periods. Moreover, the influence of investment horizon is more significant when dealing with higher returns.

The Impact of Deferral of Taxes on Investment Returns

Certain types of investment income, such as capital gains, are subject to deferred taxes. Capital gains taxes are typically incurred when an asset is sold, and they are applied to the realized gain, which is calculated as the difference between the selling price and the basis. In most cases, the basis refers to the initial investment made when acquiring the asset. Although it is uncommon for unrealized capital gains to be taxed, it happens in some tax jurisdictions. Additionally, tax-advantaged investment accounts can help defer capital gains taxes. In these cases, investment returns and income from capital gains accumulate for a time without tax drag and are only subject to taxation when they are withdrawn from the account.

If the tax on an investment's return is deferred until the end of its investment horizon T and taxed as a capital gain at rate t_{CG}, then the after-tax future accumulation can be represented as

$$FVIF_{CG} = (1 + R)^T - [(1 + R)^T - 1] \times t_{CG}$$

$$= (1 + R)^T (1 - t_{CG}) + t_{CG} \tag{3}$$

The term $(1 + R)^T$ represents the pretax accumulation. The $[(1 + R)^T - 1] \times t_{CG}$ term is the tax on the capital gain. Viewed differently, $(1 + R)^T(1 - t_{CG})$ represents the future accumulation if the entire amount was subjected to tax. Here, the t_{CG} term returns the tax of the untaxed cost associated with the initial investment; these calculations are explained in detail in the case study on Nataliia Kozlowska's deferral of tax liability.

CASE STUDY

Nataliia Kozlowska: Deferral of Tax Liability

Assume the same facts as in the previous case study. Ms. Kozlowska invests EUR100,000 at 7%. However, the return comes in the form of deferred capital gains that are not taxed until the investment is sold in 20 years' time.

Questions:

1. What is Ms. Kozlowska's expected wealth at the end of 20 years?

   Answer:

   $$FV_{CG} = 100,000 \, (1 + 0.07)^{20} - \left\{ \left[(1 + 0.07)^{20} - 1 \right] \times 0.20 \right\}$$

   $$= 100,000 \, [3.8697 - (2.8697 \times 0.20)]$$

   $$= 100,000 \times 3.2958 = EUR329,576$$

2. What proportion of potential investment gains were consumed by taxes?

   Answer:

   Ignoring taxes, FV = EUR100,000 × $(1 + 0.07)^{20}$ = EUR386,968. The difference between this and the after-tax amount accumulated from above is EUR57,392 (EUR386,968 – EUR329,576). The proportion of potential investment gains consumed by taxes was EUR57,392/EUR286,968 = 20%. This result compares favorably to the potential investment gains consumed by taxes in the previous case study, in which 31% of investment gains were consumed by taxes.

The deferral of taxes demonstrates that when tax deferrals are available, the percentage of potential investment growth consumed by taxes is equal to the tax rate, which is lower than the impact of annual taxation. Essentially, the value of capital gain tax deferral offsets a portion of tax drag, and both increase with investment return and time horizon. For long-term taxable investors, maximizing tax deferrals is an essential investment consideration.

While tax drag on after-tax accumulations subject to annual taxes compounds over time, the tax drag from deferred capital gains remains a fixed percentage regardless of investment return or time horizon. The longer the tax deferral, the lower the present value of the tax liability, allowing more capital accumulation to be protected from the ravaging effects of taxation. The case study below expands on the example of Nataliia Kozlowska and provides a more detailed illustration, emphasizing that for long-term taxable investors, maximizing after-tax capital accumulation is a key investment consideration.

CASE STUDY

Nataliia Kozlowska: Comparing Taxable Investment Alternative with Tax-Deferred Investment Alternative

Assume the same facts as in the previous two case studies. Ms. Kozlowska has a choice between a taxable investment alternative (i.e., taxed annually) and tax-deferred investment alternative.

In the taxable alternative, at the end of the 20-year horizon the initial investment of EUR100,000 has grown to

$$FV_t = \text{EUR}100,000 \times [1 + 0.07 \times (1 - 0.20)]^{20}$$

$$= \text{EUR}100,000 \times [1 + 0.07 \times 0.80]^{20}$$

$$= \text{EUR}100,000 \times (1 + 0.056)^{20}$$

$$= \text{EUR}297,357$$

The proportion of potential investment gains consumed by taxes was EUR89,611/ EUR286,968 = 31% (recall that, ignoring taxes, FV = EUR100,000 × (1 + 0.07)^{20} = EUR386,968).

In the tax-advantaged alternative, at the end of the 20-year horizon the initial investment of EUR100,000 has grown to

$$FV_{CG} = \text{EUR}100,000 \left[(1 + 0.07)^{20} - \left[(1 + 0.07)^{20} - 1\right] \times 0.20\right]$$

$$= \text{EUR}100,000 \left[(1 + 0.07)^{20} \times 0.80 + 0.20\right]$$

$$= \text{EUR}100,000 \left[(1.07)^{20} \times 0.80 + 0.20\right]$$

$$= \text{EUR}100,000 \left[3.8697 \times 0.80 + 0.20\right]$$

$$= \text{EUR}100,000 \left[3.0958 + 0.20\right]$$

$$= \text{EUR}329,576$$

The proportion of potential investment gains consumed by taxes was EUR57,394/ EUR286,968 = 20%.

The benefit from the tax deferral leads to an additional EUR32,218 (EUR329,575 − EUR297,357) investment growth. The tax drag is reduced from 31% to 20%.

One crucial implication of tax deferral value is that investments with deferred capital gains taxation can be more tax efficient than those with annual taxed returns even if the marginal tax rates applied on both returns are the same. The advantage of tax deferral compounds over time. Furthermore, even if deferred capital gains or tax-advantaged investments have higher tax rates than annually taxed (accrual) investment income, the deferral value can outweigh a lower annually applied tax rate over time.

The relative accumulations can be significantly larger when gains can be deferred over long time horizons, particularly for high returns. These models assume investors earn a fair risk-adjusted return. The benefits of tax deferral, however, can be diminished or even completely extinguished if investments taxed on an accrual basis offer sufficiently large risk-adjusted returns (i.e., pretax alpha). In other words, purchasing securities sufficiently below their intrinsic value (or short selling securities sufficiently above intrinsic value) can overcome tax drag even if the investment is taxed heavily on an annual basis. For taxable investments with lower returns, there may not be benefits from delaying taxes.

Lastly, many tax systems have lower capital gains tax rates compared to other investment or ordinary income tax rates, providing a dual benefit for capital gains returns. First, there is the tax deferral advantage and a favorable tax rate upon realization of gains. Second, capital gains tax rates on longer holding periods may receive lower tax rates to encourage long-term investments over short-term ones.

The Impact of Basis on Capital Gains

Basis or **cost basis** is the original cost of an investment including any additional expenses incurred to acquire it and is used to calculate capital gains or losses when the asset is sold. In some circumstances, this basis may be increased or decreased. For calculating capital gain taxes, the selling price minus the calculated cost basis is multiplied with the applicable tax rate.

Often, an asset purchased earlier will have a cost basis differing from the current market value. If the asset's value has increased since its purchase, the cost basis might be less than the market value. This cost basis impacts after-tax accumulation, as it sets the taxable capital gain. An asset with a low cost basis has an embedded tax liability because of potential capital gains tax from selling it today even without considering future growth. In contrast, recent investments and cash do not carry this immediate tax liability.

If the cost basis is expressed as proportion B of the current market value of the investment, then the future after-tax accumulation value can be expressed by simply subtracting this additional tax liability from the expression in Equation 3, or

$$FVIF_{CG,\,B} = (1+R)^T(1-t_{CG}) + t_{CG} - (1-B) \times t_{CG}$$

$$= (1+R)^T(1-t_{CG}) + t_{CG}B \tag{4}$$

This equation resembles Equation 3, $(1+R)^T(1-t_{CG}) + t_{CG}$, and the last term, $t_{CG}B$, represents the after-tax basis at the end of investment horizon.

An investment with an initial low cost basis has a greater current embedded tax liability than an investment with a higher cost basis because, if it were liquidated today, tax on the embedded gain would be due. Hence, when selling an appreciated asset, the potential tax liability must be weighed against the potential for return as the case study on Nataliia Kozlowska and the cost basis shows.

CASE STUDY

Nataliia Kozlowska: Cost Basis

Continuing with the facts in this series of case studies, Ms. Kozlowska has a current investment with a market value of EUR100,000 and cost basis of EUR80,000. The stock price grows at 7% per year for 20 years. The applicable tax rate is 20%.

Questions:

1. Express the cost basis as a percent of the current market value.

   Answer:

   Cost basis/Current market value = B = EUR80,000/ EUR100,000 = 0.80.

2. What is Ms. Kozlowska's expected wealth after 20 years?

   Answer:

   $$FVIF_{CB,\ G} = EUR100,000 \times [(1 + 0.07)^{20}(1 - 0.20) + 0.20(0.80)]$$

   $$= EUR325,575.$$

   This amount is EUR4,000 smaller than Ms. Kozlowska's expected wealth in the earlier example about deferral of tax liability (EUR329,575), in which it was assumed that the cost basis equaled the current market value.

Inflation

Inflation, which represents the rate at which the general price level for goods and services in an economy changes over time, diminishes the future purchasing power of money and can impact the composition of the consumption basket throughout an individual's life cycle. Factors such as changes in income, priorities, lifestyle, and family dynamics drive these shifts. For instance, younger adults tend to spend more on leisure, entertainment, and clothing, whereas retired individuals are more likely to allocate their funds towards health-related expenses, housing, and transportation. These variations in consumption patterns hold significant implications for long-term savings, including retirement planning.

By considering the joint effects of accrual taxes and inflation on long-term wealth accumulation, investors can make informed decisions and choose investments that offer the most favorable long-term outcomes. Concentrating solely on nominal returns can result in a distorted perception of an investment's real, after-tax, long-term performance.

As periodic taxes and inflation gradually erode accumulated capital, then the future after-tax inflation-adjusted accumulation on capital, $FVIF_{t,infl}$ can be calculated as in Equation 5:

$$FVIF_{t,infl} = \left[\frac{1 + R(1 - t_X)}{1 + infl}\right]^{T} \tag{5}$$

In this equation, the nominal after-tax returns from Equation 2 are reduced by the inflation rate. The nominator, $1 + R(1 - t_x)$, is the after-tax return, and the denominator, $1 + infl$, is the inflation adjustment. The case study on Nataliia Kozlowska's wealth accumulation considering taxes and inflation demonstrates the joint effects of tax and inflation.

CASE STUDY

Nataliia Kozlowska: The Effects of Tax and Inflation on Wealth Accumulation

Continuing with the facts in this series of case studies, Ms. Kozlowska is determining the impact of inflation and annual taxes on her wealth accumulations. Ms. Kozlowska expects to earn a nominal 7% per year on her investment over a 20-year time horizon and has an initial portfolio of EUR100,000. The anticipated inflation is 3% annually.

Questions:

1. What is Ms. Kozlowska's expected inflation adjusted wealth at the end of 20 years without the impact of taxes?

   Answer:

   $$FV_{t=0,infl} = EUR100,000 \left[\frac{1 + 0.07\,(1 - 0)}{(1 + 0.03)} \right]^T$$

   $$= EUR100,000 \left[\frac{1.07}{1.03} \right]^{20}$$

   $$= EUR100,000 \times 1.0388^{20}$$

   $$= EUR100,000 \times 2.1411$$

   $$= EUR214,110$$

   Ms. Kozlowska's expected inflation-adjusted wealth at the end of 20 years without the impact of taxes is EUR214,110. The purchasing power of EUR386,968 in nominal terms and ignoring taxes equals the purchasing power of EUR214,110 in real terms ignoring taxes.

2. What is Ms. Kozlowska's expected inflation adjusted wealth at the end of 20 years with the impact of taxes?

   Answer:

   $$FV_{t,infl} = EUR100,000 \left[\frac{1 + 0.07\,(1 - 0.20)}{(1 + 0.03)} \right]^T$$

   $$= EUR100,000 \left[\frac{1.056}{1.03} \right]^{20}$$

   $$= EUR100,000 \times 1.0252^{20}$$

   $$= EUR100,000 \times 1.6450$$

   $$= EUR164,500$$

   Ms. Kozlowska's expected after-tax inflation-adjusted wealth at the end of 20 years with the impact of annual taxes is EUR164,500.

3. How much purchasing power have taxes eroded?

   Answer:

   Taxes eroded the equivalent of EUR49,601 in purchasing power.

4. How much purchasing power would taxes erode if the return were 4% with no inflation (i.e., a similar real return to the 7% nominal return and 3% inflation presented earlier)?

   Answer:

   $$FV_{t=0,infl} = EUR100,000 \left[\frac{1 + 0.04\,(1 - 0)}{(1 + 0)}\right]^{20} = EUR219,112$$

   $$FV_{t=0.20,infl} = EUR100,000 \left[\frac{1 + 0.04\,(1 - 0.20)}{(1 + 0)}\right]^{20} = EUR187,756$$

   In this case, taxes eroded the equivalent of EUR31,356 in purchasing power. Although the erosion of purchasing power was less when the nominal returns were higher in the above example, the real returns are similar. This demonstrates that inflation, in conjunction with taxes, can decrease purchasing power even when there is no change in the real pretax returns.

Adapting Equation 3, where capital accumulates on a tax-advantaged basis with tax assessed on the accumulation upon sale or at liquidation (i.e., deferred capital gain), inflation can be incorporated, arriving at the relationship shown in Equation 6:

$$FVIF_{CG, B, infl} = \frac{(1 + R)^T(1 - t_{CG}) + t_{CG}B}{(1 + infl)^T} \tag{6}$$

The inflation adjustment reduces the after-tax value. Taxes are paid in nominal terms and not in purchasing power–adjusted values; however, it is the purchasing power of the after-tax wealth that is relevant from a wealth management perspective. The case study comparing increase in purchasing power of taxable accounts with tax-deferred accounts shows the effect of the time horizon, the inflation rate, and the return.

CASE STUDY

Nataliia Kozlowska: Comparing Increases in Purchasing Power of Taxable Accounts with Tax-Deferred Accounts

Continuing with the facts in this series of case studies, Ms. Kozlowska has a current investment with a market value of EUR100,000 and cost basis of EUR80,000. The stock price grows at 7% per year for 20 years. Inflation is 3%, and the applicable tax rate is 20%.

Questions:

1. What is Ms. Kozlowska's expected wealth in real, inflation-adjusted, and after-tax terms after 20 years?

   Answer:

   $$FV_{CG, B, infl} = EUR100,000 \left[\frac{(1 + R)^T\,(1 - t_{CG}) + t_{CG}B}{(1 + infl)^T}\right.$$

$$= \text{EUR}100,000 \frac{(1+0.07)^{20}(1-0.20)+0.20 \times 0.80}{(1+0.03)^{20}}$$

$$= \text{EUR}100,000 \frac{1.07^{20} \times 0.80 + 0.16}{1.03^{20}}$$

$$= \text{EUR}100,000 \times 1.8027$$

$$= \text{EUR}180,270.$$

This amount is EUR15,770 greater than Ms. Kozlowska's after-tax, purchasing power–adjusted wealth in the previous case study (EUR 164,500), where taxes were applied annually.

2. How would the answer change if the basis were EUR100,000?

Answer:

$$FV_{CG,B,infl} = \text{EUR}100,000 \left[\frac{(1+R)^T (1-t_{CG}) + t_{CG}B}{(1+infl)^T} \right]$$

$$= \text{EUR}100,000 \frac{(1+0.07)^{20}(1-0.20)+0.20 \times 1}{(1+0.03)^{20}}$$

$$= \text{EUR}100,000 \frac{1.07^{20} \times 0.80 + 0.20}{1.03^{20}}$$

$$= \text{EUR}100,000 \times 1.8248 = \text{EUR}182,480.$$

This amount is EUR2,210 greater than Ms. Kozlowska's after-tax, purchasing power–adjusted wealth when the basis was EUR80,000, illustrating the additional tax liability associated with a lower cost basis.

An important insight is that tax liabilities are levied on nominal price appreciation rather than real price appreciation. As a result, inflation exacerbates the eroding impact of taxes on the long-term increase and preservation of real purchasing power.

The Impact of Different Sources of Returns with Taxes

The prior examples demonstrate the basic mechanics of tax calculations in a simplified manner, with a single constant return exposed to a single, uniform, unchanging tax rate. In reality, portfolio returns often originate from various sources and may be subject to different tax rates. These rate of return and tax rate issues have implications for portfolio management.

A more comprehensive return model incorporates annual income component, R_{INC}, taxed yearly at the tax rate, t_X, and capital appreciation, $R_{CAPITAL}$, taxed upon liquidation at the capital gains rate, t_{CG}. Incorporating the after-tax effects on annual returns and the capital gains tax upon investment liquidation on the capital gains portion of an investment's return, we arrive at Equation 7 below as a future value accumulation factor:

$$\begin{aligned} \text{FVIF}_{INC,CAPITAL,TX,TCG} = & \left[1 + \left(R_{INC} \times (1-t_X) \right) + R_{CAPITAL} \right]^T \\ & - \left[\frac{R_{CAPITAL}}{R_{INC} \times (1-t_X) + R_{CAPITAL}} \times \left[\left[1 + \left(R_{INC} \times (1-t_X) \right) + R_{CAPITAL} \right]^T - 1 \right] \times t_{CG} \right] \end{aligned} \quad (7)$$

Equation 7 may be explained as consisting of two primary elements as described below:

- The first bracketed term is the future value of the investment after incorporating the annual tax on income gains.

- The second term in brackets consists of three intermediate terms.

  - The first intermediate term is the ratio of the capital gain return to the total after-tax annual return on income and capital gains.

  - The second intermediate term is a computation of the total gain on the investment.

  - The third intermediate term is the tax rate on capital gains.

  - Multiplying the three intermediate terms comprising the second primary element provides the total capital gains tax which is deducted from the investment's future value after incorporating annual taxes on income gains.

An application of Equation 7 is demonstrated in the following case study.

CASE STUDY

Nataliia Kozlowska: Comparing After-Tax Returns on Different Return Sources and Tax Rates

Continuing with the facts in this series of case studies, Ms. Kozlowska's EUR100,000 investment in the stock expects to generate 5% in nominal annual price appreciation and 2% in nominal annual dividend income. The dividend income is taxed at 20% annually, while the price appreciation is also taxed at 20% upon investment liquidation. Ms. Kozlowska has an investment time horizon of 20 years. For purposes of this example, we assume no inflation.

Questions:

1. Calculate Ms. Kozlowska's expected wealth in after-tax terms after 20 years.

   Answer:

   Ms. Kozlowska's expected wealth is expected to equal EUR319,792.40 after 20 years as described below.

   Equation 7 is shown below and the solution process discusses the different components of the calculation.

$$FVIF_{INC,CAPITAL,TX,TCG} = \left[1 + \left(R_{INC} \times \left(1 - t_X\right)\right) + R_{CAPITAL}\right]^T$$

$$- \left[\frac{R_{CAPITAL}}{R_{INC} \times \left(1 - t_X\right) + R_{CAPITAL}} \times \left[\left[1 + \left(R_{INC} \times \left(1 - t_X\right)\right) + R_{CAPITAL}\right]^T - 1\right] \times t_{CG}\right]$$

   As a starting point, we compute that the after-tax annual rate of return implied by RINC and RCAPITAL is 6.6% per year.

   Annual after tax rate of return $= 2\% \times (1 - 20\%) + 5\% = 6.6\%$

   Thus, the future value accumulation factor for an investment generating 6.6% per year for 20 years is 3.5904104. This is the first bracketed term in the equation above.

$$[1 + (2\% \times (1 - 20\%) + 5\%]^{20} = 3.5904104$$

Next, we compute the amount of the capital gains tax by employing the three components of the second primary element of the equation.

- Ratio of the capital gain return to the total after-tax annual return on income and capital gains = 5% ÷ 6.6% = 75.76%
- Total gain on the investment = 2.5904104
- Capital gains tax rate = 20%

Total capital gains tax = 0.7576 *x* 2.59041 *x* 0.20 = 0.3924864

$\text{FVIF}_{\text{INC,CAPITAL,TX,TCG}}$ = 3.5904104 − 0.3924864 = 3.197924

Multiplying the above result by the initial investment of EUR100,000 provides Ms. Kozlowska's expected wealth in after-tax terms after 20 years of EUR319,792.40.

2. Suppose that Ms. Kozlowska has a different investment opportunity which expects to generate 2% in nominal annual price appreciation and 5% in nominal annual dividend income. Calculate Ms. Kozlowska's expected wealth in after-tax terms after 20 years.

   Answer:

   Following the same process as illustrated in the calculations to the prior scenario, we find that Ms. Kozlowska's expected after-tax wealth for this investment is EUR306,001 as shown below.

   In this case, the after-tax annual rate of return implied by RINC and RCAPITAL is 6.0% per year.

   Annual after tax rate of return = 5% × (1 − 20%) + 2% = 6.0%

   The future value accumulation factor for an investment generating 6.0% per year for 20 years is 3.20713547.

   $$[1 + (5\% \times (1 - 20\%) + 2\%]^{20} = 3.20713547$$

   The three components of the second primary element of the equation are as follows:

   - Ratio of the capital gain return to the total after-tax annual return on income and capital gains = 2% ÷ 6% = 33.33%
   - Total gain on the investment = 2.20713547
   - Capital gains tax rate = 20%

   Total capital gains tax = 0.3333 *x* 2.20713547 *x* 0.20 = 0.14712765

   $\text{FVIF}_{\text{INC,CAPITAL,TX,TCG}}$ = 3.20713547 − 0.14712765 = 3.06001

   Multiplying the above result by the initial investment of EUR100,000 provides Ms. Kozlowska's expected wealth in after-tax terms after 20 years of EUR306,001.

3. Contrast the after-tax wealth implications of the two investments above by discussing the tax drag associated with the two investments considered in the two prior questions.

Answer:

To assess the tax drag of these two investments, we first note that, in the absence of taxes, both investments generate 7% in annual return. Without taxes, the after-tax wealth of EUR100,000 invested for 20 years at 7% is equal to EUR386,968.44 as shown below.

$$100,000 \times [1 + 0.07]^{20} = 386,968.44$$

The tax drag is reflected by the difference between the after-tax wealth compared to the wealth in the absence of taxes as a percentage of the total gain in the absence of taxes. Ms. Kozlowska is clearly better off from an after-tax perspective with the investment opportunity implied by the first question in which income taxed annually generates the lower return of 2% per year while the higher capital gains return of 5% is not taxed until the end of the 20-year investment horizon.

$$Tax\ drag\ of\ first\ scenario\ = \frac{386,968.44 - 319,792.40}{286,968.44} = 23.4\%$$

$$Tax\ drag\ of\ second\ scenario\ = \frac{386,968.44 - 306,001}{286,968.44} = 28.2\%$$

Effectively, the second scenario creates a larger total tax burden because more of each year's return is taxed. The first scenario featured 6.6% annual return after-tax while the second scenario only generated 6.0% annual return after-tax. Despite lower capital gains taxes in the second scenario, the compounding power of the additional 60 basis points of after-tax annual return sufficiently offsets the additional capital gains taxes paid in the first scenario.

Comparing Nominal and After-Tax Nominal with Real and After-Tax Real Returns

Examining long-term returns as represented by the S&P 500 Total Return, S&P 500 Price Return, and US inflation rates, we can illustrate the combined impact of taxes and inflation. The difference between S&P 500 Total Return and S&P 500 Price Return indicates the dividend yield, while the S&P 500 Price Return only reflects the capital appreciation. Both the dividend yield and the capital appreciation are taxed, but they are taxed at different rates. By applying different tax rates to these components and timing the realization of the capital appreciation that triggers capital gains taxation, we can demonstrate the impact of taxes on capital accumulation. Exhibit 26 below presents the wealth accumulation in nominal returns for four different investment alternatives:

- A tax-exempt investment alternative in which neither income nor capital accumulation is taxed

- A tax-advantaged investment alternative with a 25% tax rate on income but no tax on capital appreciation

- A taxable investment alternative in which both income and capital appreciation are taxed at 25%

- A high-tax taxable investment alternative with a 50% tax rate on both income and capital appreciation

To compute these returns, taxes were applied at the end of each month. While this example streamlines the calculations, it underscores that tax-advantaged investment options significantly reduce the impact of taxes on wealth accumulation over time. The process of accumulating USD1 million for each of the four investment alternatives is summarized below:

Exhibit 26: Accumulation of USD1 Million in Nominal Terms from 1988–2022

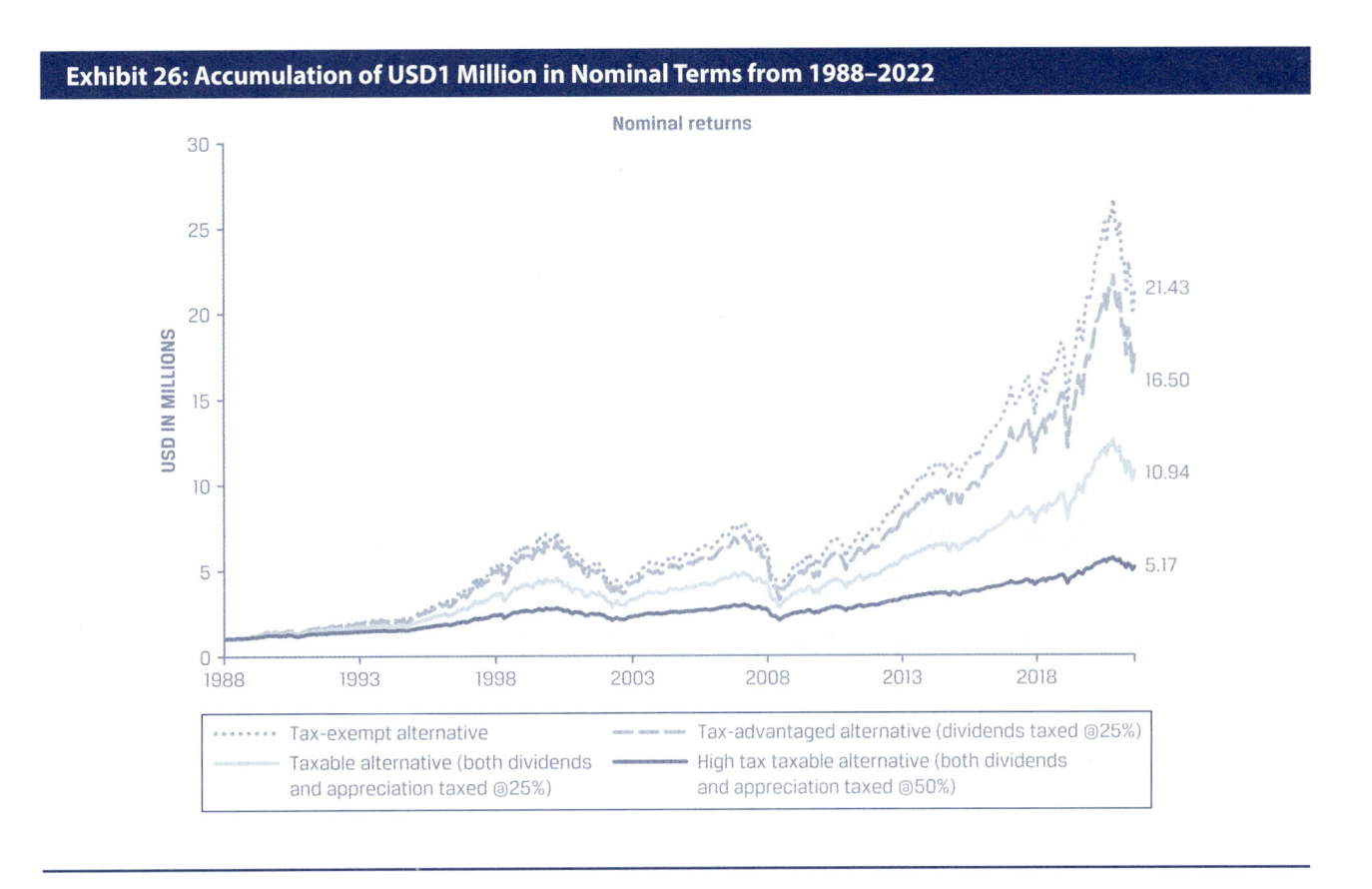

Considering the impact of the monthly consumer inflation rate, which is an important consideration for private wealth clients aiming to build wealth and enhance their purchasing power, the wealth accumulation results in Exhibit 27 are observed (illustrated on the same scale):

Exhibit 27: Accumulation of USD1 Million in Real Terms from 1988–2022

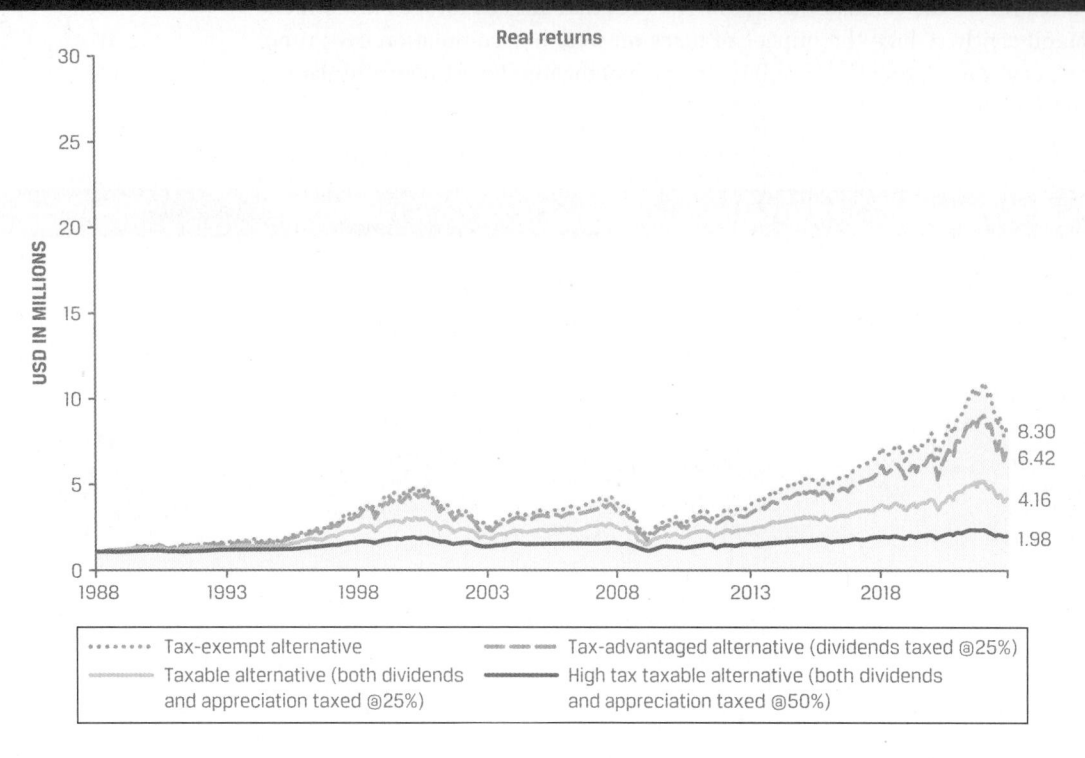

The growth in purchasing power is notably lower than in nominal terms. Exhibit 28 presents the real and nominal accumulation of an initial USD1 million invested in each of the four investment alternatives, highlighting the effects of both taxes and inflation:

Exhibit 28: The Accumulation of USD1 Million Invested

	Accumulation in millions of USD	
	Nominal terms	Real terms
Tax-exempt alternative	21.43	8.30
Tax-advantaged alternative (dividends taxed at 25%)	17.78	6.88
Taxable alternative (both dividends and appreciation taxed at 25%)	10.74	4.16
High-tax taxable alternative (both dividends and appreciation taxed at 50%)	5.12	1.98

A substantial portion of wealth accumulation can be lost to inflation, especially in long-term investments. Inflation can be particularly detrimental to fixed-income investments, as it devalues the returns on these investments in real terms. At the same time, tax-advantaged investment vehicles can help mitigate the impact of taxes on investment returns. By offering tax deferrals, reduced tax rates, or even tax exemptions, these investment alternatives enable investors to retain a larger portion of their returns, which can then be reinvested to compound and grow over time.

QUESTION SET

1. An investor plans to invest GBP25,000 in an investment opportunity expected to generate 6% in taxable income per year over the next 10 years. The appropriate tax rate is 40%, and taxes on the returns are paid annually. Demonstrate that the tax drag of this investment is greater than the tax rate.

   Solution:

   Using

   $$FV = GBP25,000 \times [1 + 0.06 \times (1 - 0.40)]^{10}$$

   $$= GBP25,000 \times (1 + 0.036)^{10} = GBP25,000 \times 1.4243 = GBP35,607$$

   Comparing the result with the no-tax alternative, the investment would have grown to

   $$FV = GBP25,000 \times (1 + 0.06)^{10} = GBP25,000 \times 1.06^{10}$$

   $$= GBP25,000 \times 1.7908 = GBP44,771$$

   The additional growth due to the absence of taxes, GBP44,771 – GBP35,607, is GBP9,164. The tax drag is

   $$\frac{GBP9,164}{GBP44,771 - GBP25,000} = 46\%,$$

   which is greater than the 40% tax rate. The negative impact of taxes on the investment's net returns reduced the overall performance and growth of an investment by 46%.

2. An investor plans to invest GBP50,000 in an investment opportunity expected to generate a return of 8% per year, which is taxed as a deferred capital gain only after 10 years. The tax rate is 20%. Compare the impact of taxes on the after-tax return relative to if taxes were paid annually at a 20% rate.

   Solution:

   The investment using deferred taxation grows to

   $$FV = GBP50,000\big[(1 + 0.08)^{10} - [(1 + 0.08)^{10} - 1] \times 0.20\big]$$

   $$= GBP50,000\big[(1 + 0.08)^{10}(1 - 0.20) + 0.20\big]$$

   $$= GBP50,000\big[(1 + 0.08)^{10} \times 0.80 + 0.20\big]$$

   $$= GBP50,000\big[(1.08)^{10} \times 0.80 + 0.20\big]$$

   $$= GBP50,000[2.1589 \times 0.80 + 0.20]$$

   $$= GBP50,000[1.7271 + 0.20] = GBP96,355.$$

   The investment using annual taxation grows to

   $$FV = GBP50,000 \times [1 + 0.08 \times (1 - 0.20)]^{10}$$

$$= \text{GBP50,000} \times 1.064^{10} = \text{GBP92,979}.$$

The deferred taxation provides a higher accumulation of GBP3,376.

3. Discuss how the benefits of tax deferral can be overcome by finding mispriced investment opportunities.

Solution:

The benefits of tax deferral can be overwhelmed if investments taxed on an accrual basis offer sufficiently high risk-adjusted returns. That is, purchasing securities sufficiently below their intrinsic value (or short selling securities sufficiently above intrinsic value) can overcome tax drag even if the investment is taxed heavily on an annual basis.

6   INDIVIDUAL INVESTORS AND INVESTMENT POLICY STATEMENTS

☐   discuss the differences between private and institutional clients and formulate an appropriate Investment Policy Statement for private clients

An **investment policy statement (IPS)** outlines the client's unique investment objectives, risk tolerance, investment time horizon, and other applicable constraints and guides the wealth manager when constructing and implementing the client's portfolio and asset allocation. The IPS evolves through the conversation between the client and the wealth manager.

The IPS should be reviewed routinely as the client's circumstances or market conditions change. An IPS benefits both the client and the manager because it promotes discipline and commitment to the strategy, particularly during adverse or volatile market conditions, while describing the investment process and the advisor's fiduciary responsibility to the client. Additionally, an IPS focuses on achieving short-, medium-, and long-term financial goals rather than just short-term performance. By offering a clear, mutual understanding of the manager's mandate, an IPS helps ensure, but does not guarantee, that the client's financial objectives are met.

The IPS contains information about the client's investment objectives, asset base, and the overall asset allocation. Together with the wealth manager's capital market assumptions, these define the inputs needed for a capital sufficiency analysis. **Capital sufficiency analysis** is the process of evaluating whether a client has sufficient capital resources to achieve their financial goals and objectives, and it considers the client's assets, liabilities, income, expenses, risk tolerance, time horizon, and other relevant factors to determine if their current and future capital resources can adequately support their lifestyle, financial goals, and long-term financial stability. Whenever the capital sufficiency analysis does not support the investment objective, the manager must work with the client to revise objectives and create those that the manager judges to be achievable.

An IPS may further specify whether the assets are managed using strategic asset allocation, tactical asset allocation, or a combination of both.

- **Strategic asset allocation** is a long-term strategy that establishes target allocations for various asset classes and aims to optimize the balance between risk and reward by diversifying investments, considering an investor's financial objectives, risk tolerance, and investment timeline. The target allocation relies on historical data, projected returns, and correlations between asset classes.

- **Tactical asset allocation** is a more proactive strategy that adjusts asset class allocations within a portfolio based on short-term market trends, economic conditions, or valuation changes to capitalize on temporary market inefficiencies or opportunities to improve returns or manage risk more effectively. Unlike strategic asset allocation's long-term focus, tactical asset allocation allows for more frequent portfolio adjustments in response to market conditions and expectations. Consequently, this method entails higher trading costs and increased complexity and requires consistent monitoring of market conditions and asset performance. Additionally, tactical asset allocation demands a higher level of skill and experience.

The case study below provides a practical example of how these asset allocation strategies affect a portfolio's management.

CASE STUDY

C.Y. Lee: Combining Strategic and Tactical Asset Allocation

Mr. C.Y. Lee, the managing director for the investment firm Acme & Bass located in the Asia-Pacific region, is working with his wealth manager to combine strategic and tactical asset allocation in his IPS.

In establishing the portfolio asset allocation, the wealth manager considers Mr. Lee's assets, expected cash needs, risk tolerance, and financial goals. To achieve higher long-term risk-adjusted returns, the manager combines both strategic and tactical asset allocation approaches while incorporating rebalancing limits for the strategic allocation. A potential strategic asset allocation plan with target allocations and rebalancing limits for various asset classes can be as follows:

	Lower rebalancing limit	Strategic allocation	Upper rebalancing limit
Cash	3%	**5%**	7%
Cash and equivalents		5%	
Fixed income	25%	**30%**	35%
Short-term debt investments		20%	
Intermediate-term bonds		10%	
Equities	45%	**50%**	55%
Domestic, Singapore		10%	
International, Asia Pacific only		10%	

	Lower rebalancing limit	Strategic allocation	Upper rebalancing limit
International, ex-Asia Pacific		30%	
Alternatives	8%	**10%**	12%
Private equity	3%	**5%**	7%

The rebalancing limits ensure that the portfolio remains aligned with Mr. Lee's long-term financial goals, risk tolerance, and investment horizon. If any asset class allocation drifts beyond the specified limits, the portfolio manager will rebalance the portfolio, typically to bring it back in line with the target strategic allocations. As we shall see shortly, there are several methods for triggering portfolio rebalancing: one method is based on time, so the portfolio is rebalanced at set time intervals (i.e., quarterly or semi-annually, etc.), and the other method is based on thresholds, so the portfolio is rebalanced whenever specified limits are breached.

Additionally, the IPS allows for tactical asset allocation adjustments specifically in international equities to capitalize on short-term market trends or opportunities. For example, the wealth manager might have the discretion to temporarily increase the allocation to international equities by up to 10%, or a total of 50% of the portfolio, if they identify an attractive investment opportunity in a specific market or sector and by selling some of the domestic equity holdings. This tactical adjustment would be subject to the following conditions, such as the overall equities allocation should remain within the rebalancing limit (i.e., should not exceed 55% or fall below 45%).

The manager must provide a rationale for a tactical adjustment, including the anticipated duration and expected impact on the portfolio's risk and return profile.

The tactical allocation must be reviewed periodically, at least quarterly, to assess its ongoing appropriateness and potential need for further adjustment.

This hybrid approach allows Mr. Lee to benefit from the stability and diversification provided by strategic asset allocation while also leveraging tactical adjustments in international equities to enhance returns or manage risk more effectively.

Parts of an IPS

The IPS lays the foundation for the client–wealth manager relationship and details how the wealth manager will make investment decisions. As such, it guides the management of an investment portfolio by outlining the investment goals, risk tolerance, and constraints for an individual or an organization. It provides a framework for making investment decisions and helps ensure that the investment strategy aligns with the investor's objectives.

The IPS includes the client's background and investment objectives, the key parameters of the investment program, the portfolio asset allocation, and some discussion of the duties and responsibilities of relevant parties. It is developed by the wealth manager, reflects conversations and discussions with the client, and serves as a guidance document. An IPS is a dynamic document that should be reviewed regularly to capture changing conditions, preferences, goals, objectives, and time horizons. Exhibit 29 depicts the typical components of an IPS.

Exhibit 29: Components of an IPS

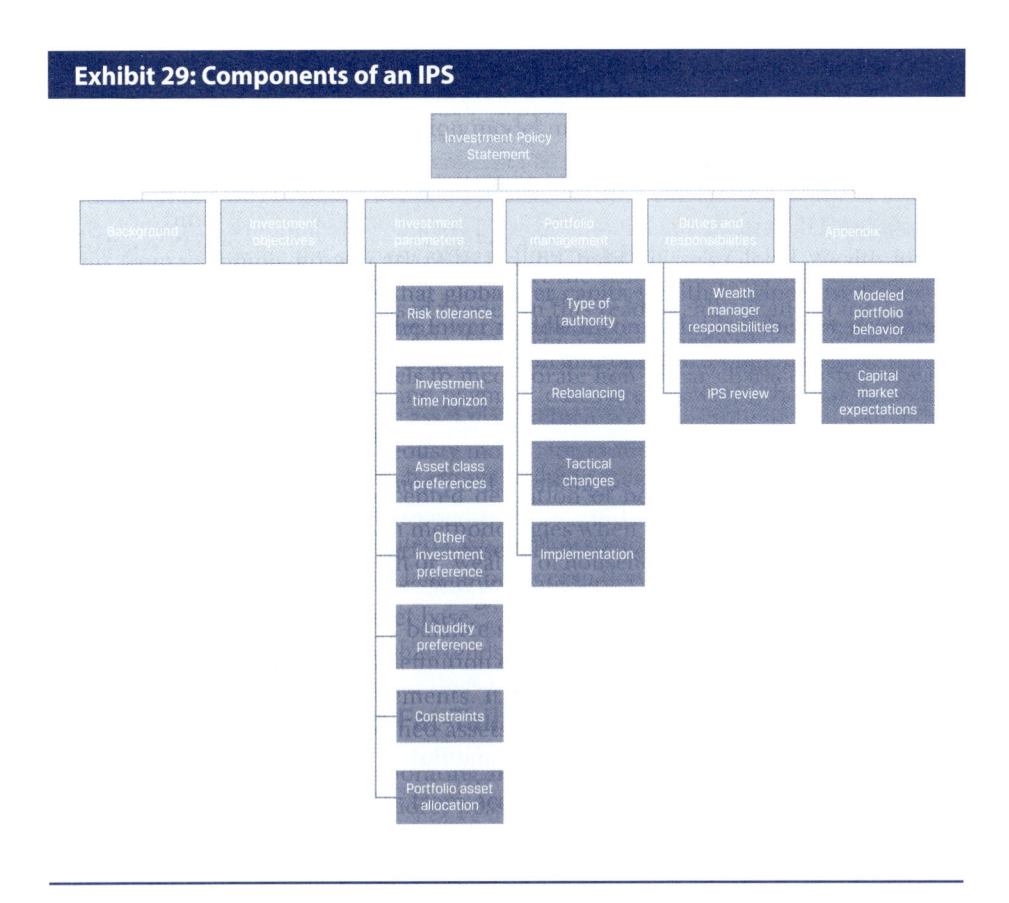

Background

The background section of the IPS usually contains the client's name, age, personal details, and pertinent financial information. This should include the portfolio's personal and business assets' market value and individual accounts within the portfolio, as well as the tax status of these accounts, and delineate substantial financial or nonfinancial assets not managed by the wealth manager. Such assets might encompass privately held business interests, real estate portfolios, and other valuable privately held assets. This section should also include a description of the family, its members, its sources of wealth (e.g., family business), and if appropriate, its core values. Specifics about tax jurisdictions where income and capital gains are taxed should be included here.

Investment objectives

The investment objectives section of the IPS typically outlines various short-term and long-term goals. Clients often have multiple, conflicting objectives they want to achieve with the same portfolio, which emerge during discussions between the client and the manager about financial matters.

Investment objectives should include overall portfolio return and risk objectives. Specific investment objectives should be detailed and quantifiable whenever possible. For example, a client might have specific amounts in mind for future bequests such as funds for their children or charitable donations. Investment objectives should avoid being oversimplified and vague. When dealing with multiple competing objectives, the manager should identify the primary goal, especially when the client has difficulty assigning specific amounts to future objectives. For instance, if a client wants to support their retirement lifestyle while preserving an inheritance for their children, the main objective would be retirement security, with the inheritance as a secondary consideration.

Investment objectives should also account for cash flows that affect capital sufficiency analysis. If a client plans to make regular contributions to the investment portfolio before starting withdrawals, the objective should reflect these future contributions. Similarly, if a client expects a significant future liquidity inflow, such as proceeds from a settlement, business sale, or inheritance, this information should be included. Likewise, if a client anticipates a considerable liquidity outflow, such as meeting spousal maintenance, it should also be listed as an objective.

Investment parameters

The investment parameters section of the IPS outlines preferences that influence each individual client's investment program and reflect the specific client's individual needs. Investment parameters include:

- *Risk tolerance*: This section outlines the client's ability and willingness to withstand portfolio volatility, as described earlier, and can reflect the score on a risk tolerance questionnaire as well as discussions that include risk preference, risk tolerance, and overall risk–return trade-offs.

- *Investment time horizon*: This section lists the time horizon for the agreed-upon goals and objectives across a range of years. It reflects discussions with the client. Typically, for a client with a long horizon, the IPS may state it as "exceeds 15 years"; for a shorter horizon, the IPS may state it as "less than 10 years." When there are multiple or parallel goals, each specific goal may be listed with its own time horizon, some of which, such as bequests and philanthropic activities, may exceed the client's lifetime.

- *Asset class preference*: This section lists the main asset classes included in the client's portfolio. These asset class preferences are often described in the context of risk, return, and income characteristics.

- *Liquidity preferences*: This section addresses liquidity considerations for clients who maintain cash in their portfolios and outlines a specific cash balance that the wealth manager must maintain. If a preference for cash constrains the asset class selection or implementation decisions, this should be discussed and then documented in the IPS. For instance, if a client's cash needs dictate that the entire portfolio should be held in relatively liquid assets, then there may be a cap on holding less liquid private equity and similarly illiquid asset classes.

- *Other investment preferences*: This section contains client-specific information such as specific "legacy" holdings that a client wishes to retain, like equity in a former employer, or an investment that the client wishes to make countering the wealth manager's advice. Some clients may hold a substantive proportion of their portfolio in their current or former employer's equity. This may create portfolio concentration risk, which can adversely impact the risk–return characteristics of the portfolio. Environmental, social, and governance (ESG)-related constraints should normally appear in this section. When a client expresses preferences for investments that meet socially responsible investing (SRI), ESG investment standards, or are otherwise acceptable or unacceptable due to religious, ethical, or personal preferences or beliefs, they should be noted here. Additionally, investment preferences may include portfolio turnover policy detailing how and when realization of potential gains should be conducted. Moreover, a preference for investing in actively or passively managed funds could also be added. Finally, any special tax or legal considerations should be noted. These might include issues of dual citizenship, legal residence in multiple countries, and the like.

- *Constraints*: This section lists investment constraints that may restrict the wealth manager from implementing certain investments or strategies. For example, a client may be constrained by an investment with large unrealized capital gains, which would create significant tax liabilities if sold. Such constraints should be clearly and unambiguously documented in the IPS, outlining the specific policy or programs for managing the effects of such a concentration. This may include a range of preferences from keeping to liquidating the investment over time. The choice of appropriate tax mitigation strategy should also be included here. For clients expressing preferences for SRI, ESG, religious, or ethical investment standards, the constraints imposed by these should be noted here. Finally, the process for client approval should also be unambiguously documented.

- *Portfolio asset allocation*: This section contains the target allocation or range for each asset class in the client's portfolio. Wealth managers who use a strategic asset allocation typically define a target allocation for each asset class as well as upper and lower bounds. Wealth managers who use a tactical asset allocation approach may list asset class target "ranges" rather than specific target allocation percentages.

Portfolio management

The portfolio management section of the IPS typically incorporates portfolio management topics such as the extent of any discretionary authority, the frequency and method of rebalancing, and, if relevant, changes to tactical asset allocation. The wealth manager may be granted discretionary authority to manage assets without explicit client approval. There are, however, different levels of such authority:

- A wealth manager *with full discretion* is free to implement rebalancing trades and replace fund managers without prior client approval.

- A wealth manager with less than full discretion has received authority to make certain specific changes such as rebalancing.

- A wealth manager *in a nondiscretionary capacity* makes recommendations to the client but is not able to take action without a client's consent.

Wealth managers may follow different methods of rebalancing a portfolio to realign the portfolio to the target allocation. Rebalancing may be included in the asset allocation section of an IPS. Expectations regarding the frequency of portfolio revisions may be stated a number of ways:

In a **time-based rebalancing policy**, the wealth manager rebalances client portfolios regularly, at a certain given time interval such as quarterly, semi-annually, or annually, regardless of any difference between prevailing asset class weights and target asset class weights.

Time-based rebalancing is a straightforward, simple, easy to understand and easy to implement policy. Its predictable rebalancing schedule ensures regular portfolio reassessment, keeping the strategic asset allocation on track, thereby reducing the risk of portfolio drift from their target allocations due to market fluctuations. Effectively, the systematic nature of rebalancing serves as an inherent risk management mechanism. However, the time-based rebalancing strategy is somewhat unresponsive to significant and sudden market changes, which may expose the portfolio to higher risks or cause missed investment opportunities between scheduled rebalancing times. Furthermore, it may lead to unnecessary transactions, which is particularly burdensome when the difference between prevailing asset class weights and target asset class weights is small (i.e., when the portfolio has not deviated much from its target allocations). Additionally, rebalancing transactions may incur extra costs both in terms of transaction fees and potential tax liabilities. Finally, the deterministic nature of time-based rebalancing means that buying or selling assets is dictated by the calendar rather than the prevailing market conditions. This could sometimes result in transacting at less than favorable prices.

In a **threshold-based rebalancing policy**, the wealth manager rebalances the portfolio when asset class weights deviate from their target weights by a prespecified percentage, for example, upper and lower rebalancing limits, regardless of timing and frequency.

Threshold-based rebalancing reacts to changing market conditions: the portfolio is rebalanced whenever there is a significant deviation from its target allocation, that is, whenever upper or lower rebalancing limits are breached. This strategy is sensitive to market volatility and sudden shifts. This approach could potentially be more efficient than the time-based rebalancing because it involves rebalancing only when necessary. This minimizes transaction costs and tax liabilities. Furthermore, because it allows for swift adjustments in response to volatile markets, it may offer better risk management, but at potentially higher cost.

However, threshold-based rebalancing is inherently complex, often requiring more sophisticated monitoring and automation systems to keep track of portfolio drift and execute rebalancing when needed. Also, the timing of rebalancing can be inconsistent. During stable markets, there may not be an adjustment for long periods. However, during periods of volatility, there may be frequent rebalancing in response to sudden periods of persistent volatility, which can create a more short-term focus. Because the rebalancing trigger is tied closely to market fluctuations, there is a risk of overreacting to short-term market events, potentially skewing away from long-term investment goals.

Both time-based rebalancing and threshold-based rebalancing require defining the target rebalancing weight, which is typically the strategic asset allocation. Exhibit 30 presents a comparison of time-based and threshold-based portfolio rebalancing.

Exhibit 30: Comparison of Time-Based and Threshold-Based Portfolio Rebalancing

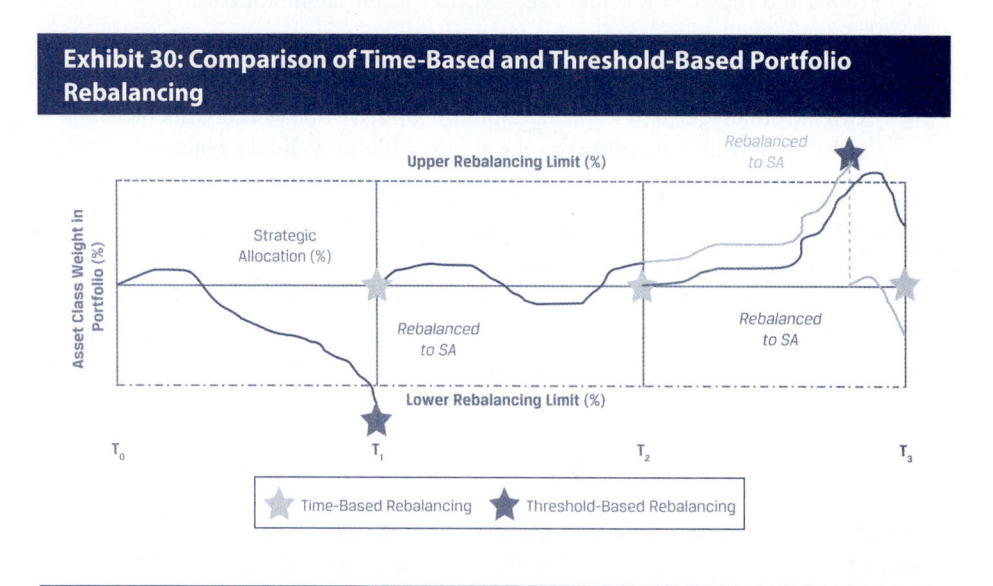

In a hypothetical portfolio, the asset class weights are initially set (at T_0) to those of the strategic allocation. At the end of period 1 (T_1), which could be a quarter, for example, portfolio rebalancing occurs both on a time and threshold basis to bring the asset class back to its strategic allocation. At the end of T_2, rebalancing would be performed on a time basis but not on a threshold basis because no threshold limit has been reached. During T_3, threshold-based rebalancing would be implemented when the upper rebalancing limit was breached. However, time-based rebalancing would only be performed at the end of period 3.

The section on tactical changes lists the specific parameters wealth managers must consider when making periodic adjustments, tactical changes, or other adjustments to a client's asset allocation. If target allocation ranges have been established in the earlier portfolio asset allocation section, this section of the IPS indicates whether, when, and how the manager can break those ranges when executing a tactical change.

This section includes information about the timeline over which the new portfolio will be created and the asset classes, investment alternatives, investment products, and derivatives the wealth manager anticipates using. Typically, it includes any specific third-party funds or money managers recommended by the wealth manager, the proprietary investment offerings managed by the wealth manager's firm, or some combination of these approaches. This section indicates whether the wealth manager prefers to invest in mutual funds, ETFs, private equity, hedge funds, or individual securities. When using third-party money managers, some additional relevant information includes the incremental costs, the specific selection and retention criteria the wealth manager uses to vet and pick third-party managers, and the extent, frequency, and steps included in the wealth manager's due diligence process to vet external managers.

Duties and responsibilities

The duties and responsibilities section of the IPS typically discusses the wealth manager's overall responsibilities, including expectations about the ongoing review of an IPS.

The wealth management responsibilities section helps the client in understanding how the wealth manager assists the client to reach their investment objectives and may include the following information:

- Developing an appropriate asset allocation
- Recommending or selecting investment options such as pooled investment vehicles or individual securities
- Monitoring the asset allocation and rebalancing
- Using derivatives, leverage, short sales, and repurchase agreements (repos) in an appropriate manner that is consistent with the client's investment and risk objectives
- Monitoring strategy implementation costs
- Monitoring the activities of third-party service providers (e.g., asset managers and/or custodians)
- Drafting and maintaining the IPS
- Reporting of performance, including an indication of the base currency
- Reporting of taxes and financial statements
- Voting proxies
- Assisting with the preparation of agreements associated with private fund offerings
- When the manager uses third-party providers, the IPS might also list their responsibilities. The distinct and important role of an asset custodian that maintains segregated client accounts, values the investment assets, collects income, and settles transactions is typically included.

The *IPS review* section sets expectations for how frequently the client and wealth manager will review the IPS and affirm that the investment objectives remain accurate and that the prevailing strategy is likely to meet those objectives.

IPS appendix

The appendix to the IPS often includes details that typically change more frequently than the main portion of the IPS, such as:

- *Modeled portfolio behavior*: This section describes a range of possible performance outcomes over various holding periods and can provide more value to the client than merely stating the return objective or the "expected compound return." The wealth manager may provide a modeled distribution of returns at various percentile ranges, which enables the wealth manager to quantify portfolio downside risk, particularly over short time periods. This can help to confirm what level of downside risk the client is able to accept.

- *Capital market expectations*: This section contains the modeled, simulated, or calculated portfolio statistics, including expected returns, standard deviations, and correlations. The section may also include historical returns both on a portfolio and individual asset class basis.

The case study below provides an example of how investment objectives are formulated for an HNWI.

CASE STUDY

Huang Zhuo Wei: Background and Investment Objectives

Huang Zhuo Wei, age 51, is a private investor in Singapore. Wei is an engineer by trade but has also been a successful real estate developer. His portfolio consists of SGD50 million in a liquid securities portfolio, including common stock positions in which he has large, embedded capital gains, and several real estate investments valued at approximately SGD90 million (combined). He expects to make additional real estate investments in the coming years. He estimates that he can invest approximately SGD1,000,000 per year, inflation-adjusted, in real estate until retirement.

He has a much higher than average risk tolerance and, historically, his liquid portfolio has consisted mostly of large-cap technology companies. He has stated that his time horizon is 10 years because he anticipates retiring in approximately 10 years. He estimates that he will need approximately SGD3 million per year, inflation-adjusted, to support his lifestyle in retirement. He wishes to grow his investment resources and create a significant inheritance for his children.

Questions:

1. Discuss how Wei's wealth manager should create the investment objectives section of Wei's IPS.

Solution:

The purpose of this portfolio is to support Wei's lifestyle in retirement and to provide an inheritance for his children. Aside from the investment assets in his portfolio, Wei has private real estate investments valued at approximately SGD90 million and is likely to add to this segment of his net worth over the next several years. Wei does not anticipate needing distributions from this portfolio for at least 10 years.

Wei estimates an annual, inflation-adjusted lifestyle need of approximately SGD3 million per year beginning at his retirement in 10 years. His cash needs will be satisfied in part through portfolio distributions and in part from his real estate portfolio. The wealth manager will continue to work

> with Wei to quantify his bequest objective and ensure that his portfolio distribution rate is sustainable throughout his retirement.

2. Discuss how his wealth manager should reflect Wei's investment horizon in the IPS.

Solution:

Given his desire to create a significant inheritance for his children, Wei's true investment horizon is through retirement, a period that likely will be much longer than 10 years. His wealth manager should describe his time horizon as exceeding 10 years. The life expectancy in Singapore for a male is around 81 years; hence, the time in retirement can be approximately 20 years.

Sample Investment Policy Statement

The following case study demonstrates a sample IPS for a private client couple, David and Amelia King. The Kings' wealth manager does not use a tactical asset allocation approach for the couple, so the section on tactical changes is not relevant in this case.

CASE STUDY

David and Amelia King: Sample Investment Policy Statement

Background and Investment Objectives

This IPS is designed to assist David and Amelia in meeting their financial objectives. It contains a summation of their objectives and expectations, sets forth an investment structure for attaining these objectives, and outlines ongoing responsibilities.

The purpose of this portfolio is to support the continuation of David and Amelia's current lifestyle, provide for their family's needs, and fund their philanthropic objectives. Maintenance of their current lifestyle is their primary objective, followed by support for family members and charitable aspirations, in that order. To meet these objectives, they anticipate needing approximately USD350,000 per year in inflation-adjusted portfolio distributions. Furthermore, they intend to purchase a second residence within the next two years. They expect the purchase price for the second residence to be approximately USD1.5 million. David and Amelia have not articulated a specific dollar amount that they intend to leave to their children, nor a specific dollar amount that they wish to leave to charity at their death. These amounts must be quantified as soon as possible.

In establishing their asset allocation, David and Amelia have considered their total assets and expected cash needs. They are seeking to achieve a higher long-term rate of return and are willing to assume the associated portfolio volatility.

Portfolio accounts

1. Taxable joint account for David and Amelia
2. Tax-deferred account for David
3. Tax-deferred account for Amelia

Current combined market value = USD12,250,000

Investment Parameters

Risk tolerance

David and Amelia are able and willing to withstand short- and intermediate-term portfolio volatility. They recognize and acknowledge the anticipated level of portfolio volatility associated with their asset allocation (as illustrated in the Modeled Portfolio Behavior section of the Appendix).

Investment time horizon

David and Amelia have an investment time horizon that exceeds 15 years.

Asset class preferences

The following asset classes are selected:

- Short-term debt investments
- Intermediate-term bonds
- US stocks
- Non-US stocks
- Global real estate securities

Liquidity preferences

David and Amelia wish to maintain within their portfolio a minimum cash balance of USD50,000. They typically maintain a more sizable cash balance at their primary bank.

Other investment preferences

The Kings wish to maintain their positions in Acme Manufacturing, Inc., which Amelia received through inheritance, and Artful Publishing, Ltd., which is her former employer. Neither position represents significant concentration risk in the context of their broader portfolio.

David has an interest in a private real estate limited partnership that invests primarily in office buildings throughout Asia. This exposure has been taken into consideration in designing the asset allocation.

Constraints

Amelia's position in Artful Publishing, Ltd., has significant embedded capital gains.

Portfolio Asset Allocation

	Lower rebal-ancing limit	Strategic allocation	Upper rebal-ancing limit
Short-term debt investments	8%	10%	12%
Intermediate-term bonds	16%	20%	24%
US stocks	30%	35%	40%
Non-US stocks	20%	25%	30%
Global real estate securities	8%	10%	12%

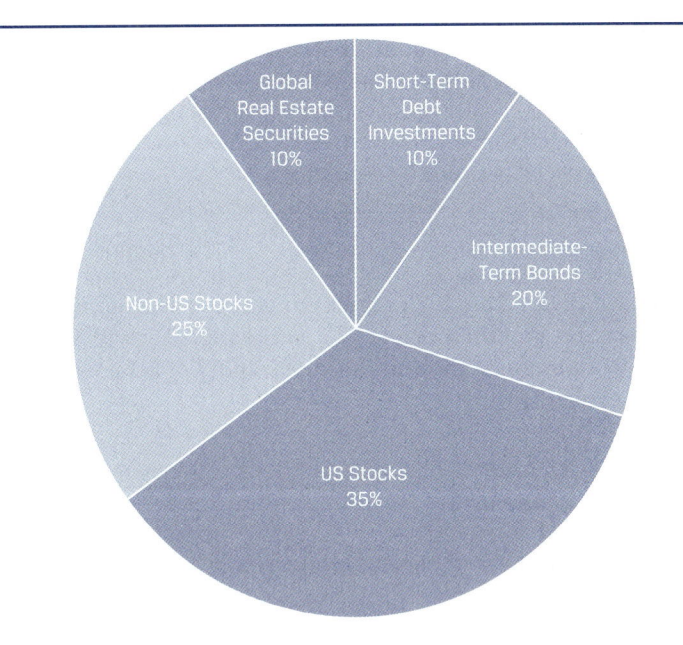

Portfolio Management

Discretionary authority

The wealth manager has full discretion to implement portfolio changes related to rebalancing the portfolio, investing new funds in existing positions, and generating liquidity to meet withdrawal requests from existing positions.

The wealth manager will receive approval prior to establishing new positions or eliminating existing positions.

Rebalancing

The wealth manager will review the portfolio on at least a monthly basis. Rebalancing will be determined by the lower and upper asset class limits set forth in the Portfolio Asset Allocation section of the IPS.

Implementation

The wealth manager will use third-party money managers via mutual funds, ETFs, and separate accounts of individual securities to implement the investment strategy. The wealth manager conducts a quarterly due diligence process to evaluate recommended managers as well as the universe of other available managers. This process involves quantitative risk and return comparisons to appropriate indexes and peer groups, as well as qualitative assessments of other factors that may impact a manager's ability to perform in the future. More information about this process is available at the client's request.

Duties and Responsibilities

Wealth manager responsibilities

The wealth manager is responsible for the following:

- Developing an appropriate asset allocation
- Selecting investment options
- Implementing the agreed-upon strategy
- Monitoring the asset allocation and rebalancing when necessary
- Monitoring the costs associated with implementing the investment strategy

- Monitoring the activities of other service vendors (e.g., custodians)
- Drafting and maintaining the IPS
- Performance reporting
- Tax and financial accounting reporting
- Proxy voting
- IPS reviews

The client will review this IPS at least annually to determine whether the investment objectives are still accurate. The wealth manager will review this IPS at least annually to evaluate the continued feasibility of achieving the client's investment objectives.

IPS Appendix

Modeled portfolio behavior

Modeled compound (inflation-adjusted) return: 6.23%

Modeled distribution of returns

Year	10th percentile	25th percentile	50th percentile	75th percentile	90th percentile
1	−10.45	−2.89	6.23	16.21	26.01
3	−3.75	0.86	6.23	11.88	17.24
5	−1.58	2.05	6.23	10.58	14.66
10	0.64	3.25	6.23	9.29	12.12
15	1.65	3.79	6.23	8.72	11.02
25	2.66	4.34	6.23	8.15	9.92

Portfolio downside risk, 1-year horizon:

- 25% likelihood of a return less than −2.89%
- 10% likelihood of a return less than −10.45%

Portfolio downside risk, 15-year horizon:

- 25% likelihood of a compound annual return less than 3.79%
- 10% likelihood of a compound annual return less than 1.65%

Capital market assumptions

Modeled Portfolio Statistics

	Expected return (%) *	Standard deviation (%)	Modeled compound return (%) *
Short-term debt investments	2.5	2.0	2.5
Intermediate-term bonds	3.5	8.0	3.2
US stocks	8.5	22.0	6.1
Non-US stocks	10.0	26.0	6.6
Global real estate securities	7.5	23.0	4.9

* Inflation-adjusted

		(1)	(2)	(3)	(4)	(5)
Modeled correlations						
1	Short-term debt investments	1.00				
2	Intermediate-term bonds	0.79	1.00			
3	US stocks	−0.08	−0.03	1.00		
4	Non-US stocks	−0.29	−0.27	0.76	1.00	
5	Global real estate securities	−0.15	0.08	0.42	0.39	1.00

QUESTION SET

1. Contrast strategic and tactical asset allocation in forming investment strategy.

   Solution:

   Strategic asset allocation focuses on target allocations across asset categories and is a long-term strategy, whereas tactical asset allocation is a proactive strategy to adjust asset allocations reflecting short-term market trends, economic conditions, or valuation changes.

2. A client's limited partnership stake in a venture that invests in office buildings throughout Asia has been revalued such that this stake is now worth 30% less than estimated at the time the IPS was written. Assume that, prior to the revaluation, this stake accounted for 10% of the total market value of the portfolio and was worth EUR10 million, the target strategic allocation for global real estate securities. The lower bound for rebalancing is 8%. The next annual review of the IPS is scheduled in nine months. Which response below best describes the next IPS review?

   A. The next IPS review should take place in nine months as scheduled.

   B. The next IPS review should be rescheduled as soon as possible with a focus on capital sufficiency analysis.

   C. The next IPS review should be rescheduled as soon as possible to review the asset allocation of the portfolio.

   Solution:

   C is the correct response.

   Given the assumption on the initial size of the limited partnership stake, the decline in the total portfolio value is just 3%, so a capital sufficiency analysis is unnecessary. Moreover, the allocation to Global Real Estate Securities declines to 7.2% (from 10%), so it is just below the 8% lower rebalancing limit for this asset class — see calculations below. Therefore, the next IPS review should be rescheduled as soon as possible to review the asset allocation of the portfolio with a view towards rebalancing.

   Decline in total portfolio value:

   $$\frac{\text{USD}10{,}000{,}000 - (0.10 \times 0.30 \times \text{USD}10{,}000{,}000) - \text{USD}10{,}000{,}000}{\text{USD}10{,}000{,}000}$$

   $= -0.03 \; or - 3\%$

   Allocation to global real estate securities:

$$\frac{0.10 \times 0.70 \times USD10,000,000}{USD10,000,000 - (0.10 \times 0.30 \times USD10,000,000)} = 0.072 \; or \; 7.2\%$$

A is incorrect because significant changes in market conditions, such as the revaluation of the limited partnership stake, can create the need for an IPS review earlier than a scheduled once per year review.

B is incorrect because the couple can tolerate portfolio volatility, and the decline in total portfolio value is just 3%, so a focus on the capital sufficiency analysis should not be a necessary aspect of the next IPS review.

---

3. A client of a private wealth manager has specifically stated a long-term time horizon. This client wants to achieve a goal of EUR4,000,000 to fund retirement in 20 years. Additionally, with no dependents of her own, the client would like to contribute towards her young niece's eventual university expenses. Which of the following best describes the priority of client goals within the investment objectives section of an IPS?

   A. Both goals reflect primary objectives.

   B. The educational funding goal is a primary objective, while the retirement goal is a secondary objective.

   C. The retirement goal is a primary objective, while the educational funding goal is a secondary objective.

Solution:

C is the correct response. Because the retirement goal is quantified and has a time frame that is consistent with the client's long-term time horizon, it is the primary objective. Funding the niece's education is a secondary objective since no amount or timing is specified for it.

A is incorrect because both goals cannot be primary objectives.

B is incorrect because the client's time horizon is for the long term, so individual retirement goals should take precedence over the funding of the niece's education, for which no amount or timing is specified.

PRACTICE PROBLEMS

The following information relates to questions 1-6

Henriette Zhao is a private wealth manager and is meeting with a new client, Nestor Cree, to plan a wealth management strategy. To begin this meeting, Zhao seeks additional background information from Cree necessary as part of preparing the IPS. Zhao learns that Cree is 45 years old and is married with three children (ages 8, 5, and 1). Cree is currently employed as an attorney with annual salary of EUR300,000. Cree has several specific financial goals that he wishes to achieve in the future but has no particular return objective for his portfolio currently valued at EUR2,500,000. Because he has been investing for 20 years, Cree is comfortable with moderate levels of market volatility. His employment provides for his current expenses, so Cree's liquidity requirements are minimal. Cree prefers to have his environmental and social concerns reflected in his investment choices.

Zhao then focuses on Cree's financial goals. Cree plans to retire in 17 years and expects to need EUR200,000 per year on an inflation-adjusted basis to fund a desired retirement lifestyle for himself and his spouse. However, he is also concerned about how increasing medical expenses might affect his portfolio's ability to fund their retirement. As a potential solution to this concern, Cree hopes to purchase an apartment building within the next three years and use the rental income from this investment property to help fund medical expenses during retirement. Cree wants to fund university expenses for his three children, with the first payment starting in 10 years and continuing for 12–15 years. Cree's wife enjoys donating to philanthropic causes. She currently donates EUR10,000 per year, but by the time Cree retires, she hopes to increase this amount to EUR30,000 per year. Cree collects antique furniture and budgets EUR15,000 per year for additions to his collection. He mentions that this year's antique purchase will be his next large expense and currently has the highest priority of all his goals.

Zhao continues the discussion with Cree in order to evaluate his degree of risk tolerance. Cree considers retirement a long-term goal and is willing to endure a 10% drop in expected retirement spending. However, he is very concerned with having sufficient funds to cover medical expenses and views purchasing an investment property as a source of stable income to cover these expenses, so it is very important to him to purchase the building.

1. Which of the following investment parameter categories of the IPS is *least likely* to include Cree's preference for investments that reflect his environmental and social concerns?

   A. Asset class preference

   B. Other investment preferences

   C. Constraints

2. Identify and discuss at least one important missing component of Cree's financial background necessary to preparing the IPS.

3. Which one of the following would most likely be described as an unplanned goal

for Cree?

A. Medical expenses

B. Apartment building purchase

C. University expenses

4. Identify and discuss two areas in which Cree needs to improve goal quantification.

5. Discuss how a capital sufficiency analysis may assist Zhao in helping Cree with goal prioritization across his identified goals.

6. Determine Cree's degree of risk tolerance (lower versus higher) with respect to his retirement goal. Justify your response.

The following information relates to questions 7-9

Sharl Zik, a private wealth manager, is meeting with a 60-year-old client, Edmundo Patel, in order to create an IPS for Patel's upcoming retirement in the next year. Patel estimates that he will require EUR200,000 per year, with annual increases for inflation, during retirement. Patel's primary spending goals during retirement are to provide for his family's needs and maintain his retirement lifestyle. His secondary goals are to fund his philanthropic activities and leave a significant inheritance to his children.

During his retirement, Patel will receive union pension payments of EUR50,000 per year with annual increases for inflation. In his spare time, Patel runs a small business that provides him with an annual income of EUR120,000 and is valued at EUR1 million. He will continue running his business during retirement.

Patel holds a portfolio of securities valued at approximately EUR4 million with a cost basis of EUR1 million. Patel expects an annual pretax capital gains return of 6.5% per year on his securities portfolio. The capital gains tax rate is 20%. The portfolio primarily contains dividend-paying stocks and interest-bearing bonds, and the yield on the portfolio is 2%. Both stock dividend and bond interest are taxed annually at a rate of 40%. In the past, Patel has reinvested all these distributions back into his portfolio but anticipates that after retirement he may need to use some of the distributions to fund his expenses.

Additionally, Patel plans to buy a vacation home to enjoy his early retirement years and expects to hold the home for 10 years. His budget for the vacation home is approximately EUR1.7 million. He expects an 8% annual pretax appreciation in the value of his vacation home and expects to pay capital gains tax of 20% on the sale of this vacation home. Patel is considering selling half of his securities portfolio to fund the vacation home purchase.

Patel is also worried about the effects of inflation. While his pension income will adjust for inflation, he is concerned that the income from his small business is unlikely to adjust with inflation. He asks Zik to do an analysis to assess whether his income sources are expected to be sufficient in 10 years to cover the effects of inflation of 5% per year.

7. Determine whether the distributions from Patel's portfolio are expected to be sufficient to cover the expected shortfall between his retirement needs and his

anticipated income.

8. Determine whether Patel should sell half of his securities portfolio to buy the vacation home.

9. Evaluate Patel's ability to generate his retirement needs in 10 years after accounting for the effects of inflation on his small business income and his securities portfolio value.

The following information relates to questions 10-14

Val Sili, age 22, has just graduated from university and begins making ambitious plans for her future. She has accepted a position as a data science analyst in a start-up company starting next month. Her starting annual salary is USD96,000 per year (after tax), and as part of her compensation, will also receive stock options in the company annually worth USD50,000. She expects to be able to set aside 25% of her after-tax salary into investments in a taxable account while also maximizing her investment contributions to a defined-contribution account.

Sili believes that by the age of 28, she will be earning several times more than her starting salary at the age of 22. She further believes that she will have realized a payoff from her company stock options of at least USD5 million and plans to use her option proceeds to purchase real estate and make selected investments in other start-up ventures. She expects the value of her financial assets to be approximately USD300,000.

By the age of 35, Sili is expecting to be a top executive at a technology firm, with personal investable net worth in excess of USD20 million and a net worth of at least USD100 million.

Between the ages of 35 and 40, Sili expects to have gained sufficient experience and access to financial capital to start her own technology company, with an initial public offering several years later that will generate a payoff of at least USD1 billion. After serving as chair and CEO of the company for two years while it transitions to being a public company, Sili plans to retire from life as a technology company senior executive. She plans to live a relatively minimalist lifestyle financially in retirement while using her vast wealth to invest in young technology startups and provide advisory services for startup managers. As her abilities to provide such services decline, she plans to gradually donate her wealth to fund endowments to nonprofit scientific organizations devoted to solving important world problems with a specific focus on targeted investments in countries with high Gini coefficients.

10. Which of the following investments would be most appropriate for Sili during the beginning years of her career?

   A. Technology equity funds

   B. Lower-risk equity funds and fixed-income funds

   C. Fixed-income funds

11. Discuss the expected roles of Sili's financial asset portfolio and her plan to purchase real estate at the age of 30 in terms of the value of her future wealth.

12. Explain the assumptions that Sili is making regarding the change in her wealth

between the ages of 28 and 35.

13. Discuss the implications of Sili's retirement plan with respect to the value of her human capital, financial capital, and total wealth, as well as with respect to the decumulation phase of her economic life cycle.

14. Which of the following is most likely considered investable wealth for an individual?

    A. Checking account used for day-to-day expenses

    B. Savings account representing funds not needed for day-to-day needs

    C. Defined benefit pension plan participation with payments only after reaching age 60

15. A client reports the following assets and liabilities in thousands:

Checking account	50
Savings account	100
Taxable investment account	200
Tax-advantaged investment account	150
Vehicles	80
Primary residence	500
Business assets	800
Short-term credit card debt	25
Business liabilities	250

The client's investable net worth in thousands is closest to:

    A. 475

    B. 975

    C. 1,175

16. A Gini wealth coefficient of 0.50 most likely indicates that there is:

    A. perfect wealth equality.

    B. greater inequality compared to a Gini coefficient of 0.35.

    C. less inequality compared to a Gini coefficient of 0.35.

17. Longevity risk is most likely associated with which phase in the wealth life cycle?

    A. Preretirement

    B. Early retirement

    C. Later retirement

18. The estimation of the value of human capital, the future income, is discounted at the:

    A. real risk-free rate.

    B. nominal risk-free rate plus a premium for inflation.

C. nominal risk-free rate plus a premium associated with occupational income volatility.

19. The value of human capital tends to:

   A. increase over time until retirement.

   B. stay the same until retirement.

   C. decrease over time until retirement.

20. Suppose a client has taxable income of EUR1,500,000. Based on the tax rate schedule, what is the client's average tax rate?

Taxable income (EUR)		Tax on column 1	Percentage on excess over column 1
Over	Up to		
0	30,000	—	5
30,000	60,000	1,500	10
60,000	90,000	6,000	15
90,000	250,000	13,500	20
250,000	500,000	50,000	30
500,000	1,000,000	150,000	40
1,000,000		400,000	50

   A. 27%

   B. 43%

   C. 50%

21. Deferred taxes on income, relative to accrual taxes,

   A. decrease tax drag.

   B. do not affect tax drag.

   C. increase tax drag.

22. Which of the following investment parameters categories of an IPS is least likely to include a client's preferences for investments that reflect his environmental and social concerns?

   A. Asset class preferences

   B. Other investment preferences

   C. Constraints

SOLUTIONS

1. The correct answer is B because this "Other investment preferences" category typically includes legacy holdings such as shares of stock of a former employer or an investment that the client wishes to make countering the wealth manager's advice.

   A is incorrect because it represents a category that may include a client's preference for environmental and socially oriented investments. C is incorrect because it represents a category that may include a client's preference for environmental and socially oriented investments. In fact, depending on the strength of Zhao's preference, it could potentially be included in investment objectives, as well.

2. Two potentially important missing pieces of Cree's financial background needed to prepare the IPS are the following:

   - The financial background omits the tax status (i.e., taxable versus tax deferred) of the portfolio. As the taxation of the portfolio will have a significant impact on the after-tax return performance necessary to conduct capital sufficiency analysis, this is a vitally important aspect that needs to be included in the IPS.

   - Another financial factor omitted from the financial background discussion is whether Cree's employment provides a pension and the expected amount of pension income. Future pension income may provide an important component with respect to Cree's financial background in the IPS.

3. The correct answer is A because medical expenses are more difficult to quantify, since either the funding need or the timing of the financial need, or both, may not be estimated. B is incorrect because the apartment building purchase can be reasonably estimated or quantified at the onset and can be achieved within an expected time horizon. C is incorrect because university expenses can be reasonably estimated or quantified at the onset and can be achieved within an expected time horizon.

4. Cree has neglected to quantify goals related to

   1. His children's university expenses, and
   2. The scope of the planned apartment building purchase.

   Given Cree's goal of funding university expenses for his three children beginning in 10 years, these amounts may compete for funds with his planned retirement in 17 years. By better quantifying amounts expected, Zhao can help determine whether the education-funding goal is consistent with the retirement-funding goal.

   The apartment building purchase presents a short-term financial need in that Cree must budget for how much he is willing to spend on the building, and furthermore, the amount of future rental income that will be available from the purchased building (along with budgeted expenses to maintain the building). A specific plan will assist Cree in assessing whether the building purchase will be consistent with the longer-term goals of funding retirement and his children's education.

5. Capital sufficiency analysis is the process of evaluating whether a client has sufficient capital resources to determine if their current and future capital resources can adequately support their lifestyle, financial goals, and long-term financial

stability. Whenever the capital sufficiency analysis does not support the investment objective, the wealth manager must work with the client to revise objectives and create those that the wealth manager judges to be achievable. After quantifying his children's education goals and the apartment building purchase goal, a capital sufficiency analysis would allow Cree to assess the likelihood of being able to achieve each of the stated quantified goals (retirement, children's education, apartment building purchase, philanthropy, and antique furniture collection). If his capital resources appear to be insufficient based on Zhao's capital sufficiency analysis, then Cree can choose to prioritize which goals should be adjusted downward or eliminated and which are most important to maintain.

6. Retirement goal: Higher risk tolerance.

   Retirement is a long-term goal with a very long time horizon given that his planned retirement date is in 17 years, so this time frame reflects the beginning of his financial needs for this goal. Cree is willing to incur a moderate drop in his planned expenses, so he likely has a higher risk tolerance for that goal. Cree is concerned about paying future medical expenses in retirement, and since his retirement is still 17 years in the future, he likely has a higher risk tolerance with the medical expenses goal, especially given that he views the planned investment property purchase as providing a stable income stream.

7. The solution below shows that the expected distributions of EUR48,000 are greater than the expected shortfall of EUR30,000. Thus, the distributions are expected to be more than sufficient to help Patel meet his annual income needs in retirement.

   The expected shortfall between Patel's retirement needs and his anticipated income is equal to EUR30,000 (=200,000 − 50,000 − 120,000).

   The expected after-tax distributions from his portfolio are EUR48,000, as shown below:

   $$FVA = B \left\{ [1 + r (1 - t_x)]^T \right\} - 1 =$$

   $$4,000,000 \left\{ [1 + 0.02 (1 - 0.40)]^1 - 1 \right\} = 48,000$$

   The current value of the portfolio or basis, B, is EUR4,000,000. The before-tax return, r, is the 2% yield from dividends and interest. The tax rate, t_x, is 40%, and T equals 1 to reflect the annual cash distributions to augment the shortfall. Note that this return ignores the after-tax return from capital appreciation, which would add to the excess of after-tax earnings over annual income needs.

8. To determine whether Patel should sell the securities, an analysis can be done to compare the expected after-tax value of the home purchase and the expected after-tax value of the securities portfolio at the end of the 10-year time horizon. To avoid additional complexity, the analysis may initially avoid considering the cash distributions of the securities portfolio.

   If half of the securities portfolio (i.e., EUR2,000,000) is sold, then Patel will realize a capital gain of EUR1,500,000 (i.e., half of the capital gain of the full portfolio). Thus, the tax on the sale of the securities will be EUR300,000 (=20% x 1,500,000), and Patel will have EUR1,700,000 (=2,000,000 − 300,000) to buy the house. Alternatively, Patel could choose to forego buying the vacation home and maintain his securities portfolio for another 10 years (i.e., continue to invest EUR2,000,000).

   For both alternatives, use the following equation to calculate the after-tax values:

   $$FVA_{cgb} = B \left[(1 + r)^T (1 - t_{cg}) + t_{cg} (B) \right]$$

   For the vacation home purchase alternative, the basis (B) is equal to EUR1,700,000 and the expected pretax rate of return r is equal to 8%. If the vacation home is foregone and the portfolio is fully reinvested, the basis is equal to EUR2,000,000 and the expected pretax rate of return is equal to 6.5%. In both cases, the time horizon (T) is 10 years and the capital gains tax rate (t_{cg}) is 20%.

After-tax value of vacation home =

$$1,700,000 \, [(1 + 0.08)^{10} \, (1 - 0.20) + 0.20 \, (1,700,000/1,700,000)] = 3,276,138$$

After-tax value of reinvesting =

$$2,000,000 \, [(1 + 0.065)^{10} \, (1 - 0.20) + 0.20 \, (2,000,000/2,000,000)] = 3,403,420$$

Thus, although the pretax investment return on the securities portfolio is lower than the pretax return on the vacation, the higher-value solution on an after-tax basis is to keep the securities portfolio in place. This is because a return can be earned on the capital gains tax amount that would have to be paid if the securities were liquidated. Patel should consider an alternative source of funding for the vacation home.

9. Patel requires EUR200,000 of real purchasing power throughout retirement. His pension income will adjust for inflation, so this amounts to EUR50,000 of real income. So, he needs EUR150,000 of real income from his securities portfolio and his small business income.

The effects of inflation on his small business income are as follows if it remains at a nominal amount of EUR120,000 per year:

Real business income in 10 years = $120,000 \times (1 - 0.05)^{10} = 71,848$

So, in 10 years, the inflation of 5% annually is expected to reduce the purchasing power of Patel's small business income to EUR71,848. Deducting this amount from EUR150,000 gives a subtotal of EUR78,152.

Can the securities portfolio provide this amount of income in 10 years? Applying the following formula to the value of the securities portfolio:

$$FVIF_{tx, inflation} = [1 + r \, (1 - t_x)]^T - (1 - \pi)^T$$

Using the capital gains appreciation of 6.5% for r, 0% for the annual tax rate, 10 for T, and 5% for inflation (π), we can determine the future value of the securities portfolio in real purchasing power terms currently.

$$FVIF_{tx, inflation} = [1 + r \, (1 - t_x) \,]^T - (1 - \pi)^T =$$

$$[1 + 0.065 \, (1 - 0)]^{10} - (1 - 0.05)^{10} = 1.27840$$

Multiplying this amount by the current portfolio value of EUR4 million gives EUR5,113,600. The securities portfolio generates a 2% pretax cash distribution taxed annually at a 40% rate; thus, the after-tax distribution is 1.2% of the portfolio value.

Cash distribution in real terms in 10 years = $0.012 \times 5,113,600 = EUR61,363$

Thus, Patel faces an income shortfall in 10 years of EUR16,789 (= 78,152 − 61,363). To cover the shortfall, Patel may have to consider liquidating small portions of his securities portfolio to generate additional cash flow each year. Of course, such reductions will cause a decline in the value of his portfolio, thus also reducing future cash distributions from the portfolio, so these would have to be considered as well.

10. The correct answer is B. In her early career stage, the value of Sili's human capital is significant, and she plans to begin building financial capital. Her option position in her employer's stock creates an undiversified equity position, and her early-career stage in a high-income job suggests that she would benefit from additional equity exposure as long as it provides diversification relative to

her employer's stock. Because of the start-up nature of her new employer, her compensation is riskier, implying that she may benefit from some fixed-income exposure.

A is incorrect because this investment would ensure that Sili's financial capital is quite high risk, thus not providing much diversification to her employment compensation. C is incorrect because of her early career stage. The diversification benefit of fixed-income investments ignores the potential for adding some additional equity exposure, as the value of her human capital is very high and she is able to take reasonable amounts of investment risk.

11. As Sili progresses in her career, the value of her human capital is likely to begin declining. To help offset the decline in her human capital, the value of her financial assets and real estate is likely to increase over time. Thus, these assets help protect the value of her future total wealth.

12. The most important assumption that Sili is making reflects a belief that one or more of the start-up ventures in which she invests will become quite valuable, but these investments will not yet be liquid during this seven-year time frame. The value of these business interests will account for the USD80 million difference between Sili's net worth and investible net worth.

    A second assumption is that the value of Sili's financial assets will continue to grow significantly during the stated time period in order for investible net worth to reach USD20 million.

    A secondary assumption that Sili may be making is that the equity in her real estate assets increases in value significantly.

13. While Sili's human capital value likely declines in retirement as she ages, her ability to earn money from her investments and advisory work for start-ups may negate significant declines in the value of her human capital. However, eventually she may decide to make fewer investments and take on fewer advisory assignments, and at this stage, her human capital will decline in value more significantly.

    Sili's financial capital is likely to continue to increase as long as she remains effective at identifying good candidate start-ups in which to invest. As these companies succeed financially, Sili will continue to realize profits from these investments.

    Eventually, she will begin converting some of her financial capital into donations to her philanthropic interests during the decumulation phase of her economic life. At this point in time, her total wealth may finally begin to decline.

14. The correct answer is B. The savings account can be used for investments, especially if the checking account is sufficient to meet ordinary expenses.

    A is incorrect because this is a transactions account and may not be considered investable. C is incorrect because the individual does not make the investment decisions until payments begin, and the individual may then invest the payments once living expenses are covered.

15. The correct answer is A. The investable net worth in thousands is calculated as

    Investable net worth = 100 + 200 + 150 − 25 = 475.

    B is incorrect because it includes the business assets and liabilities:
    Investable net worth = 100 + 200 + 150 + 800 − 25 − 250 = 975. C is incorrect because it includes a checking account and business assets and liabilities, as well as nonliquid personal assets: Investable net worth = 50 + 100 + 200 + 150 + 80 + 800 − 25 − 250 = 1,175

16. The correct answer is B. Gini coefficients range from 0 (perfect equality) to 1 (perfect inequality). Because 0.50 is greater than 0.35, this indicates that there is greater inequality for the situation with a coefficient of 0.50.

    A is incorrect because perfect equality would have a Gini coefficient equal to 0. C in incorrect because 0.50 is closer to perfect inequality (that is, a coefficient equal to 1.0) than a coefficient of 0.35.

17. The correct answer is C. Longevity risk is the risk of outliving one's financial resources. A is incorrect because longevity risk is the risk of outliving one's financial resources. B is incorrect because longevity risk is the risk of outliving one's financial resources.

18. C is correct. A premium associated with the occupational income is added to the nominal interest rate. The numerator in the human capital valuation is the anticipated income. A is incorrect because the income that is being discounted is in nominal terms. B is incorrect because the nominal risk-free rate includes an inflation premium.

19. The correct answer is C. The value of human capital diminishes over time because this value includes projected income, so as time progresses, there is less of this future income included in the valuation. B is incorrect. The value of human capital diminishes over time because this value includes projected income, so as time progresses, there is less of this future income included in the valuation. A is incorrect. The value of human capital diminishes over time because this value includes projected income, so as time progresses, there is less of this future income included in the valuation.

20. The correct answer is B. The tax is

    $$\text{Tax} = 400{,}000 + 0.50(1{,}500{,}000 - 1{,}000{,}000) = 650{,}000$$

    And the average tax rate is

    $$\text{Average tax rate} = \frac{650{,}000}{1{,}500{,}000} = 0.4333 \text{ or } 43.33\%$$

    A is incorrect because the income over 1,000,000 is not included in the tax: $\text{Average tax rate} = \frac{400{,}000}{1{,}500{,}000} = 02667$ or 26.67%. C is incorrect because this is the marginal tax rate corresponding to the highest income bracket.

21. The correct answer is A. Deferred taxes, with taxes on gains, are deferred until the end of the investment horizon, and the tax rate equals the tax drag on capital accumulation. C is incorrect because with accrual taxation, the tax drag on capital accumulation compounds over time. B is incorrect because accrual taxes create more tax drag relative to deferred taxes.

22. The correct answer is B. The "Other investment preferences" category typically includes legacy holdings such as shares of stock of a former employer or an investment the client wishes to make countering the wealth manager's advice. A is incorrect because it represents a category that may include a client's preference for environmentally and socially oriented investments. C is incorrect because it represents a category that may include client's preferences for environmentally and socially oriented investments.

5

Portfolio Management for Institutional Investors

by Arjan Berkelaar, PhD, CFA, Kate Misic, CFA, and Peter C. Stimes, CFA.

Arjan Berkelaar, PhD, CFA, is at KAUST Investment Management Company (USA). Kate Misic, CFA, is at Telstra Super Pty Ltd (Australia). Peter C. Stimes, CFA, is a private investor in Fallbrook, California (USA).

LEARNING OUTCOMES

Mastery	The candidate should be able to:
☐	discuss common characteristics of institutional investors as a group
☐	discuss investment policy of institutional investors
☐	discuss the stakeholders in the portfolio, the liabilities, the investment time horizons, and the liquidity needs of different types of institutional investors
☐	describe the focus of legal, regulatory, and tax constraints affecting different types of institutional investors
☐	evaluate risk considerations of private defined benefit (DB) pension plans in relation to 1) plan funded status, 2) sponsor financial strength, 3) interactions between the sponsor's business and the fund's investments, 4) plan design, and 5) workforce characteristics
☐	evaluate the investment policy statement of an institutional investor
☐	evaluate the investment portfolio of a private DB plan, sovereign wealth fund, university endowment, and private foundation
☐	describe considerations affecting the balance sheet management of banks and insurers

CFA Institute would like to thank Karl Mergenthaler, CFA, for his contributions to earlier drafts of this reading.

1   INSTITUTIONAL INVESTORS: TYPES AND COMMON CHARACTERISTICS

☐ | discuss common characteristics of institutional investors as a group

Institutional investors are corporations, trusts, or other legal entities that invest in financial markets on behalf of groups or individuals, including both current and future generations. On a global basis, the total value of assets under management (AUM) by the global asset management industry as of 2020 reached more than USD100 trillion, and, as such, wields significant influence over capital markets.

The universe of institutional investors includes, but is not limited to, defined benefit and defined contribution pension plans, sovereign wealth funds, endowments, foundations, banks, and insurance companies. Pension plans, which account for approximately US$57 trillion in investable assets or roughly half of global institutional assets under management, include both defined benefit plans, in which the sponsor (employer) assumes investment risk, and defined contribution plans, in which the individual makes investment decisions and assumes the investment risk. Sovereign wealth funds, which account for about US$8 trillion in assets as of the end of 2020, are government-owned investment funds that invest in financial and/or real assets. Endowments and foundations, which account for approximately US$1.6 trillion in assets, manage assets on behalf of educational institutions, hospitals, churches, museums, and other charitable organizations. Banks and insurance companies, comprising net financial assets on the order of US$9 trillion, are financial intermediaries that balance portfolios of securities, loans, and derivatives for the purposes of (i) meeting the claims of depositors, counterparties, policyholders, and creditors and (ii) providing adequate returns to their contractual capital holders. The universe of institutional investors is comprised of large, complex, and sophisticated investors that must contend with a multitude of investment challenges and constraints.

There has been an important shift in the asset allocation of institutional investors over the last half century. In the 1970s, most pensions and endowments invested almost exclusively in domestic, fixed-income instruments. In the 1980s, many institutional investors began to invest in equity markets and often pursued a long-term strategic allocation of 60% equities/40% fixed income. In the 1990s, investors recognized the benefits of diversification and many made their first forays into international equity markets. At the turn of the 21st century, many of the world's largest pension funds and endowments further diversified their portfolios and increased investments in alternative asset classes, including private equity, hedge funds, real estate, and other alternative or illiquid assets.

Meanwhile, institutional investors have seen broad shifts in their strategic investment behavior. The trend toward Liability Driven Investing (LDI), long a mainstay of banks and insurance companies, has taken hold among many defined benefit pension plans, particularly US corporate and public pension funds. Sovereign wealth funds have amassed significant assets over the past several decades, and many have implemented innovative investment approaches characterized by active management. Many endowments have adopted the "Endowment Model" of investing that involves significant exposure to alternative investments. Meanwhile, banks and insurers must navigate a complex and ever-changing economic and regulatory environment.

In this reading, we endeavor to put the numerous factors that affect investment by institutional investors into context. Section 1 discusses common characteristics of institutional investors as a group. Section 2 provides an overview of investment policies for institutional investors. Detailed coverage by institutional investor type begins with Sections 3–7, pension funds, where we discuss various factors that influence investments, including: stakeholders, liability streams, investment horizons, and liquidity needs; major legal, regulatory, accounting, and tax constraints; investment objectives and key components of Investment Policy Statements; and, finally, asset allocation and investment portfolios that emanate from the foregoing factors and constraints. Sections 8–10 follow the same approach for sovereign wealth funds, and Sections 11–15 do the same for university endowments and private foundations. Sections 16–19 covers banks and insurers and includes balance sheet management considerations. A summary of key points concludes the reading.

Institutional Investors: Common Characteristics

For the purposes of this reading, institutional investors include pension plans, sovereign wealth funds, endowments, foundations, banks, and insurance companies. As we will see in upcoming sections where we cover each of these six institutional types in detail, their objectives and constraints can vary widely. First, in this section we discuss important defining characteristics of institutional investors as a group, characteristics that set them apart from individual (retail and high-net-worth) investors. The common defining characteristics of institutional investors include the following:

1. **Scale (i.e., asset size):** The issue of scale is relevant for institutional investors because it may impact investment capabilities, access to investment strategies, liquidity, trading costs, and other key aspects of the investment process.

2. **Long-term investment horizon:** Institutional investors generally have a long-term investment horizon that is often determined by a specific liability stream, such as the benefit obligation of a pension plan, the spending policy of an endowment, or other obligations.

3. **Regulatory frameworks:** Institutional investors must contend with multiple regulatory frameworks that frequently vary by jurisdiction and complexity and are often evolving.

4. **Governance framework:** Institutional investors typically implement their investment programs through an investment office that often has a clearly defined governance model.

5. **Principal–Agent issues:** As institutional investors manage assets on behalf of others, principal–agent issues must be recognized and managed appropriately.

We discuss these five common characteristics in more detail next.

Scale

Institutional investors' assets under management can range from relatively small (e.g., less than US$25 million) to relatively large (e.g., more than US$10 billion). Smaller institutions may face challenges in building a diversified portfolio spanning public and private asset classes because they may be unable to access certain investments that have a high minimum investment size. For example, smaller institutions are less likely to be able to invest in private equity or real estate assets (i.e., property). Small institutional investors may also face challenges in hiring skilled investment professionals. As a result, they are more likely to outsource investments to external asset managers and rely on investment consultants. Larger institutional investors experience scale benefits that allow them access to a wider investment universe, and they can readily hire investment professionals. They may potentially manage part of their portfolios in-house if benefits outweigh costs. The largest institutional investors, however, may experience dis-economies of scale. For example, they might be unable to invest in certain niche investments like venture capital ("VC"). Given the huge asset size of investments under management, a small allocation to VC may not generate sufficient returns to justify the position (including due diligence costs). The largest institutional investors may also be unable to deploy as much capital as desired with some external managers as certain investment strategies are capacity constrained. External managers who want to avoid jeopardizing their ability to generate superior returns will close the strategy to new investors. To overcome these constraints, some of the largest institutions buy private companies, property, and infrastructure assets directly and manage their traditional asset-class portfolios in-house. Large institutional investors also face the costs of market impact given their sizable trading orders.

Rapidly growing institutional investors may experience high cash inflow relative to the size of their portfolios, which requires them to continuously invest inflows and to maintain the appropriate asset mix (strategic asset allocation). Ensuring access to investments capable of absorbing their growth in assets under management may be challenging when investing in capacity-constrained strategies, such as small-cap equity or venture capital.

Long-Term Investment Horizon

Pension funds, sovereign wealth funds, endowments, and foundations all typically have long investment horizons and relatively low liquidity needs. Cash outlays are relatively modest as a percent of assets under management, with net payouts typically around 5% or less. However, there are exceptions: For example, frozen defined benefit plans might be in a de-risking mode that increases their liquidity needs. Relatively low liquidity needs allow these institutions to invest in a broad range of alternative asset classes, including private equity, private real estate, natural resources, infrastructure, and hedge funds. Banks and insurance companies, however, tend to be much more asset/liability focused while operating within tight regulations designed to ensure adequacy of capital.

Regulatory Frameworks

Institutional investors are typically subject to different legal, regulatory, tax, and accounting frameworks than individual investors. These frameworks define the set of rules an institutional investor must follow to qualify for reduced tax rates or tax-exempt status. Importantly, these frameworks and rules typically differ by national jurisdiction in which the institutional investor operates. Some examples of important relevant legal, regulatory, taxation, and accounting frameworks and organizations include the following:

- United States:

    - Employee Retirement Income Security Act (ERISA)
    - Pension Protection Act (PPA)
    - Uniform Prudent Management of Institutional Funds Act (UPMIFA)
    - Uniform Prudent Investor Act (UPIA)
    - Freedom of Information Act (FOIA)
    - Governmental Accounting Standards Board (GASB)
    - Generally Accepted Accounting Principles (GAAP) set by the Financial Accounting Standards Board (FASB)
    - Statutory Accounting Principles (SAP) set by the National Association of Insurance Commissioners (NAIC)
- United Kingdom:

    - Pensions Act

- Finance Acts (various)
■ European Union:

- Institutions for Occupational Retirement Provision (IORP) II
■ South Korea:

- Employee Retirement Benefit Security Act
■ Australia:

- Superannuation Industry (Supervision) Act (SIS Act)
■ International:

- International Financial Reporting Standards (IFRS) set by the International Accounting Standards Board (IASB)
- International Organization of Securities Commissions (IOSCO)

Many relevant regulatory bodies govern and supervise institutional investors and their portfolios globally. The International Organization of Securities Commissions (IOSCO) is the international body that brings together the world's securities regulators, and it has 217 members. Ordinary members (127) include the national securities commissions or similar governmental bodies. Associate members (24) are supranational governmental regulators, subnational governmental regulators, intergovernmental international organizations, and other international standard-setting bodies. Affiliate members (66) include self-regulatory organizations, securities exchanges, and other financial market infrastructure and international regulatory bodies.

The key drivers of the legal and regulatory frameworks faced by institutional investors are investor protection, safety and soundness of financial institutions, and integrity of financial markets. Changes to these frameworks following the 2007–2009 global financial crisis focused on leverage limits, enhanced collateral requirements, increased liquidity requirements, central clearing, proprietary trading limits, private equity limits, trading tax implementation, brokerage fee limits, compensation limits, and requirements for more transparent reporting. Examples of regulations focusing on such reforms include the following:

■ United States:

- Dodd-Frank Wall Street Reform and Consumer Protection Act (Dodd-Frank)
- Section 619 (12 U.S.C. Section 1851) of the Dodd-Frank Act (Volcker Rule)
- Foreign Account Tax Compliance Act (FATCA), which has international implications
■ United Kingdom:

- Retail Distribution Review (RDR)
■ European Union (with most adopted by the United Kingdom):

- Undertakings for the Collective Investment of Transferable Securities V (UCITS V)
- Alternative Investment Fund Managers Directive (AIFMD)
- Solvency II Directive (Solvency II)
- Markets in Financial Instruments Directive II (MIFID II)
- European Market Infrastructure Regulation (EMIR)
- Financial Transaction Tax (FTT)

- Packaged Retail Investment and Insurance Products (PRIIPs)
- International:

  - Third Basel Accord / Capital Requirements Directive (Basel III / CRD IV)
  - Santiago Principles (Generally Accepted Principles and Practices for Sovereign Wealth Funds)
  - Principles of the Linaburg-Maduell Transparency Index (Sovereign Wealth Funds)

Governance Framework

Institutional investors typically operate under a formal governance structure. The governance structure generally includes a board of directors and an investment committee. The board may comprise company representative directors, employee representative directors, and independent directors. Independent directors are usually selected to increase the board's overall investment expertise. Investment committees can be sub-committees of the board with delegated authority to oversee investment policy. Alternatively, investment committees can be internal and consist of investment staff tasked with implementing the investment policy set by the board. The board and/or investment committee provide a key role in establishing the organization's investment policy, defining the risk appetite, setting the investment strategy, and monitoring the investment performance.

The board often sets the long-term strategic asset allocation and can delegate the setting of medium-term tactical asset allocation to its investment staff. It may also delegate manager selection to investment staff. Notably though, many institutional investor boards will seek to retain control through overseeing hiring and firing of managers. Best practice suggests, however, that it is better to delegate the hiring and firing of external managers to investment staff to ensure that the board focuses on such broader issues as governance, investment policy, and strategic asset allocation.

Institutional investors typically implement their investment strategy through an investment office. The investment office can be structured in different ways, but the most common model involves a Chief Investment Officer, who is supported by a team of asset-class specialists or a team of generalists working across asset classes. Institutional investors may manage investments in-house (e.g., some large Canadian pension plans and Australian superannuation funds) or outsource investment management partially or entirely to external assets managers. The factors affecting the decision to manage assets internally include the size of assets under management, capability of internal resources, or a desire to pursue custom strategies not readily offered by external managers. It can be costly to build the capability to manage assets internally, so in most cases asset owners need to achieve a certain threshold of assets under management before the benefits outweigh the costs of internalization.

For pension funds, sovereign wealth funds, endowments, and foundations, outsourcing elements of the investment function to external asset managers—or even outsourcing the entire investment operation to an outsourced chief investment officer (CIO) firm—is much more common than managing investments in-house. Such asset owners typically rely on specialized consultants to assist with asset allocation decisions and investment manager selection. These consultants often provide macro-economic forecasts and capital market assumptions for asset classes that are integral to determining the investor's optimal asset allocation. In addition, the consultant assists in monitoring the large universe of external asset managers. Finally, the consultant may provide independent performance attribution and reporting and may monitor any internally managed investments and benchmark them against the external asset manager universe.

In contrast, banks and insurance companies undertake most of their investing, risk budgeting, compliance, and balance sheet management activities internally.

Principal–Agent Issues

Institutional investors frequently experience conflicts of interest that stem from principal–agent issues. The principal–agent issue arises if one person, the agent, makes decisions on behalf of another person or institution, the principal, and their interests are not aligned. A dilemma exists for the agent when he/she may be motivated to act in his/her own best interests and not in the best interests of the principal. Because of operational and investment complexity, institutional investors generally rely on various parties (i.e., agents) to act on their behalf. Agents may be internal or external. Internal agents include investment committee members and investment staff. External agents include third-party asset managers, broker/dealers, consultants, and board members. A typical example of the principal–agent problem is where performance fee structures are designed by external fund managers to provide attractive compensation to them via a high base fee, which is due regardless of fund performance. This fee structure gives little incentive for the fund manager to produce superior performance. Such fee arrangements are common among hedge funds and have led to greater demand for fee transparency and alignment of interest between hedge fund managers and their clients. To manage principal–agent issues, institutional investors will typically have highly developed governance models and high levels of accountability with a board and/or investment committee typically overseeing the investment office. Such models should be designed to explicitly acknowledge and manage conflicts of interest and align the interests of all agents with those of the principals.

OVERVIEW OF INVESTMENT POLICY

2

☐ | discuss investment policy of institutional investors

Institutional investors codify their mission, investment objectives, and guidelines in an Investment Policy Statement (IPS). The IPS establishes policies and procedures for the effective administration and management of the institutional assets. A well-crafted IPS can help minimize principal–agent challenges by providing clear guidance on day-to-day management of the assets. Besides mission and investment objectives (i.e., return and risk tolerance), the IPS should cover any constraints that affect the asset allocation, asset allocation policy with ranges and asset class benchmarks, rebalancing policy, guidelines affecting the implementation of the asset allocation policy, and reporting requirements. The IPS should be reviewed annually; however, revisions should be infrequent, such as when material changes occur in investor circumstances and/or the market environment, as the IPS serves as the foundation for the investment program. The asset allocation policy and investment guidelines are typically included in an appendix that can be modified more easily.

Investment objectives flow from the organization's overall mission. For banks and insurance companies, the investment objective is to maximize net present value by balancing (i) the expected returns on assets, (ii) the expected cost of liabilities, (iii) the overall risks of assets and liabilities, and (iv) the economic relationships between and among assets and liabilities.

The investment objectives are more straightforward for the other types of institutions covered in this reading. For example, the overall objective of a DB pension fund might be to maintain a funded ratio in excess of 100%; for an endowment, it may be to maintain long-term purchasing power while providing needed financial support to its university. Investment objectives are typically expressed as a desired return target over the medium-to-long term (which should be clearly specified) with an acceptable level of risk. This return target should be evaluated in the context of the organization's overall mission and should be tied to the evaluation of liabilities (e.g., discount rate used to value DB pension plan liabilities or spending rate for an endowment). When expressing the return target in real terms, the relevant inflation metric must be defined. For example, GIC—Singapore's sovereign wealth fund—uses global inflation defined as G3 (the US, Japan, and Eurozone) inflation, while some US endowments use the Higher Education Price Index (HEPI) published by Commonfund (an independent asset management firm serving non-profit organizations and promoting best practices among institutional investors).

Investment objectives and return targets must be consistent with an organization's risk tolerance and other constraints. Risk tolerance can be expressed in different ways, such as for:

- DB pension funds: surplus volatility (standard deviation of asset returns in excess of liability returns);

- Sovereign wealth funds (SWFs): probability of investment losses (or probability of not maintaining purchasing power) over a certain time period;

- Endowments and foundations: volatility of total returns (standard deviation of total returns); and

- Banks and insurance companies: value at risk (VaR) or conditional VaR (CVaR) and comprehensive, scenario-based stress tests.

Finally, constraints (legal, regulatory, tax, and accounting) have a bearing on investment objectives and should be incorporated into the design of an investment policy. For example, constraints might limit the scope of acceptable risk and available asset classes.

Once the investment objectives—the desired risk and return characteristics—have been established, a strategic asset allocation or policy portfolio is designed. The investment portfolio of an institutional investor is designed to meet its objectives and should reflect the appropriate risk and liquidity considerations addressed in the IPS. For example, a large allocation to private equity is probably not appropriate for institutions with a relatively short investment horizon and high liquidity requirements. Similarly, a large fixed-income allocation might not be appropriate for an institution with a long investment horizon and low liquidity requirements. While institutional investors each have unique liability characteristics, several investment approaches have emerged over the past couple of years. Broadly speaking, these can be grouped into four different approaches:

1. **Norway model** popularized by Norway's global pension fund, Government Pension Fund Global (GPFG). The Norway model is characterized by an almost exclusive reliance on public equities and fixed income (the traditional 60/40 equity/bond model falls under the Norway model), with largely passively managed assets and with very little to no allocation to alternative investments. Investments are usually managed with tight tracking error limits. The advantages of this approach are that investment costs/fees are low, investments are transparent, the risk of poor manager selection is low, and there is little complexity for a governing board. The disadvantage is that there is limited potential for value-added (i.e., alpha from security selection skills) above-market returns. However, Norway's GPFG has begun to seek additional value over market-capitalization benchmarks by attempting to capture systematic risk factors.

2. **Endowment model** popularized by the Yale Endowment. The endowment model is characterized by a high allocation to alternative investments (private investments and hedge funds), significant active management, and externally managed assets. This investment approach stands in almost direct contrast to the Norway model. Although labeled 'endowment model,' this investment approach is not only followed by many university endowments and foundations but also by several sovereign wealth funds and defined benefit pension funds. The endowment model is appropriate for institutional investors that have a long-term investment horizon, high risk tolerance, relatively small liquidity needs, and skill in sourcing alternative investments (the nature of alternative investments is such that there is large variation between the worst and best performing asset managers, and selecting the right manager is therefore critically important). The endowment model is difficult to implement for small institutional investors as they might not be able to access high quality managers. It might also be difficult to implement for very large institutional investors because of their very large footprint. The endowment model is more expensive in terms of costs/fees compared to the Norway model.

3. **Canada model** popularized by the Canada Pension Plan Investment Board (CPPIB). The Canada model, just like the endowment model, is characterized by a high allocation to alternatives. Unlike the endowment model, however, the Canada model relies more on internally managed assets. The innovative features of the Canada model are the: a) reference portfolio, b) total portfolio approach, and c) active management. The reference portfolio is a passive mix of public equities, fixed income, and cash that represents a cheap and easily implementable portfolio that is expected to achieve the long-term expected return consistent with the institution's investment objectives and risk appetite. The reference portfolio effectively defines a transparent, risk-equivalent benchmark for the investment portfolio, and serves as a low-cost alternative to the fund's actual portfolio. The reference portfolio might be different from the institution's strategic asset allocation or policy portfolio. Importantly, the reference portfolio is typically made up of only publicly traded securities (in the form of common public market indices in equities and fixed income) that can be more easily understood by the governing board, while the strategic asset allocation may include target allocations to private markets and hedge funds. The total portfolio approach is the method of constructing the portfolio to ensure that planned risk exposures at the total portfolio level are maintained as individual investments enter, leave or change in value. It is an approach that is aimed at minimizing the unintended exposures and uncompensated risks that may arise as added value is sought by extending investments beyond the reference portfolio. For example, if private equity is added, management considers that it is leveraged equity and as a result the exposure to public equities needs to be reduced by more than the proposed allocation to private equity and the allocation to fixed-income needs to be increased to offset the leverage. Although the Canada model starts with a passive reference portfolio, it is important to note that the Canada model employs active management from tilting asset allocation through to stock selection. A good example of a sovereign wealth fund that has embraced the concept of the reference portfolio is the New Zealand Superannuation Fund.

4. **Liability Driven Investing (LDI) Model** has gained significant importance, particularly among corporate defined benefit pension plans in the United States, although some of the European pension funds—particularly in Denmark and in the Netherlands—adopted the LDI concept even prior to

the 2007–2009 global financial crisis. In the LDI model, the primary investment objective is to generate returns sufficient to cover liabilities. As such, the investor's focus shifts away from operating in an asset-only context, to a focus on maximizing expected surplus return (excess return of assets over liabilities) and managing surplus volatility. Although the implementation and resultant asset allocation may vary significantly, LDI portfolios—other than for banks and insurance institutions—typically have a significant exposure to long duration fixed-income securities. In some LDI implementations, institutional investors separate their portfolios into a hedging portfolio (this portfolio usually hedges the main risk factor in the liabilities, which is interest rate risk) and a return-generating portfolio (this portfolio needs to generate sufficient returns to offset the growth rate of liabilities, other than changes in the discount rate). The hedging portfolio for defined benefit pension funds, sovereign wealth funds, and endowments/foundations usually consists of long duration fixed-income securities and may entail the use of derivatives, such as interest rate swaps, to extend the duration of the portfolio. The return-generating portfolio usually includes public equities and alternative investments.

Exhibit 1 summarizes these four investment approaches.

Exhibit 1: Common Investment Approaches Used by Institutional Investors

Investment Approach	Description
Norway Model	Traditional style characterized by 60%/40% equity/fixed-income allocation, few alternatives, largely passive investments, tight tracking error limits, and benchmark as a starting position. *Pros*: Low cost, transparent, suitable for large scale, easy for board to understand. *Cons*: Limited value-added potential.
Endowment Model	Characterized by high alternatives exposure, active management and outsourcing. *Pros*: High value-added potential. *Cons*: Expensive and difficult to implement for most sovereign wealth funds because of their large asset sizes.
Canada Model	Characterized by high alternatives exposure, active management, and insourcing. *Pros*: High value-added potential and development of internal capabilities. *Cons*: Potentially expensive and difficult to manage.
LDI Model	Characterized by focus on hedging liabilities and interest rate risk including via duration-matched, fixed-income exposure. A growth component in the return-generating portfolio is also typical (exceptions being bank and insurance company portfolios). *Pros*: Explicit recognition of liabilities as part of the investment process. *Cons*: Certain risks (e.g., longevity risk, inflation risk) may not be hedged.

3

PENSION FUNDS: TYPES AND STAKEHOLDERS

Pension funds are long-term saving and investment plans designed to accumulate sufficient assets to provide for the financial needs of retirees. There are two main types of pension plans: **defined benefit**, in which a plan sponsor commits to paying a specified retirement benefit, and **defined contribution**, in which contributions are defined but the ultimate retirement benefit is not specified or guaranteed by the plan sponsor. Globally, there are many variations and nuances of these two broad categories of pension plans. Exhibit 2 compares the key features of defined benefit and defined contribution pension plans.

Exhibit 2: Comparison of Defined Benefit and Defined Contribution Pension Plan Features

Characteristics/Features	Defined Benefit Pension Plan	Defined Contribution Pension Plan
Benefit payments	Benefit payouts are defined by a contract between the employee and the pension plan (payouts are often calculated as a percentage of salary).	Benefit payouts are determined by the performance of investments selected by the participant.
Contributions	The employer is the primary contributor, though the employee may contribute as well. The size of contributions is driven by several key factors, including performance of investments selected by the pension fund.	The employee is typically the primary contributor—although the employer may contribute as well or may have a legal obligation to contribute a percentage of the employee's salary.
Investment decision making	The pension fund determines how much to save and what to invest in to meet the plan objectives.	The employee determines how much to save and what to invest in to meet his/her objectives (from the available menu of investment vehicles selected by the plan sponsor).
Investment risk	The employer bears the risk that the liabilities are not met and may be required to make additional contributions to meet any shortfall.	The employee bears the risk of not meeting his/her objectives for this account in terms of funding retirement.
Mortality/Longevity risk	Mortality risk is pooled. If a beneficiary passes away early, he/she typically leaves a portion of unpaid benefits in the pool offsetting additional benefit payments required by beneficiaries that live longer than expected. As a result, the individual does not bear any of the risk of outliving his/her retirement benefits.	The employee bears the risk of not meeting his/her objectives for this account in terms of funding retirement. The employee bears longevity risk.

Source: World Economic Forum, "Alternative Investments 2020: The Future of Alternative Investments" (2015).

Pension funds are significant players in the global investment landscape. Over the past 20 years, there has been a move away from defined benefit (DB) plans (especially non-government DB plans) to defined contribution (DC) plans. Among drivers of this shift are DC plans' lower financial risk for plan sponsors, absence of risk of becoming underfunded, and ease of portability (simplifies job mobility). Willis Towers Watson reports in its "Global Pension Assets Study 2018" covering the seven largest pension markets, the "P7" (Australia, Canada, Japan, the Netherlands, Switzerland, the United Kingdom, and the United States) that during the past 20 years DC pension plans have risen from 33% to 49% of total plan assets.

The split between DB and DC plans can vary significantly from country to country. One of the challenges of classifying countries by this split is that many countries offer hybrid pension plans, such as that in Switzerland where defined contribution connotes a cash balance plan in which all assets are pooled and the plan sponsor shares the investment risk. There are basically no pure DC plans in Switzerland. Exhibit 3 presents the split between DB and DC plans for the P7 countries. Together these countries comprise more than 90% of worldwide pension assets. Note that a substantial difference exists between countries. Some countries (such as Australia) rely almost exclusively on DC plans, while others (such as Japan and the Netherlands) predominantly use DB plans.

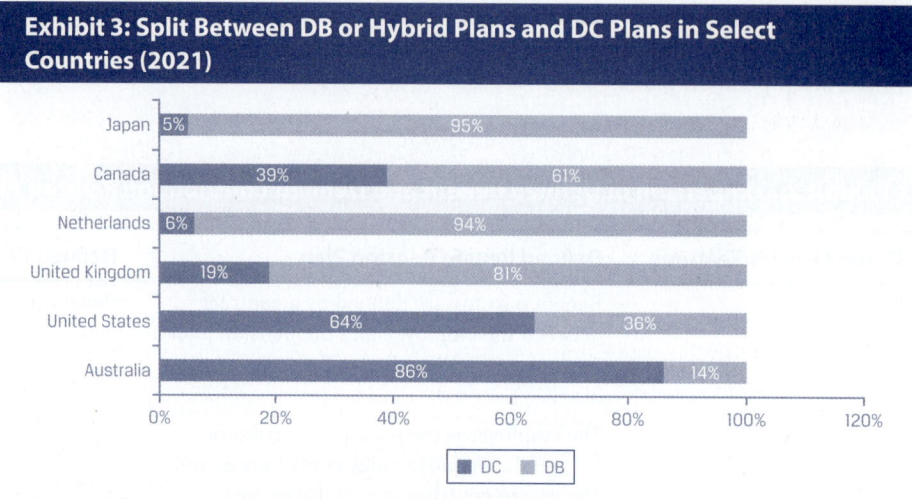

Exhibit 3: Split Between DB or Hybrid Plans and DC Plans in Select Countries (2021)

Source: Willis Towers Watson Thinking Ahead Institute (2021).

Stakeholders

Many entities are involved with institutional retirement plans. These include the employer, employees, retirees, unions, management, the investment committee and/or board, and shareholders. Governments have generally encouraged pension plans as a tool to assist individuals to build sufficient financial resources to fund their retirement needs. Government support typically comes in the form of favorable tax treatment for both companies and individuals who contribute to or manage pension plans, provided they operate according to local pension plan regulations. The government and taxpayers will bear some of the shortfall risks (in terms of added welfare or social security payments) in instances of employers failing to pay agreed on defined benefit payments and where individuals fail to accumulate sufficient wealth for retirement.

Defined Benefit Pension Plans

The stakeholders of a defined benefit pension plan are the employer [typically referred to as the plan sponsor and usually represented by management and the Chief Financial Officer (CFO)]; plan beneficiaries (employees and retirees); the Chief Investment Officer (CIO) and investment staff; the investment committee and/or board; and the government, unions, and shareholders in the case of corporate DB plans. Defined benefits promised to beneficiaries create liabilities for the plan sponsor. In operating the pension plan, the sponsor and investment staff must make investment decisions in the interest of the ultimate beneficiaries (employees and retirees). Defined benefit pension liabilities are typically funded from two sources: 1) employer and employee contributions and 2) investment returns on funded assets. Employee contributions can be fixed or variable, but employer contributions usually vary depending on the plan's funded status. Although each of the stakeholders has a strong interest in plan assets being invested appropriately, opinions might differ over the acceptable level of investment risk and the magnitude of employer contributions to the plan.

The plan sponsor may have an interest in 1) minimizing employer contributions due to budget constraints and/or 2) managing the volatility of employer contributions (by aiming for less volatility in investment returns). This allows management to plan future contributions with less uncertainty. Management and the CFO may also want to manage the impact of pension assets and liabilities on the sponsor's balance sheet. Employees and retirees, however, want to maximize the probability that plan liabilities are met and thus want the sponsor to make timely and sufficient plan contributions. Finally, the CIO and investment staff should be interested in meeting the investment objectives and constraints of the investment policy statement.

In a defined benefit pension plan, the sponsor bears the ultimate risk of the portfolio falling short of meeting liabilities. This risk manifests itself in the form of higher contributions from the plan sponsor when the plan becomes underfunded. In the extreme case of default, however—when the plan sponsor can no longer meet its legal obligations and cannot contribute further to the plan—the employee bears the ultimate risk and may need to find alternative means to meet financial needs in retirement. Some of this risk may be shared by taxpayers via additional social security or welfare payments, making the government a stakeholder in a defined benefit pension plan.[1]

The investment office of the DB pension plan is tasked with investing assets appropriately and may have variable compensation (bonuses) tied to investment performance. The investment committee or board will consider recommendations from investment staff, such as setting strategy and investment manager selection. In setting and executing strategy, all stakeholders' positions must be considered, including the sponsor's ability to make plan contributions. Ultimately, however, the board has a fiduciary duty to employees and retirees.

Finally, for corporate DB plans the company's shareholders are stakeholders. They are interested in the sustainability of the pension plan because if it is underfunded, any shortfall becomes a liability on the balance sheet, reducing the value of the company. Contributions to an underfunded plan also reduce net income. Underfunded status also increases financial risk, which may cause higher volatility in the stock price.

Defined Contribution Pension Plans

The main stakeholders of a defined contribution pension plan are the plan beneficiaries, the employer, the board, and the government.

A key stakeholder in a DC plan is the participant. Each participant has an individual account into which contributions are made on a regular basis—either by the employee, the employer, or both. Plan participants must ensure that 1) adequate contributions are made and 2) appropriate investment options are selected to generate sufficient investment returns. For a DC pension plan, the individual participant bears the investment risk of the portfolio failing to meet future liabilities (i.e., retirement needs). If plan participants outlive their savings, they will need to find other ways to meet their financial needs in retirement. In that case, the government (via taxpayers) may need to provide additional social welfare benefits, making the government another stakeholder in a DC plan.

Although DC plan participants control the investment decisions for their individual accounts, perhaps acting upon the advice of their financial adviser, the plan sponsor still has important fiduciary responsibilities, including overseeing the appropriate investment of plan assets (either by internal staff or by third-party asset managers or a combination thereof), offering suitable investment options, and selecting administrative providers. The plan sponsor, therefore, is an important stakeholder in a DC plan. The plan sponsor typically has an obligation to contribute to the DC plan on behalf of the employee as specified by the employment contract or through a government-mandated system. In some countries, a plan sponsor may also have an obligation to provide employees with a choice of different investment options within the employer-sponsored DC plan or even the choice of different DC plans. The sponsor typically must ensure that the investment options provide appropriate

---

1 Some risk is also shared by other plan sponsors through agencies as the Pension Benefit Guaranty Corporation (PBGC) in the United States. It is not funded by the government; rather, PBGC's funding comes primarily from insurance premiums paid by DB plan sponsors, the assets of failed pension plans that the PBGC takes over, and investment income.

levels of diversification. It may also need to provide investment education and communications so that employees can make well informed investment choices. Running DC plans can be more expensive than DB plans given their increased complexity of administration and meeting regulatory compliance, all of which may result in higher fees for DC plan participants.

The board of a DC plan sponsor must consider the differing levels of sophistication among participants and provide adequate disclosure in communications to ensure participants are well informed. The board may be required to select a default investment option when participants do not explicitly make an investment choice. In such cases, the board has a higher obligation because by entering the default option, the participant is indicating that he/she either does not have sufficient understanding to make an informed choice or that he/she trusts the board of the pension plan to make the best choice.

4 PENSION FUNDS: LIABILITIES, INVESTMENT HORIZON, AND LIQUIDITY NEEDS

> ☐ | discuss the stakeholders in the portfolio, the liabilities, the investment time horizons, and the liquidity needs of different types of institutional investors

Liabilities and Investment Horizon

Defined Benefit Pension Plans

The liabilities of a DB pension plan are the present value of the future payments it will make to beneficiaries upon retirement, disability, or death. Calculating DB liabilities is complex and typically undertaken by actuaries employed by the plan sponsor or by external actuaries. Here we will highlight some key elements and focus on the discount rate used in calculating the present value of future benefit payments.

The first step in determining DB liabilities is to calculate the expected future cash flows (i.e., retirement benefits). These depend on the design and specifics of the pension plan. Some of the key elements common among DB plans in the calculation of expected cash flows are:

1. **Service/tenure:** The number of years the employee has been with the company or organization (or service years) determines the defined benefit the employee is expected to receive upon retirement. The higher the service years, the higher the retirement benefit. Sometimes a minimum number of service years is required before retirement benefits become vested (i.e., the employee becomes eligible to receive a pension).

2. **Salary/earnings:** The salary or earnings level of the employee affects the calculation of the defined benefit the employee is expected to receive upon retirement. The defined benefit may be a function of the average earnings over the entire career or the average earnings over the last several years prior to retirement (e.g., last three years).

3. **Mortality/longevity:** The length of time that retirement benefits are expected to be paid to plan participants is important in calculating expected cash flows. This requires assumptions about employees' and retirees' life

expectancies. Importantly, ever-increasing life expectancies is a key factor in making DB pension plans less affordable from the sponsor's perspective. Longevity risk is the risk to the plan sponsor that participants will live longer than assumed in the pension liabilities calculations.

In estimating future benefits, the plan sponsor must make several key assumptions, such as the growth rate of salaries, expected vesting, and mortality and disability assumptions. **Vesting** means that employees only become eligible to receive a pension after meeting certain criteria, typically a minimum number of years of service. In measuring defined benefit obligations, the plan sponsor must consider the likelihood that some employees may not satisfy the vesting requirements. Under both International Financial Reporting Standards (IFRS) and US generally accepted accounting principles (GAAP), pension obligations are determined as the present value of future benefits earned by employees for service provided to date. Assumptions about future salary increases, expected vesting, and life expectancy change over time and will change the estimated pension obligation. Given the importance of these factors, pension plans require periodic actuarial reviews to determine the value of the liabilities and the sponsor's annual required contribution rate.

Once expected future benefits are calculated, they must be discounted to determine their present value. Practices of marking-to-market liabilities using market discount rates can vary considerably based on country, or even within a country, between private and public pension plans. Typical discount rates include government bond yields or swap rates, corporate bond yields, and constant actuarial discount rates (long-term expected rate of return). Plan sponsors might be inclined to use a higher discount rate that will, all else equal, result in lower pension liabilities, a better funded status, and potentially lower contributions. Beneficiaries prefer to see a lower discount rate being used that will, all else equal, result in higher pension liabilities, a worse funded status, and potentially higher contributions. There is a delicate balance, however, because if contributions become unsustainable, the plan sponsor might decide to shut down its DB plan and substitute it with a less risky DC plan.

Over the past 15 years, a shift has occurred in many countries toward tying the discount rate to market rates. As a result, many pension plans have adopted a more liability-driven investment approach to partially or fully hedge the interest rate risk in their liabilities. Given the low interest rate environment since the 2007–2009 financial crisis, this has posed tremendous challenges for pension funds globally.

Discount Rates for Defined Benefit Plans in the US

In the United States, private and corporate DB pension plans may discount liabilities at rates based on high-grade bond yields averaged over 25 years. This was allowed under the 2012 update to the Pension Protection Act (PPA), part of broader legislation known as MAP-21. The change effectively raised the applicable discount rates (and reduced DB pension liabilities), providing some relief to defined benefit plans given what were perceived to be 'artificially' low interest rates. Prior to the PPA, corporate DB plans had to discount liabilities using current investment-grade corporate bond yields, not a historical average.

US public DB pension plans use actuarial discount rates which, as required by the US Governmental Accounting Standards Board (GASB), are based on the expected return of the pension plan asset portfolio. These are typically far higher than bond rates. The higher discount rates lower their liabilities and raise their funded status. However, this may cause such pension plans to potentially make inadequate plan contributions and take on excessive risk by investing heavily in equities and alternatives in hope of generating an expected rate of return that supports the high discount rate.

Exhibit 4 summarizes the key elements in the calculation of defined benefit pension plan liabilities.

Exhibit 4: Factors Affecting Calculation of Defined Benefit Liabilities

Factor	Impact on Liabilities
Service/tenure	Depending on plan design, often the longer the period of service or tenure, the larger the benefit payments.
Salary/earnings	The faster salaries or earnings grow, the larger the benefit payments.
Additional or matching contributions	Additional or matching contributions are often rewarded by a step change increase in benefit payments.
Mortality/Longevity assumptions	If life expectancy increases, the obligations or liabilities will increase.
Expected Vesting	If employee turnover decreases, expected vesting will increase.
Expected Investment Returns	In some cases, increases in expected returns will result in a higher discount rate being used—hence, lower obligations or liabilities.
Discount Rate	A higher (lower) discount rate results in lower (higher) liabilities.

The main objective of a DB plan is to have sufficient assets to cover future benefit payments. A common pension industry metric used to gauge asset sufficiency is the funded ratio, also known as the vested benefit index (VBI) in some countries. The funded ratio is defined as:

Funded ratio = Fair value of plan assets/PV of Defined benefit obligations

In some countries, if the funded ratio is less than 100%, the sponsor must increase contributions until it exceeds 100%. Improving the plan's funded ratio can transform the pension obligation from a liability to an asset on the plan sponsor's balance sheet. It is important to note that in some cases, underfunded pension plans may take more investment risk in the hope of achieving higher returns and growing assets sufficiently to return to fully funded status. In other cases, underfunded pension plans reduce investment risk and rely on other actions to improve their funded status, such as increasing contributions or reducing benefits.

Additional considerations in DB pension design are:

1. the size of the pension plan relative to the size of the sponsor's balance sheet; and

2. the cyclicality of the plan sponsor's core business.

If plan assets and liabilities are small relative to the sponsor's balance sheet, then there may be more flexibility in taking investment risk and more tolerance for volatility in employer contributions. If, on the other hand, plan asset and liabilities are large in relation to the sponsor's balance sheet, then there may be less appetite for volatility of employer contributions and hence a reduced desire for taking investment risk.

Another important factor is the core business of the plan sponsor. If the plan sponsor's revenues are highly cyclical, it will not want plan funded status to deteriorate when the core business suffers from a cyclical downturn. In such cases, the DB plan's asset allocation would be modified to ensure adequate diversification so as not to have significant exposure to assets highly correlated with the sponsor's core business or industry. In sum, it is desirable for plan assets to have low (high) correlations with the sponsor's operating assets (liabilities).

The plans sponsor's ability to tolerate volatility of contribution rates may impact the investment horizon, and hence the pension plan's appetite for such illiquid investments as private equity and venture capital. Another important factor determining the investment horizon is the mix of active plan participants (i.e., current employees) versus retirees. The higher the proportion of retirees (so the higher the liability associated with retirees only) relative to the proportion of active participants (or the liability associated with active participants), the more mature the plan—hence, the lower its risk tolerance. Some mature DB pension plans have been frozen (closed to new participants) as they typically experience negative cash flow where benefit payments exceed contributions. Generally, the more mature a pension fund, the shorter its investment horizon, which directly affects risk tolerance and the allocation between fixed-income assets and riskier assets.

Defined Contribution Pension Plans

In a DC plan, participants' pension benefits are based on amounts credited to their individual accounts in the form of contributions (from the employee and possibly the employer) and investment returns. Consequently, the liabilities of a DC pension plan sponsor are equal only to its required contributions. DC plan assets are typically pooled, and the sponsor invests according to the investment choices selected by plan participants. Often the DC plan may invest in a broadly diversified portfolio that may include investments not generally offered to retail investors, such as private equity and hedge funds. This is possible since pooling of assets gives rise to scale and the long-term horizon of the aggregate beneficiaries. In such case, the plan sponsor takes on the residual investment risk of its asset allocation. Once invested in such alternative asset types, the DC plan sponsor bears liquidity risk if any event occurs that causes a significant proportion of its participants to exit the plan. The asset allocation may be impacted to such an extent that the plan sponsor is unable to provide the asset allocation promised to its participants. Such a circumstance will have regulatory and reputational consequences for the DC plan sponsor.

Individuals in a DC plan are at different stages of their careers, so each has a different investment time horizon (the time period from his/her current age until expected death or expected death of a spouse, whichever is longer) as well as different risk tolerances. Therefore, key considerations for most DC plans are participants' ages and invested balances. If the plan has a larger proportion of older (younger) participants with large (small) invested balances, the investment options might reflect a shorter (longer) investment horizon. Many DC plans offer investment options that allow participants to select the investment horizon that best aligns with their own investment horizon. Examples are life-cycle options or target date options, which feature a glide path that manages the asset mix based on a desired retirement date. In the United States, most DC plans offer target-date options as default options; in Hong Kong SAR it is mandated that every default option plan have a life-cycle option.

There are two main types of life-cycle options. **Participant-switching life-cycle options** automatically switch members into a more conservative asset mix as their age increases. There may be several automatic de-risking switches at different age targets. A **participant/cohort option** pools the participant with a cohort that has a similar target retirement date. For example, if a participant is 40 years old in 2020 and plans to retire at the age of 65, he/she could invest in an option with a target date of 2045 and the fund would manage the appropriate asset mix over the next 25 years. In

2020, the assets might be 90% invested in equities and 10% in bonds. As time passes, however, the fund would gradually change the asset mix (less equities and more bonds) to reflect an appropriate allocation given the time to retirement.

Liquidity Needs

Although pension plans typically have long investment time horizons, they still must maintain sufficient liquidity relative to their projected liabilities. Liquidity needs are driven by:

- Proportion of active employees relative to retirees—The former contribute to the plan, while the latter receive benefit payments. More mature pension funds have higher liquidity needs. Frozen DB pension plans, often facing negative cash flow, must hold even more cash and other liquid investments compared to open mature plans.

- Age of workforce—Liquidity needs rise as the age of the workforce increases, since the closer participants are, on average, to retirement, the sooner they will switch from the contribution phase to benefit payment stage. This is true for both DB and DC plans.

- DB plan funded status—If the plan is well funded, the plan sponsor may reduce contributions, generating a need to hold higher balances of liquid assets to pay benefits.

- Ability of participants to switch/withdraw from plan—If pension plan participants can switch to another plan or withdraw on short notice, then higher balances of liquid assets must be held to facilitate these actions. This applies to DB and some DC plans.

A pension plan with lower liquidity needs can hold larger balances in private investments—such as real estate, infrastructure, private equity, and hedge funds—and can invest a higher proportion in equities and credit. A pension plan with higher liquidity needs, however, must invest a higher proportion of its assets in cash, government bonds, and highly liquid, investment-grade corporate bonds.

It is important for pension plans to regularly perform liquidity stress tests, which may include stressing the value of their assets and modelling reduced liquidity of certain asset classes in a market downturn. Such stress-testing may also help DC plans anticipate whether participants might switch out of more volatile investment options during market downturns.

EXAMPLE 1

Comparing Defined Benefit (DB) and Defined Contribution (DC) Pension Plans

1. Geoff Albright is 35 years old and has been working at Henley Consulting in Melbourne, Australia, for 10 years. Henley Consulting offers a defined benefit (DB) pension plan for its employees. The defined benefit plan is fully funded. Geoff Albright's benefit formula for monthly payments upon retirement is: final monthly salary × benefit percentage (=1.5%) × number of years of service, where final monthly salary equals his average monthly earnings for the last three financial years immediately prior to retirement date. Hav-

ing been at Henley Consulting for 10 years, his benefits have vested and can be transferred to another pension plan.

Geoff has been offered a job at rival Australian firm, Horizon Ventures Consulting, which is offering a similar salary; however, Horizon Ventures Consulting offers a defined contribution (DC) pension plan for its employees. Horizon Ventures Consulting will pay 15% of annual salary into the plan each year. Employees can choose to invest in one of three diversified portfolios offered by the plan sponsor—Horizon Growth, Horizon Balanced, and Horizon Conservative—based upon their risk appetite, and employees can elect to make additional contributions to the plan. The monthly pension payments will depend on what has accumulated in Geoff's account when he retires.

Discuss the features that Geoff should consider in evaluating the two plans. Please address benefit payments, contributions, shortfall risk, and mortality/longevity risks.

Solution:

- Geoff notes his benefits at Henley Consulting have vested and can be transferred to Horizon Ventures Consulting's DC plan.

- Henley Consulting's plan provides a defined benefit payment linked to years of service and final salary, whereas Horizon Ventures Consulting's plan provides an uncertain benefit payment linked to the company's and Geoff's contribution rates and investment performance of plan assets. The benefits he can achieve in Henley Consulting's DB plan increase both by time employed as well as by growth in his wages. Geoff considers his capacity to achieve wage growth and compares this to the return objectives of his chosen option in Horizon Ventures Consulting's DC plan. Geoff notes his risk appetite and time horizon are suited to the Horizon Growth option.

- Although Henley Consulting's contribution rate is not known, Geoff is aware that the plan is currently fully funded and that it is Henley Consulting's obligation to maintain a fully funded status. Horizon Ventures Consulting's contribution rate is known (15% of annual salary), and Geoff can also make additional contributions himself.

- Geoff notes that the shortfall risk of plan assets being insufficient to meet his retirement benefit payments falls to his employer in the case of Henley Consulting's DB plan. But, for Horizon Ventures Consulting's DC plan, the shortfall risk falls to Geoff and depends on the contribution rate (15% from the company plus any additional contributions he chooses to make) and the performance of his chosen investments.

- Henley's DB plan pools mortality risk such that those in the pool who die prematurely leave assets that help fund benefit payments for those who live longer than expected. Horizon Venture Consulting's DC plan pays out the amount accumulated in Geoff's account, and he bears the risk of outliving his savings.

5   PENSION FUNDS: EXTERNAL CONSTRAINTS

☐ describe the focus of legal, regulatory, and tax constraints affecting different types of institutional investors

In this section, we take a high-level view of some of the legal and regulatory constraints faced by pension funds. In the next section, we consider tax and accounting constraints that may affect investing by pension funds.

Legal and Regulatory Constraints

Regulatory bodies supervising pension funds typically cover financial services licensing and regulation, prudential supervision, capital adequacy, market integrity, and consumer protection. Breeching key regulations may result in loss of operating licenses and/or loss of tax benefits, where applicable, which provides a strong incentive to comply. Regulations do vary from country to country; for example, some countries specify minimum and maximum percentage allocations to certain asset classes, while other countries require a minimum contribution rate by employers, particularly if the plan's funded ratio falls below 100%. However, despite national differences, there are similar themes in regulation globally.

Reporting and transparency are heavily influenced by regulatory requirements, as some regulators now require extensive reporting, not only on direct investment fees and costs incurred by pension plans but also on indirect fees and costs of external commingled vehicles. Drivers of more detailed reporting and transparency are avoidance of corruption by government officials involved with public pension plans and increased consumer protection for private pension plans so participants and stakeholders make appropriate investment choices. Many countries have increased personal liability for pension trustees to ensure they act in the best interests of ultimate beneficiaries. For example, DC plan participants must choose their contribution rates and the investment risk they are willing to bear. However, regulators are aware that many DC plan participants have little understanding of how to invest for retirement. Although regulators may require the plan sponsor to provide investor education to their employees, DC plan trustees, as fiduciaries, are still required to operate with prudence and as if they were the asset owners.

In Australia, for example, most employees are covered by the DC Superannuation Guarantee, under which employers must contribute 9.5% of an employee's salary. Since many participants do not actively make investment decisions, the government applies strict licensing and other obligations for trustees when offering the default option (MySuper), including: providing a single diversified investment strategy as a default option suitable for the majority of participants; avoiding unnecessary or excessive fees; and delivering value for money (measured by long-term net returns). A similar default DC plan account exists in the United States (known as the Qualified Default Investment Alternative), which must also be diversified.

In Europe the updated Institutions for Occupational Retirement Provision (IORP II) will lead to regulatory changes for pension plans. Although each country will interpret the provisions slightly differently, the changes relate to governance, risk management, and disclosure. A number of key functions are defined, such as an internal audit, and standards are applied to those executing these key functions, including a requirement that such a person does not carry out a similar function for the plan sponsor. Many pension plans will need to document their risk management policies and procedures. For example, each fund must document its "own risk assessment" covering items such as the risk of not meeting benefit obligations and operational risk, including administrative error or fraud. For disclosure, there will also be greater harmonization of pension benefit statements with certain items required to be included.

US corporate pension plans are subject to significant regulatory oversight. The Employee Retirement Income Security Act of 1974 (ERISA) regulates vesting, funding requirements, and payouts. ERISA includes a fiduciary code of conduct and required disclosures. ERISA established the Pension Benefit Guaranty Corporation, a US government agency that collects premiums from pension plan sponsors and pays benefits to participants (approximately 630,000) in terminated plans. Although ERISA protects benefits that workers have earned, an employer may still terminate a plan, essentially freezing a worker's ability to earn additional benefits. Moreover, the US Pension Protection Act of 2006 established minimum funding standards for DB plans, while later revisions raised the rates corporations could use to discount their liabilities (high-grade bond yields averaged over 25 years). Importantly, a potential consequence of using higher discount rates is these DB plans must generate higher returns for their funding status to remain sustainable, which typically requires taking on greater investment risk.

Tax and Accounting Constraints

Governments around the world encourage citizens to save for retirement by typically providing favorable tax treatment to retirement savings. Favorable tax treatment may come in different forms: reduced taxes on retirement plan contributions, favorable tax rates on investment income and/or capital gains, and lower tax rates on benefit payments drawn throughout retirement (versus higher taxes on lump sum payments). Foregone tax revenues from such favorable tax treatment are costly, so to ensure pension plans actually reduce tax burdens for retirement savers, governments typically place restrictions on plan design, governance, and investment activities in order for plans to qualify for the favorable tax treatment.

In the United States, 401(k) plans are tax deferred as participants make pre-tax contributions and do not pay tax on investment earnings; benefit payments, however, are taxed as ordinary income. To encourage savings retention within the pension plan, early withdrawals before age 59½ are taxed an additional 10%. In the United Kingdom, private pension plans are also tax deferred, with no tax on contributions or on investment earnings. The first 25% of benefit payments are tax free, and the remaining 75% is taxed as ordinary income after a tax-free personal allowance. In China, companies providing occupational pensions (known as Enterprise Annuities) are given tax relief amounting to 4% of wages; however, there are taxation differences between regions.

Pension plans taxed on investment earnings must be aware of tax implications of their investment activities. For example, there may be favorable capital gains tax treatment for investments held over 1 year, which should incentivize investing in lower turnover strategies. Also, pension plans must consider tax implications when returns from investing via futures and other derivatives are treated as income and taxed at higher rates than returns from investing in the underlying securities, which are typically taxed at lower capital gains and dividend rates. When investing internationally, double taxation may occur when the same income or capital gain is taxed both by the jurisdiction in which it is earned *and* in the jurisdiction where the pension fund resides. To achieve tax efficiency, pension plans should invest via legal structures that provide access to double taxation treaties, whereby taxes paid in the country of residence are exempt in the country where they arise (alternatively, the plan receives a foreign tax credit in its country of residence to reflect taxes withheld in the country where the income/gain arose).

Accounting treatment is another important external factor that drives investment decision making by pension funds. These treatments may differ across countries, so it is important to be fully aware of them. Here we focus on the United States to illustrate how accounting treatment may influence investment choices. Corporate DB pension plans must follow generally accepted accounting principles—notably, Accounting Standards Codification (ASC) 715, Compensation—Retirement Benefits, which requires that an overfunded (underfunded) plan must appear as an asset (liability) on the balance sheet of the corporate sponsor. Such plan sponsor must also report gains, losses, and service costs as part of net income. This accounting treatment significantly increased the transparency of US plans' funded status, and it prompted many corporate plans to implement liability-driven investing techniques to reduce the effect of funded ratio volatility on their financial statements.

Public pension plans in the US must follow Governmental Accounting Standards Board (GASB) rules. Under GASB rules, public plan sponsors must report fair market values of plan assets and can use a blended approach to valuing plan liabilities. The latter involves discounting the funded portion of pension liabilities using the (higher) expected return on plan assets as well as discounting the unfunded portion of liabilities based on the (lower) yield on tax-exempt municipal bonds. Using a higher discount rate for the funded portion of liabilities skews the risk tolerance of public pension plans and incentivizes them to allocate relatively large proportions of assets to equities and alternative investments.

6 PENSION FUNDS: RISK CONSIDERATIONS

> ☐ | evaluate risk considerations of private defined benefit (DB) pension plans in relation to 1) plan funded status, 2) sponsor financial strength, 3) interactions between the sponsor's business and the fund's investments, 4) plan design, and 5) workforce characteristics

Despite the long-term trend in the shift away from DB plans toward DC plans, as previously demonstrated, DB plans (and their hybrids) are still a key part of the pension landscape in several P7 countries, such as Canada, Japan, the Netherlands, and Switzerland. As such, it is important to review risk management considerations of private defined benefit pension plans—a topic that has intensified following the global financial crisis of 2007-2009. Key risk considerations of such plans must be measured and managed.

1. Plan funded status

   When a defined benefit pension plan is fully funded, the value of assets is greater than or equal to the present value of the liabilities. If the value of the assets falls below the present value of the liabilities, the pension plan is considered to be underfunded and the plan sponsor is left with a financial liability. The plan sponsor can take several approaches in order to minimize the risk of generating a financial liability:

   a. Seek to match assets to liabilities in terms of quantity, timing, and risk using a Liability Driven Investing (LDI) approach. Duration gap management or cash flow–matching suits plans that are close to fully funded and seek to maintain that status.

   b. Seek to grow assets at a higher rate of return than the expected growth in liabilities—which typically involves taking on more investment risk. This form of investment suits plans that are underfunded and wishing to return to a fully funded status. It may also suit fully funded plans that are seeking to lower their contribution rate over time and are willing to endure the increased volatility in funded status that this approach entails.

   c. Seek to invest in more defensive assets expected to deliver less volatile returns. This may suit defined benefit pension plans where the plan sponsor is willing to make higher contributions over time in exchange for less variability in the plan funded status.

In cases where a plan is adequately funded, the sponsoring corporation may seek to remove pension-driven balance sheet volatility by engaging pension risk transfer through such mechanisms as:

- offering lump sum payments to beneficiaries in exchange for voluntarily leaving the plan; or
- negotiating a transfer of the risk to an insurance provider.

2. Sponsor financial strength

When a defined benefit pension plan sponsor is not financially strong, there is a considerable risk that it may fail to make the necessary contributions to the plan. The plan sponsor may not be able to meet its defined benefit pension plan liabilities if there is a funding shortfall. If the plan sponsor files for bankruptcy protection, an underfunded pension plan is in the same difficult position as other creditors, having to join the queue claiming the firm's remaining assets.

The relative size of the plan also influences the sponsor's ability to assume risk. If the pension plan is small (large) relative to the size of the sponsor, then volatility in pension assets, liabilities, and/or contributions will have a smaller (larger) effect on the sponsoring company's balance sheet.

3. Interactions between the sponsor's business and the fund's investments

In the past, many private defined benefit pension plans have held significant stakes in the equity of the sponsor company. However, due to the risk involved, many regulators have restricted how much a plan may invest in the stock of the sponsor company. This risk materializes in circumstances in which the company performs poorly and its share price falls, thereby increasing the risk that pension plan assets fall below liabilities. This may coincide with a point in time when the sponsor's financial strength is poor, constraining its ability to make additional contributions necessary to address the developing funding shortfall. For this reason, it is advisable for the plan to diversify out of the sponsor company's stock. It is also prudent to diversify away from companies operating in the same industry, because their risk and return are expected to be highly correlated with those of the sponsor company's stock.

4. Plan design

Poor plan design can contribute many risks for the private defined benefit pension plan sponsor. When setting out the formula for calculation of defined benefit payments, the plan sponsor must balance adequacy (will the benefit payment be sufficient to meet income needs in retirement) and sustainability (what contribution rate is sustainable, and what investment return can realistically be achieved) within the context of its risk tolerance.

There is a significant risk that a company will be overly optimistic in predicting its ability to make contributions to its pension plan decades into the future.

The plan design is informed by its purpose as an employee retention tool to mitigate the risk of losing employees to a competitor. The company/sponsor may also wish to increase future defined benefit payments to address worker unrest, which may otherwise lead to strike action or lengthy negotiations with unions. If a company does not have immediate excess cash flow, it may prefer to increase future defined benefit payments instead of granting immediate pay raises.

5. Workforce characteristics

The nature of the workforce is an important risk consideration for companies because it impacts what the duration of the assets should be. The younger the workforce, the longer the duration of assets and the greater risk tolerance the plan will have. If a company's workforce has high turnover, it may have few employees whose entitlements to defined benefit payments will vest. On the other hand, if the average tenure of the workforce increases, then more liabilities will vest, thereby reducing the plan's funded status. If the workforce is older and nearer to retirement age, an important risk consideration is keeping sufficient liquidity so the plan can meet liabilities when they become due. Conversely, in a plan where the workforce is younger, on average, the sponsor may take on more liquidity risk. A workforce with a high level of vested benefits may constrain the company in terms of flexibility in managing its workforce. For example, a company may prefer to downsize its workforce, but doing so might require it to pay out excessive vested benefits.

Retired workers also influence the longevity risk of DB plans. Longevity risk is the risk that an individual will live longer than expected and draw more in benefit payments than the amount determined in the calculation of plan liabilities. In private DB pension plans, longevity risk is pooled such that if a participant dies earlier than expected, he/she leaves more assets in the pool that can then cover additional payments for those who live longer than expected. However, this pooling of longevity risk does not mitigate the effect of rising life expectancies, which implies, all else equal, an increase in total DB plan liabilities.

In setting a risk objective, plan sponsors must consider plan status, sponsor financial status and profitability, sponsor and pension fund common risk exposures, plan features, and workforce characteristics, as shown in Exhibit 5.

Exhibit 5: Factors Affecting Risk Tolerance and Risk Objectives of Defined Benefit Plans

Category	Variable	Explanation
Plan status	• Plan funded status (surplus or deficit)	• Higher pension surplus or higher funded status implies potentially greater risk tolerance.
Sponsor financial status and profitability	• Debt to total assets • Current and expected profitability	• Lower debt ratios and higher current and expected profitability imply greater risk tolerance.
	• Size of plan compared to market capitalization of sponsor company	• Large sponsor company size relative to pension plan size implies greater risk tolerance.

Category	Variable	Explanation
Sponsor and pension fund common risk exposures	▪ Correlation of sponsor operating results with pension asset returns	▪ The lower the correlation, the greater the risk tolerance, all else equal.
Plan features	▪ Provision for early retirement ▪ Provision for lump-sum distributions	▪ Such options tend to reduce the duration of plan liabilities, implying lower risk tolerance, all else equal.
Workforce characteristics	▪ Age of workforce ▪ Active lives relative to retired lives	▪ The younger the workforce and the greater the proportion of active lives, the greater the duration of plan liabilities and the greater the risk tolerance.

EXAMPLE 2

Andes Sports Equipment Corporation—Defined Benefit Plan

1. Frank Smit, CFA, is chief financial officer of Andes Sports Equipment Company (ADSE), a leading Dutch producer of winter and water sports gear. ADSE is a small company based in Amsterdam, and all of its revenues come from Europe. Product demand has been strong in the past few years, although it is highly cyclical. The company has rising earnings and a strong (low debt) balance sheet. ADSE is a relatively young company, and as such, its defined benefit pension plan has no retired employees. This essentially active-lives plan has €100 million in assets and an €8 million surplus in relation to the projected benefit obligation (PBO). Several facts concerning the plan follow:

   - The duration of the plan's liabilities (which are all Europe-based) is 20 years.
   - The discount rate applied to these liabilities is 6 percent.
   - The average age of ADSE's workforce is 39 years.

   Based on the information provided, discuss ADSE's risk tolerance.

Solution:

   ADSE appears to have above average risk tolerance for the following reasons:

   a. The plan has a small surplus (8 percent of plan assets); that is, the plan is overfunded by €8 million.
   b. The company's balance sheet is strong (low use of debt).
   c. The company is profitable despite operating in a cyclical industry.
   d. The average age of its workforce is low.

2. Smit must set risk objectives for the ADSE pension plan. Because of excellent recent investment results, ADSE has not needed to make a contribution to the pension fund in the two most recent years. Smit considers it very important to maintain a plan surplus in relation to PBO. Because an €8 million surplus will be an increasingly small buffer as plan liabilities increase, Smit

decides that maintaining plan funded status, stated as a ratio of plan assets to PBO at 100 percent or greater, is his top priority.

Based on the information provided, state an appropriate risk objective for ADSE.

Solution:

Given Smit considered it very important to maintain a plan surplus in relation to PBO, an appropriate risk objective for ADSE relates to shortfall risk with respect to the plan's funded status falling below 100 percent. For example, ADSE may want to minimize the probability that funded status falls below 100 percent, or it may want the probability that funded status falls below 100 percent to be less than or equal to 10 percent. If a plan surplus is maintained, ADSE may experience more years in which it does not need to make a contribution. Indeed, a major motivation for maintaining a plan surplus is to reduce the contributions ADSE needs to make in the future. As such, another relevant type of risk objective would be to minimize the present value of expected cash contributions.

7   PENSION FUNDS: INVESTMENT OBJECTIVES AND ASSET ALLOCATION

☐ evaluate the investment policy statement of an institutional investor

☐ evaluate the investment portfolio of a private DB plan, sovereign wealth fund, university endowment, and private foundation

Investment Objectives

Defined Benefit Pension Plans

Defined benefit pension plans ultimately need to meet pension liabilities through a combination of investment returns and contributions. In practice, the investment objective of a DB pension plan is often to achieve a long-term rate of return on plan assets that exceeds the assumed rate of return used by the pension plan actuaries, typically the discount rate used in valuing pension liabilities. Importantly, targeting a long-term return based on the discount rate may be inappropriate in some cases. For example, when the discount rate is set using yields on government bonds, the target return is likely too low. In such a case, it may be preferable to fully hedge interest rate risk by adopting a liability-driven investing approach.

In determining an appropriate target return, it is worth noting that, ideally, the asset base should grow—through investment returns and contributions—in line with the growth of liabilities. If a plan is underfunded, the asset base must grow faster than liabilities. Because the growth of liabilities is met through investment returns and contributions (from the plan sponsor and/or employees), the DB plan's board and investment committee must consider the appropriate level of portfolio risk relative to the plan sponsor's willingness and ability to raise contribution rates should investment returns fall short of expectations.

In summary, the primary objective for DB pension plans is to achieve a long-term target return (usually defined in nominal terms) over a specified investment horizon (3–5 years or even as long as 10 or 25 years) with an appropriate level of risk that allows the plan to meet its contractual liabilities. The secondary objective could be to minimize the present value of expected cash contributions.

In setting overall investment strategy, many DB pension plans engage in detailed Asset Liability Management studies every 3–5 years. These studies include Monte Carlo simulations of thousands of scenarios for asset returns and factors driving pension liabilities (importantly, the discount rate) aimed at producing probability distributions for funded ratios and contribution rates at different horizons. These distributions are useful for determining key metrics, such as the expected funded ratio in 10 or 15 years, surplus volatility, surplus-at-risk, and volatility of contribution rates. Additionally, many pension funds engage in detailed liquidity modeling and stress testing that involve modeling contributions, benefit payments, capital calls for funding private equity investments, stressed asset values, and reduced liquidity of certain asset classes in market downturns. Besides providing an assessment of the appropriateness of the pension fund's liquidity profile, such stress testing provides insights into meeting liquidity needs during a financial crisis.

Defined Contribution Pension Plans

The main objective of defined contribution pension plans is to prudently grow assets that will support spending needs in retirement. Defined contribution plans usually offer a variety of investment options with differing investment objectives to suit participants of different ages, asset balances, and risk appetites. The investment options offered by the DC plan sponsor can be managed either in-house or externally as well as passively or actively. Most DC pension plans also provide a default option for disengaged participants. Plan trustees/boards must set an appropriate investment objective of the default option after reviewing the characteristics of existing default participants. Unsurprisingly, many DC plans end up with a balanced asset allocation mix as the default option—frequently in the form of a life-cycle fund. In cases where a DC plan provides participants a balanced asset allocation option with active management, a secondary objective may be to outperform the long-term policy benchmark consisting of the weighted average of individual asset class benchmarks and the policy weights defined by the strategic asset allocation. Finally, for some DC plans it is important their investment options outperform those of other DC pension plans, which is particularly relevant in countries where participants can voluntarily switch between DC plan providers.

Sample Investment Objectives of Different Pension Plans

Public DB Pension Plan:

1. The assets of Public Plan will be invested with the objective of achieving a long-term rate of return that meets or exceeds the Public Plan actuarial expected rate of return.

2. Public Plan will seek to maximize returns for the level of risk taken.

3. Public Plan will also seek to achieve a return that exceeds the Policy Index.

4. Public Plan will seek to achieve its objectives on an after fees basis.

Corporate DB Pension Plan:

The Trustee wishes to ensure that the Corporate Plan can meet its obligations to the beneficiaries while recognizing the cost implications to the Company of pursuing excessively conservative investment strategies. The objectives of the Plan are defined as: wishing to maximize the long-term return on investments subject to, in its opinion, an acceptably low likelihood of failing to achieve an ongoing 105% funding level.

Corporate DC Pension Plan:

The Fund currently offers a range of investment options to its participants and has adopted an age-based default strategy for participants who do not choose an investment option.

The investment strategy of the Fund is to put in place portfolios to achieve the objectives of its stakeholders over a reasonable period of time with a reasonable probability of success.

In establishing each option's investment objectives, the Trustee takes into account the average participant's age, account balance, and risk appetite. The participant's choice of investment option indicates his/her risk appetite.

For example, a participants selecting the growth option indicates a higher risk tolerance over a longer investment time horizon. The investment objective for the growth option is to build an investment portfolio to outperform inflation + 4% per annum over 7-year periods while accepting a high level of risk that is expected to generate 4–6 negative annual returns over any 20-year period.

Asset Allocation by Pension Plans

An examination of pension fund asset allocations shows very large differences in average asset allocations by country. Moreover, examining pension fund asset allocations within a country also typically shows large differences despite these plans seeking to achieve similar goals. Such inter- and intra-national differences are driven by many factors discussed earlier in this reading, including the differences in legal, regulatory, accounting, and tax constraints; the investment objectives, risk appetites, and investment beliefs of the stakeholders; the liabilities to and demographics of the ultimate beneficiaries; the availability of investment opportunities; and the expected cost of living in retirement.

Exhibit 6 presents the average asset allocation of pension funds in the world's largest pension fund markets. The data are an aggregation of both DB and DC plans as presented (the split between DB and DC plans for each of the P7 countries is shown in Exhibit 3).

Note the category 'Other' includes hedge funds, private equity funds, loans, structured products, other mutual funds (i.e., not invested in equities, bonds, or cash), land, buildings, and other miscellaneous investments.

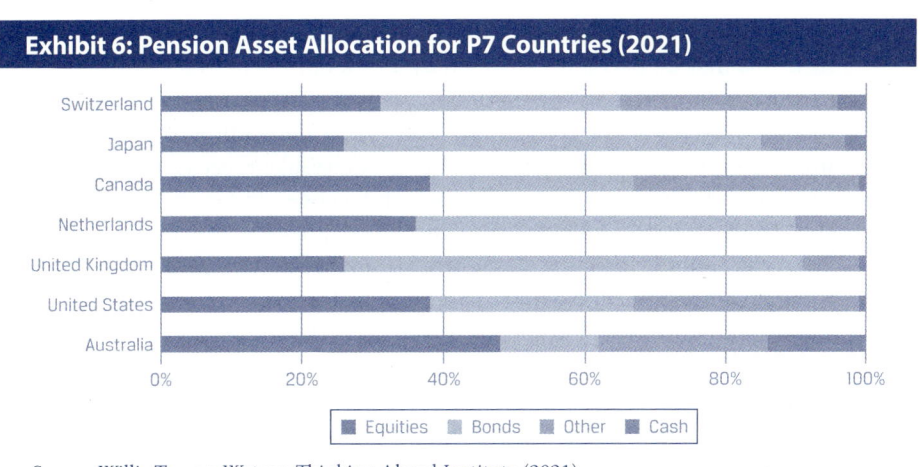

Exhibit 6: Pension Asset Allocation for P7 Countries (2021)

Source: Willis Towers Watson Thinking Ahead Institute (2021).

The key observations regarding the data presented in Exhibit 6 are as follows:

- *Equities*: Equities provide a long-term risk premium over bonds and cash and are typically viewed as the asset class of choice for long-term investors, like pension plans because of the higher expected returns they offer. Traditionally, equities are also viewed as an inflation hedge, as opposed to bonds that do not perform well in an inflationary environment. However, over the past decade, there has been a decrease in the equity allocation in several countries, particularly in Japan, Canada, and Australia. In aggregate, the resulting reallocation has been to the category 'Other,' which includes such alternatives as private equity and debt, real assets, and hedge funds, as well as to bonds (and fixed income, generally) as DB pension funds have reduced their risk appetite to lower the volatility of their funded ratios. Australia and the US have the largest proportions of DC pension assets and also the largest allocations to equities. Although not shown in Exhibit 6, it is worth noting that the United States, Australia, and the Netherlands have the highest proportions of their equities allocations invested in their local markets. Given the size of the domestic equities markets in Australia and the Netherlands, this implies significant home bias.

- *Fixed Income*: Fixed income plays a defensive role in pension fund portfolios, because during times of financial market stress, equity markets and interest rates tend to fall. Fixed-income investments also help DB pension plans hedge the interest rate risk relative to their pension liabilities. Many regulators, in fact, require DB pension plans to hold a minimum allocation in fixed-income investments. Over the last decade, US corporate pension plans have increased their allocations to fixed-income investments, despite low expected returns, driven by the desire to reduce their funded ratio volatility. Conversely, US public pension plans have reduced their fixed-income allocations overall while increasing their allocations in the fixed-income space to high yield (riskier) bonds. The reallocation and repositioning are driven by the large gap that has opened between their expected rate of return and the yield available on long-term government securities.

- *Alternatives (Other)*: This category includes private equity and debt markets, real estate, hedge funds, and real assets. As a group, these alternative assets tend to have low, or negative, correlations with traditional investments as well as lower drawdowns. In the case of hedge funds, this may be explained by the lower volatility of these strategies versus equity markets. Private asset classes have historically also exhibited lower drawdowns compared to equities. This may be partially explained by a lack of fully marking-to-market because of limited market transactions as well as appraisal-based valuations that lag changes in market pricing. Overall, the perception of institutional investors is that alternatives can produce equity-like returns over the long run with relatively low drawdowns, which has been the motivation for the shift from equities to alternatives over the past decade and a half. However, given the complexity and skill required to manage alternative investments, these investments come with high fees; thus, fee-sensitive institutions with significant liquidity needs may be unable to make sizable allocations to alternatives. Furthermore, attractive investment opportunities in private markets and in hedge fund strategies may be scarce. Increased competition and the huge amounts of capital deployed on a global scale by institutional investors may put downward pressure on future returns. Although still a smaller part of most institutional portfolios, allocations to real assets have increased significantly because they are considered an attractive way to hedge inflation. Japan has been slowest among the select countries to increase allocations to alternatives; however, the transition is underway with the country's largest pension plan, Government Pension Investment Fund (GPIF), which is reducing its allocation to domestic bonds in favor of alternatives.

EXAMPLE 3

Asset Allocation by a Public Defined Benefit Plan

1. Susan Liew, CFA, is the chief investment officer of the Lorenza State Pension Plan (LSPP), a public DB plan. The plan maintains an asset allocation of 30% US equities, 30% international equities, 30% US fixed income, and 10% international fixed income. Liew's investment team developed the following long-term expected real returns for the asset classes in which the LSPP has traditionally invested. The outlook for US and international equities is slightly below long-term averages, while the outlook for US and international fixed income is well below long-term averages.

Asset Class	Expected Long-Term (10-Year) Annual Return
US equities	4.0%
International equities	5.0%
US fixed income	1.0%
International fixed income	−0.5%

Given the poor prospects for fixed income and the mediocre expectations for equities, Liew is exploring making allocations to various alternatives and has asked LSPP's asset consultant to provide comments on considerations for each alternative asset class, as shown here:

Asset Class	Comments
Alternative debt	Represents a diverse range of high yielding and floating-rate debt expected to return 300 bps annually over traditional fixed income (default-adjusted basis). The additional returns are compensation for increased liquidity risk in private debt, added credit risk in high yield and EM debt, and non-performing loans.
Infrastructure funds	Strong income-like characteristics given contracted cash flows for most underlying infrastructure projects. This asset class entails increased liquidity risk but offers some inflation protection (many contracted cash flows are linked to inflation).
Hedge funds	Provide access to various diversifying strategies, including those with potential to generate gains in both rising and falling markets. Expected to return 250 bps annually over traditional long-only equities. Careful manager selection and underlying strategy selection (especially exposure to equity market beta) are important factors.

Liew recommends to LSPP's Board of Trustees the following change in asset allocation:

Asset Class	Current Asset Allocation	Recommended Asset Allocation
US equities	30%	25%
International equities	30%	25%
US fixed income	30%	15%
International fixed income	10%	5%
Alternative debt	—	10%
Infrastructure funds	—	10%
Hedge funds	—	10%

How would the recommended change in asset allocation be expected to affect LSPP's funded status?

Solution:

The recommended changes in asset allocation would likely affect LSPP's funded status as follows:

- The changes would increase expected returns, implying higher expected asset values for LSPP over time.

- Given that both alternative debt and hedge funds have higher projected long-term returns than traditional debt and equities, respectively, the discount rate applied to LSPP's liabilities can be increased, thereby reducing their present value.

- On balance, LSPP's funded status would be expected to improve because of the recommended changes in asset allocation. In addition to generating higher asset values and lower present value of liabilities, the volatility of assets (and therefore the risk to funded status) should be reduced because of the lower correlation among asset returns.

Note that although these alternative investments entail reduced liquidity, this does not impact funded status; in fact, funded status improves because of the factors mentioned previously. However, the reduced liquidity must be considered to ensure sufficient coverage of prospective liabilities. Alternative investments entail greater manager selection risk and larger dispersion of returns around the policy benchmark relative to a passive allocation to public markets. Careful manager selection would likely require resources that would increase internal costs, and also require paying higher fees to access skilled alternative asset managers.

Exhibit 7 shows the evolution of pension fund asset allocation trends from 2000–2020 for the P7 countries. It is apparent that the allocation to equities has decreased from about 60% in 2000 to about 43% in 2020, while allocations to the 'Other' category of alternatives has increased from about 7% to 26% over the same time period. This is consistent with the general trend among institutional investors of diversifying out of equities and into alternative investments, including private equity, natural resources, real estate, and hedge funds.

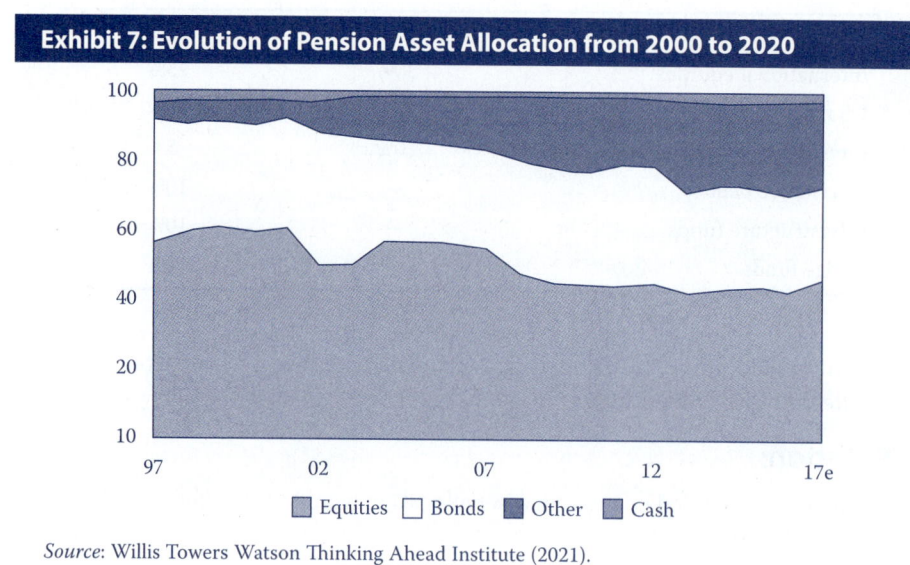

Exhibit 7: Evolution of Pension Asset Allocation from 2000 to 2020

Source: Willis Towers Watson Thinking Ahead Institute (2021).

SOVEREIGN WEALTH FUNDS: TYPES AND STAKEHOLDERS

8

☐ discuss the stakeholders in the portfolio, the liabilities, the investment time horizons, and the liquidity needs of different types of institutional investors

Sovereign wealth funds (SWFs) are state-owned investment funds or entities that invest in financial or real assets. Sovereign wealth funds have increased significantly in number and size over the past two decades. Governments have established SWFs from budget surpluses to meet different objectives. The International Monetary Fund (IMF) has defined five broad types of sovereign wealth funds, and each pursues different investment objectives. Exhibit 8 summarizes these five types with their main objective and some notable examples.

Exhibit 8: Major Types of Sovereign Wealth Funds

Type	Objective	Examples
Budget stabilization funds	Set up to insulate the budget and economy from commodity price volatility and external shocks.	Economic and Social Stabilization Fund of Chile; Timor-Leste Petroleum Fund; Russia's Oil Stabilization Fund
Development funds	Established to allocate resources to priority socio-economic projects, usually infrastructure.	Mubadala (UAE); Iran's National Development Fund; Ireland Strategic Investment Fund; Temasek (Singapore)
Savings funds	Intended to share wealth across generations by transforming non-renewable assets into diversified financial assets.	Abu Dhabi Investment Authority; Kuwait Investment Authority; Qatar Investment Authority; Russia's National Wealth Fund
Reserve funds	Intended to reduce the negative carry costs of holding reserves or to earn higher return on ample reserves.	China Investment Corporation; Korea Investment Corporation; GIC Private Ltd. (Singapore)
Pension reserve funds	Set up to meet identified future outflows with respect to pension-related contingent-type liabilities on governments' balance sheets.	National Social Security Fund (China); New Zealand Superannuation Fund; Future Fund of Australia

Source: International Monetary Fund, "Sovereign Wealth Funds—A Work Agenda" (29 February 2008).

Exhibit 9 shows some of the largest sovereign wealth funds, which manage a total of about US$3.6 trillion in assets—close to 50% of all SWF assets (more than US$7.3 trillion).

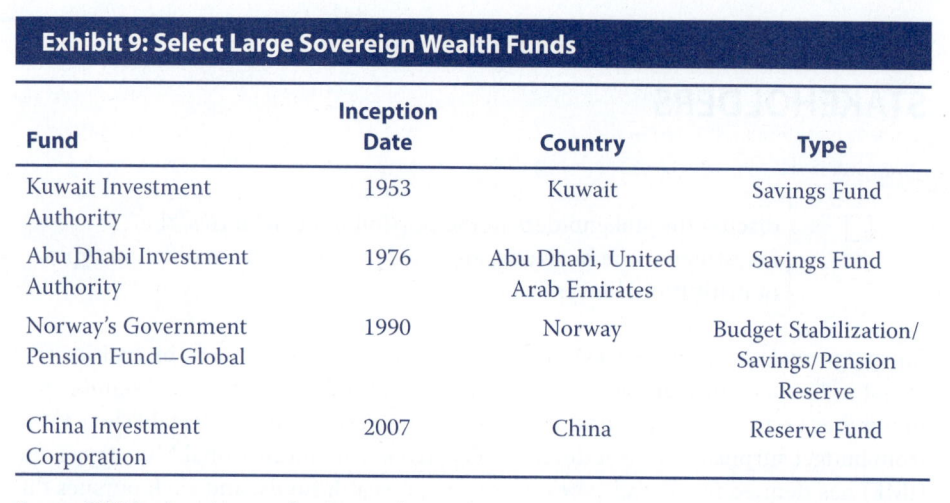

Exhibit 9: Select Large Sovereign Wealth Funds

Fund	Inception Date	Country	Type
Kuwait Investment Authority	1953	Kuwait	Savings Fund
Abu Dhabi Investment Authority	1976	Abu Dhabi, United Arab Emirates	Savings Fund
Norway's Government Pension Fund—Global	1990	Norway	Budget Stabilization/ Savings/Pension Reserve
China Investment Corporation	2007	China	Reserve Fund

Source: SWF Institute (www.swfinstitute.org).

Stakeholders

SWF stakeholders include the citizens, the government, and external asset managers as well as the SWF management, investment committees, and boards.

The ultimate SWF stakeholders are the current and future citizens (or residents) of the country. Depending on the objectives of the SWF, these stakeholders either benefit directly in the form of payments (e.g., for pension reserve funds) or indirectly through stabilization of government budgets, lower taxes, or investments by the SWF in the domestic economy. If the SWF fails to meet its objectives, citizens/residents might be impacted through higher future taxes. Several SWFs are explicitly set up to benefit not only the current generation but also future generations. When such intergenerational wealth transfer is part of the objective, significant transparency and communication are required by the SWF and government to gain support from all stakeholders. This also requires long-term thinking by the government, which can be challenging when some governments have tenures of only a few years and when fiscal budgets vary significantly over the economic cycle.

The management or investment office of an SWF is tasked with investing its assets according to the investment policy and objectives of the fund. They monitor assets, make recommendations on investment strategy, and either select external asset managers or manage assets in-house. Appointment to an SWF's board, which oversees the management or investment office, is typically executed through a formal process that may include appointment by the current ruling government. In any case, the board has a fiduciary duty to the ultimate beneficiaries, the nation's current and future generations.

9 SOVEREIGN WEALTH FUNDS: OTHER CONSIDERATIONS

Liabilities and Investment Horizons

There is a wide variety in investment objectives, liabilities, investment horizons, and liquidity needs among the five types of SWFs, so we will discuss each type separately. As a group, however, SWFs are different from the other institutional investors covered in this reading when it comes to liabilities. The liabilities of DB pension funds, endowments and foundations, insurance companies, and banks are clearly defined, which facilitates asset/liability management (ALM) processes. SWFs, however, do not generally have clearly defined liabilities given their mission of intergenerational wealth transfer. It is also worth noting that SWFs do not necessarily fit neatly into one of the five different types discussed in this section. For example, Norway's Government Pension Fund Global (formerly known as Norway's Petroleum Fund) undertakes elements of stabilization and sterilization, accumulating pension reserves, and saving for future generations.

Budget Stabilization Funds

Budget stabilization funds are established to insulate the fiscal budget from commodity price volatility and other external shocks, particularly if a nation's revenue is tied to natural resource production or other cyclical industries. These funds have uncertain liabilities and relatively short investment horizons. Their main purpose is risk management because such funds may be needed on a short-term basis to help support the government budget. The investment objective is usually to deliver returns in excess of inflation with a low probability of a negative return in any year. Budget stabilization funds typically avoid assets that are highly correlated with the main sources of government revenue, and they may engage in hedging against declines in prices of commodities that are important revenue generators for the local economy. These funds mainly invest in government bonds and other debt securities. Examples of budget stabilization funds include the Economic and Social Stabilization Fund of Chile and Russia's Oil Stabilization Fund.

Development Funds

Development funds are established to support a nation's economic development through investing in essential infrastructure, innovation, or by supporting key industries. Liabilities are not clearly defined and typically uncertain for development funds, but their overall objective is to raise a country's economic growth or to diversify the economy. As such, these funds have an implicit real return target: to increase real domestic GDP growth and productivity. Some initiatives, such as infrastructure/industrial development, may be ongoing and long-term, while others may have a fixed, medium-term horizon, such as a medical research fund. Examples of development funds include Mubadala Development Corp. (UAE) and the National Development Fund of Iran.

Savings Funds

Savings funds are typically established to transform proceeds from the sale of non-renewable natural resources into long-term wealth and a diversified portfolio of financial assets. The mission of a savings fund is wealth transfer to future generations after the sources of natural wealth have been depleted. As such, their liabilities are long-term. Some savings funds have a real return objective or an explicit spending policy (like endowments). Norway's Government Pension Fund Global (GPFG) uses a fiscal spending rule whereby it intends to withdraw 3% of the fund's value annually with the goal of gradually phasing oil revenue into the Norwegian economy. This spending rate is linked to the expected real return earned by the GPFG. A special case of savings funds involves government investment holding companies, which are funded from the privatization proceeds of national companies (e.g., Singapore's Temasek Holdings). Because of their long-term horizons, savings funds invest in risky and illiquid assets, including equities and a wide range of alternative investments. Of course, savings funds should avoid investing in assets highly correlated with the non-renewable resources from which the government is trying to diversify.

Reserve Funds

Reserve investment funds are established from central bank excess foreign currency reserves. The objective is to achieve a return higher than that on FX reserves (usually invested in low-duration, high-grade debt instruments) and to reduce the negative cost-of-carry of holding FX reserves. Reserve funds are common in export-intensive economies that have built up large FX reserves. Central banks accumulate such reserves as they print local currency to buy FX (like US dollars or euros) from local firms selling export goods. The central banks then issue monetary stabilization bonds to absorb the excess local currency. So, the central banks typically end up with FX reserves invested in low-yielding US Treasury or other high-quality sovereign debt instruments, while their liabilities (monetary stabilization bonds) pay much higher yields that create the negative cost-of-carry. Countries mitigate this cost by creating sovereign wealth reserve funds, placing excess FX reserves in these funds, and investing them globally in higher yielding, risky assets. Although their true liabilities are the central bank's monetary stabilization bonds, in practice, reserve funds operate somewhat similarly to endowments and foundations by having either a nominal or real return target. Also, their investment horizons are very long, with typically no immediate or interim pay-out expectation. Consequently, reserve funds generally invest in diversified portfolios with significant exposure to equities and other high-yielding alternative investments. Examples of reserve funds include China Investment Corporation (CIC), Korea Investment Corporation (KIC), and GIC Private Limited (GIC), formerly known as Government of Singapore Investment Corporation.

Pension Reserve Funds

Pension reserve funds are established to help prefund contingent pension-related liabilities on the government's balance sheet. Pension reserve funds are usually funded from fiscal surpluses during economic booms. The goal is to help reduce the burden on future taxpayers by prefunding social security and health care costs arising from aging populations, so these funds generally have long-term investment horizons. There is usually an **accumulation phase** (**decumulation phase**) where the government predominantly contributes to (withdraws from) the fund. However, additional uncertainty also exists around expected cash flows, particularly in the case of funding health care because those costs are quite volatile. The investment objective of pension reserve funds is to earn returns sufficient to maximize the likelihood of meeting future pension, social security, and/or health care costs as they arise. Therefore, such funds will typically invest in a diversified portfolio with the majority in such equities and alternative investments as property, infrastructure, hedge funds, and private markets. An example of a pension reserve fund is Future Fund of Australia (FFA). Its goal is to meet unfunded pension liabilities (retirement payments or superannuation payments in Australia) that will be owed to former public employees starting in 2020. FFA was funded from budget surpluses and privatization proceeds of Telstra, an Australian telecommunications company that was formerly a state-owned enterprise. The investment mandate for FFA is to achieve an average annual return of at least the Consumer Price Index (CPI) + 4% to 5% per year over the long term with an acceptable level of risk.

Liquidity Needs

Budget Stabilization Funds

Stabilization funds must maintain a high level of liquidity and invest in assets that have a low risk of significant losses over short time periods. For example, in the event of a negative commodity price shock, the government might experience a significant budget deficit caused by lower commodity-based revenues. To stabilize the budget and meet spending needs, the stabilization fund's assets must be readily accessible. As a result, budget stabilization funds invest a significant portion of their portfolios in cash and high-grade, fixed-income instruments that are very liquid and carry little risk of significant drawdown.

Development Funds

A development fund supports national economic development. Liquidity needs depend on the particular strategic economic development initiatives the fund was created to support. For example, infrastructure investments are very long-term, so funds established to develop infrastructure would have low liquidity needs. Development funds designed to promote research and innovation may also require long time periods to see the fruits of investments in innovation and research and are likely to have low liquidity needs as well.

Savings Funds

Savings funds have a very long-term investment horizon and low liquidity needs. Their main objective is to grow wealth for future generations, so their liquidity needs, being long-term in nature, are comparable to those of endowments and foundations. In instances where the savings fund was established to transform the proceeds from the sale of non-renewable commodities into long-term wealth, the fund's liquidity needs may change once the nation's natural resources have been depleted because the government is more likely to begin withdrawing money from the fund to support its budgetary needs.

Reserve Funds

Reserve funds operate to offset negative carry effects of holding FX reserves, and consequently, excess reserves are invested in higher growth investments. The liquidity needs of reserve funds are lower than those of stabilization funds but higher than those of savings funds. Reserve funds typically hold 50%–70% in equity or equity-equivalent investments to achieve their return targets. The remainder, however, is likely to be invested in liquid fixed-income securities that could be readily sold should a dramatic change in the balance of trade require additional central bank reserves.

Pension Reserve Funds

Pension reserve funds need to meet future pension or health care liabilities when they come due. Depending on when significant fund withdrawals are expected, liquidity needs change over time. During the accumulation phase, reserve funds can hold a significant part of their portfolios in equities and relatively illiquid investments. Once the decumulation phase begins, the asset allocation will gradually shift toward more liquid, high-quality, fixed-income investments.

External Constraints Affecting Investment

In this section and the next, we briefly highlight some legal/regulatory and tax constraints, respectively, that sovereign wealth funds must consider when investing.

Legal and Regulatory Constraints

Sovereign wealth funds are typically established by national legislation that contains details on: the fund's mission; contributions to the fund; circumstances allowing withdrawals from the fund; and governance structure, including selection of board members, their roles, and the level of board independence. Some SWFs are set up with clear rules on asset allocation. For example, a technology development fund may be required to be 100% invested in offshore technology assets to provide diversification (versus local economic drivers) and eventual technology transfer. Alternatively, an industrial development fund may be required to invest 100% locally to support the development of key industries in the domestic economy. In any case, SWFs should operate in a transparent and accountable manner as they are ultimately established for the benefit of a nation's people and future generations. Sound governance, independence, transparency, and accountability are all essential to ensure that SWFs are protected from political influence.

The International Forum of SWFs (IFSWF) is a self-governing body established to promote best practices among SWFs. All IFSWF members have endorsed a set of generally accepted principles and practices (GAPP). Known as the "Santiago Principles" for the city where they were drafted, the GAPP provide a best practices framework by which SWFs should operate that addresses such key elements as sound legal framework, well-defined mission, independence, accountability, transparency, disclosure, ethics and professionalism, effective risk management, and regular review for compliance with the Santiago Principles.

Tax and Accounting Constraints

Typically, sovereign wealth funds are given tax-free status by the legislation that governs them. However, SWFs may be ineligible to claim withholding taxes or tax credits that are ordinarily available to taxable investors. As SWFs invest in offshore markets, they also need to consider any tax treaties that may exist between the countries in which they are investing and their own country. Some regulators allow SWFs to be exempt from domestic tax rules that have been put in place to deter tax avoidance by corporations and individuals. To prevent any international diplomatic issues, SWFs should be sensitive to ensuring they are not perceived as trying to avoid paying taxes in any offshore jurisdictions where they operate or invest.

10   SOVEREIGN WEALTH FUNDS: INVESTMENT OBJECTIVES AND ASSET ALLOCATION

> ☐ evaluate the investment policy statement of an institutional investor
>
> ☐ evaluate the investment portfolio of a private DB plan, sovereign wealth fund, university endowment, and private foundation

Investment Objectives

Budget Stabilization Funds

The investment objective of budget stabilization funds is capital preservation. This is achieved by endeavoring to deliver returns in excess of inflation with a low probability of a negative return in any given year. In addition, budget stabilization funds should avoid cyclical assets whose returns are highly correlated to the main sources of government revenue (such as natural resources industries). According to the stated investment objectives of Chile's Economic and Social Stabilization Fund, *"the main aim of its investment policy is to maximize the fund's accumulated value in order to partially cover cyclical reductions in fiscal revenues while maintaining a low level of risk. Its risk aversion is reflected by the choice of an investment portfolio with a high level of liquidity and low credit risk and volatility, thereby ensuring the availability of the resources to cover fiscal deficits and preventing significant losses in the fund's value."*

Development Funds

Development funds are established to support a nation's economic development with the ultimate goal of raising a country's long-term economic growth. The implicit investment objective of development funds is therefore to achieve a real rate of return in excess of real domestic GDP or productivity growth.Accordingly, Khazanah Nasional Berhard, the strategic investment fund of the government of Malaysia, *"strives to create sustainable value and cultivate a high-performance culture that helps contribute to Malaysia's economic competitiveness. Utilizing a proactive investment approach, we aim to build true value through management of our core investments, leveraging on our global footprint for new growth, as well as undertaking catalytic investments that strategically boost the country's economy. We also actively develop human, social and knowledge capital for the country."*

Savings Funds

The mission of savings funds is to ensure wealth transfer to future generations. Therefore, their primary objective is to maintain purchasing power of the assets in perpetuity while achieving investment returns sufficient to sustain the spending necessary to support ongoing governmental activities. According to Alaska Statutes 37.13.020, the Alaska Permanent Fund, *"should provide a means of conserving a portion of the state's revenue from mineral resources to benefit all generations of Alaskans; the fund's goal should be to maintain safety of principal while maximizing total return; the fund should be used as a savings device managed to allow the maximum use of disposable income from the fund for purposes designated by law."*

Reserve Funds

The investment objective of reserve funds is usually to achieve a rate of return above the return the government must pay on its monetary stabilization bonds, thereby eliminating the negative cost-of-carry of holding excess FX reserves (that are typically invested in low duration, high-grade, fixed-income instruments). For example, Singapore's Government Investment Corporation (GIC) has a clearly defined purpose: *"We aim to achieve good long-term returns for the Government—a reasonable risk-adjusted rate above global inflation over a 20-year investment horizon. By achieving these returns, we meet our responsibility to preserve and enhance the international purchasing power of Singapore's foreign reserves. The reserves provide a stream of income that can be spent or invested for the benefit of present and future generations."*

Pension Reserve Funds

The investment objective of pension reserve funds is to earn sufficient returns to maximize the likelihood of being able to meet future unfunded pension, social security, and/or health care liabilities of plan participants as they arise. Accordingly, among its mandates, the Australian government states that its Future Fund should *"maximise the return earned on the Fund over the long term; ... adopt an average return of at least the Consumer Price Index (CPI) +4 to +5 per cent per annum over the long term as the benchmark return on the Fund; [and] in targeting the benchmark return, the Board must determine an acceptable but not excessive level of risk for the Fund...."*

> **EXAMPLE 4**
>
> ## The People's Fund of Wigitania—A Pension Reserve Fund
>
> The People's Fund is a pension reserve fund established by the government of Wigitania by setting aside current government surpluses. Its objective is to meet future unfunded social security payments caused by an aging population. The following is an extract from the People's Fund IPS.
>
> Effective from 2030, the government will have the ability to withdraw assets to meet pension and social security liabilities falling due each year. Actuarial projections estimate annual payouts to be about 5% of the total fund value at that time. Given this level of cash flow, the Fund is expected to maintain most of its asset base for the foreseeable future. As such, 2030 does not represent an 'end date' for measurement purposes. A long-term investment horizon remains appropriate at present. However, the appropriate timeframe, risk tolerance, portfolio construction and liquidity profile may change.
>
> 1. What are the liquidity needs of the People's Fund?
>
> **Solution:**
>
> From the extract, we see that the unfunded pension and social security liabilities that the Fund is meant to cover are expected to be about 5% of total fund value per year, starting in 2030. Management of the fund will need to ensure that they have sufficient liquidity at that time to meet those ongoing liabilities. Until that time, liquidity needs are very low, which should allow the People's Fund to invest a significant part of its portfolio in less-liquid alternative asset classes.
>
> 2. What factors does the Board need to consider when reviewing the Fund's investment horizon?
>
> **Solution:**
>
> The Board should consider two separate phases when reviewing the Fund's investment horizon and investment policy: an accumulation phase and a decumulation phase. The accumulation phase lasts until 2030 and allows the Fund to invest with little to no liquidity needs and little concern for interim volatility. The decumulation phase starts after 2030, when the government expects to withdraw about 5% of the assets on an annual basis. The investment horizon, liquidity needs, and risk tolerance will need to be modified during the decumulation phase, which will affect the investment policy.

Asset Allocation by Sovereign Wealth Funds

Each of the five types of sovereign wealth funds have very different objectives and purposes. Not surprisingly then, these funds have very different asset allocations. Development funds usually have little flexibility with their asset allocations as they operate within a limited investment universe as part of their mandate (e.g., they are required to invest in local infrastructure development projects). Given that national development projects can be different in nature and purpose between countries, it would be difficult to envision a 'typical' asset allocation for a development fund. The other four types of sovereign wealth funds are more homogeneous within their respective groups, for which Exhibit 10 provides illustrative asset allocations.

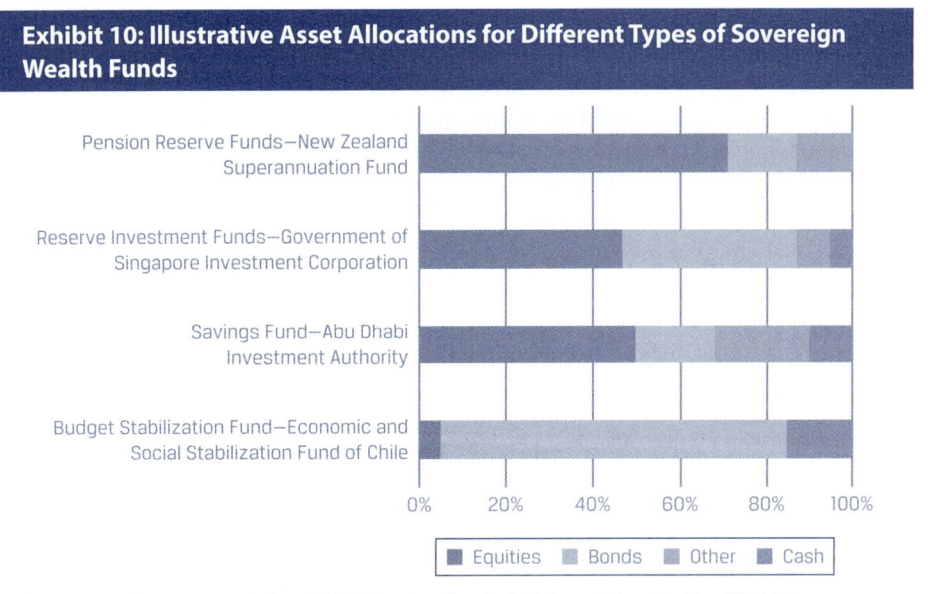

Exhibit 10: Illustrative Asset Allocations for Different Types of Sovereign Wealth Funds

Sources: 1. Economic and Social Stabilization Fund of Chile website; 2. Abu Dhabi Investment Authority (ADIA), *2020 Review*; 3. Government Investment Corporation (GIC), *Report on the Management of the Government's Portfolio for the Year 2020/21*; 4. NZSUPERFUND, *New Zealand Superannuation Fund Annual Report2021*.

Several key points stand out from the data in Exhibit 10:

- The portfolios of budget stabilization funds are dominated by fixed-income investments because of their defensive nature, relatively stable investment returns, and diversification against cyclically sensitive factors (such as commodity prices) that drive government budget revenues in some countries. The conservative asset allocation may be partly explained by the fact that several major stabilization funds are managed by their countries' central bank or Ministry of Finance; these entities tend to be relatively risk averse.

- The portfolios of savings funds are shown to be tilted toward growth assets, equities, and alternatives (the "Other" category). Due to their very long investment horizons, these funds can take on more equity-related risks, and they consequently hold relatively high allocations to such alternative investments as real assets, private equity and debt (loans), and hedge funds.

- Reserve investment funds have a similar allocation to savings funds but they tend to allocate less to alternatives. This may be partially explained by reserve funds having potentially higher liquidity needs compared to savings funds because of central bank activities. Public equities are typically the most liquid growth asset available and help counter the negative carry generated by foreign exchange reserves, while bonds and other fixed-income investments help to reduce reserve funds' portfolio volatility.

- The portfolios of pension reserve funds are relatively heavily tilted toward equities with a significant allocation to alternative assets, such as real assets and infrastructure, private equity and debt markets, and hedge funds. Pension reserve funds generally have long-term investment horizons (but not necessarily inter-generational as with savings funds) and low liquidity needs during their accumulation phases, which can explain their high allocation to alternatives compared with other SWFs.

Sovereign wealth funds with savings or pension reserve objectives typically follow the endowment investment model. Some also adopt the Canada reference portfolio model. An example of the latter is the New Zealand Superannuation Fund (NZSF). As noted previously, this model makes use of a reference portfolio comprising passive investment in stocks and bonds that are expected to meet the fund's investment objectives. The total portfolio is then invested to replicate the risk factors of the reference portfolio, while individual investments are benchmarked against a combined stock and bond benchmark representing the risk factors driving the individual investments. Both models result in higher allocations to alternative investments, as observed in Exhibit 10.

In the Asia Pacific region, sovereign wealth funds are the largest institutional investors. Some examples include China Investment Corporation (CIC), State Administration of Foreign Exchange (SAFE) Investment Company (China), Hong Kong Monetary Authority Investment Portfolio (HKMAIP) and Government Investment Corporation of Singapore (GIC). Given the huge size of their assets, these SWFs tend to dominate the regional investment landscape. They typically have fewer investment constraints than other Asia Pacific institutional investors. These SWFs also have broader investment mandates, minimal investment management fee constraints, and longer time horizons as compared to (for example) pension funds. Such flexibility allows these SWFs to implement higher allocations to alternative assets.

11   UNIVERSITY ENDOWMENTS AND PRIVATE FOUNDATIONS

☐ | describe the focus of legal, regulatory, and tax constraints affecting different types of institutional investors

This section introduces university endowments and private foundations. As will be seen shortly, these two types of institutional investors have some similarities but also important differences that affect their investing activities.

University Endowments

Many institutions have endowments, including universities, churches, museums, and hospitals. These endowments are typically funded through gifts and donations and are intended to help the institutions provide for some of their main services. Endowment funds invest in capital markets to provide a savings and growth mechanism that allows the institution to meet its mission in perpetuity. The main objective is to provide intergenerational equity. As James Tobin wrote in 1974: "The trustees of an endowed institution are the guardians of the future against the claims of the present. Their task is to preserve equity among generations."

Throughout this reading, for simplicity we will focus on university endowments. The investment objectives and philosophies of the endowments of other institutions are typically not very different from those of university endowments. Exhibit 11 shows some large (by assets) university endowments.

Exhibit 11: Select US University Endowments

University	Assets (US$ bn)
Harvard University	40.5
University of Texas System	31.9
Yale University	31.2
Stanford University	28.9
Princeton University	26.6

Source: TIAA and the National Association of College and University Business Officers (NACUBO), *2020 NACUBO–TIAA Study of Endowments (NCSE).*

Private Foundations

Foundations are nonprofit organizations that typically make grants to outside organizations and persons who carry out social, educational and other charitable activities. Many foundations are located in the United States, but some large foundations are outside the United States, such as the Wellcome Trust in the United Kingdom. Foundations are more common in the United States because of favorable tax treatment. Outside the United States, charitable giving is typically undertaken by family offices.

There are four different types of foundations:

1. *Community foundations*: These are charitable organizations that make social or educational grants for the benefit of a local community (e.g., the New York Community Trust). These foundations are usually funded by public donations.

2. *Operating foundations*: Organizations that exist to operate a not-for-profit business for charitable purposes. They are typically funded by individual donors or donor families.

3. *Corporate foundations*: These are established by businesses and funded from profits.

4. *Private grant-making foundations*: These are established by individual donors or donor families to support specific types of charities. Most of the largest foundations in the US fall into this category.

Community foundations are a type of public charity associated with such community organizations as hospitals, schools, and churches. They are funded by many relatively small donors, and they typically provide charitable support in the region or community where they are located. Private operating foundations are established to provide funding and support for related programs and activities (e.g., operating a museum) rather than giving grants to outside organizations or activities.

Private grant-making foundations (also called private non-operating foundations) are by far the largest group (in number of foundations and in total assets), so they are our primary focus. Private grant-making foundations support different types of charities and usually run a large grant-making operation in addition to an investment office. The main objective of most private grant-making foundations is to maintain purchasing power into perpetuity, so that the organization can continue making grants. In recent years, however, there has been a trend toward limited-life foundations as original donors seek to maintain control over foundation spending during their lives.

The focus of grants varies widely and includes issues such as health, education, environment, arts, and culture. Some foundations make large and targeted grants to very specific causes while others make many smaller grants to a wide variety of causes. Exhibit 12 shows some large US foundations and their missions.

Exhibit 12: Select US Foundations

Foundation	Mission
Bill & Melinda Gates Foundation	Focus on global health and poverty. In US focus on education.
Ford Foundation	Focus on inequality.
Robert Wood Johnson Foundation	Improve health and health care of all Americans.
Lilly Endowment Inc.	Support religion, education, community development.
William and Flora Hewlett Foundation	Help people build measurably better lives by focusing on education, the environment, global development, performing arts, philanthropy, and population. Also supports disadvantaged communities in San Francisco.

Source: Foundation Center (www.foundationcenter.org).

External Constraints Affecting Investment

In this section and the next we briefly touch on some legal/regulatory and tax constraints, respectively, that affect investing by university endowments and private foundations.

Legal and Regulatory Constraints

Charitable organizations, including endowments and foundations, are typically subject to rules and regulations in their country of domicile that: 1) require investment committees/officers/boards to invest on a total return basis and consider portfolio diversification when managing assets (i.e., follow the principles of modern portfolio theory, MPT); and 2) require investment committees/officers/boards to exercise a duty of care and prudence in overseeing the assets and making investment decisions (i.e., fiduciary duty).

In the United States, endowments and foundations are governed by the Uniform Prudent Management of Institutional Funds Act of 2006 (UPMIFA). Two important features of UPMIFA include:

1. Allowing charitable organizations flexibility in spending decisions, which could be adjusted for fluctuations in the market value of assets. Endowments, particularly, could meet the fiduciary standard of prudence by maintaining purchasing power of the fund.

2. Modernizing the standard of prudence for the management of charitable funds by adopting the principles of MPT established by the Uniform Prudent Investor Act (1994).

UK endowments and foundations are typically organized as trusts. Until 2000, UK trusts were limited to spending only income earned from investments (not capital gains). The Trustee Act (2000) changed that and, like UPMIFA in the United States, required trustees to manage trust assets based on MPT principles. The act also imposed a duty of care upon trustees. The shift toward managing portfolios using MPT principles has enabled endowments and foundations to embrace a broader range of asset classes compared to the traditional 60/40 equity/bond mix. It has also allowed them to focus on total return rather than solely on income return (high coupon bond and/or high-dividend-yield stocks).

Tax and Accounting Constraints

Endowments and foundations typically enjoy tax-exempt status. Tax-exempt status has three elements:

1. *Taxation of gifts and donations to endowments and foundations*: Gifts and donations to endowments and foundations are usually tax-deductible (up to a certain percentage of adjusted gross income) for the person or entity making the gift or donation.

2. *Taxation of income and capital gains on assets*: Income and capital gains on assets are usually tax-exempt in countries that have endowments and charitable organizations, which are tied to such non-profit, tax-exempt organizations as universities, religious organizations, or museums.

3. *Taxation on payouts from endowments and foundations*: Payouts are tax exempt if the receiving institution is exempt from income tax. If payouts are made to support the operating budget of a for-profit business, then that business is required to treat the payout as taxable income.

In the United States, private grant-making foundations enjoy the same tax-exempt status as endowments. But unlike endowments, such private foundations are subject to minimum payout (spending) requirements, whereby they must distribute a minimum of 5% of their asset value on an annual basis in grants that support their mission. Failing to meet this spending requirement subjects such foundations to 30% tax on undistributed income. Most tax-exempt private foundations also have an excise tax of 2% on their net investment income. In the United Kingdom, charitable organizations do not pay taxes on most of their income and gains if these are used for charitable purposes; however, taxes must be paid on funds that are not used for charitable purposes.

UNIVERSITY ENDOWMENTS: OTHER CONSIDERATIONS

12

☐ | discuss the stakeholders in the portfolio, the liabilities, the investment time horizons, and the liquidity needs of different types of institutional investors

Stakeholders of a university endowment include current and future students, alumni, current and future university faculty and administrators, and the larger university community. Each of these stakeholders has a strong interest in seeing the endowment invested prudently. There is potential, however, for tension between increasing spending to meet current needs versus preserving sufficient funds to serve future generations. Endowment boards or investment committees, therefore, need to determine an appropriate balance.

University endowments are generally funded by gifts and donations from alumni. It is common that donors specify the handling and use of their gifts—for example, that only the income portion be spent or that only specific scholarships, programs, or departments benefit. Other gifts may be unrestricted and can be spent for general purposes. Alumni are concerned about current students and faculty and also future generations, so they expect endowment assets to be invested for the long-run. Endowment payouts support the university's operating budget and provide an important source of income. Endowments provide stability and continuity when other revenues sources, such as tuition and government funding, fluctuate. Endowments also allow universities to more readily undertake long-term capital projects, knowing required resources are available to meet those future commitments.

Stakeholders of a university endowment often have representation on the endowment's board or investment committee, including alumni who are investment professionals running or working for financial services organizations.

University Endowments—Liabilities and Investment Horizon

Although most endowments operate on an asset-only basis, their main purpose is to support the university's operating budget based on the principle of intergenerational equity. The investment horizon for endowments is thus perpetuity, and their main objective is to maintain long-term purchasing power. An endowment's liabilities are the future stream of payouts to the university, which are typically codified in an official spending policy. The spending policy serves two important purposes: 1) to ensure intergenerational equity; and 2) to smooth endowment payouts to partially insulate contributions to the university from capital market volatility.

Although the spending policy defines how much of the endowment's assets are paid out annually, several other liability characteristics should be considered when designing an appropriate investment policy, including:

a. What is the university's capacity for fund-raising: How much in gifts and donations are contributed (on average) each year?

b. What percentage of the university's operating budget is supported by the endowment?

c. Balance sheet health: Does the endowment or university have the ability to issue debt?

We first discuss different types of spending policies and then discuss other important liability-related characteristics. Broadly speaking, there are three different types of endowment spending policies:

1. *Constant Growth Rule*: The endowment provides a fixed amount annually to the university, typically adjusted for inflation (the growth rate). The inflation rate is usually based on the Higher Education Price Index (HEPI)[2] in the United States or a more general consumer price index elsewhere, possibly with an additional spread. A shortcoming of constant growth spending rules is that spending does not adjust based on the endowment's value. If the endowment experiences weak (strong) average returns, the spending amount expressed as a percentage of assets may become very high (low). This spending rule is therefore commonly complemented with caps and floors, typically between 4% and 6% of average assets under management (AUM) over one or three years.

2. *Market Value Rule*: The endowment pays a pre-specified percentage (the spending rate) of the moving average of asset values, typically between 4% and 6%. Asset values are usually smoothed using a 3- to 5-year moving average. A disadvantage of this spending rule is that it tends to be pro-cyclical; when markets have performed well (poorly), the overall payout increases (decreases).

---

2 The HEPI is calculated annually by Commonfund and tracks the most important components in the cost of higher education. More information can be found at https://www.commonfund.org/commonfund -institute/higher-education-price-index-hepi.

3. *Hybrid Rule*: Spending is calculated as a weighted average of the constant growth and market value rules. Commonly referred to as the Yale spending rule, weights can range from 30% to 70%. This spending rule was designed to strike a balance between the shortcomings of the respective spending rules.

All three spending rules can be summarized by the following formula:

Spending Amount in Year $t + 1$

$= w \times$ [Spending Amount in Year $t \times (1 + $ Inflation Rate)] $+ (1 - w) \times$ Spending Rate $\times$ Average AUM,

where w denotes the weight put on the prior year's spending amount. When $w = 1$, the formula simplifies to a constant growth rule; when $w = 0$, it simplifies to a market value rule. For any other choice of w ($0 < w < 1$), the formula represents a hybrid spending rule. Most US endowments use a market value spending rule, but some of the larger ones use a hybrid rule. As noted, a market value spending rule is pro-cyclical: This may not be an issue for universities that receive only a small percentage of their operating budgets from their endowment, but this may be more problematic otherwise. The goal of providing intergenerational equity means university endowments aim to maintain their purchasing power. Therefore, endowments target a real rate of return (after inflation) equal to or greater than their spending rates. Given that endowments pay out (on average) between 4% and 6% of assets annually, they typically target a 5% to 5.5% real, long-term rate of return.

Other liability-related factors must be considered when managing an endowment. Universities regularly raise money from donors. Depending on the wealth of their alumni base, such fund-raising activity may be more or less successful. Because of gifts and donations, endowments' net spending rate tends to be lower than the headline spending of 4% to 6% of assets previously discussed. On average, net spending is closer to 2% to 4% of assets. Another important distinction between endowments is how much the university relies on its endowment to support the operating budget. Such support may be less than 5% for some universities, while in other cases, 40% to 50% of the university's operating budget is provided by its endowment. All else equal, endowments that support a smaller percentage of the overall budget should be able to tolerate more market, credit, and liquidity risk. In practice, however, this important distinguishing factor is typically insufficiently incorporated in the design of investment policies. It is common for university endowments to be benchmarked against each other, which creates herding behavior even though the organizations might have very different liability characteristics. A final consideration is the debt issuance capability of the endowment (or university). Some endowments access the public and private debt markets on a regular basis. The capability to access debt markets, especially during periods of market stress, affects the levels of risk and illiquidity endowments can accept in their investments.

University Endowments—Liquidity Needs

The liquidity needs of university endowments are relatively low (compared to foundations). On average, endowments' annual net spending is 2% to 4% of assets, after factoring in gifts and donations. Low liquidity needs combined with long investment horizons allow endowments to accept relatively high short-term volatility in pursuit of superior long-term returns. Consequently, many university endowments have relatively high allocations to equity markets and illiquid private asset classes and small allocations to fixed income. Having significant allocations to illiquid asset classes, such as private equity and private real estate, creates additional liquidity needs to meet annual net capital calls from general partners managing these assets. Finally, to the extent that endowments use derivatives for rebalancing or portable alpha strategies, there may be further liquidity needs—particularly during times of financial market stress—to meet margin calls or to cover higher collateral demands.

13   PRIVATE FOUNDATIONS

Stakeholders of a foundation include the founding family, donors, grant recipients, and the broader community that may benefit indirectly from the foundation's activities. Each has a strong interest in seeing the foundation's assets invested appropriately. As with university endowments, a tension may exist between increasing current grant spending versus preserving sufficient funds to serve future generations of grant recipients. The founding family and donors typically want their donations to support grant recipients in perpetuity. There is a trend, however, toward limited-life foundations as donors seek to maintain control over foundation spending during their lives. Finally, the government (Internal Revenue Service in the United States) may also be a stakeholder because of the favorable tax treatment that foundations enjoy. The government's main concern is that foundations remain engaged strictly in charitable work.

The boards of foundations tend to be different in terms of skill sets than the boards of endowments. University endowments typically have alumni sitting on their boards—people with a special relationship to the university and who may have significant financial market skills (for example, in private equity or hedge funds). Board members for foundations, however, are typically individuals involved with grant making and not necessarily investment professionals. This difference in skill sets may affect the quality of board oversight, the level of delegation of decision making to investment staff, and the quality of investment decisions.

Mission-related investing (also known as "**impact investing**"), which aims to direct a significant portion of assets in excess of annual grants into projects promoting the foundation's mission, is becoming increasingly important. For example, the Ford Foundation has allocated up to US$1.0 billion (more than 8% of assets) over 10 years to investments related to its mission of addressing global inequality. The challenge for foundations is to ensure that mission-related investments generate financial returns commensurate with risks assumed. As typically lower yielding mission-related investments are undertaken at the expense of higher return investment opportunities, portfolio returns (expected and realized) may decline, which could result in foundation assets being spent down sooner and annual grant-making activities being reduced.

Private Foundations—Liabilities and Investment Horizon

In practice, the investment philosophy of private foundations is typically similar to that of university endowments, despite important differences between them in terms of liabilities and liquidity needs. Foundations and endowments both typically have perpetual investment horizons (although, as noted shortly, some foundations may have finite lives) and both invest to maintain purchasing power; however, foundations generally have higher liquidity needs. In the United States, private grant-making foundations are legally required to pay out 5% of assets (on a trailing 12-month basis) plus investment expenses, while university endowments have more-flexible spending rules. In addition, foundations must spend any donations in the year received, known as flow-through (but this is not necessarily the case outside the United States). Foundations typically use a smoothing formula similar to that of university endowments to ensure payouts do not fluctuate with the market volatility of assets. The constant growth spending rule and the hybrid spending rule, discussed previously for university endowments, are rarely used by foundations.

Foundations sometimes issue bonds. The capability to access debt markets, especially during periods of market stress, is positively associated with the levels of investment risk and liquidity risk that foundations can accept in their investments. The Wellcome Foundation (United Kingdom), with a credit rating of AAA, has occasionally issued bonds. For example, in early 2018, it issued £750 million of century bonds (i.e., 100-year maturity) with a coupon of 2.517%.[3] Proceeds from such bonds have been used to support charitable work, and bondholders are repaid by the returns generated on the investment portfolio.

Spending Rate and Investment Expenses of Foundations

Costs of running a foundation are included in the 5% required payout, excluding investment expenses, which means the investment office is considered a cost center. Consequently, the investment office of a foundation will typically be much smaller compared to that of a similar-sized (by AUM) endowment, leading to potentially different investment behavior. For example, many small foundations have limited investment staff and therefore rely on an outsourced CIO model, whereby assets are managed by an external organization that assumes fiduciary duty and takes responsibility for the strategic asset allocation and investments across various asset classes. Although many outsourced CIOs do offer allocations to alternative asset classes, the result of such outsourcing may typically be a heavier allocation to public markets, more-intensive use of passive strategies, and a heavier reliance on beta as a driver of returns.

Many foundations typically receive a one-time gift from the founding family. Some foundations are allowed to raise money on an ongoing basis, but in the US, any such donations must be spent on a flow-through basis. Unlike universities that derive revenues from other sources besides their endowments, such as tuition and research grants, foundations rely almost exclusively on their investment portfolios to support operating budgets. This high dependency has important implications for risk tolerance, and as a result, foundations (on average) have more conservative, more-liquid investment portfolios compared to endowments.

Typically, the original gift must be maintained in perpetuity (principal protection). There is, however, a trend toward **limited-life foundations**, as some founders seek to maintain control of spending while they (or their immediate heirs) are still alive. For example, the Bill and Melinda Gates Foundation is mandated to spend down assets to zero within 30 years of the Gates' death. There is risk—and concern by some founding donors—that as the foundation's leadership changes over time, the mission may move away from the founder's vision. Thus, to minimize this risk, more limited-life foundations are being established. Importantly, a limited-life foundation faces a different investment problem than a perpetual foundation: As the investment horizon of a limited-life foundation shortens, its liquidity needs increase and risk tolerance decreases.

Real-Life Example of a Limited-Life Foundation

The Atlantic Philanthropies, set up by Chuck Feeney in 1982, is among the largest limited-life foundations to complete its grant-making activities. After giving a total of US$8 billion over 35 years to human rights, health care, and education

---

3 In late 2017, Oxford University issued a century bond with the same size and similar coupon.

causes, the last grant was made in 2016 and the Atlantic Philanthropies expects to close in 2020. All stakeholders have been informed of the spend-down process and critical challenges are being addressed, including: 1) choosing who will oversee the portfolio wind-down process with staff departing for other employment opportunities; and 2) deciding how best to liquidate private investments. As a limited-life foundation gives away its assets, liquidity needs increase and risk tolerance decreases, resulting in lower financial returns and thus limiting the size of the grants that can be made. The de-risking process requires a very "hands-on" investment approach and includes liquidating private portfolios by reducing/stopping commitments, selling private portfolios in the secondary markets, and reinvesting distributions. This becomes increasingly challenging as talented investment staff depart the organization. Actions taken and lessons learned by The Atlantic Philanthropies provide a great case study for other limited-life foundations.

Private Foundations—Liquidity Needs

The liquidity needs of foundations are relatively low but still higher than those of university endowments. US foundations are legally required to spend 5% of assets or face a tax penalty. They must set aside monies to pay one-year grants and to meet annual installments for longer-term (typically two- to five-year) grants. Having a significant allocation to such relatively illiquid asset classes as private equity and private real estate creates additional liquidity needs to meet general partners' annual net capital calls. Also, derivatives use for such activities as portfolio rebalancing or implementing portable alpha strategies may result in added liquidity demands to meet increased margin calls or to cover higher collateral demands (especially during times of financial market stress).

Exhibit 13 presents a summary comparison of foundations and endowments.

Exhibit 13: Comparison Between Private US Foundations and US University Endowments

	US Foundation	US University Endowment
Purpose	Grant-making for social, educational, and charitable purposes; principal preservation focus.	General support of institution or restricted support; principal preservation focus.
Stakeholders	Founding family, donors, grant recipients, and broader community that may benefit from foundation's activities.	Current/future students, alumni, university faculty and administration, and the larger university community.
Liabilities/Spending	Legally mandated to spend 5% of assets + investment expenses + 100% of donations (flow-through).	Flexible spending rules (headline spending rate between 4% and 6% of assets) with smoothing.
Other liability considerations	Future gifts and donations, or just one-time gift?	Gifts and donations, percentage of operating budget supported by endowment, and ability to issue debt.
Investment time horizon	Very long-term/perpetual (except limited-life foundations).	Perpetual
Risk	High risk tolerance with some short-term liquidity needs.	High risk tolerance with low liquidity needs.
Liquidity needs	Annual net spending is at least 5% of assets.	Annual net spending is typically 2% to 4% of assets, after alumni gifts and donations.

UNIVERSITY ENDOWMENTS: INVESTMENT OBJECTIVES AND ASSET ALLOCATION

14

☐ evaluate the investment policy statement of an institutional investor

☐ evaluate the investment portfolio of a private DB plan, sovereign wealth fund, university endowment, and private foundation

We now consider the investment objectives and investment policy statement for university endowments and the investment objectives of private foundations.

University Endowments

A university endowment's mission is to maintain the purchasing power of the assets into perpetuity while achieving investment returns sufficient to sustain the level of spending necessary to support the university budget. For a university endowment, investment policy and spending policy are intertwined, so the IPS should cover spending policy. As discussed previously, endowments use different spending rules. In general, endowments target a spending rate of about 5% of (average) assets. The effective spending rate will, however, be reduced after accounting for gifts and donations. An endowment's primary investment objective is typically to achieve a total real rate of return (after inflation) of $X\%$ with an expected volatility of $Y\%$ over the long term (K years). A common target for $X\%$ is 5%, with inflation being measured using the Higher Education Price Index (HEPI), to be achieved over 3 to 5 years (i.e., $K = 3$ or 5). The expected volatility of returns, $Y\%$, is typically in the range of 10% to 15% annually. Note that the target rate of return may also be expressed as a nominal (as opposed to real) return.

Endowments sometimes have secondary and tertiary investment objectives. A secondary objective might be to outperform the long-term policy benchmark. A third objective might be to outperform a set of pre-defined peers (e.g., outperform the average of the 20 largest university endowments). Peer comparison can lead to herding behavior and be detrimental to long-term success if the focus moves away from managing investments based on each organization's unique liability characteristics to exploit their own comparative advantages. To achieve their objectives, endowments invest in a broad range of asset classes, including fixed income, public equities, hedge fund strategies, private equity, private real estate, and natural resources (e.g. energy and timber). Given that endowments aim to maintain the purchasing power of their assets, they tend to have significant allocations to real assets that are expected to generate returns commensurate with inflation.

The following box provides two examples of investment objectives found in IPSs for real-life endowments.

Investment Objectives of University Endowments

Oxford University Endowment: *"The specific investment objective of the Oxford Endowment Fund is to grow our investors' capital by an average of 5% per annum in real terms, and to achieve this at a lower volatility than would be experienced by investing solely in the public equity markets."*

Source: Oxford Endowment Fund, www.ouem.co.uk/the-oxford-endowment-fund/.

Note: The Oxford Endowment Fund defines its investors as the University of Oxford, including 23 of its colleges and five associated foundations and trusts.

Massachusetts Institute of Technology Endowment: *"Our primary long-term goal is to generate sufficient investment returns to maintain the purchasing power of the endowment after inflation and after MIT's annual spending. Assuming inflation will average around 3% over the long-term and MIT's spending rate will average around 5%, we need to earn approximately 8% to meet this goal. As a secondary check on the quality of our performance, we compare our returns to other endowments and to passive benchmark alternatives."*

Source: www.mitimco.org/wp-content/uploads/2017/03/MITIMCo-Alumni-Letter.pdf.

One of the lessons from the 2007–2009 global financial crisis is that liquidity risk must be managed carefully, particularly for institutions that invest heavily in illiquid assets. Most endowments now engage in detailed cash flow modeling for the illiquid portions of their portfolios, and some use a liquidity risk band as part of their overall risk profile. The liquidity risk band is defined as total NAV allocated to illiquid investments plus uncalled commitments to total fund AUM. If the liquidity band is violated (i.e., when the total allocation to illiquid investments exceeds a pre-specified upper bound), this may trigger a reduction (or even a stoppage) of commitments or possibly a sale of some illiquid investments in secondary markets to bring the overall illiquid allocation back to within the liquidity risk band.

EXAMPLE 5

Investment Objectives of the Ivy University Endowment

The hypothetical Ivy University Endowment was established in 1901 by Ivy University and supports up to 40% of the university's operating budget. Historically, the endowment has invested in a traditional 20% public US equities and 80% US Treasury portfolio, entirely implemented through passive investment vehicles. The investment staff at the endowment is relatively small. With the appointment of a new chief investment officer, the investment policy is being reviewed. Endowment assets are US$250 million, and the endowment has an annual spending policy of paying out 5% of the 3-year rolling asset value to the university.

An investment consultant hired by the new CIO to assist with the investment policy review has provided the following 10-year (nominal) expected return assumptions for various asset classes: US equities: 7%, Non-US equities: 8%, US Treasuries: 2%, hedge funds: 5%, and private equity: 10%. Additionally, the investment consultant believes the endowment could generate an extra 50 bps per year in alpha from active management in equities. Expected inflation for the next ten years is 2% annually.

1. Draft the investment objectives section of the IPS of the Ivy University Endowment.

Solution:

The mission of the Ivy University Endowment is to maintain purchasing power of its assets while financing up to 40% of Ivy University's operating budgeting in perpetuity. The investment objective, consistent with this mission, is to achieve a total real rate of return over the Higher Education Price Index (HEPI) of at least 5% with a reasonable level of risk; the volatility of returns should not to exceed 15% annually.

2. Discuss whether the current investment policy is appropriate given the investment objectives of Ivy University Endowment.

Solution:

Given the expected returns provided by the consultant, a portfolio of 80% fixed income and 20% public equities, invested passively, is expected to provide a nominal expected return of 3% per year (= 0.8 × 2% + 0.2 × 7%). Given, expected inflation of 2%, this implies a 1% real rate of return, which falls well short of the 5% spending rate and the stated objective of a 5% real rate of return. The endowment will see its purchasing power deteriorate over time if it continues with its current asset mix and spending rate.

3. What decisions could the CIO and board of the Ivy University Endowment take to align the investment policy and the spending policy?

Solution:

The CIO and board could either change the investment policy by adopting an asset mix that has a more reasonable probability of achieving a 5% real rate of return (an asset allocation including non-US equities and private equity); they could change the spending rate to more accurately reflect the expected real rate of return of the current investment policy; or the new CIO may want to recommend a combination of both.

Below is an example of a university endowment Investment Policy Statement. In this case the university endowment has clearly articulated primary and secondary investment objectives.

University Endowment Investment Policy Statement

A. Introduction

The hypothetical Ivy University Endowment Fund (the "Endowment") has been established to fund scholarships, fellowships, faculty salaries, programs, activities, and facilities designed to promote and advance the mission of Ivy University (the "University"). This investment policy statement (IPS) is established by the Investment Committee of the Board of Trustees (the "IC") for the guidance of the IC, the Investment Office, the Endowment's investment managers, and other fiduciaries in the course of investing the monies of the Endowment. This IPS establishes policies and procedures for the administration and investment of the Endowment's assets. This document formally defines the goals, objectives, and guidelines of the Endowment's investment program.

B. Mission and Investment Objectives

The Endowment provides financial support for the operations of the University. Investment and spending policies are designed to balance the current goals of the University with its future needs, in order to achieve parity in supporting both current and future generations of Ivy students. The goal for the Endowment is to provide a real total return that preserves the purchasing power of the Endowment's assets while generating an income stream to support the academic activities of the University.

The primary investment objective of the Endowment is to earn an average annual real total return (net of portfolio management fees) of at least 5% per year over the long term (rolling five-year periods), within prudent levels of risk. Attainment of this objective will be sufficient to maintain, in real terms, the purchasing power of the Endowment's assets and support the defined spending policy.

A secondary investment objective is to outperform, over the long term, a blended custom benchmark based on a current asset allocation policy of: 30% MSCI World Index, 20% Cambridge Associates LLC US Private Equity Index, 10% NCREIF Property Index, 10% Consumer Price Index for All Urban Consumers (annualized CPI-U) + 5%, 20% HFRI Fund of Funds Index, and 10% Citigroup US Treasury Index.

C. Spending Policy

The Endowment's spending policy was developed to meet several objectives, namely to: (a) provide a sustainable level of income to support current operations, (b) provide year-to-year budget stability, and (c) meet intergenerational needs by protecting the future purchasing power of the Endowment against the impact of inflation. Under this policy, spending for a given year equals 80% of spending in the previous year, adjusted for inflation (CPI within a range of 0% and 6%), plus 20% of the long-term spending rate (5.0%) applied to the 12-quarter rolling average of market values. This spending policy has two implications. First, by incorporating the previous year's spending, the policy eliminates large fluctuations and so enables the University to plan for operating budget needs. Second, by adjusting spending toward a long-term rate of 5.0%, the policy ensures that spending levels will be sensitive to fluctuating market value levels, thereby providing stability in long-term purchasing power.

D. Asset Allocation Policy, Allowable Ranges, and Benchmarks

The single most important investment decision is the allocation of the Endowment to various asset classes. The primary objective of the Endowment's asset allocation policy is to provide a strategic mix of asset classes that produces the highest expected investment return within a prudent risk framework. To achieve this, the Endowment will allocate among several asset classes with a bias toward equity and equity-like investments caused by their higher long-term return expectations. Other asset classes may be added to the Endowment to enhance returns, reduce volatility through diversification, and/or offer a broader investment opportunity set.

To ensure broad diversification among the major categories of investments, the Endowment has adopted the following capital allocation policy ranges for each asset class within the overall portfolio set forth in the Annex. This asset allocation framework is reviewed annually by the IC, but because of the long-term nature of the Endowment, changes to the framework are expected to be infrequent:

Asset Class	Policy Range	Benchmark
Global equity	20%–40%	MSCI World Index
Private equity & venture capital	15%–25%	Cambridge Associates LLC US Private Equity Index
Private real estate	5%–15%	NCREIF Property Index

Asset Class	Policy Range	Benchmark
Real assets	5%–15%	Consumer Price Index for All Urban Consumers (annualized CPI-U) + 5%
Absolute return strategies	15%–25%	HFRI Fund of Funds Index
Fixed income & cash	5%–15%	Citigroup US Treasury Index

The following core investment principles provide the foundation for the asset allocation policy:

- Equity dominance: Equities are expected to be the highest-performing asset class over the long term and thus will dominate the portfolio.

- Illiquid assets: In general, private illiquid investments are expected to outperform more-liquid public investments by exploiting market inefficiencies.

- Global orientation: The Endowment will consider the broadest possible set of investment opportunities in its search for attractive risk/return profiles.

- Diversification: Thoughtful diversification within and between asset classes by region, sector, and economic source of return can lower volatility and raise compound returns over the long term.

E. Rebalancing

The IPS establishes the long-term asset allocation targets for the endowment and policy ranges for the various asset classes approved by the IC. The role of the capital allocation ranges is to allow for short-term fluctuations caused by market volatility or near-term cash flows, to recognize the flexibility required in managing private investments, and to provide limits for tactical investing. The IC will rely on investment staff to determine allocations within the stated ranges and to regularly manage actual asset class allocations to be within the ranges where possible. In addition, the IC will review actual asset allocations relative to this asset allocation framework at each quarterly meeting.

F. Reporting

The Investment Team, with the oversight of management, must provide adequate reporting to the Board of Trustees, the IC, and other stakeholders. The reporting structure should include the following:

- Performance measurement and attribution for the quarter and trailing periods for the portfolio both in absolute terms and relative to the established benchmarks

- Asset allocation of the total portfolio

- Market value of the total portfolio

Asset Allocation

We now consider asset allocation, investment portfolios, and investment performance of university endowments. We follow with a similar discussion focusing on private foundations.

University Endowments

Most large endowments follow the endowment investment model and rely heavily on alternative investments to achieve their long-term investment objectives. This approach is not without risks. During the global financial crisis, several large endowments faced significant liquidity challenges and were forced to either sell portions of their private investment portfolios in the secondary markets, reduce payouts to their universities, or issue bonds to bridge their liquidity needs. The rapid post-crisis recovery arguably bailed out many endowments, but had the crisis lasted longer, the pain would have been substantially worse. David Swensen, the longtime CIO of the Yale Endowment, and his colleagues have regularly warned against a blanket application of the endowment model. Yale and some of the other large endowments have enjoyed a first-mover advantage in their private investments, and their alumni networks have provided access to investment opportunities that may not be as easily accessible to other institutions.

Exhibit 14 shows the average asset allocation for US endowments by size at the end of June 2020 using data from a study in which more than 800 colleges and universities participated. Here alternatives include private equity and venture capital, hedge funds and other marketable alternative strategies, private real estate, energy and natural resources (e.g., oil, gas, timber, commodities, and managed futures), and distressed debt.

These data reveal several important points. First, the larger endowments have a significantly higher allocation to alternatives. Larger endowments have achieved better returns over the past 10 years, and their larger allocation to alternatives has played an important role. Second, the larger endowments do not face the "home bias" issue that smaller endowments seem to suffer. The allocation of smaller endowments to US equities is significantly larger than their allocation to non-US equities. Finally, the larger endowments hold a significantly smaller amount of their assets in fixed-income securities. This might pose a challenge during liquidity crises—such as in the 2007–2009 global financial crisis when some larger endowments struggling to meet their liquidity needs pressured managers of private investment funds to delay any calls (i.e., demands) for additional capital. Some universities also issued bonds during the crisis to help relieve the liquidity pressures faced by their endowments.

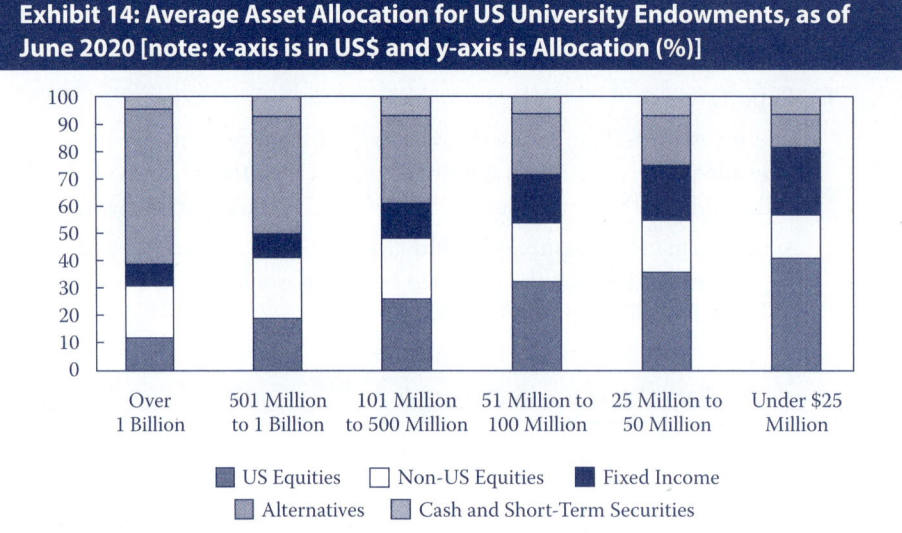

Exhibit 14: Average Asset Allocation for US University Endowments, as of June 2020 [note: x-axis is in US$ and y-axis is Allocation (%)]

Source: TIAA and the National Association of College and University Business Officers (NACUBO), *2020 NACUBO–TIAA Study of Endowments*.

Exhibit 15 shows the average asset allocation at the end of June 2005 and June 2017 for university endowments of more than US$1 billion in size. During this period, the largest endowments significantly increased their allocation to alternatives from 39% to 60%. This increased allocation to alternatives has come at the expense of public equities (reduced from 45% to 30%) and fixed income (reduced from 14% to 11%).

Exhibit 15: Average Asset Allocation for the Largest (> US$1 billion) US Endowments: FY2005 versus FY2020 [note: y-axis is Allocation (%)]

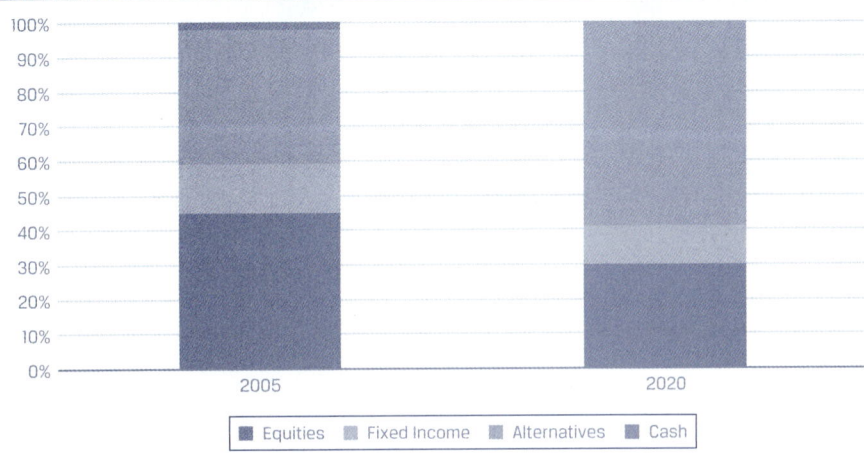

Sources: Commonfund and the National Association of College and University Business Officers (NACUBO), *2005 NACUBO–Commonfund Study of Endowments* and TIAA and the NACUBO, *2020 NACUBO–TIAA Study of Endowments.*

Given asset allocations that are tilted toward alternative investments, how have endowments fared over the past 10 years? Exhibit 16 shows the average annual 10-year return (net of fees) for US endowments by size as of end-June 2020. The mean US Consumer Price Index was about 1.8% over the same period, while the mean Higher Education Price Index (HEPI) was 2.0%. Note: Larger endowments have generally been able to generate higher returns during this period. Endowments of more than US$1 billion have generated anywhere between 50 bps to 60 bps higher returns (annually) compared to the smaller endowments (with less than US$500 million). This difference compounds to a significant gap over a 10-year period. These higher returns have allowed the larger endowments to pay out a larger part of their assets to support their universities. It is worth noting that the 10-year period ending 30 June 2020 is time-period specific. A different 10-year period might lead to a different conclusion. However, this 10-year period is reasonably representative of long-term asset class returns because capital markets have generally rewarded growth assets over the period.

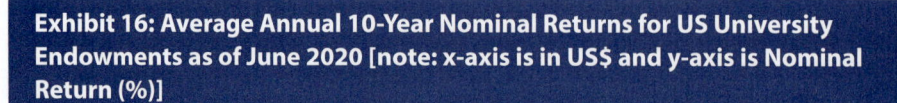

Exhibit 16: Average Annual 10-Year Nominal Returns for US University Endowments as of June 2020 [note: x-axis is in US$ and y-axis is Nominal Return (%)]

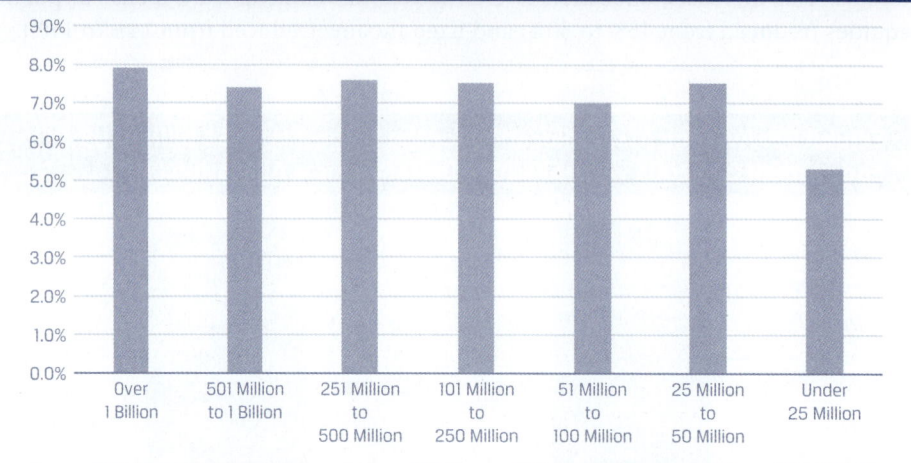

Source: TIAA and the National Association of College and University Business Officers (NACUBO), *2020 NACUBO–TIAA Study of Endowments.*

EXAMPLE 6

Investment Portfolio of the Ivy University Endowment

The hypothetical Ivy University Endowment was established in 1901 and supports Ivy University. The endowment supports about 40% of the university's operating budget. Historically, the endowment has invested in a traditional 20% public US equities, 80% US Treasury portfolio, and it is entirely implemented through passive investment vehicles. The investment staff at the endowment is relatively small. With the appointment of a new chief investment officer, the investment policy is being reviewed. Endowment assets are US$250 million, and the endowment has a spending policy of paying out 5% of the 3-year rolling asset value to the university.

The new CIO has engaged an investment consultant to assist her with the investment policy review. The investment consultant has provided the following 10-year (nominal) expected return assumptions for various asset classes: US equities: 7%, Non-US equities: 8%, US Treasuries: 2%, hedge funds: 5%, private equity: 10%. In addition, the investment consultant believes that the endowment could generate an additional 50 bps in alpha from active management in equities. Expected inflation for the next 10 years is 2%.

The new CIO was at a previous endowment that invested heavily in private investments and hedge funds and recommends a change in the investment policy to the board of Ivy University Endowment. She recommends investing 30% in private equity, 30% in hedge funds, 30% in public equities (15% US and 15% non-US with *active* management), and 10% in fixed income. This mix would have an expected real return of 5.1% based on the expected return assumptions provided by the investment consultant.

1. Given the expected return assumptions from the investment consultant, provide an asset mix that would be more appropriate for Ivy University Endowment?

Solution:

To achieve a 5% real rate of return, the endowment will need to accept significantly more equity risk, diversify its assets internationally, allocate some of its assets to hedge funds and private equity, and engage in active management. There are several possible combinations that could result in a portfolio with a 5% expected real rate of return. Here are two possible asset mixes:

I: 40% in US equities with active management (7.5% expected return), 40% in non-US equities with active management (8.5% expected return), 10% in US Treasuries (2% expected return), 10% in hedge funds (5% expected return). This asset mix would result in an expected nominal return of 7.1% or an expected real return of 5.1%.

II: 50% in US equities with passive management (7% expected return), 30% in non-US equities with active management (8.5% expected return), 10% in US Treasuries (2% expected return), 10% in private equity (10% expected return). This asset mix would result in an expected nominal return of 7.25% or an expected real return of 5.25%.

2. Should the board approve the new CIO's recommendation? Provide your reasoning.

Solution:

The board should reject the CIO's recommendation. This is a very significant departure from the current practice. The size of the investment team is small, and they have no prior experience in managing hedge fund and private equity portfolios (except for the new CIO). Additionally, given the size of the endowment, it is unlikely to have access to top quartile managers in the hedge fund and private equity spaces. The CIO should explain why the recommended asset mix with 60% in alternatives is preferable over asset mixes that deliver the same or higher expected real return (such as I and II in Solution 1).

PRIVATE FOUNDATIONS: INVESTMENT OBJECTIVES AND ASSET ALLOCATION

15

☐　evaluate the investment policy statement of an institutional investor

☐　evaluate the investment portfolio of a private DB plan, sovereign wealth fund, university endowment, and private foundation

As discussed previously, private foundations in the United States are legally required to pay out a minimum of 5% of assets annually to be eligible for tax-exempt status. Foundations strive to be capable of making grants that support their overall missions in perpetuity while meeting the minimum 5% payout requirement. The primary investment objective for foundations is typically to generate a total real return over consumer price inflation of 5%, plus investment expenses, with a reasonable expected volatility (approximately 10%–15% annual standard deviation) over a 3- to 5-year period. A secondary investment objective may include outperforming the policy benchmark with a specified tracking error budget. Monte Carlo-based modeling for generating expected returns and risk distributions as well as liquidity modeling and asset stress testing mentioned earlier for DB pension plans are also used by management and consultants to develop cogent investment objectives and policies for foundations and endowments. Foundations, like endowments, invest in a broad range of asset classes, including fixed income, public equities, hedge fund strategies, and private equity.

The following box provides two real-life examples of investment objectives for foundations.

Investment Objectives for Private Foundations

Wellcome Trust (UK):

"Our overall investment objective is to generate 4.5% real return over the long term. This is to provide for real increases in annual expenditure while preserving the Trust's capital base to balance the needs of current and future beneficiaries. We use this absolute return strategy because it aligns asset allocation with funding requirements and provides a competitive framework in which to judge individual investments."

Note: Wellcome Trust's IPS mentions that the real return is based on an average of US and UK consumer price inflation.

Source: Wellcome Trust, wellcome.ac.uk/about-us/investments.

Robert Wood Johnson Foundation:

"The Robert Wood Johnson Foundation is working to improve the health and well-being of everyone in America. Reflecting our Guiding Principles, 'we act as good stewards of private resources, using them to advance the public's interest with a focus on helping the most vulnerable'... Achieving comprehensive and meaningful change in health and health care will require sustained attention over many years to come. The Foundation therefore seeks to earn an investment return that, over time, equals or exceeds the sum of its annual spending, as a percentage of the Foundation's assets plus the rate of inflation. This balance of investment return and spending is designed to spread risk and promote a steady, stable flow of support for our grantees."

Source: Robert Wood Johnson Foundation, www.rwjf.org/en/about-rwjf/financials.html.

The IPS of a private foundation is not very different from that of a university endowment and follows a similar format as outlined in the previous section. The mission statement would be framed slightly differently, but the IPS would cover the same elements.

Private Foundations

Foundations tend to follow a similar investment approach compared to endowments, despite important differences in their liability structures. Two of the most notable differences between foundations and endowments that should have a bearing on their asset allocation are that:

1. foundations support the entire budget of their organization, while universities have significant other sources of financing available besides the endowment; and

2. foundations (in the United States) are mandated to pay out at least 5% of their assets to maintain tax-exempt status and typically receive no additional inflows in the form of gifts and donations (or, if there are gifts/donations, these need to be spent in the same year that they are received and do not count against the 5% mandated payout), whereas university endowments typically have a net payout of less than 5%.

Exhibit 17 shows the average asset allocations for US foundations by size and type at year-end 2016. The underlying data cover 203 institutions (123 private foundations and 80 community foundations). Here, alternative investments include private equity and venture capital, hedge funds and other marketable alternative strategies, private real estate, energy and natural resources, and distressed debt.

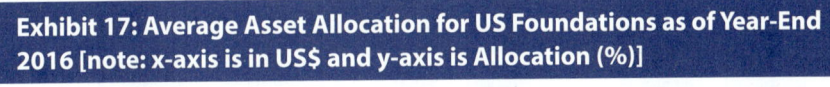

Exhibit 17: Average Asset Allocation for US Foundations as of Year-End 2016 [note: x-axis is in US$ and y-axis is Allocation (%)]

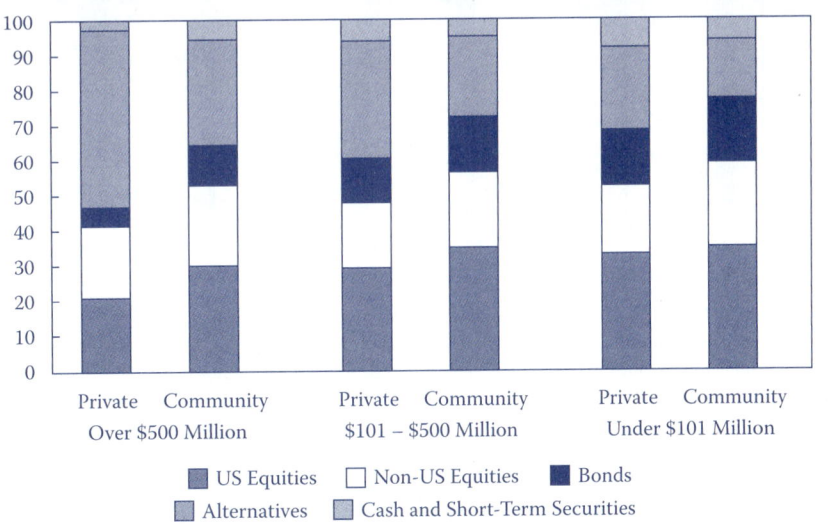

Source: Council on Foundations–Commonfund, *2016 Council on Foundations–Commonfund Study of Investment of Endowments for Private and Community Foundations (CCSF)*: www.cof.org/content/2016-council-foundations-commonfund-study-investment-endowments-private-and-community.

These data highlight several key points. The larger foundations have a significantly higher allocation to alternatives, and private foundations have higher allocations to alternatives compared to community foundations. The largest private foundations (more than US$500 million) have about half of their assets invested in alternatives. Although not shown, the largest private and community foundations have similar allocations to marketable alternatives (hedge funds), but the private foundations have significantly higher allocations to the higher-return-generating, illiquid alternatives—such as private equity, venture capital, private real estate, and distressed debt. Smaller foundations seem generally to have a higher allocation to US equities compared to the larger foundations. Finally, the larger private foundations hold a smaller amount of their assets in fixed-income securities.

Foundations must generate real (net of fee) returns above 5% to maintain their purchasing power. Exhibit 18 shows that over the 10-year period to year-end 2016 (when US CPI averaged 1.8%), US foundations have fallen well short of this minimum target. As a result, their purchasing power has deteriorated. However, during this period larger private foundations (more than US$500 million) have been able to generate higher returns—anywhere between 10 bps to 60 bps higher returns (annually)—compared to medium/small private foundations. Their larger allocation to alternatives likely played a key role in this outperformance. Note that the effective spending rate in 2016 was 5.8% for private foundations.

Exhibit 18: Average Annual 10-Year Nominal Return for US Foundations as of Year-End 2016 [note: x-axis is in US$ and y-axis is Nominal Return (%)]

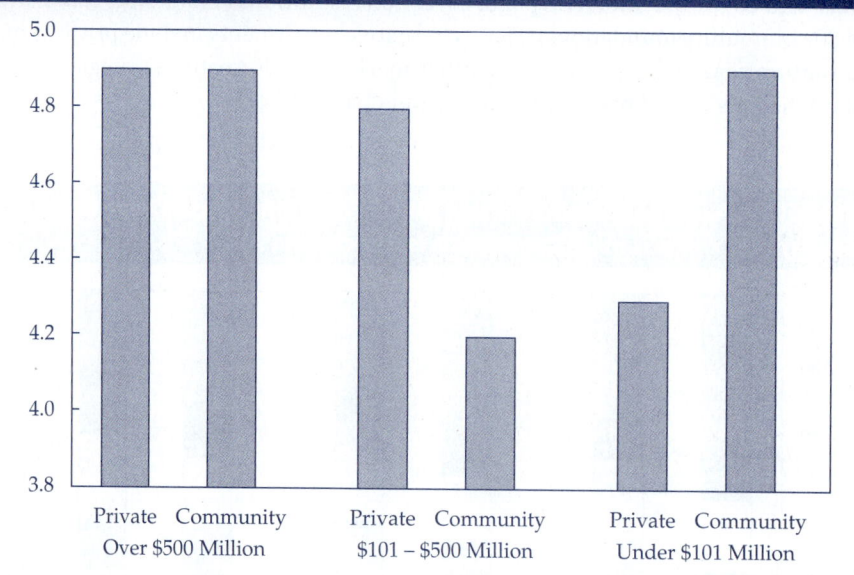

Source: Council on Foundations–Commonfund, *2016 Council on Foundations–Commonfund Study of Investment of Endowments for Private and Community Foundations (CCSF)*: www.cof.org/content/2016-council-foundations-commonfund-study-investment-endowments-private-and-community.

Real-Life Case Study: Wellcome Trust (UK)

Wellcome Trust ("the Trust") provides a historical example of how a foundation transformed its investment approach and asset allocation and, in the process, significantly improved its investment performance. The Wellcome Trust was founded in 1936 and managed about £23 billion in its investment portfolio (as of end-September 2017). The investment portfolio supported all of the charitable work of the Trust, which provides funding for scientific and medical research to improve health worldwide. During FY2016–17, charitable grants were more than £1 billion.

Between 1936 and 1986, the Trust was the sole owner of Burroughs Wellcome, the pharmaceutical company founded by Henry Wellcome. In 1986, the Trust began selling shares in the company and used the proceeds to diversify its assets. Over the two decades leading up to 2017, the portfolio generated an average annual (nominal) return of 14%. The overall investment objective was to generate a 4.5% real return over the long term. The Trust used to target a payout rate of 4.7% of the weighted average value of the portfolio over the previous three years. Historically, this resulted in an average annual payout of 4.3%.

Daniel Truell joined the Trust as CIO in 2005 and initiated radical changes to its investment approach and asset mix, shifting from short-term, liquid, and low-risk assets to longer-term, less-liquid, and higher risk assets. The most notable changes were an increase in the allocation to private equity (including buyout and venture capital funds) and hedge funds as well as reduced allocations to public equities and cash. In addition to radically changing its allocations, the decision was made to concentrate assets with fewer managers and in fewer, higher quality investments, such that by 2017 less than 100 investments represented nearly 85% of the portfolio's value. The Trust also shifted to more direct investments, and active management in public equities was brought predominantly in-house and conducted by an investment team of more than 30 professionals.

At end-September 2017, the Trust's investment portfolio consisted of 53% in public equities, 9% in hedge funds, 24% in private equity, 9% in property and infrastructure, 1% in commodity futures and options, and 4% in cash. The Trust has issued bonds totaling £2 billion—representing about 8% of total assets. Proceeds from the bond issuance are used for investments.

In 2017, the Trust adopted a new approach to determine how much to fund its charitable activities. According to the October 2017 IPS, the Trust *"targets an annual real cash spend in the Primary Fund (based on UK CPI) of £900 million in 2017 prices. This level of spending will be reviewed in 2022, or earlier in the event of declines in the investment portfolio below £20 billion in 2017 prices."*

The Trust managed risk by ongoing monitoring of the following key risk factors: 1) 95% value-at-risk at a one-year horizon (if more than 20%, then this is highlighted to the Investment Committee), 2) foreign currency exposure (if more than 85%, then this is highlighted to the Investment Committee), 3) forecast of cash levels (unencumbered cash should exceed 2% of gross assets within a 5-year forecast period), and 4) estimated equity beta for the portfolio should be in the range of 0.4 to 0.8.

Sources: 1. Wellcome Trust, "Investment Policy" (October 2017): https://wellcome.ac.uk/sites/default/files/investment-policy-october-2017.pdf. 2. Wellcome Trust, *Annual Report and Financial Statements 2016* (https://wellcome.ac.uk/sites/default/files/WellcomeTrustAnnualReportFinancialStatements_160930.pdf). 3. Wellcome Trust, Annual Report and Financial Statements 2017 (https://wellcome.ac.uk/sites/default/files/wellcome-trust-annual-report-and-financial-statements-2017.pdf). 4. World Economic Forum, "Alternative Investments 2020: The Future of Alternative Investments" (2015). 5. Steve Johnson, "Uncovering Little Investment Gems among the Shrunken Heads," *Financial Times* (12 April 2014): www.ft.com/content/c49bb40c-be63-11e3-b44a-00144feabdc0.

BANKS AND INSURERS 16

This section focuses on institutional investors that are also financial intermediaries, namely banks and insurance companies.

Banks

Banks are financial intermediaries that take deposits, lend money, safeguard assets, execute transactions in securities and cash, act as counterparties in derivatives transactions, provide advisory services, and invest in securities. The universe of banks is quite large and diverse, ranging from small community banks to global diversified financial services institutions. A precise estimate of total worldwide banking assets is difficult to obtain; nevertheless, using publicly available data from such sources as the Bank for International Settlements (BIS), Reuters, and individual balance sheets for the largest public banks, an estimate of more than US$100 trillion seems reasonable.[4] An order-of-magnitude estimate for bank equity capitalization works out to US$7 trillion. Our focus here is on the largest, most globally important banks—the two to three dozen banks that account for the great majority of international commercial bank assets and liabilities. Exhibit 19 shows some of these banks, all of which are designated as global systemically important banks by the Financial Stability Board, an international body that monitors the global financial system.

Exhibit 19: Select Large Global Banks

Bank	Country/Region
Industrial & Commercial Bank of China	China
China Construction Bank Corp.	China
Agricultural Bank of China	China
Bank of China	China
HSBC Holdings Plc	Hong Kong SAR/United Kingdom
JPMorgan Chase & Co.	United States
Wells Fargo	United States
Mitsubishi UFJ Financial Group	Japan
Bank of America	United States
CitiGroup	United States

Source: Marie Kemplay, "Top 1000 World Banks 2021," *The Banker*, https://top1000worldbanks.com/ (20 October 2021).

Insurers

The universe of insurance companies can be divided into two broad categories:

- Life insurers
- Property and casualty (P&C) insurers

According to the OECD (Organisation for Economic Co-Operation and Development) data on 35 large countries (ex-China and India), aggregate direct-insurance assets for both types of insurers had combined totals of more than US$22 trillion, with equity capitalization of more than US$2.2 trillion.[5]

---

4 Inter-company and cross-border transactions, non-contemporaneous reporting dates, differing accounting treatment (IFRS vs. GAAP, for example), and currency exchange rate conversions are inescapable complications.
5 OECD (2016).

The life insurance product set includes traditional whole and term insurance, variable life insurance and annuity products, as well as health insurance. The P&C product suite encompasses insurance against a wide range of perils—covering commercial property and liability, homeowner's property and liability, and automotive as well as such multiple specialty coverage lines as marine, surety, and workers' compensation. Exhibit 20 lists some of the largest global insurance companies.

Exhibit 20: Select Large Global Insurance Companies

Entity	Country/Region
AXA	France
Zurich Insurance Group	Switzerland
China Life Insurance	China
Ping An Insurance	China
Berkshire Hathaway	United States
Prudential plc	United Kingdom
Nippon Life Insurance	Japan
Munich Re Group	Germany
Assicurazioni Generali S.p.A.	Italy
Japan Post Holding Co., Ltd.	Japan
Allianz SE	Germany

Source: "Commercial Insurance," Insurance Information Institute, www.iii.org/publications/commercial-insurance/rankings (accessed 20 October 2021).

External Constraints Affecting Investment

The legal and regulatory environments, as well as tax and accounting constraints, faced by banks and insurers are complex and may vary according to the national and local jurisdictions in which these institutional investors do business. In this section, we take a high-level view of some of the major legal and regulatory constraints within which banks and insurers must operate. In the following section, we consider tax and accounting constraints that affect investing by banks and insurers.

Legal and Regulatory Constraints

For banks and insurance companies, the liabilities to depositors, the claims of policyholders, and the amounts due to creditors are clearly and contractually defined. This is different from the other types of institutions discussed previously where there typically can be a great deal of discretion in the timing and amounts due and paid to stakeholders. Furthermore, banks and insurance companies carry out important functions with respect to the underlying economies in which they operate. These include facilitation of individual and commercial payments, extensions of credit, safeguarding of assets, and transfers of risk—to name the more important. The activities of companies in the financial industry not only are deeply intertwined with the non-financial, or *real,* economy, but their activities also are deeply intertwined with each other. Thus, a disturbance in the operation of individual banks and insurance companies can spread through the entire financial industry with great speed and with compounding damage; significant adverse effects can easily overflow into the real economy. Such negatives can include depositor runs on a banking system, credit crunches whereby companies or governments cannot obtain funding for maintaining operations, or the failure of insurance companies that undermine the viability of large sectors of the economy, such as residential housing or the health care markets. Consequently, banking and insurance regulators in most jurisdictions are intensely focused on capital adequacy, liquidity, and leverage to mitigate systemic or contagion risk.

Banks and insurance companies are primarily regulated at national and state levels and are increasingly overseen by supranational regulatory and advisory bodies. The need to regulate banks and insurance companies at high, rather than local, levels stems from the fact that financial institutions are mainly large and spread across many local and national jurisdictions. At its most essential, the regulation of financial institutions centers on making sure banks and insurance companies have adequate capitalization to absorb losses rather than allowing losses to be borne by the rest of the financial system or the real economy—including depositors, insurance policyholders, creditors, or taxpayers.

Lowering the risk of assets through regulation is the first way to lower the potential strains on bank and insurance company capitalization. This can be through requirements for diversification, asset quality (including adequate reserve provisioning for credit, market, and operational risk losses) and liquidity maintenance. Likewise, setting requirements on liabilities can lower potential stress on bank and insurance capital resources. Such regulation of liabilities may include requirements for funding sources to be diversified over time and among different groups of depositors and debtholders. In the case of insurance companies, potential losses from liabilities can be regulated through rules limiting the size and concentration of potential policy claims. In addition to limiting potential losses from assets and liabilities—or from other operational risks—regulators may mandate certain minimum required capitalization.

Turning to insurers, the US insurance industry is regulated by individual states, each having its own administrative agency; the federal government does not play a major role in oversight. The National Association of Insurance Commissioners (NAIC), of which every state is a member, provides a forum for industry issues and sets accounting policies and financial reporting standards for the industry. In Europe, regulators have developed the Solvency II framework to standardize insurance regulation across member states.

The size and diversity of financial institutions result from powerful economies of scale. These economies of scale arise because most activities of banks and insurance companies (such as extension of credit, underwriting health or property risks, or taking of deposits) are made in large numbers, where the successes and failures of individual transactions are not normally highly correlated among each other. By the law of large numbers, the volatility of the weighted sum of independent risks decreases as a function of the square root of the number of independent risks assumed. This diversification effect would be a benefit to a financial firm that grows larger than its competitors. In fact, it would represent increasing returns to scale because the largest institution could hold a portfolio of assets with less capital than its competitors, because asset and liability volatility would be much less and would result in a higher and less volatile return on capital for the largest institution. Of course, offsetting factors keep this effect from dominating. Other marginal costs of operation, communications, and management keep the industry from eventually evolving into one giant financial firm. Nevertheless, the powerful impacts of diversification in terms of credit defaults, deposit funding, casualty insurance claims, and life-and-health mortality/morbidity claims are very strong factors in contributing to the existence of a small number of large national and international financial firms that comprise most of the financial industry's assets and earnings.

These few large firms are regarded as systemically important financial institutions (SIFIs). Since the worldwide financial system meltdown of 2008–2009, legislators and regulators worldwide have moved in the direction of bolstering the financial system by raising capital requirements—directly, by requiring higher absolute amounts of primary capital, and indirectly, by (1) effectively increasing the amount of capital needed to support the holding of certain investments, (2) limiting the payout of dividends and repurchases of common equity, and (3) making subordinated debt and preferred shareholders less able to assert their claims in the event of bankruptcy or regulator-mandated restructuring. Furthermore, regulators' actions have resulted in tightening regulations on the use of derivatives, proprietary trading, and off-balance-sheet liabilities/guarantees. These actions require institutions through stress testing to show how they can survive severe economic and financial market turbulence, and they impose more stringent accounting/disclosure rules and reserving requirements. The consequences of a relatively small number of SIFIs dominating the financial industry and the existence of regulatory cycles mean that the management of a financial institution must take into account the actions of its SIFI competitors and must integrate its asset and liability portfolio decisions with a view to where the rules are today *and* where they are likely heading.

Accounting and Tax Considerations

Three different types of accounting systems apply for every financial institution. For the enterprise and its subsidiaries, the first is standard financial accounting, whether in the form of GAAP or IFRS, and which is used for communicating results to shareholders (or members), deposit or policyholders, and suppliers of debt capital. Regulators of banks and insurance companies, in addition, impose a second type of accounting in various forms and known as *statutory* accounting. Statutory accounting rules can be very different across different national and local regulatory jurisdictions. Although statutory results are normally available to the public, they mostly are utilized by regulators. Finally, the third type, true economic accounting, marks all assets and liabilities (net of imputed income taxes) to current market values.

Each accounting system is designed with a particular objective in mind, and it is incumbent upon financial institution managers and investment analysts to understand the purposes of all three. Economic or mark-to-market (MTM) accounting provides the best picture of an entity's assets, liabilities, and changes in economic well-being. MTM earnings are the most volatile of all because they reflect all value changes contemporaneously rather than being smoothed over time. The results of MTM reporting are likely to differ from those from financial reporting, where the reporting rules are consistently and conservatively applied over time (but where asset and liability values may depart from reported balance sheet amounts). Financial reporting has moved increasingly in the direction of MTM accounting over the past several decades, although changes in asset and liability values often are reported by way of balance sheet comprehensive income accounts rather than directly through an income statement. On balance, financial reporting will provide the smoothest reporting of income and asset/liability valuations.

Statutory accounting represents essentially a system of adjustments to standard financial accounting. For both bank and insurance regulators, this means most significantly the subtracting of intangible assets from asset and common equity accounts and/or the acceleration of certain expenses, such as policy underwriting and sales costs. In other cases, it is the recognition and assignment of additional reserves against losses on assets or unexpectedly large losses on guarantees or insurance claims. Statutory accounting usually results in lower earnings and lower common equity capital than in financial accounting. Capital requirements for both banks and insurance companies are predicated on one or another version of statutory reporting.

In terms of taxation, banks and insurance companies typically are taxable entities, and the industry-specific tax rules can be quite complicated. As taxable entities, banks and insurance companies must manage their investment programs with consideration of after-tax returns.

17   BANKS: OTHER CONSIDERATIONS

☐ | describe considerations affecting the balance sheet management of banks and insurers

Bank stakeholders include external parties (such as shareholders, creditors, customers, credit rating agencies, regulators, and even the communities where they operate) as well as internal parties (such as employees, management, and boards of directors). A bank's investment program must meet the needs and expectations of multiple parties. Most large, international banks are typically companies with publicly issued securities, which are expected to maximize the net present value of shareholders' capital. As will be seen shortly in greater detail, this hinges importantly on the ability of banks to manage the volatility of the value of shareholders' capital.

On the liability side, bank customers are comprised of a variety of depositors, including individuals, corporations, and municipalities. Individuals deposit cash and depend on banks to safeguard their assets over time. Legal entities, ranging from small privately held companies to large publicly listed corporations, often have multiple banking relationships and depend on banks to provide financing throughout economic cycles. Similarly, municipalities and other public entities deposit funds and rely on banks' safekeeping and transaction services. In addition, both for their own account and for the benefit of customers, banks are important counterparties to both publicly traded and over-the-counter derivatives transactions. Finally, most global banking institutions are significant issuers of fixed-income securities, either directly or via such other means as asset-backed trusts.

On the asset side, bank customers include both retail and commercial borrowers. Individuals borrow money from banks to finance large purchases, such as houses that are often financed with mortgages. On the corporate side, real estate developers often require bank financing through commercial real estate loans. Additionally, large companies require commercial and industrial loans from banks in order to finance working capital, ongoing operations, or capital improvements.

Internal stakeholders include a bank's employees, management, and board of directors. Notably, the largest banks may each have more than 200,000 employees around the globe. At banks with a national or global presence, management teams are often highly visible in regulatory and economic affairs. At the regional and local level, bank management teams are often integrated within the local business community.

Banks—Liabilities and Investment Horizon

Banks are unique in that they originate assets (loans), liabilities (deposits, derivatives, fixed-income securities), and capital (preferred and common stock) in the normal course of business. The ability to originate and manage both assets and liabilities has implications for the management of a bank's interest rate risk exposure (i.e., asset/liability gap management) and the volatility of equity capitalization.

The largest component of bank assets is loans, typically comprising up to 50% or more of the assets of the large, international banks that dominate the sector. The next largest component of assets is debt securities, typically accounting for 25% or more of total assets. The largest remaining portion of assets consists of currency, deposits with central banks (e.g., Bank of Japan or Bank of England), receivables, and bullion.

Banks' liabilities are comprised of deposits and also include short-term funding, such as commercial paper, as well as longer term debt. Deposits are the largest component of liabilities, usually more than half of total liabilities. Bank deposits include the following:

- **Time deposits** or **term deposits** – These interest-bearing accounts have a specified maturity date. This category includes savings accounts and certificates of deposit (CDs). Banks have visibility on the duration of these deposits because they require advance notice prior to withdrawal.

- **Demand deposits** – These accounts can be drawn upon regularly and without notice. This category includes checking accounts and certain savings accounts that are often accessible through online banks or automated teller machines (ATMs). Consequently, banks have limited visibility on the expected lives of these accounts and tend to assume they are short-term in duration.

In addition to deposits, banks can access wholesale funding, sources of which include Federal Funds, public funds, and other government-supported, short-term vehicles. Banks must actively monitor the expected cash outlays and timing of their liabilities. For time deposits, the amount and timing of the cash outlay are known, while for demand deposits, the amount is known but the timing is uncertain. Other liabilities comprise (1) long-term debt, 10%–15% of total balance sheet; and (2) such items as trading/securities payables and repurchase finance payables, also on the order of 10%–20% of balance sheet liabilities.

The tactical investment horizon for a bank's investment portfolio is directly impacted by the nature and maturities of its asset base and liability structure.[6] Although commercial banks, as corporations, have a perpetual time horizon (possibly longer than the other institutions in this reading), the instruments held in a bank portfolio tend to have far shorter maturities than those held by other financial institutions.

SUSTAINABILITY LINKED LOANS: PROMOTING SUSTAINABLE DEVELOPMENT WHILE ALSO MANAGING RISK

As per the Sustainability Linked Loan Principles, "Sustainability linked loans are any types of loan instruments and/or contingent facilities (such as bonding lines, guarantee lines or letters of credit) which incentivize the borrower's achievement of ambitious, predetermined sustainability performance objectives." These loans aim to support environmentally and socially sustainable economic activity and growth and look to improve the borrower's sustainability profile by aligning loan terms to the borrower's performance against the relevant predetermined targets.

As some environmental and social issues such as carbon emissions, deforestation, water scarcity, and occupational health and safety become increasingly material for certain sectors, they could affect a company's ability to generate sustainable returns in the long term. Therefore, ensuring that corporates are managing such issues sufficiently well and avoiding any large negative impact on their ability to repay the loan is in the interest of providers of capital such as banks. In this context, a product such as a sustainability-linked loan provides the right incentive for corporates viz. a lower cost of capital, if they can manage the said risk(s) well. For banks, it is a way to manage and mitigate their credit risk exposure.

---

6 Its strategic horizon is perpetuity because of its corporate structure, which makes it as long, or longer, than many defined benefit plans, endowments, foundations, and sovereign wealth funds.

Example:

During Q1 2021, ING together with Santander coordinated one of the largest sustainability-linked revolving credit facilities ever issued. Anheuser-Busch InBev (AB InBev), a multinational drinks and brewing company, was provided a USD10.1 billion revolving credit facility with a five-year term by a consortium of 26 leading global financial institutions.

The pricing mechanism incentivizes AB InBev to address four key performance areas that are aligned with its sustainability goals:

1. Further improving water efficiency at AB InBev's breweries globally
2. Increasing PET recycled content in PET primary packaging
3. Sourcing purchased electricity from renewable sources as outlined in the RE100 commitment
4. Reducing greenhouse gas emissions as part of the science-based Climate Action Goal

The difference between the long time horizon of the institution and the much shorter maturity of most of its assets and liabilities may seem counterintuitive. Suppose that in the current market, the credit spreads on loans are narrow and the economy is nearing recession. The long-term horizon of the bank is evidenced by it: (1) cutting back new lending, (2) selling part of its existing loan portfolio, (3) increasing allocations to short-maturity, liquid securities, and (4) decreasing leverage through fewer large wholesale time deposits. The bank is sacrificing current earnings while looking forward to an uncertain time horizon when it can aggressively expand in the more favorable future environment. The long-term time horizon means that it expects to apply similar tactics—with medium to short-term maturity assets and liabilities—many more times over the indefinite future.

Banks—Liquidity Needs

Liquidity management is a core consideration in the management of bank portfolios. Given the short duration of deposits, as well as the potential need for increased liquidity in adverse market conditions, management and regulators have developed a robust framework around liquidity management for bank portfolios. Apart from asset or cash flow securitization, banks must have the ability to liquidate their investment portfolios within a certain period to generate adequate cash in the event of a crisis.

Bank liquidity needs have evolved since the global financial crisis of 2007–2009. Prior to that period, deficiencies in liquidity from deposits were made up with wholesale funding; banks would use their portfolios as a source of return so were invested in lower quality, less liquid securities. In the post-crisis environment, however, bank portfolios are increasingly comprised of higher quality, more liquid securities. This trend to more conservative management of investment portfolios has largely been driven by increased regulatory scrutiny on a global basis, most noticeably through the introduction of mandated liquidity coverage ratios (LCRs) and net stable funding ratios (NSFRs).[7]

---

7 LCRs require that highly liquid assets must constitute more than 100% of highly probable near-term expected cash outflows. NSFRs set minimum requirements for stable funding sources relative to assets; such stable sources include capital, long-term debt, and non-volatile deposits.

In general, contrasting commercial banks and retail-oriented banks, commercial banks have a higher cost of funds and lower liquidity because of wholesale funding of loan commitments and other contingent commitments. Conversely, retail banks have a lower cost of funds and better liquidity because their retail deposits are relatively low cost and tend to be more stable.

INSURERS 18

The stakeholders of insurers include such external parties as shareholders, derivatives counterparties, policyholders, creditors, regulators, and rating agencies as well as such internal parties as employees, management, and boards of directors. Insurance companies are organized as either companies with publicly listed securities or mutual companies.

In North America and Europe, most large insurers are companies with publicly issued securities, with the inherent shareholder concerns and pressures. As such, there is significant interest and scrutiny on quarterly investment performance, corporate earnings, and balance sheet strength. Within this context, as with banks, optimal management must focus on the long-term maximization of net present value of shareholders' capital. Concretely, this requires balancing expected returns on investments and policy writing in such a way that all insurance liabilities will be met. This requires a very strong focus by management and regulators on maintaining tight control over the volatility of the value of shareholder capital. Capital must be maintained at all investment horizons and under all scenarios so that the company will be able to honor its obligations, especially to policyholders.

Mutual companies are owned by policyholders. Mutual companies either retain profits as surplus or rebate excess cash to policyholders in the form of dividends or premium reductions.[8] Although mutual companies are free from the shareholder pressure for earnings performance, they have less access to capital markets than peers with publicly issued securities. Mutual companies remain quite prevalent in the United States, Canada, Japan, and many European countries. To provide certainty that policyholders are paid under all economic conditions, the need to control and maintain capital surplus is fundamentally the same as in the case of for-profit insurers.

Customers are primarily policyholders who have a need to protect themselves against specific risks. The main objective of any insurance company investment program is to fund policyholder benefits and claims.

Given the nature and requirements of their product suite, life insurers maintain both a **general account** and **separate accounts**. For traditional life insurance products and fixed annuities, insurers bear all the risks—particularly mortality risk and longevity risk, respectively—so they maintain a general account of assets to fund future liabilities from these products. However, in the case of variable life and variable annuity products, customers make investment decisions from a menu of options and themselves bear investment risk. Consequently, insurers invest the assets arising from these products within separate accounts. Exhibit 21 summarizes the main bearers of investment risk and the account structure for the major categories of insurance and annuity products.

---

8 Mutual companies can also increase the amount of "paid up insurance" for whole-life policies.

Exhibit 21: Main Investment Risk Bearers for Different Insurance Products

Products	Bearer of Investment Risk	Account
Whole and term life insurance	Company	General
Universal life insurance	Company	General
Fixed annuities	Company	General
Variable life insurance	Policyholder	Separate
Variable annuities	Policyholder	Separate

The insurance industry is tightly regulated in most countries, usually by state or national authorities. The regulatory environment, including constraints impacting insurance asset management, will be discussed shortly. The rating agencies—including A.M. Best, Standard & Poor's, Moody's, and Fitch—are stakeholders in the management of insurance investment portfolios because they monitor the financial stability of insurance companies and provide credit ratings and data on the industry to the investment community globally.

An insurance company's management team and employees are also direct stakeholders. The large global insurance companies may have thousands of employees spread over many countries. Their management teams are often highly visible in terms of regulatory and economic affairs. Clearly, the employees are impacted by the amount of risks taken on an insurance company's balance sheet.

Insurers—Liabilities and Investment Horizon

Insurance companies manage their investment portfolios with an intense focus on asset/liability management (ALM). Within the insurance industry, the business line is critical because it determines the nature and structure of the liabilities. Further, effective management of liabilities is crucial to the long-term viability of any insurance company.

Life Insurers

Broadly speaking, life insurers face a liability stream and time horizon with a long duration. Life insurance involves a range of products, including Individual Life, Group Life and Disability, Individual Annuity, and Retirement Plan products. Life insurance portfolios are comprised of asset accumulation products, with some nuances in the associated liability stream. The liability stream is driven by the predictability of claims, which can vary based on the specific product line. For example, Term Life products have a one-time payout and the predictability is relatively high using statistical and actuarial analyses on large portfolios with many policies. Meanwhile, annuity products involve an ongoing payout with shorter duration that is subject to longevity risk. The nature of the liability stream has important implications for the amount of investment risk that can be tolerated.

Within life insurance, product features and resulting liabilities as well as policyholder behavior are key determinants of the associated portfolios' investment horizons. Historically, life insurance companies set portfolio return objectives with long time horizons of 20 to 40 years.

Property & Casualty Insurers

In general, P&C insurers face a shorter duration liability stream and investment horizon than life insurers. Further, P&C insurance involves events with lower probability of occurrence and potentially higher cost (especially in the case of natural disasters), leading to highly volatile business claims. This results in a liability stream with short duration and high uncertainty.

For example, a P&C insurance company may initiate policies against catastrophic events, such as hurricanes or other natural disasters. By definition, this insurance involves unpredictable and infrequent events that are difficult to hedge against. Insurance companies utilize statistical and actuarial analyses to forecast liability cash flows on a probabilistic (scenario) basis. P&C insurers may benefit from developing global, diversified portfolios that are more applicable to statistical analysis because of the law of large numbers. In any case, P&C insurers face a liability stream with a shorter duration and more potential volatility than life insurers.

MEASURING AND MANAGING PHYSICAL CLIMATE RISKS

Environmental risks such as the physical impacts of climate change (e.g., floods, droughts, wildfires) are affecting our day-to-day lives both more frequently and on a larger scale than ever imagined. Physical risks might have financial implications for organizations, such as direct damage to assets and indirect impacts from supply chain disruption. Wildfires in California, the Amazon Forest, and Australia that caused billions of dollars in financial losses, in addition to the loss of life and to megacities such as Cape Town and Chennai almost running out of water, are just a few recent examples of how climate change and related global warming are accelerating the frequency and magnitude of such erratic weather patterns.

For insurance companies, this increase in frequency of the hitherto infrequent and low-probability events poses a new set of modeling challenges. AXA S.A., a French multinational insurance company, for example, states that as of the end of 2020, the annual average losses (AAL) for its real estate portfolio are estimated to be EUR4.3 million due to floods and EUR6.2 million due to windstorms. To manage these physical climate risks, AXA's models that assess the risk of natural hazards consider three components: the hazard (as defined by its severity and frequency), the exposure (as characterized by the building's physical properties), and the vulnerability (as defined by destruction rates, function of the hazard, and the exposure). These risk evaluation and management efforts would naturally evolve to consider potential financial impacts under various climate scenarios that are published by the Intergovernmental Panel on Climate Change, such as the Representative Concentration Pathways 2.6 and 8.5 scenarios, which make predictions of how concentrations of greenhouse gases in the atmosphere (and thus global temperature rise) will change in the future because of human activities.

As these physical climate risks become more and more material, insurance companies will have to better understand their exposure to physical risk and chart appropriate adaptation efforts to limit such exposures.

With both life and P&C insurers, as with banks, the nature and timing of expected policy claims strongly influence the time horizon and nature of investments held. Even so, the ultimate management time horizon is perpetuity. A natural and frequently occurring example for both types of insurers is the case of underwriting cycles. Such cycles relate to the pricing of newly issued policies relative both to then-existing expected security returns and to the actuarial outlook for life and casualty loss claims. Long-term strategic investment and balance-sheet management policies result in modifications to portfolios and overall company leverage at different points in time to adjust to the varying relative attractiveness of bearing investment risk versus bearing underwriting risk and/or financial (leverage) risk.

Insurers—Liquidity Needs

Insurance companies must actively manage and monitor the liquidity of their portfolios. The level of liquidity required has important implications across the portfolio management process, including the insurer's ability to utilize leverage. Further, liquidity needs can vary greatly based on the business line.

Both life and P&C insurers need a sound, two-part liquidity plan that includes internal and external components. An insurer's internal liquidity includes cash and cash equivalents maintained on the balance sheet. Insurers must actively manage cash from operations (including investment income) that involves steady inflows and outflows. Further, insurers manage and project the cash flows from investment portfolio income and principal repayments. An insurer's external liquidity includes the ability to issue bonds in the capital markets and to access credit lines through syndicated commercial bank credit lines or other lines of credit. Finally, insurers manage short-term liquidity by actively buying and selling repurchase agreements. In this way, insurers consistently manage both internal and external sources of liquidity.

The liquidity needs of life insurance companies must also be considered in the context of the interest rate environment. In periods of rising/high interest rates, insurance companies may face the risk of significant net cash outflow as policies are surrendered by customers searching for higher yields in other investments. P&C insurers face uncertainty regarding both the value and timing of the payment of benefits. This significant cash flow uncertainty necessitates maintaining ample liquidity and results in P&C portfolios comprised of high proportions of cash and cash substitutes as well as short-term fixed-income instruments.

Insurers segment general account investment portfolios into two major components: **reserve portfolio** and **surplus portfolio**. Insurance companies are typically subject to specific regulatory requirements to maintain a reserve portfolio that is intended to ensure the company's ability to meet its policy liabilities. The surplus portfolio is intended to realize higher expected returns. Insurance companies manage reserve assets relatively conservatively. The size of the reserve portfolio is typically dictated by statute, and assets must be highly liquid and low risk. Meanwhile, insurance companies have more of an ability to assume liquidity risk in the surplus portfolio. Insurance companies are often willing to manage these assets aggressively with exposure to alternative assets, including private equity, hedge funds, and non-security assets.

19 | BANKS AND INSURERS: INVESTMENT OBJECTIVES

☐ | describe considerations affecting the balance sheet management of banks and insurers

We now consider the investment objectives of banks followed by a discussion of investment objectives and an investment policy statement for insurers.

Banks

The investment securities portfolio of a bank is an integral component of the overall banking enterprise. The primary objective of a bank's securities investment portfolio is to manage the bank's liquidity and risk position relative to its non-securities assets, derivatives positions, liabilities, and shareholders' capitalization. Given the highly regulated nature of the industry, banks typically have formally documented investment policies as well as multiple levels of oversight in the form of internal committees and external regulators.

What follows provides a real-life example of how investment objectives are framed at banks.

Bank Investment Objective

JPMorgan Chase & Co., Treasury and Chief Investment Officer Overview

"Treasury and CIO is predominantly responsible for measuring, monitoring, reporting and managing the Firm's liquidity, funding, capital, structural interest rate and foreign exchange risks. The risks managed by Treasury and CIO arise from the activities undertaken by the Firm's four major reportable business segments to serve their respective client bases, which generate both on- and off-balance sheet assets and liabilities.

Treasury and CIO achieve the Firm's asset-liability management objectives generally by investing in high-quality securities that are managed for the longer-term as part of the Firm's investment securities portfolio. Treasury and CIO also use derivatives to meet the Firm's asset-liability management objectives."

Source: JPMorgan Chase & Co., *Annual Report 2020*, www.jpmorganchase.com/content/dam/jpmc/jpmorgan-chase-and-co/investor-relations/documents/annualreport-2020.pdf.

Banks establish an asset/liability management committee ("ALCo") that provides direction and oversight of the investment portfolio. The ALCo has significant visibility with the bank's management and board of directors, as well as with external regulators. This ALCo sets the investment policy statement (IPS), monitors performance on an ongoing basis, and has the ability to mandate adjustments on the asset and liability sides of the balance sheet. The ALCo also ensures that market (interest rate and FX), credit, liquidity, and solvency (capital adequacy) risk positions are within the limits of the bank's specified risk tolerances. Once the overall investment objectives and risk levels are set, the investment team establishes policy benchmarks. The investment team monitors performance and such portfolio characteristics as duration and convexity relative to the benchmark for each asset class. Further, the investment team may monitor performance relative to a set of peers with comparable business models and investment objectives. Finally, the investment team makes periodic presentations to senior management and the board of directors regarding performance and characteristics of the investment portfolio.

Insurers

Given the highly regulated nature of the insurance industry, a detailed and well-documented Investment Policy Statement is of paramount importance. It is a best practice for an IPS to take a holistic approach and include the parent company's strategic enterprise risk management framework. Similar to banks, insurers manage their investment portfolios with a focus on liquidity as well as interest rate, foreign exchange, credit, and other risk factors.

The investment oversight function is a critical part of an insurer's overall governance. Insurers typically have a committee on the board of directors that maintains oversight of all investment policies, procedures, strategies, and performance evaluation. Insurers provide significant transparency to their underlying portfolios—including showing the inherent duration, credit, and other risks to regulators and other external stakeholders.

The IPS should encompass the insurer's appetite for market risk, credit risk, and interest rate risk. An insurer's risk tolerance may vary relative to the competitive environment for various product lines, regulatory and tax changes, market conditions, and other factors. Moreover, the IPS should be a "living document" that evolves as market, regulatory, and business conditions change.

Hypothetical Life Insurance Company—Investment Policy Statement

i.   Introduction

XYZ Life Insurance Company ("the Company") underwrites and markets life insurance and annuity products. The Company is licensed to provide insurance products in all 50 US states, as well as several foreign countries. This investment policy statement ("IPS") documents the policies and procedures that govern the Company's general account securities portfolio. There are detailed policy statements for each asset segment within the portfolio that provide a more granular breakdown of investment guidelines.

ii.   Governance and Stakeholders

The Company's investment policies, including investment objectives and constraints, are the responsibility of the Investment and Finance Committee ("IFC") of the board of directors ("BoD"). The insurer's senior management team ("Mgmt") is responsible for implementation of the investment program consistent with this policy. In turn, the investment team ("InvTeam") manages the investment portfolio on a day-to-day basis.

The IFC will review the investment policy on an annual basis. The IFC must consider changes to the Company's strategic direction, regulatory changes, tax changes, financial market conditions, and any other relevant factors that may arise. The IFC proposes adjustments to the IPS to the BoD, and all material changes must be approved by the BoD in their entirety.

The IFC has responsibility to employ appropriate resources for the management of the investment portfolio. The IFC may retain or dismiss InvTeam personnel at its discretion. Further, the IFC may retain investment consultants or other advisers to manage specific asset classes or other sub-components of the portfolio. All consultant, external investment managers, and other advisers are required to comply with this IPS.

iii. Mission and Investment Objective

The core mission of the general account is twofold:

1. Provide liquidity for the payment of policyholder claims in the normal course of insurance operations.
2. Grow the Company's surplus over the long-term.

The investment objective must follow prudent investing practices and achieve an appropriate balance between maintaining short-term liquidity and contributing to long-term asset growth.

iv. Risk Tolerance and Constraints

The Company is subject to significant scrutiny from internal and external stakeholders, including shareholders, regulators, and others. The general account investment program must take into account the following key factors:

- **Liquidity.** The investment portfolio must maintain sufficient liquidity to meet all policyholder claims that may arise on a short-term and long-term basis. The InvTeam monitors investment cash flow to ensure the Company's ability to meet all obligations in a timely manner. Further, the InvTeam may liquidate publicly traded securities as a secondary source of liquidity.
- **Interest Rate Risk.** The InvTeam monitors the portfolio's exposure to changes in interest rates, including the relative exposure of both assets and liabilities.
- **Credit Risk.** The InvTeam monitors the credit (default) risk inherent in the portfolio and must continually monitor the financial health of key counterparties.
- **Foreign Exchange Risk.** The Company is subject to foreign exchange risk in the normal course of business. The InvTeam monitors the aggregate foreign exchange risk of the portfolio.
- **Regulatory Requirements.** All investments must adhere to the insurance code of the Company's state of domicile as well as all other applicable domestic and foreign guidelines. Further, the investment program must comply with risk-based capital considerations and rating agency requirements.
- **Tax Considerations.** Further, the securities portfolio must account for tax considerations, and all investment decisions should be evaluated on an after-tax basis. The income tax planning of the Company may impact the timing of realization of capital gains and losses.

v. Asset Allocation Policy, Allowable Ranges, and Benchmarks

The primary investment vehicles within the Company's investment portfolio will consist of highly liquid instruments, including US and foreign government obligations, corporate debt, and other fixed-income instruments. Further, the Company may invest in private placement bonds, commercial mortgage loans, and other less liquid instruments within the parameters specified. Further, the Company may invest in real estate and private equity in order to enhance long-term returns and contribute to the surplus growth of the company. However, strict guidelines apply for less liquid asset classes.

The IFC establishes the strategic asset allocation that is consistent with the long-term constraints of the Company. The IFC will review the strategic asset allocation annually and may make adjustments as appropriate. Further, the IFC sets out allowable ranges of allocation for each asset class. Further, the IFC approves appropriate benchmarks for each asset class upon consultation with the InvTeam.

vi. Investment Guidelines

The InvTeam should seek to diversify holdings in terms of economic exposure, counterparty, and other applicable attributes to the extent possible. Securities that are guaranteed by the US government or its agencies must constitute at least 25% of the portfolio.

vii. Reporting

The InvTeam, with the oversight of Mgmt, must provide adequate reporting to the BoD and other stakeholders. The reporting structure should include the following:

- Daily Flash Report: Summary of market values, yield, and interest rate position of entire portfolio
- Monthly Investment Performance Detail: Detailed investment performance by asset class, including market values, yields, and interest rate position
- Quarterly Investment Summary: Detailed analysis of market values, yield, and interest rate exposure, including long-term performance metrics and attribution

20   BANKS AND INSURERS: BALANCE SHEET MANAGEMENT AND INVESTMENT CONSIDERATIONS

> ☐ describe considerations affecting the balance sheet management of banks and insurers

We turn now to the portfolio investment strategy for banks and insurance companies. The objectives and constraints are very different from what we have seen with respect to pensions, sovereign wealth funds, endowments, and foundations. In the case of banks and insurance companies, the need is to fund deposits, policy claims, derivatives payoffs, and debtholders. A financial institution's fundamental purpose is to assure such contractual parties the full and timely payment of claims when they come due. A firm can only hope to earn a profit if it can provide counterparties assurance it will be able to meet all claims with extremely high probability.

The financial claims against banks and insurers may not always be known with certainty, but they are, at any point in time, measurable. Such measurement may require the use of probabilistic methods to account for such outcomes as: (1) the liquidation of bank deposits; (2) insurance policy claims and surrenders; (3) losses on derivatives, guarantees, or forward purchase commitments; and (4) returns on variable annuities, among other outcomes. Thus, in the case of banks and insurers, the well-defined, contractual nature of the financial claims, along with their measurability, imply that—unlike with defined benefit and defined contribution pension plans, sovereign wealth funds, endowments, and foundations—the underlying investment strategy is mainly liability driven investing (LDI as earlier defined).

We can obtain insight about both investment strategy and regulation of financial institutions by applying a fairly simple but intuitive economic model. The model's first two equations define the relationship between an institution's assets A, liabilities (claims) L, and residual equity of the institution's shareholders or members E:

$$A = L + E \tag{1}$$

$$\Delta A = \Delta L + \Delta E \tag{2}$$

Assets are equal to the sum of contractual claims and residual ownership. Likewise, all changes in assets must equal the sum of changes in the value of contractual claims and ownership interest (equity capitalization). These equations are set forth in terms of current market—or economic—values, which will not necessarily coincide with GAAP, IFRS, or regulatory/statutory values. However, using current market values will facilitate the subsequent application of these other accounting valuations.

These equations can be used to understand not just market value changes but also the impact of earnings, the consequences of adding or selling off assets in total, and changes in an institution's capital structure. All of these are relevant to investment strategy and are additional layers of complexity as compared with the other portfolio strategies in this reading.

By multiplying the various terms by 1 (i.e., $A \div A$ or $L \div L$), dividing both sides by E, and doing a little regrouping, we obtain a useful expression, namely:

$$\frac{\Delta A}{A}\left(\frac{A}{E}\right) = \frac{\Delta L}{L}\left(\frac{L}{E}\right) + \frac{\Delta E}{E} \tag{3}$$

Using Equation 1 and moving liabilities and assets to the same side of the equation, we rewrite this as:

$$\frac{\Delta E}{E} = \frac{\Delta A}{A}\left(\frac{A}{E}\right) - \frac{\Delta L}{L}\left(\frac{A-E}{E}\right) = \frac{\Delta A}{A}\left(\frac{A}{E}\right) - \frac{\Delta L}{L}\left(\frac{A}{E}-1\right) \tag{4}$$

Equation 4 provides an easy way to see how percentage changes in market value of both assets and liabilities are magnified by the leverage factors.

To demonstrate this point, Exhibit 22 presents the effects on the market value of the institution's equity capital as a function of (i) declines in underlying asset value,[9] and (ii) beginning degree of leverage. Asset values can decline for several reasons, such as deterioration in credit quality and/or liquidity of loans or securities held. The value of assets can also be hurt by rising interest rates in the case of fixed-rate loans or securities.

Exhibit 22: Effects on Market Value of Equity Due to Change in Market Value of Assets (Given Beginning Degree of Leverage)

Beg. Equity to Assets Ratio	Leverage (x)	Percentage Change in Institution's Equity Value Due to Change in Asset Value of:			
(E÷A)	(A÷E)	−0.5%	−1.0%	−1.5%	−2.0%
20%	5.0	−2.5%	−5.0%	−7.5%	−10.0%
15%	6.7	−3.3%	−6.7%	−10.0%	−13.3%

9 Which, for our analysis, focuses on the investment portfolio assets. The net equity described here is net financial equity. The portion of an institution's equity associated with financing other assets, such as buildings and equipment, are not a focus of this reading.

Beg. Equity to Assets Ratio	Leverage (x)	Percentage Change in Institution's Equity Value Due to Change in Asset Value of:			
(E÷A)	(A÷E)	−0.5%	−1.0%	−1.5%	−2.0%
10%	10.0	−5.0%	−10.0%	−15.0%	−20.0%
5%	20.0	−10.0%	−20.0%	−30.0%	−40.0%

This analysis reveals that even small losses in the market value of assets can have a pronounced negative effect on the institution's equity capital account because of the leverage factor. Naturally, it works in reverse; Small gains in assets can have a very positive impact for equity capital holders. These relationships give rise to a conflict of interest: Because equity capital holders can only lose the value of their investment but also can make extremely large gains if assets perform well, liability holders require some form of protection against the potential inclination of the institution to take excessive risks. Contractual, regulatory, and reputational methods all come into play to provide such protection. In one form or another, they relate to limiting the volatility of assets and providing for a capital cushion so that equity capital holders, rather than liability holders, are expected to absorb unforeseen losses on assets.

Similarly, financial institutions face the possibility of loss from adverse changes in the market value of liabilities. In the case of insurance companies, unexpectedly high policy loss claims are the most notable cause of expanding liabilities. For banks, it could be having to make a forward-funding commitment to a struggling company, the exercise of a guarantee, or a loss on forward currency purchase contracts. Exhibit 23 uses Equation 4 to illustrate the effect on the market value of the institution's equity capital as a function of (i) increases in its liabilities and (ii) beginning degree of leverage.

Exhibit 23: Effects on Market Value of Equity Due to Change in Market Value of Liabilities (Given Beginning Degree of Leverage)

Beg. Equity to Assets Ratio	Leverage (x)	Percentage Change in Institution's Equity Value Due to Change in Liability Value of:			
(E÷A)	[(A÷E) − 1]	+0.5%	+1.0%	+1.5%	+2.0%
20%	4.0	−2.0%	−4.0%	−6.0%	−8.0%
15%	5.7	−2.8%	−5.7%	−8.5%	−11.3%
10%	9.0	−4.5%	−9.0%	−13.5%	−18.0%
5%	19.0	−9.5%	−19.0%	−28.5%	−38.0%

Exhibit 23 bolsters the conclusions reached in Exhibit 22. Mainly, liability holders, regulators, and owners (equity shareholders) of a financial institution all are motivated to limit the volatility and magnitude, relative to the base capital level, of market value changes in the institution's liabilities.

Now we must integrate the analysis of both sides of the balance sheet with the capital management strategy of the financial institution. To do this, we would like to have a framework for understanding various interactions in a more rigorous manner. A customary starting point is with an analysis of interest rate risk. Our framework comfortably accommodates the standard duration-based model of value changes with respect to interest rate changes. In order to find the percentage change in the value of the institution's equity capital associated with a change in the reference yield, y, on the asset holdings, we divide Equation 4 by the change in such yield, thereby obtaining:

$$\frac{\Delta E}{E \Delta y} = \frac{\Delta A}{A \Delta y}\left(\frac{A}{E}\right) - \frac{\Delta L}{L \Delta y}\left(\frac{A}{E} - 1\right) \tag{5}$$

Likewise, we want to understand how this relates to the change in the effective yield on the liabilities, i. Multiplying by $1 = \Delta i \div \Delta i$ in the appropriate location, we restate Equation 5 as:

$$\frac{\Delta E}{E \Delta y} = \frac{\Delta A}{A \Delta y}\left(\frac{A}{E}\right) - \frac{\Delta L}{L \Delta i}\left(\frac{\Delta i}{\Delta y}\right)\left(\frac{A}{E} - 1\right) \tag{6}$$

Recall that the modified duration of asset W with respect to its yield-to-maturity, r, (D_W^*) is defined as:

$$D_W^* = -\frac{\Delta W}{W \Delta r} \tag{7}$$

This allows us to revise Equation 6 to a practical and intuitive analytical tool, namely,

$$D_E^* = \left(\frac{A}{E}\right)D_A^* - \left(\frac{A}{E} - 1\right)D_L^*\left(\frac{\Delta i}{\Delta y}\right) \tag{8}$$

Over reasonably modest yield changes, Equation 8 provides a useful way to break down the volatility of a financial institution's equity capital as a function of degree of leverage, comparative (modified) duration of assets and liabilities, and correlation (or sensitivity) of changes in yields of assets and liabilities.

Exhibit 24 and Exhibit 25 show how sensitive the valuation of equity is to changes in the security portfolio yield for differing degrees of mismatching of asset and liability durations. In both these exhibits, the x-axis shows the duration of the financial institution's liabilities, the y-axis shows the duration of its security portfolio assets, and the z-axis (vertical axis) shows the resulting duration of the institution's shareholders' equity. The yields on liabilities are assumed to move only 90% as much as the yields on portfolio assets. That is,

$$\frac{di}{dy} = \frac{\Delta i}{\Delta y} = 0.90$$

Exhibit 24 and Exhibit 25 show results for differing initial degrees of leverage, as measured by the equity-to-assets ratio, which is 20% and 10%, respectively.

Exhibit 24: Duration of Shareholders' Equity as a Function of Asset and Liability Durations (Given Equity/Assets = 20% and Sensitivity of Yield Changes = 0.90)

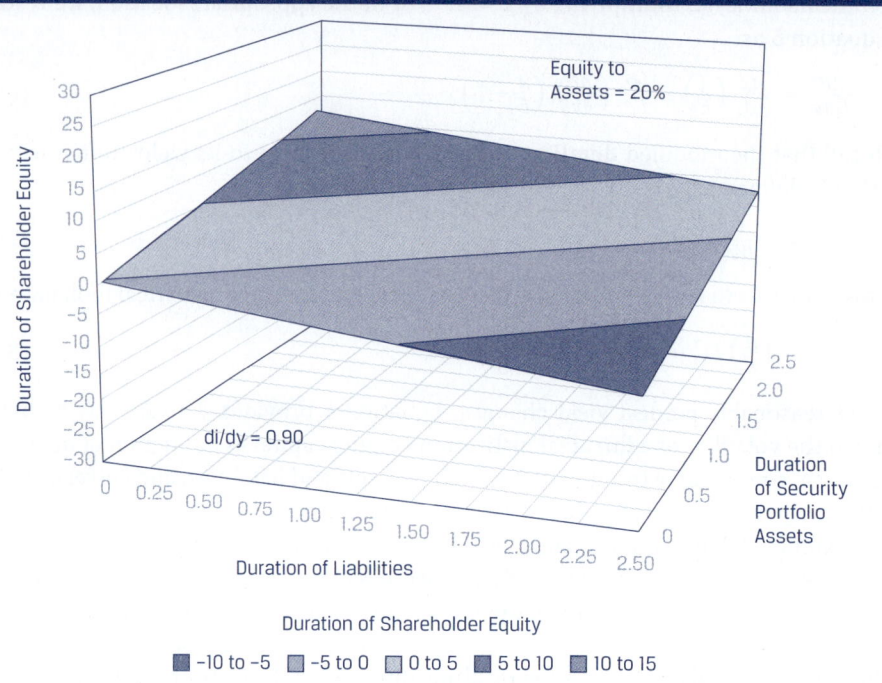

Duration of Shareholder Equity

■ −10 to −5   ■ −5 to 0   □ 0 to 5   ■ 5 to 10   ■ 10 to 15

Exhibit 24 indicates that, even at relatively high capital ratios of 20%, moderate differences between asset and liability durations can imply durations for equity that can be sizable in either a positive or negative direction. Remember that, by definition, the modified duration of a zero-coupon bond is its final maturity divided by one plus its yield. Thus, by comparison, a 10-year zero coupon bond would have a modified duration around 9.75. Utilizing Equation 7, a +/− 100 basis point change in interest rates when multiplied by a modified duration of 9.75 implies an approximate +/− 10% change in value. It is highly unlikely that regulators would like to see large asset/liability duration mismatches, since regulators want equity capital to remain stable in periods of large adverse interest rate changes.

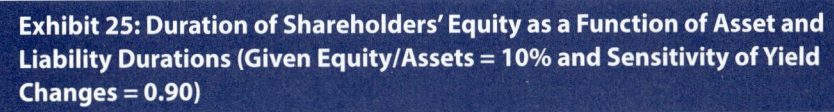

Exhibit 25: Duration of Shareholders' Equity as a Function of Asset and Liability Durations (Given Equity/Assets = 10% and Sensitivity of Yield Changes = 0.90)

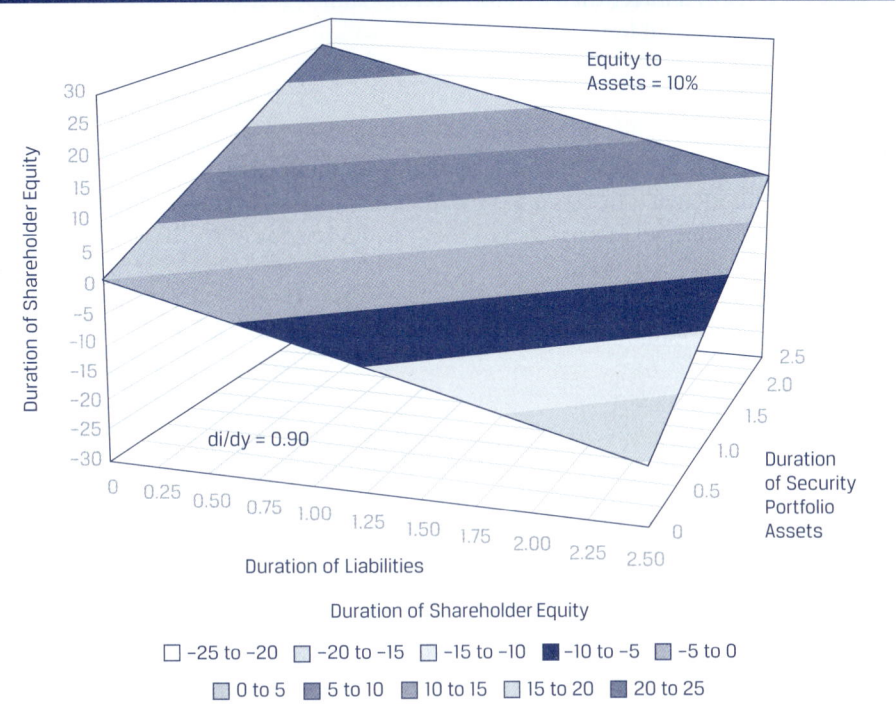

In Exhibit 25, we see that lowering the equity capital ratio to 10% means that in order to avoid very high durations for equity capitalization, it is all the more necessary to keep assets and liabilities from having large differences in duration. It is often mistakenly thought that banks (and to a lesser degree, insurance companies) climb the yield curve by raising capital through the issuance of short maturity deposits that they then invest in longer duration loans and securities. The foregoing exhibits indicate the potential dangers of such an asset/liability mismatch. In Exhibit 25, assuming a liability duration of close to zero (very short-term deposits and overnight borrowing), even if the security portfolio duration is only 2.5 years, the duration of shareholder's equity reaches 25 years (about the equivalent of a 26-year zero coupon bond). In such a case, a +/− 100 basis point change in asset yields would produce a +/− 25% change in shareholder equity value. The loss potential is a danger that neither deposit holders, creditors, stockholders, nor regulators would be keen to embrace.

In actuality, in order to lower asset duration, financial institutions hold cash, deposits at central banks, foreign currency reserves, and other highly liquid (zero duration) assets. Also, as a means of lowering effective asset durations, banks typically make business loans that float according to market reference rates, which are expected to move in line with the variable cost of deposits. Likewise, credit card and many real estate loans are tied to variable rate indexes in order to minimize the sensitivity of values to interest rates. Moreover, many fixed-rate mortgage loans are securitized and sold off to private investors. All these foregoing techniques are ways of limiting the duration of asset portfolios.

On the liability side, there are many ways in which the duration of liabilities can be extended far beyond the implicit zero duration of demand deposits. These include issuance of intermediate and longer-term debt instruments, deeply subordinated capital securities, and perpetual preferred stock. Finally, banks can and do utilize financial futures and interest rate swaps to alleviate asset/liability mismatches.

In the light of persistent low interest rates since the global financial crisis of 2007–2009, many large international banks have an asset/liability structure where earnings are poised to benefit from a rise in interest rates. In such cases, the duration of assets is actually shorter than the duration of liabilities. This is clearly not the naïve "borrow short and lend long" strategy.

EXAMPLE 7

MegaWorld Bancorp has an equity capital ratio for financial assets of 9%. The modified duration of its assets is 2.0 and of its liabilities is 1.5. Over small changes, the yield on liabilities is expected to move by 85 bps for every 100 bps of yield change in its asset portfolio.

1. Compute the modified duration of the bank's equity capital.

Solution:

Using Equation 8, $A \div E = 1/0.09 = 11.11$; $(A \div E) - 1 = 10.11$; $D_A^* = 2.0$; $D_L^* = 1.5$; and $\Delta i \div \Delta y = 0.85$.

Therefore, the modified duration of shareholders' capital is:

$$D_E^* = (11.11 \times 2) - (10.11 \times 1.50) \times 0.85 = 9.33$$

---

2. What would be the impact on the value of shareholder capital of a 50 basis point rise in the level of yields on its asset portfolio?

Solution:

Using the implications of Equation 7, the change in equity capitalization value is computed as:

$$0.5\% \times -9.33 = -4.67\%.$$

---

3. Management is considering issuing common stock, selling investment portfolio assets, and paying off some liabilities in order to achieve an equity capitalization ratio of 10%. Assuming no change in the durations of assets and liabilities and assuming no change in the sensitivity of liability yields to asset yields, what is the resulting modified duration of the bank's equity capital?

Solution:

With this less leveraged balance sheet, $A \div E = 1/0.1 = 10$; $(A \div E) - 1 = 9$; and the duration of shareholders' equity is:

$$D_E^* = (10 \times 2) - (9 \times 1.50) \times 0.85 = 8.53$$

---

4. Using the facts in question 3 but assuming the bank rebalances its investment portfolio to achieve a modified duration of assets of 1.75, what happens to the duration of the bank's equity capital?

Solution:

The duration of shareholders' capital now declines to:

$$D_E^* = (10 \times 1.75) - (9 \times 1.50) \times 0.85 = 6.03$$

BANKS AND INSURERS: INVESTMENT STRATEGIES AND ASSET AND LIABILITY VOLATILITY

21

Our previous discussion has given us some insight into the effects of leverage and the volatility of underlying assets and liabilities on the value of a financial institution's equity. The degree of leverage was given; the sensitivity of changes in liability to asset yields (di/dy) was constant; and the durations of assets and liabilities varied. Although quite useful in many circumstances, such duration analysis captures the effects of only small changes in overall levels of interest rates and only over short time intervals.[10] Although of great significance, changes in the overall levels of interest rates are only one source of volatility. An expansion of Equation 4 is therefore necessary. A natural step is to extend it in a probabilistic way. We can thereby capture the volatility of the market value change in the financial institution's equity capital as shown in Equation 9. Volatility is defined here as standard deviation, where $\sigma_{\frac{\Delta E}{E}}$, $\sigma_{\frac{\Delta A}{A}}$, and $\sigma_{\frac{\Delta L}{L}}$ represent the standard deviations of the percentage changes in market value of equity capital, asset holdings, and liability claims, respectively.[11] Furthermore, $-1 \leq \rho \leq 1$ denotes the correlation between percentage value changes of assets and liability claims.[12]

$$\sigma_{\frac{\Delta E}{E}}^2 = \left(\frac{A}{E}\right)^2 \sigma_{\frac{\Delta A}{A}}^2 + \left(\frac{A}{E} - 1\right)^2 \sigma_{\frac{\Delta L}{L}}^2 - 2\left(\frac{A}{E}\right)\left(\frac{A}{E} - 1\right)\rho\,\sigma_{\frac{\Delta A}{A}}\,\sigma_{\frac{\Delta L}{L}} \tag{9}$$

Equation 9 states the relationship in precise mathematical terms. It also incorporates the concept of correlation, which is an essential element of liability-driven investing. Exhibit 26 is a graphical representation of Equation 9 and illustrates the magnitude of the asset/liability correlation effect (ρ is measured on the x-axis) on the volatility of the financial institution's equity capital ($\sigma_{\frac{\Delta E}{E}}$ is measured on the y-axis) for various levels of leverage (the downward-sloping dotted lines). For purposes of this exhibit, the volatilities of asset and liability percentage value changes ($\sigma_{\frac{\Delta A}{A}}$, $\sigma_{\frac{\Delta L}{L}}$) are both assumed to be constant at 1.5%.

Exhibit 26 demonstrates that over the range of leverage shown (equity/assets ratios from 5% to 20%), the volatility of the financial institution's equity capital decreases as the correlation between asset and liability *value changes* (ρ) increases toward +1.0. This beneficial effect is most pronounced when the financial institution is highly leveraged.

For example, assuming leverage of 20% (assets/equity = 5x) and correlations (ρ) of 0.5 and then 0.9, the volatility of equity declines from 6.9% to 3.5%. However, if higher leverage is assumed, at 5% equity/assets, and ρ takes the same two values, then the decrease in volatility of equity from 29.3% to 13.2% is more dramatic.

If the correlation between assets and liabilities is 1.0, the volatility of shareholders' equity capital shrinks to minimal amounts, even for high leverage (equity to assets = 5.0%). However, the flip side is that any divergence in correlations—such as can often occur in turbulent markets—causes equity volatility to increase and especially dramatically when leverage is high.

---

10 Most notably, the duration model does not reflect well on non-linear factors, such as convexity and embedded options in many fixed-income securities and derivatives.

11 The variance of any random variable is equal to the square of the standard deviation of the variable.

12 Transforming Equation 4 into Equation 9 follows the basic statistical property that, for any random variable Z, which is a linear sum of two other random variables X and Y (specifically, $Z = AX + BY$), the variance of Z is $\sigma_Z^2 = A^2 \sigma_X^2 + B^2 \sigma_Y^2 + 2AB\rho\,\sigma_X\sigma_Y$. This expression does not depend on the nature and shape of the underlying probability distributions of either X or Y.

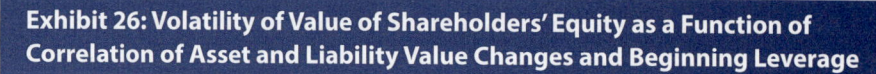

Exhibit 26: Volatility of Value of Shareholders' Equity as a Function of Correlation of Asset and Liability Value Changes and Beginning Leverage

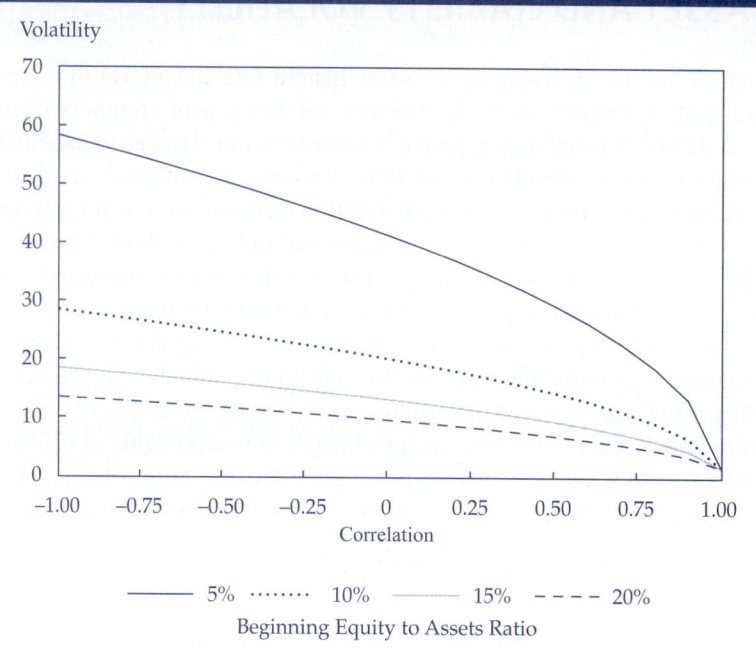

With the comprehensive framework provided by Equation 9, we next turn to a brief catalogue, shown in Exhibit 27, of how differing portfolio strategies and actions affect the inputs and thus the results of the volatility paradigm in Equation 9. Before doing so, however, it is important to note that hedging with derivatives, duration-based portfolio management and funding, and other techniques for raising the correlation between asset and liability values are not a cure-all. High correlations between assets and liabilities are not easy to achieve in practice, and often breakdown during periods of financial industry stress or stress in an individual institution. In the final analysis, techniques for raising correlations are not a pure substitute for maintaining adequate capitalization buffers.

Exhibit 27: Investment Strategies and Effects on Bank/Insurer Asset and Liability Volatility

Portfolio Strategy Considerations	Main Factors Affected	Explanation/Rationale	Additional Regulatory Concerns
Diversified fixed-income investments	Decreases $\frac{\sigma_{\Delta A}}{A}$	Debt securities are less volatile than common equities, real estate, and other securities.	Effective diversification involves a multiplicity of issuers and industries, both domestic and foreign.
High-quality bond/debt investments	Decreases $\frac{\sigma_{\Delta A}}{A}$	Overall, higher quality securities are less likely to be downgraded or default, thereby lessening the probability of significant loss of value through either losses or widening of credit spreads.	Regulatory structures and central banks favor sovereign issuers most for this reason.

Portfolio Strategy Considerations	Main Factors Affected	Explanation/Rationale	Additional Regulatory Concerns
Maintain reasonable balance between asset and liability durations, key rates durations, and sensitivity to embedded borrower and claimant options	Increases ρ	Requires more in-depth analysis than simple duration-matching strategy, because must account for convexity and asymmetric payoffs due to (i) defaults, (ii) principal payoffs prior to maturity, and (iii) annuity, life-insurance policy, and bank CD surrenders in high interest rate scenarios.	Regulatory structures penalize institutions with unjustifiable asset/liability mismatches.
Common Stock Investments	Increases $\sigma_{\frac{\Delta A}{A}}$, typically decreases ρ	Equity and other high-volatility assets provide only slight diversification benefits while adding to volatility. Also, common stock returns do not correlate well with financial institution returns, which pushes correlation, ρ, away from 1.0 toward 0.0.	Most regulatory structures require 100% or more risk weighting for common stock investments thus, such investments are ineligible for backing financial liability issuance.
Derivatives transparency, collateralization	Decreases both $\sigma_{\frac{\Delta A}{A}}$ and $\sigma_{\frac{\Delta L}{L}}$ and increases ρ	Whether derivatives are used to hedge or synthesize (i) assets or (ii) liabilities, the more "plain vanilla" (and protected against counterparty default) they are, the less likely they will revalue in unexpected directions.	Transparency fosters regulatory "financial stress test" confidence. It also allows regulators and claimants to ascertain whether derivatives are being used in a justifiable manner.
Liquidity of portfolio investments	Decreases $\sigma_{\frac{\Delta A}{A}}$	Includes short-maturity debt securities of highly rated issuers, currency reserves, access to credit lines, and access for banks to emergency central bank borrowing.	Problems occur for regulators when financial contagion extends beyond just a few institutions.
Surrender penalties	Decreases $\sigma_{\frac{\Delta L}{L}}$	For typical life insurance, annuities, and bank deposits, such penalties cushion losses to financial institutions for having to pay back liabilities "at par" when rising interest rates would otherwise have reduced the discounted present value of the obligations.	Properly computed surrender penalties must account for interest rate volatility and slope of the yield curve. Typically, regulators/customers do not tolerate economically justified surrender penalties (they are usually priced too low to offset the institution's risk).
Prepayment penalties on debt investments	Increases ρ	When interest rates are declining, borrowers must incur a penalty to repay loans at par to refinance. Also, prepayment penalties help institutions offset rising values of their fixed-rate liabilities in falling rate environments.	None.
Catastrophic insurance risks	Increases $\sigma_{\frac{\Delta L}{L}}$	By definition, these losses faced by insurance companies are less predictable and possibly very large.	Regulators and insurance customers usually expect (i) higher capital ratios, (ii) higher quality and liquid investment portfolios, and (iii) strong reinsurance agreements compared with typical home, health, auto, and fire insurance.

Portfolio Strategy Considerations	Main Factors Affected	Explanation/Rationale	Additional Regulatory Concerns
Predictability of underwriting losses	Decreases $\frac{\sigma \Delta L}{L}$	High frequency, low cost loss events caused by law of large numbers make total insurance liabilities less uncertain.	Adverse changes in legal or regulatory systems cannot be offset by actions on the asset side of the financial institution. These are risks borne by owners of the institution's equity capital.
Diversifying insurance business	Decreases $\frac{\sigma \Delta L}{L}$	Diversifying across several business lines increases aggregate risk-reduction potential (due to law of large numbers).	None.
Variable annuities	Increases ρ, and $\frac{\sigma \Delta A}{A}$, $\frac{\sigma \Delta L}{L}$ diminish in relevance	Where equity/bond market risks are fully borne by policyholders, the correlation between asset and liability returns approaches 1.0, independent of investment performance of the underlying, segregated account assets.	Assuming adequate risk disclosure to policyholders, and sufficient asset custody protections, regulators permit greater investment flexibility than in insurer's standard business lines.

The last key implication of the aggregate risk framework in Equation 9 relates to the importance of raising equity capitalization externally. The ability to raise capital is not just the key to expanding operations; more importantly, it is a way of buffering financial uncertainty. It diminishes both the probability of default to liability holders and the total volatility of equity capitalization values.[13] Over the past several decades, the financial industry has moved increasingly to publicly traded, for-profit, corporations, rather than mutual or membership co-ops. This is primarily because publicly traded companies can issue new common stock capital in cases of either opportunity or emergency. Mutual and membership co-ops (for example, credit unions) are restricted by the growth of their membership, which usually cannot change much over short periods of time.

> ### EXAMPLE 8
>
> Foresight International Assurance is an international multiline insurance conglomerate. Under its overall strategic financial plan, it computes the annualized standard deviation of returns on investment assets as 5.0% and on liabilities as 2.5%. The bulk of its liabilities are constituted by the net present value of expected claims payouts. The correlation between asset and liability returns is therefore a very low 0.25. Foresight's common equity to financial assets ratio is 20.0%.

---

13 Although raising equity ratios negatively impacts return on common equity (ROCE) and earnings per share of financial companies, the diminished volatility of earnings and economic value acts toward raising price-earnings and market-to-book ratios. Perhaps somewhat counterintuitively, the issuing of common stock by financial companies can be neutral or even a net benefit to pre-existing shareholders.

1. What is the standard deviation of changes in the value of Foresight's shareholder capitalization?

Solution:

We use Equation 9 recognizing that $A \div E = 1/0.20 = 5$; $(A \div E) - 1 = 4$; the standard deviation of asset returns $(\sigma_{\Delta A/A}) = 0.05$; the standard deviation of changes in liability values $(\sigma_{\Delta L/L}) = 0.025$; and the correlation between asset and liability value changes $(\rho) = 0.25$.

First, we compute the variance of shareholders' capital value changes:

$$\sigma^2_{\frac{\Delta E}{E}} = 5^2 \times 0.05^2 + 4^2 \times 0.025^2 - 2 \times 5 \times 4 \times 0.25 \times 0.05 \times 0.025 = 0.06.$$

The standard deviation of shareholder capital valuation change is the square root of the variance. Thus,

$$\sigma_{\frac{\Delta E}{E}} = \sqrt{\sigma^2_{\frac{\Delta E}{E}}} = \sqrt{0.06} = 0.245 = 24.5\% \text{ per year.}$$

2. Management believes the overall risk profile of the company is too high and desires to increase the common equity ratio by issuing additional shares of common equity and listing such shares on several international stock market exchanges. The new target equity ratio will be 25.0%. All other things being equal, how does this impact the volatility of value changes in shareholder capitalization?

Solution:

The new asset to equity ratio is $A \div E = 1/0.25 = 4$, and so $(A \div E) - 1 = 3$. Using the existing values of the other variables in Equation 9, we obtain

$$\sigma^2_{\frac{\Delta E}{E}} = 4^2 \times 0.05^2 + 3^2 \times 0.025^2 - 2 \times 4 \times 3 \times 0.25 \times 0.05 \times 0.025 = 0.038125.$$

from which we see $\sigma_{\frac{\Delta E}{E}} = \sqrt{\sigma^2_{\frac{\Delta E}{E}}} = \sqrt{0.038125} \approx 0.195 = 19.5\%$ per year.

3. Management believes it also needs to lower the volatility of its assets. It shifts out of low-quality bonds into higher quality, more liquid government securities and, by doing so, expects to lower the standard deviation of asset returns to 4.0% per year without having any impact on the correlation ratio between assets and liabilities. Along with the stronger capital ratios premised in question 2, what does this do to the volatility of shareholder equity value?

Solution:

Equation 9 now produces the following results:

$$\sigma^2_{\frac{\Delta E}{E}} = 4^2 \times 0.04^2 + 3^2 \times 0.025^2 - 2 \times 4 \times 3 \times 0.25 \times 0.04 \times 0.025 = 0.025225$$

from which we obtain $\sigma_{\frac{\Delta E}{E}} = \sqrt{\sigma^2_{\frac{\Delta E}{E}}} = \sqrt{0.025225} \approx 0.159 = 15.9\%$.

4. What is the impact of the various portfolio and capitalization changes on the value of Foresight's common shares outstanding? Explain your answer.

Solution:

We note that the proposed changes are likely to reduce earnings per share, first by having a greater number of shares outstanding and second by lowering the expected returns on assets (because there will now be a greater percentage of safer, lower yielding assets). All other things being equal, this would pressure the common stock price. However, Foresight is also lowering its overall equity risk exposure while strengthening its reputation as a more soundly operated and capitalized insurance company. The lower risk profile might well result in a higher credit rating and a lower discount rate at which the lower earnings per share trajectory is valued. Also, the improved long-term survivability and underwriting strength could result in a higher *long-term* growth outlook. In sum, the impact on common equity prices cannot be predicted merely by a change in capital structure and near-term reduction in earnings and portfolio expected returns.

22   BANKS AND INSURERS: IMPLEMENTATION OF PORTFOLIO DECISIONS

> ☐ | describe considerations affecting the balance sheet management of banks and insurers

With sovereign wealth funds, endowments, foundations, and employee benefit plans (DB and DC), the investment adviser must primarily focus on the investment of assets. In the case of financial institutions, optimal management must simultaneously focus on liabilities, particularly the volatility and convexity of asset and liability payouts. Consequently, the investment strategy of financial institutions must also consider the appropriate degree of leverage and total amount of common equity capital. Returning to the basic framework of Equations 2 and 4, the proper way to maximize long-term economic earnings thus might be to raise (lower) leverage through: (a) the acquisition (disposal) of portfolio assets; (b) the underwriting (retirement) of liabilities; or (c) the repurchase (issuance) of capital stock.

The financial management of a bank or insurer has not only to deal with the level and direction of interest rates, credit spreads, derivatives markets, economic cycles, and stock markets as they impact the investment portfolio, but we also now see it needs to have a keen understanding of the valuation of its own common equity and debt capital securities. Financial management also requires a view on the actions of competitors. For example, will they create a housing bubble through excessive lending to low-quality borrowers? Will they drive down insurance policy premiums through overly aggressive underwriting? Finally, financial management must satisfy all existing regulations as well as the ones that may evolve with changes in global economic circumstances and other political pressures.

In sum, financial and portfolio management of banks and insurance companies is an attempt to create positive net present value for capital holders by solving simultaneously several different conditions with several different variables. Consequently, key decisions are typically made at the highest levels of the institution's management. Specific analysts and investment managers are typically assigned only to specialized subsets of the institution's varied assets and liabilities.

In such dynamically changing economic and regulatory environments, it is difficult to specify particular portfolio investment rules and policies. Therefore, the following mini-case studies are offered to provide illustrations of the types of high-level portfolio decisions that are required.

EXAMPLE 9

Mini-Case A:

A bank considers reducing its ownership of commercial loans in smaller businesses. These loans pay interest quarterly at various contractually pre-specified spreads above the floating market reference rate (MRR). The runoff of the loan portfolio through repayments, together with proceeds of outright sales and securitizations of other loans, are to be reinvested in a portfolio of fixed-rate government securities of comparable maturities. The securities will be hedged fully against general interest rate risk through the use of publicly traded options and futures on government securities. Additionally, hedging interest rate risk completely would create a synthetic variable rate asset. If interest rates rise, gains on hedges can be reinvested to raise overall portfolio income; if interest rates fall, losses on hedges will require some assets to pay counterparties, thereby lowering overall portfolio income.

1. How would this portfolio restructuring affect the asset/liability profile of the bank?
2. What is the expected impact on the volatility of bank shareholder equity valuation?
3. What is the likely impact on bank earnings?
4. What are reasons that argue in favor of this portfolio redeployment?

Solution to 1:

Switching from variable rate to fixed-rate assets of similar maturities increases the duration of the bank's overall portfolio. However, entering into hedging positions with futures and options on fixed-rate assets has the effect of shortening overall duration. As described, the net effect of the portfolio alteration likely should have little effect on the bank's existing asset/liability duration profile, because floating-rate corporate loans also have little price exposure in the event of rising or falling interest rates.

Solution to 2:

The overall volatility of assets and bank capitalization should decrease, because a hedged portfolio of government securities is more liquid than a portfolio of individual small business loans and also less subject to volatility arising from changes in credit default spreads on corporate loans.

Solution to 3:

Bank earnings would be expected to decline, independent of subsequent changes in the overall level of interest rates. This is because the yields on business loans, adjusting for expected default rates, are higher than on government securities, adjusting for the costs of hedging the government securities. Furthermore, if overall interest rates subsequently rise, the business loan portfolio would generate higher income to the bank. However, hedges on the government securities generate gains when interest rates rise—offsetting losses on the underlying securities and thus permitting more money to be reinvested in now higher yielding government securities. Similarly, a decline in interest rates would lead to a loss on the hedges and a sale of appreciated underlying government securities to cover these hedge losses. The portfolio value is approximately unchanged, but the (reduced) ability to generate income has tracked interest rates downward. In sum, *changes* in overall interest rates impact income-generating ability similarly for both the loan portfolio and the hedged securities portfolio. This is the flip side of the coin; in other words, the two portfolios have similar modified durations. In any environment, the net yields on the hedged government securities are lower than on the business loans. Thus, bank net income is unambiguously lower because of the portfolio rebalancing.

Solution to 4:

Although the proposed redeployment is expected to lower bank earnings, there are at least three good reasons for this action, any of which would justify the decision: (a) the bank believes it needs to have a more liquid investment portfolio because of the risk of unexpected claims against assets; (b) the bank needs to raise its regulatory "equity to risky assets" ratio (by substituting low credit-risk for high credit-risk assets); and (c), the bank believes it will be able to reverse the trade in the future after a recession has driven up the effective default-adjusted spreads (i.e., driven down the prices) on small business loans. In all three rationales, overall volatility is expected to decline and the reduction in volatility is expected to provide a benefit that more than offsets the anticipated reduction in earnings. That is, the risk-adjusted return is projected to rise.

Mini-Case B:

A medium size insurance company plans to sell a large portion of its diversified, fixed-rate, investment-grade-rated securities in order to redeploy proceeds into a special purpose trust holding a diversified portfolio of automobile loans with original loan lives of 5 years. The loans are collateralized by direct liens on the vehicles, and the underlying borrowers meet minimum consumer credit scores set by a national credit rating agency. The underlying loans were randomly selected for the trust, and the collateral constitutes a nationwide sample of automobiles of different foreign and domestic manufacturers.

1. What does this transaction reveal about the regulatory capital of this insurer?

2. What key information must the insurer know about the automobile loans held by the trust in order to manage its asset/liability duration profile?

3. What external factors might the insurer need to consider with respect to the duration of trust assets?

4. What is the expected impact from the proposed investment transaction on (a) the insurer's earnings, and (b), the overall volatility of the insurer's common equity capitalization?

Solution to 1:

The portfolio redeployment reduces the insurer's liquidity. Given that the insurer is able to undertake this action, the company has excess regulatory capital, because the underlying illiquid loans require more regulatory capital than high-quality/investment-grade, marketable, fixed-income securities.

Solution to 2:

The insurer must make actuarial projections of contractual cash flows from the auto loans, which must take into account full and partial pre-payments because of accidents, auto trade-ins, and loan defaults. The acceptable credit quality of the borrowers and the geographical and brand diversity contribute to the accuracy of such predictions. The overall asset/liability profile for the insurer might well change depending on how the projected modified duration of the auto loan receivables compares with the investment-grade marketable securities to be sold. A material difference might require management to undertake (a) changes in the modified duration of the insurance company's liabilities, such as by altering the maturities of future debt issuances; or (b), implementation of interest rate-hedging transactions.

Solution to 3:

The insurer must be concerned about an adverse change in the economic cycle, changes in technology, and/or energy prices—all of which could adversely impact the value of the auto loan receivables (as compared with the marketable securities portfolio to be sold) and which could undermine the cash flow assumptions made with respect to setting the company's overall asset/liability profile.

Solution to 4:

The portfolio redeployment is likely to raise the insurer's earnings, because the expected yield on the auto loans, net of credit losses, is higher than for investment-grade, liquid securities. However, the company is taking on more credit risk, which should translate into higher volatility of the value of assets and, thus, higher volatility of equity capitalization.

Mini-Case C:

Floating-rate securities, paying a fixed spread over the floating MRR, are trading at historically narrow yield spreads over MRR. In addition, issuers of these securities tend to be concentrated disproportionately in a small number of industries—notably in banks, insurers, and other financial services companies. A bank's investment manager considers selling the bank's portfolio holdings of these floating-rate securities, which have a 5-year maturity and trade at 0.1% over MRR. The proceeds will be used to buy more-diversified (by issuer type), investment-grade, fixed-rate securities that are selling at more normal spreads versus government bond yields of comparable duration (which trade at 1.0% over 5-year US Treasury bond yields). The fixed-rate securities portfolio is to be combined with pay-fixed/receive-floating interest rate swaps under standard mark-to-market collateralization terms. The 5-year interest rate swap terms permit one to receive MRR while paying 0.4% over Treasury yields.

1. What does the portfolio alteration do to required regulatory risk-based capital?
2. What might indicate that the bank's senior managers are more concerned about risks to equity capitalization than are regulators?
3. What is the expected effect on the bank's asset/liability profile?
4. What is the expected effect on expected earnings?
5. Summarize the rationale for the portfolio alteration.

Solution to 1:

To a first approximation, substituting one kind of marketable security for another should have little effect on regulatory risk-based capital requirements, because there is little apparent change in average credit quality. The new portfolio will have more issuer and industry diversification than the securities being sold. Thus, under robust scenario simulation testing, the new portfolio should be somewhat more resistant to loss than the more-concentrated portfolio assets being sold.

Solution to 2:

The bank's senior managers appear to be concerned about systemic risk in the financial sector, especially since the securities the bank plans to sell are concentrated in the financial sector and are trading at unusually high prices (narrow spreads to MRR). Apart from interest rate risk, the probability of underperformance for financial company securities is higher than for a diversified portfolio of fixed-rate securities. In the bank's view, the prospective volatility of floating-rate bank assets—and thus, the company's own equity capital—is higher than what is reflected in the regulatory risk-weight framework, because the latter does not take into account relative price risk. Thus, from the bank's perspective, the proposed trade lowers asset and equity volatility.

Solution to 3:

Substituting fixed-rate securities in place of variable-rate securities tends to increase the modified duration of the bank's assets. However, entering into a pay-fixed/receive-floating swap is equivalent to creating a synthetic liability, which becomes (i) smaller as interest rates rise and (ii) greater as interest rates fall. The interest rate swap can be tailored to offset the tendency of the newly acquired fixed-rate securities to lose value as interest rates rise and gain value as interest rates fall. Said differently, the synthetic liability increases the duration of the bank's liabilities to counterbalance the rise in asset duration from replacing variable-rate with fixed-rate debt securities.

Solution to 4:

Earnings are expected to rise. The securities sold pay a low spread over MRR. The new package (fixed-rate securities plus pay-fixed/receive-floating interest rate swap) pays a higher expected spread over MRR. The high yield received on the fixed-rate securities, net of the fixed-rate leg of the interest rate swap paid, represents the new built-in spread that is then added to the MRR received in the floating-leg of the interest rate swap. Specifically, the new portfolio will (i) receive 5-year Treasury yield plus 1.0% on the fixed-rate securities, (ii) pay 5-year Treasury yield plus 0.4% on the fixed leg of the interest rate swap, and (iii) receive MRR on the floating side of the interest rate swap. The net result is that the hedged, fixed-rate holdings will pay the bank the 5-year Treasury yield (T) + 1.0% − (T + 0.4%) + MRR = MRR + 0.6%. This synthetic floating-rate portfolio compares with the original floating-rate portfolio that paid just MRR + 0.1%.

Solution to 5:

A pay-fixed/receive-floating interest rate swap is "plain vanilla"; it is easy to value and unwind. The trade would thus not have any major adverse impact on the institution's liquidity. The bank, by selling securities in the banking and financial services industry, can lower its own exposure to systemic financial risk. In essence, the trade achieves better diversification while creating cheap (i.e., higher yielding) synthetic MRR floaters in place of true MRR floaters. The regulatory system in which the bank operates likely has a statistical system that penalizes excessive use of derivatives by deeming worst-case liabilities in a stress test. This should not be an issue assuming the proposed trade is small enough, relative to the institution's size, to have no significant impact on stress test results. Overall, the trade would be a duration-neutral trade, achieving higher net earnings and lower asset and equity risk without significantly impacting the bank's regulatory capital ratios.

Mini-Case D:

In the aftermath of prolonged financial turmoil and a recession, a large pan-European life insurance company believes that corporate debt securities and asset-based securities are now very attractive relative to more-liquid government securities. The yield spreads more than compensate for default and credit downgrade risk. Interest rates for government securities are near cyclical lows. The insurance company is concerned that rates may rise and that, as a result, many outstanding annuities might be surrendered. The insurer believes the probability of a large, adverse move in interest rates is much higher than is currently reflected by the implied volatility of traded options on government securities in the eurozone. The insurer's regulatory capital and reserves are deemed to be healthy.

1. What are the consequences of lowering allocations to government securities and raising allocations to corporate and asset-backed securities?

2. Are there steps that the insurer should take on the liability side?

Solution to 1:

These proposed asset reallocations have several implications. First, corporate debt securities have higher yields and thus shorter durations than government securities of similar maturity. Asset-backed securities tend to have lower effective durations than corporate and government bonds. Thus, the proposed rebalancing would likely lower the overall duration of the investment portfolio, which is consistent with the insurer's concerns about rising interest rates and the expected consequences. Second, the change in portfolio allocation would likely lower the company's overall liquidity and lower regulatory risk-based capital measures, because the new securities are treated less favorably for regulatory purposes (less liquid, higher credit risk corporate debt and asset-backed securities require a higher equity charge than liquid, low credit risk government securities, so regulatory "equity to risky assets" is reduced). Thus, the proposed portfolio moves make sense only if the regulatory capital position of the insurer is already ample and if the existing liquidity elsewhere in the portfolio is enough to fund an uptick of annuity surrenders in the case of rising interest rates. Finally, the reallocation would increase expected earnings (from higher interest income) and set the stage for price gains if credit spreads versus government securities contract to more normal levels.

Solution to 2:

Because overall interest rates are low, the company must also deal with an asymmetric risk separate and apart from the reallocation of its investment portfolio. In other words, the insurer must alter its liability profile in order to minimize potential adverse changes in its common equity capitalization. A spike up in interest rates could result in a rise in surrenders of annuities during a time when asset values are coming under pressure. Because the company is more concerned about higher interest rate volatility than is reflected in current option prices, the insurer might consider purchasing out-of-the-money puts on government securities and/or purchasing swaptions with the right to be a fixed-payer/floating-receiver. Sharp rises in rates would make both positions profitable[14] and offset some of the burden of premature annuity surrenders. If time passes without any substantial rise in interest rates, the cost of purchasing option protection would detract from the incremental benefits from the proposed switch into higher yielding securities.

SUMMARY

This reading has introduced the subject of managing institutional investor portfolios. The key points made in this reading are as follows:

- The main institutional investor types are pension plans, sovereign wealth funds, endowments, foundations, banks, and insurance companies. Common characteristics among these investors include a large scale (i.e., asset size), a long-term investment horizon, regulatory constraints, a clearly defined governance framework, and principal–agent issues.

- Institutional investors typically codify their mission, investment objectives, and guidelines in an Investment Policy Statement (IPS).

- Four common investment approaches to managing portfolios used by institutional investors are the Norway model, the Endowment model, the Canada model, and the Liability Driven Investing (LDI) model.

- There are two main types of pension plans: defined benefit (DB), in which a plan sponsor commits to paying a specified retirement benefit; and defined contribution (DC), in which contributions are defined but the ultimate retirement benefit is not specified or guaranteed by the plan sponsor.

- Pension plan stakeholders include the employer, employees, retirees, unions, management, the investment committee and/or board of directors, and shareholders.

- The key elements in the calculation of DB plan liabilities are as follows:

  - Service/tenure: The higher the service years, the higher the retirement benefit.

  - Salary/earnings: The higher the salary over the measurement period, the higher the retirement benefit.

  - Mortality/longevity: The longer the participant's expected life span, the higher the plan sponsor's liability.

  - Vesting: Lower turnover results in higher vesting, increasing the plan sponsor's liabilities.

  - Discount rate: A higher discount rate reduces the present value of the plan sponsor's liabilities.

- DB plan liquidity needs are driven by the following:

  - Proportion of active employees relative to retirees: More mature pension funds have higher liquidity needs.

---

14 A put option becomes valuable to the holder if prices of the underlying asset fall. A swaption with the right to enter a swap paying fixed and receiving floating is economically analogous to a put option on a bond. If rates rise, the swaption owner has the right to receive a rising stream of floating payments in exchange for what will have then become a stream of reasonably low fixed payments. The swaption contract will have gained in value.

- Age of workforce: Liquidity needs rise as the age of the workforce increases.

- Plan funded status: If the plan is well funded, the sponsor may reduce contributions, generating a need to hold higher balances of liquid assets to pay benefits.

- Flexibility: Ability of participants to switch among the sponsor's plans or to withdraw from the plan.

■ Pension plans are subject to significant and evolving regulatory constraints designed to ensure the integrity, adequacy, and sustainability of the pension system. Some incentives, such as tax exemption, are only granted to plans that meet these regulatory requirements. Notable differences in legal, regulatory, and tax considerations can lead to differences in plan design from one country to another or from one group to another (e.g., public plans vs. corporate plans).

■ The following risk considerations affect the way DB plans are managed:

- Plan funded status

- Sponsor financial strength

- Interactions between the sponsor's business and the fund's investments

- Plan design

- Workforce characteristics

■ An examination of pension fund asset allocations shows very large differences in average asset allocations by country and within a country despite these plans seeking to achieve similar goals. Such inter- and intra-national differences are driven by many factors, including the differences in legal, regulatory, accounting, and tax constraints; the investment objectives, risk appetites, and investment views of the stakeholders; the liabilities to and demographics of the ultimate beneficiaries; the availability of suitable investment opportunities; and the expected cost of living in retirement.

■ The major types of sovereign wealth funds (SWFs) follow:

- Budget Stabilization funds: Set up to insulate the budget and economy from commodity price volatility and external shocks.

- Development funds: Established to allocate resources to priority socio-economic projects, usually infrastructure.

- Savings funds: Intended to share wealth across generations by transforming non-renewable assets into diversified financial assets.

- Reserve funds: Intended to reduce the negative carry costs of holding foreign currency reserves or to earn higher return on ample reserves.

- Pension Reserve funds: Set up to meet identified future outflows with respect to pension-related, contingent-type liabilities on governments' balance sheets.

■ Stakeholders of SWFs include the country's citizens, the government, external asset managers, and the SWF's management, investment committee and board of directors.

■ Given their mission of intergenerational wealth transfer, SWFs do not generally have clearly defined liabilities, so do not typically pursue asset/liability matching strategies used by other institutional investor types.

- Sovereign wealth funds have differing liquidity needs. Budget stabilization funds require the most liquidity, followed by reserve funds. At the other end of the spectrum are savings funds with low liquidity needs, followed by pension reserve funds.

- The investment objectives of SWFs are often clearly articulated in the legislative instruments that create them. They are often tax free in their home country, though must take foreign taxation into consideration. Given their significant asset sizes and the nature of their stakeholders, SWFs have aimed to increase transparency regarding their investment activities. In this regard, the Santiago Principles are a form of self-regulation.

- The typical asset allocation by SWF type shows budget stabilization funds are invested mainly in bonds and cash given their liquidity needs. Reserve Funds invest in equities and alternatives but maintain a significant allocation of bonds for liquidity. Savings funds and pension reserve funds hold relatively higher allocations of equities and alternatives because of their longer-term liabilities.

- Endowments and foundations typically invest to maintain purchasing power while financing their supporting university (endowments) or making grants (foundations) in perpetuity—based on the notion of intergenerational equity. Endowments and foundations usually have a formal spending policy that determines how much is paid out annually to support their mission. This future stream of payouts represents their liabilities. For endowments, other liability-related factors to be considered when setting investment policy are: 1) the ability to raise additional funds from donors/alumni, 2) the percentage of the university's operating budget provided by the endowment, and 3) the ability to issue debt.

- Foundations and endowments typically enjoy tax-exempt status and face relatively little regulation compared to other types of institutional investors.

- Foundations face less flexible spending rules compared to endowments; foundations in the US are legally mandated to pay out 5% of their assets annually to maintain tax-exempt status. Endowments and foundations have relatively low liquidity needs. However, foundations have somewhat higher liquidity needs (vs. endowments), because they 1) typically pay out slightly more as a percentage of assets, and 2) finance the entire operating budget of the organization they support.

- Endowments and foundations typically have a long-term real return objective of about 5% consistent with their spending policies. This real return objective, and a desire to maintain purchasing power, results in endowments and foundations making significant allocations to real assets. In general, endowments and foundations invest heavily in private asset classes and hedge funds and have relatively small allocations to fixed income.

- Banking and insurance companies manage both portfolio assets and institutional liabilities to achieve an extremely high probability that obligations on deposits, guarantees, derivatives, policyholder claims, and other liabilities will be paid in full and on time.

- Banking and insurance companies have perpetual time horizons. Strategically, their goal is to maximize net present value to capital holders; tactically, this may be achieved by liability driven investing (LDI) over intermediate and shorter horizons.

- Financial institutions are highly regulated because of their importance to the non-financial, or real, sectors of the economy. Such institutions are also regulated in order to minimize contagion risk rippling throughout the financial and real sectors.

- The underlying premise of regulation is that an institution's capital must be adequate to absorb shocks to both asset and liability values. This implies limiting the volatility of value of the institution's shareholder capital.

- The volatility of shareholder capital can be managed by (a) reducing the price volatility of portfolio investments, loans, and derivatives; (b) lowering the volatility from unexpected shocks to claims, deposits, guarantees, and other liabilities; (c) limiting leverage; and (d) attempting to achieve positive correlation between changes in the value of assets and liabilities.

- Ample liquidity, diversification of portfolio and other assets, high investment quality, transparency, stable funding, duration management, diversification of insurance underwriting risks, and monetary limits on guarantees, funding commitments, and insurance claims are some of the ways management and regulators attempt to achieve low volatility of shareholder capital value.

REFERENCES

OECD. 2016. *OECD Insurance Statistics 2008–2016.* https://read.oecd-ilibrary.org/finance-and
-investment/oecd-insurance-statistics-2016_ins_stats-2016-en#page1.

Willis Towers Watson Thinking Ahead Institute. 2021. *"Global Pension Assets Study 2021"*
(February). https://www.thinkingaheadinstitute.org/research-papers/global-pension-assets
-study-2021.

PRACTICE PROBLEMS

The following information relates to questions 1-5

Bern Zang is the recently hired chief investment officer of the Janson University Endowment Investment Office. The Janson University Endowment Fund (the Fund) is based in the United States and has current assets under management of $12 billion. It has a long-term investment horizon and relatively low liquidity needs. The Fund is overseen by an Investment Committee consisting of board members for the Fund. The Investment Office is responsible for implementing the investment policy set by the Fund's Investment Committee.

The Fund's current investment approach includes an internally managed fund that holds mostly equities and fixed-income securities. It is largely passively managed with tight tracking error limits. The target asset allocation is 55% equities, 40% fixed income, and 5% alternatives. The Fund currently holds private real estate investments to meet its alternative investment allocation.

1. **Identify** the investment approach currently being used by the Investment Committee for managing the Fund. **Justify** your response.

Identify the investment approach currently being used by the Investment Committee for managing the Fund.
(circle one)

Norway Model	Endowment Model	Canadian Model	LDI Model

Justify your response.

2. **Discuss** the advantages and the disadvantages of the investment approach currently being used by the Investment Committee.

	Discuss the advantages and the disadvantages of the investment approach currently being used by the Investment Committee.
Advantages	
Disadvantages	

3. **Describe** how *each* of the following common characteristics of institutional investors supports the Fund's allocation to private real estate:

   i.   Scale

   ii. Investment horizon

   iii. Governance framework

	Describe how *each* of the following common characteristics of institutional investors supports the Fund's allocation to private real estate.
Scale	
Investment Horizon	
Governance Framework	

4. After a thorough internal review, Zang concludes that the current investment approach will result in a deterioration of the purchasing power of the Fund over time. He proposes a new, active management approach that will substantially decrease the allocation to publicly traded equities and fixed income in order to pursue a higher allocation to private investments. The management of the new investments will be outsourced.

   Identify the new investment approach proposed by Zang for managing the Fund. **Justify** your response.

Identify the new investment approach proposed by Zang for managing the Fund. (circle one)

Norway Model	Endowment Model	Canadian Model	LDI Model
Justify your response.			

5. After a thorough internal review, Zang concludes that the current investment approach will result in a deterioration of the purchasing power of the Fund over time. He proposes a new, active management approach that will substantially decrease the allocation to publicly traded equities and fixed income in order to pursue a higher allocation to private investments. The management of the new investments will be outsourced.

   Discuss the advantages and the disadvantages of the new investment approach proposed by Zang.

	Discuss the advantages and the disadvantages of the new investment approach proposed by Zang.
Advantages	
Disadvantages	

The following information relates to questions 6–12

William Azarov is a portfolio manager for Westcome Investments, an asset management firm. Azarov is preparing for meetings with two of Westcome's clients and obtains the help of Jason Boulder, a junior analyst. The first meeting is with Maglav Inc., a rapidly growing US-based technology firm with a young workforce and high employee turnover. Azarov directs Boulder to review the details of Maglav's defined benefit (DB) pension plan. The plan is overfunded and has assets under management of $25 million. Boulder makes the following two observations:

Observation 1 Maglav's shareholders benefit from the plan's overfunded status.

Observation 2 The funded ratio of Maglav's plan will decrease if employee turnover decreases.

Maglav outsources the management of the pension plan entirely to Westcome Investments. The fee structure requires Maglav to compensate Westcome with a high base fee regardless of performance. Boulder tells Azarov that outsourcing offers small institutional investors, such as Maglav's pension plan, the following three benefits:

Benefit 1: Regulatory requirements are reduced.

Benefit 2: Conflicts of interest are eliminated from principal–agent issues.

Benefit 3: Investors have access to a wider range of investment strategies through scale benefits.

In the meeting with Maglav, Azarov describes the investment approach used by Westcome in managing the pension plan. The approach is characterized by a high allocation to alternative investments, significant active management, and a reliance on outsourcing assets to other external asset managers. Azarov also explains that Maglav's operating results have a low correlation with pension asset returns and that the investment strategy is affected by the fact that the pension fund assets are a small portion of Maglav's market capitalization. Azarov states that the plan is subject to the Employee Retirement Income Security Act of 1974 (ERISA) and follows generally accepted accounting principles, including Accounting Standards Codification (ASC) 715, *Compensation—Retirement Benefits*.

Azarov's second meeting is with John Spintop, chief investment officer of the Wolf University Endowment Fund (the Fund). Spintop hired Westcome to assist in developing a new investment policy to present to the Fund's board of directors. The Fund, which has assets under management of $200 million, has an overall objective of maintaining long-term purchasing power while providing needed financial support to Wolf University. During the meeting, Spintop states that the Fund has an annual spending policy of paying out 4% of the Fund's three-year rolling asset value to Wolf University, and the Fund's risk tolerance should consider the following three liability characteristics:

Characteristic 1 The Fund has easy access to debt markets.

Characteristic 2 The Fund supports 10% of Wolf University's annual budget.

Characteristic 3 The Fund receives significant annual inflows from gifts and donations.

The Fund has a small investment staff with limited experience in managing alternative assets and currently uses the Norway model for its investment approach. Azarov suggests a change in investment approach by making an allocation to externally managed alternative assets—namely, hedge funds and private equity. Ten-year nominal expected return assumptions for various asset classes, as well as three proposed allocations that include some allocation to alternative assets, are presented in Exhibit 1.

Exhibit 1: 10-Year Nominal Expected Return Assumptions and Proposed Allocations

Asset Class	Expected Return	Allocation 1	Allocation 2	Allocation 3
US Treasuries	4.1%	45%	10%	13%
US Equities	6.3%	40%	15%	32%
Non-US Equities	7.5%	10%	15%	40%
Hedge Funds	5.0%	0%	30%	5%
Private Equity	9.1%	5%	30%	10%

Expected inflation for the next 10 years is 2.5% annually.

6. Which of Boulder's observations regarding Maglav's pension plan is correct?

   A. Only Observation 1

   B. Only Observation 2

   C. Both Observation 1 and Observation 2

7. Which of the benefits of outsourcing the management of the pension plan suggested by Boulder is correct?

   A. Benefit 1

   B. Benefit 2

   C. Benefit 3

8. Westcome's investment approach for Maglav's pension plan can be *best* characterized as the:

   A. Norway model.

   B. Canadian model.

   C. endowment model.

9. The risk tolerance of Maglav's pension plan can be *best* characterized as being:

   A. below average.

   B. average.

   C. above average.

10. Based on Azarov's statement concerning ERISA and ASC 715, which of the following statements is correct?

    A. Maglav is not allowed to terminate the plan.

    B. Maglav can exclude the plan's service costs from net income.

    C. Maglav's plan must appear as an asset on Maglav's balance sheet.

11. The risk tolerance of the Wolf University Endowment Fund can be *best* characterized as:

    A. below average.

B. average.

C. above average.

12. Which proposed allocation in Exhibit 1 would be *most appropriate* for the Fund given its characteristics?

A. Allocation 1

B. Allocation 2

C. Allocation 3

The following information relates to questions 13-15

The Prometheo University Scholarship Endowment (the Endowment) was established in 1950 and supports scholarships for students attending Prometheo University. The Endowment's assets under management are relatively small, and it has an annual spending policy of 6% of the five-year rolling asset value.

13. **Formulate** the investment objectives section of the investment policy statement for the Endowment.

14. Prometheo University recently hired a new chief investment officer (CIO). The CIO directs her small staff of four people to implement an investment policy review. Historically, the endowment has invested 60% of the portfolio in US equities and 40% in US Treasuries. The CIO's expectation of annual inflation for the next 10 years is 2.5%.

The CIO develops nominal 10-year return assumptions for US Treasuries and US equities, which are presented in Exhibit 1.

Exhibit 1: Asset Class Return Assumptions	
Asset Class	**10-Year Return Assumptions (Nominal)**
US Treasuries	4.0%
US Equities	7.4%

Discuss whether the current investment policy is appropriate given the Endowment's annual spending policy.

15. Upon completion of the investment policy review by her four-person staff, the CIO makes some recommendations to the Endowment's board regarding the investment objectives and asset allocation. One of her recommendations is to adopt the endowment model as an investment approach. She recommends investing 20% in private equity, 40% in hedge funds, 25% in public equities, and 15% in fixed income.

Determine whether the board should accept the CIO's recommendation. **Justify** your response.

Determine whether the board should accept the CIO's recommendation. (circle one)	Justify your response.
Accept	
Reject	

16. Fiona Heselwith is a 40-year-old US citizen who has accepted a job with Lyricul, LLC, a UK-based company. Her benefits package includes a retirement savings plan. The company offers both a defined benefit (DB) plan and a defined contribution (DC) plan but stipulates that employees must choose one plan and remain with that plan throughout their term of employment.

    The DB plan is fully funded and provides full vesting after five years. The benefit formula for monthly payments upon retirement is calculated as follows:

    - Final monthly salary × Benefit percentage of 2% × Number of years of service
    - The final monthly salary is equal to average monthly earnings for the last five financial years immediately prior to the retirement date.

    The DC plan contributes 12% of annual salary into the plan each year and is also fully vested after five years. Lyricul offers its DC plan participants a series of life-cycle funds as investment choices. Heselwith could choose a fund with a target date matching her planned retirement date. She would be able to make additional contributions from her salary if she chooses.

    Discuss the features that Heselwith should consider in evaluating the two plans with respect to the following:

    i. Benefit payments
    ii. Contributions
    iii. Shortfall risk
    iv. Mortality/longevity risks

Discuss the features that Heselwith should consider in evaluating the two plans with respect to the following:
Benefit Payments
Contributions
Shortfall Risk
Mortality/ Longevity Risks

17. Dianna Mark is the chief financial officer of Antiliaro, a relatively mature textile production company headquartered in Italy. All of its revenues come from Europe, but the company is losing sales to its Asian competitors. Earnings have been steady but not growing, and the balance sheet has taken on more debt in the past few years in order to maintain liquidity. Mark reviews the following facts concerning the company's defined benefit (DB) pension plan:

    - The DB plan currently has €1 billion in assets and is underfunded by €100 million in relation to the projected benefit obligation (PBO) because of investment losses.

- The company to date has made regular contributions.
- The average employee age is 50 years, and the company has many retirees owing to its longevity.
- The duration of the plan's liabilities (which are all Europe based) is 10 years.
- The discount rate applied to these liabilities is 6%.
- There is a high correlation between the operating results of Antiliaro and pension asset returns.

Determine whether the risk tolerance of the DB plan is below average or above average. **Justify** your response with *two* reasons.

Determine whether the risk tolerance of the DB plan is below average or above average. (circle one)	Justify your response with *two* reasons.
Below Average	1.
Above Average	2.

18. Meura Bancorp, a US bank, has an equity capital ratio for financial assets of 12%. Meura's strategic plans include the incorporation of additional debt in order to leverage earnings since the current capital structure is relatively conservative. The bank plans to restructure the balance sheet so that the equity capitalization ratio drops to 10% and the modified duration of liabilities is 1.90. The bank also plans to rebalance its investment portfolio to achieve a modified duration of assets of 2.10. Given small changes in interest rates, the yield on liabilities is expected to move by 65 bps for every 100 bps of yield change in the asset portfolio.

Calculate the modified duration of the bank's equity capital after restructuring. **Show** your calculations.

SOLUTIONS

1.

Identify the investment approach currently being used by the Investment Committee for managing the Fund.
(circle one)

Norway Model	Endowment Model	Canadian Model	LDI Model

Justify your response.

The investment approach currently used to manage the Fund's assets is the Norway model. This approach is characterized by a heavy allocation to public equities and fixed-income securities with little allocation to alternatives and largely passively managed assets with tight tracking error limits.

2.

	Discuss the advantages and the disadvantages of the investment approach currently being used by the Investment Committee.
Advantages	Advantages of using the Norway model are that investment costs/fees are low, investments are transparent, manager risk is low, and there is little complexity for a governing board (the model is easy to understand).
Disadvantages	The disadvantage of using the Norway model is that there is limited potential for value-added (i.e., alpha from security selection skills), above-market returns.

3.

	Describe how *each* of the following common characteristics of institutional investors supports the Fund's allocation to private real estate.
Scale	The Fund has $12 billion of assets under management. Its relatively large size allows it access to a broad investment universe and to investments that have a high minimum investment size, such as private real estate.
Investment Horizon	Alternative investments, such as private real estate, require a long-term investment horizon. Janson, like most university endowments, has a long-term investment horizon and relatively low liquidity needs. This makes private real estate an appropriate investment and also helps the endowment maintain long-term purchasing power.
Governance Framework	Institutional investors usually operate under a formal governance framework. Janson has a well-structured governance framework that includes an Investment Committee that is part of the board overseeing the endowment's investment portfolio. This framework also includes an Investment Office that implements the investment policy approved by the Investment Committee. The decision to invest in private real estate had to go through an approval process that is set and maintained by the governance structure in place.

4.

Identify the new investment approach proposed by Zang for managing the Fund. (circle one)

| Norway Model | Endowment Model | Canadian Model | LDI Model |

Justify your response.

The new investment approach proposed by Zang is the endowment model. This model is characterized by significant active management, a high allocation to alternative investments, and externally managed assets (which distinguishes it from the Canadian model, an approach that relies more on internally managed assets).

5.

	Discuss the advantages and the disadvantages of the new investment approach proposed by Zang.
Advantages	The primary advantage of using the endowment model is a higher potential for value-added, above-market returns.
Disadvantages	The endowment model can be difficult to implement for small institutional investors because they might not be able to access high-quality managers. The endowment model may also be difficult to implement for a very large institutional investor because of the institutional investor's very large footprint. Furthermore, relative to the Norway model, the endowment model is more expensive in terms of costs/fees.

6. C is correct. Both observations are correct. For a corporate defined benefit plan, Maglav's shareholders are stakeholders. These stakeholders are interested in the sustainability of the pension plan, and the overfunded status is an asset on the balance sheet, potentially increasing the value of Maglav's stock. The overfunded status also allows management to potentially lower employer contributions to the plan and increase net income. It also lowers financial risk, which may reduce volatility in the stock price. In addition, decreasing employee turnover will increase plan liabilities and worsen the funded ratio. With high turnover, fewer workers will be vested and entitled to defined benefit payments. Conversely, if employee turnover decreases, expected vesting will increase, leading to higher plan liabilities and a lower funded ratio.

7. C is correct. Scale (asset size) is a defining characteristic for institutional investors since it affects key aspects of the investment process. Maglav's pension plan is small, with $25 million in assets under management. Smaller institutions may be unable to access certain investments that have a high minimum investment, such as private equity and real estate assets. These smaller institutions may also have difficulty in hiring skilled investment professionals. As a result, small institutional investors, such as Maglav's pension plan, are more likely to outsource all or most of the investment operations to external asset managers or investment consultants.

8. C is correct. The endowment model operates in an asset-only context and is characterized by a high allocation to alternative investments, including private investments and hedge funds; significant active management; and outsourcing to external managers. These characteristics describe the investment approach used by Westcome. The skill in sourcing alternative investments is critically important given the large variation in performance among asset managers, especially for alternative investments.

9. C is correct. The risk tolerance for Maglav's defined benefit plan is high and thus above average. Several factors influence the plan sponsor's ability to assume risk. For Maglav, the overfunded status of the pension fund allows the plan to withstand more volatility, and its small size relative to the company size implies greater risk tolerance. The low correlation of Maglav's operating results with pension asset returns also results in greater risk tolerance. Finally, the workforce characteristics imply greater risk tolerance. The younger workforce increases the duration of the plan liabilities and enables the sponsor to take on more liquidity risk. The high turnover of the workforce means fewer employees may be vested, reducing the number of employees entitled to receive defined benefit payments. All these factors contribute to an above average risk tolerance for Maglav's defined benefit plan.

10. C is correct. ASC 715, *Compensation—Retirement Benefits* requires that an overfunded (underfunded) plan appear as an asset (liability) on the balance sheet of the corporate sponsor. Maglav's plan is overfunded, so it appears as an asset on Maglav's balance sheet.

11. C is correct. The risk tolerance of the Wolf University Endowment Fund is above average since endowments that support a small percentage of the university's operating budget (10% in this case) should be able to tolerate more market, credit, and liquidity risk. In addition, the Fund's ability to access debt markets, especially during periods of market stress, increases the level of risk the endowment can accept in its investments. Finally, because of the significant inflows from gifts and donations, the effective spending rate will be lower than the annual spending policy of paying out 4% of the Fund's three-year rolling asset value. Thus, the Fund can rely less on investment returns to generate the income stream needed to support the university and can accept higher-risk investments.

12. C is correct. Allocation 3 is the most appropriate allocation for the Fund. The annual expected returns for the three allocations are as follows:

$$\text{Allocation 1 exp. return} = (0.45 \times 4.1\%) + (0.40 \times 6.3\%) + (0.10 \times 7.5\%) + (0.05 \times 9.1\%)$$

$$= 5.57\%.$$

$$\text{Allocation 2 exp. return} = (0.10 \times 4.1\%) + (0.15 \times 6.3\%) + (0.15 \times 7.5\%) + (0.30 \times 5.0\%) + (0.30 \times 9.1\%)$$

$$= 6.71\%.$$

$$\text{Allocation 3 exp. return} = (0.13 \times 4.1\%) + (0.32 \times 6.3\%) + (0.40 \times 7.5\%) + (0.05 \times 5.0\%) + (0.10 \times 9.1\%)$$

$$= 6.71\%.$$

The real return for Allocation 1 is 3.07% (= 5.57% − 2.50%), and the real return for Allocation 2 and Allocation 3 is 4.21% (= 6.71% − 2.50%).

Therefore, Allocation 1 is not appropriate because the expected real rate of return is less than the annual spending rate of 4%. With expected spending at 4%, the purchasing power of the Fund would be expected to decline over time with Allocation 1.

Allocations 2 and 3 both offer an expected real rate of return greater than the annual spending rate of 4%. Thus, the purchasing power of the Fund would be expected to grow over time with either allocation. However, Allocation 3 is more appropriate than Allocation 2 because of its lower allocation to alternative assets (hedge funds and private equity). The total 60% allocation to alternative assets in Allocation 2 is well above the 15% allocation in Allocation 3 and is likely too high considering the Fund's small investment staff and its limited experience with managing alternative investments. Also, given the Fund's relatively small size of assets under management ($200 million), access to top hedge funds and private equity managers is likely to be limited.

13. The mission of the Prometheo University Scholarship Endowment is to provide scholarships for students attending the university. In order to achieve this mission, the Endowment must maintain the purchasing power of the assets in perpetuity while achieving investment returns sufficient to sustain the level of spending necessary to support the scholarship budget. Therefore, the investment objective of the endowment should be to achieve a total real rate of return (after inflation) of at least 6% with a reasonable level of risk.

14. GUIDELINE ANSWER:

   - The policy is not appropriate.
   - The expected real return of 3.54% is less than the spending policy rate of 6%.
   - Therefore, the current allocation and investment objectives are not sustainable.

   The nominal expected return on the current portfolio, according to the nominal return assumptions in Exhibit 1, is 6.04% per year ($0.6 \times 7.4\% + 0.4 \times 4.0\% = 6.04\%$). The expected real return is approximately 3.54% ($6.04\% - 2.5\% = 3.54\%$), which is below the 6% spending rate and the stated objective of a 6% real return. Therefore, this real return is not sufficient to meeting the spending policy, which makes the Endowment's goals unsustainable. The Endowment will need to change its asset allocation to earn higher returns and/or lower its spending policy rate.

15.

Determine whether the board should accept the CIO's recommendation. (circle one)	Justify your response.
Accept Reject	The board should reject the CIO's recommendation. This recommendation is a significant departure from current practice and entails a much higher level of risk. The size of the investment team is small, with only four people, and it may not have adequate access to or experience in alternative investments. Given the relatively small size of the Endowment, it is unlikely that it has access to top managers in the hedge fund and private equity spaces.

16.

	Discuss the features that Heselwith should consider in evaluating the two plans with respect to the following:
Benefit Payments	Heselwith notes that the vesting schedule with regard to the company's contributions is the same in both plans, although her contributions in the DC plan are vested immediately. The DB plan provides a defined payment linked to final salary and years of service, whereas the DC plan provides an uncertain benefit based on Lyricul's and Heselwith's contributions as well as the investment performance of the plan assets.
Contributions	Lyricul's contribution rate to the DB plan is not known, but the plan is fully funded. However, there is no guarantee that it will remain fully funded or that Lyricul is committed to maintaining the DB plan's fully funded status. The rate for the DC plan is stated to be 12% of annual salary.
Shortfall Risk	Heselwith notes that the shortfall risk of plan assets being insufficient to meet her retirement benefit payments falls to her employer, Lyricul, with the DB plan. However, for the DC plan, the shortfall risk falls to her and depends on the 12% contribution rate from the company, plus any additional contributions she chooses to make, as well as the performance of the chosen investments.
Mortality/ Longevity Risks	The DB plan pools mortality risk such that those in the pool who die prematurely leave assets that help fund benefit payments for those who live longer than expected. Heselwith bears the risk of outliving her savings with the DC plan.

17.

Determine whether the risk tolerance of the DB Plan is below average or above average. (circle one)	**Justify your response with *two* reasons.**
Below Average	• The plan is underfunded, and the discount rate being used is fairly aggressive. 1. The DB plan already has a deficit, despite regular contributions, and is suffering from investment losses. The discount rate is already aggressive and should not be increased to lower the contribution. • The uncertain financial condition of the company. 2. The uncertain condition of Antiliaro may constrain its ability to make contributions to the DB plan. Lack of earnings growth and increasing debt on the balance sheet over the last few years imply below-average risk tolerance.

Determine whether the risk tolerance of the DB Plan is below average or above average. (circle one)	Justify your response with *two* reasons.
Above Average	• The plan suffers from investment losses. 3. Often, investment losses can lead a DB plan to take on more investment risk to achieve higher returns, but the other constraints, such as the plan's underfunded status and the company's financial condition, prevent this approach.
	• The older age of employees necessitates liquidity. 4. The average employee age is 50 years, and the company has many retirees because of its longevity. These characteristics generate a need for liquidity, which lowers the amount of risk the plan can assume.
	• The high correlation between the operating results of Antiliaro and pension asset returns lowers the risk tolerance of the pension plan. 5. The high correlation between the operating results of Antiliaro and the pension asset returns suggests a low risk tolerance. If Antiliaro is performing poorly as a company, this will constrain its ability to make additional contributions that may be necessary to address the shortfall in the pension's funding.

18. The modified duration of the bank's equity capital after restructuring is 9.89 years:

$$D_E^* = \left(\frac{A}{E}\right)D_A^* - \left(\frac{A}{E} - 1\right)D_L^*\left(\frac{\Delta i}{\Delta y}\right)$$
$$= \left(\frac{1}{0.10}\right) \times 2.10 - \left(\frac{1}{0.10} - 1\right) \times 1.90 \times 0.65$$
$$= 9.89 \text{ years}$$

6

Trading Costs and Electronic Markets

by Larry Harris, PhD, CFA.

Larry Harris, PhD, CFA, is at the USC Marshall School of Business (USA).

LEARNING OUTCOMES

Mastery	The candidate should be able to:
☐	explain the components of execution costs, including explicit and implicit costs
☐	calculate and interpret effective spreads and VWAP transaction cost estimates
☐	describe the implementation shortfall approach to transaction cost measurement
☐	describe factors driving the development of electronic trading systems
☐	describe market fragmentation
☐	identify and contrast the types of electronic traders
☐	describe characteristics and uses of electronic trading systems
☐	describe comparative advantages of low-latency traders
☐	describe the risks associated with electronic trading and how regulators mitigate them
☐	describe abusive trading practices that real-time surveillance of markets may detect

This reading draws from *Trading and Electronic Markets: What Investment Professionals Need to Know,* by Larry Harris, PhD, CFA, Research Foundation of CFA Institute. © 2015 CFA Institute. All rights reserved.

1 COSTS OF TRADING

☐ | explain the components of execution costs, including explicit and implicit costs

Securities research, portfolio management, and securities trading support the investment process. Of the three, trading is often the least understood and least appreciated function. Among the questions addressed in this reading are the following:

- What are explicit and implicit trading costs, and how are they measured?
- How is a limit order book interpreted?
- How have trading strategies adapted to market fragmentation?
- What types of electronic traders can be distinguished?

This reading is organized as follows: Section 2 discusses the direct and indirect costs of trading.[1] Section 3 discusses developments in electronic trading and the effects they had on transaction costs and market fragmentation. Section 4 identifies the most important types of electronic traders. Section 5 describes electronic trading facilities and some important ways traders use them. Section 6 discusses risks posed by electronic trading and how regulators control them. Finally, Section 7 summarizes the reading.

Costs of Trading

Understanding the costs of trading is critical for ensuring optimal execution and transaction cost management for portfolios. Because trading costs are a significant source of investment performance slippage, investment sponsors and their investment managers pay close attention to trading processes.

The costs of trading include fixed costs and variable costs. For buy-side institutions, fixed trading costs include the costs of employing buy-side traders, the costs of equipping them with proper trading tools (electronic systems and data), and the costs of office space (trading rooms or corners). Small buy-side institutions often avoid these costs by not employing buy-side traders. Their portfolio managers submit their orders directly to their brokers. Variable transaction costs arise from trading activity and consist of explicit and implicit costs.

Explicit costs are the direct costs of trading, such as broker commission costs, transaction taxes, stamp duties, and fees paid to exchanges. They are costs for which a trader could receive a receipt.

Implicit costs, by contrast, are indirect costs caused by the market impact of trading. Buyers often must raise prices to encourage sellers to trade with them, and sellers often must lower prices to encourage buyers. The price concessions that impatient traders make to complete their trades are called the market impacts of their trades. For small orders, market impact often is limited to buying at bid prices and selling at lower ask prices. Small market orders generally have small market impact because these orders often are immediately filled by traders willing to trade at quoted bid and offer prices, or even better prices. Larger orders have greater market impact when traders must move the market to fill their orders. In these cases, traders must accept larger price concessions (less attractive prices) to execute their orders in entirety. Although no receipt can be given for implicit costs, they are real nonetheless.

---

1 CFA Institute would like to thank Ananth Madhavan, PhD, at BlackRock (USA) for his contribution to this section, which includes material first written by him.

Implicit costs result from the following issues:

- The **bid–ask spread** is the ask price (the price at which a trader will sell a specified quantity of a security) minus the bid price (the price at which a trader will buy a specified quantity of a security). Traders who want to trade quickly buy at higher prices and sell at lower prices than those willing to wait for others to trade with them.

- **Market impact** (or price impact) is the effect of the trade on transaction prices. Traders who want to fill large orders often must move prices to encourage others to trade with them.

- **Delay costs** (also called slippage) arise from the inability to complete the desired trade immediately. Traders fail to profit when they fill their orders after prices move as they expect.

- **Opportunity costs** (or unrealized profit/loss) arise from the failure to execute a trade promptly. Traders fail to profit when their orders fail to trade and price move as they expect.

Dealer Quotes

Dealers provide liquidity to other traders when they allow traders to buy and sell when those traders want to trade. Those traders may be the clients known to the dealers, or they may be unknown traders whose orders exchanges assign to standing dealer orders and quotes.

Unlike brokers, dealers trade for their accounts when filling their customers' orders. When dealers buy or sell, they increase or reduce their inventories. Dealers profit by selling at ask prices that are higher than the bid prices at which they buy. If buying interest is greater than selling interest, dealers raise their ask prices to discourage buyers and raise their bid prices to encourage sellers. Likewise, if selling interest is greater than buying interest, dealers lower their ask prices to encourage buyers and lower their bid prices to discourage sellers.

Dealers help markets function well by being continuously available to take the other side of a trade when other traders want to trade. Dealers thus make markets more continuous. They are especially important in markets for infrequently traded securities in which buyers and sellers rarely are present at the same time. For example, most bond markets are overwhelmingly dealer markets because most bonds rarely trade. If an investor wants to sell a rarely traded bond, the investor might have a long wait before another investor interested in buying that bond arrives. Instead, a dealer generally will buy the bond and then try to market it to potential buyers. Practitioners say that dealers "make market" when they offer to trade.

Bid–Ask Spreads and Order Books

The prices at which dealers will buy or sell specified quantities of a security are, respectively, their **bid prices** and **ask prices**. (Ask prices are also known as offer prices.) The excess of the ask price over the bid price is the dealer's **bid–ask spread**.

When several dealers offer bid prices, the **best bid** is the offer to buy with the highest bid price. The best bid is also known as the **inside bid**. The **best ask**, also known as the **best offer** or **inside ask**, is the offer to sell with the lowest ask price.

The spread between the best bid price and the best ask price in a market is the market bid–ask spread, which is also known as the **inside spread**. It will be smaller (tighter or narrower) than the individual dealer spreads if the dealer with the highest bid price is not also the dealer with the lowest ask price.

For example, suppose that a portfolio manager gives the firm's trading desk an order to buy 1,000 shares of Economical Chemical Systems, Inc. (ECSI). Three dealers (coded A, B, and C) make a market in those shares. When the trader views the market in ECSI at 10:22 a.m. on his computer screen, the three dealers have put in the following limit orders to trade at an exchange market:

- Dealer A: *bid*: 98.85 for 600 shares; *ask*: 100.51 for 1,000 shares
- Dealer B: *bid*: 98.84 for 500 shares; *ask*: 100.55 for 500 shares
- Dealer C: *bid*: 98.82 for 700 shares; *ask*: 100.49 for 200 shares

The bid–ask spreads of Dealers A, B, and C are, respectively,

- 100.51 − 98.85 = 1.66
- 100.55 − 98.84 = 1.71
- 100.49 − 98.82 = 1.67

The best bid price, 98.85 by Dealer A, is lower than the best ask price, 100.49 by Dealer C. The market spread is thus 100.49 − 98.85 = 1.64, which is lower than any of the dealers' spreads.

The trader might see the quote information organized on his screen as shown in Exhibit 1. In this display, called a **limit order book**, the bids and asks are separately ordered from best to worst with the best at the top. The trader also notes that the **midquote price** (halfway between the market bid and ask prices) is (100.49 + 98.85)/2 = 99.67.

Exhibit 1: The Limit Order Book for Economical Chemical Systems, Inc.

	Bids				Asks		
Dealer	Time Entered	Price	Size	Dealer	Time Entered	Price	Size
A	10:21 a.m.	98.85	600	C	10:21 a.m.	100.49	200
B	10:21 a.m.	98.84	500	A	10:21 a.m.	100.51	1,000
C	10:19 a.m.	98.82	700	B	10:19 a.m.	100.55	500

Note: The bids are ordered from highest to lowest, while the asks are ordered from lowest to highest. These orderings are from best bid or ask to worst bid or ask.

If the trader on the firm's trading desk submits a market buy order for 1,000 shares, the trader would purchase 200 shares from Dealer C at 100.49 per share and 800 shares from Dealer A at 100.51 per share.

Note that filling the second part of the order cost the trader 0.02 per share more than the first part because Dealer C's ask size was insufficient to fill the entire order. Large orders have price impact when they move down the book as they fill. The price impact of an order depends on its size and the available liquidity.

If this market were not an exchange market, the trader might choose to direct the buy order to a specific dealer—for example, to Dealer A. The trader may do so for many reasons. The trader may believe that Dealer A more likely will honor her quote than would Dealer C. Alternatively, the trader may believe that Dealer A more likely will settle the trade than Dealer C. Such considerations are especially important in markets for which no clearinghouse guarantees that all trades will settle—for example, most currency markets. Institutions active in such markets may screen counterparties on credit criteria. Finally, the trader might fear that Dealer A will cancel her quote when she (or a computer managing her quote) sees that a trade took place at 100.49. Sending the order first to Dealer A thus could produce a better average price.

Implicit Transaction Cost Estimates

Investment managers and traders measure transaction costs so that they can better predict the cost of filling orders and so that they can better manage the brokers and dealers who fill their orders. Buyers, of course, want to trade at low prices, while sellers want to trade at high prices. Expensive trades are purchases arranged at high prices or sales arranged at low prices.

To estimate transaction costs, analysts compare trade prices to a benchmark price. Commonly used price benchmarks include the midquote price at the time of the trade, the midquote price at the time of the order submission, and a volume-weighted average price around the time of the trade. These three benchmarks, respectively, correspond to the effective spread, implementation shortfall, and VWAP methods of transaction cost estimation.

EFFECTIVE SPREADS AND VOLUME-WEIGHTED COST ESTIMATES

2

☐ calculate and interpret effective spreads and VWAP transaction cost estimates

☐ describe the implementation shortfall approach to transaction cost measurement

The market spread is a measure of trade execution costs. It is how much traders would lose per quantity traded if they simultaneously submitted buy and sell market orders that respectively execute at the ask and bid prices. The loss is the cost of trading, because this strategy otherwise accomplishes nothing. Given that two trades generated the cost, the cost per trade is one half of the quoted spread.

The prices that traders receive when trading often differ from quoted prices. Smaller orders sometimes fill at better prices; larger orders often fill at worse prices. Standing orders offering liquidity fill at same-side prices (buy at bid, sell at ask), if they fill at all.

The effective spread provides a more general estimate of the cost of trading. It uses the midquote price (the average, or midpoint, of the bid and the ask prices at the time the order was entered) as the benchmark price:

Effective spread transaction cost estimate =

$$\text{Trade size} \times \begin{cases} \text{Trade price} - \left(\frac{\text{Bid} + \text{Ask}}{2}\right) & \text{for buy orders} \\ \left(\frac{\text{Bid} + \text{Ask}}{2}\right) - \text{Trade price} & \text{for sell orders} \end{cases}$$

For a buy order filled at the ask, the estimated implicit cost of trading is half the bid–ask spread, because Ask − [(Bid + Ask)/2] = [(Ask − Bid)/2]. Multiplying this midquote price benchmark transaction cost estimate by 2 produces a statistic called the **effective spread**. It is the spread that traders would have observed if the quoted ask (for a purchase) or the bid (for a sale) were equal to the trade price.

The effective spread is a sensible estimate of transaction costs when orders are filled in single trades. If an order fills at a price better than the quoted price (e.g., a buy order fills at a price below the ask price), the order is said to receive **price improvement** and the spread is effectively lower. Price improvement occurs when trade execution prices are better than quoted prices. An order that fills at a price outside the quoted spread has an effective spread that is larger than the quoted spread. Such results occur when trade execution prices are worse than quoted prices.

The effective spread is a poor estimate of transaction costs when traders split large orders into many parts to fill over time. Such orders often move the market and cause bid and ask prices to rise or fall. The impact of the order on market prices, called **market impact**, makes trading expensive—especially for the last parts to fill—but the effective spread will not fully identify this cost if it is computed separately for each trade.

For example, suppose that a buy order for 10,000 shares fills in two trades. The prices and sizes of these trades and the best bids and offers in the market when the trades occurred appear in the following table:

Trade	Trade Price	Trade Size	Prevailing Bid	Prevailing Offer
#1	10.21	4,000	10.19	10.21
#2	10.22	6,000	10.20	10.22

For this buy order, the effective spread transaction cost per share is 0.01, or [(10.21–10.19)/2] and [(10.22 – 10.20)/2], for both trades (the effective spreads are both 0.02). Thus, the total transaction cost estimate measured using the midquote price benchmark is 100 = 0.01 × 10,000. This estimate is problematic because it reflects the higher price of the second trade, which was likely caused by the market impact of the trader's first trade.

Effective spreads also do not measure **delay costs** (also called slippage) that arise from the inability to complete the desired trade immediately because of its size in relation to the available market liquidity. Delay costs also arise when portfolio managers or their traders fail to create and route orders quickly to the markets where they will fill most quickly. Analysts often measure delay costs on the portion of the order carried over from one day to the next. Delay is costly when price moves away from an order (up for a buy order, down for a sell order), often because information leaks into the market before or during the execution of the order.

When delays in execution cause a portion of the order to go unfilled, the associated cost is called **opportunity cost**. For example, suppose a futures trader places an order to buy 10 contracts with a limit price of 99.00, good for one day, when the market quote is 99.01 to 99.04. The order does not execute, and the contract closes at 99.80. If the order could have been filled at 99.04, the difference (99.80 – 99.04 = 0.76) reflects the opportunity cost per contract. By trading more aggressively, the trader might have avoided these costs. Opportunity costs are difficult to measure. In the example, the one-day time frame is arbitrary, and the assumption that the order could fill at 99.04 may be suspect. The estimate usually is sensitive to the time frame chosen for measurement and to assumptions about the prices at which orders could trade.

Implementation Shortfall

The implementation shortfall method of measuring trading costs addresses the problems associated with the effective spread method. Implementation shortfall is also attractive because it views trading from an investment management perspective and measures the total cost of implementing an investment decision by capturing all explicit and implicit costs. The implementation shortfall method includes the market impact costs and delay costs as well as opportunity costs, which are often significant for large orders.

Implementation shortfall compares the values of the actual portfolio with that of a paper portfolio constructed on the assumption that trades could be arranged at the prices that prevailed when the decision to trade is made. The prevailing price—also called the decision price, the arrival price, or the strike price—is generally taken to be the midquote price at the time of the trade decision. The excess of the paper value over the actual value is the **implementation shortfall**. The coverage of implementation shortfall is continued at Level III.

VWAP Transaction Cost Estimates

Volume-weighted average price (VWAP) is one of the most widely used benchmark prices that analysts use to estimate transaction costs. Analysts typically compute the VWAP using all trades that occurred from the start of the order until the order was completed, a measure that is often referred to as "interval VWAP." The VWAP is the sum of the total dollar value of the benchmark trades divided by the total quantity of the trades. The VWAP transaction cost estimate formula is as follows:

VWAP transaction cost estimate =

$$\text{Trade size} \times \begin{cases} \text{Trade VWAP} - \text{VWAP benchmark} & \text{for buy orders} \\ \text{VWAP benchmark} - \text{Trade VWAP} & \text{for sell orders} \end{cases}$$

The VWAP transaction cost estimate is popular in part because it is easy to interpret. It answers this question: Did you get a better or worse average price than all traders trading when you were trading?

Interpreting VWAP transaction cost estimates is problematic when the trades being evaluated are a substantial fraction of all trades in the VWAP benchmark, or, more generally, when the trades took place at the same rate as other trades in the market. In both cases, the Trade VWAP and the VWAP benchmark will be nearly equal, which would suggest that the evaluated trades were not costly. But this conclusion would be misleading if the trade had substantial price impact. For example, if a large trader were the only buyer for a given trading period (or interval), the VWAP transaction cost estimate would be zero regardless of the market impact.

This bias toward zero helps explain why the measure is so popular. Investment managers like to show their investment sponsors transaction cost estimates that suggest that trading is not expensive.

EXAMPLE 1

Transaction Cost Analyses for an Illiquid Stock

Arapahoe Tanager, portfolio manager of a Canadian small-cap equity mutual fund, and his firm's chief trader, Lief Schrader, are reviewing the execution of a ticket to sell 12,000 shares of Alpha Company, limit C$9.95. The order was traded over the day.

Schrader split the ticket into three orders that executed that day as follows:

A. A market order to sell 2,000 shares executed at a price of C$10.15. Upon order submission, the market was C$10.12 bid for 3,000 shares, 2,000 shares offered at C$10.24.

B. A market order to sell 3,000 shares executed at a price of C$10.11. Upon order submission, the market was C$10.11 bid for 3,000 shares, 2,000 shares offered at C$10.22.

C. Toward the end of the trading day, Schrader submitted an order to sell the remaining 7,000 shares, limit C$9.95. The order executed in part, with 5,000 shares trading at an average price of C$10.01. Upon order submission, the market was C$10.05 bid for 3,000 shares, 2,000 shares offered at C$10.19. This order exceeded the quoted bid size and "walked down" the limit order book (i.e., after the market bid was filled, the order continued to sell at lower prices). After the market closed, Schrader allowed the order to cancel. Tanager did want to sell the 2,000 unfilled shares on the next trading day.

Only two other trades in Alpha Company occurred on this day: 2,000 shares at C$10.20 and 1,000 shares at C$10.15. The last trade price of the day was C$9.95; it was C$9.50 on the following day.

1. For each of the three fund trades, compute the quoted spread. Also, compute the average quoted spreads prevailing at the times of each trade.

Solution:

The quoted spread is the difference between the ask and bid prices. For the first order, the quoted spread is C$10.24 – C$10.12 = C$0.12. Similarly, the quoted spreads for the second and third orders are C$0.11 and C$0.14, respectively. The average quoted spread is (C$0.12 + C$0.11 + C$0.14)/3 = C$0.1233.

2. For each of the three fund trades, compute the effective spread (use the average fill price for the third trade). Also, compute the average effective spread.

Solution:

The effective spread for a sell order is 2 × (Midpoint of the market at the time of order entry – Trade price). For the first order, the midpoint of the market at the time of order entry is (C$10.12 + C$10.24)/2 = C$10.18, so that the effective spread is 2 × (C$10.18 – C$10.15) = C$0.06.

The effective spread for the second order is 2 × [(C$10.11 + C$10.22)/2 – C$10.11] = C$0.11.
The effective spread for the third order is 2 × [(C$10.05 + C$10.19)/2 – C$10.01] = C$0.22.
The average effective spread is (C$0.06 + C$0.11 + C$0.22)/3 = C$0.13.

3. Explain the relative magnitudes of quoted and effective spreads for each of the three fund trades.

Solution:

The first trade received price improvement because the shares sold at a price above the bid price. Therefore, the effective spread is less than the quoted spread. No price improvement occurred for the second trade because the shares sold at the bid price. Also, the second trade had no price impact beyond trading at the bid; the entire order traded at the quoted bid. Accordingly, the effective and quoted spreads are equal. The effective spread for the third trade is greater than the quoted spread because the large order size, which was greater than the bid size, caused the order to walk down the limit order book. The average sale price was less than the bid so that the effective spread was higher than the quoted spread.

4. Calculate the VWAP for all 13,000 Alpha Company shares that traded that day and for the 10,000 shares sold by the mutual fund. Compute the VWAP transaction cost estimate for the 10,000 shares sold.

Solution:

The VWAP for the day is the total dollar volume divided by the total number of shares traded. The dollar volume is 2,000 shares × C$10.15 + 3,000 shares × C$10.11 + 5,000 shares × C$10.01 + 2,000 shares × C$10.20 + 1,000 shares at C$10.15 = C$131,230. Dividing this by the 13,000-share total volume gives a VWAP of C$10.0946. A similar calculation using only the sales made by the mutual fund gives a trade VWAP of C$10.0680. The VWAP transaction cost estimate for the sale is the difference multiplied by the 10,000 shares sold: C$266.15 = 10,000 shares × (C$10.0946 − C$10.0680) [differences due to rounding].

DEVELOPMENT OF ELECTRONIC MARKETS

3

☐ | describe factors driving the development of electronic trading systems

☐ | describe market fragmentation

The application of new information technologies to trading processes produced radical changes in how investment managers trade. Automated trading systems and trading strategies replaced manual processes. New electronic exchanges, alternative trading systems, electronic traders, and securities dramatically changed trading in most markets. The resulting efficiencies generally improved market quality, but electronic trading also produced new regulatory concerns. High levels of fragmentation and electronification now characterize most global trading markets.

Electronic Trading

Trading at organized exchanges now depends critically on automated electronic systems used both by exchanges and by their trader clients. The exchanges use electronic systems to arrange trades by matching orders submitted by buyers with those submitted by sellers. Traders use electronic systems to generate the orders that the exchanges process. The most important electronic traders are dealers, arbitrageurs, and buy-side institutional traders who use algorithmic trading tools provided by their brokers to fill their large orders.

The two types of systems are co-dependent: Traders need high-speed order processing and communication systems to implement their electronic trading strategies, and the exchanges need electronic exchange systems to process the vast numbers of orders that these electronic traders produce. The adoption of electronic exchange systems led to huge growth in automated order creation and submission systems.

The widespread use of electronic trading systems significantly decreased trading costs for buy-side traders. Costs fell as exchanges obtained greater cost efficiencies from using electronic matching systems instead of floor-based, manual trading systems. These technologies also decreased costs and increased efficiencies for the dealers and arbitrageurs, who provide much of the liquidity offered at exchanges. Competition forced them to pass along many of the benefits of their new technologies to buy-side traders in the form of narrower spreads quoted for larger sizes. New electronic buy-side order management systems also decreased buy-side trading costs by allowing a smaller number of buy-side traders to process more orders and to process them more efficiently than manual traders.

Advantages of Electronic Trading Systems

Compared with floor-based trading systems, electronic order-matching systems enjoy many advantages:

- Most obviously, electronic systems are cheap to operate once built. Operating in server rooms, they require less physical space than trading floors. Also, in contrast to floor-based trading systems, electronic trading systems do not require exchange officials to record and report prices.

- Electronic exchange systems do exactly what they are programmed to do. When properly programmed, they precisely enforce the exchange's trading order precedence and pricing rules without error or exception.

- Electronic exchange systems can also keep perfect audit trails so that forensic investigators can determine the exact sequence and timing of events that may interest them.

- Electronic exchange systems that support hidden orders keep those orders perfectly hidden. Unlike floor brokers, they never inadvertently or fraudulently reveal their clients' hidden orders to others.

- In contrast to floor-based brokers and exchange officials, electronic order-matching systems can operate, for the most part, on a continuous, "around-the-clock" basis.

- Finally, electronic exchanges can operate when bad weather or other events would likely prevent workers from convening on a floor.

These efficiencies led to great growth. Electronic trading systems have largely displaced floor-based trading systems in all instruments for which order-driven markets are viable. Order-driven markets—markets in which orders submitted by traders are arranged based on a rules-based, order-matching system run by an exchange, a broker, or an alternative trading system (ATS)—are now organized by most exchanges and electronic communication networks (ECNs).

Additionally, computers have come to dominate the implementation of many trading strategies because they are so efficient and so unlike human traders:

- Computers have infinite attention spans and a very wide attention scope. They can continuously watch and respond to information from many instruments and many markets simultaneously and essentially forever.

- Their responses are extraordinarily fast.

- Computers are perfectly disciplined and do only what they are instructed (programmed) to do.

- Computers do not forget any information that their programmers want to save.

Electronification of Bond Markets

The electronic market structures of equity, futures, and options markets have attracted tremendous attention throughout the world. Much less attention has been given to the market structures of corporate and municipal bond markets, most of which, from the customer's point of view, have changed little since the late 19th century. Despite the efforts of many creative developers of electronic bond trading systems, most public investors in these markets still trade largely over the counter with dealers. The potential for electronic trading systems in these markets—and the attendant growth in electronic trading strategies—is quite large. Such systems undoubtedly will reflect the fact that bond issues—especially municipal bonds—vastly outnumber stock issues. Accordingly, except for the most actively traded bonds, limit order book trading systems will not be successful because buyers and sellers rarely will be present at the same time.

However, systems can be built that would allow public investors to trade with each other when both sides are present in the market. These systems would provide order display facilities, where public investors and proprietary traders could post limit orders so that all traders could see them. Like marketable orders, limit orders seek to obtain the best price immediately available; additionally, they instruct not to accept a price higher than a specified limit price when buying or a price lower than a specified limit price when selling. If these facilities also had automatic execution mechanisms and regulations or legal decisions to prevent dealers from trading through displayed orders when arranging their trades, bond transaction costs would drop substantially and bond trading would become much more active. Many such electronic bond order-matching systems already exist, but they primarily serve dealers and not public investors. Recent empirical research suggests that public investors would greatly benefit if their brokers provided them with direct access to these systems as they presently do in the equity markets. Instead, most broker/dealers commonly interpose themselves.

Market Fragmentation

Markets for many asset classes have become increasingly fragmented throughout the world because venues trading the same instruments have proliferated and trading in any given instrument now occurs in multiple venues. Available liquidity for an instrument on any one exchange now often represents just a small fraction of the aggregate liquidity for that instrument. **Market fragmentation**—trading the same instrument in multiple venues—increases the potential for price and liquidity disparities across venues because buyers and sellers often are not in the same venues at the same time.

For example, in the United States, order flow in exchange-listed equities is now divided among 11 exchanges, 40 alternative trading systems, and numerous dealers. In the late 20th century, however, trading mainly occurred on three primary exchanges, a few minor regional exchanges, and in the offices of some large institutional broker/dealers. Alternative trading systems (ATSs), also known as electronic communication networks (ECNs) or multilateral trading facilities (MTFs), are increasingly important trading venues. They function like exchanges but do not exercise regulatory authority over their subscribers except concerning the conduct of their trading in their trading systems.

With increasing market fragmentation, traders filling large orders now adapt their trading strategies to search for liquidity across multiple venues and across time to control the market impacts of their trades. Electronic algorithmic trading techniques, such as liquidity aggregation and smart order routing, help traders manage the challenges and opportunities presented by fragmentation. Liquidity aggregators create "super books" that present liquidity across markets for a given instrument. These tools offer global views of market depth (available liquidity) for each instrument regardless of which trading venue offers the liquidity. For example, the best bid, or highest price a buyer is willing to pay, for a Eurodollar future may be on the Chicago Mercantile Exchange (CME) and the second best on ELX Markets, a fully electronic futures exchange. Smart order-routing algorithms send orders to the markets that display the best-quoted prices and sizes.

Effects on Transaction Costs

Numerous studies show that transaction costs declined with the growth of electronic trading over time. Some studies also show that at a given point in time, lower transaction costs are found in those markets with the greatest intensity of electronic trading. These time-series and cross-sectional results are not surprising. They result from the greater cost efficiencies associated with electronic trading.

With the growth of electronic trading, bid–ask spreads decreased substantially. These decreases lowered transaction costs for retail traders and institutions trading small orders.

Overall transaction costs also decreased for large orders, many of which are now broken into smaller parts for execution. A study of the execution costs of tens of thousands of equity orders for US stocks involving tens of millions of dollars of principal value shows that the implementation shortfall cost of filling those orders dropped with the growth of electronic trading. This evidence suggests that any profits obtained by parasitic traders from front running orders are smaller than the cost savings obtained by buy-side traders from trading in electronic markets using algorithms.

4   TYPES OF ELECTRONIC TRADERS

☐ | identify and contrast the types of electronic traders

The proliferation of electronic exchange trading systems has led to the adoption of electronic trading by proprietary traders, buy-side traders, and the electronic brokers that serve them. Proprietary traders include dealers, arbitrageurs, and various types of front runners—all of whom are profit-motivated traders. In contrast, buy-side traders trade to fill orders for investment and risk managers who use the markets to establish positions from which they derive various utilitarian and profit-motivated benefits. Electronic brokers serve both types of traders.

Electronic traders differ in how they send orders to markets. Those proprietary traders who are registered as broker/dealers usually send their orders directly to exchanges. Those who are not broker/dealers must send their orders to brokers, who then forward them to exchanges. These brokers are said to provide sponsored access to their proprietary electronic trader clients. Brokers who provide sponsored access have very fast electronic order processing systems that allow them to forward orders to exchanges as quickly as possible while still undertaking the regulatory functions necessary to protect the markets and themselves from various financial and operational risks associated with brokering orders for proprietary electronic traders.

Electronic trading strategies are most profitable or effective when they can act on new information quickly. Accordingly, proprietary traders and electronic brokers build automated trading systems that are extremely fast. These systems often can receive information of interest to the trader, process it, and place a trading instruction at an exchange in less than a few milliseconds—and sometimes much faster.

The events that interest electronic traders include:

- trade reports and quote changes in the securities or contracts that they trade;

- similar data for instruments that are correlated with the securities or contracts that they trade;

- indexes that summarize these data across markets and for various instrument classes;

- changes in limit order books; and

- news releases from companies, governments, and other producers and aggregators of information.

Electronic traders typically receive information about these events via high-speed electronic data feeds. Not all electronic traders analyze all these different information sources, but many do.

Electronic proprietary traders include high-frequency traders and low-latency traders. High-frequency and low-latency (i.e., extremely fast) traders must often trade very quickly in response to new information to be profitable. They are distinguished by how often they trade.

High-frequency traders (HFTs) generally complete round trips composed of a purchase followed by a sale (or a sale followed by a purchase) within a minute and often as quickly as a few milliseconds. During a day, they may trade in and out of an actively traded security or contract more than a thousand times—but usually only in small sizes.

Low-latency traders include news traders who trade on electronic news feeds and certain parasitic traders. Parasitic traders are speculators who base their predictions about future prices on information they obtain about orders that other traders intend, or will soon intend, to fill. Parasitic traders include front runners, who trade in front of traders who demand liquidity, and quote matchers, who trade in front of traders who supply liquidity. When trying to open or close positions, low-latency traders often need to send or cancel orders very quickly in response to new information. In contrast to HFTs, low-latency traders may hold their positions for as long as a day and sometimes longer.

The distinction between HFTs and low-latency traders is relatively new. Many commentators do not make any distinction, calling all electronic traders who need to trade quickly HFTs.

The Major Types of Electronic Traders

Electronic news traders subscribe to high-speed electronic news feeds that report news releases made by corporations, governments, and other aggregators of information. They then quickly analyze these releases to determine whether the information they contain will move the markets and, if so, in which direction. They trade on this information by sending marketable orders—instructions to fill the order at the best available price—to wherever they expect they may be filled. News traders profit when they can execute against stale orders—orders that do not yet reflect the new information.

For example, stock prices usually rise when a company announces earnings of 25 pence a share when the consensus forecast is only 10 pence. Electronic news traders who receive the initial press release will use their computers to parse the text of the release to find the earnings number. The computers then will compare that number with the consensus forecast, which they have stored in their memory rather than on disk to reduce access time. If the 15 pence difference is sufficiently large, news traders may send one or more marketable buy orders to exchanges for execution. News traders must be very quick to ensure that they get to the market before others do. If they are too late, the price may have changed already or liquidity suppliers may have canceled their quotes.

Some news traders also process news releases that do not contain quantitative data. Using natural language-processing techniques, they try to identify the importance of the information for market valuations. For example, a report stating that "our main pesticide plant shut down because of the accidental release of poisonous chemicals" might be marked as having strong negative implications for values. Electronic news traders would sell on this information. If they are correct, the market will drop as other, slower traders read, interpret, and act on the information. If they are wrong, the market will not react to the information. In that case, news traders will reverse their position and lose the transaction costs associated with their round-trip trades. (Note that these transaction costs could be high if many news traders made the same wrong inference.) Because round-trip transaction costs usually are lower than the profits that electronic news traders can occasionally make when significant news arrives, news traders often may trade with the expectation of being right only occasionally.

Electronic dealers, like all dealers, make markets by placing bids (prices at which they are willing to buy) and offers (prices at which they are willing to sell) with the expectation that they can profit from round trips at favorable net spreads. Those who trade at the highest frequencies tend to be very wary. On the first indication that prices may move against their inventory positions (i.e., price decreases if they are long or own the asset; price increases if they are short or sold an asset they do not own), they immediately take liquidity by executing on the opposite side to reduce their exposure. They generally will not hold large inventory positions in actively traded stocks. As soon as they reach their inventory limit on one side of the market or the other, they cease bidding or offering on that side. Electronic dealers often monitor electronic news feeds. They may immediately cancel all their orders in any security mentioned in a news report. If the news is material, they do not want to offer liquidity to news traders to whom they would lose. If the news is immaterial, they merely lose whatever opportunity to trade may have come their way while out of the market.

Electronic dealers, like all other dealers, also keep track of scheduled news releases. They cancel their orders just before releases to avoid offering liquidity to traders who can act faster than they can. They also may try to reduce their inventories before a scheduled release to avoid holding a risky position.

Electronic arbitrageurs look across markets for arbitrage opportunities in which they can buy an undervalued instrument and sell a similar overvalued one. The combination of these two positions is called an arbitrage portfolio, and the positions are called legs. Electronic arbitrageurs try to construct their arbitrage portfolios at minimum cost and risk.

Electronic front runners are low-latency traders who use artificial intelligence methods to identify when large traders, or many small traders, are trying to fill orders on the same side of the market. They will purchase when they believe that an imbalance of buy orders over sell orders will push the market up and sell when they believe the opposite. Their order anticipation strategies try to identify predictable patterns in order submission. They may search for patterns in order submissions, trades, or the relations between trades and other events.

In most jurisdictions, dealers and brokers cannot legally front run orders that their clients have submitted. These orders include large orders that they know their clients are breaking up to fill in small pieces. But dealers and brokers can study records of their clients' past orders to identify patterns in their behavior that would allow them to predict orders not yet submitted.

Some front runners also look for patterns in executed trades. For example, suppose that a trader sees that trades of a given size have been occurring at the offer every 10 minutes for an hour. If the trader has seen this pattern of trading before, the trader may suspect that the activity will continue. If so, the trader may buy on the assumption that a trader is in the market filling a large buy order by breaking it into smaller pieces.

Buy-side traders, and the brokers who provide them with algorithms to manage large orders, are aware of the efforts that electronic traders make to detect and front run their orders. Accordingly, they randomize their strategies to make them more difficult to detect. They submit orders at random times instead of at regular intervals, and they submit various sizes instead of the same size. Although these techniques make detection more difficult, hiding large, liquidity-demanding trades is always challenging because sophisticated traders can ultimately identify them by the inevitable relation between prices and volumes that they create. Electronic front runners look for these patterns, often using very advanced, automated data-mining tools.

Finally, some front runners examine the relation between trades and other events to predict future trades. Traders who identify these events quickly may be able to profit by buying ahead of retail or institutional traders. Because many traders initiate trades in response to common stimuli or in response to predictable situations, traders who can identify patterns in the relations between trades and events may profit from trading ahead. When the time between the stimulus and the response is short, electronic traders have a clear advantage.

Electronic quote matchers try to exploit the option values of standing orders. Standing orders are limit orders waiting to be filled. Options to trade are valuable to quote matchers because they allow them to take positions with potentially limited losses. Quote matchers buy when they believe they can rely on standing buy orders to get out of their positions, and they sell when they can do the same with standing sell orders. Traders say that quote matchers lean on these orders. If prices then move in the quote matchers' favor, they profit for as long as they stay in the security or contract. But if the quote matchers conclude that prices are moving against them, they immediately try to exit by trading with the standing orders and thereby limiting their losses.

For example, a fast quote matcher may buy when a slow trader is bidding at 20. If the price subsequently rises, the quote matcher will profit. If the quote matcher believes that the price will fall, the quote matcher will sell the position to the buyer at 20 and thereby limit his losses. The main risk of the quote-matching strategy is that the standing order may be unavailable when the quote matcher needs it. Standing orders disappear when filled by another trader or when canceled.

Most large buy-side traders use electronic order management systems (OMSs) to manage their trading. These systems keep track of the orders that their portfolio managers want to be filled, which orders have been sent out to be filled, and which fills have been obtained. Buy-side OMSs generally allow the buy-side trader to route orders to brokers for further handling, along with instructions for how the orders should be handled. These entities may include exchanges, brokers, dealers, and various alternative trading systems. The OMSs typically have dashboards that allow the buy-side trader to see summaries of all activity of interest so that the trader can better manage the trading process. Finally, the OMSs help the buy-side traders report and confirm the trades to all interested parties.

Buy-side traders often employ electronic brokers to arrange their trades. In addition to supporting standard order instructions, such as limit or market orders, these brokers often provide a full suite of advanced orders, trading tactics, and algorithms. The broker's electronic trading system generally manages these advanced orders, tactics, and algorithms, but in some cases, exchange computers may perform these functions.

ELECTRONIC TRADING SYSTEM: CHARACTERISTICS AND USES

5

☐ describe characteristics and uses of electronic trading systems

☐ describe comparative advantages of low-latency traders

Traders value speed because it allows them to act before other traders can act. This section identifies the three situations where speed is valuable, how exchanges and traders build and use fast trading systems, and some select examples of how electronic trading changed trading strategies.

Why Speed Matters

Electronic traders must be fast to trade effectively, regardless of whether they are proprietary traders or buy-side traders. Electronic traders have three needs for speed:

1. **Taking**. Electronic traders sometimes want to take a trading opportunity before others do. A new trading opportunity may attract many traders, and an existing trading opportunity may attract many traders when market events cause it to become more valuable (e.g., a standing limit order to sell becomes much more attractive when the prices of correlated securities rise). Often only the first trader to reach the attractive opportunity will benefit. Thus, electronic traders must be fast so they can beat other traders to attractive trading opportunities.

2. **Making**. Market events often create attractive opportunities to offer liquidity. For example, at most exchanges when prices rise, the first traders to place bids at improved prices acquire time precedence at those prices that may allow them to trade sooner or at better prices than they otherwise would be able to trade. Therefore, electronic traders must be fast so they can acquire priority when they want it and before other traders do.

3. **Canceling**. Frequently, traders must quickly cancel orders they no longer want to fill, often because market events have increased the option values of those orders. For example, if traders have limit buy orders standing at the best bid and large trades take place at other exchanges at the same price, these traders may reasonably conclude that prices may drop and that they may obtain better executions at a lower price. They must cancel their orders as quickly as possible to reduce the probability that they will trade.

Note that electronic traders do not simply need to be fast to trade effectively: They must be faster than their competitors. Little inherent value comes from being fast; the value lies in being faster. The reason electronic trading systems have such low latencies (i.e., are extremely fast) is because electronic traders have been trying for years to be faster than their competitors.

Electronic order-handling systems used by exchanges also have grown faster as exchanges compete for order flows from electronic traders. Electronic traders often will not send orders to exchanges where they cannot quickly cancel them, especially if other exchanges have faster trading systems. Accordingly, exchanges with slow order-handling systems have lost market share.

Latency is the elapsed time between the occurrence of an event and a subsequent action that depends on that event. For example, the event might be a trade at one exchange, and the action might be the receipt by another exchange of an instruction to cancel a standing order that a trader has sent upon learning of the trade. Electronic traders measure these latencies in milliseconds or microseconds (millionths of a second).

The latency of a linear multi-step process is the sum of the latencies of each step in the process. The submission of an order instruction by a trader in response to an event consists of three major steps, each of which involves many smaller steps beyond the scope of this discussion:

1. The trader must learn that the event took place.

2. The trader must respond to the new information with a new order instruction.

3. The trader must send, and the exchange must receive, the new instruction.

Traders must use very fast communication systems to minimize the latencies associated with steps 1 and 3 (communicating in and out), and they must use very fast computer systems to minimize the latency associated with step 2 (responding).

Fast Communications

Electronic traders and brokers use several strategies to minimize their communication times. These strategies involve minimizing communication distances and maximizing line speeds. Note that the relevant measure of communication distance is the total of two distances that signals must travel. The first distance is from where the event is reported (often an exchange but sometimes another type of news source) to the computer that will process the information. The second distance is from the computer to the exchange trading system where the trader wants to deliver an order instruction.

Electronic traders and brokers locate their computers as close as possible to the exchanges at which they trade to minimize latencies resulting from physics: No message can travel faster than the speed of light. At 300,000 kilometers (186,000 miles) per second in a vacuum, light travels 300 kilometers in a millisecond. Although the speed of light is incredibly fast, a fast computer with a clock speed of 5 GHz (billion cycles per second) can do 5 million operations in a millisecond—which often is more than required to receive information, process it, and send out an order instruction in response.

Communication latencies are particularly important when messages must travel significant distances. For example, the great circle (shortest) distances between Chicago and New York and between New York and London are, respectively, 1,146 kilometers and 5,576 kilometers. Thus, round-trip communications between these two pairs of cities have minimum latencies of approximately 8 and 37 milliseconds simply because of the speed of light. (The actual minimum latencies are longer because the speed of light in standard optical fiber is 31% slower than the speed of light in a vacuum.) Such delays illustrate that no electronic trader located at any significant distance from where information is created or must be delivered can effectively compete with traders who have minimized these combined distances.

Many exchanges allow electronic traders to place their servers in the rooms where the exchange servers operate, a practice called collocation. Exchanges charge substantial fees for collocation space and related services, such as air conditioning and power. Note that even within collocation centers, concerns about fairness dictate that the communication lines connecting proprietary servers to exchange servers all be of the same length for all customers buying the same class of collocation service.

Electronic traders and brokers also use the fastest communication technologies they can obtain to collect and transmit information when any distance separates the places where information events occur from the places where they act on those events. To that end, they use the fastest and most direct communication lines that are available. For example, they prefer line-of-sight microwave channels to fiber-optic and copper channels because of the differences in speed of electromagnetic wave propagation through these materials. (Microwaves travel through air at just slightly below the speed of light, whereas signals travel through fiber-optic channels and copper wires only two-thirds as quickly.) They also ensure that their communications pass through the fewest electronic routers and switches possible because passage through each of these devices adds its latency to the total latency of the line.

Finally, electronic traders and brokers subscribe to special high-speed data feeds directly from exchanges and other data vendors. The vendors charge premium prices for these services, which are delivered over very high-speed communication lines. Some exchanges provide multiple classes of data services that vary by speed to price-discriminate among their clients.

Fast Computations

Once electronic traders receive information about an event of interest, they must decide whether to act on that information and how. Those traders who can make decisions faster than their competitors will trade more profitably. Electronic traders minimize the latencies associated with their decision making by using several strategies.

First and most obviously, they use very fast computers. They overclock their processors (i.e., run them faster than the processor designers intended) and use liquid cooling systems to keep them from melting. They store all information in fast memory to avoid the latencies associated with physical disk drives, which cannot deliver information while their heads are seeking the right track and can only deliver information as fast as their disks spin once the right track is found. They sometimes use specialized processors designed to solve their specific trading problems quickly, and they may even use processors etched on gallium arsenide rather than silicon.

Electronic traders also must run very efficient software. They often use simple and specialized operating systems to avoid the overhead associated with supporting operating system functions they do not use. Remarkably, many electronic trading systems run under variants of the original MS-DOS operating system because of its simplicity.

Electronic traders optimize their computer code for speed. They often write important functions that they repeatedly use in assembler language to ensure that they run quickly. (Code written in high-level languages, such as C++, tends to be slower because their compilers are designed to handle all types of code, not just code written to solve trading problems.) And they avoid using such languages as Python because they are interpreter languages that compile (create executable machine code) as they run, rather than compiling only once when first written.

Some electronic trading problems change so frequently that speed of coding is more important than speed of execution. For example, some problems depend on ever-changing sets of conditions or exceptions that present or constrain profit opportunities. For such problems, traders use high-level languages (e.g., Python), because they can code faster and more accurately in these languages than in lower-level languages, such as C++. If they expect that the software will remain useful, they may later recode their routines in other languages to make them run faster.

Some electronic traders also reduce latency by creating contingency tables that contain prearranged action plans. For example, suppose that a bid rises in a market in which electronic traders are active. In response to the increased bid, traders may want to raise their bids or offers. The decision to do so may depend on their inventory positions and perhaps on many other factors as well. To decide what to do following an increased bid may require substantial analyses, which take time. Traders can reduce their decision latencies by doing these analyses before the bid increases instead of afterward. Seeing the increased bid, they can respond by simply looking up the optimal response in a contingency table stored in memory. To be most useful, the contingency tables must be kept up to date and must include responses for most-likely events. In this example, traders presumably would also have precomputed responses for a decrease in the bid, among many other contingencies.

EXAMPLE 2

Latency

1. Explain why low-latency is important to electronic traders.

Solution:

Electronic traders need a comparative speed advantage to 1) take advantage of market opportunities before others do, 2) receive time precedence that would allow them to trade sooner when offering liquidity to others, and 3) ensure order cancellation when they no longer want to fill the order. To gain a comparative advantage relative to others, electronic traders try to minimize latency—the time between an event occurring and a subsequent action, typically the submission of an order instruction, based upon that event. To minimize latency, electronic traders invest in very fast communication systems and very fast computer systems.

Advanced Orders, Tactics, and Algorithms

Buy-side traders often use electronic brokers and their systems for advanced orders, trading tactics, and algorithms provided by their electronic brokers to search for liquidity.

Advanced order types.

Advanced orders generally are limit orders with limit prices that change as market conditions change. An example would be a pegged limit order for which the trader would like to maintain a bid or an offer at a specified distance relative to some benchmark. Suppose that a trader wants to peg a limit buy order two ticks below the current ask. A broker who supports this instruction may forward it to an exchange that supports the instruction if the probability of the order's filling at that exchange is favorable compared with other exchanges. When the ask rises or falls, the exchange system will immediately cancel the order and replace it with a new limit order to keep the order at two ticks below the current ask. If the exchange does not support this instruction, the broker's computer will manage the order by submitting a limit order priced two ticks below the current ask and adjusting it as necessary to maintain the peg when the market moves. Effective management of a pegged limit order requires an electronic trading system with very low latency. If the order is not adjusted quickly enough, it risks being executed at an unfavorable price (in this example, if prices drop) or being resubmitted after other orders have been placed at the new price so the probability of execution at that price will be lower (if prices rise). Traders sometimes call pegged limit orders floating limit orders.

Trading tactics.

A trading tactic is a plan for executing a simple function that generally involves the submission of multiple orders. Note that the distinction between advanced orders and tactics can be arbitrary, and not all traders will use the same language to describe various trading functions. An example of a trading tactic is an instruction to sweep through every market at a given price to find hidden trading opportunities.

Suppose that the best exposed bid among all trading venues is 20.00 and the best exposed offer is 20.02. Because many trading systems permit traders to hide their orders, hidden buyers or sellers may be willing to trade at the 20.01 midpoint. Depending on the exchange, at least three types of orders could permit a trade at the midpoint. First, among exchanges that permit hidden orders, one or more exchanges may be holding a hidden limit order at 20.01. Second, among exchanges that permit discretionary limit orders, one or more exchanges may be holding a discretionary limit order that can be filled at the midpoint. For example, suppose that an exchange is holding a limit order to buy at 19.99 with 0.02 discretion. This order can be filled at 20.01 if a suitable sell limit order arrives at that price. Finally, among exchanges and dark pools that permit midspread orders, one or more exchanges or dark pools may be holding such an order. Dark pools are trading venues that do not publish their liquidity and are only available to selected clients. A midspread order is a limit order that is pegged to the midpoint of the quoted bid–ask spread.

To find such hidden liquidity, an electronic trading system may submit an immediate or cancel (IOC) order priced at 20.01 to the exchange that the trader expects will most likely have hidden liquidity on the needed side of the market. If such liquidity exists, the order will execute up to the minimum of the sizes of the two orders. If not, the exchange will immediately cancel the order and report the cancellation. If the order has any remaining unfilled size, the electronic trading system will search for liquidity at another exchange. This process will continue until the order is filled or until the trader decides that further search is probably futile. This sweeping tactic is most effective when the electronic trading system managing it has very low latency. A slow system may lose an opportunity to trade if someone else takes it first. Also, a slow system that obtains one or more partial fills may lose opportunities to trade at other exchanges if the proprietary electronic trading systems managing the standing orders that provide those opportunities cancel their standing orders when they suspect someone is sweeping the market, as they might if they see trade reports inside the quoted spread.

An example of another trading tactic is placing a limit order at some price with the hope that it will fill at that price. If the order does not fill after some time period (which might be random or based on information), the electronic trading system will cancel the order and resubmit it with an improved price (i.e., a higher price for a buy order or a lower price for a sell order). The process is repeated until the order fills.

Algorithms.

Algorithms ("algos" for short) are programmed strategies for filling orders. Algorithms may use combinations or sequences of simple orders, advanced orders, or multiple orders to achieve their objectives. Buy-side traders use algorithms, often provided by brokers, extensively to trade small orders and to reduce the price impacts of large trades. For example, many algorithms break up large orders and submit the pieces to various markets over time. Breaking up orders makes it difficult for other traders to infer that a trader is trying to fill a large order. The algorithms typically submit the orders at random times, in random sizes, and sometimes to randomly selected exchanges to hide their common origin.

The rates at which algorithms try to fill large orders may depend on market volumes or on elapsed time. For example, VWAP algorithms attempt to obtain a volume-weighted average fill price that is close to (or better than) the volume-weighted average price (VWAP) of all trades arranged within a prespecified time interval. To minimize the variation between the actual average fill price and the VWAP over the interval, these algorithms try to participate in an equal fraction of all trading volume throughout the interval. To do so, they forecast volumes based on the historical volume profile and on current volumes. The algorithm trades more during periods of historically high volume (e.g., around market open and close) and when the market has been more active than normal. It trades less during periods of relatively low volume. In practice, the execution rate will vary because volumes will differ from expectations. Buy-side traders use VWAP algorithms when spreading the order over time and when obtaining the average market price within an interval is acceptable to them or their portfolio managers.

Many algorithms use floating limit orders with the hope of obtaining cheap executions. If they fail to fill after some time period, they may switch to more-aggressively priced orders or to marketable orders to ensure that they fill. Large traders who use algorithms to manage their orders are especially concerned about hiding their intentions from front runners. Many electronic traders use artificial intelligence systems to detect when large traders are present in the market. In particular, they look for patterns that large traders may leave. For example, a poorly designed algorithm may submit orders exactly at the same millisecond within a second whenever it submits an order. A clever trader who is aware of this regularity may detect when a large trader is in the market and, equally important, when the trader has completed filling his order. To avoid these problems, algorithm designers often randomize order submission times and sizes to avoid producing patterns that might give them away. They also sometimes try to hide their orders among other orders so that front runners cannot easily identify their intentions.

Developing good algorithms requires extensive research into the origins of transaction costs. Algorithm authors must understand transaction costs well so that they can design algorithms that will trade effectively. To that end, algorithm providers build and estimate models of the costs of trading orders of various sizes, models of the impact trades of a given size or frequency will have on prices, and models of the probabilities that limit orders will fill under a variety of conditions. They must also predict volumes accurately. The most effective algorithms are based on the best research and implemented on the fastest and most capable electronic systems.

Good algorithms generally obtain low-cost executions by knowing when and where to offer liquidity via limit orders, when to use market orders, and how to most effectively keep the market from being aware of their efforts. They reduce the price impacts of large trades and greatly reduce the costs of managing many small trades.

EXAMPLE 3

Use of Electronic Brokers

1. You have recently been hired recently as a junior buy-side analyst. Part of your training (on-boarding) has been to sit with the trading desk to learn how the desk trades through its electronic brokers. In a meeting with your manager, she asks you to explain the use of electronic brokers for advanced orders, trading tactics, and algorithmic trading tools that your electronic brokers provide. What would you say?

Solution:

The use of electronic brokers and their systems is valuable for such advanced order types as pegged or floating limit orders, whose limit prices change as market conditions change. Traders use these order types to supply liquidity at a specified distance from the market. These orders require continuous real-time evaluation to determine if an order cancellation or replacement is needed as market conditions change. The use of electronic brokers relieves the need for the trader to continuously monitor the market to cancel and resubmit orders when prices change. An electronic broker is also valuable for orders placed a few ticks outside the best market that will be among the last orders to supply liquidity to a large trader, hopefully at a good price.

Electronic brokers also allow their clients to access order execution tactics (presented as another complex order type) that involve multiple submissions that may "sweep" through markets to uncover hidden liquidity. These tactics allow traders to submit multiple orders with a single instruction.

Finally, electronic brokers also provide algorithmic trading tools. Algorithms are automated (programmed trading strategies for combinations of simple and single, advanced, or multiple orders and various trading tactics) to fill small orders efficiently based on various criteria. They often break up large orders into smaller pieces to minimize the market impact of filling the order. They may route the orders to multiple venues at the same time or to the same venue at various times. For example, VWAP algorithms attempt to fill orders at the volume-weighted average price (or better) of all trades over a specified interval. The systems running algorithms that place standing limit orders must be very fast to cancel orders in trading. In these cases, low latency is critical to ensure order cancellation before unfavorable executions occur. Fast systems also help ensure that traders are first to respond when market conditions change and to maintain time precedence.

Select Examples of How Electronic Trading Changed Trading Strategies

The growth in electronic trading systems changed how traders interact with the market. Proprietary traders, buy-side traders, and brokers adapted their trading strategies to use new electronic tools and facilities. Select characteristics of electronic trading are described below.

Hidden orders.

Hidden orders are very common in electronic markets. Hidden orders are orders that are exposed (or shown) only to the brokers or exchanges who receive them. Traders—especially large traders—submit them when they do not want to reveal the existence of the trading options that their standing orders provide to the markets. Traders concerned about quote matchers can protect themselves to some extent by submitting hidden limit orders. Note that hidden limit orders are the electronic equivalent of giving orders to floor brokers to fill with the understanding that the floor brokers may expose the orders only if they can arrange trades. Such orders work better at electronic exchanges than at floor-based exchanges because computers never inadvertently or intentionally display these orders improperly. In electronic markets, the most common type of order by far is the immediate or cancel (IOC) limit order. Traders use these orders to discover hidden orders that may stand in the spread between a market's quoted bid and ask prices. Because they cancel immediately if they do not find liquidity, these orders are also hidden and thus do not reveal trade intentions.

Some electronic traders try to discover hidden orders by pinging the market: They submit a small IOC limit order for only a few shares at the price at which they are looking for hidden orders. If the pinging order trades, they know that a hidden order is present at that price; however, they do not know the full size of the order (which they can discover only by trading with it). Traders then may use this information to adjust their trading strategies.

All traders who subscribe to a complete trade feed that includes odd-lot transactions (substandard transaction sizes) can see the results of a ping that discovers liquidity. At almost all exchanges, however, only the pinger will know on which side of the market the hidden liquidity lies. Nonetheless, the information produced by someone else's successful ping can be useful to various traders. It indicates that someone in the market is concerned enough about liquidity conditions that pinging is worthwhile and that hidden liquidity is available on one side of the market.

Leapfrog.

When bid–ask spreads are wide, dealers often are willing to trade at better prices than they quote. They quote wide spreads because they hope to trade at more favorable prices. When another trader quotes a better price, dealers often immediately quote an even better price. For example, if the market is 20 bid, offered at 28, and a buy-side trader bids at 21, a dealer might instantly bid at 22. (The improved price might also come from a quote matcher.) This behavior frustrates buy-side traders, who then must quote a better price to maintain order precedence. If the spread is sufficiently wide, a game of leapfrog may ensue as the dealer jumps ahead again.

Flickering quotes.

Electronic markets often have flickering quotes, which are exposed limit orders that electronic traders submit and then cancel shortly thereafter, often within a second. Electronic dealers and algorithmic buy-side traders submit and repeatedly cancel and resubmit their orders when they do not want their orders to stand in the market; rather, they want other traders to see that they are willing to trade at the displayed price. Traders who wish to trade with a flickering quote can place a hidden limit order at the price where the quote is flickering. If the flickering order returns, it will hit their hidden limit order, and then they will trade with it.

Electronic arbitrage.

Electronic arbitrageurs use electronic trading systems to implement three types of arbitrage trading strategies:

1. **Take liquidity on both sides**. The costliest and least risky arbitrage trading strategy involves using marketable orders to fill both legs, or positions (i.e., buying an undervalued instrument and selling a similar overvalued instrument), of the arbitrage portfolio. This strategy is profitable only if the arbitrage spread is sufficiently large, but competition among arbitrageurs ensures that such large arbitrage spreads are quite rare. Arbitrageurs can seldom simultaneously take liquidity in two markets for identical instruments and make a profit. To effectively execute this strategy, arbitrageurs must use very fast trading systems so that they can lock in the arbitrage spread before prices in one or both markets change.

2. **Offer liquidity on one side**. In this strategy, arbitrageurs offer liquidity in one or both markets in which they trade. When they obtain a fill in one market, they immediately take liquidity in the other market to complete the construction of their arbitrage portfolio. This strategy produces lower-cost executions, but it is a bit riskier than the first strategy.

   For example, suppose that Markets A and B are both quoting 20 bid, offered at 21 for the same instrument. An arbitrageur may place a bid at 19 in Market A with the hope that a large seller will come along who takes all liquidity at 20 (i.e., fills all bids at 20) in Market A and then proceeds to fill the arbitrageur's order at 19. If so, the arbitrageur will immediately try to sell to the 20 bid in Market B. If the arbitrageur is quick enough, he may be able to fill his order before the bidder at 20 in Market B cancels that bid and before any other trader—particularly the large trader—takes it. If successful, the arbitrageur realizes a profit of 1. Of course, the arbitrageur will immediately cancel his 19 bid in Market A if the 20 bid in Market B disappears.

3. **Offer liquidity on both sides.** The final arbitrage strategy involves offering liquidity in both markets. In this strategy, after the first order to execute fills, the arbitrageur continues to offer liquidity to complete the second trade. This strategy is the riskiest strategy because arbitrageurs are exposed to substantial price risk when one leg is filled and the other is not. Moreover, if prices are moving because well-informed traders are on the same side in both markets—as they might be if the well-informed traders possess information about common risk factors—the leg providing liquidity to the informed traders will fill quickly, whereas the other leg probably will not fill.

Arbitrageurs using this strategy trade much like dealers—switching from offering (supplying) liquidity to taking (demanding) liquidity when they believe that offering liquidity may be too risky. They may also often cancel and resubmit their orders when market conditions change. Thus, they are most effective when they use fast trading systems.

When the arbitrage spread reverts, as the arbitrageurs expect, the arbitrageurs will reverse their trades, often using the same strategy they used to acquire their arbitrage portfolios. Of course, if the spread never reverts, arbitrageurs will lose regardless of how they trade. They will lose less, however, if they can trade their arbitrage portfolio by offering liquidity in one or both legs.

Machine learning.

Machine learning, also known as data mining, uses advanced statistical methods to characterize data structures, particularly relations among variables. These methods include neural nets, genetic algorithms, classifiers, and other methods designed to explain variables of interest using sparse data or data for which the number of potential explanatory variables far exceeds the number of observations.

Machine-learning methods produce models based on observed empirical regularities rather than on theoretical principles identified by analysts. These methods can be powerful when stable processes generate vast amounts of data, such as occurs in active financial markets.

Many trading problems are ideally suited for machine-learning analyses because the problems repeat regularly and often. For such problems, machine-based learning systems can be extraordinarily powerful.

However, these systems are often useless—or worse—when trading becomes extraordinary (e.g., when volatilities shoot up). Machine-learning systems frequently do not produce useful information during volatility episodes because these episodes have few precedents from which the machines can learn. Thus, traders often instruct their electronic trading systems to stop trading—and sometimes to close out their positions—whenever they recognize that they are entering uncharted territory. Many traders shut down when volatility spikes, both because high-volatility episodes are uncommon and thus not well understood and because even if such episodes were well understood, they represent periods of exceptionally high risk.

6   ELECTRONIC TRADING RISKS

☐ | describe the risks associated with electronic trading and how regulators mitigate them

The advent of electronic trading affected securities markets in many ways. Investors now benefit from greater trade process efficiencies and reduced transaction costs, but electronic trading also creates new systemic risks for market participants.

The HFT Arms Race

The competition among high-frequency traders (HFTs) has created an "arms race" in which each trader tries to be faster than the next. Consequently, the state-of-the-art, high-frequency trading technologies necessary to compete successfully are now very expensive, making entry quite costly. These costs form barriers to entry that can create natural monopolies. Although substantial evidence suggests that electronic trading benefits the markets, these benefits may erode if only a few HFTs survive and can exploit their unique positions. Already, many HFTs are quitting the markets because they cannot compete effectively.

More generally, many commentators have observed that most of the costly technologies that high-frequency traders acquire do little to promote better or more-liquid markets. HFTs primarily incur these costs so they can beat their competitors. The utilitarian traders who demand liquidity ultimately pay these costs. Concerns about the costs of the HFT arms race have led to calls for changes in market structure that would diminish the advantages of being faster. Some commentators suggest that markets be slowed by running call markets once a second or more often instead of trading continuously. Others suggest that the order processing be delayed by random intervals to reduce the benefits of being fast and thus the incentives to invest in speed.

Systemic Risks of Electronic Trading

Electronic trading created new systemic risks that concern regulators and practitioners. A systemic risk is a risk that some failure will hurt more than just the entity responsible for the failure. Systemic risks are particularly problematic when the responsible entity is not required or is unable to compensate others for the costs its failure imposes on them. When people do not bear the full costs of their behaviors, they tend not to be as careful in avoiding damaging behaviors as they otherwise would be.

Systemic risks associated with fast trading may be caused by electronic exchange trading system failures or excessive orders submitted by electronic traders. Electronic exchange trading system failures occur when programmers make mistakes, exchange servers have insufficient capacity to handle traffic, or computer hardware or communication lines fail.

The 18 May 2012 Facebook IPO at NASDAQ is an example of a trading system failure caused by a programming error that unexpectedly high demands on capacity revealed. In this case, two software processes locked into an infinite loop as they took turns responding to each other.

Examples of systemic risks caused by excessive orders submitted by electronic traders include the following:

- *Runaway algorithms* produce streams of unintended orders that result from programming mistakes. The problems sometimes occur when programmers do not anticipate some contingency. The Knight Capital trading failure on 1 August 2012 may be the most extreme example of a runaway algorithm incident. Owing to a software programming mistake, Knight sent millions of orders to the markets over a 45-minute period when it intended only to fill 212 orders, some of which normally might have been broken up but none of which would have generated so many orders. These orders produced 4 million executions involving 397 stocks. Knight lost $400 million in the incident.

- *Fat finger errors* occur when a manual trader submits a larger order than intended. They are called fat finger errors because they sometimes occur when a trader hits the wrong key or hits a key more often than intended. These types of errors are not unique to electronic trading systems, but their consequences are often greater in electronic systems because of the speed at which they operate and because clerks often catch these errors in manual trading systems before they cause problems.

- *Overlarge orders* demand more liquidity than the market can provide. In these events, a trader—often inexperienced—will try to execute a marketable order that is too large for the market to handle without severely disrupting prices in the time given to fill the order. The 6 May 2010 Flash Crash occurred as a result of such an order. The crash was triggered when a large institutional trader tried to sell $4.1 billion in E-mini S&P 500 futures contracts using an algorithm over a short period. The algorithm was designed to participate in a fixed fraction of the market volume. When the initial trades depressed S&P 500 futures prices, trading volumes increased substantially as arbitrageurs and others started to trade. The increase in trading volumes caused the algorithm to increase the rate of its order submissions, which exacerbated the problem. The market reverted to its former levels after the Chicago Mercantile Exchange briefly halted trading in the E-mini S&P 500 futures contract, and the large order eventually was filled.

- *Malevolent order streams* are created deliberately to disrupt the markets. The perpetrators may be market manipulators; aggrieved employees, such as traders or software engineers; or terrorists. Traders conducting denial-of-service attacks designed to overwhelm their competitors' electronic trading systems with excessive quotes also may create malevolent order streams.

The solutions to the systemic risk problems associated with electronic trading systems are multifold:

- Most obviously, traders must test software thoroughly before using it in live trading. Exchanges often conduct mock trading sessions to allow developers to test their software.

- Rigorous market access controls must ensure that only those orders coming from approved sources enter electronic order-matching systems.

- Rigorous access controls on software developers must ensure that only authorized developers can change software. Best practice mandates that these controls also include the requirement that all software be read, understood, and vouched for by at least one developer besides its author.

- The electronic traders who generate orders and the electronic exchanges that receive orders must surveil their order flow in real time to ensure that it conforms to preset parameters that characterize its expected volume, size, and other characteristics. When the order flow is different than expected, automatic controls must shut it off immediately.

- Brokers must surveil all client orders that clients introduce into electronic trading systems to ensure that their clients' trading is appropriate. Brokers must not allow their clients to enter orders directly into exchange trading systems—a process called sponsored naked access—because it would allow clients to avoid broker oversight.

- Some exchanges have adopted price limits and trade halts to stop trading when prices move too quickly. These rules stop trading when excess demands for liquidity occur. They also prevent the extreme price changes that can occur in electronic markets when market orders arrive and no liquidity is present. Most brokers now automatically convert market orders into marketable limit orders to ensure that they do not trade at unreasonable prices.

HISTORICAL EVENT: THE FLASH CRASH

The 6 May 2010 Flash Crash was the most notable market structure event in recent memory. During the crash, which started at about 2:42 p.m. ET, the E-mini S&P 500 futures contract dropped approximately 5% in 5 minutes and then recovered nearly fully in the next 10 minutes. The price volatility spilled from the equity futures market into the stock market, where some stocks traded down more than 99% or up more than 1,000%. In the immediate aftermath of the crash, regulators decided that more than 20,000 trades in more than 300 securities that occurred more than 60% away from earlier prices would be broken (canceled).

This extraordinary event raised many concerns about security market structure—in particular, how the adoption of electronic trading may have increased potential systemic risks. This subsection describes the events that led up to the crash, what happened during the crash, and the regulatory responses to the crash.

The Event and Its Causes

On Thursday, 6 May 2010, the stock market traded down throughout the day at an accelerating rate. By 2:30 p.m., it had lost about 4% from its previous close. Contemporaneous commentators attributed the fall to concerns about Greek sovereign debt and the implications of a Greek default for other markets. During the day, many traders who had been providing liquidity to the market were accumulating substantial long positions as people demanded to sell. As the day wore on, their willingness to continue to accumulate additional inventory decreased. Moreover, day traders, who do not normally carry inventory overnight, also were considering how and when they would sell their losing positions.

Presumably, in response to the European concerns and perhaps other concerns, portfolio managers at Waddell & Reed Financial Inc. (W&R) decided to reduce US equity exposure in their $27 billion Asset Strategy Fund by selling 75,000 June 2010 E-mini S&P 500 futures contracts with a nominal value of approximately $4.1 billion. They gave this order to their buy-side trader, who proceeded to fill it using an algorithm that split the order into small pieces for execution. Although the order was the largest single order submitted to the E-mini futures market that year, it was not without precedent. Two earlier orders in the previous year were of similar size or larger, one of which had been submitted by W&R. Those orders had been filled in more stable markets and over longer periods of time than W&R's 6 May order. The order started to execute at 2:32 p.m.

W&R's head trader, who normally would have handled such a large order, was out of the office that day. Instead, a less-senior trader in his office handled the order.

The trader set parameters on the algorithm to target an execution rate of 9% of the trading volume calculated over the previous minute without regard to price or time. This trading strategy was more aggressive than the one W&R had used to fill its large order from the previous year. The trader probably set an aggressive rate because he feared that the firm would obtain a worse execution if prices continued to fall. The more aggressive strategy contributed to the crash.

When the initial trades depressed S&P 500 futures prices, trading volumes increased substantially as arbitrageurs and others started to trade, many of them trading with each other as they normally did. The arbitrageurs bought the futures and sold equities and equity ETFs (exchange-traded funds), such as the SPDR S&P 500 Trust (ticker SPY). Some arbitrageurs also sold call option contracts and bought put option contracts. The increase in trading volumes caused the algorithm to increase the rate of its order submissions as it tried to keep up with its mandate to participate in 9% of the market volume. The increasing order submission rate exacerbated the problem.

Initially, high-frequency traders and other liquidity suppliers in the E-mini futures markets supplied liquidity to W&R's order and accumulated long positions. Between 2:41 p.m. and 2:44 p.m., these short-term traders sold these positions as the algorithm continued to pump more orders into the market. During this 4-minute period, the E-mini dropped 3%. By the end of this period, buy-side depth (total size of standing buy orders) in the E-mini contract dropped to only 1% of the average depth observed earlier in the day. The E-mini contract then dropped 1.7% in the next 15 seconds.

The arbitrage trades caused the equity markets to drop. In many securities—especially the ETFs—falling prices triggered stock loss market orders, which further depressed prices. The levered ETFs were particularly affected because their high volatilities make them popular with technical traders and retail traders, many of whom routinely place stop orders to protect their positions.

As the prices changed quickly, many traders who were providing liquidity in the futures and equity markets dropped out because they were unwilling to trade in the face of such extreme volatility. Many also had already accumulated large inventory positions from earlier in the day and did not want to buy more. Interestingly, researchers later discovered that the largest and most active high-frequency trading firms did not withdraw. Nonetheless, limit order books thinned out—especially on the buy side—as traders canceled standing orders and as sellers filled those buy orders still standing.

In some stocks, all standing buy orders were exhausted and trading stopped. In other stocks, all buy orders except those placed with a limit price of only a cent or two were exhausted. In these stocks, exchange trading systems blindly filled market sell orders at extraordinarily low prices. In a few other stocks, the withdrawal of liquidity suppliers from the market also removed essentially all liquidity from the sell side of the market. Some stocks then traded at prices as high as $100,000 when market buy orders were filled against sell orders placed at extraordinarily high prices.

The slide stopped at 2:45:28 p.m. when a Chicago Mercantile Exchange trading rule called Stop Logic Functionality caused the exchange's computers to halt trading briefly in the E-mini S&P 500 futures contract and to clear the limit order book of all standing limit orders. The rule is triggered when it becomes apparent that pending order executions would cause prices to jump too far. The futures contract dropped about 5% from when the algorithm started to trade at 2:32 p.m. to the market halt at 2:45 p.m. The algorithm sold about 35,000 contracts during this period.

When trading resumed 5 seconds later, the buy-side algorithm continued to trade, but many liquidity suppliers were now willing to provide liquidity. Prices rose quickly in orderly markets.

The episode largely ended when the big W&R order completed filling at around 2:51 p.m., about 20 minutes after it started. However, the market remained quite volatile during the remainder of the day as traders adjusted their positions and responded to the extreme volatility.

Following the crash, regulators broke all trades that had occurred more than 60% away from the previous close.

Implications for Traders

The Flash Crash provided three important lessons for observant traders:

- First, market orders are incompatible with electronic order-matching systems that do not curb trading when prices move too quickly. Had traders priced all their orders, no trades would have taken place at unreasonably high or low prices. Following the crash, many retail brokers adopted a policy of converting all customer market orders into marketable limit orders with limit prices set about 10% above the current ask for buy orders and 10% below the current bid for sell orders.

- Second, institutional traders using algorithms must be careful not to demand more liquidity than orderly markets can provide. Most buy-side investors probably immediately recognized that W&R lost a substantial amount of its clients' money owing to the extraordinarily high transaction costs associated with the trade. To obtain a crude estimate of this loss, assume that the algorithm traded all $4.1 billion of its order at a uniform rate throughout the 5% price reversal. The average market impact of the trade would have been 2.5%, which implies total transaction costs of about $100 million, or 0.37% of the $27 billion in assets of the W&R Asset Strategy Fund. Such significant losses attract attention. Within a week, many algorithm writers probably coded limits into their algorithms to help prevent them from being used irresponsibly.

- Finally, algorithm writers and the traders who use algorithms must pay much more attention to the dangers of using algorithms that can create destructive feedback loops. They particularly must understand how algorithms respond to market conditions that they may create themselves.

Regulatory Responses

Following the Flash Crash, regulators adopted new rules to prevent a similar crash from happening again. They placed curbs that halt trades in a stock for 5 minutes if prices move up or down by more than 10% for large stocks and 20% for smaller stocks. This rule ensures that prices cannot move too quickly, but it does not prevent traders from behaving foolishly. Had it been in effect during the Flash Crash, the rule would have stopped trades from occurring at ridiculously low or high prices, but it would not have stopped the W&R trader from submitting an unrealistically aggressive order.

Regulators also adopted rules to establish when and which trades will be broken in the event of another extreme price change. Such rules should help ensure that liquidity suppliers who are afraid that their trades may be broken do not withdraw from the market prematurely.

EXAMPLE 4

Electronic Trading and Transaction Costs

1. Describe the impact of electronic trading on transaction costs.

Solution:

Growth in electronic trading has resulted in greater trade process efficiencies and reduced transaction costs for investors. Electronic systems are

> much cheaper to operate than floor-based systems (requiring less physical space and fewer exchange personnel). These systems can operate on a close-to-continuous basis at far greater scale and scope and at much faster speeds than humans. Process efficiencies from electronic trading have led to significant decreases in bid–ask spreads, which have lowered transaction costs for investors.

7 DETECTING ABUSIVE TRADING PRACTICES

☐ | describe abusive trading practices that real-time surveillance of markets may detect

Regulators around the world recognize that real-time market monitoring and surveillance systems allow faster responses to potential crises and market abuses with the potential for rapid intervention to prevent or minimize damages. Many trading venues have long used real-time surveillance technologies, but their use is not consistent across all markets. The goal of real-time market surveillance is to detect potential market abuse while it is happening. Real-time surveillance often can detect the following damaging behaviors:

Front running.

Front running involves buying in front of anticipated purchases and selling in front of anticipated sales. In most jurisdictions, front running is illegal if the front runners acquire their information about orders improperly—for example, by a tip from a broker handling a large order.

Some traders use electronic artificial intelligence systems to identify when traders are filling large orders over time by breaking them up into small pieces. When these traders suspect that buyers or sellers are working large orders, they will trade ahead on the same side with the hope of benefiting when the large traders move prices as they fill their orders. This front-running strategy is legal if the information on which it is based is properly obtained— for example, by watching a market data feed.

Front running increases transaction costs for the traders whose orders are front run because the front runners take liquidity that the front-run traders otherwise would have taken for themselves.

Market manipulation.

In general, market manipulation consists of any trading strategy whose purpose is to produce misleading or false market prices, quotes, or fundamental information to profit from distorting the normal operation of markets. Market manipulators are parasitic traders who attempt to fool or force others into making disadvantageous trades. Many market manipulation strategies exist—including bluffing, squeezing, cornering, and gunning.

In most jurisdictions, market manipulation strategies are illegal. Enforcement is often difficult, however, because the exact infractions can be hard to define and because prosecutors generally must prove scienter (a legal term meaning intent or knowledge of wrongdoing), which can be difficult when defendants suggest alternative explanations for their behavior.

Market manipulation strategies usually involve one or more of the following improper market activities:

- *Trading for market impact* involves trading to raise or lower prices deliberately. A market manipulator often is willing to incur substantial transaction costs to raise or lower the price of a security to influence other traders' perceptions of value.

- *Rumormongering* is the dissemination of false information about fundamental values or about other traders' trading intentions to alter investors' value assessments. Financial analysts must be careful to ensure that they base their analyses on valid information and not on false information designed to fool them into making poor decisions. Note that although rumormongering is illegal in most jurisdictions, simply reporting one side of an issue is not illegal. Financial analysts, therefore, must also be careful to ensure that they base their analyses on balanced information and not on information that is true but selectively presented to them with the purpose of distorting their analyses.

- *Wash trading* consists of trades arranged among commonly controlled accounts to create the impression of market activity at a particular price. The purpose of wash trading is to fool investors into believing that a market is more liquid than it truly is and to thereby increase investors' confidence both in their ability to exit positions without substantial cost and in their assessments of security values. Manipulators also can achieve these purposes by falsely reporting trades that never occurred, which is essentially what happens when they arrange trades among commonly controlled accounts.

- *Spoofing*, also known as *layering*, is a trading practice in which traders place exposed standing limit orders to convey an impression to other traders that the market is more liquid than it is or to suggest to other traders that the security is under- or overvalued. For example, suppose that a spoofer wants to buy stock cheaply or quickly. The spoofer might place a hidden buy order in the market. The spoofer then places one or more exposed sell limit orders in the market to convey the impression that prices may soon fall. Seeing the spoofing sell orders, one or more traders may conclude that values may be lower than market prices suggest. On that basis, they may sell into the spoofer's buy order, enabling the spoofer to obtain a quick and possibly cheaper purchase than the spoofer otherwise would have obtained had the spoofer not placed the spoofing sell orders. Of course, immediately following the execution of the buy order, the spoofer will cancel the sell orders.

  Spoofing is risky because the spoofing orders that spoofers submit might execute before their intended orders execute. Spoofers can manage this risk by keeping track of the orders in the limit order book ahead of their spoofing orders. If these orders fill before the spoofers' intended orders fill, spoofers will cancel their spoofing orders to prevent them from executing. To effectively manage these processes, spoofers use electronic systems to monitor trading and to ensure that they can quickly cancel their orders as soon as they no longer want them to stand.

Market manipulators often use these improper market activities singly or in combination when they try to fool or force other traders into trades that will ultimately prove to be disadvantageous to them. Market manipulation strategies include:

- **Bluffing**. Bluffing involves submitting orders and arranging trades to influence other traders' perceptions of value. Bluffers often prey on momentum traders, who buy when prices are rising and sell when prices are falling. For example, consider typical "pump-and-dump" schemes in which bluffers buy stock to raise its price and thereby encourage momentum traders to buy. The bluffers then sell the stock to the momentum traders at higher prices. To further the scheme, bluffers may engage in such activities as rumormongering or wash trading. Note also that bluffers may time their purchases to immediately follow the release of valid positive information about the security and thereby fool traders into overvaluing the material significance of the new information.

In a pump-and-dump manipulation, the bluffer tries to raise prices. Similar manipulations can occur on the short side, though they are less common. In such manipulations, manipulators take short positions and then try to repurchase shares at lower prices. These manipulations are often called "short and distorts."

To avoid falling into these traps, financial analysts must ensure that they base their analyses on independent assessments of value. Their analyses must have a proper foundation as required by Standard V(A): Diligence and Reasonable Basis, of the CFA Institute Code of Ethics and Standards of Professional Conduct.

- **Gunning the market**. Gunning the market is a strategy used by market manipulators to force traders to do disadvantageous trades. A manipulator generally guns the market by selling quickly to push prices down with the hope of triggering stop-loss sell orders. A stop-loss (or stop) sell order becomes valid for execution once the specified stop price condition is met by a trade occurring at or below the stop price. For example, suppose that a market manipulator believes that traders have placed many stop-loss sell orders at 50. These sell orders would become valid upon a trade occurring at 50 or below. The manipulator may sell aggressively to push prices down from 51 to 50 and thereby trigger the stop-loss sell orders. The manipulator then may be able to profit by repurchasing at lower prices.

- **Squeezing and cornering**. Squeezing, cornering, and gunning the market are all schemes that market manipulators use to force traders to do disadvantageous trades. In a squeeze or corner, the manipulator obtains control over resources necessary to settle trading contracts. The manipulator then unexpectedly withdraws those resources from the market, which causes traders to default on their contracts, some of which the manipulator may hold. The manipulator profits by providing the resources at high prices or by closing the contracts at exceptionally high prices.

For example, in short squeezes, manipulators obtain control of a substantial fraction of all available lendable stock shares or bonds. If the securities are overvalued, as they might be if the manipulators are also engaging in a pump and dump, many speculators may be short selling the securities by unknowingly borrowing them from the manipulators. The manipulators then will recall the security loans. If the short sellers ("shorts") cannot borrow the securities from others, they will be forced to buy securities in the market to cover their stock loans. Their purchases will raise prices and allow the manipulators to sell their securities at overvalued prices. Manipulators also may profit by raising the rates they charge to lend their securities. To avoid being caught in a short squeeze, short sellers must be sure that the market for lendable securities has many participants and is not concentrated in the hands of one or more entities acting in concert.

In commodity market corners, manipulators buy many futures contracts while simultaneously buying in the spot markets much of the deliverable supply of the commodity. When the contract approaches expiration, the manipulators then demand delivery from the shorts, most of whom will not own the deliverable commodity. The shorts then must buy the deliverable supply from the manipulators at exceptionally high prices. Alternatively, they may repurchase their contracts from the manipulators, again at very high prices.

Corners can occur in commodity markets because most participants in commodity futures contracts do not demand to receive or make delivery when the contract expires. Instead, they close their positions by arranging offsetting trades in the futures market, either because they are simultaneously accepting or making delivery elsewhere or because they are rolling their positions into future contract months. Accordingly, most short sellers neither expect nor intend to make delivery. When forced to make delivery, they are caught short.

Corners are illegal in most jurisdictions, and they always violate the rules of the exchanges on which futures contracts trade. In general, long holders cannot demand delivery if they do not have a valid business reason for doing so. However, enforcement is complicated by the fact that manipulators may offer plausible reasons for requesting unexpected deliveries. Note also that sometimes, unexpected supply shortages coupled with unexpected legitimate demands for delivery can result in inadvertent short squeezes. Thus, short sellers who do not intend to make delivery should try to close their positions early to ensure that they are not caught in an intentional corner or an inadvertent squeeze.

SUMMARY

This reading explains the implicit and explicit costs of trading as well as widely used methods for estimating transaction costs. The reading also describes developments in electronic trading, the main types of electronic traders, their needs for speed and ways in which they trade. Electronic trading benefits investors through lower transaction costs and greater efficiencies but also introduces systemic risks and the need to closely monitor markets for abusive trading practices. Appropriate market governance and regulatory policies will help reduce the likelihood of events such as the 2010 Flash Crash. The reading's main points include:

- Dealers provide liquidity to buyers and sellers when they take the other side of a trade if no other willing traders are present.

- The bid–ask spread is the difference between the bid and the ask prices. The effective spread is two times the difference between the trade price and the midquote price before the trade occurred. The effective spread is a poor estimate of actual transaction costs when large orders have been filled in many parts over time or when small orders receive price improvement.

- Transaction costs include explicit costs and implicit costs. Explicit costs are the direct costs of trading. They include broker commissions, transaction taxes, stamp duties, and exchange fees. Implicit costs include indirect costs, such as the impact of the trade on the price received. The bid–ask spread, market impact, delay, and unfilled trades all contribute to implicit trading costs.

- The implementation shortfall method measures the total cost of implementing an investment decision by capturing all explicit and implicit trading costs. It includes the market impact costs, delay costs, as well as opportunity costs.

- The VWAP method of estimating transaction costs compares average fill prices to average market prices during a period surrounding the trade. It tends to produce lower transaction cost estimates than does implementation shortfall because it often does not measure the market impact of an order well.

- Markets have become increasingly fragmented as venues trading the same instruments have proliferated. Trading in any given instrument now occurs in multiple venues.

- The advantages of electronic trading systems include cost and operational efficiencies, lack of human bias, extraordinarily fast speed, and infinite span and scope of attention.

- Latency is the elapsed time between the occurrence of an event and a subsequent action that depends on that event. Traders use fast communication systems and fast computer systems to minimize latency to execute their strategies faster than others.

- Hidden orders, quote leapfrogging, flickering quotes, and the use of machine learning to support trading strategies commonly are found in electronic markets.

- Traders commonly use advanced order types, trading tactics, and algorithms in electronic markets.

- Electronic trading has benefited investors through greater trade process efficiencies and reduced transaction costs. At the same time, electronic trading has increased systemic risks.

- Examples of systemic risks posed by electronic traders include: runaway algorithms that produce streams of unintended orders caused by programming mistakes, fat finger errors that occur when a manual trader submits a larger order than intended, overlarge orders that demand more liquidity than the market can provide, and malevolent order streams created deliberately to disrupt the markets.

- Real-time surveillance of markets often can detect order front running and various market manipulation strategies.

- Market manipulators use such improper activities as trading for market impact, rumormongering, wash trading, and spoofing to further their schemes.

- Market manipulation strategies include bluffing, squeezing, cornering, and gunning.

PRACTICE PROBLEMS

The following information relates to questions 1-10

Brian Johnson is a senior manager at Star Asset Management (SAMN), a large asset management firm in the United States. Tim Martin has just earned his advanced degree in statistics and was hired to support the trading team at SAMN. Martin meets with Johnson to undergo a training relating to SAMN's trading activities.

Johnson begins the training with a review of the limit order book for Light Systems, Inc., which is presented in Exhibit 1. Three dealers make market for the shares of Light Systems. Based on these prices, SAMN's trading desk executes a market sell order for 1,100 shares of Light Systems.

Exhibit 1: Limit Order Book for Light Systems, Inc.

	Bid				Ask		
Dealer	Time Entered	Price	Size	Dealer	Time Entered	Price	Size
B	10.10 a.m.	$17.15	900	C	10.11 a.m.	$17.19	1,200
C	10.11 a.m.	$17.14	1,500	B	10.10 a.m.	$17.20	800
A	10.11 a.m.	$17.12	1,100	A	10.12 a.m.	$17.22	1,100

Johnson then discusses a market buy order for 5,000 shares of an illiquid stock. The order was filled in three trades, and details about the three trades are presented in Exhibit 2.

Exhibit 2: Buy Trade Order Details

Trade #	Time	Trade Price	Trade Size	Bid Price	Ask Price
1	9.45 a.m.	$25.20	1,200	$25.17	$25.20
2	9.55 a.m.	$25.22	1,300	$25.19	$25.22
3	11.30 a.m.	$25.27	2,500	$25.22	$25.26

Johnson explains to Martin that the number of venues trading the same instruments has proliferated in recent years, and trading in any given instrument has now been distributed across these multiple venues. As a result, the available liquidity on any one of those exchanges represents just a small portion of the aggregate liquidity for that security. As a result, SAMN has had to adapt its trading strategies, particularly for large trades.

Johnson asks Martin about his views on how the introduction of electronic trading might have impacted SAMN. Martin tells Johnson:

Statement 1   Once built, electronic trading systems are more efficient and cheaper to operate than floor-based trading systems.

Statement 2   Electronic trading systems have attracted a lot of new buy-side traders, and the increased competition has resulted in narrower bid–ask spreads.

Statement 3   The introduction of electronic markets has had a much greater impact on the trading of corporate and municipal bonds than on the trading of equities.

Johnson tells Martin that communication speed is SAMN's current highest priority. All of SAMN's competitors have increased their communication speeds in recent months, and Johnson says management wants SAMN to be faster than its competitors. SAMN's trading desk is located in a residential area far from downtown where the exchanges it works with are located. SAMN's trading team is relatively large with experienced investment professionals, and the firm recently invested in fast computers with the latest algorithms.

At the end of the training, Johnson gives Martin his first assignment. The assignment is for Martin to use the vast amount of data that SAMN has collected to design a machine learning (ML) model using advanced statistical methods to characterize data structures and relations. Then he has to build a trading algorithm based on the same model. Since electronic trading has added systemic risk to the market, Johnson asks Martin to suggest ways to minimize the systemic risk introduced by his algorithm. Martin offers two suggestions:

Suggestion 1   Perform extensive testing of the algorithm before its launch.

Suggestion 2   Impose mandatory trading halts if prices change outside a threshold range.

A month into the job, Johnson sends Martin to an investment conference focused on abusive trading practices. Based on what he learned at the conference, Martin recommends to Johnson that SAMN incorporate a new rule that news be validated before a trade triggered by news is executed.

1. Based on Exhibit 1, the inside bid–ask spread for the limit order book for Light Systems is *closest* to:

   A. $0.04.

   B. $0.07.

   C. $0.10.

2. Based on Exhibit 1, the total amount that SAMN will receive, on a per share basis, for executing the market sell order is *closest* to:

   A. $17.14.

   B. $17.15.

   C. $17.22.

3. Based on Exhibit 2, the market impact relating to Trade 2, on a per share basis, is *closest* to:

   A. $0.02.

   B. $0.03.

   C. $0.07.

4. Based on Exhibit 2, the average effective spread of the three trades is *closest to*:

   A. $0.0333.

   B. $0.0367.

   C. $0.0400.

5. The reason for SAMN having to adapt its trading strategies is a result of:

   A. latency.

   B. market fragmentation.

   C. high frequency trading.

6. Which of Martin's statements relating to the introduction of electronic markets is correct?

   A. Statement 1

   B. Statement 2

   C. Statement 3

7. Which of the following changes should SAMN make to address its key priority?

   A. Hire more investment professionals

   B. Upgrade to more complex operating systems

   C. Move the trading desk physically closer to the exchanges it works with

8. The model that Martin is tasked with designing will likely be *most* effective:

   A. for testing new markets.

   B. in a well-understood market environment.

   C. during periods of higher than normal market volatility.

9. Which of Martin's suggestions will *most likely* be effective in limiting the systemic risk introduced by his algorithm?

   A. Only Suggestion 1

   B. Only Suggestion 2

   C. Both Suggestion 1 and Suggestion 2

10. Which market manipulation strategy is *most likely* the target of the new rule suggested by Martin?

    A. Rumormongering

    B. Gunning the market

    C. Trading for market impact

The following information relates to questions 11-16

Michael Bloomfield is a trader at 2Fast Trading, a proprietary trading company that uses machine learning and algorithms to execute trades. He works with Amy Riley, a junior trader at the company. Bloomfield and Riley meet to review the company's trading systems and several trades in Bloomfield's trading account.

They discuss the increasing impact of market fragmentation on available liquidity for the company's trading strategies. Riley makes the following comments regarding market fragmentation:

Comment 1   Liquidity aggregation and smart order routing help traders manage the challenges and opportunities presented by fragmentation.

Comment 2   With increasing market fragmentation, traders who fill large orders now search for liquidity across multiple venues and across time to control market impact.

Bloomfield tells Riley that he noticed trades of 500 shares of BYYP stock were executed every 20 minutes for an hour. Bloomfield saw the same pattern of trading in the stock during the previous trading day. He instructs Riley to submit an order to purchase BYYP shares on the assumption that a trader seeks liquidity and is executing a large buy order by breaking it into pieces. The prices of these trades and the best bids and offers in the market when the BYYP trades occurred are presented in Exhibit 1.

Exhibit 1: BYYP Trade Details

Trade	Trade Price	Prevailing Bid	Prevailing Offer
1	41.50	41.45	41.50
2	41.75	41.73	41.75

Bloomfield shifts the conversation to AXZ Corp. Bloomfield notes that AXZ's bid–ask spread is narrow, even though AXZ's share price has been experiencing a period of high volatility. After extensive research, Bloomfield will purchase AXZ shares using a trading strategy that does not include standing orders.

Bloomfield then assesses the risks that 2Fast's electronic trading strategies introduce into the market. He is concerned that these risks may bring on more regulation. Bloomfield claims that the risks can be reduced by changing the structure of the market, and those structural changes can maintain 2Fast's primary competitive advantage, which is trading faster than competitors.

Bloomfield mentions that a regulatory body is investigating a competitor's trading practices. The investigation involves a tip that the competitor is manipulating markets by submitting orders and arranging trades to influence other traders' perceptions of value. Specifically, regulators were informed that the competitor has been buying stock to raise its price, thereby encouraging momentum traders to buy, and then selling the stock to them at higher prices. The regulator confirmed that the competitor did not use standing limit orders or commonly controlled accounts for the trades under investigation.

11. Which of Riley's comments related to market fragmentation is accurate?

    A. Only Comment 1

    B. Only Comment 2

    C. Both Comment 1 and Comment 2

12. Bloomfield's strategy to purchase BYYP shares is *best* classified as electronic:

    A. arbitrage.

    B. front running.

    C. quote matching.

13. Based on Exhibit 1, the average effective spread of the BYYP trades is *closest* to:

    A. $0.018.

    B. $0.035.

    C. $0.070.

14. Bloomfield's trading strategy for the purchase of AXZ shares *most likely* includes the use of:

    A. flickering quotes.

    B. machine learning.

    C. leapfrogging quotes.

15. Which structural change for the market associated with electronic trading systems is *most* consistent with Bloomfield's claim?

    A. Delaying order processing by random intervals

    B. Exchanges using trade halts when prices move too quickly

    C. Slowing markets by running call markets once a second or more often instead of trading continuously

16. The competitor company's trading is *best* described as:

    A. bluffing.

    B. spoofing.

    C. wash trading.

SOLUTIONS

1. A is correct. The inside bid–ask spread, or market bid–ask spread, is the difference between the highest bid price and the lowest ask price. The highest bid price for Light Systems is $17.15, and the lowest ask price is $17.19. Therefore, the inside bid–ask spread = $17.19 – $17.15 = $0.04.

2. B is correct. SAMN's trading desk executes a market sell order for 1,100 shares. Based on the limit order book, the trader would first sell 900 shares at $17.15 (highest bid, Dealer B) and then sell the remaining 200 shares at $17.14 (second highest bid, Dealer C). Therefore, the approximate price per share received by SAMN for selling the 1,100 shares is equal to [(900 × $17.15) + (200 × $17.14)] / 1,100 = $17.1482 per share ($17.15 rounded).

3. A is correct. Market impact, or price impact, is the effect of a trade on transaction prices. After the first trade (Trade 1) was executed at $25.20, Trade 2 was executed at $25.22, which is $0.02 per share higher than the trade price of Trade 1. So, the execution of Trade 1 led to a price impact of $0.02 per share on Trade 2.

4. C is correct. The effective bid–ask spread for buy orders is calculated as:

   Effective bid–ask spread (buy order) = 2 × {Trade price − [(Ask price + Bid price) / 2)]} or

   = 2 × (Trade price − Midpoint of the market at the time an order is entered).

   So, the effective bid–ask spreads for the three buy trades are calculated as:

   Effective spread of Trade 1 = 2 × {$25.20 − [($25.20 + $25.17)/2]} = $0.0300.

   Effective spread of Trade 2 = 2 × {$25.22 − [($25.22 + 25.19)/2]} = $0.0300.

   Effective spread of Trade 3 = 2 × {$25.27 − [($25.26 + $25.22)/2]} = $0.0600.

   The resulting average effective spread is then calculated as:

   Average effective spread

   = (Effective spread of Trade 1 + Effective spread of Trade 2 + Effective spread of Trade 3)/3.

   Average effective spread = ($0.0300 + $0.0300 + $0.0600)/3 = $0.0400.

5. B is correct. According to Johnson, markets have become increasingly fragmented as the number of venues trading the same instruments has proliferated and trading in any given instrument has been split (or fragmented) across these multiple venues. As a result, the available liquidity on any one exchange represents just a small portion of the aggregate liquidity for that instrument. This phenomenon is known as market fragmentation and creates the potential for price and liquidity disparities across venues. As a result, SAMN has had to adapt its trading strategies to this fragmented liquidity to avoid intensifying the market impact of a large trade.

6. A is correct. Once built, electronic systems are indeed cheaper to operate than floor-based trading systems. They require less physical space than do trading floors, and in contrast to floor-based trading systems, they do not require exchange officials to record and report prices. Furthermore, the widespread use

of electronic trading systems significantly decreased trading costs for buy-side traders. Costs fell as exchanges obtained greater cost efficiencies from using electronic matching systems instead of floor-based manual trading systems. These technologies also decreased costs and increased efficiencies for the dealers and arbitrageurs who provide much of the liquidity offered at exchanges. Competition forced them to pass along much of the benefits of their new technologies to buy-side traders in the form of narrower spreads quoted for larger sizes. New electronic buy-side order management systems also decreased buy-side trading costs by allowing a smaller number of buy-side traders to process more orders and to process them more efficiently than manual traders.

While electronic trading has had a significant effect on equity markets, it has not had as much of an effect on the markets for corporate and municipal bonds. The market structures of corporate and municipal bond markets have hardly changed since the late 19th century. Despite the efforts of many creative developers of electronic bond trading systems, most public investors in these markets still trade largely over the counter with dealers.

7. C is correct. The speed required by electronic traders is affected by fast communication and fast computations. The shorter the distance between the trader and the exchange, the faster the communication. Many exchanges allow electronic traders to place their servers in the rooms where the exchange servers operate, a practice called collocation.

8. B is correct. Many trading problems are ideally suited for machine learning analyses because the problems repeat regularly and often. For such problems, machine-based learning systems can be extraordinarily powerful. However, these systems are often useless—or worse—when trading becomes extraordinary, as when volatilities shoot up. Machine learning systems frequently do not produce useful information during volatility episodes because they have few precedents from which the machines can learn. Thus, traders often instruct their electronic trading systems to stop trading—and sometimes to close out their positions—whenever they recognize that they are entering uncharted territory. Many traders shut down when volatility spikes—both because high-volatility episodes are uncommon and thus not well understood and because even if such episodes were well understood, they represent periods of exceptionally high risk.

9. C is correct. Both suggestions will likely be effective in minimizing the systemic risk introduced by electronic trading. First, exhaustive testing of the algorithm prior to its launch can minimize risk relating to programming errors, which could result in an extreme market reaction that could trigger an even more extreme market reaction. Second, imposing mandatory trade halts in case of large price changes (outside a given threshold) would limit potential undesired results and help minimize systemic risk.

10. A is correct. Rumormongering is the dissemination of false information about fundamental values or about other traders' trading intentions in an attempt to alter investors' value assessments. Martin's suggested news validation rule would reduce the likelihood that SAMN would be adversely affected by this market manipulation strategy.

11. C is correct. Both of Riley's comments are correct. Electronic algorithmic trading techniques, such as liquidity aggregation and smart order routing, help traders manage the challenges and opportunities presented by fragmentation. Liquidity aggregators create "super books" that present liquidity across markets for a given instrument. These tools offer global views of market depth (available liquidity) for each instrument regardless of the trading venue that offers the liquidity. Smart

order-routing algorithms send orders to the markets that display the best quoted prices and sizes. Additionally, with increasing market fragmentation, traders filling large orders adapt their trading strategies to search for liquidity across multiple venues and across time to control the market impacts of their trades.

12. B is correct. Bloomfield noticed a pattern of trading in BYYP and decided to front run shares on the assumption that a trader is in the market filling a large buy order by breaking it into pieces. Electronic front runners trade in front of traders who demand liquidity. They identify when large traders or many small traders are trying to fill orders on the same side of the market. The order anticipation strategies of electronic front runners try to identify predictable patterns in order submission. They may search for patterns in order submissions, trades, or the relations between trades and other events.

   A is incorrect because electronic arbitrageurs look across markets for arbitrage opportunities in which they can buy an undervalued instrument and sell a similar overvalued one. His decision to purchase BYYP shares is based on the pattern of trading that Bloomfield observed.

   C is incorrect because quote matchers trade in front of traders who supply (not demand) liquidity. Bloomfield decides to purchase BYYP shares on the assumption that a trader is in the market seeking (not supplying) liquidity, which is consistent with front running (not quote matching). Quote matchers trade in front of traders who supply liquidity and try to exploit the option values of standing orders. Quote matchers buy when they believe they can rely on standing buy orders to get out of their positions, and they sell when they can do the same with standing sell orders.

13. B is correct. The effective spread is calculated as follows:

   $$\text{Effective spread} = 2 \times (\text{Trade price} - \text{Midpoint of market at time of order entry})$$

   $$\text{Effective spread of Trade 1} = 2 \times (\$41.50 - \$41.475) = \$0.05$$

   $$\text{Effective spread of Trade 2} = 2 \times (\$41.75 - \$41.74) = \$0.02$$

   $$\text{Average Effective Spread} = (\$0.05 + \$0.02)/2 = \$0.035$$

14. A is correct. Flickering quotes are exposed limit orders that electronic traders submit and then cancel shortly thereafter, often within a second. Electronic dealers and algorithmic buy-side traders submit and repeatedly cancel and resubmit their orders when they do not want their orders to stand in the market; rather, they want other traders to see that they are willing to trade at the displayed price. Bloomfield does not want his orders to stand in the market; using flickering quotes to purchase AXZ shares would satisfy that objective.

   B is incorrect because AXZ shares are currently in a period of high volatility, so Bloomfield would not likely use machine learning to execute his trades. Machine-learning systems frequently do not produce useful information during volatility episodes because these episodes have few precedents from which the machines can learn. Machine-learning methods produce models based on observed empirical regularities rather than on theoretical principles identified by analysts. Many traders shut down when volatility spikes, both because high-volatility episodes are uncommon and thus not well understood and because even if such episodes were well understood, they represent periods of exceptionally high risk.

   C is incorrect because market participants use leapfrogging quotes when spreads are wide (not narrow), and Bloomfield noted that the bid–ask spread for AXZ shares is narrow. When bid–ask spreads are wide, dealers often are willing to trade at better prices than they quote. They quote wide spreads because they hope to trade at more favorable prices. When another trader quotes a better price, dealers often immediately quote an even better price. If the spread is sufficiently wide, a game of leapfrog may ensue as the dealer jumps ahead again.

15. B is correct. To reduce the systemic risks associated with fast trading, some exchanges have adopted trade halts when prices move too quickly. These rules stop trading when excess demand for liquidity occurs. They also prevent the extreme price changes that can occur in electronic markets when market orders arrive and no liquidity is present. 2Fast Trading's competitive advantage will be maintained despite exchange trading halts because the company will be free to trade faster than its competitors once trading resumes. Therefore, exchanges using trade halts to stop trading is the risk reduction strategy that most likely maintains 2Fast Trading's competitive advantage and is consistent with Bloomfield's claim that risks can be reduced by changing the structure of the market.

A is incorrect because delaying order processing by random intervals reduces the benefits of high-frequency traders being faster than their competitors and investing in speed. Therefore, delaying order processing by random order intervals does not maintain 2Fast Trading's primary competitive advantage, which is trading faster than competitors, because that advantage will be reduced.

C is incorrect because slowing markets by running call markets once a second or more often instead of trading continuously diminishes the benefits of high-frequency traders being faster than their competitors and investing with speed. Therefore, slowing markets once a second or more often instead of trading continuously does not maintain 2Fast Trading's primary competitive advantage, which is trading faster than competitors, because that advantage will be reduced.

16. A is correct. Bluffing involves submitting orders and arranging trades to influence other traders' perceptions of value. Bluffers often prey on momentum traders, who buy when prices are rising and sell when prices are falling. Similarly, Bloomfield mentioned that regulators were informed that 2Fast's competitor has been submitting orders and arranging trades to influence other traders' perceptions of value; regulators were informed the competitor has been buying stock to raise its price, thereby encouraging momentum traders to buy, and then selling the stock to them at higher prices.

B is incorrect because the competitor did not use standing limit orders—those orders that are used in a spoofing strategy—for the trades the regulator is investigating. Spoofing is a trading practice in which traders place exposed standing limit orders to convey an impression to other traders that the market is more liquid than it is or to suggest to other traders that the security is under- or overvalued.

C is incorrect because the competitor did not use commonly controlled accounts—those accounts that are used in a wash trading strategy—for the trades that regulators are investigating. Wash trading consists of trades arranged among commonly controlled accounts to create the impression of market activity at a particular price. The purpose of wash trading is to fool investors into believing that a market is more liquid than it truly is and to thereby increase investors' confidence both in their ability to exit positions without substantial cost and in their assessments of security values.

7

Case Study in Portfolio Management: Institutional (SWF)

by Steve Balaban, CFA, Arjan Berkelaar, PhD, CFA, Nasir Hasan, and Hardik Sanjay Shah, CFA.

Steve Balaban, CFA, is at Mink Capital Inc. (Canada). Arjan Berkelaar, PhD, CFA, is at KAUST Investment Management Company (USA). Nasir Hasan is at Ernst & Young (UAE). Hardik Sanjay Shah, CFA, is at GMO LLC (Singapore).

LEARNING OUTCOMES	
Mastery	The candidate should be able to:
☐	discuss financial risks associated with the portfolio strategy of an institutional investor
☐	discuss environmental and social risks associated with the portfolio strategy of an institutional investor
☐	analyze and evaluate the financial and non-financial risk exposures in the portfolio strategy of an institutional investor
☐	discuss various methods to manage the risks that arise on long-term direct investments of an institutional investor
☐	evaluate strengths and weaknesses of an enterprise risk management system and recommend improvements

INTRODUCTION

1

The focus of this reading is a fictional "case study." The case itself will focus on the portfolio of a sovereign wealth fund (SWF) specifically looking at risk in terms of the SWF's long-term investments. There are three Learning Outcome Statements (LOS) within the case. Prior to the case, we provide two LOS outside the case. These LOS will provide some background information that will be helpful to the candidate in understanding the case.

2   FINANCIAL RISKS FACED BY INSTITUTIONAL INVESTORS

☐ | discuss financial risks associated with the portfolio strategy of an institutional investor

Long-Term Perspective

Institutional investors (also referred to as *asset owners*) such as pension funds, sovereign wealth funds, endowments, and foundations are distinct from other institutional investors such as banks and insurance companies in terms of the time horizon over which they invest their assets. This long-term perspective allows these institutions to take on certain investment risks that other institutional investors simply cannot bear and to invest in in a broad range of alternative asset classes, including private equity, private real estate, natural resources, infrastructure, and hedge funds. This section will focus on the financial risks associated with the portfolio strategy of long-term institutional investors and in particular will focus on investments in illiquid asset classes. Banks and insurance companies are excluded from the discussion because they are typically much more asset/liability focused and face much tighter regulatory constraints to ensure capital adequacy.

This section will not cover the quantitative aspects of risk management or the mechanics behind various risk metrics, such as standard deviation and conditional value at risk, or risk management techniques, such as Monte Carlo simulation and factor modelling. Those topics are covered in other parts of the CFA Program curriculum. Instead, this reading will cover key risk considerations faced by long-term institutional investors as they invest in a range of traditional and alternative asset classes, including private equity and infrastructure. An important distinguishing feature of long-term institutional investors is their ability to invest in illiquid asset classes. Since the late 1990s, such asset classes have become an ever more important part of the investment portfolios of pension funds, sovereign wealth funds, endowments, and foundations. In this reading, we put particular emphasis on the financial risks that emanate from illiquid investments because these risks tend to be least well quantified but can pose an existential threat to long-term investors if not addressed and managed carefully. The focus is on how market and liquidity risk interact to create potential challenges at the overall portfolio level and affect the institutional investor's ability to meet its long-term objectives.

Section 2.2 briefly discusses the various lenses through which risk management can be viewed. Risk management is a very broad topic, and the goal is to simply provide the reader with a frame of reference. Section 2.3 focuses on the key financial risks that institutional investors face. The focus is on portfolio-level, top-down, long-term financial risk. Risk management for long-term institutional investors should primarily be concerned with events that may jeopardize the organization's ability to meet its long-term objectives. The interaction between market and liquidity risk plays a critical role. In Section 2.4 we discuss the challenges associated with investing in illiquid asset classes from a risk management perspective. We discuss two important aspects of illiquid asset classes: the uncertainty of cash flows and return-smoothing behavior in the return pattern. Section 2.5 describes how institutional investors address and manage liquidity risk at the overall portfolio level.

Dimensions of Financial Risk Management

The aim of risk management is to avoid an existential threat to the organization. In other words, risk management should focus on what types of events can jeopardize the organization's ability to meet its long-term objectives. Existential threats can arise from both financial risks (e.g., market losses and liquidity risk in the form of the inability to meet cash flows) and non-financial risks (e.g., reputational risks). In this reading, we solely focus on financial risk. Financial risk needs to be viewed through multiple lenses. There is no simple template to financial risk management. It is not simply a matter of calculating, for example, the value at risk of a portfolio. There are several dimensions to sound financial risk management, and we cover them briefly in the following subsections. Our goal is to simply provide a frame of reference for the reader because risk management is a very broad topic.

Top-down vs. bottom-up risk analysis

Risk management requires both a top-down and a bottom-up perspective. From a top-down perspective, the board and chief investment officer (CIO) set overall risk guidelines for the portfolio that serve as guardrails within which the investment team is expected to operate. Risk management involves measuring, monitoring, and reporting portfolio results versus the guidelines. The investment team is tasked with implementing the overall investment strategy either through hiring external asset managers or by directly purchasing and managing securities and assets. The investment team takes a more bottom-up, sub-portfolio approach to managing the risks of each individual portfolio or asset class, while assessing and monitoring their interaction and impact on the risk level of the overall portfolio.

Portfolio-level risk vs. asset-class-specific risk

Although risk management for an institutional investor is ultimately about controlling overall portfolio-level risk, risks also need to be managed and controlled at the asset-class or strategy level so that no particular asset class or strategy will have an undue adverse effect on the overall portfolio. Different asset classes require different risk management techniques. Some risk metrics and methods make sense for publicly traded asset classes, but they may not be meaningful when assessing the risk of, for example, illiquid asset classes or hedge fund investments. For some asset classes, such as public equities, detailed security-level information might be available, whereas for other asset classes, such as hedge funds, only monthly manager returns may be available. In the case of a public equity portfolio, risk analysis might be very granular and rely on sophisticated factor models, whereas risk analysis for hedge fund investments might simply involve calculating the historical volatility of observed returns. Because of differences in data transparency, data frequency, and risk methods used, it is difficult—if not impossible—to aggregate these results at the overall portfolio level. It is not uncommon for institutional investors to have an overall risk management system for portfolio-wide risk metrics in addition to asset-class-specific systems or approaches that provide a more in-depth risk view tailored to a particular asset class.

Return-based vs. holdings-based risk approaches

Financial risk management systems are typically described as being return based (risk estimation relies on the historical return streams of an external manager or a portfolio of securities) or holdings based (risk estimation relies on individual security holdings and the historical returns of those securities in the portfolio). Both approaches have their pros and cons, and they are not mutually exclusive. Return-based systems are relatively easy to implement but may produce risk estimates that are biased because they rely on past returns from a strategy that may be very different today compared with, for example, five years ago. Holdings-based risk systems, in contrast, tend to be more costly and time-consuming to implement. For many institutional investors that invest in hedge funds and illiquid asset classes, holdings-based risk systems for the entire portfolio are typically not feasible because of a lack of transparency on holdings and their related investment strategy (a multi-strategy fund may maintain a long position in a security within one strategy book and a short position in another strategy book), data being available with a one-month to three-month lag, and significant turnover in certain types of hedge fund investments.

Absolute vs. relative risk

Investors are interested in both absolute risk and relative risk. Absolute risk concerns the potential for overall losses and typically relies on overall portfolio-level metrics, such as standard deviation, conditional value at risk, and maximum drawdown. Relative risk concerns underperformance versus policy benchmarks and relies on such metrics as tracking error (the standard deviation of returns relative to a benchmark).

Long-term vs. short-term risk metrics

Modern risk systems used by institutional investors typically focus on calculating volatility, value at risk, and conditional value at risk using sophisticated risk factor techniques. Given the heavy reliance on the current portfolio composition and the granular modeling of each component in the portfolio, these risk systems are most useful in providing an estimate for the potential for near-term losses. Institutional investors are also interested in calculating longer-term risks, such as the probability of losses, the probability of not being able to meet cash flows, and the probability of maintaining purchasing power or meeting a certain return target over longer time periods, such as 5 years, 10 years, 20 years, and so forth.

These long-term risk metrics are typically calculated using Monte Carlo simulation, where asset-class returns are simulated on the basis of a set of forward-looking capital market assumptions (typically expected returns, volatilities, and correlations) and total assets are calculated including cash flows, such as benefit payments and contributions in the case of pension funds and payouts (spending amounts) in case of endowments and foundations. These methods, although typically much less granular than a risk management system, are better able to incorporate future portfolio changes, different rebalancing methods, and cash flows.

Quantitative vs. qualitative risks

At the end of the day, risk management is not simply a quantitative endeavor. Quantitative risk management techniques are backward looking by nature and typically parametric (i.e., they rely on historical data to estimate parameters). Although history can serve as a guide, it does not provide a prediction of the future. Risk management is about assessing the potential for future losses, and quantitative tools need to be complemented with qualitative assessments. However, with qualitative assessments, it is important for risk managers to be aware of their own biases because they are basing these assessments on their own past experience. Thus, it is important for risk managers to recognize and mitigate the backward-looking bias in both quantitative (explicit) and qualitative (implicit) risk analysis.

Pre- and post-investment risk assessment

Finally, although risk management efforts typically focus on measuring the risks of existing investments, a sound risk management philosophy ensures a proper assessment of financial risks prior to making investments. Institutional investors typically put a lot of effort into operational and investment due diligence prior to making investments. In addition to analyzing past investment performance, it is critical when hiring external managers to evaluate the character of the key decision makers, the business ethics of the firm, the investment experience of the team, the quality of operations (such as accounting and trade settlements), and the risk management practices of the external manager. As part of their investment due diligence, institutional investors also look at the quality of the non-executive directors of the fund, the integrity and independence of external auditors, fee structures, master fund and feeder fund structure, custodians, and safekeeping on assets. These considerations are even more important for illiquid investments because it is very difficult to exit from them (investors cannot easily change their mind). After investing, risk management might take on a more quantitative role, but continued due diligence and monitoring are of equal importance. In the case of external managers, this obligation resides with the team responsible for the hiring and firing of the managers. In the case of internal management, an in-house risk management team may be tasked with the ongoing due-diligence and monitoring responsibilities.

The various risk dimensions we have described should provide a sense of the wide-ranging nature of risk management as a discipline. For this reading, we focus exclusively on the key financial risks that long-term institutional investors face. We take a portfolio-level, top-down perspective and are primarily concerned with how illiquid asset classes and the interaction between market and liquidity risk affect an institutional investor's ability to meet its long-term objectives. This risk is unique to long-term institutional investors. The next section will provide a more in-depth description of this risk.

Risk Considerations for Long-Term Investors

Long-term institutional investors have the ability to invest a significant part of their portfolio in risky and illiquid assets because of their long-term investment horizon and relatively low liquidity needs. The past two decades have seen a steady increase in the allocation to illiquid asset classes, such private equity, private real estate, and infrastructure, by pension funds, sovereign wealth funds, endowments, and foundations. These asset classes create unique risk management challenges and can pose an existential threat if the risks are not addressed and managed carefully. As stated before, the ultimate objective of risk management is to ensure that the organization survives and can meet its long-term objectives.

We start with briefly describing and reviewing the main objectives of long-term institutional investors and their key risk considerations. Exhibit 1 provides an overview by institutional investor type. The ultimate risk consideration for each of these institutional investors is their ability to meet the payouts that they were set up to provide. This risk is largely affected by how the overall investment portfolio performs over time. On the one hand, a very low-risk portfolio that consists primarily of fixed-income investments is unlikely to cause a problem in providing the required payouts in the short run but will almost certainly jeopardize the organization's ability to provide the required payouts in the long run. On the other hand, a very risky and illiquid portfolio is expected to provide high expected returns in the long run but could cause significant pain in the short run during a significant market downturn or financial crisis. Long-term institutional investors aim to strike the right balance between these two extremes in designing their investment policy or strategic asset allocation.

Exhibit 1: Objectives and Risk Considerations by Institutional Investor Type

Institutional Investor	Main Objective	Key Risk Consideration
Pension funds	Provide retirement income to plan participants	Inability to meet pension payouts to beneficiaries
Sovereign wealth funds	Varies by type of SWF but most have been set up to provide some future financial support to the government	Inability to provide financial support to the government
Endowments and Foundations	Provide financial support in perpetuity while maintaining intergenerational equity	Inability to provide financial support to the institution or to the mission

This process usually involves a Monte Carlo simulation exercise where asset-class returns are simulated on the basis of a set of forward-looking capital market assumptions and total assets are calculated including cash flows, such as benefit payments and contributions in the case of pension funds and payouts (spending amounts) in the case of endowments and foundations. Monte Carlo simulation allows institutional investors to calculate such metrics as the probability of maintaining purchasing power and the probability of a certain loss or drawdown (e.g., 25%) over a specific time period (e.g., 5 or 10 years) and to determine the appropriate trade-off between two such metrics. What is often ignored in this type of analysis, however, is the important interaction between potential market losses and liquidity. Pension funds, SWFs, endowments, and foundations are unique in that they can often tolerate significantly more market and liquidity risk than other investors. Their long-term investment horizon allows them to survive a significant market correction and even operate in a counter-cyclical way during a market crisis. As institutional investors invest more in such illiquid asset classes as private equity, private real estate, and infrastructure, however, their ability to tolerate market losses may diminish.

Institutional investors need liquidity to meet payouts (retirement payments in the case of pension plans, payouts to the university or foundation in the case of endowments and foundations, etc.), meet capital calls on their illiquid investments, and rebalance their portfolios. During a significant market downturn, these needs can become stretched and impact the institution's ability to meet cash flows, particularly if a large part of the portfolio is invested in illiquid asset classes, such as private equity, real estate, and infrastructure. Exhibit 2 shows the main liquidity needs and the main sources of liquidity for long-term institutional investors. Each of these liquidity needs and sources may be adversely affected during a financial crisis.

Exhibit 2: Liquidity Needs and Sources for Institutional Investors

Liquidity Needs	Liquidity Sources
Outflows (e.g., pension payouts to beneficiaries, university payouts, and financial support to the government)	Inflows (e.g., pension contributions, gifts, donations, government savings)
Capital calls for illiquid investments	Distributions from illiquid investments
Portfolio rebalancing	Investment income and proceeds from selling liquid asset classes (cash, fixed income, public equities)

We first start with discussing how liquidity needs may increase during a crisis. First, payouts might increase as the beneficiary requires additional financial support. For example, a university may need additional funds from its endowment to support its operations as other sources of income dry up, or a government might require additional financial support from the sovereign wealth fund to mitigate the crisis situation. Second, there might be an acceleration of capital calls as attractive investment opportunities present themselves during a crisis. Finally, rebalancing flows will be more significant during a crisis because of significant market movements. Good governance and best practice suggest that investors rebalance their portfolios at regular intervals. Sticking to rebalancing practices is particularly important during a financial crisis because failure to rebalance may prevent investors from fully participating in the rebound after the crisis.

Having discussed how the needs for liquidity may increase during a significant market downturn, we next turn to how sources of liquidity might dry up under those circumstances. First, inflows might decrease in a crisis. For example, donors might be struggling financially and donate less to their alma mater, or plan sponsors might be faced with budgetary challenges and, therefore, less inclined to contribute to the pension fund. Second, distributions from illiquid investments might be reduced because there are no attractive exit points due to depressed prices or lower profitability. Finally, investments that are otherwise liquid might become less liquid or simply undesirable to exit from. The main sources of liquidity during a financial crisis are typically cash and fixed-income investments. And most long-term institutional investors hold relatively low allocations to cash and fixed income in their portfolios.

Illiquid asset classes (such as private equity, real estate, and infrastructure) are not available to meet liquidity needs during a crisis. These asset classes cannot be rebalanced or redeemed because they are long term in nature and the assets can be locked up for 5–10 years or even longer. Semi-liquid asset classes, such as hedge fund investments, should not be expected to be liquid and available to meet liquidity needs during a financial crisis because many of these managers might impose redemption gates or have lockups in place or their investments might turn out to be less liquid than anticipated. Finally, although public equity investments are technically liquid, investors may be reluctant to sell part of their public equity portfolio to meet liquidity needs because the market value of these investments may have gone down significantly in a crisis. In addition, investors might not want to redeem from certain active external managers, even if the investments are liquid, because it may impact the future relationship with that manager (particularly for high-demand active managers with limited available capacity).

In conclusion, the main risk that long-term institutional investors face is having insufficient liquidity during a significant market downturn to meet their obligations and rebalance their portfolios. Liquidity needs tend to increase in a crisis while sources of liquidity dry up. This risk increases as institutional investors allocate more to illiquid asset classes. The combination of financial losses and not being able to meet cash flows or rebalance the portfolio because of insufficient liquidity can become a matter of survival. Managing this risk is, therefore, very important for long-term institutional investors. In the next section, we will discuss in more detail the risks associated with illiquid asset classes. In Section 2.5, we will discuss the various ways in which institutional managers manage liquidity risk.

Risks Associated with Illiquid Asset Classes

Illiquid asset classes, such as private equity, real estate, and infrastructure, offer the potential for returns in excess of those on publicly traded asset classes, such as public equity and fixed income. The higher expected return of these asset classes comes at a cost to investors in the form of illiquidity. Illiquid asset classes are typically subject to a drawdown structure where committed capital is called at an unknown schedule and investors receive profits at an unknown schedule. As a result, investors need to hold sufficient liquid assets to meet capital calls from their private fund managers. The uncertain pattern of cash flows poses both a liquidity and a risk management challenge for investors in illiquid asset classes.

In addition to the importance of adequately managing liquidity needs when investing in illiquid assets, these asset classes tend to be subject to stale pricing, appraisal-based valuations, and a lagged response to movements in public markets. As a result, illiquid asset classes exhibit returns that are smooth, understating the true volatility and correlation with publicly traded asset classes. For example, the standard deviation of observed returns for private equity is often smaller than that of public equity. Although this feature may be appealing for institutional investors, it causes traditional asset allocation models, such as mean–variance optimization, to over-allocate to private asset classes because the Sharpe ratios of observed returns are superior to those of publicly traded asset classes.

Finally, illiquid asset classes cannot be rebalanced easily and costlessly. Although investors could potentially, for example, sell their private equity stakes in the secondary market, this cannot be done instantaneously and investors may have to accept a significantly lower price compared with the true market value.

Cash flow modeling

Illiquid asset classes are subject to a drawdown structure. The investor (typically the limited partner, or LP, in the partnership agreement) commits capital, and this capital gets drawn down over time at the discretion of the general partner, or GP. Investors need to figure out both the commitment strategy (i.e., how much to commit each year) to reach a certain target allocation to illiquid assets and the liquidity needs to meet capital calls when required. Committing too much can pose severe liquidity risk because the percentage allocation to illiquid asset classes may soar due to the so-called denominator effect (total assets under management, or AUM, falls by a larger amount than the repricing of illiquid asset classes). Committing too little may prevent the investor from reaching the target allocation and may result in falling short of return expectations.

In managing liquidity needs and determining the appropriate commitment strategy to illiquid asset classes, investors need to be able to predict future cash flows.

Addressing return smoothing behavior of illiquid asset classes

To calculate the true underlying economic risks of illiquid asset classes as part of their risk management efforts, institutional investors typically use one of two approaches: (1) Use public market proxies in place of private asset classes—for example, use small-cap public equities as a proxy for private equity—or (2) unsmooth observed returns of private asset classes. The objective of the latter is to remove the serial correlation structure of the original return series. The implicit assumption is that the serial correlations in reported returns are entirely due to the smoothing behavior funds engage in when reporting results. A common and simple technique to unsmooth the returns of illiquid asset classes and hedge funds is a method developed by Geltner (1993) to address appraisal-based valuations in real estate. The method proposed by Geltner removes only the first-order serial correlation in observed returns. Okunev and White (2003) extended the method of Geltner (1993) to include higher-order serial correlations. An alternative to the Geltner method is the GLM method proposed by Getmansky, Lo, and Makarov (2004). They assumed that observed returns for illiquid asset classes and hedge funds follow a moving-average process.

To show the effect of these different methods on the annualized volatility of various illiquid asset classes, we use quarterly historical returns for global buyouts, global venture capital, global private real estate, and global private natural resources for the period from Q1 1990 until Q4 2019. Exhibit 3 shows the annualized volatility of the observed returns and the volatility of adjusted returns using the three methods briefly discussed earlier. For the Okunev–White and GLM methods, we use up to four lags. Exhibit 4 shows the beta to global equity returns. For global equity returns, we use quarterly returns for the MSCI World Index from 1990 to 2019.

Exhibit 3: Impact of Unsmoothing on Annualized Volatility

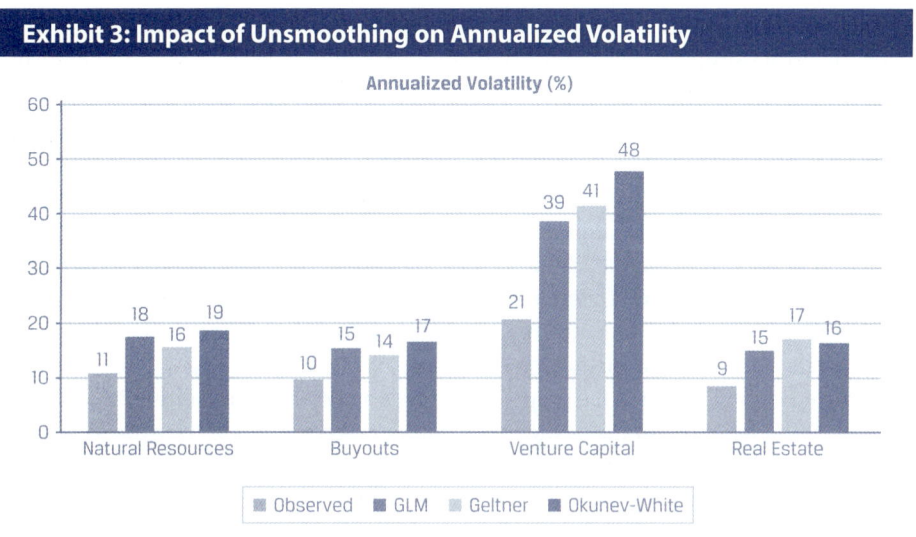

Source: Data is from Cambridge Associates.

Exhibit 4: Impact of Unsmoothing on Beta to Public Equities

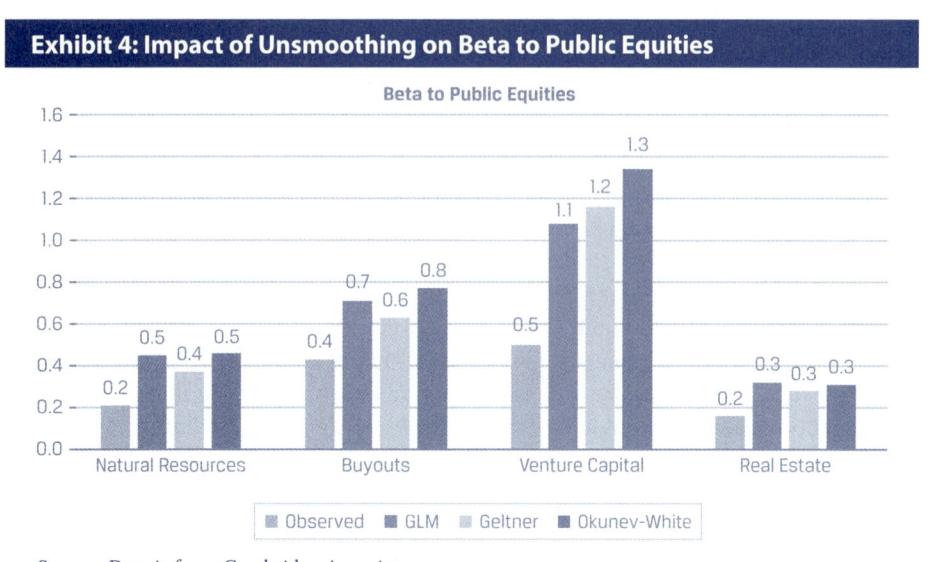

Source: Data is from Cambridge Associates.

As illustrated in Exhibit 3 and Exhibit 4, after applying unsmoothing techniques, the resulting returns exhibit higher volatility and are typically more correlated with public equity markets. These unsmoothed return series can then be used along with returns on publicly traded asset classes to determine the covariance matrix to be used in a mean–variance optimization exercise when determining the appropriate allocation to illiquid asset classes and hedge funds. Mean–variance optimization, however, still falls short as an adequate asset allocation tool for institutional investors because it is not able to take into account the illiquid nature of some asset classes. Illiquid asset classes cannot be rebalanced easily without a potential significant price concession. Single-period optimization methods, such as mean–variance optimization, fail when illiquid asset classes are introduced, because such techniques implicitly assume that investors keep portfolio weights constant over time (i.e., portfolio weights are rebalanced perfectly) and they ignore the drawdown structure of illiquid asset classes and the uncertainty of cash flows. Currently, there are not any widely accepted alternatives. Most investors simply constrain the allocations to illiquid asset classes in the mean–variance optimization to achieve reasonable and practical portfolios.

Direct vs. fund investments in illiquid asset classes

In recent years, large pension funds and sovereign wealth funds have increasingly opted to invest directly in illiquid asset classes rather than through the more typical limited partner (LP)–general partner (GP) setup. Some large pension funds and SWFs have built up a large team of merchant banking professionals who are equally capable as a large private equity fund team. The main motivation behind such a move is to save on the high fees that institutional investors typically pay to GPs (2% base fee on committed capital and 20% fee on profits or over a certain hurdle rate). Being able to save on these fees should make the investments more profitable over the long term. Direct investments provide an institutional investor with control over each individual investment. This situation puts the investor in a better position to manage liquidity. In the case of direct investments, there are no unfunded commitments, making it easier to manage capital. The investor also has full discretion over the decision when to exit investments and will not have to be forced to sell in a down market. As a result, direct investments partially alleviate some of the liquidity challenges typically associated with private asset classes and resolve some of the principal–agent issues associated with fund investing.

There are also disadvantages to direct investments in private asset classes. Direct investments in private equity, real estate, or infrastructure require a dedicated and experienced in-house team. In some instances, rather than building out an in-house team for private investments, large pension funds and sovereign wealth funds acquire a general partner. For example, Ontario Teachers' Pension Plan purchased Cadillac Fairview, a large operating company for real estate. Managing and assembling an in-house team adds several challenges compared with the more nimble setup in the case of fund investing. The sourcing of deals may be constrained by the talent and network of the in-house team. As a result, it may be more difficult to diversify the portfolio across geography and industries. Direct investment portfolios may have higher concentration risk because direct investors opt for larger investments due to staffing issues and scalability. This risk could adversely affect the liquidity of these investments because they might be harder to sell and, therefore, potentially less liquid. If the investor relies on external managers for deal sourcing or a partnership agreement, there is a risk of adverse selection. Finally, the governance structure is not set up as well in the case of direct investing compared with fund investments. In contrast to fund managers, employees of a pension fund or sovereign wealth fund may not be able to sit on the board of a private company. Institutional investors may not be able to afford the liability issues associated with direct investing. For fund investments, the investor is a limited partner and has limited liability, whereas with direct investments, the investor may be considered a general partner, with additional liability risks. Finally, institutional investors may find it difficult to adequately compensate internal staff to ensure that they hire and retain talent. This is usually a problem for public pension funds because there is public pressure to keep compensation down.

Managing Liquidity Risk

In this section, we discuss some of the tools used by institutional investors to manage overall liquidity risk in their portfolios.

Liquidity management steps:

1. **Establish liquidity risk parameters.**

   Institutional investors typically create liquidity guidelines regarding what percentage of assets needs to be liquid and available on a daily or monthly basis. In addition, given the drawdown structure of illiquid asset classes, institutional investors need to keep track of uncalled commitments, not simply invested capital. It is typical for institutional investors to have internal guidelines or bands around the sum of invested capital and uncalled commitments as a percentage of total assets. In addition to such bands, they may have automatic or semiautomatic escalation triggers, such as reducing commitments to illiquid asset classes or even actively seeking to reduce investments through secondary sales once the sum of invested capital plus uncalled commitments reaches a certain level (expressed as a percentage of total assets). These liquidity risk parameters can either be internal or be included in an investment policy statement approved by the board.

2. **Assess the liquidity of the current portfolio and how it evolves over time.**

   The second step in managing liquidity risk at the overall portfolio level is to have a clear sense of the liquidity of the portfolio and measure liquidity parameters versus guidelines. Most institutional investors have an internal report that shows what percentage of the portfolio can be liquidated within a day, within a week, within a month, within a quarter, and within a year and what percentage of the portfolio takes more than a year to be liquidated. It is important not only to have a snapshot of that report at a given point in time but also to understand how it evolves over time as the portfolio changes. A good starting point for developing these statistics is to simply look at the legal terms that are in place with external managers. This is particularly relevant for active managers and hedge funds that have redemption notices and lockups included in the investment agreement. In the case of internal management, an even more granular assessment can be made depending on the types of securities being held and using market liquidity measures to gauge how much of these securities can be sold over different time frames during a financial crisis. As discussed in Section 2.3, investors may also want to take into account how redeeming from certain external managers during a crisis may impact the future relationship with that manager (in other words, they may not want to redeem even if the investments are liquid and instead include these investments in a less liquid category).

3. **Develop a cash flow model and project future expected cash flows.**

   The third step is to understand and model the various cash flows. As discussed in Section 2.3, institutional investors make payouts (retirement payments, foundation spending, etc.), they receive inflows (gifts and donations for an endowment, pension contributions for a pension plan, etc.), they have to meet capital calls for illiquid asset classes and receive distributions, and they have to rebalance their portfolios. Most institutional investors model each of those cash flows and project future expected cash flows. Section 2.4 briefly discussed how capital calls and distributions are modeled for illiquid asset classes.

4. **Stress test liquidity needs and cash flow projections.**

The standard cash flow modeling and projections assume business as usual, but it is important to stress test these cash flow projections and liquidity needs. As discussed in Section 2.4, cash flows are affected by market movements. For example, donations might be lower in a crisis and payouts might be higher. Institutional investors stress test their cash flow projections and liquidity needs. It is important to point out that this process is more of an art than a science and there is no universally accepted method for stress testing (as there are universally accepted methods for market risk calculations).

5. **Put in place an emergency plan.**

   Finally, institutional investors should put in place an emergency action plan. Such an action plan should include what to liquidate—and in what order—in a crisis to meet cash flows and how to rebalance the portfolio in a crisis. Having such a plan in place can help avoid the risk of panicking in a crisis. Sharing the emergency action plan with the board to get buy-in can also help when a crisis occurs and mitigate the risk of board members pressuring the investment team to make sub-optimal short-term decisions.

Exhibit 5 summarizes the five steps in developing a liquidity management plan.

Exhibit 5: Liquidity Management Steps

1. Establish liquidity risk parameters.
2. Assess the liquidity of current portfolio, and monitor the evolution over time.
3. Develop a cash flow model and project future cash flows.
4. Stress test liquidity needs and cash flow projections.
5. Develop an emergency action plan.

Long-term institutional investors are able take on certain investment risks that other institutional investors simply cannot bear. Since the late 1990s, they have increasingly invested in a broad range of alternative asset classes, including private equity, private real estate, natural resources, infrastructure, and hedge funds. In this reading, we focus on the financial risks that emanate from illiquid investments because these risks tend to be less well quantified but can pose an existential threat to long-term investors if not addressed and managed carefully. The focus has been on how market and liquidity risk interact to create potential challenges at the overall portfolio level and affect the institutional investor's ability to meet its long-term objectives. We propose several steps institutional investors can take to better manage liquidity at the overall portfolio level.

Enterprise Risk Management for Institutional Investors

Exhibit 6 provides a high-level view of a risk management framework in an enterprise context:

Exhibit 6: Risk Management Framework in an Enterprise Context

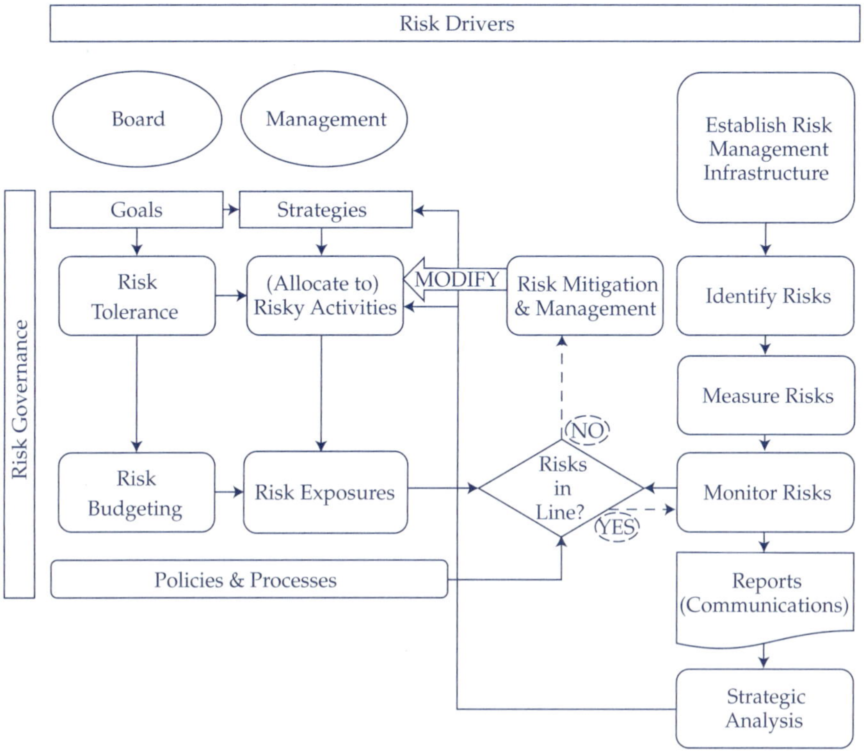

Source: "Risk Management: An Introduction," CFA Program Level I curriculum reading (2021).

We can apply this framework to the setting of an institutional investor in the following manner. The risk management process for an institutional investor starts with the board setting the overall risk tolerance for the organization that is consistent with its objectives and constraints. Risk tolerance should capture the amount of market risk that an institutional investor is willing and able to take in order to maximize expected returns, and it informs the most important investment decision that is made by the board—namely, the strategic asset allocation. Risk tolerance can be expressed in asset-only (for sovereign wealth funds, endowments, and foundations) or asset/liability terms (for pension funds and insurance companies). Typical risk measures used for setting the risk tolerance of institutional investors include volatility, maximum drawdown, and value at risk or conditional value at risk (sometimes referred to as *expected tail loss*, or *ETL*).

In addition to setting the overall risk tolerance (for market losses), the board usually approves additional risk parameters, limits, requirements, and guidelines (some quantitative and others procedural) that are codified in an investment policy statement (IPS). These may include liquidity risk parameters if the institutional investor has a significant allocation to illiquid asset classes, an active risk budget to limit and control the amount of active management pursued by investment staff, restrictions on leverage and the use of derivatives, ethical investment guidelines, and possibly credit risk parameters and constraints in the case of significant fixed-income investments (for example, for an insurance company). These additional guidelines and constraints are put in place to ensure that the investment activities are consistent with the board's risk tolerance and expectations (and with regulatory requirements if applicable).

Management (i.e., the investment team) is tasked with implementing the strategic asset allocation (SAA) and investing the assets either internally or through external managers across the various asset classes included in the SAA. The investment team is also responsible for managing and monitoring the risks associated with the implementation of the SAA and reporting to the board. The objective is not to minimize or eliminate risk but to measure and attribute risk to various risk exposures and factors to ensure that the investments adequately compensate the institution for the risks being taken. Institutional investors typically perform risk factor analysis to better understand the fund's risk exposures, such as exposure to equity risk, interest rate risk, credit risk, inflation risk, currency risk, and liquidity risk. This analysis includes both quantitative modeling and qualitative risk assessments. Quantitative tools may involve sophisticated risk management systems based on returns or holdings, scenario analysis, and stress testing. Other risks are more qualitative in nature, such as potential reputational risk from certain types of investments.

For public equity investments, active risk versus a benchmark needs to be measured and monitored. Institutional investors may have an explicit active risk budget in place. Part of the risk budgeting effort involves ensuring that the active risk budget accurately reflects the areas where most excess return can be expected. In addition, the investment team will want to ensure that most of the active risk in public equities comes from stock picking and not simply from loading on certain equity risk factors, such as growth, momentum, or quality.

For private equity investments, the board may want to understand whether the returns achieved on the investment adequately compensated the fund for giving up liquidity. One way to answer that question is by comparing the returns on the private equity investment with the return of public equities. Currency risk tends to sometimes be overlooked by institutional investors. This risk can have an outsized and unexpected impact on the overall return. Although currency risk can be hedged in some cases, doing so is typically costly or even impossible when investing in emerging and frontier markets. The risk of currency devaluation needs to be acknowledged and assessed prior to making investments. Another risk that gets overlooked is asset allocation drift. The investment portfolio should be rebalanced on a regular basis to bring it back in line with the strategic asset allocation that was approved by the board.

The risk management infrastructure of the institutional investor should be set up to identify and measure the aforementioned risks and monitor how they change over time and whether they are in line with the guidelines set up by the board in the IPS and with additional—more granular—internal guidelines set by the Chief Investment Officer and risk team. The risk team is usually tasked with risk reporting to the various stakeholders, which may include an internal investment committee and the board to ensure adequate risk oversight. The investment team should recognize when risk exposures are not aligned with the overall risk tolerance and guidelines and take action to bring them back into alignment. These actions may involve hedging, rebalancing, and secondary sales or in the case of illiquid investments, reducing commitments.

3   ENVIRONMENTAL AND SOCIAL RISKS FACED BY INSTITUTIONAL INVESTORS

☐ discuss environmental and social risks associated with the portfolio strategy of an institutional investor

Universal Ownership, Externalities, and Responsible Investing

In this section, we define universal owners as large institutional investors that effectively own a slice of the whole economy and hence are generally managing their total market exposure, instead of focusing on a subset of issuers. Institutional investors such as sovereign wealth funds and public pension funds usually have large portfolios that are highly diversified and built with a long-term focus. Such portfolios are representative of global capital markets, thereby making such investors "universal owners."

Investing long term in widely diversified holdings inevitably exposes such portfolios to increasing costs related to negative environmental and social externalities. An externality is an impact that an individual's or a corporation's activities have on a third party. If everyone acts in their own self-interest, it could lead to an overall negative outcome for society. Examples of negative environmental externalities include plastic pollution in the ocean, poor air quality due to industrial and vehicular emissions, and water toxicity due to improper effluent management.

Universal owners find it challenging to effectively diversify risks arising from negative environmental and social externalities. Costs that are externalized by one portfolio company can negatively affect the profitability of another portfolio company, thereby adversely affecting the overall portfolio return. For example, a sovereign wealth fund invests in a plastic manufacturer that is saving waste treatment and disposal costs by directly releasing waste pellets and other chemical residues into a nearby river. Water toxicity arising as a result of these actions causes reduced productivity in the agriculture operations downstream, which the asset owner is also invested in. In addition, strengthening regulations related to environmental protection, for example, may lead to monetary fines and penalties, thereby leading to financial risks for a company causing such negative externalities.

According to the UN-backed Principles for Responsible Investment (PRI), environmental costs for universal owners are reflected in portfolio impacts via insurance premiums, taxes, inflated input prices, and the physical costs associated with weather-related disasters (PRI Association 2017). Also, the cost of remediating environmental damage is often significantly higher than the cost of preventing it. Given these facts, it is imperative for large institutional investors to internalize the price of such negative externalities by considering the impact of their investments on society and future generations.

Exhibit 7 provides a non-exhaustive list of environmental and social issues that we have introduced in Level I of the CFA Program curriculum.

Exhibit 7: Examples of Environmental and Social Factors

Environmental Issues	Social Issues
Climate change and carbon emissions	Customer satisfaction and product responsibility
Air and water pollution	Data security and privacy
Biodiversity	Gender and diversity
Deforestation	Occupational health and safety
Energy efficiency	Community relations and charitable activities
Waste management	Human rights
Water scarcity	Labor standards

In the next section, we share examples of how some of these environmental and social issues could impact the portfolio strategy for large institutional investors that have a long-term focus toward their investments.

Systemic risks have the potential to destabilize capital markets and lead to serious negative consequences for financial institutions and the broader economy. The unpredictable nature of such megatrends as climate change and their related impacts, both environmental and socioeconomic, pose clear systemic risks to global financial markets. A study carried out by researchers at the Grantham Research Institute on Climate Change and the Environment (2016) at the London School of Economics and Political Science and Vivid Economics projected that climate change could reduce the value of global financial assets by as much as $24 trillion—resulting in permanent damage that would far eclipse that from the 2007–09 financial crisis.

Material Environmental Issues for an Institutional Investor

For an institutional investor, such as a sovereign wealth fund, such megatrends as climate change and their related risks—both physical and transition risks—have the potential to cause significant harm to a portfolio's value over the medium to long term, particularly for investments in real assets (real estate, infrastructure) and private equity, neither of which are easily divestible. Next, we will discuss the impact of climate-related risks on an institutional investor's portfolio from the perspective of private equity and real asset investments.

Physical climate risks

As we have observed since the beginning of the current century, climate change has profoundly affected the physical world we live in. Annual average temperatures across the globe are continuously rising, and 19 of the 20 warmest years have occurred since 2001 (NASA 2019). Erratic weather patterns, such as heavy precipitation, droughts, and hurricanes, are both more frequent and of higher magnitude. Similarly, wildfires are causing more and more devastation every year. In addition, the chronic issue of sea-level rise is causing coastal flooding. As shown in Exhibit 8, an increase in extreme weather events has occurred.

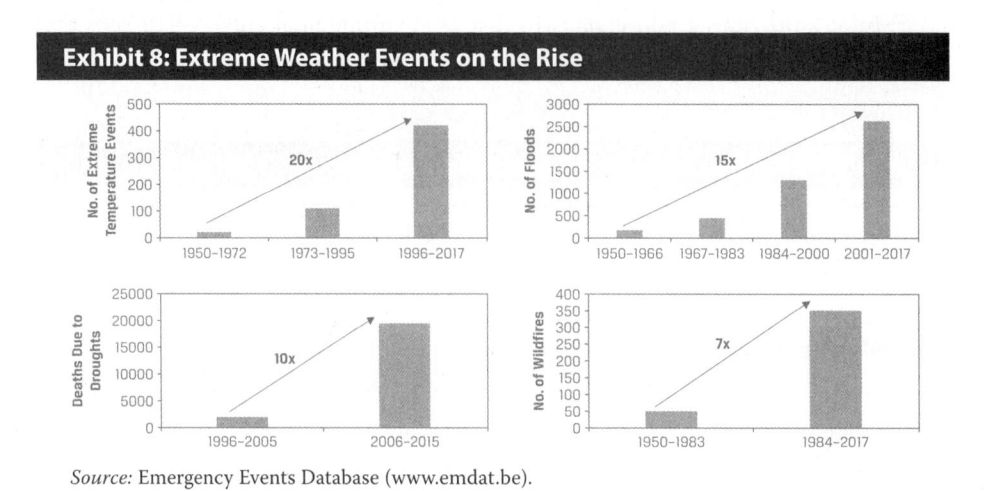

Exhibit 8: Extreme Weather Events on the Rise

Source: Emergency Events Database (www.emdat.be).

With continued climate change, all these physical climate risks could become more severe in the future and, to a certain extent, become the new normal for the world. Depending on global responses to climate change in the coming decade, the degree of their impact on our economies and investments may be alleviated.

So, what does this mean for the portfolio strategy of large institutional investors with private equity and real asset investments?

Impact on real assets

Should these trends continue, the physical risks that we have discussed could create increased levels of stress on such assets as residential and commercial real estate and infrastructure, such as roads and railways. Rising sea levels that lead to flooding would impact both rents and property valuation for hitherto prime coastal properties. Prolonged exposure to extreme heat would negatively affect the useful life of roads and train tracks, which would lead to accelerated depreciation of such assets and, therefore, more frequent replacement costs for companies and governments (CFA Institute 2020).

Similarly, physical damage caused by frequent, large-scale weather-related events, such as hurricanes or even wildfires—once considered too irregular to insure against— could not only lead to large-scale drawdowns in the portfolio's asset value but also make it difficult or expensive to insure such assets. Most of the flooding-related losses around the world are uninsured, thereby causing additional stress on a country's economy and its people (see Exhibit 9).

Exhibit 9: Global Flood Losses and Insurance Levels

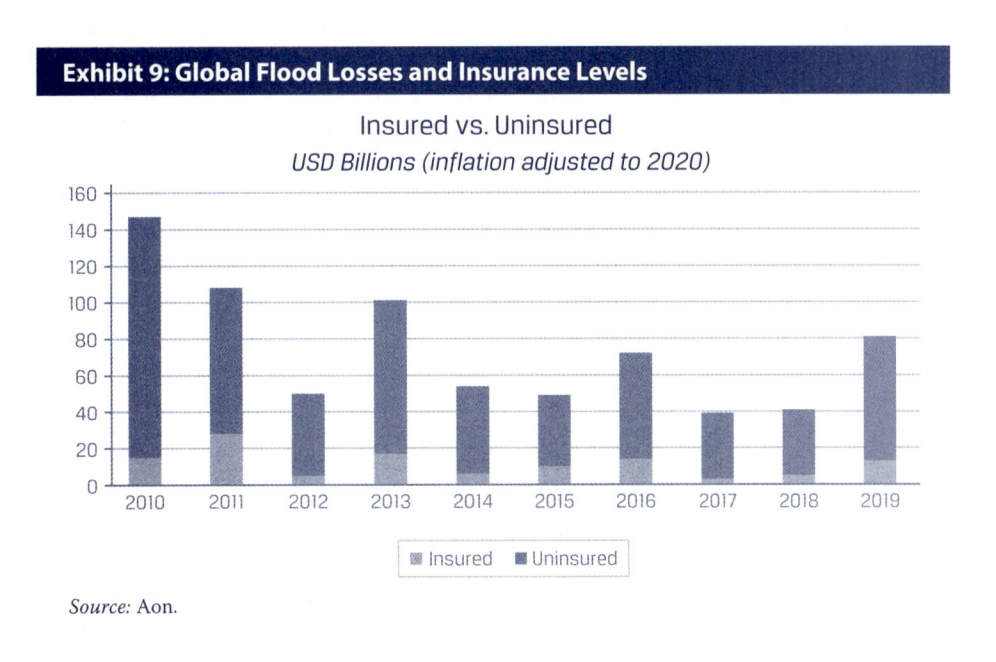

Insured vs. Uninsured
USD Billions (inflation adjusted to 2020)

Source: Aon.

Because these physical climate-related risks continue to play out in a much larger and more frequent manner than previously anticipated, they will continue to bring down prices and rental yields of prime real estate, leading to permanent impairments of asset valuations. For a large institutional investor that is looking to preserve capital and provide growth benefits to multiple generations, it is imperative that these risks be factored into the portfolio construction strategies.

Climate transition risks

In line with the 2015 Paris Climate Agreement, countries and companies around the world are already making efforts to dramatically reduce or eliminate their CO_2 emissions in order to limit the global temperature increase in this century to 2 degrees Celsius above preindustrial levels. To keep global warming less than 2°C, scientists project that energy-related CO_2 emissions need to fall 25% by 2030 and reach "net zero" by 2070 (Intergovernmental Panel on Climate Change 2018; IEA 2020).

One of the most ambitious efforts to incentivize decarbonization is the European Union's sustainable finance taxonomy, which helps investors understand whether an economic activity is environmentally sustainable. As of October 2020, looking at the scientific evidence about the current and potential impacts of climate change, it has become clear that the world needs to move toward a low-carbon future if we are to cap global warming at less than 2°C and prevent the negative effects that not doing so would bring to our climate, our ecosystems, and human life. What is currently unclear is the pace at which this decarbonization will happen.

Rapid decarbonization will lead to restrictions on carbon emissions, implementation of some form of carbon pricing, introduction of new technologies, and changes in the consumer behavior. All these effects can create massive disruptions in certain sectors, such as electricity generation (with the increasing cost competitiveness of renewable energy sources as compared with coal) and automobiles (with the impending widespread switch from internal combustion engines to electric vehicles. The International Energy Agency has forecast that in order to reach carbon neutrality by 2050, half of all cars in the world should be electric by 2030 (Lo 2020).

The PRI's Inevitable Policy Response (IPR) project aims to prepare financial markets for climate-related policy risks that are likely to emerge in the short to medium term. The IPR forecast a response by 2025 that will be forceful, abrupt, and disorderly because of the delayed action (see Exhibit 10). The PRI argues that markets have inefficiently priced climate transition risks, but its policy forecast is that a forceful policy response to climate change in the near term is a highly likely outcome, leaving portfolios of institutional investors exposed to significant risks that need to be mitigated.

Exhibit 10: IPR Key Policy Forecasts

Coal phase-outs	Sales ban on Internal Combustion Engines (ICE)	Carbon Pricing (Emission Allowances)	Zero carbon power
Early coal phase-out for first mover countries by 2030	Early sales ban for first mover countries by 2035	US$40-80/tCO$_2$ prices by 2030 for first movers	Significant ramp-up of renewable energy globally
Steady retirement of coal-fired power generation after 2030 in lagging countries	Other countries follow suit as automotive industry reaches tipping point	Global convergence accelerated by Border Carbon Adjustment (BCA) to >=$100/tCO$_2$ by 2050	Policy support of nuclear capacity increase in a small set of countries, nuclear phased out elsewhere

Carbon Capture and Storage (CCS) & industry decarbonisation	Energy efficiency	Green House Gas (GHG) removal (Land use-based)	Agriculture
Limited CCS support in power,	Increase in coverage and stringency of performance standards	Improved forestry and nature-based solutions	Technical support to improve agricultural yields
Policy incentives primarily for industrial and bioenergy CCS	Utility obligation programs	Stronger enforcement of zero deforestation	Increasing public investment in irrigation and AgTech
Public support for demonstration, and then deployment of hydrogen clusters	Financial and behavioral incentives	Controlled expansion of bioenergy crops	Incremental behavioural incentives away from beef

Source: PRI IPR (www.unpri.org/the-inevitable-policy-response-policy-forecasts/4849.article).

Given the uncertainty around the precise timing and magnitude of the impact of climate change, organizations are increasingly using climate-related scenario analysis to better understand how their businesses might perform under a variety of global warming scenarios—for example, in a world that is 2°C, 3°C, or 4°C warmer. The Task force on Climate-Related Financial Disclosures (TCFD) recommends organizations, including banks, asset managers, and asset owners, use scenario analysis to estimate the implications of such risks and opportunities for their businesses over time and also to inform their strategic thinking. The International Energy Agency and the Intergovernmental Panel on Climate Change both publicly offer a set of climate-related scenarios that are widely used. To learn more about climate-related scenario analysis, refer to the technical supplement issued by the TCFD.

Climate opportunities

Although most of the investor focus in dealing with climate change has been on managing physical and transition risks, exciting investment opportunities are arising in companies focused on climate change mitigation and adaptation. These opportunities exist in secondary markets and, in some cases, investments in real assets and infrastructure projects, such as wind and solar farms and smart grids.

Because the levelized cost of energy for renewable energy generation technologies has considerably decreased since 2010, these have become cost competitive with some conventional generation technologies, such as coal-based power generation, as shown in Exhibit 11.

Exhibit 11: 2019 Levelized Cost of Energy, Unsubsidized

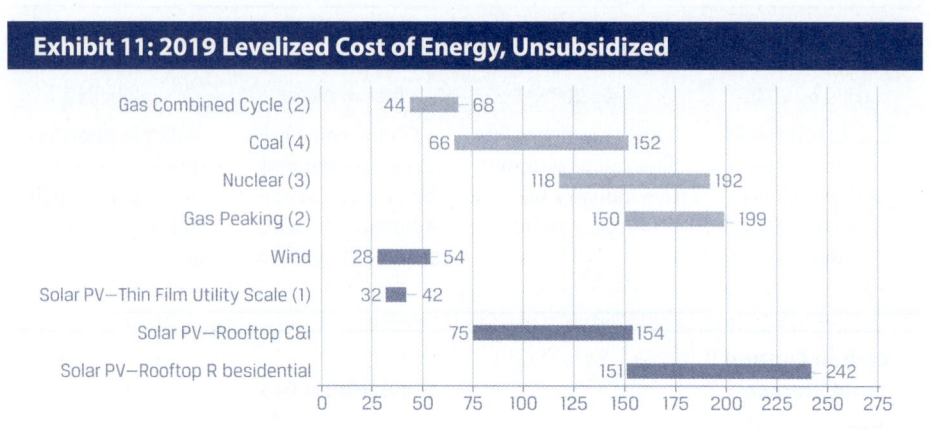

Note: Levelized cost of energy is a measure of the average net present cost of electricity generation for a power plant over its lifetime.

(1)   Unless otherwise indicated herein, the low end represents a single-axis tracking system and the high end represents a fixed-tilt system.

(2)   The fuel cost assumption for Lazard's global, unsubsidized analysis for gas-fired generation resources is $3.45/MMBTU.

(3)   Unless otherwise indicated, the analysis herein does not reflect decommissioning costs, ongoing maintenance-related capital expenditures or the potential economic impacts of federal loan guarantees or other subsidies.

(4)   High end incorporates 90% carbon capture and compression. Does not include cost of transportation and storage.

Sources: Data is from Lazard (www.lazard.com/perspective/lcoe2019).

This cost competitiveness, coupled with the urgency to decarbonize our economies to avoid the potentially catastrophic physical impacts of climate change, has created secular growth opportunity for such businesses and assets, thereby attracting increasingly large investor attention.

A summary of the business segments where such opportunities may lie follows.

Climate mitigation

This category includes companies that are positioned to benefit, directly or indirectly, from efforts to curb or mitigate the long-term effects of global climate change, to address the environmental challenges presented by global climate change, or to improve the efficiency of resource consumption.

Exhibit 12: Climate Mitigation Opportunity Examples

Business Segment	Description
Clean energy	Companies in this segment are involved in the generation of clean energy from such sources as wind, solar, and small hydro. This segment also includes manufacturers of such equipment as windmills and solar panels, as well as related service providers.
Energy efficiency	This segment comprises businesses that provide products and services to improve the efficiency of energy consumption in a variety of processes. Examples include energy efficient transportation and building solution providers and recycling technology.

Business Segment	Description
Batteries and storage	This segment includes companies that help improve battery storage capacity and efficiency. These improvements are critical, for instance, to sustainable growth and wider penetration of some of the previously mentioned technologies, such as clean energy generation and distribution and electric vehicles.
Smart grids	Smart grids are digitally enhanced versions of the conventional electricity grid, with a layer of communication network overlaying the traditional grid. They are a key enabler for energy security and reliability and integration of clean energy resources.
Materials	Such materials as copper and battery-grade lithium are key ingredients in the clean energy value chain because they are required in clean energy power generation, storage solutions, and electric vehicles, resulting in a projected demand rise as the world transitions toward a low-carbon future.

Climate adaptation

This category includes companies that would help better adjust to actual or expected future change in climate with an aim to reduce vulnerability to the harmful effects of climate change, such as food insecurity, sea-level rise, and frequent extreme weather events.

Exhibit 13: Climate Adaptation Opportunity Examples

Business Segment	Description
Sustainable agriculture	Companies in this segment are involved in providing products that improve agriculture productivity and reduce the resource consumption in the entire process. Sustainable fish farming and timber production are other activities included here.
Water	This This segment consists of businesses that provide products and services to improve the efficiency of water consumption in a variety of processes, including wastewater treatment and reuse.

Many institutional investors are increasing allocations to such sectors as part of their real-asset allocation or as a potential equity alpha opportunity with the expectation that companies in these sectors will outperform the broad equity market over a long period of time as the world transitions to a low carbon future. Evaluating and sufficiently managing both physical and transition climate risks in the portfolio and capturing some of the aforementioned secular growth opportunities could position large institutional investor portfolios to outperform and grow in value in the long term.

Material Social Issues for an Institutional Investor

Environmental issues, such as climate change and air pollution, are reasonably mature and quite well understood, making them easier to accommodate in discounted cash flow models. Social issues, such as community relation, occupational health and safety, privacy and data security, modern slavery and other human right violations in the supply chain, and inequality, however, are relatively challenging to quantify and integrate into financial models. Most social issues have largely qualitative data reported by companies, such as health and safety policies and initiatives, lists of product quality certifications, and human capital management policies, rather than metrics on which long-term performance can be judged. Nevertheless, these issues have the potential to cause reputational and financial damage to a company and its investors if not managed sufficiently well.

Managing community relations and the social license to operate

For large institutional investors, such as sovereign wealth funds and public pension funds, their investments may have positive social impacts, such as improving essential public infrastructure and services or providing better access to medicine and technology, or negative social impacts, via poor labor standards or forceful relocation and improper rehabilitation of communities by their portfolio companies. Good corporate behavior is usually well received by the community relations, leading to a sustainable and mutually beneficial long-term relationship. In many ways, these aspects are essential to keeping a company's social license to operate.

Let's take a hypothetical example of a sovereign wealth fund (SWF) that has invested in a dam-based hydroelectric power plant in an economically less developed part of its country. Although there will be a positive environmental impact of the project because it will generate electricity from a renewable source, the social impacts of the project could be mixed. On the positive side, rural electrification arising from this project will lead to economic development in the region, thereby improving the standard of living. Dam-based hydroelectric power plants require large-scale land acquisition, often leading to relocation and rehabilitation of indigenous communities. Some locals protest that they have not been sufficiently consulted by the government before issuing consent to establish this project. Moreover, there are allegations of acquisition of land for the project at unfair/poor valuations. In some instances, protesting locals were forcefully removed and relocated by local government authorities, leading to unrest. Eventually, the SWF decides to cease the project implementation owing to this wide variety of instances of pushback from the society.

This example highlights the importance of considering social risks when investing. Despite having the positive intent of supporting development of renewable power generation in a less economically developed part of the country, the SWF faced pushback and reputational damage for not holistically considering the interests of all the stakeholders involved, especially local communities that were the most affected by the project. Some of the best practices in community relation management include extensive stakeholder consultation meetings to better understand their needs and address their concerns, providing alternative employment opportunities to those affected, and ensuring fair land acquisition, rehabilitation, and resettlement practices.

Labor issues in the supply chain

Another increasingly important social topic is the one related to poor labor practices, especially in the supply chain. Driven by globalization, a consumption boom across developed and emerging markets, and the availability of cheap labor in certain parts of the world, a large portion of the manufacturing and assembling activities across such key sectors as technology and garments has been outsourced to developing and frontier markets, such as India, Vietnam, and Malaysia. Although access to cheap, semi-skilled labor has led to better bottom lines for multinational companies, it has also come at the cost of exploitation of workers in such supply chains. Labor rights are being compromised in the form of heavy reliance on temporary workers, excessive or forced overtime, and low wages. Moreover, lax regulations in many countries allow legal prevention of unionization or any form of collective bargaining, thereby making such workers more vulnerable.

Large brands in the apparel industry, such as Nike and Gap, and in the technology space, such as Apple and Samsung, have all been accused of various levels of lapses in their supply chain related to the aforementioned labor management issues. Apart from suffering significant damage to their brands and reputations, which could lead to consumer boycotts, such companies may also face additional costs and/or fines related to product recalls and ad hoc shifting of supply chains.

For SWFs with equity exposure to some of the largest apparel brands and branded tech hardware companies, considering such issues while making investments is of paramount importance because lack of transparency in the supply chain and lapses in labor management may weigh heavily on the resilience of such supply chains amid global-scale disruptions, such as that caused by the COVID-19 pandemic. In addition to the financial risks, reputational risks may also arise because of a view that the SWF implicitly supports such improper and unethical business practices.

The "just" transition

Sustainable development involves meeting the needs of the present generation without compromising the ability of future generations to meet their own needs. Sustainable development includes economic, social, and environmental dimensions, all of which are interrelated. In the transition to environmentally sustainable economies and societies, several challenges may arise—for example, displacement of workers and job losses in certain industries, such as coal mining, fossil fuel extraction/production, and fossil fuel-based power generation. Similarly, increased energy costs due to carbon taxes and higher costs of commodities partly resulting from sustainable production practices may have adverse effects on the incomes of poor households. Therefore, a "just" transition is necessary to ensure that there are limited negative social impacts in our pursuit of positive environmental impacts via avoiding fossil fuels and implementing sustainable agriculture and business practices. Although there is no fixed set of guidelines, the just transition encourages a dialogue between workers, industry, and governments influenced by geographical, political, cultural, and social contexts in order to tackle some of the aforementioned challenges.

CASE STUDY

4

- [ ] analyze and evaluate the financial and non-financial risk exposures in the portfolio strategy of an institutional investor
- [ ] discuss various methods to manage the risks that arise on long-term direct investments of an institutional investor
- [ ] evaluate strengths and weaknesses of an enterprise risk management system and recommend improvements

Case Study: Introduction

You are working as a Risk Analyst at a small sovereign wealth fund (SWF) and reporting to the Head of Risk. The SWF is considering making some new investments in direct private equity and direct infrastructure. You have been asked to review risk aspects of these investment opportunities, which will be discussed in an upcoming investment committee meeting. Assuming the investments will be made, you will also have the responsibility to monitor the risk of the investments as well as make recommended improvements to the SWF's risk management system. You are excited about these opportunities and look forward to putting your knowledge and skills learned from the CFA Program to work!

Case Study: Background

- Over 20 years ago, the "Republic of Ruritania" discovered an extremely large deposit of crucial rare earth metals that are key elements in the manufacturing of high-speed computers used in science and finance. The entire deposit was sold to various entities allowing Ruritania to secure its financial future. At the same time, the government of Ruritania "dollarized" the economy, moving from the domestic RRR currency to the USD.

- The government of Ruritania (R) decided to form a sovereign wealth fund, R-SWF, in order to grow the capital for future generations. This type of SWF is a "savings fund," intended to share wealth across generations by transforming non-renewable assets into diversified financial assets.

- R-SWF has built up a diversified portfolio of equities, fixed income, and alternative investments.

- In equities and fixed income, the SWF invests in developed markets, emerging markets, and frontier markets through both fund investing and direct investing.

- In alternatives, the SWF invests in private equity (PE), infrastructure, and real estate. Investment methods used include direct investing, making co-investments, and fund investing.

- The case study begins in Section 3 at an investment committee meeting to discuss two potential investments. The next scene, in Section 4, is set three years later, when the performance of the investments are discussed at another investment committee meeting. The final scene, in Section 5, is set five years later and provides additional information on investment performance.

R-SWF'S Investments: 1.0

Initial Case Facts (1.0)

Today, the investment committee of R-SWF is considering several new investments, including direct private equity and direct infrastructure investments. The investment committee will be discussing risk aspects of the investments, led by the Head of Risk and supported by *you*, a Risk Analyst.

- The investment committee meeting will open with an overview of asset allocation and a few basic discussions on the two proposed investments. However, the focus of the meeting is on the potential risks of the new investment proposals, not details on the investments themselves. (An in-depth investment committee meeting on the new investments was held last month.)

- The meeting will then move on to a discussion of the potential risks of the two specific direct investments being considered.

  1. Direct infrastructure investment in an airport

  2. Direct PE investment in a beverage manufacturer

- The investment committee meeting will discuss key risks that R-SWF should consider as it decides whether to make new direct investments in PE and infrastructure.

- All investment committee participants (and CFA Program Level III candidates) are provided with a background memo with the following information:

Memo A: Background on R-SWF's asset allocation and performance

Memo B: Details on the proposed direct infrastructure investment

Memo C: Details on the proposed direct private equity investment

INVESTMENT COMMITTEE MEETING MEMO 1.0

To: R-SWF Investment Committee Members

From: R-SWF Chief Investment Officer

Re: Investment Committee Meeting Agenda

Distribution: Head of Risk, Head of PE, Head of Infrastructure, Head of Equities, and Level III Candidates in the CFA Program

An agenda for today's meeting is as follows:

Agenda

- Opening Remarks and Review of Asset Allocation: Chief Investment Officer
- Review of Infrastructure Investment Opportunity: Head of Infrastructure
- Review of Private Equity Investment Opportunity: Head of PE
- Discussion of Risk—Infrastructure Investment: Head of Risk + Everyone
- Discussion of Risk—PE Investment: Head of Risk + Everyone
- Closing Remarks: Chief Investment Officer

The investment committee meeting will discuss key risks that R-SWF should consider as it determines whether to make new direct investments in PE and infrastructure.

Memo 1A: Asset Allocation and Performance

- Since its inception, over a 25+ year period, R-SWF has built a diversified portfolio of investments. As of last month, the fund had AUM of $50 billion USD, with the fund outperforming its overall benchmark by 150 bps net of fees since inception. Of course, there have been short-term periods of underperformance as the fund pursued its long-term strategy.
- Asset allocation as of last month for the overall fund was as follows:

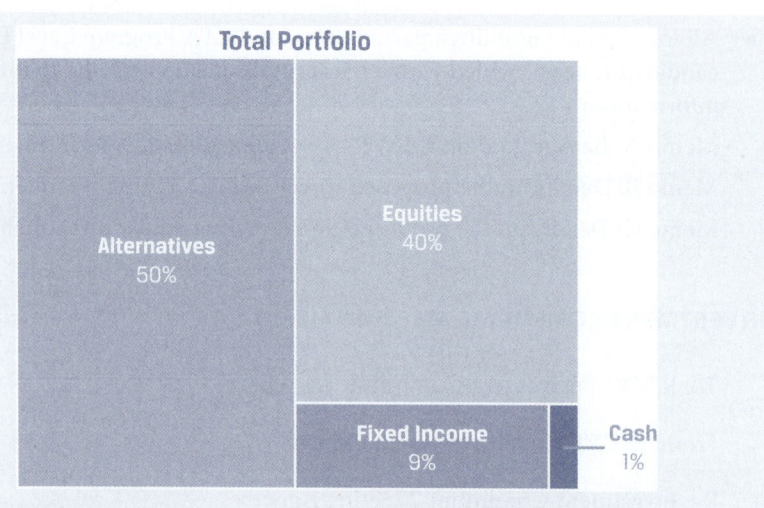

- As of last month, R-SWF had approximately 50% of assets invested in alternative investments, consistent with its long-term objectives.

- In today's investment committee meeting, R-SWF is considering two new investments in alternative investments—specifically, in direct private equity and direct infrastructure investments. *(Note: Funding for these two investments will come from a combination of cash, dividends, receivables, and fixed income. The mix will be determined by the Asset/Liability Committee, or ALCO).*

- Because today's investment committee meeting will focus on alternative investments, we will break the allocation of alternatives down further, as follows:

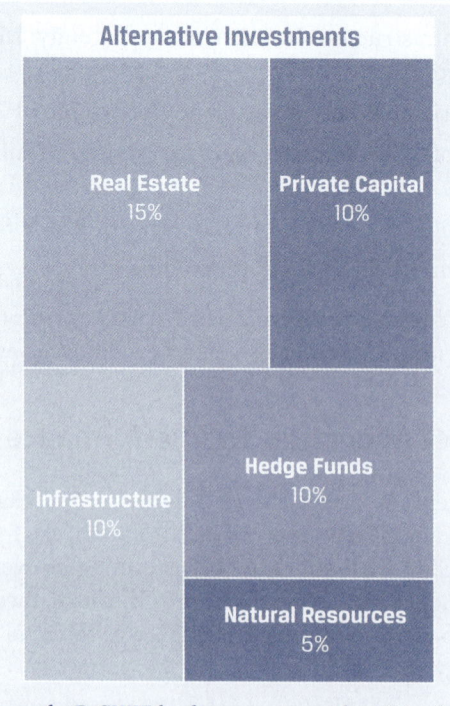

- As of last month, R-SWF had approximately 10% of assets invested in private capital and 10% of assets invested in Infrastructure.
- Next, we provide a breakdown of private capital and infrastructure:

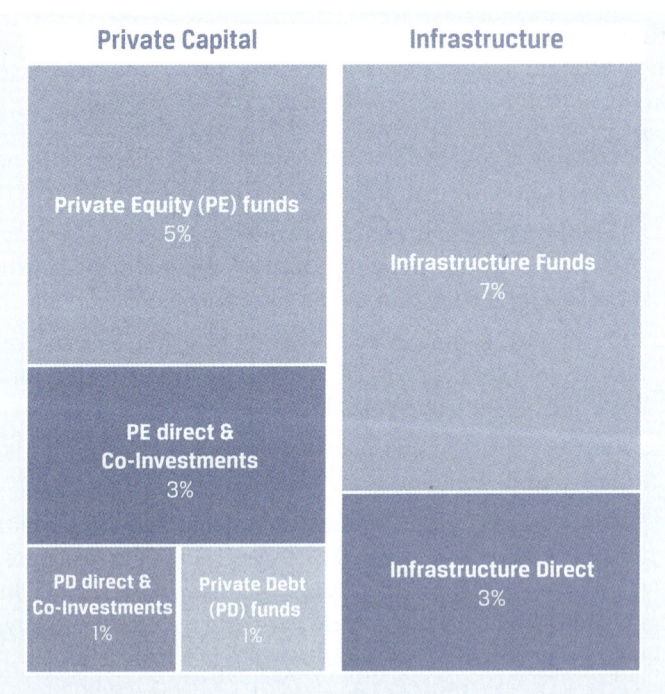

- As of last month, R-SWF had approximately 3% of assets invested in private equity direct and co-investment and 3% of assets invested in direct Infrastructure.

- The investment committee will be discussing risk aspects of the cases, led by the Head of Risk and supported by the Risk Analyst.

- Details on the proposed infrastructure investment are found in Memo 1B.

- Details on the proposed private equity investment are found in Memo 1C.

Memo 1B: Proposed Direct Infrastructure Investment

- The infrastructure direct investment opportunity is an investment in helping modernize an airport in the frontier market island nation of "Sunnyland."

- Sunnyland has beautiful beaches and several hotels, ranging from 3–star to 5–star. However, the Sunnyland Airport has only one small runway that can support airplanes of only up to 10 passengers.

- The Sunnyland government is keen on expanding the airport with a new terminal and new runway. Doing so will allow much larger aircraft to land (up to 150 passengers) and be a major boost to tourism.

- The airport is located about 2 km from the sea, providing scenic views on takeoff and landing. The new runway will be built 1 km from the sea, providing even nicer views.

- R-SWF has been approached by the Sunnyland Airport Authority (SAA) to consider a $100 million investment in a public–private partnership (PPP) on a build–operate–transfer (BOT) basis.

- For R-SWF (with assets of $50 billion), this is a small investment (0.2% of total assets). The investment will be about 2% of total infrastructure assets—$100 million/($100 million + $5,000 million)—which includes investments in funds and direct investments.

- Other facts about this infrastructure investment that are important for the investment committee to understand: *(Note: The focus of the case and investment committee discussion is risks.)*

  - Total project cost of $500 million for new 5 million passenger per annum (pax) terminal

  - $33 million investment to be provided by Airport Operating Group (AOG), which will operate the airport under a management agreement (with fixed fee plus/minus performance incentive)

  - $300 million funding to be provided through non-recourse project finance debt (i.e., approx. 70/30 debt/equity) with 15–year tenor following 3-year grace period

  - 2–year construction period, with fixed price construction contract awarded under tender

  - 25–year concession (including 2–year construction period), with investor consortium entitled to collect all regulated airport charges (e.g., passenger departure charge, landing charges) and commercial revenue (duty free, retail, F&B, car parking), subject to payment of quarterly concession fee of 35% of all revenue to SAA

  - Airport charges (70% of all revenue) are regulated by concession contract—that is, schedule of charges set and then subject to stated formula for future changes (e.g., CPI)

  - Concession agreement includes quality and performance standards to be met for design/construction/development (including timely delivery of new terminal) and operations, respectively

  - Expected IRR for full investment term of 25 years of 15%

Risk Discussion: Infrastructure Investment

The Head of Infrastructure believes the potential return on this project far outweighs the potential risk(s). However, she is happy to discuss potential risks with the investment committee.

Memo 1C: Proposed Direct Private Equity Investment

- The private equity direct investment opportunity is an investment in a local beverage company (Atsui Beverage Company Limited (ABC)) that manufactures and sells carbonated beverages. The investment will be used to modernize the plant.

- ABC is an unlisted beverage company located in the tropical, land-locked nation of "Atsui." Atsui has a developing economy and can be considered a frontier market.

- ABC is the only local manufacturer of carbonated beverages in Atsui. All other beverages are imported.

- ABC's factory is located near a river that allows for transport to the port. Also, the river is known for its unique biodiversity.

- R-SWF's Head of Private Equity has been on several vacations to Atsui and saw an investment opportunity.

- ABC is keen on modernizing its plant, but the founder is worried about giving up control. Thus, the founder is willing to sell only a minority stake of 35% in exchange for $25 million.

- For R-SWF (with assets of $50 billion), this is a small investment (0.05% of total assets). The investment will be about 0.4% of total PE assets—$25 million/($25 million + $6,000 million)—which includes investments in funds, co-investments, and direct investments.

- Other facts about this direct PE investment that are important for the investment committee to understand: *(Note: The focus of the case and investment committee discussion is risks.)*

  - R-SWF has been investing in PE for many years in funds. Over the years, R-SWF has developed direct investing capabilities through its co-investments and is now expanding its direct investing program.

  - Because of the increased direct investing capabilities of R-SWF and recent outperformance in returns, R-SWF is looking to increase its private equity allocation to direct investments over the next five years.

  - The government of Atsui has implemented tariffs on all soft drink imports. There is an upcoming election that could change this stance.

  - The cost to modernize the ABC plant is estimated to be $20 million.

  - Over the last 12 months, ABC had a revenue of $50 million. Revenue is expected to increase significantly over the next 10 years—with a modernized plant.

  - Over the last 12 months, ABC had an EBITDA of $7 million. This is an EBITDA margin of 14% and a 10× EBITDA multiple. The Head of PE feels that there is significant room for improvement.

  - With the new technology from the plant modernization, ABC will be able to expand into non-carbonated drinks, such as sports drinks and juices.

  - Once the plant is modernized, productivity will improve significantly, allowing ABC to reduce factory staff headcount by 40%, from 500 employees to 300 employees, which will drive a higher EBITDA margin in the future.

  - With a significant minority, R-SWF will be allowed to have two seats on the board of ABC. So, the board will expand from five members to seven members. R-SWF is planning to have the Head of PE join the board of ABC but hasn't decided on the other board seat.

Risk Discussion: Private Equity Investment

The Head of PE believes the potential return on this project far outweighs the potential risk(s). However, he is happy to discuss potential risks with the Investment Committee.

IN-TEXT QUESTION:

Please respond to the following question based on **Investment Committee Memo 1.0**.

As R-SWF's Risk Analyst, do you anticipate liquidity risk will likely be highlighted as a significant financial risk in the upcoming risk discussions for either investment? Explain your thinking.

Guideline Answer:

No. I do not anticipate the Head of Infrastructure or the Head of PE to highlight liquidity risk as a significant risk for either investment. Although liquidity risk is the main risk that long-term institutional investors face, particularly during a significant market decline, each of these investments represents a small portion of R-SWF's total assets. R-SWF does not have cash flow pressure, unlike many institutional investors that face pressure from the regular payment of liabilities. In addition, R-SWF has been growing over time and is making a concerted effort to expand its direct investment program.

Direct investments typically help mitigate some of the liquidity issues commonly experienced when investing in a fund because direct investment provides a greater amount of control and discretion over when to exit investments. Furthermore, as the direct investment program grows and the proportion of direct investments as part R-SWF's total assets increases, R-SWF's ability to manage capital should improve. I believe there are other financial risks that are more likely to be highlighted as a significant risk for each investment.

Investment Committee Meeting 1.0

Participants

Chief Investment Officer (CIO)

Head of Infrastructure

Head of PE

Head of Risk

Head of Equities

Analysts [no speaking role]

Chief Investment Officer:

Good morning, everyone. Welcome to today's investment committee meeting of the sovereign wealth fund of the Republic of Ruritania. After running this money on behalf of our citizens and future generations since its inception, the fund has outperformed our benchmark by 150 basis points, net of fees, and we've grown AUM to $50 billion over 25 years. We are very blessed.

At last month's investment committee meeting, our **Head of Infrastructure** and our **Head of PE** got together to discuss the financials and particulars of two investment opportunities. As they both deserve our attention, today we are joined by our **Head of Risk**, along with our **Head of Equities**, to review them through the lens of risk. Our esteemed junior analysts are in the room with us to observe and provide additional analysis as required.

For now, as we consider our opportunities, I'm mostly here as a facilitator, to pave the way for a robust discussion of investment risk.

Memo A shows us our asset allocation as of mid-June, and we've got 50% in alternatives. We believe in alternatives because our liabilities are negligible and we take a long-term view of things. About 40% of our allocation is in listed equities, with a large portion of that in emerging markets, which we're also big believers in. If we do fund one or both of the two investments on the table, we'll do it with a mix of cash, dividends receivable, and fixed income, but that's not for this committee to decide; the ALCO will go over that at a later date.

In any event, our focus here is private capital, the private equity side. We've got about 3% of our investments in direct private equity and co-investments and about 3% in direct infrastructure.

Again, this meeting is primarily about risk. Let's go to Memo B and ask our **Head of Infrastructure** to talk us through the first investment. It's usually the depth of her infrastructure experience that gives R-SWF the comfort to proceed in the face of risk.

Infrastructure Investment Discussion

Head of Infrastructure:

Thank you for the kind words, **CIO**. I'm glad everyone's here so we can apply the full breadth of the investment committee's expertise.

This is an airport BOT project, a PPP in the frontier island nation of Sunnyland, whose primary industry is tourism. The members of our hard-working analyst team who are new to infrastructure have been briefed on the build-operate-transfer models that private developers often adopt under private-public partnerships so they can operate the facilities they have designed and built for a number of years before handing them over to government agencies.

[**Head of Infrastructure** looks around the room to see a few polite nods from the assembled analysts.]

Funds are needed for an airport upgrade: A new terminal and a new, bigger runway will accommodate larger planes. Sunnyland needs to get rid of the passenger bottleneck to allow for an all-important boost in tourism. We're thinking $500 million and two years of construction time should be enough.

Ruritania is prepared to contribute $100 million, and we're insisting on bringing in AOG, a properly experienced airport operator, which will also be investing private equity—about $33 million. The rest of the capital will be no-recourse debt, about $300 million, and an equity injection from the government and other infrastructure investors for the remainder. The debt will be 15-year with a 3-year grace period.

With the BOT arrangements, of course, we take over the airport from the beginning under a 25-year concession agreement for all the cash flows from the terminal. So that's airport charges, like aircraft landing and passenger departure fees, as well as the commercial revenue from duty-free concessions, retail, and so forth, and we remit 35% of what we collect to the Sunnyland Airport Authority on a quarterly basis. If we want to charge more, any increases—say, for CPI adjustments—are worked out according to fixed formulas.

CIO has set the stage for this discussion of risk, and in that spirit, everyone should note the standards and conditions of our agreement with the government. You already know we've got a two-year development program—that's two years to see the revamped airport up and running—so if there are delays or shortfalls in quality, the concession agreement sets out the consequences.

Finally, our expected return for the full 25-year term given our fund's $100 million investment is a 15% IRR.

Chief Investment Officer:

Thank you, **Head of Infrastructure**. That's a sufficient return, to be sure, but let's also understand that our involvement can help our friends down in Sunnyland. If we execute this project carefully, it means a boost to the wealth of all Sunnylanders.

You've been there recently, right?

Head of Infrastructure:

I have. All indications are that it's an attractive tourist destination. Tourism is key to them now; they lack natural and other resources to diversify the economy. That's what they're depending on to build the economy.

Things are constrained because of the airport. The runway allows only for short, smaller aircraft, so just by increasing runway size and the associated facilities, you're paving a path for the whole nation to grow.

Chief Investment Officer:

I ask the assembled team to consider for a minute the responsibilities we have to ourselves, to Ruritania; we all feel partly responsible for its success. When we invest in another sovereign country, such as Sunnyland, we may carry over a similar sense of responsibility, and we take that seriously. While our proposed $100 million investment is just 0.2% of our AUM, this single investment in transportation infrastructure will have an outsized impact on our investees.

With that in mind, let's move to the other proposal on the table. Our **Head of PE** has recently returned from Atsui, the site of the proposed private equity investment outlined in Memo C. Over to you, **Head of PE**.

Private Equity Investment Discussion

Head of PE:

Yeah, I just got back. The company is called Atsui Beverage Company or ABC for short, and it was kind of "love at first sight"—or sip. I was on the beach, and a waiter brought me a drink and said it was called the "Mango Special." I thanked him but I was barely listening. You know how it is; my mind was elsewhere. But after the third sip, I was paying less attention to my leisure and more attention to just how good this drink was: refreshing, perfectly sweet, and unlike anything I'd tasted before. You know I'm always thinking about investments, ladies and gents, and I began to think I'd stumbled onto a winner.

I've been back to Atsui three times, and I introduced R-SWF to the team at the ABC plant that makes the Mango Special. I explained how sovereign wealth funds usually partner for the long term, and I built some trust while learning about their business. I know how small this is compared to the rest of our portfolio, but I'm still obsessed with this drink, so I figured out that we can invest $25 million for 35% of the business. They've got $50 million in revenue and $7 million in EBITDA. For those on the team who can't do math quickly like I can, that's a 14% EBITDA margin. And we're looking at a company valuation of roughly 10× EBITDA.

So, wait: Is this a good deal or not?

Well, let's think about it. ABC markets the only locally sourced carbonated beverage in Atsui, *and* tariffs are imposed on foreign competitors. That alone seems pretty great. And they'd use $20 million of our $25 million to modernize the plant. That way, they can turn out product way faster while also gearing up to make non-carbonated drinks like sports drinks and juices. We'd drive efficiency enough to cut headcount from 500 to 300, and that's even better for the EBITDA margin: new equipment, big changes.

I've got the most knowledge on the ground, so I could take a board seat along with someone else from our team. We've gotten pretty comfortable with co-investing, making some money, and developing our skills, and since we're expanding our direct investing effort anyway, this seems like a good fit. It's just $25 million out of our $50 billion pool, so it's a good way to learn, even if some of us think it's risky.

And, you know, sun, mango drinks, and the beach—I bet everyone wants to join the board!

Chief Investment Officer:

So, the plant modernization allows for both a meaningful expansion of the product line *and* significant cost savings. But you said that a cut of 200 people underpins those savings?

Head of PE:

Yeah.

Chief Investment Officer:

OK. Any further questions for **Head of PE**?

Head of Risk:

A question from me for **Head of PE**. You mentioned that these guys are the sole beverage manufacturer in Atsui and that there are entry barriers on foreign manufacturers coming in. You've been on the ground, so are local competitors raising their voices about giving ABC some competition?

Head of PE:

I've done a lot of local research, and I'm not seeing anyone. When ABC thinks about threats, they think of the big international drink players, who are still scared off by the government's import tariffs.

Chief Investment Officer:

A lot of senior officials are keen to grow the local industry. It's a small country, and there's a common emotional investment in ABC's success.

Head of Risk:

These do seem like heavy tariffs. **CIO** mentioned they're as high as 100% if you try to buy Coke or Pepsi. The memo says there's an election coming up. Surely there's a risk those entry barriers fall away?

Head of PE:

A mango drink is much better than cola, I promise!

Chief Investment Officer:

I've done a little outreach myself to people in the know. Combining that with **Head of PE**'s research, I'd say a relaxing of tariffs after the election is a fair assumption.

Head of Equities:

I have a question. Will this investment allow for ABC to start exports? Is that part of the expansion plan?

Head of PE:

The markets nearby are also tropical, frontier nations. Business relations are decent, and the plant is next to a river that connects to a big port.

Chief Investment Officer:

Head of PE has explained that the plant workers fish on the freshwater river during their lunch and during breaks, and the river does indeed connect to Atsui's major port. I see good potential for connecting to neighbouring buyers.

Head of Risk:

But let's remember that this is a frontier market with a developing economy.

Chief Investment Officer:

Quite right. Beverages are still somewhat of a luxury item. Nevertheless, there's plenty of growth potential for us and for them.

Head of Equities:

Sure, that's encouraging on exports, but **Head of PE** said that ABC sees its competition as the big international drink players, who are still scared off by the government's tariffs. If the election brings in a government keen on foreign investment, that could completely overturn the advantage this particular business has.

Let's apply a probability to a tariff reduction and to import markets opening up. Pepsi and Coca-Cola have much deeper pockets for waiting out a price war.

Head of PE:

I hear you, but maybe I went too far by saying ABC sees them as competitors. Products like the Mango Special and their other drinks don't actually exist in the Coke and Pepsi product lines, and the Mango Special recipe is so proprietary that if we protect it, it's a real competitive advantage. The other ABC beverages use tropical fruit the multinationals don't have supply chains for, and we believe—I mean, *ABC* believes they have a way of mixing things that no one else can figure out. If that's the case, a path to exports is still there.

With investment, they still have time to get into other juices and diversify. And we're always talking to government officials and to people who could make up the government, and everyone's pretty aligned.

Chief Investment Officer:

These risks are tied to the modernization program we're investing in, which means job cuts. In frontier markets, this is very sensitive: Unions may protest, and politicians may make it part of their election agenda, especially given that we're talking about one of the country's more popular companies. We're veering into reputational risk here.

Look, this is a rather small investment, of $25 million, but even a small investment can have an outsized negative impact on us if we don't manage the risk properly.

Thoughts?

Head of PE:

We're not just investing and then forgetting things, folks. We're going to be proactive. Before modernization starts, we're going to do some research that shows us what issues are in the minds of all the people of Atsui, not just our workers, and we're going to design new community programs around that. We'll try to make a positive impact first.

We know that cutting employees is sensitive. But by helping many more people than we let go and by giving employees proper training so they have the skills for whatever they're doing next, we're going to be part of a sensible transition.

Head of Equities:

That's going to be critical. Community relations is a key component of our social license to operate.

Chief Investment Officer:

My dialogue with the **Head of PE** on the ground in Atsui has been ongoing, and he wants us to do right by the community. It's almost an impact investment in and of itself.

Any other questions on the PE investment?

Head of Risk:

How comfortable are you with ABC's management? We'll only have a minority stake, and founders are sometimes not the best people to run a business.

So are these people reliable? Do they have the right skill set? The right education? Any worry about potential corruption?

Head of PE:

Our due diligence is thorough, and we don't think corruption is an issue. We're new to direct investing, and so we'll be tracking progress extra carefully. And also we're the ones implementing a lot of the modernization, so there'll be more monitoring built in than ever before.

Do we keep management or not? You always have this question in private equity. With all the co-investing we've done, the directors of the funds we partner with find management teams and then keep them and then work *with* them to help them grow.

I see your point that we'd only hold 35% of ABC, but we'll also hold two board seats. I can't predict the future, but we've done a lot of due diligence and we've done a lot of interviews with management, customers, and suppliers. We've interviewed a lot of people who know the management.

We're paying $25 million, and $20 million goes to modernizing the plant. Management will take a little money off the table, and we'll structure it so that they are incentivized in alignment with growth and good oversight. After all, they'll still hold 65%.

We think they'll see that working with us will create success and that willful mismanagement or corruption or taking too much money out of the business works against them in the long run. We're coming to them with our track record through the co-investments we've made, our expertise, and our channels to other markets.

There's always risk, but that's my point of view.

Head of Equities:

I support the PE investment. With management having this much skin in the game, their interests are aligned with ours.

Chief Investment Officer:

This is a $25 million investment out of our $50 billion fund, and there are impact elements as well that make it more interesting.

Head of PE:

Yeah, and to build our direct investment program, we must learn by doing. We've gotten really comfortable with co-investing, and that's great, but to me, it's the people who do this a lot on their own who tend to be really successful.

Yes, there's some risk with management and the government, but a lot of those are risks we're willing to take with one of our first direct investments, where we can get our hands dirty. It's a simple business, right? It's carbonated beverages, and then maybe we go into juices and non-carbonated stuff, right? We can really build the experience of working with management and the other skills that our direct program is going to need.

Hey, maybe our next committee meeting should be in Atsui!

General Discussion on Risk

Chief Investment Officer:

I won't argue, but let me ask the committee about a risk that applies to both of these investments. We're an open forum, and so I ask the entire room: What bears more scrutiny?

Head of Risk:

The first thing that comes to my mind when we're investing in frontier markets like these is, "How do we deal with the currency risk?" It's hard to hedge these currencies. Meanwhile, they can move wildly against the dollar, turning a really good investment into a really bad investment.

What's your read on this, **Head of PE**?

Head of PE:

I'm not stressed about it. When it comes to me and most other visitors to Atsui, we're using US dollars.

Head of Infrastructure:

I can speak to the currency risk in Sunnyland. When we're talking about the aviation industry and airports, a lot of revenues for infrastructure investors come in the form of regulated charges. Look at our own concession contract: 70% of the revenues are airport charges. It's typical with these arrangements to outsource the collection of these charges to international organizations like IATA. They collect the revenue from the airline, and almost all of that is paid in dollars, so we're comfortable there.

That leaves the 30% of our revenue coming from commercial sources—retail revenue in the terminal and past the gate and all that duty free and parking. In the big international airports, those transactions take place in the local currency, but we're in a locale that's expressly seeking international tourism. Pricing will be geared to international markets, so we'll have the freedom to price everything in dollars and benchmark the pricing against the affluent traveler.

Head of Risk:

I'm glad to hear that.

What about the borrowing side, though? To keep people happy and the logistics simple, I assume any borrowings will come from local banks that use their country's currency.

Head of Infrastructure:

It's a good thought, but no. The lenders are big international banks. The in-country banks may participate, but given the size of the loans and how long term these arrangements are—at least in Sunnyland—the local banks just don't have the capacity yet.

Whoever the lenders are, they'll be comfortable knowing the investors are getting their returns mostly in US dollars, which is what the $300 million of debt is denominated in.

Head of Risk:

Which brings me to defaults.

Head of Infrastructure:

Right, well, this is non-recourse financing, and the concession agreement outlines the terms of default and termination. These are matters that impinge on the direct arrangement between the government and the banks, so while it's something to be aware of, I don't see us getting dragged in.

Head of Risk:
Thanks.

Head of Equities:
I know the **Head of Risk** was coming to this, but the topic is coming up very often recently.

If you look at the World Economic Forum's "Global Risk Report" since 2017, climate risk and extreme weather feature in the top risks every time. Year over year, the weather gets more erratic. Sea-level rise may be gradual, but it doesn't stop. And while I understand the need to support Sunnyland's economy by expanding the airport, the memo says that the new runway is less than a kilometer from the sea.

Sure, you get a fantastic view when you take off and land, but the sea *is* rising, and the risk of flooding could become real even just during high tide. Running an airport in those conditions would not be possible.

It's a 25-year infrastructure investment. That's long enough for climate risks to materialize and impact operations. We've got to factor this in.

Head of Infrastructure
These points are well taken, but keep in mind that to even get as far as finding interested lenders for the airport, it means we've gone through the due diligence process. The big banks need environmental-impact statements before they jump on board, and even just in our role as equity investors, we had to satisfy ourselves that these kinds of issues were thought through.

Head of Risk:
Sure, and naming risks is necessary and commendable, but—

Head of Infrastructure:
—But that doesn't mean the risk goes away. Of course.

I'm obviously not an engineer or a contractor, but what I'd say to the committee is that the experts tells us, in the time frame we're looking at, environmental risks are unlikely to materialize, and even so, they're accounted for during the design process. The drainage systems are modified to handle increases in groundwater levels, and the engineers are building in once-in-50-years and once-in-100-years flood scenarios. Those are risks they're confident they can build for.

Chief Investment Officer:
None of us are experts here, but my perspective is that we can take comfort from the fact that these kinds of challenges have been around for decades. Consider Kansai International Airport in Japan: People are always saying that it's sinking—and it *has* gone down a tiny bit—but it's been around for over 25 years and it's been fine.

It's important to be aware of it, and I'm glad you brought it up, but indications are that there's nothing really stopping us on this front.

Head of Infrastructure:
That's right. We've come to rely on the reports from the technical adviser, and that's a fairly standard approach for us with these sorts of investments.

Head of PE:
Agreed.

Head of Risk:
What about previous foreign investment in Sunnyland? Did political risk come into play for other investments? What's the general feeling?

Head of PE:

Head of Infrastructure called me from Sunnyland when I was on the beach in Atsui planning the ABC upgrades, and he asked me to look into it. Investment in Sunnyland has mostly been on the tourism side. There's a mixture of three- and five-star hotels, so major international hotel operators are around. And they're still arriving, but they feel the transportation bottleneck. Those who are there and the ones who are thinking about coming in are happy about the airport project.

Head of Infrastructure:

And I haven't heard any horror stories about investors in Sunnyland getting burned because of unfair rule changes. Plus, relations are good. The Sunnyland authorities approached us as a fellow government institution, so we're comfortable on a sort of government-to-government basis.

Chief Investment Officer:

One nice thing about an island nation is that it *is* an island. There's less political interference from the neighbours. From what **Head of Infrastructure** was telling me, we can feel positive that our investment in the airport will help the economy and stabilize the local political situation more than the contrary.

Head of Risk:

Good to hear. Let's dig a little deeper on the modeling we've done for the airport investment. We expect a 15% IRR over 25 years. That is our base case. Have we done any stress tests to those baseline expectations? What if there are delays and we have to pay a penalty? What if construction costs overrun the budget? What if revenues fall short? Give us an idea of how bad the IRR could get if we don't achieve the base case.

Head of Infrastructure:

Sure. I like how you've framed the question, because it covers some key risks.

From our perspective, the biggest risk is traffic—comparing the actual number of visitors and tourists coming in and out of the airport against our projections. We're not experts here, either, but we hired an established traffic consultant who looks at the global tourism numbers and the particulars of our development to make a determination.

The consultant produced a low case and a high case based on different traffic forecasts. The low case is also of interest to the banks, of course, which want confidence that they'll be paid.

Our analysis of the reasonable low case puts IRR down to around 10% or 11%. The high case pushes the return out into the high teens.

There are some sensitivities around CapEx, and we're looking to manage this risk through a fixed-price contract, the language of which says that whatever penalties we'd face for delayed or subpar construction will be passed down to the contractor. We've applied a ±10% sensitivity around that, and it does impinge on the IRR a little bit but not as much as the low-traffic case. If we run into real cost overruns or delays, we're looking at about a 13% IRR.

Head of PE:

The airport's key source of revenue is tourist numbers, and we've got an exotic luxury destination on our hands, folks.

Head of Equities:

Agreed. And therefore, we need to consider the risk of a prolonged global recession when discretionary vacations and spending take a nosedive. For a small island like Sunnyland, this is a big risk. Some scenario analysis that considers the impact of a downturn that lasts for two or three or even four years seems necessary.

Head of Infrastructure:

We've done some work on those scenarios, and it's influenced by a specific responsibility of the government, which they have explicitly accepted, to aggressively promote tourism as soon as, if not before, a recession hits.

Think of the aviation industry, which has been through shocks again and again. With downtimes like the global financial crisis around 2009 and the few instances where travelers were spooked by crashes, the airlines came out with attractive deals and recovery was quick.

Sunnyland's government is used to adjusting and always reduces pricing to attract tourists when they need to. Our sense is that even a prolonged recession isn't a deal killer, because the authorities and the industry will react quickly.

Head of PE:

I like your optimism.

Chief Investment Officer

Well, beyond optimism, we're starting from a low base; there's enormous room for growth in Sunnyland.

Head of Risk:

If I may, **CIO**, just a follow-up question to the **Head of Equities**' point on the recession: We all experienced the coronavirus pandemic in 2020, and plenty of scientists have warned us that pandemics are going to be more likely—

Head of Equities:

—Helped along by climate change!

Head of Risk:

Yes, thank you, because of how we're damaging the environment, and again, this investment has a 25-year horizon. What if another pandemic causes rampant restrictions and people are simply not allowed to travel? Has that been factored into our scenario analysis?

Head of Infrastructure:

To a limited extent, yes. We pass through 35% of whatever revenue we take on, so our payments to the government are handled that way in the concession agreement. That leaves the crucial aspect of defaults to lenders and what would trigger them.

The built-in debt-service reserve covers us for a period of time, and if travel is on hold for too much longer, then we turn to restructuring or rescheduling the financing.

But let's understand that the COVID-19 pandemic in 2020 was a game-changer, and the language and dynamics of certain contractual agreements were adjusted to avoid straight defaults in these cases. And the concern here is about short-term impact, whereas over 25 years, we expect things to gradually recover, so our concerns are more about keeping the project going and avoiding default during the problem period.

Voting on Infrastructure Investment

Chief Investment Officer:

OK, I'm grateful for the expertise we have around this table. I think that's probably good for a committee vote. Let's start with our **Head of Infrastructure**: yes or no?

Head of Infrastructure:

Yes.

Chief Investment Officer:

How about our **Head of Risk**?

Head of Risk:

I have my doubts, but because it is a $100 million investment on AUM of $50 billion, we'll give it a shot. I'll say "yes."

Chief Investment Officer:

We have to take a little bit of risk, after all.

Head of PE, how about you?

Head of PE:

Before we ultimately pull the trigger, we should take another look at our other investments and similar memos to see if they're related to tourism and it would mean too much correlation. Besides that, I'm a "yes."

Chief Investment Officer:

OK. **Head of Equities**?

Head of Equities:

Yes from me as well. Given the size of the investment, I think it's worth taking the risk.

Chief Investment Officer:

And I vote "yes."

As a sovereign wealth fund, beyond our responsibility to manage risks and returns well, we want to give back, and where our participation helps nations develop, we feel a responsibility there as well.

Voting on Private Equity Investment

Chief Investment Officer:

All right, very good. Let's move on to our direct private equity investment in ABC. **Head of PE**, what say you?

Head of PE:

I'm in. Yes.

Chief Investment Officer:

Very good. How about you, **Head of Equities**?

Head of Equities:

I'm supportive of this. For one thing, it presents much less risk than the airport in Sunnyland. Yes.

Chief Investment Officer:

OK. And our resident infrastructure expert, what say you?

Head of Infrastructure:

Well, you might expect me to disagree with **Head of Equities** in terms of the risk—we have a minority position, for one thing. But the investment is small, so I'm fine. Yes.

Chief Investment Officer:

OK. And finally, **Head of Risk**?

Head of Risk:

Head of PE made some very good points. It *is* indeed a simple investment to understand and a chance to gain some experience in direct investment. Even if it doesn't work out financially, there's upside to building our experience and to having a positive impact on the wider community, to name but two areas of non-financial return. Yes from me.

Chief Investment Officer:

OK, we have two investments that I'm excited to proceed with. I'd like **Head of Infrastructure** and **Head of PE** to run with those and keep us posted, and now it's time—

Head of PE:

—To fight for the open board seat!

Head of Risk:

Sounds fun, but actually, let's do this the old-fashioned way by filling the other board seat on the basis of experience?

Head of PE:

One free Mango Special to our wise, risk-averse colleague!

Chief Investment Officer:

And with that, we'll see everyone for the next investment committee meeting, in a month's time.

—The End—

IN-TEXT QUESTIONS

Please respond to the following questions based on **Investment Committee Meeting 1.0**.

1. The Head of Infrastructure identified a key risk to the Sunnyland airport investment. Explain what analysis could be shared with you to increase your confidence that the key risk is properly managed prior to making the investment in the Sunnyland airport.

2. Explain how the upcoming election most likely exposes the R-SWF's investment in ABC to financial risk. Discuss whether or not you believe the Head of PE's approach to managing this particular risk is sufficient.

Guideline Answers:

1. During the investment committee meeting, the Head of Infrastructure identified traffic as the key risk to the Sunnyland airport investment. The island might not draw an increased number of tourists simply because the airport can accommodate larger planes and more passengers. Although the Head of Infrastructure alluded to the fact that he has quantified the financial risk should the level of tourists not meet expectations after the completion of the new airport, I would like to review his scenario analysis to feel comfortable with his assumptions. Scenario analysis would be the best way to manage this financial risk prior to making the investment in Sunnyland.

2. I do not think the Head of PE's approach to managing the financial risk due to the upcoming election is sufficient. My understanding is that the upcoming election will expose ABC to financial risk because the current government has imposed large tariffs on foreign competitors that would like to export their products to Atsui. In the event a different political party, specifically one that opposes such tariffs, wins

> the upcoming election in Atsui, it could have a significant effect on the profitability of ABC because the company would need to compete for local customers.
>
> Of course, a change in government is not something that ABC can control. Although I believe the steps the Head of PE has taken to manage this particular risk are good, including building rapport with the current government, it is not clear to me that he has conducted a thorough analysis to illustrate the potential financial impact on ABC should the tariffs be reduced or eliminated after the upcoming election. This analysis should be done using scenario analysis. Despite this being a relatively small investment for R-SWF, the financial risk of a change in the tariff policy should be thoroughly modeled and assessed prior to making the investment.

R-SWF'S Investments: 2.0

Extension of Case Facts (2.0)

After Investment Committee Meeting 1.0, the investment committee of the sovereign wealth fund of Ruritania, R-SWF, added two new significant investments to its portfolio. These investments were direct infrastructure and direct private equity investments—the investments in the airport in Sunnyland and the beverage manufacturer in Atsui, respectively.

- Three years have passed, and the investment committee of R-SWF has decided to conduct an investment review of the two projects.

- Note: The focus of the meeting is on the risks (current and potential) of the new investment proposals, not details on the financial performance of the investments. (An in-depth meeting on the financial performance of the investments was held in the previous month).

- All investment committee participants (and Level III candidates in the CFA Program) are provided with a background memo with the following information:

  - Memo A: Update on R-SWF's asset allocation and performance
  - Memo B: Update on the direct infrastructure investment (airport expansion in Sunnyland) and a list of risks for discussion
  - Memo C: Provides details on the proposed direct private equity investment (investment in ABC) and a list of risks for discussion.

INVESTMENT COMMITTEE MEETING MEMO 2.0

To: R-SWF Investment Committee Members

From: R-SWF Chief Investment Officer

Re: Investment Committee Meeting 2.0 Agenda

Distribution: Head of Risk, Head of PE, Head of Infrastructure, Head of Equities, and Junior Staff

Agenda

- Opening Remarks and Asset Allocation CIO—5 minutes
- Infrastructure Update CIO + Head of Infrastructure—5 minutes
- PE Update CIO + Head of PE—5 minutes
- Discussion of Risk—Infrastructure: Head of Infrastructure, Head of Risk, All—10 minutes
- Discussion of Risk—PE: Head of PE, Head of Risk, All—10 minutes
- Other Risks: Head of Equities + All—5–10 minutes
- Closing Remarks: CIO—5 minutes

Memo 2A: Asset Allocation and Performance

- Since its inception, R-SWF has built a diversified portfolio of investments. As of last month, the fund had AUM of $56 billion USD, with the fund outperforming its overall benchmark by 130 bps net of fees since inception. Of course, there have been short-term periods of underperformance as the fund pursued its long-term strategy.
- The asset allocation as of last month for the overall fund was as follows:

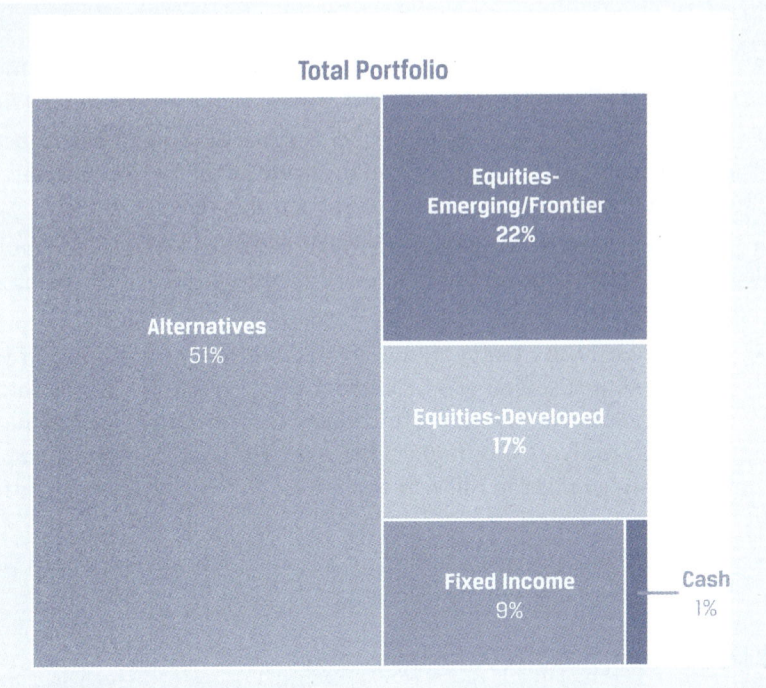

- R-SWF had approximately 51% of assets invested in alternative investments, consistent with its long-term objectives.
- Asset allocation was covered extensively in the prior month's investment committee meeting, so today's meeting will not provide any further breakdown.
- The investment committee will be discussing various points of view on risk aspects of the investments—including risk mitigation.
- The discussion will include "other risks" that were perhaps not covered well in the initial discussion. Discussion of environmental and social risks are challenging for long-term direct investing.

- Updates on the airport expansion in Sunnyland infrastructure investment are found in Memo 2B.
- Updates on the PE investment in ABC in Atsui are found in Memo 2C.

Memo 2B: Update on Infrastructure Investment in Sunnyland Airport

Investment Update

- Based on investment committee approval, the $100 million investment in Sunnyland has moved forward in accordance with agreed plans. This amount represents approximately 0.2% of total R-SWF assets.
- The Sunnyland government is happy with the progress of construction, which was completed recently. There was a delay in getting started, but that is Island life. Thankfully, there were no material cost overruns on the project.
- The new terminal is beautifully built and will be a great addition to the island nation as it further develops its tourism capabilities.
- We expect a grand opening of the new terminal in September, in time for the busy fall season. Tourist season is primarily from October through May, with the summer months being very hot (around 40°C) and humid.
- There are rumors that Airport Operating Group (AOG) is looking to renegotiate its contract for a higher fixed fee.
- One of the advantages of Sunnyland as a tourist attraction is its beautiful beaches with easy access to the airport, with the new runway, only 1 km from the sea, providing spectacular views.
- However, climate change has led to rising seas and more frequent storms. Storms are common in island nations; however, the rising seas are of concern.
- In addition, hotter temperatures are of additional concern. A few years ago, the tourist season was September through June, with only July and August being "too hot." However, in May this year, daytime highs were frequently 42°C or higher. There is a risk that the hotter temperatures lasting longer in the year will reduce tourism (and revenues for the airport project).
- Although this is a small investment in total, there are some risks we should focus on in today's discussion.

Risk Discussion: Infrastructure Investment

The following key risks are highlighted for discussion:

- Currency risk
- Expropriation risk by the Sunnyland government
- Risk that revenue from airport is less than expected
- Risk of project delays
- Risk of operating and maintenance costs being higher than projected
- Risk of default of AOG
- Risk that actual future (borrowing) interest rates will be higher than forecast

- Risk of underperformance regarding service quality–not meeting defined standards
- Other risks

Possible Mitigation of the Key Risks

- What should we do to mitigate the key risks?
- What should be our priorities? Action plan?

Memo 2C: Update on PE Investment in Atsui Beverage Company

Investment Update

- Based on investment committee approval, the $25 million investment in ABC has moved forward in accordance with agreed plans. This amount represents approximately 0.05% of total R-SWF assets.
- The modernization of the ABC plant went well, and the product expansion is starting to take shape. However, there several key updates that are unfortunately negative:

  - Atsui and surrounding nations went into a recession last year. Furthermore, a currency devaluation is anticipated. Beverages are considered a luxury item in Atsui.

  - A new government was elected in Atsui last year and took office in January. One of the first orders of business was to reduce tariffs on imported beverages from a 100% tariff to a 20% tariff. This change hurts our cost advantage over foreign brands. It is rumored that tariffs were reduced because Atsui wants to gain favor with foreign governments for potential loans.

  - Because the modern equipment will improve productivity, the original plan was to reduce headcount by 40%. In addition, due to slowing sales, management wanted to reduce staff by a total of 50%. However, labor laws are strict in Atsui. In order to terminate the employment of an Atsui citizen, significant notice (two years) is required. Plus, there is reputational risk for R-SWF for firing factory employees in a frontier market during a recession.

  - In order to make up for lower profits (due to the above reasons), plant management has started to cut corners to save on costs. Unfortunately, one way to do this was to dump waste into the nearby river rather than transport the waste for proper treatment. Although the waste is not toxic, it is starting to spoil the lovely fishing spot near the factory.

  - Another way ABC has tried to cut costs is by reducing employee breaks from one hour to 30 minutes and removing soap from the restrooms, requesting that employees bring their own.

- Although this is a small investment in total, there are some risks we should focus on in today's discussion.

Risk Discussion: Private Equity Investment

The following key risks are highlighted for discussion:

- Currency risk

- Expropriation risk by the Atsui government
- Quality control issues
- Challenges with local management (don't have a majority stake)
- Competitor pressure
- Growing trend of health foods that would result in avoidance of many carbonated beverages
- Elimination of tariffs protecting ABC from foreign-owned manufacturers
- Other risks

Possible Mitigation of the Key Risks

- What should we do to mitigate these risks?
- What should be our priorities? Action plan?

IN-TEXT QUESTIONS

Please respond to the following questions based on **Investment Committee Memo 2.0**.

The investment committee has identified several new risks that were not previously discussed (before Memos 2B and 2C). The CIO asks you to recommend how R-SWF can manage each of the following risks:

a. Risk of actual future (borrowing) interest rates will be higher than forecast (Memo 2B)

b. Growing trend of health foods that would result in avoidance of many carbonated beverages (Memo 2C)

Guideline Answers:

a: R-SWF can manage the risk that actual future (borrowing) interest rates will be higher than forecast by hedging its interest rate exposure for the Sunnyland airport project.

b: R-SWF can manage the risk of carbonated beverages falling out of favor due to an increasing preference for health foods by working to develop new healthy alternatives to carbonated, presumably sugar-filled drinks. As the production facility expands its ability to produce product, ABC could focus its new product development on healthy alternatives. The company can leverage its experience producing such beverages given the success of its natural mango drink in order to differentiate itself and increase market share.

Investment Committee Meeting 2.0

Participants

Chief Investment Officer (CIO)

Head of Infrastructure

Head of PE

Head of Risk

Head of Equities

Analysts [no speaking role]

Chief Investment Officer:

Good morning, everyone, and welcome to today's investment committee meeting of the sovereign wealth fund of the Republic of Ruritania. We're grateful for the opportunity to serve our constituents.

During last month's committee meeting, we reviewed the financial statements of the two projects in question—the airport in Sunnyland and the beverage manufacturer in Atsui. Our **Head of PE** provided the Mango Specials, so thank you for that!

It's been three years—wow, time really flies—since we unanimously approved proceeding with both investments. We'll go through some updates, but today's focus is risks and sensible mitigation measures.

First, though, the bigger picture: In those three years, AUM have grown by $6 billion. We're still outperforming our overall benchmark, but our outperformance has been dulled by difficulties with some assets, primarily real estate, because commercial real estate has underperformed. So that's hurt us a little bit, but as ever, we are long-term investors, and we may reap the benefits of those investments yet.

As we discuss risk mitigation, let's consider environmental and social risks. The greater pressure we've put on ourselves to invest responsibly and sustainably is matched by increased scrutiny from outside observers.

Whether we've decided to make an exit on our own or because of outside pressure, our rather long-term horizon doesn't make it any easier for us to step away from an investment when the time comes. As a contrast, our **Head of Equities** was telling me before the meeting started that he wasn't too happy about how much one of his portfolio companies was polluting, and so he just went ahead and sold the position. It was a liquid investment in a public market, and he was done within the hour. That's a contrast we have to keep in mind.

Allow me to read this comment about ABC from the minutes of the last meeting, as a sort of touchstone for us today: "This is a rather small investment, of $25 million, but even a small investment can have an outsized negative impact on us if we don't manage the risk properly."

But let's begin with Sunnyland airport. **Head of Infrastructure**, why don't you start us off?

Head of Infrastructure:

Thanks, **CIO**.

The good news is that the new terminal is pretty much complete and in line with specifications. We received some good reviews, both from locals and the international trade press. The downside is delays: At the outset, we expected a two-year construction program, but we're now well into the third year, unfortunately. There were noticeable cost overruns, and those were borne by the contractor, according to the contract, but there are some delay penalties that have yet to be settled.

The government, the contractor, and ourselves and AOG as investors—we're in discussions about these penalties, and the contractors are pointing to variations they say arose from our side. What they're calling "variations" we see as necessary design thinking for optimizing the commerciality of the retail outlets. The "variations" were pretty minimal, so let's see where our discussions end up. And some further disagreements center around the offices of customs and immigration within the terminal, which the contractor is laying at the foot of the government.

We should also highlight that as we're nearing the startup of terminal operations, the operator, AOG, has started complaining that the costs of training local staff are higher than expected. They haven't said anything formally yet, but I imagine they'll want to renegotiate their fixed-fee contract—nothing too serious.

Meanwhile, the grand opening of the terminal is a month away, in late August. It should be a good, high-profile event, and we should make a good showing. At least four Ruritania representatives, I think.

And then always swirling around our work is the focus of the press on the environmental movement and climate change, so we need to think about the impact on tourism. The main tourist season is September through June, historically, but it's just getting too hot, and so really the prime window for visitors will narrow to October through May.

The debate in the local press is frequently about the impact of so many tourists flying to Sunnyland, and AOG is in dialogue with the airlines about it. We have yet to see how that plays out in terms of impact on the airport operations down the road, but at the grand opening, we'll be able to celebrate the start of the upcoming season in September; bookings are in line with optimistic projections for the first year with the new terminal and runway.

Chief Investment Officer:

OK, thank you for that update.

And what can we say about ABC in Atsui?

Head of PE:

So, there are positives and negatives. A big positive is that this has been a fantastic learning experience for our direct investment program. But there's been a currency devaluation, and you could argue it's going to get worse because of the recession—the recession that started last year and that you all know so well because we're in the middle of it.

Still, is that good or bad? We do sell to tourists who bring their own currency, and we've got a lot of flexibility to shift our pricing so we can keep prices where they should be relative to our costs, which is positive.

But following the recent election, the new administration is talking about dropping all sorts of import tariffs, including the ones on food and drink. They've basically said, "For sure, we're going to cut them from 100% to 20%."

Obviously, this hurts our cost advantage over foreign brands, and the challenge here is that the new government wants to win favor with foreign governments before asking them for big loans, so the issue is about more than just carbonated drinks.

Chief Investment Officer:

There's a rumor that the new president likes Pepsi, so it's almost as if she doesn't want to pay double for a can, but 20% more is OK.

Head of PE:

ABC's new modernized equipment is ready to go, but here's the problem: Management is now saying they want to reduce headcount by 50%, instead of just 40%, because of the slowing sales. But labor laws in Atsui are strict, and to let someone go, you usually have to give as much as two years' notice.

Head of Risk:

Two years?

Head of PE:

Yeah, and the other issue is that for us as a sovereign wealth fund, there's reputational risk. Flying in from world cities and firing factory employees in frontier markets mean bad publicity, especially in Atsui and especially during the recession.

And here's another thing: In order to make up for lower profits, management has started cutting corners. They're dumping waste in the nearby river rather than paying to transport it to the treatment site. Do you remember how the plant is right next to the river and the employees fish in it during lunch? It's spoiling the fishing spot. This is a problem. And it gets worse: Scientists are saying that the plant site and the river overlap with the range of a rare reptile that is found here and only one other place on earth. So our site has attracted the attention of people with no interest in soda or mangoes.

Head of Risk:
This is a problem.

Head of PE:
Now here's another thing: ABC has tried to cut costs by reducing employee breaks from an hour to 30 minutes and—this is probably a little granular for our meeting, but risks are risks, they have removed soap from the restrooms! Everyone has to bring their own soap now.

Now, I know we're a $50 billion sovereign wealth fund—

Chief Investment Officer:
—$56 billion.

Head of PE:
I know we're a $56 billion sovereign wealth fund, and here we are talking about removing soap from a few bathrooms in the tropics where we have a $25 million direct investment, but stuff like this can have a reputational impact.

Head of Risk:
Agreed.

Chief Investment Officer:
Our focus right now is risk, and we should be talking about this. We haven't really faced any of these health and safety or social issues before at the individual investment level, and it's a learning opportunity as we expand our direct investing program. **Head of PE**, when you went to the restroom and found out there was no soap, you had to borrow some from the plant manager. Is that right? Did he give it to you for free, or did he charge you?

Head of PE:
He wanted to charge me, but I didn't need any soap because I had hand sanitizer with me. I got used to carrying hand sanitizer around with me everywhere back in the coronavirus days, so now I just do that when I'm in Atsui.

Chief Investment Officer:
OK, then let's discuss infrastructure.

Three years ago when we approved this investment, we talked potential risks, including climate, and we were comfortable with the position that the threat of rising seas was well into the future. We may have to re-evaluate that position.

Head of Risk:
Despite our comfort then, the fact is that storms have become more frequent and the sea level *has* risen measurably—in three short years.

Head of Infrastructure:

The lenders have also raised this point, as has our in-country political adviser. I still don't see any impact in the immediate term. If you remember three years ago, much of our comfort came from the environmental-impact assessments, which were required and were factored into the design. What has been constructed can deal with it sufficiently.

The bigger worry is the force of an unanticipated and rare storm that compounds the impact of some already bad flooding. Originally, the engineers planned for a once-in-50-years or once-in-100-years scenario, and it may be that the risk of those events has increased.

There's a discussion to be had with the government about architectural solutions—maybe some proper flood barriers. As for the cost of them, if they'll even work, and whose responsibility that is—those issues are unclear. It's not in anybody's interest for the airport to shut down.

Head of Equities:

My experience engaging with large public companies on climate risk tells me that a tiny island like Sunnyland can't have any meaningful impact on a global scale and hence they must focus on adaptation rather than worry too much about mitigation. **Head of Infrastructure** points to one of the more logical solutions: some sort of storm-surge barrier like the Netherlands has relied on for years.

As for who's going to pay for it, let's think beyond our own project for a minute. Rising seas aren't just going to have an impact on the airport; every five-star, beach-facing property will feel it too. The prime hotels feel it, and eventually the whole tourist ecosystem feels it, and with the country so dependent on tourism, my view is that this has to be a government-driven initiative. And a storm-surge barrier that successfully avoids damaging floods will be important enough to private interests, such as real estate and other infrastructure investors, that they'll form part of the funding circle.

Head of Infrastructure:

I think that's right. It's a question for the whole economy and for the government. Serious talks are taking place in Sunnyland about a new tax to cover the costs, a sort of climate tax that would go to a host of worsening climate issues.

How the authorities end up structuring that tax will inform whether we can avoid it.

Chief Investment Officer:

Understood, but as a sovereign institution, even if we could avoid such a tax to protect our investment value, from a reputational perspective, we should think twice.

Head of PE:

Head of Infrastructure said that AOG might be asking for a higher fixed fee to operate the new terminal. I'm not sure if this is a question for this point in the meeting, but is there anything we can do to proactively protect ourselves against a higher contract fee in the event AOG gets its renegotiation?

Head of Infrastructure:

We all signed a well-structured agreement, and that affords us some decent protection against any meddling in the fee structure, though there are break clauses if anything gets too out of line. Still, there are incentives built into the concession agreement to make sure everyone wins to a greater or lesser extent when traffic goes up.

Equally, we don't want a disgruntled operator. Happy employees, happy travelers, better experience, more traffic.

We haven't been formally approached about this, but let's not dismiss it out of hand just because we have a contract we can hide behind. AOG is a strong global operator. If they did activate a break clause in two or three years' time, that lands us with a responsibility we really don't want, which is finding a new operator. We're still satisfied with their cooperation. I recommend seeing how talks over the delays play out, and if we find that the government is liable for the delay, we'll request an extension to the concession and then sit down with AOG to positively collaborate on retooling the whole picture.

Chief Investment Officer:

OK, we've covered the environmental and reputational risks, the climate risk, and the AOG item as well. Are there any other risks we should examine at this point?

Head of Risk:

That covers the important ones. Currency risk and the risk of further delays are less of a concern. With climate change, we can't *solve* it; as **Head of Equities** insists, we have to adapt. It affects the entire nation, so hopefully the government will step in.

And I reinforce the idea of positive negotiations with AOG. We want a happy operator.

Chief Investment Officer:

Right. OK, very good.

Head of Risk, it looks like something is still on your mind.

Head of Risk:

Thanks for noticing. A little more scrutiny of ABC is warranted. I acknowledge its importance for boosting our direct investment know-how. It's been a great learning experience for **Head of PE** and his team, and it's a very small investment. Even if we lose money, it's not going to move the needle for our fund, but—and this is a substantial "but"—the reputational risk is a big concern.

We don't want to end up in the newspaper firing people during a recession, polluting the river, threatening endangered species, and being rather petty about soap.

Head of Infrastructure:

True on all counts.

Head of Risk:

Ladies and gentlemen, the writing is on the wall. I propose we exit this investment as soon as possible, if we can. Maybe we can't, and if that's the case, I would remain very concerned.

Head of PE:

No, I'm happy you mentioned it, and it's good that it's all coming out in this room. Let me tell you how we see things.

Before we jumped into this as one of our first direct investments, we co-invested and participated in many private equity funds that invest in all kinds of things, including special situations and distressed investments, and we've always gone in with third-party experts or used our own experts. Just because things get a little dicey, it doesn't mean we exit.

When we started, ABC was a conventional, if small, investment. If that's changed and it now is a problem business, we've got a team whose job it is to make lemonade out of lemons, so let's think about passing ABC over to the distressed-asset team before it becomes properly distressed. I'm not saying we keep it or some other team takes it. I'm saying let's at least see if it's a better fit for someone else.

What if we keep going? We've got risks around firing employees, dumping waste in the river, and pettiness around soap. And we're shifting our mindset, and the challenge is less about the return and more about the reputational risk.

So we really need to figure out: Can we change how this business functions to manage that risk? We have a 35% interest, we know that management has skin in the game. But in what game? With management incentivized to improve the bottom line, we're motivating them to cut employees instead of keeping employees happy and avoiding resentment.

So we're asking ourselves a new question: How do we motivate management to keep people inside and outside the plant happy? We have two board seats, and investing more money in modernization seems to make less sense now.

And we've got employees now who don't have much to do, but they're collecting a salary, so why would they leave? And if we can't fire them, it's an issue. Maybe we pay them a percentage—say, half their regular salary—while offering them good training and assistance for eight months to find another job. At the same time, we'd convince management to shift to a less profit-driven focus.

I don't know if any of that will work. Maybe we should have divested earlier, but that's our thinking if we keep holding on.

Head of Equities:

And what about the toxic stuff being released into the river?

Head of PE:

It's actually not toxic, technically, but we don't even want to be talking about whether it's toxic or not toxic. Ending that practice is an important piece of our talks with management, and so is removing incentives to cut corners.

Can we fundamentally change the way things are going? If we can't, then maybe this is an investment for someone else. Or perhaps we sell our 35% stake back to management?

Chief Investment Officer:

Thanks, **Head of PE**. We talked about this being a learning experience. We also talked about it displaying aspects of impact investment. Maybe part of the value is in education. In some less developed areas, they think it's maybe not a big deal to throw things into the river. Can we inform their thinking with the idea that wanting a beautiful river for fishing and enjoyment is a virtue and that it's not really that hard to dispose of waste properly? What can we intelligently say about impact?

Head of Equities:

This line of thinking makes sense to me. Our experience in other developing nations as well as developed nations tells us that you'll save some costs in the short term with actions like dumping waste directly into water bodies, but in the long run, regulations catch up to you and the cost of pre-treatment or appropriate handling of waste is much lower than the penalties you get for taking such shortcuts.

If we decide to stay, we have to paint the picture for management that there's a fatal flaw in our approach at the moment. Public perception is one issue, but eventually regulations will be introduced with penalties and obligations to clean up the river.

If we do try to salvage the situation and continue with our investment, there's a path that involves the government. Our pitch should be that if there are legal roadblocks for cutting 50% of the jobs, you might be putting 100% of the jobs at risk because the company won't survive if tariffs are reduced to 20%. The government doesn't want the factory to shut down because of *its* rigid labor laws, so there may well be room for a more, let's say, negotiated conclusion.

It's worth exploring, again, in consultation with the local management.

Chief Investment Officer:

Lobbying the government, reframing management's incentives—these are interesting ways to pivot. We should also consider as a committee the extent to which we want to maintain our direct investing/private equity approach or whether there is wisdom in recasting our work as more of an impact program. The committee's analysis has highlighted the difficulties faced by a sovereign wealth fund in cutting staff. It ends up being a headline risk.

The conventional private equity houses can more easily cut jobs for purely financial reasons. However, as a sovereign wealth fund, it is more complicated for us. Imagine the headline: "Government of Ruritania Cuts Jobs in XYZ during a Recession."

Head of Infrastructure:

It's not a good look.

Chief Investment Officer:

It's not a good look. Right.

Head of Risk:

From my point of view, we've covered the main risks for ABC. I like the sequence: We engage with management to change the mindset, and we lobby government on how a two-year notice period and similar restrictions could jeopardize the whole business. We give it another year, and if we're not making progress, we look for an exit option, maybe handing things over to a team that is comfortable with these thorny issues.

Chief Investment Officer:

Well summarized. I'm grateful for the focus we are putting on the risks here.

And as for Sunnyland?

Head of Equities:

I'd submit to the team that while the world's major governments have *started* taking action on climate change, we're not going to "fix" these problems easily so the planet can just go back to the way it was 30 years ago. The impact will intensify, and we have to adapt.

In my mind, the focus should be on liaising with the government. They will have to drive things because of the scale of the investment required—

Chief Investment Officer:

—And because of how long term the investment horizon is.

Team, this is the sort of experienced scrutiny of risk we needed, so thank you very much. This was a highly worthwhile meeting, and let's keep a keen focus on the risks.

—The End—

IN-TEXT QUESTIONS

Please answer the following question based on **Investment Committee Meeting 2.0**.

1. In the template provided, state the primary environmental risk that has been identified by R-SWF's investment committee for each investment. Recommend how each risk can be managed in the future.

Investment	Primary Environmental Risk	Risk Management Recommendation
Sunnyland Airport		
Atsui Beverage Company		

2. Identify one significant social risk that both investments have in common and that was not originally identified by the investment committee. Discuss whether or not this risk is easily managed once recognized.

Guideline Answers

1. In the template provided, state the primary environmental risk that has been identified by R-SWF's investment committee for each investment. Recommend how each risk can be managed in the future.

Investment	Primary Environmental Risk	Risk Management Recommendation
Sunnyland Airport	Climate change due to rising sea levels	Given the uncertainty around the precise timing and magnitude of the impact of climate change and rising sea levels specifically, R-SWF should use climate-related scenario analysis to better understand how climate change will affect its investment in Sunnyland. In addition, since R-SWF cannot mitigate climate change, it must focus on adaptation strategies. In this case, a strategy to provide protection for the airport against a storm surge or higher sea levels is the most realistic option. An adaptation strategy is consistent with the development mandate of R-SWF's investment in Sunnyland.
Atsui Beverage Company	Waste management due to dumping waste into river	R-SWF must find a way to persuade the board and local management to stop dumping waste in the river in an effort to pursue sustainable development and a "just" transition. Although it might be a cost savings in the short run, in the long run, regulations will catch up. Cleanup of improperly disposed waste is far more costly than appropriately disposing of waste up front. One of the ways to encourage prioritization of protecting the river is to educate the local community about the importance of a healthy river. Community education, the pursuit of sustainable development, and a "just" transition are consistent with the impact investing element of this investment for R-SWF.

2. Reputational risk is very significant in the case of each investment and can have an outsized effect on the performance of the investments. Social issues, such as reputational risk, are generally quite difficult to manage even once identified and understood because they are relatively challenging to quantify and integrate into financial models. Furthermore, best practices include considering the interests of all the stakeholders involved, which is not easy.

In Sunnyland, R-SWF must contribute to any effort to raise funds to implement protection against rising seas. This project will likely be expensive. However, it is not in R-SWF's best interest to appear to be avoiding contributing to the project to accommodate climate change. Doing so could significantly damage R-SWF's reputation in Sunnyland and beyond given the international attention paid to the construction of the new airport. In theory, reputational risk in this case is relatively simple to manage in that R-SWF simply needs to be a contributor to the project and overall community by supporting efforts to adapt to climate change so as to not destroy Sunnyland's tourism industry. However, execution of such a strategy to mitigate R-SWF's reputational risk in Sunnyland will need to be closely monitored in order to effectively execute it. Managing this type of risk is not easy.

Reputational risk is also very significant in the case of ABC because of two major social issues: (1) occupational health and safety and (2) labor standards. Each of these issues could significantly damage R-SWF's reputation. Removing hand soap from the restrooms is an occupational health and safety issue that could cause reputational damage. Shortening employee breaks and firing people during a recession are social issues related to labor standards.

These types of choices indicate that local management is more concerned about profitability than reputational risk. In order to manage its reputational risk, R-SWF needs to persuade the board to adjust its incentive structure in order to encourage local management to reverse course on these short-sighted, destructive social issues, even if it is expensive. R-SWF does not want to be perceived as an investor that exploits its labor force. Soap should be provided for employees, breaks should be reasonable in length, and rather than firing employees, which can't be effectively executed because of the strict labor laws, ABC should focus on retraining employees for the future of the business. This is a complicated, multifaceted course especially as a minority owner. It isn't easily implemented but can be done. Any changes will need to be monitored to ensure they continue and have the desired outcome—a sustainable and mutually beneficial long-term relationship with the local community.

R-SWF'S Investments: 3.0

Second Extension of Case Facts (3.0)

You left R-SWF at the end of Year 3 and took a position as a Senior Risk Consultant at Kiken Consulting, a risk consulting firm.

In the summer of Year 5, you are reading the newspaper and notice some commentary on two of the R-SWF investments you had been involved with. You read the following excerpts with nostalgic interest.

Update on Infrastructure Investment

- The infrastructure investment continues to perform poorly because of a combination of the following:

  - lower revenue (fewer tourists) vs. forecast (50% lower than base case)
  - higher costs (mitigating flood damage) vs. forecast (50% higher than base case)

- The medium- and long-term forecast on this investment does not look promising.

Update on PE Investment

- The PE team was able to avoid a diplomatic crisis and reputational risk damage by finding a buyer for the 35% stake. They sold the full position at $27 million.

- The stake was sold to an international beverage company that had been exporting to Atsui. The company's sales had been adversely affected by a weaker Atsui currency. Thus, producing locally is advantageous because it provides a natural foreign exchange hedge.

You set the newspaper down and start thinking about Sunnyland and Atsui when your boss suddenly interrupts you with the following news:

Kiken Consulting has a new client! R-SWF has hired the firm for a risk analysis project. Because you have prior knowledge on R-SWF's approach, your boss has assigned you to the project with a lead role. You are expected to evaluate the strengths and weaknesses of R-SWF's enterprise risk management system and to make recommendations for improvements.

IN-TEXT QUESTION

Please respond to the following question.

1. Provide key facts/inputs from the R-SWF case, use them to evaluate the strengths and weaknesses of R-SWF's enterprise risk management processes, and make recommendations for improvements.

Guideline Answer

1. One of the main strengths of R-SWF's risk management process is that R-SWF dedicated an entire internal investment committee meeting to identifying and discussing the potential risks of two relatively small investment opportunities. Ample time was taken to allow senior management of R-SWF to express their concerns and discuss mitigation strategies to reduce potential risks. The investment committee was able to identify various potential risk factors, and senior management voted on both investment opportunities.

One of the weaknesses of R-SWF's risk management process is that too little effort was made in trying to quantify the various risks and agreeing on specific actions that could be taken if some of those risk materialized. The team, with the help of the Head of Risk, could have done a better job at performing scenario analysis for both investments and presented a base case, an optimistic case, and a pessimistic case. Although the team identified and discussed several risk factors, they should have put together an action plan for risk mitigation and potential hedging tools prior to making the investments. This action plan would be conditional on certain bad outcomes materializing. Finally, since both investments were quite small in the overall scheme and had limited financial and liquidity risk implications for the fund, more consideration could have been given to identifying potential reputational risks and ESG.

REFERENCES

Geltner, D. 1993. "Estimating Market Values from Appraised Values without Assuming an Efficient Market." *Journal of Real Estate Research* 8:325–45.

Getmansky, M., A. W. Lo, and I. Makarov. 2004. "An Econometric Model of Serial Correlation and Illiquidity in Hedge Fund Returns." *Journal of Financial Economics* 74:529–609. 10.1016/j.jfineco.2004.04.001

Grantham Research Institute on Climate Change and the Environment. "*New Study Estimates Global Warming of 2.5 Centigrade Degrees by 2100 Would Put at Risk Trillions of Dollars of World's Financial Assets.*" Press release (4 April 2016). www.lse.ac.uk/GranthamInstitute/news/us2-5-trillion-of-the-worlds-financial-assets-would-be-at-risk-from-the-impacts-of-climate-change-if-global-mean-surface-temperature-rises-by-2-5c.

IEA. 2020. "*World Energy Outlook 2020*" (October). www.iea.org/reports/world-energy-outlook-2020.

Intergovernmental Panel on Climate Change. 2018. "*Special Report: Global Warming of 1.5 ºC*" (6 October). www.ipcc.ch/sr15/chapter/spm.

Lo, Joe. 2020. "*IEA Outlines How World Can Reach Net Zero Emissions by 2050.*" *Climate Home News* (13 October). www.climatechangenews.com/2020/10/13/iea-outlines-world-can-reach-net-zero-emissions-2050.

NASA. 2019. "*NASA Global Climate Change: Vital Signs of the Planet.*" https://climate.nasa.gov/vital-signs/global-temperature.

Okunev, J. and D. White. 2003. "*Hedge Fund Risk Factors and Value at Risk of Credit Trading Strategies.*" Working paper, University of New South Wales. 10.2139/ssrn.460641

Glossary

Absolute return benchmark   A minimum target return that an investment manager is expected to beat.

Accrual taxes   Taxes levied and paid on a periodic basis.

Accumulation phase   Phase where the government predominantly contributes to a sovereign wealth pension reserve fund.

Active management   A portfolio management approach that allows risk factor mismatches relative to a benchmark index causing potentially significant return differences between the active portfolio and the underlying benchmark.

Active return   The return on a portfolio minus the return on the portfolio's benchmark.

Active risk   The standard deviation of active returns.

Active risk budgeting   Risk budgeting that concerns active risk (risk relative to a portfolio's benchmark).

Active share   A measure of how similar a portfolio is to its benchmark. A manager who precisely replicates the benchmark will have an active share of zero; a manager with no holdings in common with the benchmark will have an active share of one.

Aggregate wealth   The total value of all assets owned, encompassing personal property, financial assets, real assets, and rights.

Arithmetic attribution   An attribution approach which explains the arithmetic difference between the portfolio return and its benchmark return. The single-period attribution effects sum to the excess return, however, when combining multiple periods, the sub-period attribution effects will not sum to the excess return.

Ask price   The price at which a trader will sell a specified quantity of a security. Also called *ask*, *offer price*, or *offer*.

Asset-only   With respect to asset allocation, an approach that focuses directly on the characteristics of the assets without explicitly modeling the liabilities.

Authority bias   A behavioral bias which involves groups deferring to a group member that is a subject matter expert or in a position of authority.

Aversion to complexity   A behavioral phenomenon of groups in many professional contexts, in which disproportionate attention is given to trivial issues at the expense of important but harder-to-grasp or contested topics.

Back-fill bias   The distortion in index or peer group data which results when returns are reported to a database only after they are known to be good returns.

Base   With respect to a foreign exchange quotation of the price of one unit of a currency, the currency referred to in "one unit of a currency."

Basis risk   The possibility that the expected value of a derivative differs unexpectedly from that of the underlying.

Bear spread   An option strategy that becomes more valuable when the price of the underlying asset declines, so requires buying one option and writing another with a *lower* exercise price. A put bear spread involves buying a put with a higher exercise price and selling a put with a lower exercise price. A bear spread can also be executed with calls.

Best ask   The offer to sell with the lowest ask price. Also called *best offer* or *inside ask*.

Best bid   The highest bid in the market.

Best offer   The lowest offer (ask price) in the market.

Best-in-class   An ESG implementation approach that seeks to identify the most favorable companies and sectors based on ESG considerations. Also called *positive screening*.

Bid price   In a price quotation, the price at which the party making the quotation is willing to buy a specified quantity of an asset or security.

Bid–ask spread   The ask price minus the bid price.

Buffering   Establishing ranges around breakpoints that define whether a stock belongs in one index or another.

Bull spread   An option strategy that becomes more valuable when the price of the underlying asset rises, so requires buying one option and writing another with a *higher* exercise price. A call bull spread involves buying a call with a lower exercise price and selling a call with a higher exercise price. A bull spread can also be executed with puts.

Business cycle   Fluctuations in GDP in relation to long-term trend growth, usually lasting 9-11 years.

Calendar rebalancing   Rebalancing a portfolio to target weights on a periodic basis; for example, monthly, quarterly, semi-annually, or annually.

Calendar spread   A strategy in which one sells an option and buys the same type of option but with different expiration dates, on the same underlying asset and with the same strike. When the investor buys the more distant (near-term) call and sells the near-term (more distant) call, it is a long (short) calendar spread.

Canada model   Characterized by a high allocation to alternatives. Unlike the endowment model, however, the Canada model relies more on internally managed assets. The innovative features of the Canada model are the: a) reference portfolio, b) total portfolio approach, and c) active management.

Capital market expectations (CME)   Expectations concerning the risk and return prospects of asset classes.

Capital sufficiency analysis   The process of evaluating whether a client has sufficient capital resources to achieve their financial goals and objectives; it considers the client's assets, liabilities, income, expenses, risk tolerance, time horizon, and other relevant factors.

Capture ratio   A measure of the manager's gain or loss relative to the gain or loss of the benchmark.

Carhart model   A four factor model used in performance attribution. The four factors are: market (RMRF), size (SMB), value (HML), and momentum (WML).

Carry trade   A trading strategy that involves buying a security and financing it at a rate that is lower than the yield on that security.

Cash flow matching   Immunization approach that attempts to ensure that all future liability payouts are matched precisely by cash flows from bonds or fixed-income derivatives.

Cash-secured put   An option strategy involving the writing of a put option and simultaneously depositing an amount of money equal to the exercise price into a designated account (this strategy is also called a fiduciary put).

Collar   An option position in which the investor is long shares of stock and then buys a put with an exercise price below the current stock price and writes a call with an exercise price above the current stock price. Collars allow a shareholder to acquire downside protection through a protective put but reduce the cash outlay by writing a covered call.

Contingent immunization   Hybrid approach that combines immunization with an active management approach when the asset portfolio's value exceeds the present value of the liability portfolio.

Cost basis   The initial cost of acquiring an investment including expenses incurred to acquire the investment. Also referred to as simply basis.

Covered call   An option strategy in which a long position in an asset is combined with a short position in a call on that asset.

Cross hedge   A hedge involving a hedging instrument that is imperfectly correlated with the asset being hedged; an example is hedging a bond investment with futures on a non-identical bond.

Cross-currency basis swap   A swap in which notional principals are exchanged because the goal of the transaction is to issue at a more favorable funding rate and swap the amount back to the currency of choice.

Cross-sectional consistency   A feature of expectations setting which means that estimates for all classes reflect the same underlying assumptions and are generated with methodologies that reflect or preserve important relationships among the asset classes, such as strong correlations. It is the internal consistency across asset classes.

Currency overlay programs   A currency overlay program is a program to manage a portfolio's currency exposures for the case in which those exposures are managed separately from the management of the portfolio itself.

Custom security-based benchmark   Benchmark that is custom built to accurately reflect the investment discipline of a particular investment manager. Also called a *strategy benchmark* because it reflects a manager's particular strategy.

Decision-reversal risk   The risk of reversing a chosen course of action at the point of maximum loss.

Decumulation phase   Phase where the government predominantly withdraws from a sovereign wealth pension reserve fund.

Deferred taxes   Taxes postponed until some future date.

Defined benefit   A retirement plan in which a plan sponsor commits to paying a specified retirement benefit.

Defined benefit plan   Retirement plan that is funded by the employer that guarantees a retirement benefit based on factors such as years of service, salary, and age.

Defined contribution   A retirement plan in which contributions are defined but the ultimate retirement benefit is not specified or guaranteed by the plan sponsor.

Defined contribution plan   Retirement plan in which the employer, employee, or both contribute to an account in which the employee bears the investment risk.

Delay costs   Implicit trading costs that arise from the inability to complete desired trades immediately. Also called *slippage*.

Delta   The sensitivity of the derivative price to a small change in the value of the underlying asset.

Delta hedging   Hedging that involves matching the price response of the position being hedged over a narrow range of prices.

Demand deposits   Accounts that can be drawn upon regularly and without notice. This category includes checking accounts and certain savings accounts that are often accessible through online banks or automated teller machines (ATMs).

Diffusion index   Reflects the proportion of the index's components that are moving in a pattern consistent with the overall index.

Dividend capture   A trading strategy whereby an equity portfolio manager purchases stocks just before their ex-dividend dates, holds these stocks through the ex-dividend date to earn the right to receive the dividend, and subsequently sells the shares.

Domestic asset   An asset that trades in the investor's domestic currency (or home currency).

Domestic currency   The currency of the investor, i.e., the currency in which he or she typically makes consumption purchases, e.g., the Swiss franc for an investor domiciled in Switzerland.

Domestic-currency return   A rate of return stated in domestic currency terms from the perspective of the investor; reflects both the foreign-currency return on an asset as well as percentage movement in the spot exchange rate between the domestic and foreign currencies.

Drawdown   A percentage peak-to-trough reduction in net asset value.

Drawdown duration   The total time from the start of the drawdown until the cumulative drawdown recovers to zero.

Due diligence   Investigation and analysis in support of an investment action, decision, or recommendation.

Duration matching   Immunization approach based on the duration of assets and liabilities. Ideally, the liabilities being matched (the liability portfolio) and the portfolio of assets (the bond portfolio) should be affected similarly by a change in interest rates.

Duration times spread   Weighting of spread duration by credit spread in order to incorporate the empirical observation that spread changes for lower-rated bonds tend to be consistent on a percentage, rather than absolute, basis.

Dynamic asset allocation   Dynamic asset allocation is an investment strategy premised on long-term asset allocation but employing short-term, tactical trading to maintain investment allocation targets.

Dynamic hedge   A hedge requiring adjustment as the price of the hedged asset changes.

Econometrics   The application of quantitative modeling and analysis grounded in economic theory to the analysis of economic data.

Economic balance sheet   An extended balance sheet that includes the present values of both lifetime earnings and future consumption.

Economic indicators   Economic statistics provided by government and established private organizations that contain information on an economy's recent past activity or its current or future position in the business cycle.

Effective federal funds (FFE) rate   The fed funds rate actually transacted between depository institutions, not the Fed's target federal funds rate.

Effective spread   Two times the difference between the execution price and the midpoint of the market quote at the time an order is entered.

Endowment model Characterized by a high allocation to alternative investments (private investments and hedge funds), significant active management, and externally managed assets.

Enhanced indexing approach Maintains a close link to the benchmark but attempts to generate a modest amount of outperformance relative to the benchmark.

Excess return Used in various senses appropriate to context: 1) The difference between the portfolio return and the benchmark return, which may be either positive or negative; 2) The return in excess of the risk-free rate, thus representing the return for bearing risk.

Exhaustive Covering or containing all possible outcomes.

Extended portfolio assets and liabilities Assets and liabilities beyond those shown on a conventional balance sheet that are relevant in making asset allocation decisions; an example of an extended asset is human capital.

Factor-model-based benchmarks Benchmarks constructed by examining a portfolio's sensitivity to a set of factors, such as the return for a broad market index, company earnings growth, industry, or financial leverage.

Family offices Private firms that offer a range of wealth management services tailored specifically for ultra-high-net-worth individuals.

Foreign assets Assets denominated in currencies other than the investor's home currency.

Foreign currency Currency that is not the currency in which an investor makes consumption purchases, e.g., the US dollar from the perspective of a Swiss investor.

Foreign-currency return The return of the foreign asset measured in foreign-currency terms.

Forward rate bias An empirically observed divergence from interest rate parity conditions that active investors seek to benefit from by borrowing in a lower-yield currency and investing in a higher-yield currency.

Funding currencies The low-yield currencies in which borrowing occurs in a carry trade.

Gamma A numerical measure of how sensitive an option's delta (the sensitivity of the derivative's price) is to a change in the value of the underlying.

General account Account holding assets to fund future liabilities from traditional life insurance and fixed annuities, the products in which the insurer bears all the risks—particularly mortality risk and longevity risk.

Gini coefficient A measure of inequality of wealth, or i, that ranges from 0 (perfect equality) to 1 (perfect inequality).

Goals-based With respect to asset allocation or investing, an approach that focuses on achieving an investor's goals (for example, related to supporting lifestyle needs or aspirations) based typically on constructing sub-portfolios aligned with those goals.

Goals-based investing An investment industry term for approaches to investing for individuals and families focused on aligning investments with goals (parallel to liability-driven investing for institutional investors).

Grinold–Kroner model An expression for the expected return on a share as the sum of an expected income return, an expected nominal earnings growth return, and an expected repricing return.

Groupthink A behavioral bias that occurs when a team minimizes conflict and dissent in reaching and maintaining a consensus.

Hedge ratio The proportion of an underlying that will offset the risk associated with a derivative position.

High-net-worth individuals (HNWIs) Individuals with investable assets exceeding a certain minimum level, often as low as USD1 million, but typically more.

High-water mark A measure that reflects the fund's maximum value as of a performance fee payment date net of fees.

Holdings-based attribution A "buy and hold" attribution approach which calculates the return of portfolio and benchmark components based upon the price and foreign exchange rate changes applied to daily snapshots of portfolio holdings.

Holdings-based style analysis A bottom-up style analysis that estimates the risk exposures from the actual securities held in the portfolio at a point in time.

Home bias A preference for securities listed on the exchanges of one's home country.

Home currency See *domestic currency*.

Home-country bias The favoring of domestic over non-domestic investments relative to global market value weights.

Human capital The present value of an individual's future expected labor income.

Impact investing Refers to investments made with the specific intent of generating positive, measurable social and environmental impact alongside a financial return (which differentiates it from philanthropy).

Implementation shortfall (IS) The difference between the return for a notional or paper portfolio, where all transactions are assumed to take place at the manager's decision price, and the portfolio's actual return, which reflects realized transactions, including all fees and costs.

Implied volatility The standard deviation that causes an option pricing model to give the current option price.

Implied volatility surface A three-dimensional plot, for put and call options on the same underlying asset, of days to expiration (x-axis), option strike prices (y-axis), and implied volatilities (z-axis). It simultaneously shows the volatility skew (or smile) and the term structure of implied volatility.

Inflation-linked bonds Debt instruments that link the principal and interest to inflation.

Input uncertainty Uncertainty concerning whether the inputs are correct.

Inside ask See *best ask*.

Inside bid See *best bid*.

Inside spread The spread between the best bid price and the best ask price. Also called the *market bid-ask spread*, *inside bid-ask spread*, or *market spread*.

Interaction effect The impact of overweighting and underweighting individual securities within sectors that are themselves overweighted or underweighted.

Intertemporal consistency A feature of expectations setting which means that estimates for an asset class over different horizons reflect the same assumptions with respect to the potential paths of returns over time. It is the internal consistency over various time horizons.

Intrinsic value The amount gained (per unit) by an option buyer if an option is exercised at any given point in time. May be referred to as the exercise value of the option.

Investable net worth The sum of liquid assets, such as savings and investment accounts, and less short-term liabilities such as credit card debt.

Investable wealth The sum of liquid assets such as savings and investment accounts.

Investment currencies The high-yielding currencies in a carry trade.

Investment policy statement (IPS)   A description of a client's unique investment objectives, risk tolerance, investment time horizon, and other applicable constraints.

Investment style   A natural grouping of investment disciplines that has some predictive power in explaining the future dispersion of returns across portfolios.

Key person risk   The risk that results from over-reliance on an individual or individuals whose departure would negatively affect an investment manager.

Knock-in/knock-out   Features of a vanilla option that is created (or ceases to exist) when the spot exchange rate touches a pre-specified level.

Latency   The elapsed time between the occurrence of an event and a subsequent action that depends on that event.

Leading economic indicators   Turning points that usually precede those of the overall economy; they are believed to have value for predicting the economy's future state, usually near-term.

Liability driven investing (LDI) model   In the LDI model, the primary investment objective is to generate returns sufficient to cover liabilities, with a focus on maximizing expected surplus return (excess return of assets over liabilities) and managing surplus volatility.

Liability glide path   A specification of desired proportions of liability-hedging assets and return-seeking assets and the duration of the liability hedge as funded status changes and contributions are made.

Liability-based mandates   Mandates managed to match or cover expected liability payments (future cash outflows) with future projected cash inflows.

Liability-driven investing   An investment industry term that generally encompasses asset allocation that is focused on funding an investor's liabilities in institutional contexts.

Liability-relative   With respect to asset allocation, an approach that focuses directly only on funding liabilities as an investment objective.

Limit order book   The book or list of limit orders to buy and sell that pertains to a security.

Limited-life foundations   A type of foundation where founders seek to maintain control of spending while they (or their immediate heirs) are still alive.

Longevity risk   The risk of exhausting an individual's financial resources before passing away, thereby leaving insufficient capital for living expenses and unmet needs.

Lorenz curve   A measure of the cumulative percentage of wealth owned by each percentage of the population.

Macro attribution   Attribution at the sponsor level.

Manager peer group   See *manager universe*.

Manager universe   A broad group of managers with similar investment disciplines. Also called *manager peer group*.

Marginal tax rate   The highest rate of tax applied to taxable income.

Market fragmentation   Trading the same instrument in multiple venues.

Market impact   The effect of the trade on transaction prices. Also called *price impact*.

Micro attribution   Attribution at the portfolio manager level.

Midquote price   The average, or midpoint, of the prevailing bid and ask prices.

Minimum-variance hedge ratio   A mathematical approach to determining the optimal cross hedging ratio.

Mission-related investing   Investing aimed at causes promoting positive societal or environmental change.

Model uncertainty   Uncertainty as to whether a selected model is correct.

Negative screening   An ESG investment style that focuses on the exclusion of certain sectors, companies, or practices in a fund or portfolio on the basis of specific ESG criteria.

Net worth   The difference between assets and liabilities.

Non-deliverable forwards   Cash-settled forward contracts, used predominately with respect to foreign exchange forwards. Also called *contracts for differences*.

Nonstationarity   A characteristic of series of data whose properties, such as mean and variance, are not constant through time. When analyzing historical data it means that different parts of a data series reflect different underlying statistical properties.

Norway model   Characterized by an almost exclusive reliance on public equities and fixed income (the traditional 60/40 equity/bond model falls under the Norway model), with largely passively managed assets and with very little to no allocation to alternative investments.

Offer price   The price at which a counterparty is willing to sell one unit of the base currency.

Opportunity cost   Reflects the foregone opportunity of investing in a different asset. It is typically denoted by the risk-free rate of interest, r.

Optional stock dividends   A type of dividend in which shareholders may elect to receive either cash or new shares.

Overbought   A market condition in which market sentiment is thought to be unsustainably bullish.

Oversold   A market condition in which market sentiment is thought to be unsustainably bearish.

Packeting   Splitting stock positions into multiple parts.

Parameter uncertainty   Uncertainty arising because a quantitative model's parameters are estimated with error.

Participant-switching life-cycle options   Automatically switch DC plan members into a more conservative asset mix as their age increases. There may be several automatic de-risking switches at different age targets.

Participant/cohort option   Pools the DC plan member with a cohort that has a similar target retirement date.

Passive management   A buy-and-hold approach to investing in which an investor does not make portfolio changes based upon short-term expectations of changing market or security performance.

Percent-range rebalancing   An approach to rebalancing that involves setting rebalancing thresholds or trigger points, stated as a percentage of the portfolio's value, around target values.

Performance attribution   The process of disaggregating a portfolio's return to determine the drivers of its performance.

Personal assets   Nonbusiness, on-investment assets including personal property and real property.

Personal property   Property owned by individuals that are not real property and not considered investments.

Planned goals   Financial objectives that can be reasonably estimated or quantified at the onset and can be achieved within an expected time horizon.

Position delta   The overall or portfolio delta. For example, the position delta of a covered call, consisting of long 100 shares and short one at-the-money call, is +50 (= +100 for the shares and -50 for the short ATM call).

Positive screening   An ESG implementation approach that seeks to identify the most favorable companies and sectors based on ESG considerations. Also called *best-in-class*.

Price improvement When trade execution prices are better than quoted prices.

Private wealth management Financial planning and investment management to help individual investors, particularly high-net-worth individuals (HNWIs) and ultra-high-net-worth individuals (UHNWIs), manage their wealth.

Protective put A strategy of purchasing an underlying asset and purchasing a put on the same asset.

Pure indexing Attempts to replicate a bond index as closely as possible, targeting zero active return and zero active risk.

Put spread A strategy used to reduce the upfront cost of buying a protective put, it involves buying a put option and writing another put option.

Re-base With reference to index construction, to change the time period used as the base of the index.

Realized volatility Historical volatility, the square root of the realized variance of returns, which is a measure of the range of past price outcomes for the underlying asset.

Rebalancing Adjusting the weights of the constituent securities in an index.

Rebalancing range A range of values for asset class weights defined by trigger points above and below target weights, such that if the portfolio value passes through a trigger point, rebalancing occurs. Also known as a corridor.

Rebate rate The portion of the collateral earnings rate that is repaid to the security borrower by the security lender.

Reduced form models Statistical credit models that solve for the probability of default over a specific time period, using observable company-specific and market-based variables.

Regime The governing set of relationships (between variables) that stem from technological, political, legal, and regulatory environments. Changes in such environments or policy stances can be described as changes in regime.

Relative value A concept that describes the selection of the most attractive individual securities to populate the portfolio with, using ranking and comparing.

Repo rate The interest rate on a repurchase agreement.

Repurchase agreements In repurchase agreements, or repos, a security owner agrees to sell a security for a specific cash amount while simultaneously agreeing to repurchase the security at a specified future date (typically one day later) and price.

Reserve portfolio The component of an insurer's general account that is subject to specific regulatory requirements and is intended to ensure the company's ability to meet its policy liabilities. The assets in the reserve portfolio are managed conservatively and must be highly liquid and low risk.

Resistance levels Price points on dealers' order boards where one would expect to see a clustering of offers.

Return attribution A set of techniques used to identify the sources of the excess return of a portfolio against its benchmark.

Returns-based attribution An attribution approach that uses only the total portfolio returns over a period to identify the components of the investment process that have generated the returns. The Brinson–Hood–Beebower approach is a returns-based attribution approach.

Returns-based benchmarks Benchmarks constructed by examining a portfolio's sensitivity to a set of factors, such as the returns for various style indexes (e.g., small-cap value, small-cap growth, large-cap value, and large-cap growth).

Returns-based style analysis A top-down style analysis that involves estimating the sensitivities of a portfolio to security market indexes.

Reverse repos Repurchase agreements from the standpoint of the lender.

Risk attribution The analysis of the sources of risk.

Risk aversion The dislike for risk such that compensation is required in terms of higher expected returns for assuming higher risk.

Risk budgeting The establishment of objectives for individuals, groups, or divisions of an organization that takes into account the allocation of an acceptable level of risk.

Risk capacity The ability to bear financial risk.

Risk premiums Extra returns expected by investors for bearing some specified risk.

Risk reversal A strategy used to profit from the existence of an implied volatility skew and from changes in its shape over time. A combination of long (short) calls and short (long) puts on the same underlying with the same expiration is a long (short) risk reversal.

Risk tolerance The level of risk an investor is willing and able to bear.

Seagull spread An extension of the risk reversal foreign exchange option strategy that limits downside risk.

Securities lending A form of collateralized lending that may be used to generate income for portfolios.

Selective An index construction methodology that targets only those securities with certain characteristics.

Separate accounts Accounts holding assets to fund future liabilities from variable life insurance and variable annuities, the products in which customers make investment decisions from a menu of options and themselves bear investment risk.

Sharpe ratio The ratio of mean excess return to standard deviation (excess return).

Shortfall probability The probability of failing to meet a specific liability or goal.

Shrinkage estimation Estimation that involves taking a weighted average of a historical estimate of a parameter and some other parameter estimate, where the weights reflect the analyst's relative belief in the estimates.

Special dividends Dividends paid by a company that does not pay dividends on a regular schedule, or dividends that supplement regular cash dividends with an extra payment.

Spread duration The change in bond price for a given change in yield spread. Also referred to as OAS duration when the option-adjusted spread (OAS) is the yield measure used.

Static hedge A hedge that is not sensitive to changes in the price of the asset hedged.

Stock lending Securities lending involving the transfer of equities.

Stops Stop-loss orders involve leaving bids or offers away from the current market price to be filled if the market reaches those levels.

Straddle An option combination in which one buys *both* puts and calls, with the same exercise price and same expiration date, on the same underlying asset. In contrast to this long straddle, if someone *writes* both options, it is a short straddle.

Strangle A variation on a straddle in which the put and call have different exercise prices; if the put and call are held long, it is a long strangle; if they are held short, it is a short strangle.

Strategic asset allocation A long-term strategy that establishes target allocations for various asset classes and aims to optimize the balance between risk and reward by diversifying investments.

Structural models   Models that specify functional relationships among variables based on economic theory. The functional form and parameters of these models are derived from the underlying theory. They may include unobservable parameters.

Support levels   Price points on dealers' order boards where one would expect to see a clustering of bids.

Surplus   The difference between assets and liabilities, analogous to shareholders' equity on a corporate balance sheet.

Surplus portfolio   The component of an insurer's general account that is intended to realize higher expected returns than the reserve portfolio and so can assume some liquidity risk. Surplus portfolio assets are often managed aggressively with exposure to alternative assets.

Survivorship bias   Relates to the inclusion of only current investment funds in a database. As such, the returns of funds that are no longer available in the marketplace (have been liquidated) are excluded from the database. Also see *backfill bias*.

Synthetic long forward position   The combination of a long call and a short put with identical strike price and expiration, traded at the same time on the same underlying.

Synthetic short forward position   The combination of a short call and a long put at the same strike price and maturity (traded at the same time on the same underlying).

Tactical asset allocation   A proactive strategy that adjusts asset class allocations within a portfolio based on short-term market trends, economic conditions, or valuation changes to capitalize on temporary market inefficiencies or opportunities to improve returns or manage risk more effectively.

Tax drag   The negative effect of taxes on an investment's net returns.

Taylor rule   A rule linking a central bank's target short-term interest rate to the rate of growth of the economy and inflation.

Term deposits   Interest-bearing accounts that have a specified maturity date. This category includes savings accounts and certificates of deposit (CDs). Also see *time deposits*.

Term structure of volatility   The plot of implied volatility (y-axis) against option maturity (x-axis) for options with the same strike price on the same underlying. Typically, implied volatility is not constant across different maturities – rather, it is often in contango, meaning that the implied volatilities for longer-term options are higher than for near-term ones.

Thematic investing   An investment approach that focuses on companies in a specific sector or following a specific theme, such as energy efficiency or climate change.

Theta   The change in a derivative instrument for a given small change in calendar time, holding everything else constant. Specifically, the theta calculation assumes nothing changes except calendar time. Theta also reflects the rate at which an option's time value decays.

Threshold-based rebalancing policy   The manager rebalances the portfolio when asset class weights deviate from their target weights by a prespecified percentage regardless of timing and frequency.

Time deposits   Interest-bearing accounts that have a specified maturity date. This category includes savings accounts and certificates of deposit (CDs). Also see *term deposits*.

Time value   The difference between an option's premium and its intrinsic value.

Time-based rebalancing policy   The manager rebalances the portfolio regularly, at a certain given time interval such as quarterly, semi-annually, or annually, regardless of any difference between prevailing asset class weights and target asset class weights.

Time-series estimation   Estimators that are based on lagged values of the variable being forecast; often consist of lagged values of other selected variables.

Total factor productivity   A scale factor that reflects the portion of growth unaccounted for by explicit factor inputs (e.g., capital and labor).

Total return payer   Party responsible for paying the reference obligation cash flows and return to the receiver but that is also compensated by the receiver for any depreciation in the index or default losses incurred by the portfolio.

Total return receiver   Receives both the cash flows from the underlying index and any appreciation in the index over the period in exchange for paying the MRR plus a predetermined spread.

Tracking risk   The standard deviation of the differences between a portfolio's returns and its benchmarks returns. Also called *tracking error*.

Transactions-based attribution   An attribution approach that captures the impact of intra-day trades and exogenous events such as a significant class action settlement.

Trigger points   In the context of portfolio rebalancing, the endpoints of a rebalancing range (corridor).

Ultra-high-net-worth individuals (UHNWIs)   Individuals with net worth usually exceeding USD30 million or more.

Unplanned goals   Unforeseen financial needs that are difficult to quantify because either the funding need, the timing of the financial need, or both may not be estimated.

Unsmoothing   An adjustment to the reported return series if serial correlation is detected. Various approaches are available to unsmooth a return series.

Variance notional   The notional amount of a variance swap; it equals vega notional divided by two times the volatility strike price [i.e., (vega notional)/(2 × volatility strike)].

Vega   A measure of the sensitivity of an option's price to changes in the underlying's volatility.

Vega notional   The trade size for a variance swap, which represents the average profit and loss of the variance swap for a 1% change in volatility from the strike.

Vesting   The process of an employee becoming unconditionally entitled to, and an employer becoming obligated to pay, compensation.

Volatility clustering   The tendency for large (small) swings in prices to be followed by large (small) swings of random direction.

Volatility skew   The skewed plot (of implied volatility (y-axis) against strike price (x-axis) for options on the same underlying with the same expiration) that occurs when the implied volatility increases for OTM puts and decreases for OTM calls, as the strike price moves away from the current price.

Volatility smile   The U-shaped plot (of implied volatility (y-axis) against strike price (x-axis) for options on the same underlying with the same expiration) that occurs when the implied volatilities priced into both OTM puts and calls trade at a premium to implied volatilities of ATM options.

Wealth   The value of all the assets owned by an individual.

Wealth life cycle   Stages of an individual investor's wealth in terms of human capital, financial capital, and economic net worth.